Library of Congress Cataloging-in-Publication Data

When leadership goes wrong : destructive leadership, mistakes, and ethical failures / edited by Birgit Schyns and Tiffany Hansbrough.
p. cm.
Includes bibliographical references.
ISBN 978-1-61735-067-2 (pbk.) -- ISBN 978-1-61735-068-9 (hardcover) -- ISBN 978-1-61735-069-6 (e-book)
1. Leadership. 2. Leadership--Moral and ethical aspects. 3. Business ethics. I. Schyns, Birgit. II. Hansbrough, Tiffany.
HD57.7.W4565 2010
658.4'092--dc22

2010018430

Printed in the United States of America

When Leadership Goes Wrong

Destructive Leadership, Mistakes, and Ethical Failures

When Leadership Goes Wrong

Destructive Leadership, Mistakes, and Ethical Failures

edited by

Birgit Schyns
University of Portsmouth, United Kingdom

and

Tiffany Hansbrough
Baldwin-Wallace College, Ohio, United States

Information Age Publishing, Inc.
Charlotte, North Carolina • www.infoagepub.com

CONTENTS

PART II: ABUSIVE SUPERVISION

PART III: TOXIC LEADERSHIP, NARCISSISM, AND (UN)ETHICAL LEADERSHIP

PART IV: LEADER ERRORS AND FAILURE

PREFACE

Robert C. Liden

The recent trend in the organizational sciences toward positive organizational scholarship (Cameron, Dutton, & Quinn, 2003; Luthans & Avolio, 2009), geared toward a focus on the positive qualities in people, has generated substantial research on such topics as positive organizational behavior (Dutton & Ragins, 2007; Dutton, Worline, Frost, & Lilius, 2006), servant leadership (Liden, Wayne, Zhao, & Henderson, 2008), authentic leadership (Avolio & Gardner, 2005), and spiritual leadership (Fry & Kriger, 2009). Positive, compassionate leaders place a top priority on caring for followers, and strive to be fair and honest in interactions with others. Furthermore, research has revealed that positive organizational behaviors can be contagious (Barsade, 2002; Bono & Ilies, 2006). When leaders exhibit optimism and hope and provide followers with direction toward a vision, followers tend to share this optimism and passion for reaching goals. Positively oriented leaders may groom select followers into leaders who also focus on providing help to others. Cultivating a new generation of compassionate leaders contributes toward the growth of organizational cultures in which maintaining dignity and respect for people are paramount. Organizations whose cultures are based on positive leadership find themselves in the enviable position of knowing that their employees voluntarily engage in behaviors that benefit the organization and larger society, because they trust the leaders of the organization and they know that they will benefit from the successes of the organization.

So, why is there a need for a book devoted to destructive leadership? Why are organizations based on positive, supportive leadership described above not more common? Why does there appear to be an overabundance of abusive, coercive, divisive, and toxic leaders? I contend, consistent with the views of servant leadership pioneer Robert Greenleaf (1977), that the key reason for the ubiquity of destructive leaders around the globe is *self-interest*. Leaders driven by self-interest orient their behaviors toward ends that benefit themselves at the expense of followers, whose needs and interests are either ignored or trampled upon. Such leaders engage in dominating authoritative behaviors that slow follower career growth, diminish team coordination and potency, emotionally strain employees, eventually leading to the loss of talented employees (Tepper, 2007). Self-interest explains leader exploitation of workers for the purpose of achieving the leader's personal goals. Such striving for personal glorification is exemplified in the manipulation of subordinates so that any success can be attributed to the leader. And unfortunately, just as positive emotions and moods tend to spread to others in the workplace, negative emotions and moods are contagious as well (Dasborough, Ashkanasy, Tee, & Tse, 2009; Sy, Côté, & Saavedra, 2005). Exacerbating this spread of negativism and depression at work, negative emotions are often taken home as well, where they negatively affect family members (Hoobler & Brass, 2006).

It is important to acknowledge that leaders guilty of engaging in destructive leadership, may be responding in part to deviant behaviors of subordinates. Most researchers of destructive leadership make the assumption that abusive leader behaviors are initiated by leaders due to their need for power or to reach personal goals. Although this assumption may be correct in many instances, some leaders may be motivated to engage in abusive behavior by the organizational deviance of subordinates (Tepper, 2007). Employees who engage in behaviors, such as insubordination, theft, and excessive unwarranted absenteeism, may provoke leaders to show their abusive side. These employees, like destructive leaders, are motivated by self-interest.

Situations may also breed destructive leadership. Leaders who face organizational pressure to meet unrealistic goals, threats to their job security, perceptions of unfairness in the way they have been treated by the organization, such as breaches in their psychological contracts, may consciously or unconsciously take their frustrations out on their subordinates (Tepper, 2007). Indeed, such trickle-down effects have been documented (Hoobler & Brass, 2006). Organizational cultures that are characterized by aggressiveness and a lack of respect for people may also contribute to a prevalence of destructive leadership throughout the organization. Chief executives are responsible for setting goals as well as the tone that evolves into the culture of the organization (Schneider, 1987).Ultimately, when top executives are driven by self-interest, or engage in destructive leadership themselves, a culture of destructive leadership may emerge.

Is there hope that the tendency to be driven by self-interest, which characterizes many humans, especially those raised in individualistic cultures, can be reversed? Is it possible to socialize children in school and individuals in organizations to treat others with dignity and respect, and to focus on behaviors that help others at work, in one's family, and the larger community? I certainly hope so. To answer, "no" to this question is equivalent to giving up hope for humanity.

Is it within the realm of humanity to realistically hope for such a dream to come true? I contend that world change begins in work organizations. For many people, the main exposure to the outside world comes at work. And given that people's experiences and felt emotions at work spread to home and community, changes made at work are capable of impacting larger societies. Robert Greenleaf (1977) extended his visions of leadership at work by applying them to solving world problems. He argued that the underlying cause of the world's major problems—war, poverty, and environmental destruction—is the ego (or self-interest) of leaders. When leaders are driven by self-interest, they fail to consider the interests, goals, and needs of followers. Greenleaf envisioned the growth of caring, supportive leadership in organizations, through its focus on helping others at work but also in one's community, as eventually spreading to governments, and ultimately to a universal emphasis on helping others among all of the world's people.

Making the transformation from a focus on self-interest to an emphasis on helping others is a daunting task. One formidable challenge is overcoming resistance among leaders to move toward a positive, helping, compassionate form of leadership. Beyond combating the proclivity of some individuals to interact with others in a hostile and aggressive way is the relatively benign challenge of overcoming the simple truth that behaving with a focus on self-interest is considerably easier than engaging in empathy and providing support to others. Barking orders, controlling, and directing is much easier and takes substantially less time to than listening, showing empathy, supporting, mentoring and empowering followers. The key may be to demonstrate to leaders the many positive outcomes that are possible with supportive, empathetic approaches to leadership. Although leading in this manner requires patience and perseverance, the potential benefits are great. In addition to the intrinsic satisfaction that may be derived from helping other individuals to achieve their life goals, this form of leadership also serves to develop mutual trust between leader and follower, which translates into follower attitudes and behaviors that benefit the leader, the organization, and ultimately society.

Please join in this journey to move leadership in a positive direction. Certainly, developing a solid understanding of destructive leadership is the critical first step in identifying approaches to correct the problem. So, I challenge you to read the chapters in this book with an eye toward developing and researching strategies for overcoming destructive leadership.

REFERENCES

Avolio, B. J., & Gardner, W. L. (2005). Authentic leadership development: Getting to the root of positive forms of leadership. *Leadership Quarterly, 16,* 315-338.

Barsade, S. G. (2002). The ripple effects: Emotional contagion and its influence on group behavior. *Administrative Science Quarterly, 47,* 644-675. doi: 10.2307/3094912

Bono, J. E., & Ilies, R. (2006). Charisma, positive emotions and mood contagion. *The Leadership Quarterly, 17,* 317-334. doi: 10.1016/j.leaqua.2006.04.008

Cameron, K. S., Dutton, J. E., & Quinn, R. E. (Eds.). (2003). *Positive organizational scholarship: Foundations of a new discipline.* San Francisco: Berrett-Koehler.

Dasborough, M. T., Ashkanasy, N. M., Tee, E. Y. J., & Tse, H. H. M. (2009). What goes around comes around: How meso-level negative emotional contagion can ultimately determine organizational attitudes toward leaders. *The Leadership Quarterly, 20,* 571-585. doi: 10.1016/j.leaqua.2009.04.009

Dutton, J. E., & Ragins, B. R. (Eds.). (2007). *Exploring positive relationships at work: Building a theoretical and research foundation.* Mahwah, NJ: Erlbaum.

Dutton, J. E., Worline, M. C., Frost, P. J., & Lilius, J. (2006). Explaining compassion organizing. *Administrative Science Quarterly, 51,* 59-96.

Fry, L., & Kriger, M. (2009). Towards a theory of being-centered leadership: Multiple levels of being as context for effective leadership. *Human Relations, 62,* 1667-1696. doi: 10.1177/0018726709346380

Greenleaf, R. K. (1977). *Servant leadership: A journey into the nature of legitimate power and greatness.* New York: Paulist Press.

Hoobler, J. M., & Brass, D. J. (2006). Abusive supervision and family undermining as displaced aggression. *Journal of Applied Psychology, 91,* 1125-1133. doi: 10.1037/0021-9010.91.5.1125

Liden, R. C., Wayne, S. J., Zhao, H., & Henderson, D. (2008). Servant leadership: Development of a multidimensional measure and multilevel assessment. *Leadership Quarterly, 19,* 161-177.

Luthans, F., & Avolio, B. J. (2009). The "point" of positive organizational behavior. *Journal of Organizational Behavior, 30,* 291-307. doi: 10.1002/job.589

Schneider, B. (1987). Interactional psychology and organizational behavior. *Research in Organizational Behavior, 5,* 1–31.

Sy, T., Côté, S., & Saavedra, R. (2005). The contagious leader: Impact of the leader's mood on the mood of group members, group affective tone, and group processes. *Journal of Applied Psychology, 90,* 295-305. doi: 10.1037/0021-9010.90.2.295

Tepper, B. J. (2007). Abusive supervision in work organizations: Review synthesis, and research agenda. *Journal of Management, 33,* 261-289.

OVERVIEW

Birgit Schyns and Tiffany Hansbrough

The leadership landscape has begun to shift. A growing body of inquiry has emerged with a focus on the darker side of leadership (Popper, 2001). Allowing for the possibility that leaders can also do harm, either intentionally or unintentionally, broadens the scope of leadership studies and serves to increase the practical implications of leadership research. This volume considers how leaders, followers and situational factors can make leadership go awry.

Leaders

Leadership can go wrong because of certain characteristics of leaders or because leaders are corrupt (Wesche, May, Peus, & Frey). In this regard, McFarlin and Sweeney examine narcissism in executives and the antecedents and consequences of this personality disorder. Wang and colleagues point out how leader beliefs and traits interact with stressors leading to destructive behavior. Similarly, Eubanks and Mumford outline how leaders' cognitive processes can lead to destructive behavior. Rispens, Giebels, and Jehn analyze leaders' conflict perceptions, as an antecedent of abusive supervision. Specifically, a task conflict can trigger conflict perceptions and subsequently hostile actions with all the known negative consequences. Price even argues that ethical considerations can lead to unethical leadership. He suggests that leaders tend to believe that acting in the interest of others provides moral justification for unethical behavior.

While some leaders may simply be "evil" (Delbecq, 2001) and others intentionally or unintentionally behave destructively, probably all leaders make mistakes. Hunter, Tate, Dzieweczynski, and Cushenbery propose a taxonomy of leader errors and highlight how errors could and should be avoided. Likewise, Boies, Robinson, and Robertson focus on leaders' personal experience of failure and how it can serve a learning trigger. Thus, when leadership goes wrong, it can still serve to improve leadership in the long run. Similarly, Deng, Bligh, and Kohles examine the relationship between different leadership styles and learning from mistakes.

Followers

Leadership can also go wrong due to follower factors. In this context, Van Gils, Van Quaquebeke, and Van Knippenberg examine followers' influence on ethical decision making. They suggest that leaders are open to "cues" and that followers provide such cues with respect to leaders' ethical decision making. In addition, Grandy warns that especially for young workers the experience of abusive leadership is a trigger for sense-making that can shape their future behavior and possibly diminish their productivity. Finally, Hansbrough and Schyns argue that followers' romantic conceptions of leaders may actually prevent negative attributions of bad performance to leaders.Thus, follower perceptions provide leaders with a protective halo.

Environmental Factors

Mulvey and Padilla, as well as Chandler and Fields, outline how the environment of an organization can contribute to leader destructiveness. Bardes and Piccolo refer to the specific problem of goal setting as an antecedent of destructive behavior. By contributing to leaders' stress, goal setting can lead to destructive leadership behavior. Similarly, Pawlowska Braun, Peus, and Frey argue that some types of environments, such as academia with all its attached romance, can foster perceptions of adverse leadership.

While most authors concentrate on the negative effects of bad leadership, Lindebaum takes an interesting stance to the negative emotional expression of leaders. He suggests that anger, which some might associate with bad leadership, can under some circumstances and in the right environment be considered supportive of project success.

In conclusion, this book outlines antecedents and consequences of bad leadership—be they intentional or not. We hope that this book stimulates further research in this worthwhile area. As one of our colleagues noted, he is interested in destructive leadership "because it has stronger effects than good leadership" (Einarsen, personal communication, May 2009).

REFERENCES

Delbecq, A. L. (2001). "Evil" manifested in destructive individual behavior: A senior leadership challenge. *Journal of Management Inquiry, 10*, 221-226.

Popper, M. (2001). *Hypnotic leadership: Leaders, followers and the loss of self.* Westport, CT: Greenwood Press.

ACKNOWLEDGMENTS

The editors would like to thank all contributors for their hard work on this project. While reviewing was done among contributors, some colleagues provided comments despite not being involved as contributors: Our thanks go to Tina Kiefer, Charlotte Rayner, and Jan Schilling for their review work. A big "thank you" to Nina Junker for checking all chapters regarding their compliance with the IAP style guidelines. Thanks to George Johnson from IAP for his continuous support.

PART I

DESTRUCTIVE LEADERS

CHAPTER 1

GOAL SETTING AS AN ANTECEDENT OF DESTRUCTIVE LEADER BEHAVIORS

Mary Bardes and Ronald F. Piccolo

A relatively new stream of research has emerged that examines the dark, or destructive, side of leadership. This research examines negative leader behaviors in several forms including abusive supervision, petty tyranny, destructive leadership, social undermining, workplace aggression, and workplace bullying. Recently, scholars have begun to consider the reasons *why* leaders choose to engage in these negative behaviors toward their subordinates. In this chapter, we review extant research on antecedents of negative supervisory behaviors. Then, we add to these findings by presenting a theoretical model that suggests aspects of goals and reward systems can act as contextual antecedents of destructive leader behaviors. Despite the vast literature in support of goal setting theory, a small but emerging line of research suggests that goals can have negative consequences. We draw on this research, as well as research on stress, to propose that goal difficulty and goal-contingent reward can contribute to destructive leader behaviors through the effects these characteristics have on levels of stress.

When Leadership Goes Wrong: Destructive Leadership, Mistakes and Ethical Failures, pp. 3–22

Most of the academic research on leaders and the leadership process has focused on positive, romantic conceptions of leader behaviors (e.g., transformational, charismatic, ethical leadership), and how these behaviors have positive impacts on followers (e.g., self-efficacy; Shamir, House, & Arthur, 1993) and on organizations as a whole (e.g., group potency; Sosik, Avolio, & Kahai, 1997). Literally, thousands of studies have examined supervisor-subordinate interactions and have explored the effects of various positive, socially acceptable leadership behaviors (Bass, 1990; Yukl, 1998). With few exceptions (e.g., Kellerman, 2004; Kets de Vries, 2006; Luthans, Peterson, & Ibrayeva, 1998), however, "social scientists have avoided the dark side of leadership" (Padilla, Hogan, & Kaiser, 2007, p. 177), leaving the leadership literature positively skewed in its contribution to both theory and practice.

A relatively new stream of research, however, has emerged to describe leader behaviors that are dark and overtly destructive to individual achievement and positive group functioning, such as sabotaging subordinates' success, acting physically violent or aggressive toward subordinates, and exhibiting nonphysical hostility toward subordinates. Most conceptions of negative leader behaviors take the form of nonphysical interactions between supervisors and subordinates. Destructive supervisors, for example, make angry public outbursts directed towards subordinate, openly ridicule subordinates, take credit for other's successes, and blame subordinates for organizational failures (Keashley, Trott, & MacLean, 1994). These types of destructive behaviors have fallen under a number of different headings, including *abusive supervision* (Tepper, 2000), *petty tyranny* (Ashforth, 1994, 1997), and *destructive leadership* (Einarsen, Aasland, & Skogstad, 2007). Additionally, the literature on the dark side of organizational behavior (e.g., *workplace aggression*; Schat, Desmarais, & Kelloway, 2006; *social undermining*; Duffy, Ganster, & Pagon, 2002; *workplace bullying*; Zapf & Einarsen, 2001) has given particular attention to negative behaviors by those at supervisory levels. In Table 1.1 we provide a summary of the definitions of each of these behaviors (see also, Keashley & Jagatic, 2003).

While destructive behaviors by leaders can fall into a number of categories, each varying on the level of direct contact with a victim and the extent of physical and verbal abuse, we consider destructive behaviors in this paper to be those labeled as physical/active/direct and verbal/active/direct by Keashley and Jagatic (2003), representing overt and aggressive behavior by a leader on culpable subordinates. That said, we do not see our proposed model as limited to those two categories. Indeed, destructive behavior can reveal itself in many ways, and although not yet studied in the literature, the antecedents of these diverse behaviors are likely to be similar.

Table 1.1. Constructs That Capture Destructive Leader Behaviors

Construct	*Definition*
Abusive supervision	Subordinates' perceptions of the extent to which their supervisors engage in the sustained display of hostile verbal and non-verbal behaviors, excluding physical contact (Tepper, 2000, p. 178).
Petty tyranny	Managers' use of power and authority oppressively, capriciously, and vindictively (Ashforth, 1997).
Supervisor aggression	Supervisor behavior "that is intended to physically harm a worker or workers in the work-related context" (Schat et al., 2006).
Supervisor undermining	Supervisor "behavior intended to hinder, over time, the ability to establish and maintain positive interpersonal relationships, work-related success, and favorable reputation" (Duffy et al., 2002).
Destructive leadership	Supervisor "behaviors by a leader ... that violate the ... interest of the organization by undermining and/or sabotaging the organization's goals, tasks, resources, and effectiveness and/or the motivation, well-being, or job satisfaction of subordinates" (Einarsen et al., 2007).
Workplace bullying	Occurs when an individual "persistently over a period of time, is on the receiving end of negative actions from one or several others, in a situation where the one at the receiving end may have difficulty defending him or herself against these actions" (Zapf & Einarsen, 2001, p. 369).
Victimization	"The individual's self-perception of having been exposed, either momentarily or repeatedly, to aggressive actions emanating from one or more other persons" (Aquino, 2000, p. 172).

Although destructive leader behaviors affect a relatively small portion of the workforce (Tepper, Duffy, Henle, & Lambert, 2006), these behaviors tend to be very costly for supervisors and the organizations they lead, in terms of both the psychological burden for subordinates and the tangible economic costs to the organization (e.g., missed work, lack of employee effort, and outright sabotage by those affected). A number of studies have shown these negative leader behaviors are associated with both micro- (e.g., job and life dissatisfaction, Tepper, 2000; psychological distress, Tepper, Moss, Lockhart, & Carr, 2007; deviant behavior, Mitchell & Ambrose, 2007; subordinate performance, Harris, Kacmar, & Zivnuska, 2007) and macrolevel outcomes (e.g., fraudulent accounting, Carpenter & Reimers, 2005; firm performance, Hmieleski & Ensley, 2007). In fact, Tepper et al. (2006) reported that destructive leader behaviors (e.g., abusive supervision) in U.S. corporations lead to increases in absenteeism and health care costs and decreases in productivity, which cost these organizations approximately $23.8 billion annually.

Because of the substantial costs of destructive leader behaviors, scholars have begun to consider the reasons *why* leaders choose to engage in these negative behaviors toward their subordinates. Some of these destructive behaviors appear to be the results of characteristics of the leaders themselves (e.g., trait anger, Hershcovis et al., 2007; hostility, Schaubroeck, Walumbwa, Ganster, & Kepes, 2007; threatened egotism; Baumeister, Smart, & Boden, 1996), characteristics of followers (e.g., low self-esteem, Bardes & Ambrose, 2008; negative self-evaluations, Padilla et al., 2007), and characteristics of the work environment (e.g., organizational injustice, Tepper et al., 2006; Aryee, Chen, Sun, & Debrah, 2007; psychological contract violation, Hoobler & Brass, 2006). Whereas examinations of the dispositional antecedents of transformational (Bono & Judge, 2004) and ethical leadership behaviors (e.g., Walumbwa & Schaubroeck, 2009) are well developed, similar examinations of destructive leader behaviors are only in their infancy. Thus, it is imperative for researchers to continue to investigate the factors that contribute to destructive leader behaviors.

In this chapter, we do just that. We extend research on antecedents of destructive leader behaviors by examining aspects of the supervisors' goals and reward systems as additional contextual antecedents of leader behavior. In particular, we present a theoretical model that suggests an attribute of leaders' goals (viz., goal difficulty) and a characteristic of the leaders' reward systems (viz., goal-contingent rewards—the extent to which the leaders rewards are contingent upon goal attainment) act as antecedents of destructive leader behavior. We draw on a small but emerging stream of research that proposes organizational goal-setting can have negative consequences (e.g., Barsky, 2008; Latham, 1986; Latham & Locke, 2006; Locke & Latham, 1990; Ordóñez, Schweitzer, Galinsky, & Bazerman, 2009). Our model also draws on the stress literature to consider a leaders' level of psychological stress as the mechanism by which these contextual attributes encourage negative leader behaviors.

Thus, the ideas presented in this chapter make two contributions to the literature on leadership and motivation. First, we propose two new contextual antecedents of destructive leader behaviors, namely, goal difficulty and goal-contingent rewards. Second, we add to research on goal-setting by suggesting that difficult goals and goal-contingent reward may lead to negative outcomes in the form of destructive behaviors by an organization's leader. In the next sections of this paper, we briefly review research on antecedents of destructive leader behaviors, discuss the potential negative consequences of goal-setting, and present our theoretical model of relationships between goals and leader behavior.

ANTECEDENTS OF DESTRUCTIVE LEADER BEHAVIORS

For the most part, research on antecedents of destructive leader behaviors has taken an interactionist perspective and has examined both individual and situational factors that contribute to these types of negative behaviors. Much of this research has examined characteristics of leaders, susceptible followers, and conducive work environments as antecedents (e.g., Bardes & Ambrose, 2008; Padilla et al., 2007). In what follows, we use this framework to present brief discussions of extant research on antecedents of destructive leader behaviors.

Characteristics of Leaders

Some destructive leader behaviors are a direct function of individual characteristics of the leaders themselves. For example, leaders who score high on measures of negative personality traits, such as trait anger (Bardes & Ambrose, 2008), hostility, and negative affectivity (Schaubroeck et al., 2007), are more likely to engage in destructive supervisory behaviors such as ridiculing subordinates and criticizing employees in public. Similar results are reported in research on workplace aggression, which notes individual differences, such as a hostile attribution bias (i.e., the tendency to believe others have hostile intentions, Neuman & Baron, 1998), trait anger, and negative affectivity (Hershcovis et al., 2007), are associated with aggressive behavior. Also, some have noted that leaders, who abuse power, are charismatic, are narcissistic, have experienced negative life events, or have an ideology for hate, are likely to exhibit destructive leader behaviors toward followers (Padilla et al., 2007). Taken together, this research suggests that leaders who possess socially undesirable traits are more likely to engage in destructive behaviors.

Characteristics of Followers

Beyond the stable individual differences of leaders, certain personality traits and individual dispositions of followers enhance the likelihood of destructive behavior by leaders in a work context. Similar to the suggestion that desirable traits in followers enhance the effectiveness of positive forms of supervisory behavior (e.g., charisma and follower efficacy; Howell & Shamir, 2005), passive and undesirable dispositions among followers are likely to make destructive leader behaviors more common and more accepted without recourse. Einarsen (1999), for example, found that victims of workplace bullying reported that their own shyness and lack of conflict management skills contributed to being bullied. Similarly, Aquino and Bradfield (2000) suggested that victims of aggressive behaviors in the workplace tend to have both submissive characteristics, such as shyness, nonassertiveness, and passivity, as well as provocative characteristics, such as aggressiveness and negative affectivity.

Researchers have also examined the interaction of followers' characteristics with leader and/or situational factors, emphasizing the extent to which followers' characteristics contribute to negative behavior by leaders. For example, Tepper et al. (2006) found that subordinates' negative affectivity moderated the relationship between supervisors' perceptions of procedural injustice and abusive supervision, such that the relationship between injustice and abuse emerged only when subordinates had a negative disposition. Bardes and Ambrose (2008) examined the role of subordinates' self esteem on the relationship between supervisors' trait anger and abusive supervision, noting that the relationship between anger and abusive behavior was strongest towards subordinates who had low self-esteem. Additionally, in suggesting a "toxic triangle" (i.e., the interplay of characteristics of destructive leaders, susceptible followers, and conducive situations), Padilla et al. (2007) posit that followers' characteristics of unmet needs, negative self-evaluations, psychological immaturity, and selfishness can contribute to destructive leader behaviors. Thus, research on followers' characteristics has suggested that (a) followers' characteristics provoke and/or (b) interact with aspects of the situation or with characteristics of the leader to trigger and exaggerate destructive leader behaviors.

Characteristics of Work Environments

Of course, in researching antecedents of destructive leader behaviors, scholars also acknowledge that the situation matters (Padilla et al., 2007) and have examined the extent to which contextual factors induce counterproductive behavior by organizational leaders. Perceptions of systemic procedural injustice (Tepper et al., 2006), interactional injustice (Aryee et al., 2007), and psychological contract violation (i.e., the perception that the organization did not give what was promised; Hoobler & Brass, 2006) are associated with abusive supervisory behaviors, such that leaders retaliate against the organization by being abusive to organization members. Additionally, in separate reviews on workplace aggression, Neuman and Baron (1998) suggested that provocation, frustrating events, unfair treatment, and aggressive norms may be situational antecedents of aggressive behavior, while Herschcovis et al. (2007) found that distributive injustice, procedural injustice, interpersonal conflict, and situational constraints (e.g., availability of resources) were predictors of aggressive behavior. Similarly, Salin (2003) noted that downsizing, restructuring, competition, reward systems, and perceived power imbalances are environmental factors that contribute to bullying behaviors. Finally, Padilla et al. (2007) argued that environmental instability and overt threats to financial security encourage a defensive stance among organizational managers, which often reveals itself in behaviors that are aggressive, destructive, and toxic for the organization, its members and constituents.

Summary

This brief review has identified recent research on antecedents of destructive leader behaviors. Although this research has fallen under various headings (e.g., abusive supervision, workplace aggression, destructive leadership), it all gives evidence of characteristics of leaders, followers, and situations that contribute to destructive supervisory behaviors. In what follows, we add to this research on antecedents of destructive leader behaviors and suggest additional situational antecedents by positing a theoretical model linking goal-setting to destructive acts by leaders.

UNINTENDED CONSEQUENCES OF GOAL SETTING

A central tenet of goal setting theory (Locke & Latham, 1990), one of the most dominant and enduring theories in organizational behavior (Mitchell & Daniel, 2003), is the notion that goals are precursors to actions (Latham, 2007). Goal setting theory states that specific, difficult goals serve to enhance one's self-regulation by focusing attention on specific objectives and directing effort towards goal-relevant behavior. Goals further enhance the intensity and persistence used to attain an objective while providing feedback for the success of one's effort.

There are more than 1,000 studies that report the positive effects of goal setting (Mitchell & Daniels, 2003) on performance, persistence, and motivation. In many of these studies, results suggest that specific, challenging goals yield superior results in terms of performance and persistence to goals that are vague and easy to attain. Indeed, the vast majority of studies on the goal setting process find that specific, challenging goals, when paired with commitment to those goals, have a positive influence on a host of positive outcomes (Latham, Locke, & Fassina, 2002; Locke & Latham, 1990; Locke & Latham, 2002).

Despite the strong evidence in favor of challenging goals, however, several recent papers argue that difficult goals may actually drive individuals to engage in a host of counterproductive behaviors, such as lying about one's progress towards a stated goal, undermining colleagues who have competing goals, or unethical handling of customer interactions for achievement of a narrow, goal-directed benefit (Ordóñez et al., 2009). Latham and Locke (2006), the founders of goal setting theory, have themselves suggested that there are possible "pitfalls" of goal-setting, but Schweitzer, Ordóñez, and Douma (2004) were the first to empirically study negative consequences of goal-setting. In a laboratory study, Schweitzer and his colleagues examined the effect of goal setting on ethical decision making. Participants in the study were given unmet performance goals and were provided the opportunity to overstate their performance in order to obtain specific goals. As the authors noted, participants with specific, challenging, unmet goals were more likely to lie about their performance (i.e., engage in unethical behavior) than participants who were simply asked to "do their best." This effect was strongest among participants who were just barely "falling short of goals," highlighting the potential consequences of a strong desire for goal attainment.

Following Schweitzer et al. (2004), Barsky (2008) attempted to extend the research on the goals and ethics, considering the mechanisms by which goals influence unethical behavior, the attributes of goals that are the strongest predictors of unethical behavior, and how individual differences moderate these relationships. Barsky presented a theoretical model that linked goal attributes (e.g., difficulty, specificity, content) and goal-setting practices (e.g., level of participation, rewards) to unethical behavior through two mediating mechanisms, ethical recognition and moral disengagement. Ethical recognition occurs when a decision-maker becomes morally aware such that decision processes recognize an issue as having "ethical" implications, while moral disengagement refers to the process by which one convinces himself that ethical standards do not apply to him in a particular context, most often by separating moral reactions from unethical conduct by disabling the mechanism of self-condemnation (Fiske, 2004). These are two psychological factors that serve as underpinnings of ethical behavior.

Barsky (2008) suggested that (a) performance goals can interfere with an individual's ethical recognition (i.e., the awareness that an action will harm others) by directing attention toward achieving those goals and away from assessing the ethicality of behaviors, and (b) goal-setting practices, such as assigning goals and tying rewards to goal attainment, may lead to moral disengagement (i.e., the process of rationalizing behaviors; Bandura, Barbaranelli, Caprara, & Pastorelli, 1996) by providing justifications to engage in unethical behavior. Similarly, Schweitzer and his colleagues have noted the potential "side effects" of goal setting (Ordóñez et al., 2009), such as distorted risk preferences, unethical behavior, decreases in learning, and reduced intrinsic motivation. Although the assertions by Barsky and Ordóñez et al. have been vehemently disputed by Locke and Latham (2009), on grounds that criticisms of goal setting theory are not derived from inductive assessments of existing empirical studies, a number of questions remain regarding the possible negativity of goal setting, supporting additional examination of the theory's "pitfalls" (Latham & Locke, 2006).

We address some of these questions by suggesting that goal-directed reward systems can contribute to an additional form of "bad" behavior, namely destructive leader behaviors. We integrate research on goal-setting, stress, and aggressive behavior to propose a theoretical model that links an attribute of goals (goal difficulty) and a goal-setting practice (goal-contingent reward) to destructive leader behaviors (e.g., abusive supervision, undermining, bullying). Because there is considerable research supporting the positive effects of goal setting, we were also interested in exploring why goal-setting may lead to leader aggression. As such, we also suggest the leader's level of stress can mediate the relationship between goal-setting and destructive leader behaviors.

GOALS, STRESS, AND DESTRUCTIVE LEADER BEHAVIORS

Consistent with the notion of potential negative consequences of goal setting (e.g., Barsky, 2008; Latham & Locke, 2006; Schweitzer et al., 2004), the primary purpose of this manuscript is to describe aspects of goals and reward structures that serve as contextual antecedents of destructive leader behaviors. Specifically, we suggest that the difficulty of a leader's goal and the extent to which a leader's rewards are tied to goal accomplishment contribute to destructive leader behaviors through the effects they have on a leader's level of psychological stress. Our theoretical model is shown in Figure 1.1.

Leaders' Goal Difficulty and Stress

Stress is defined as "an individual's psychological response to a situation in which there is something at stake and where the situation taxes or exceeds the individual's capacity or resource" (LePine, LePine, & Jackson, 2004, p. 883). This definition is derived from Lazarus and Folkman's (1984) cognitive theory of stress, which suggests that when an individual is exposed to a potential stressor, he or she engages in cognitive appraisals of the stressor and decides if it is something that (a) will cause harm and (b) can be managed. Lazarus and Folkman propose that stress arises when

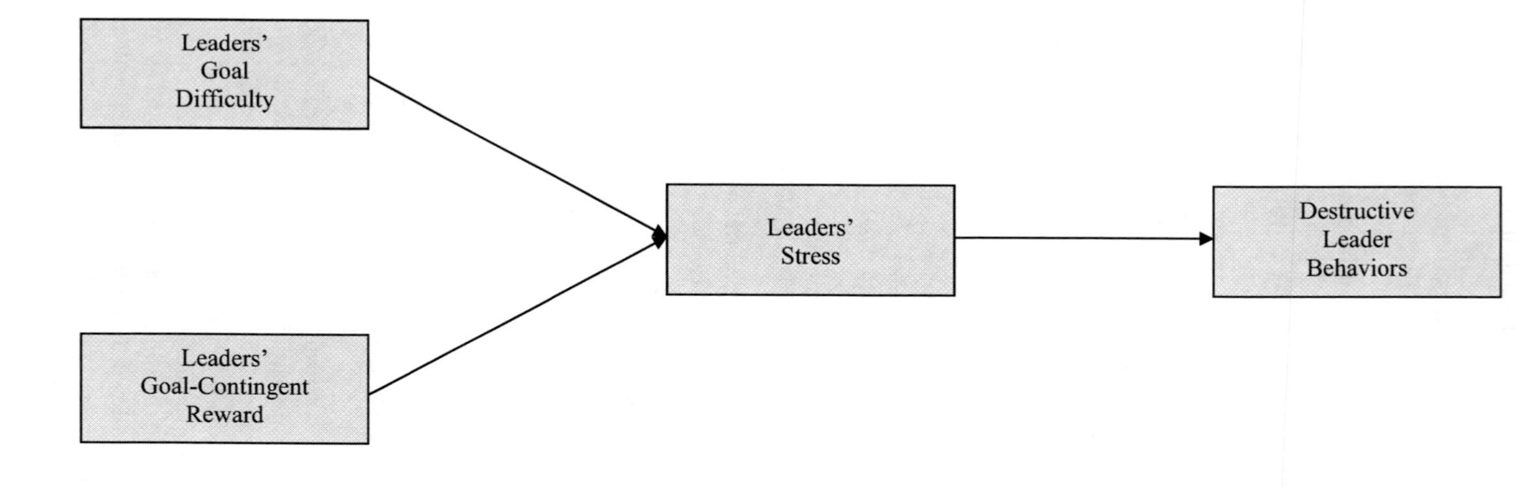

Figure 1.1. Proposed relationships among variables.

a potential stressor is deemed to be challenging (a challenge stressor, which gives opportunities for growth, learning, or success) or threatening (a hindrance stressor, which hinders growth, learning, or success) and when demands exceed available resources.

The cognitive theory of stress and its definition provide a platform for consideration of the link between difficult goals and psychological stress. There are two main reasons to propose that this relationship exists. First, difficult goals create stress because they can be perceived as threatening. Locke and Latham (1990) report that goal setting introduces a potential threat, in that the mere existence of goals creates pressure to perform and the threat of failure. All goals, but challenging and difficult goals in particular, make it apparent that there are specific, difficult standards by which performance will be evaluated, thus making salient the potential for failure to meet those standards. The threat of failure associated with difficult goals and standards make it more likely that goals will be appraised as threatening.

Second, difficult goals may create perceptions of an imbalance between demands and resources. As mentioned previously, stress arises from judgments that particular demands exceed available resources (Folkman & Lazarus, 1985). Because difficult goals create challenging demands, individuals who regard their goals as particularly difficult may feel that they do not possess the resources (e.g., skills, abilities, time) required for goal accomplishment, creating a perceived imbalance of demands and resources, an imbalance that increases feelings of stress.

Although very few studies have empirically tested the link between goals and stress reactions (Drach-Zahavy & Erez, 2002), those that have find a positive effect. For example, White, Mitchell, and Bell (1977) conducted a laboratory experiment in which they measured perceived pressure caused by goal setting. Compared to having no goals, participants with challenging goals felt more stress from greater pressure to perform and greater chances of failure. Also, Nebeker (1987) conducted a work simulation experiment in which computer operators were given various types of goals and incentives. The study found that those who were assigned goals with difficult standards experienced higher stress than those assigned easier standards. Furthermore, in a study of individuals performing a heuristic maze task, Huber (1985) found that specific, difficult goals created excessive stress, which hampered performance.

Thus, drawing on the cognitive theory of stress and empirical research that has linked difficult goals to stress, we propose when leaders are given difficult goals, they will be likely to experience higher levels of stress.

Proposition 1: Leaders' goal difficulty is positively related to leaders' levels of stress.

Leaders' Goal-Contingent Reward and Stress

Aspects of leaders' reward systems can also contribute to the leaders' levels of stress. One such attribute is goal-contingent reward, which we define as the extent to which the leaders' rewards are contingent upon goal attainment. In describing the cognitive theory of stress, Lazarus and Folkman (1984) suggest that the degree of stress an individual experiences is shaped by perceptions of the consequences tied to the stressor. When the stakes are high and explicitly tied to the stressor, psychological stress will increase.

Perceptions that the stakes are high may exist when rewards are contingent upon goal attainment. Companies vary in the methods by which they reward employees for their efforts. In many objective-oriented organizations, the distribution of rewards (e.g., salary increases, promotions, bonuses) is based primarily on goal attainment (Latham et al., 2002; Locke & Latham, 1990). We focus on this type of reward system, which we refer to as goal-contingent rewards.

There are two main reasons to expect goal-contingent reward is related to feelings of stress, both of which are based on the notions that goal-contingent rewards make it obvious that something of value is at stake and create a potential threat of failure. First, tying rewards to goal attainment can make it apparent that valued outcomes are at stake. As mentioned, stress arises in response to situations in which there is something at stake and where the demands of the situation exceed an individual's resources (LePine et al., 2004). When an individual is exposed to a potential stressor and what is at stake is extremely salient, the stressor is more likely to increase levels of stress. With goal-contingent reward, the negative consequences (or the stakes) of not attaining the goal are extremely obvious, which could also increase feelings of stress.

Second, goal-contingent rewards can increase an individual's awareness that a potential threat of failure exists. An individual involved in this type of reward system is very aware that not fulfilling the goal will result in failure to attain some type of valued outcome (e.g., compensation, promotion, bonus) and thus, may be more likely to perceive that the potential for failure exists. This may make them more likely to experience stress.

The relationship between contingent rewards and stress has been empirically supported in research on stress reactions to pay systems. Types of pay systems vary on a continuum of the extent to which an employee's compensation is based on individual job performance (Shirom, Westman, & Melamed, 1999). Piece-rate pay is the most common performance-contingent reward system, whereby employees' wages are determined exclusively on an individual job performance or output (e.g., commissions given to a sales person for meeting his quotas).

There are a limited number of studies that have examined the relationship between pay systems and stress. Those that have, however, have provided evidence that employees who receive piece-rate pay exhibit significantly higher levels of stress than those who do not (Shirom et al., 1999). For example, in a study of professional typists doing computer-based data entry, Schleifer and colleagues (Schleifer & Amick, 1989; Schleifer & Okogaba, 1990) found that levels of anxiety were higher during periods of piece-rate pay as compared to periods without piece-rate pay. Findings such as these indicate that piece-rate payment systems can lead to psychological stress and that an individual's level of anxiety is at least partially dependent on the extent to which rewards (e.g., compensation) depend on goal attainment.

Hence, drawing on the stress literature, particularly the link between contingent reward systems and stress, we suggest that leaders are more likely to experience high levels of stress when their rewards are highly contingent on goal attainment.

Proposition 2: Leaders' goal-contingent reward is positively related to leaders' levels of stress.

Leaders' Stress and Destructive Leader Behaviors

A considerable amount of research has suggested that stress and stressful events can be meaningful triggers of destructive behavior. A meta-analysis conducted by Hershcovis et al. (2007) reported individuals use workplace aggression as a way of coping with stress that results from workplace stressors, in the form of situational constraints (e.g., scarcity of resources) and interpersonal conflict. Similarly, research has found that job stress resulting from role ambiguity, role conflict, interpersonal conflict, and situational constraints is related to aggressive and counterproductive action (e.g., Chen & Spector, 1992). In addition, a number of studies have reported that workplace stressors, such as excessive workload or constraints on resources, are related to counterproductive work behaviors (e.g., Fox & Spector, 1999; Fox, Spector, & Miles, 2001; Spector & Fox, 2005).

Also, research that supports the link between stress and abusive behavior can be found in studies that relate negative emotions associated with stress to aggressive behavior. Stress is characterized by negative emotions, such as fear, anger, and anxiety (Lazarus & Folkman, 1984), and these emotions are consistently related to aggressive behavior. For example, the meta-analysis by Herschcovis et al. (2007) found that anger and negative affectivity (which captures distressing emotions such as fear and anxiety) were strong predictors of workplace interpersonal aggression.

As such, we propose that when leaders experience higher levels of stress, they will be likely to engage in destructive leader behaviors.

Proposition 3: Leaders' stress will be positively related to destructive leader behaviors.

DISCUSSION

Research on various forms of destructive leader behaviors has found that these supervisory behaviors are associated with a number of negative outcomes (e.g., employee job and life dissatisfaction, Tepper, 2000; deviant behavior, Mitchell & Ambrose, 2007; counterproductive behavior, somatic complaints, Duffy et al., 2002). Recently, scholars have begun to examine why leaders choose to engage in behaviors that are disruptive and destructive to organizational functioning (e.g., Hogan & Hogan, 2001). This chapter adds to the literature on antecedents of abusive supervision by examining situational factors that may be determinants of destructive supervisory behaviors. Specifically, we propose a theoretical model that suggests leaders' difficult goals and goal-contingent rewards contribute to destructive behaviors through the effect these factors have on leaders' feelings of stress. Below we discuss the implications of this theoretical model and mention avenues for future research.

Implications

Our theoretical model makes contributions to research on goal setting, stress, and destructive leader behaviors. First, the model contributes to the literature on goal setting. Most research on goal setting has examined the effects of attributes of goals and goal setting practices on positive outcomes. Only a few studies have examined negative outcomes (e.g., Barsky, 2008; Schweitzer et al., 2004). Our model adds to this limited research on the possible negative outcomes of goal setting by proposing that difficult goals and goal-contingent reward systems contribute to destructive leader behaviors.

Our model also adds to research on stress by suggesting the mediating effects of psychological stress on the effects of difficult goals and goal-contingent rewards on destructive leader behaviors. Research on stress suggests a sequence in which stressors lead to an appraisal process (hindrance or challenge stress), which in turn, leads to outcomes (Lazarus & Folkman, 1984). Our model proposes a similar sequence and suggests difficult goals are stressors that can lead to feelings of stress, which in turn, can lead to destructive leader behaviors. The model also suggests goal-contingent rewards can be stressors that can have the same effect.

Finally, our theoretical model contributes to the limited research on antecedents of destructive leader behaviors. The main purpose of this chapter was to suggest additional contextual antecedents of destructive supervisory behaviors. Our model suggests that difficult goals, goal-contingent rewards, and stress may contribute to destructive leader behaviors, and the relationship between difficult goals and goal-contingent reward and destructive behaviors is explained by the mediating effect of stress. These propositions add to research that has linked situational factors to various forms of destructive leader behaviors

Future Research

Of course, our theoretical model should be empirically tested. In addition, this chapter brings to light a number of avenues for future research. First, the relationship between difficult goals and destructive leader behaviors should be further examined. Much research on goal setting suggests difficult goals lead to positive outcomes such as higher performance and job satisfaction. Our theoretical model does not dispute these findings, but we suggest that difficult goals can also lead to negative outcomes, such as destructive behaviors by leaders. The next plausible step in the examination of difficult goals and negative outcomes, then, is investigations of the conditions under which difficult goals are more or less likely to lead to negative outcomes (e.g., abusive supervision, unethical behavior, counterproductive behavior). This should include examinations using the interactionist perspective and should investigate the moderating effects of characteristics of leaders and followers that may increase the likelihood that difficult goals will lead to negative behaviors. Some supervisor characteristics commonly associated with aggressive behavior could influence the goals-negative outcomes relationship, such as trait anger (e.g., Bardes & Ambrose, 2008; Herschcovis et al., 2007), hostile attribution bias (e.g., Neuman & Baron, 1998), and negative affectivity (e.g., Aquino & Bradfield, 2000). In addition, the moderating effects of attributes of the difficult goals themselves should be examined (e.g., goal commitment, participation in goal setting, number of goals).

Second, future research should continue to examine the link between difficult goals and stress. To more fully examine this effect, researchers should investigate how difficult goals are differentially related to both challenge and hindrance stress. Examining this link between difficult goals and the different types of stress will assist in our understanding of why difficult goals have been found to be related to both positive and negative outcomes. Research has found that challenge stressors are positively related to positive outcomes, such as job satisfaction and organizational commitment, and negatively related to negative outcomes, such as turnover and withdrawal behaviors, whereas hindrance stress had opposite relationships with those outcomes (Podsakoff, LePine, & LePine, 2007). Perhaps, difficult goals lead to positive outcomes when they are perceived as challenge stressors, but lead to negative outcomes when perceived as hindrance stressors. Additionally, future research should address the factors that contribute to perceptions of difficult goals as a challenge or hindrance.

Finally, additional mediators of the relationships between difficult goals and goal-contingent reward and destructive leader behaviors should be examined. The current study examined stress as the explanatory mechanism. However, it is possible that additional explanations for this relationship exist. As such, future research should attempt to explain the relationship between goals and goal-setting practices and abusive supervision by examining additional mediators. Barsky's (2008) work on the link between attributes and goals and goal-setting practices and unethical behavior sheds light on possible mediators of moral disengagement and ethical recognition. Also, Latham and Locke (2006) suggest goal setting can have negative consequences if the goals, or possibility of not attaining the goal, threatens the individual's self-esteem. Thus, threats to self-esteem may be a mediator of the relationship between goals and abusive supervision.

CONCLUSION

There is a need to understand factors that may contribute to a supervisor's destructive behavior. Our theoretical model integrates research on goal-setting, stress, and aggressive behavior and suggests stress mediates the relationship between leaders' difficult goals and destructive leader behaviors and leaders' goal-contingent reward and destructive leader behavior. This chapter is the first to suggest these relationships, and by doing so, makes theoretical contributions to research on goal setting, stress, and destructive leader behaviors. Future research should empirically examine these relationships.

REFERENCES

Aquino, K., & Bradfield, M. (2000). Perceived victimization in the workplace: The role of situational factors and victim characteristics. *Organizational Science, 11*, 525-537.

Aryee, S., Chen, Z. X., Sun, L., & Debrah, Y. A. (2007). Antecedents and outcomes of abusive supervision: Test of a trickle-down model. *Journal of Applied Psychology, 92*, 191-201.

Ashforth, B. (1994). Petty tyranny in organizations. *Human Relations, 47*, 755-778.

Ashforth, B. (1997). Petty tyranny in organizations: A preliminary examination of antecedents and consequences. *Canadian Journal of Administrative Sciences, 14*, 126-140.

Bandura, A., Barbaranelli, C., Caprara, G. V., & Pastorelli, C. (1996). Mechanisms of moral disengagement in the exercise of moral agency. *Journal of Personality and Social Psychology, 7*, 364-374.

Bardes, M., & Ambrose, M. L. (2008, August). *Abusive supervision: An examination of its antecedents.* Paper presented at the annual meetings of the Academy of Management, Anaheim, CA.

Barsky, A. (2008). Understanding the ethical cost of organizational goal-setting: A review and theory development. *Journal of Business Ethics, 81*, 63-81.

Bass, B. M. (1990). *Bass and Stogdill's handbook of leadership: Theory, research, & managerial applications* (3rd ed.). New York: Free Press.

Baumeister, R. F., Smart, L., & Boden, J. M. (1996). Relation of threatened egotism to violence and aggression: The dark side of high self-esteem. *Psychological Review, 103*, 5-33.

Bono, J. E., & Judge T. A. (2004). Personality and transformational and transactional leadership: A meta-analysis. *Journal of Applied Psychology, 89*, 901-910.

Carpenter, T. D., & Reimers, J. L. (2005). Unethical and fraudulent financial reporting: Applying the theory of planned behavior. *Journal of Business Ethics, 60*, 115-129.

Chen, P. Y., & Spector, P. E. (1992). Relationships of work stressors with aggression, withdrawal, theft, and substance use: An exploratory study. *Journal of Occupational and Organizational Psychology, 65*, 177-184.

Drach-Zahavy, A., & Erez, M. (2002). Challenge versus threat effects on the goal-performance relationship. *Organizational Behavior and Human Decision Processes, 88*, 667-682.

Duffy, M. K., Ganster, D., & Pagon, M. (2002). Social undermining in the workplace. *Academy of Management Journal, 45*, 331-351.

Einarsen, S. (1999). The nature and causes of bullying at work. *International Journal of Manpower, 20*, 16-26.

Einarsen, S., Aasland, M. S., & Skogstad, A. (2007). Destructive leader behaviour: A definition and conceptual model. *The Leadership Quarterly, 18*, 207-216.

Fiske, S. (2004). *Social Beings: A core motives approach to social psychology.* Hoboken, NJ: Wiley.

Folkman, S., & Lazarus, R. S. (1985). If it changes it must be a process: A study of emotion and copying during three stages of a college examination. *Journal of Personality and Social Psychology, 48*, 150-170.

Fox, S., & Spector, P. E. (1999). A model of work frustration-aggression. *Journal of Organizational Behavior, 20*, 915-932.

Fox, S., Spector, P. E., & Miles, D. (2001). Counterproductive work behavior (CWB) in response to job stressors and organizational justice: Some mediator and moderator tests for autonomy and emotions. *Journal of Vocational Behavior, 59*, 291-309.

Harris, K. J., Kacmar, K. M., & Zivnuska, S. (2007). An investigation of abusive supervision as a predictor of performance and the meaning of work as a moderator of the relationship. *The Leadership Quarterly, 18*, 252-263.

Hershcovis, S. M., Turner, N., Barling, J., Arnold, K. A., Dupre, K.E., Inness, M., et al. (2007). Predicting workplace aggression: A meta-analysis. *Journal of Applied Psychology, 92*, 228-238.

Hmieleski, K. M., & Ensley, M. D. (2007). The effects of entrepreneur abusive supervision. *Academy of Management Proceedings*, 1-6.

Hogan, R., & Hogan, J. (2001). Assessing leadership: A view from the dark side. *International Journal of Selection & Assessment, 9*, 40-51.

Hoobler, J., & Brass, D. (2006). Abusive supervision and family undermining as displaced aggression. *Journal of Applied Psychology, 91*, 1125-1133.

Howell, J. M., & Shamir, B. (2005). The role of followers in the charismatic leadership process: Relationships and their consequences. *Academy of Management Review, 30*, 96-112.

Huber, V. L. (1985). Effects of task difficulty, goal setting, and strategy on performance on a heuristic task. *Journal of Applied Psychology, 70*, 492-504.

Keashley, L., & Jagatic, K. (2003). By any other name: American perspectives on workplace bullying. In S. Einarsen, H. Hoel, D. Zapf, & C. Cooper (Eds.), *Bullying and emotional abuse in the workplace: International research and practice perspectives* (pp. 31-61). London: Taylor & Francis.

Keashley, L., Trott, V., & MacLean, L. M. (1994). Abusive behavior in the workplace: A preliminary investigation. *Violence and Victims, 9*, 341-357.

Kellerman, B. (2004). *Bad leadership: What it is, how it happens, why it matters.* Boston: Harvard Business School Press.

Kets de Vries, M. (2006). The spirit of despotism: Understanding the tyrant within. *Human Relations, 59*, 195-220.

Latham, G. P. (1986). Job performance and appraisal. In C. L. Cooper & I. T. Robertson (Eds.), *Review of industrial and organizational psychology.* Chichester, England: Wiley.

Latham, G. P. (2007). *Work motivation: History, theory, research, and practice.* Thousand Oaks, CA: SAGE.

Latham, G. P., & Locke, E. A. (2006). Enhancing the benefits and overcoming the pitfalls of goal setting. *Organizational Dynamics, 35*, 332-340.

Latham, G. P., Locke, E. A., & Fassina, N. E. (2002). The high performing cycle: Standing the test of time. In S. Sonnentag (Ed.), *The psychological management of individual performance. A handbook in the psychology of management in organizations* (pp. 201-228). Chichester, England: Wiley.

Lazarus, R. S., & Folkman, S. (1984). *Stress, appraisal, and coping*. New York: Springer.

LePine, J. A., LePine, M. A., & Jackson, C. (2004). Challenge and hindrance stress: Relationships with exhaustion, motivation to learn, and learning performance. *Journal of Applied Psychology, 89*, 883-891.

Locke, E. A., & Latham, G. P. (1990). *A theory of goal setting & task performance.* Englewood Cliffs, NJ: Prentice Hall.

Locke, E. A., & Latham, G. P. (2002). Building a practically useful theory of goal setting and motivation: A 35-year odyssey. *American Psychologist, 57*, 705-717.

Locke, E. A., & Latham, G. P. (2009, *August*). Has goal setting gone wild, or have its attackers abandoned good scholarship? *Academy of Management Perspectives*, 17-23.

Luthans, F., Peterson, S., & Ibrayeva, L. (1998). The potential for the "dark side" of leadership in post-communist countries. *Journal of World Business, 33*, 185-201.

Mitchell, M. S., & Ambrose, M. L. (2007). Abusive supervision and workplace deviance and the moderating effects of negative reciprocity beliefs. *Journal of Applied Psychology, 92*, 1159-1168.

Mitchell, T. R., & Daniels, D. (2003). Motivation. In W. C. Borman, D. R. Ilgen, & R. J. Klimoski (Eds.), *Comprehensive handbook of psychology: Industrial organizational psychology* (Vol. 12, pp. 225-254). New York: Wiley.

Neuman, J. H., & Baron, R. A. (1998). Workplace violence and workplace aggression: Evidence concerning specific forms, potential causes, and preferred targets. *Journal of Management, 24*, 391-419.

Nebeker, D. M. (1987). *Computer monitoring, feedback, and rewards: Effects of workstation operators' performance, satisfaction and stress* (unpublished manuscript). San Diego, CA: Navy Personnel Research and Development Center.

Ordóñez, L. D., Schweitzer, M. E., Galinsky, A. D., & Bazerman, M. H. (2009, February). Goals gone wild: The systematic side effects of overprescribing goal setting. *Academy of Management Perspectives*, 6-16.

Padilla, A., Hogan, R., & Kaiser, R. (2007). The toxic triangle: Destructive leaders, susceptible followers, and conducive environments. *Leadership Quarterly, 18*, 76-194.

Podsakoff, N. P., LePine, J. A., & LePine, M. A. (2007). Differential challenge stressor-hindrance stressor relationships with job attitudes, turnover intentions, turnover, and withdrawal behavior: A meta-analysis. *Journal of Applied Psychology, 92*, 438-454.

Salin, D. (2003). Ways of explaining workplace bullying: A review of enabling, motivating, and precipitating structures and processes in the work environment. *Human Relations, 56*, 1213-1232.

Schat, A. C. H., Desmarais, S., & Kelloway, E. K. (2006). *Exposure to workplace aggression from multiple sources: Validation of a measure and test of a model.* Unpublished manuscript, McMaster University, Hamilton, Canada.

Schaubroeck, J., Walumbwa, F. O., Ganster, D. C., & Kepes, S. (2007). Destructive leader traits and the neutralizing influence of an "enriched" job. *The Leadership Quarterly, 18*, 236-251.

Schleifer, L. M., & Amick, B. C. (1989). System response time and methods of pay: Stress effects in computer-based tasks. *International Journal of Human-Computer Interaction, 1*, 23-39.

Schleifer, L. M., & Okogaba, O. G. (1990). System response time and methods of pay: Cardiovascular effects in computer-based tasks. *Ergonomics, 33*, 1495-1509.

Schweitzer, M. E., Ordóñez, L., & Douma, B. (2004) Goal setting as a motivator of unethical behavior. *Academy of Management Journal, 47*, 422-432.

Shamir, B., House, R. J., & Arthur, M. A. (1993). The motivational effects of charismatic leadership: A self-concept based theory. *Organization Science, 4*, 577-594.

Shirom, A., Westman, M., & Melamed, S. (1999). The effects of pay systems on blue-collar employees' emotional distress: The mediating effects of objective and subjective work monotony. *Human Relations, 52*, 1077-1097.

Sosik, J. J., Avolio, B. J., & Kahai, S. S. (1997). Effects of leadership style and anonymity on group potency and effectiveness in a group decision support system environment. *Journal of Applied Psychology, 82*, 89-103.

Spector, P. E., & Fox, S. (2005). The stressor-emotion model of counterproductive work behavior. In P. E. Fox & S. Spector (Eds.), *Counterproductive work behavior: Investigations of actors and targets* (pp. 151-174). Washington, DC: American Psychological Association.

Tepper, B. J. (2000). Consequences of abusive supervision. *Academy of Management Journal, 43*, 178-190.

Tepper, B. J., Duffy, M. K., Henle, C. A., & Lambert, L. S. (2006). Procedural injustice, victim precipitation, and abusive supervision. *Personnel Psychology, 59*, 101.

Tepper, B. J., Moss, S. E., Lockhart, D. E., & Carr, J. C. (2007). Abusive supervision, upward maintenance communication, and subordinates' psychological distress. *Academy of Management Journal, 50*, 1169-1180.

Walumbwa, F. O., & Schaubroeck, J. (2009). Leader personality traits and employee voice behavior: Mediating roles of ethical leadership and work-group psychological safety. *Journal of Applied Psychology, 94*, 1275-1286.

White, S. E., Mitchell, T. R., & Bell, C. H. (1977). Goal setting, evaluation apprehension, and social cues as determinants of job performance and satisfaction in a simulated organization. *Journal of Applied Psychology, 62*, 665-673.

Yukl, G. A. (1998). *Leadership in organizations* (4th ed.). Englewood Cliffs, NJ: Prentice Hall.

Zapf, D., & Einarsen, S. (2001). Bullying in the workplace: Recent trends in research and practice—an introduction. *European Journal of Work and Organizational Psychology, 10*, 369-373.

CHAPTER 2

DESTRUCTIVE LEADERSHIP

The Role of Cognitive Processes

Dawn L. Eubanks and Michael D. Mumford

Destructive leaders can cause hardship not only to immediate followers, but to the broader population. For example when a large company struggles financially, it is not only employees, but customers, suppliers, and shareholders that are negatively affected. The cognitive processes employed by the leader play a large role in how he or she gathers information, interprets it, and makes decisions toward a course of action. In this chapter, we offer a discussion of motives behind these destructive acts based on dispositional and situational influences. Previous research on violent leadership, leader errors, and leader responses to criticism will be incorporated in this discussion about cognitive processes and destructive leadership.

The influence of leaders may be felt within an organization or across boundaries and may endure long after they have left power. Leaders may act in ways that create changes in organizations or societies that facilitate prosperity or they may seek to change organizations or societies to promote their own personal agendas and move their inner circles toward advancement. Therefore, leaders have great potential for using their

When Leadership Goes Wrong: Destructive Leadership, Mistakes and Ethical Failures, pp. 23–47

power for positive or negative purposes (Strange & Mumford, 2002). In this chapter, we will explore dispositional and situational factors and their subsequent influence on cognitive processes that may allow a leader to act destructively. Dispositional factors include cognitive processes such as the manner that a leader gathers information, interprets it, and makes decisions to influence those around him or her. Situational factors include follower actions and the environment. In essence we will seek to explain under what conditions leaders behave destructively. These factors will be discussed using a model of leader cognition. Activities leaders engage in such as environmental scanning and monitoring models will be discussed along with how conditions for cognition can influence decisions made and actions taken. Throughout the chapter we will discuss the motives behind these destructive actions. Destructive actions can take many forms and exist at varying degrees so to start we must have a clear understanding of destructive leadership.

Defining Destructive Leadership

We will be using the definition by Illies and Reiter-Palmon (2008) who wrote that destructive leadership can be defined as "harming organizational members or striving for short term gains over long-term organizational goals" (p. 251). This definition was selected because the focus of this piece is on sustained destructive acts with profound implications rather than minor slip-ups. This definition is inclusive of those leaders who cause damage within organizations through fraud or deceit, leaders who engage in violent acts to harm people, and leaders who cause destruction through a series of bad decisions. Examples of destruction in the corporate world can be found among leaders like Kenneth Lay of Enron or Martha Stewart of Martha Stewart Living as the lure of quick financial gain led to negative outcomes. In the political arena destruction can be found in leaders such as Saddam Hussein who sentenced to death those around him that stood in his way (Karsh & Rautsi, 1991) and Joseph Stalin who sent his two sons and wife to death and sent his daughter and her child onto the street with no possessions (Tucker, 1990). The behaviors of leaders in these organizations and governments promote the short term gains versus long-term gains of the organization or government. Although this short sighted perspective may be to the detriment of the organization or society, it does not necessarily imply intent to be destructive. Nevertheless, regardless of intent, destructive outcomes can clearly result. It is the complex interaction of many dispositional and situational variables that can lead to these destructive outcomes. A framework for understanding the relationships between these variables can be found in the model of leader cognition. Through this model we can begin to understand how the interaction of dispositional and situational variables result in destructive actions taken by the leader.

MODEL OF LEADER COGNITION

The model of leader cognition described by Mumford, Friedrich, Caughron, and Byrne (2007) is helpful in explaining the ways that leaders process information and how this can be related to destructive acts. This model assumes that the way leaders think about crisis is externally driven, as these leaders are constantly scanning the environment for relevant information. The question remains then, in their scanning, how do leaders determine what information to attend to? According to the model of leader cognition, the search for information begins with environmental scanning in which leaders look for change events that are related to crises.

Environmental scanning is an activity that leaders frequently engage in to gather information relevant to their particular situation. While environmental scanning is a process driven by the leader, the information in existence is not within the leader's control. As described in the article on violent leadership by Mumford, Espejo et al. (2007), external factors play a large role in the tendency for leaders to act in a violent manner which is clearly an extreme form of destructive leadership. In this study, 80 historically notable leaders were assessed using academically based biographies written about them. Through this, comparisons were made between violent and nonviolent nonideological leaders, and violent and nonviolent ideological leaders. In this project researchers examined factors that might predispose ideological leaders to take violent action. Variables were assessed for leaders at individual, group, organization, and environmental levels. Results of this study indicated that when influence is based on the articulation of a distinct and powerful ideology and the leader has violent tendencies, destruction can occur. This is illustrated in examples such as Pol Pot who brought about the deaths of tens of thousands of people. We can observe similar, more recent destruction incited by Usama Bin-Laden. It is not only the individual characteristics that lead to destructive behavior, and may have some sort of intent associated with them. It is also of note that these characteristics interact with characteristics of the group, organization, and environment (Klein & House, 1998; Mumford, Dansereau, & Yammarino, 2000). The leader then interprets the information and reactions he or she gathers from the group, organization, and environment through scanning activities which make up the first component of the model for leader cognition.

Once environmental scanning activities have occurred, monitoring models provide an interpretation of information gathered through these multiple sources. Illies and Reiter-Palmon (2008) argued that values could play a role in how leaders view, perhaps unconsciously, the attractiveness of a destructive behavior. Values are then activated internally or from the environment to influence behavior (Williams, 1979). Mumford, Friedrich, Caughron, and Byrne (2007) described how information gathered will be influenced by the mental model that is being used. Past experiences and values could play a role in the mental model that is used. Once a mental model is activated, case-based or experiential knowledge will be accessed. Analysis of these cases then leads to the construction of a prescriptive mental model including an idealized image of operations relating to the current crisis (Mumford, Friedrich et al., 2007). As past experiences and values can play a role in mental models that are used, these experiences and values also influence leadership style. There are many ways to view and categorize a leader based on behaviors, traits, and skills, and describe positive and negative ways of behaving. While much attention has been drawn to the positive aspects of leadership, several researchers have also drawn attention to the negative aspects of leadership, particularly in the area of the dark side of charisma (Bass & Steidlmeier, 1999; Conger, 1989; Conger & Kanungo, 1998; Hogan, Raskin, & Fazzini, 1990; House & Howell, 1992; Kets de Vries & Miller, 1985; Mumford, Gessner, Connelly, O'Connor, & Clifton, 1993; O'Connor, Mumford, Clifton, Gessner, & Connelly, 1995; Sandowsky, 1995).

Leader styles. The theory of outstanding leadership described by Mumford (2006) states that leaders emerge when social systems are experiencing a crisis (Rivera, 1994). This theory is one related to sensemaking. It states that leaders differ in the ways that they cognitively process information and make sense out of these crisis situations and thus fall into different leadership styles. Subsequently, the manner that a leader responds to crisis events is particularly indicative of the leader's style (Mumford, 2006). The leadership styles described by Mumford are charismatic, ideological, and pragmatic. While much research has been conducted on charismatic leaders, less is known about ideological and pragmatic leaders. To provide a brief description, charismatic leaders have a future oriented vision and have a great deal of enthusiasm in their communication of a grand future. Researchers have found that charismatic leaders tend to make riskier decisions that can result in devastating consequences. The excessive optimism and enthusiasm held by charismatic leaders can make them blind to warning signs and reduce their ability to view situations objectively (Yukl, 2006). Similarly, followers may be in such awe of a charismatic leader that they also have reduced ability to view leader decisions and actions objectively (Finkelstein, 2003). Through this combination of variables, charismatic leaders may turn to the dark side leading their people into destructive situations because followers are convinced by the charismatic figure. The path to destruction may be unintentional in this type of instance as the leader may not necessarily have devious motives, but the outcome can still be devastating. Conversely, the leader may have devious motives and simply use his or her charisma to gather support for the destructive agenda. However, charismatic leaders are not the only leaders that can cause destruction.

Although much research has focused on charismatic leadership and the potential dangers associated with this style, recent research has shown that there are other styles that can cause dangerous outcomes, ideological in particular (Mumford, 2006). Ideological leaders have a vision that is past oriented. These visions are often tied to strong beliefs and values. When acting destructively, ideological leaders can use these strong beliefs and values to rally followers to a cause and marginalize those opposing their beliefs. It is this idea of marginalizing those in the outgroup and building a strong base around beliefs and values that can potentially incite violence. Lastly, pragmatic leaders do not have a vision. Rather they are focused on the present and the problem at hand. They have great insight into complex social systems and are able to bring together the right people to solve these complex problems (Mumford, 2006). The way that leaders make sense of information gathered based on their preexisting mental models, in turn influences the course of action selected. However, there is still a question of motive behind the actions.

Motives. Given that leaders may engage in destructive behavior as a result of applying preexisting mental models, the question may arise as to whether destructive behavior on the part of the leader is intentional or not. According to House and Howell (1992) there are two ways leaders can use their power motives. The first class of leaders act in a way that is personalized in nature and therefore they do not have the interests of humankind in mind. They are merely hoping to pursue agendas that will benefit them and their inner circles. Whether their actions result in positive outcomes for humankind is another matter. We argue that these leaders are somewhat intentional in bringing about destruction because the well-being of humanity is not a central interest. The second class of leaders are socialized in nature meaning they work for the greater good of society. This is not to say that these leaders never cause destruction, but the motive may be different. While their intentions may be noble, the outcomes may prove disastrous as a result of cognitive failures such as focusing on positive, simplistic, controllable causes while overemphasizing emotionally salient, short-term feedback (Dörner & Schaub, 1994). When cognitive failures such as this occur, decisions are made without thorough consideration of all the relevant information which can lead to a negative outcome.

Dispositional characteristics. According to House and Howell (1992) power motives are generally nonconscious, but not exclusively and are relatively stable dispositions. Leaders may act in a personalized manner working for their own self-aggrandizement or leaders may act in a socialized manner working towards the greater good of society. This may be attributed in part to expression of dispositional characteristics like narcissism, power motives, negative life themes, outcome uncertainty, and object beliefs (the belief that others could be used to help the leader achieve personal gain) (Mumford, 2006; Strange & Mumford, 2002). Motives can then be activated by a leader's beliefs about a situation (Binswanger, 1986; Locke, 1991). For example in the case of outcome uncertainty, leaders may have a predisposition to view ambiguous events and the associated uncertain outcomes as negative thus increasing attempts to act in controlling ways that allow them to engage in destructive behaviors (e.g. racist activities, discrimination against lower-class individuals, acceptance of acts committed by others against their opponents) (House & Howell, 1992). These dispositional characteristics in turn have been shown to predict aggression, damage done to individuals, and destruction caused to society (Mumford, 2006; Strange & Mumford, 2002). Baumeister (1996) points to egotism and sense of superiority as influences on destructive behavior. Last, Staub (1999), Ligon, Hunter, and Mumford (2008), and Sternberg (2003) have suggested that contributing factors to destructive leadership include tendency to devalue others, selectively processing information due to hate, and specific anchoring events or life experiences. Thus these dispositional characteristics may lead to destructive acts that would appear to be intentional.

Entering into this destructive style of leadership is not something that happens as a singular occurrence; rather it becomes a pattern of behavior for the leader because it is tied into his or her values and mental models constructed in his or her mental library. There is additional influence of tacit knowledge on leader performance in the formation of experiences that shape a leader's thoughts and actions (Mumford, Friedrich, Caughron, & Byrne, 2007). Therefore, once a leader has acted in a destructive manner, it is likely to reoccur if he or she is acting with intention because they are accessing those mental models that are tightly tied to their values. Their destructive actions and experiences may become part of their implicit knowledge, thus creating a reinforcing loop of destructive behaviors.

This idea of a consistent behavior pattern is congruent with the research conducted by Ligon, Hunter, and Mumford (2008) on developmental influences of outstanding leadership. In this paper, researchers reviewed

120 leader biographies to identify how similar life events may influence a leader's style (charismatic, ideological, or pragmatic) and power orientation (personalized or socialized). They found that contaminating events were observed more frequently in personalized leaders' biographies. Contaminating events are associated with disappointment and humiliation. These events are those that initially had emotionally positive attributes, but had negative downstream consequences (Ligon et al., 2008). An example of a contaminating event is when Carla Fiorina of Hewlett Packard, the only female CEO of a company in the Dow industrial average, was forced out after making a controversial deal to buy Compaq. While initially she was in the spotlight for holding this notable position, this focused attention turned negative when the Compaq deal was not the successful venture that was expected. Also, personalized leaders experienced *fewer* anchoring events that signal what is to be valued and avoided (Ligon et al., 2008) and would shape their belief systems. The result is a leader that has a weakly formed belief system with a fuzzy perception of what is to be valued and avoided. The discussion to this point has been of dispositional characteristics such as the environmental scanning activities employed, monitoring models, and the influence of leader style on decisions that are made. Next we will turn to situational factors to understand how contextual factors can play a role in destructive behavior.

Conditions for Cognition

It is not only dispositional variables that influence cognitive processes among leaders, it is also situational variables. Mumford, Friedrich, Caughron, and Byrne (2007) identified five conditions that are critical in influencing need for cognition among leaders. They are choice optimization, complexity and ambiguity, novelty, cognitive resource accessibility, and lack of social/structural support. The first, choice optimization is related to decisions a leader must make where one course of action will produce a different result than another course of action. The leader has some degree of discretion here in identifying the direction he or she deems appropriate. Although the leader determines what direction is appropriate, this does not necessarily imply intent if an unexpected result occurs. For example, a leader may choose a course of action that they believe will benefit the wider population, but the outcome could end up being negative. Conversely, a leader may choose a direction that will benefit a small group of people, but will add to the suffering of many more. Choice optimization can be illustrated by a study of response strategies used by leaders receiving criticism.

Regardless of whether a leader is intentionally or unintentionally destructive, followers also play a role in determining how a leader might proceed with his or her agenda. Leaders frequently encounter crisis situations where they must make controversial or unpopular decisions (Watkins, 2001). These decisions are often criticized as a result. Criticizing a leader is other people's way of attempting to prevent a leader from becoming destructive. This gives followers or others around the leader a chance to provide information to the leader and perhaps change his or her behavior. In effect, the more powerful a leader becomes, the greater his or her opportunity for widespread destruction.

It is during times of crisis or change events that leaders have significant opportunities for influence and impact. Therefore it is often during these crisis events that criticism of the leader may occur. These criticisms may help to direct or influence future actions or response strategies taken by the leader (Eubanks et al., 2010). These criticisms provide information to the leader that they may attend to when engaging in environmental scanning activities. In turn, decisions taken may change as a result of this information. The conditions created through these criticisms may shape a leader's tendency to act destructively in the future.

In a study looking at criticisms made toward leaders, researchers found that criticisms were sometimes able to direct a leader's behavior and sometimes were not (Eubanks et al., 2010). In some instances leaders were criticized on the same topic multiple times or by multiple people. This would be an example of when case-based knowledge about previous encounters would be activated in the model of leader cognition. Leaders may then choose to respond in the same or different manner as they previously had. If previous strategies were successful, they may take the same course of action the next time. However, if past strategies did not produce a desirable ending, they may search for alternative ways of handling the criticism.

Leaders and others around them may proceed through several different stages once the leader has been criticized (Eubanks et al., 2010). Once a hostile criticism has been directed at the leader, the leader appraises the criticism and determines the most appropriate course of action. Next, the leader responds to the criticism. Determining a response strategy illustrates choice optimization in the model of leader cognition. The leader's choice of response strategy was found to be critical to the follower perceptions of the leader as well as overall future success of the leader (Eubanks et al., 2010). The success of the leader was described from the leader's perspective meaning that the leader was able to continue forward with his or her agenda items and goals. However, this may not always be positive for followers. In fact, the continuation of the leader's goals may be detrimental to followers.

The following example from a biography about Nelson Mandela illustrates the path followed in the text leading through the criticism event. This particular passage describes his attempt to prevent the onset of civil war in South Africa (Meredith, 1997). The passage starts with a criticism from Black individuals claiming that Mandela was showing favoritism to the Whites over Blacks. Mandela somewhat ignored this criticism, believing that the grievances of Whites needed to be addressed first in order to facilitate a smooth transition. Therefore, after engaging in choice optimization, his response strategy was to ignore this criticism and focus on the Rugby World Cup tournament, which was generally ignored by Blacks. This was intentional as he knew that this new focus on rugby might be a way to build unity between the races. South Africans supported this response strategy and began to form a strong national identity for their team. They not only learned the words to the team song but chanted Mandela's name at the final game. When the South African team won, Blacks and Whites began celebrating together illustrating the national pride and united spirit that Mandela had created. While this provides one example, these criticism events fell into a variety of topic areas where others believed the leader was acting destructively, with a wide range of response strategies and reactions from others. The response strategy is a noteworthy element in the criticism event because it is this that most significantly influences the reactions of followers and the future success of the leaders as related to this issue being criticized. Therefore, the response strategy used by a leader can contribute to whether a destructive outcome occurs.

In the study of leader criticisms it was found that response strategies that initially appear positive may not always yield positive results (Eubanks et al., 2010). Specifically, it was found that response strategies related to a successful resolution of the criticism event included collaboration, confrontation, and diversion of attention. One would expect collaboration to yield positive results as this has been supported by past literature (Delerue, 2005; Hanson, 2006; and Malici, 2005). However, it was somewhat surprising to find that confrontation would be related to a successful resolution of the criticism event. Schütz (1998) found that when an opponent was attacked in a focused manner the person delivering the attack was perceived as competent. This provides an explanation for why a strategy of confrontation is related to a successful resolution of the criticism event. Interestingly, confrontation was negatively related to supportive reactions by others. It is apparent that others do not respond favorably to confrontation, but they are pleased with the end result that confrontation strategies are able to achieve. The relationship between diversion of attention and successful resolution of the criticism event exists because the critic was successfully distracted from the issue and the leader was able to successfully pursue his or her agenda. As leaders select the response strategy based on preexisting mental models, they clearly have some control here over the future course of actions and thus some intent is associated with the response strategy selected and the resulting outcome.

Followers do generally play a role in the actions of the leader as there was a relationship found between others' supportive reactions to the leader response and successful resolution of the criticism. Similarly, others' unsupportive reactions to the leader response was related to unsuccessful resolution of the criticism. Therefore, in the sample used in the study of leader criticisms by Eubanks et al. (2010) others were able to influence the leader's agenda based on their reactions to the leader's response to the initial criticism. It is noteworthy to mention that only leaders for which criticism events were documented in a biography were used in this study. Hence, leaders that were not criticized in biographies due to the time the leader was in power or cultural influences may not be held in check in the same manner as the leaders used for the study of leader criticisms. This poses an interesting point however in that there may be some leader's that remain unchecked, a condition making it easier for him or her to follow a path of destruction.

There are some leaders that do not respond well to criticism and take harsh action and immobilize their followers. For example, Saddam Hussein was intolerant of political dissidents. A joke or derogatory comment about the government and its' leadership could cost the critic his or her life. Less severe punishments included detainment or torture (Karsh & Rautsi, 1991). Interestingly during the Iran-Iraq War initially Saddam Hussein was not challenged by the military or politicians. When he was eventually challenged by the military, some 300 high-ranking officers were executed (Karsh & Rautsi, 1991). It is of note that this type of destruction and intolerance is rare.

Obviously Saddam Hussein exhibited destruction at a different level from Kenneth Lay and Martha Stewart. Therefore, it becomes clear that there are varying levels of destructive leadership. In essence conditions need to be perfectly in place for extreme destruction to occur. Although the behaviors on the part of Saddam Hussein are much more harsh and overt than the destructive influences of a CEO they can still be felt by many people. Some appear to have distorted morals and ethics while others engage in more minor ethical infractions or perhaps unintentionally pursue a path that leads to destruction.

In some instances those surrounding the leader are able to enact some degree of influence on the actions and decisions made by the leader. In the case of Stalin, he was somewhat kept in check by those surrounding him. For example when a district party secretary in Moscow wrote an appeal against Stalin, he sought to execute the man as a terrorist. The majority of those around Stalin opposed the action and managed to have the man's sentence reduced to a 10-year prison term. Stalin did eventually order the man killed as well as his wife and two sons. He was unsuccessful however in his demand that the death of this man should be recorded as an enemy to Stalin and the Revolution (Tucker, 1990). Although a small consolation, at least on that occasion, those around Stalin were able to push back against him and his destructive acts.

Choice optimization is just the first condition for cognition. Next, Mumford, Friedrich, Caughron, and Byrne (2007) identified complexity and ambiguity of the situation as influencing leader cognition. More complex and ambiguous situations increase the difficulty of anticipating the outcomes of an action and thus the importance of cognition increases (Uhl-Bien, Marion, & McKelvey, 2007). This has the potential to produce unintended negative consequences as errors could occur. These errors then can lead to destructive outcomes. Similarly, the degree of novelty of the situation, the third condition identified, also increases the importance of leader cognition (Mumford & Connelly, 1991). This is due to the alternative actions that must be generated and the evaluation of these alternatives (Mumford, Friedrich et al., 2007). The increased importance of cognitive activity makes errors and negative outcomes more likely to occur in novel situations.

Cognitive resource accessibility, the fourth condition for cognition identified (Mumford, Friedrich et al., 2007) is important for cognitive activities because there are many conditions that can take away resources such as stress (Reeves & Weisberg, 1994), time pressure (Runco, 2002), stretched cognitive carrying capacity (Sternberg, 2007), and role demands (Finkelstein, 2002) all of which are experienced by leaders. Deficiencies in cognitive resource accessibility could increase the likelihood of unintended negative outcomes which could lead to destruction.

Finally, social structure and the support of followers in particular their skill levels (Hersey & Blanchard, 1984) can compensate for poor leader cognition (Mumford, Friedrich et al., 2007). When there is a lack of social structure or support from those around the leader, cognition becomes increasingly important. Conversely, when followers are highly skilled and compensate for leader cognition, this cognition in effect becomes less critical (Hersey & Blanchard, 1984). If leaders do not have social structures in place to compensate for poor leader cognition, then errors are more likely to occur that could lead to destruction. These five conditions heavily influence the importance of leader cognition. When these conditions are not considered by the leader, decisions that are made can easily lead to destructive outcomes, although the result may be entirely unintended.

Cognitive Leader Errors

While in some instances, destruction may be intentional as seems to be the case with personalized leaders, leaders may not always have deviant intentions, regardless of attributions made toward them, and may be destructive without meaning to cause harm. However, the results can still be devastating. In this instance it may be that the leader has good intentions, but his or her goals are not reached. They are not necessarily deviant, rather they make errors. Cognition plays a central role in the performance of a leader (Mumford, Campion, & Morgeson, 2007). In the study on leader errors by Eubanks and Mumford (2010), researchers observed common cognitive errors and were able to identify that it is often what an individual is *not* focused on that leads to negative performance outcomes. As this is the case, it is important to realize the influence of being overly focused on a set of issues. This could come about by a leaders own obsession, environmental factors leading to heightened awareness of one particular issue (e.g., focusing on security issues while the economy falters), or focus being drawn to one issue due to continued criticism.

Often information is not evaluated as it should or could have been for a multitude of reasons ranging from dispositional to situational factors resulting in flawed cognitive processing activities which lead to errors being committed (Eubanks & Mumford, 2010). The definition of errors by Hunter, Tate, Dzieweczynski, and Cushenbery (this volume) is "an action or inaction, performed by a leader which results in undesired or unintended outcomes." From this definition we can interpret that some errors may influence performance more negatively than others. Eubanks and Mumford (2010) found that it is important to consider errors and work conditions in combination to realize the effects on performance. In essence it is the combination of work condition (e.g., excessive information, information falling outside general framework) paired with specific errors (e.g., failure to identify causes and goals, truncated information processing), that influences performance levels. If a leader continues to make the same error under the same work condition, depending on the combination, this could have a destructive influence on performance. The impact may initially be small and increase as the cumulative effect of errors is felt. While the devastating effects of these destructive influences can certainly be felt by followers, they may be unintentional. They may also form a pattern of behavior if the leader continues to find him or herself in the same work conditions and commit the same errors. In most instances, eventually organizational controls will come into play to remediate the situation. However other times this does not happen or happens too late, and the results are disastrous such as the case of Kenneth Lay and Martha Stewart mentioned earlier in the piece.

Past research on errors in creative thought has illustrated the hazards of relying solely on familiar causal relationships rather than conducting a more thorough information search. Causal models are useful when leaders are interpreting problems and making decisions. Creativity is also often used when solving complex problems. Several researchers have found that relying on familiar causal relationships when interpreting problems may lead to case based errors in creative thought (Blair & Mumford, 2007; Dailey & Mumford, 2006; Dörner & Schaub, 1994; Hogarth & Makridakis, 1981; Licuanan, Dailey, Mumford, 2007; Mumford, Blair, Dailey, Leritz, & Osburn, 2006; Woodman, Sawyer, & Griffin, 1993) resulting in unintended detrimental outcomes. The danger of relying on these familiar causal models is that while they are being attended to, information falling outside of the extant model will be discounted (Kuhn, 1970; Watkins, 1983). The effects can be destructive because leaders will not be considering all relevant information to make decisions. Experts in particular tend to have multiple well-structured exemplars from which to access relevant cases that can decrease the impact of new information. However, if exemplars are less well formulated, new information may have a stronger influence. This can therefore have a particularly profound effect on experienced leaders.

Leaders, particularly those that have advanced in their positions, are constantly handling vast quantities of information making cognitive resource accessibility particularly problematic. It is therefore understandable that leaders make errors that can lead to unintended outcomes. This can happen because cognitive shortcuts such as heuristics are used to overcome the limitations of working memory. These shortcuts allow a leader to recall personal experiences as they access information to build an interpretive framework (Hambrick, Finkelstein, & Mooney, 2005; Hambrick & Mason, 1984; Wright, 1974). Relying on these heuristics increases the likelihood that experts overlook new information in idea generation (Mumford, Blair, Dailey, Leritz, & Osburn, 2006) that may result in less comprehensive solutions and possible negative outcomes (Shah & Oppenheimer, 2008). The strategies leaders have learned to use as they process information as well as the work conditions the leaders experience when engaging in planning and decision-making activities may contribute to errors being made and subsequent negative performance outcomes. The negative performance from these errors committed may be unintentional on the part of the leader, but the decisions and actions can still be considered destructive and the results devastating.

Eubanks and Mumford (2010) measured performance outcomes when four types of cognitive errors occurred under four types of work conditions.

This was to determine under what types of conditions destructive outcomes may occur. The first type of cognitive error measured was when leaders showed reliance on known causal relationships that may not be relevant in the current setting. The second type of cognitive error was related to inaccurate framing of actions necessary to be successful as well as not understanding barriers to success. In essence, this error related to not understanding keys to success and barriers necessary to overcome. The third type of cognitive error measured was a disregard for relevant information falling outside of the interpretive framework of the leader. Leaders have a framework they use as they approach problems. If relevant information is excluded from this framework as they solve a problem the solutions will be incomplete as not all relevant factors are considered. This can result in an error. The last type of cognitive error measured was settling on the first relevant exemplar rather than engaging in an extended search of relevant cases. In this situation, not all information is thoroughly explored thus making the problem solution incomplete. As leaders often find themselves in different types of work conditions, there were also four experimental conditions where different work conditions were experienced. The first experimental condition was one in which work scenarios were presented emphasizing the relationship between causes and goals. This work condition was called *causal relationships*. The second experimental condition was one in which work scenarios were presented that emphasized the contingencies and restrictions present in a work setting. This work condition was called *understanding constraints*. In the third experimental condition, work scenarios contained additional information presented as an anomaly falling outside the core case framework. This work condition was called *incongruent information*. In the last experimental condition time pressure was induced and additional case information was provided in the work scenario. This work condition was called *processing overload*. The types of errors studied in this project varied in their level of impact on performance outcomes.

This study indicates that the error and work condition pairings that appear to be particularly detrimental to performance outcomes were the *understanding constraints* work conditions paired with errors related to reliance on known causal relationships, *processing overload* work conditions paired with errors related to settling on the first relevant exemplar, *irrelevant information* work conditions paired with errors related to inaccurate framing of contingencies and restrictions, and *causal relationships* work conditions paired with errors related to settling on the first relevant exemplar. All of the errors indicated a lack of intentionality in that the negative performance outcome was unintended. For this first combination, where understanding constraints were emphasized in work conditions, and errors were made where there was over-reliance on known causal relationships, intricate understanding of the situation is critical. In this work condition, not only will leaders need to understand what is required for success, but also what barriers are present. Errors related to reliance on known causal relationships where they may not be relevant, are particularly detrimental in this situation as cognitive capacity is already overwhelmed by work condition and therefore not understanding the relations between various elements of the situation will lead to negative performance outcomes. Social structure and having close advisors onboard that have an in-depth understanding of the issues involved may help to avoid these detrimental outcomes (Mumford, Friedrich et al., 2007).

Next, in work conditions where there is irrelevant information present and leaders have a poor understanding of what is required for success and barriers to success, negative performance outcomes occur. Once again, having competent advisors that can assist with sifting through this irrelevant information should help in reducing these negative outcomes. Last, in work conditions where causal relationships are emphasized and leaders make errors related to settling on the first relevant exemplar, there is a particularly negative influence on performance outcomes. This may be because cognitive capacity is taken up by focusing on the causal relationships present in the work condition and leaders truncate their information processing making rushed decisions that lead to negative performance outcomes. All of these negative performance outcomes can result in destructive leadership.

When working under conditions of processing overload or those emphasizing causal relationships, errors where leaders settled on the first relevant exemplar had the most detrimental effect on performance. These errors were consistently related to performance problems highlighting the dangers many leaders face in terms of committing errors. When leaders are working under conditions where they need to analyze causal relationships, capacity becomes restricted from the intense cognitive activity involved in synthesizing the information into a coherent form. Errors made by relying on the first relevant exemplar may be particularly damaging to performance in these situations because of mental fatigue. Solutions arrived upon are not as comprehensive or creative as they could be. However, errors that result from inaccurate framing of contingencies and restrictions proved most detrimental to performance when working in conditions where irrelevant information is present. Exceptional leaders may focus more naturally on contingencies and restrictions and this natural tendency is inhibited by thinking about irrelevant information. All of these situations illustrate how leaders' failed cognitive activities may cause destructive acts, but they are not intentionally carried out as they might be in other circumstances.

Additionally, Eubanks and Mumford (2010) found that not all leadership errors are created equally because there are some that have more of a negative impact on performance than others. Because errors have differential levels of influence on performance, it may be necessary to tolerate some types of error because they do not have the strong negative impact on performance that another type of error might, thus reducing the extent of destruction. However, when leaders make errors that reflect a restricted mental capacity, they tend to have a negative influence on performance regardless of work condition.

Last, from the leader error study it was found that it is important to realize what the leader is *not* focused on can cause performance problems. In general errors are made due to what leaders are *not* thinking about rather than what they *are* thinking about. When participants were in processing overload work conditions, errors related to inaccurate framing of contingencies and restrictions and over-reliance on known causal relations were committed most frequently. Additional time is necessary to engage in an adequate search and active analysis of cases which was not available in this time pressured work condition (Licuanan, Dailey, & Mumford, 2007). When these easily accessible more familiar causal relationships were not relevant, errors were made. Lastly, in processing overload work conditions leaders may not have the time to carefully assess restrictions to use in framing the problem. When there is insufficient time to correctly frame the problem, task performance suffers (Baughman & Mumford, 1995). This is an easy trap for leaders to fall into, for example focusing on increasing productivity levels while a competitor is developing a new and innovative product. The way that leaders process information and frame problems proves critical in the actions that they will take. While in the case of leader errors, negative outcomes are unintended, in the case of violent leaders, however, they are not concerned with the well-being of humanity and thus may cause destruction and devastation. However, both instances are influenced by cognitive processes and help us to understand the conditions under which leaders behave destructively.

Extreme Destructive Leadership

Although focusing solely on violence as a form of destructive leadership, the results of a study on violent ideological leaders provides information about the multi-level influences that shape a leader's tendency toward destruction in the extreme form (Mumford, Espejo, et al., 2007). These multi-level influences provide information that the leader must process after engaging in environmental scanning activities. A central finding of this study was that ideological leaders and their respective groups were particularly susceptible to violence although all types of leaders may become violent. Overall, Mumford, Espejo, et al. argued that ideological leaders may be particularly prone to destruction that may be intentional because their focus on shared values allows for the denigration of those who do not share those values. These values become activated by internal or external influences to drive behavior. These values then play a role in what mental model becomes activated during cognitive processing activities. This, in turn, can incite social violence (Fromm, 1973; Moghaddam, 2005; Staub, 1999). O'Connor, Mumford, Clifton, Gessner, & Connelly (1995) found that ideological leaders have a tendency to express uncertainty about outcomes and negative life themes because they reflect on failed case models when engaging in their search of relevant cases that can in turn promote destructive acts. The values described by ideological leaders can allow them to hold a sense of superiority allowing them to justify violent acts (Baumeister, 1996; Sternberg, 2003). Last, this sense of injustice coupled with a sense of superiority can lead ideologues to endorsing violent acts against those to be of lower status (Mumford, Espejo, et al., 2007).

There were three individual level functions that provided discrimination between violent ideological, violent nonideological, nonviolent ideological, and nonviolent, nonideological leaders. Functions at all levels (individual, group, organizational, and environmental) influence what a leader would attend to when engaging in environmental scanning activities and thus provide an understanding of the conditions under which a leader may act destructively. Additionally they will influence the mental model that is activated. Violent leaders regardless of strength of ideology scored high on *selective information processing* which included variables such as reality distortion, entitlement, low openness, information distrust, channeled social commitment, and selective interpretation of information (Mumford, Espejo, et al., 2007). This indicates how information the leader attends to can relate to violent actions. Nonviolent ideological leaders scored substantially higher on the function called *just world commitments* than nonideological leaders, or even violent ideological leaders perhaps to achieve some sort of abstract justice. Variables in this function included sensitivity to injustice, value crystallization, asceticism, negative life themes, and personal self sacrifice (Mumford, Espejo, et al., 2007). In this instance ideology would appear to be related to *just world commitments*. Violent and nonviolent ideological leaders displayed differences in scores on the function called *ideological extremism*. This function was comprised of interest in ideological material, information distrust, and exposure to ideological leaders. This indicates that extremism acts to facilitate violent ideologies (Mumford, Espejo, et al., 2007). These individual level functions indicate specific cognitive processes that can lead to destructive behavior and outcomes. Although these outcomes are clearly extreme examples of destructive leadership, there could certainly be radical or ideological leaders in organizations that would engage in nefarious behavior under the right circumstances.

To illustrate the multilevel nature of these influences, there were three group-level functions that exhibited discrimination between violent ideological leaders, violent nonideological leaders, nonviolent ideological leaders, and nonviolent, nonideological leaders. The function called *group insularity* comprised of group feelings of superiority, negative mental models, strong group boundaries, group rivalry, extensive socialization, and group exclusivity illustrates that violent leaders regardless of level of ideology scored higher on this function than non-violent leaders. This indicates that groups that are insular and in conflict with broader society are drawn to violence and violent leaders. The second group level function that yielded discrimination was *oppositional bonding*. This function made up of victimization, submergence of individuals, strong group affect, peer group influence, value based recruitment, and group sacrifice demonstrated higher scores for both violent and non-violent ideological leaders received higher scores for this function than non-ideological leaders regardless of level of violence (Mumford, Espejo, et al., 2007). This indicates that variables associated with *oppositional bonding* relate to levels of ideology rather than violence. The last group-level function demonstrating discrimination was *value-based identity*. This function was comprised of strength of group values, group feelings of superiority, victimization, and symbolism. Nonviolent ideological leaders received the highest scores on this function compared to all leaders, with nonideological violent leaders falling close behind. This may be due to the tendency of personalized charismatics to use symbolism to influence those around them (Mumford, 2006). These group level influences are related to information gathering activities and the cases that are activated. Considering group level variables certainly provides a more complete picture of the influencing variables on destructive behaviors.

There were also three functions discriminating among leader types at the organizational level. The first included *institutional sanctioning of violence* which was comprised of violence as a control, use of punishment as a control, and denigration of other institutions. The findings indicated that violent leaders regardless of level of ideology were found in organizations that condoned violence. The second function that discriminated among these leader types was *imposition of interpretive structures* which was made up of sense-breaking, sense-making, and centralization. As there were differences in the scores found between violent ideologues and violent nonideologues, this was interpreted this as meaning that extremist ideological organizations that are isolated engage in sense-breaking activities followed up by sense-making or providing new interpretive structures (Mumford, Espejo, et al., 2007). The third function showing discrimination was *value-based control.* This function was comprised of resource control and rewards for value convergence. Nonviolent ideological leaders received the highest scores on this function implying that nonviolent leaders of ideological organizations rely on shared cultural values as a method for directing followers (Mumford, Espejo, et al., 2007). These organizational level functions apply to the influence attempts employed by the leader. This is relevant because by having the right organizational systems in place, a leader can spread the destructive behavior throughout the organization.

When looking at the environmental functions, there were three found to discriminate among leader types. The first function was *corruption* which contained only one variable—violence as control that had higher scores for violent leaders than nonviolent leaders regardless of ideology. The second function, *social disruption,* containing the variables threats to traditional culture, globalization, and middle class marginalization was higher for ideological leaders than nonideological leaders regardless of levels of violence. This indicates that social disruption is related to the emergence of ideological leaders. These two functions in combination indicate that corruption coupled with social disruption could lead to the emergence of violent ideologues. In the last function, *economic difficulties* comprised of globalization, economic displacement, and loss of social institutions, non-violent ideological leaders received the highest scores. This indicates that non-violent ideological leaders tend to emerge when there is a search for improvements in the economy (Mumford, Espejo, et al., 2007). These environmental functions influence environmental scanning activities and information leaders attend to. Thus, it is important to understand how multilevel variables can influence destructive leadership behaviors. Although leaders cannot necessarily control their environment, the way that events are interpreted may be dispositional and the resulting destructive actions may be taken with intention. From this study on extreme destructive behavior we can see the dangers associated with violent ideological leaders.

When leaders are operating in stressful situations, as is often the case, they may have difficulty using schematic information leading them to turn to case-based or autobiographical information (Mumford, Friedrich et al., 2007). This knowledge from past experiences then allows a leader who has experienced perceived success to continue forward with the same successful policies or actions. When a leader has experienced the functions described above, the information they attend to in environmental scanning activities will differ along with the mental models they activate. This in turn will contribute to the destructive nature of their actions. This application of cases in a somewhat automatic manner results in less drain on cognitive resources (Charness & Schultetus, 1999; Mumford, Friedrich et al., 2007). If this continues to occur however, there may be a way to break this pattern. Perhaps this pattern of quick automatic processing will be broken when an extremely novel situation is encountered that cannot be linked with cases stored in the leader's library. In these instances, when leaders reflect on cases, they identify key elements, improve case indexing, and make note of any negative outcomes resulting from the case (Eliam & Shamir, 2005).

CONCLUSION

Before turning to the broader implications of these observations, we will note some limitations. First, the leaders discussed in this piece hold a high level of expertise in their particular domains allowing them to progress through the same cognitive framework. However, these observations would not necessarily apply to leaders at lower levels of organizations. The levels of expertise would not allow them to flow through this same cognitive framework. For example, a midlevel manager would not have the vast mental library of cases to be able to reference when facing a complex problem so this model of leader cognition may not be appropriate for them.

Second, little has been said about the leaders who appeared not to receive criticisms. In the study by Eubanks et al. (2010) we mentioned that there were leaders that appeared to not be criticized and therefore may go unchecked. However, leaders that do seem to have run amuck like Hitler were criticized. Therefore, the reactions of followers may not provide enough of a check on leaders. Similarly leaders that were not criticized such as Ataturk were not creating widespread destruction like Hitler. Therefore, while followers may have some influence on the actions of their leaders, the leader's morals and values, and environmental influences may provide more of a driving force for their actions.

Even considering these limitations, we believe the present effort has noteworthy contributions to our understanding of destructive leadership. First, this piece takes the view that while the actions of a leader may have the same destructive outcomes, the intent may differ based on whether the destructive outcome was one they actually wanted or if it was an unintended outcome, the result of leader errors. Ultimately it may not matter to the followers if the outcome was intentional or not if in both scenarios they are suffering or their lives are worse off as a result. Similarly, in both cases, intentional or unintentional destructive actions, the leader may continue to take the same destructive actions based on previous behavior. Although the reasons for this may be different based on whether actions are intentional or unintentional, the pattern will still exist. In the case of intentionally destructive behavior and power motives, leaders are shaped by early life experiences (Ligon, Hunter, & Mumford, 2008). Conversely, in the case of leader errors, if the work context remains the same and thought processes consistent, they are likely to continue experiencing the same destructive outcomes of their actions until disciplinary action is taken (Eubanks & Mumford, 2010).

Next, our observations about leader cognition prove noteworthy in that having poor cognitive processes will lead to destructive outcomes, but may be able to be compensated for by social systems in the form of close aides or advisors. Based on the level or type of difficulty the leader faces, these aides or advisors may require varying levels of involvement. This is particularly noteworthy given our understanding of destructive behavior becoming a pattern regardless of intent.

Emphasis has been placed on the importance of environmental scanning in leader cognition activities. As a starting point, this activity must take place with speed and frequency. We see the significant influence of external activities (group, organizational, and environmental) on leaders' actions. It is the combinations of specific variables at multiple levels that influence cognitive processing and can lead to devastating outcomes (Mumford, Espejo, et al., 2007).

Our hope is that realizing the path to destructive leadership may allow us to minimize its occurrence. While destructive leadership that occurs intentionally as a result of a twisted belief and value system may be more challenging to minimize, perhaps we could focus on minimizing the unintentional destructive actions that occur. Perhaps this could happen by sharing more responsibility with close colleagues in the leader's social system. By relieving some of the burden, leaders may be able to minimize the cognitive overloading that can occur. Additionally, by maintaining focus on multiple issues rather than becoming fixated on one, leaders are less likely to make errors leading to detrimental outcomes (Eubanks & Mumford, 2010). Keeping multiple issues at the forefront is therefore essential to minimizing the negative outcomes that can result from errors. While a range of distinctive dispositional and situational influences have been discussed in this piece, it is our hope that understanding the underlying cognitive processes underlying these behaviors can help to minimize these occurrences.

REFERENCES

Bass, B. M., & Steidlmeier, P (1999). Ethics, character, and authentic transformational leadership behavior. *The Leadership Quarterly, 10,* 181-217.

Baughman W. A., & Mumford, M. D. (1995). Process analytic models of creative capacities: Operations involved in the combination and reorganization process. *Creativity Research Journal, 8,* 37-62.

Baumeister, R. F. (1996). *Evil: Inside human cruelty and violence.* New York: W. H. Freeman/Times Books/Henry Holt.

Binswanger, H. (1986). The goal-directedness of living action. *The Objectivist Forum,* 7(4), 1-10.

Blair, C. S., & Mumford, M. D. (2007). Errors in idea evaluation: Preference for the unoriginal? *Journal of Creative Behavior, 41,* 197-222.

Charness, N., & Schultetus, R. S. (1999). Knowledge and expertise. In F. T. Durso (Ed.), *Handbook of applied cognition* (pp. 57-81). New York: Wiley.

Conger, J. A. (1989). *The charismatic leader.* San Francisco: Jossey-Bass.

Conger, J. A., & Kanungo, R. N. (1998). *Charismatic leadership in organizations.* Thousand Oaks, CA: SAGE.

Dailey, L., & Mumford, M. D. (2006). Evaluative aspects of creative thought: Errors in appraising the implications of new ideas. *Creativity Research Journal, 18,* 367-384.

Delerue, H. (2005). Conflict resolution mechanisms, trust and perception of conflict in contractual agreements. *Journal of General Management, 30,* 11-26.

Dörner, D., & Schaub, H. (1994). Errors in planning and decision-making and the nature of human information processing. *Applied Psychology: An International Review, 43,* 433-453.

Eliam, G., & Shamir, B. (2005). Organizational change and self-concept threats: A theoretical perspective and case study. *Journal of Applied Behavioral Science, 4,* 399-421.

Eubanks, D. L., Antes, A. L., Friedrich, T. L., Caughron, J. J., Blackwell, L. V., Avers-Bedell, K. E., et al. (2010). Criticism and outstanding leadership: An evaluation of leader reactions and critical outcomes. *The Leadership Quarterly, 21*(3).

Eubanks, D. L., & Mumford, M. D. (2010). Leader errors and the influence on performance: An investigation of differing levels of impact. *The Leadership Quarterly, 21*(5).

Finkelstein, S. (2002). Planning in organizations: One vote for complexity. In F. J. Yammarino & F. Dansereau (Eds.), *The many faces of multi-level issues* (pp. 73-80). Oxford, England: Elsevier Science/JAI Press.

Finkelstein, S. (2003). *Why smart executives fail.* London, England: Penguin Books.

Fromm, E. (1973). *The anatomy of human destructiveness.* New York: Holt, Rinehart & Winston.

Hambrick, D. C., Finkelstein, S., & Mooney, A. C. (2005). Executive job demands: New insights for explaining strategic decisions and leader behaviors. *Academy of Management Review, 30,* 472-491.

Hambrick, D. C., & Mason, P. (1984). Upper echelons: The organization as a reflection of its top managers. *Academy of Management Review, 9,* 193-206.

Hanson, M. P. (2006). Make-or-break roles in collaboration leadership. In S. Schuman (Ed.), *Creating a culture of collaboration: The International Association of Facilitators handbook* (pp. 129-148). San Francisco: Jossey-Bass.

Hersey, P., & Blanchard, K. H. (1984). *The management of organizational behavior* (4th ed.). Englewood Cliffs, NJ: Prentice-Hall.

Hogan, R., Raskin, R., & Fazzini, D. (1990). The dark side of charisma. In K. E. Clark & M. B. Clark (Eds.), *Measures of Leadership* (pp. 343-354). West Orange, NJ: Leadership Library of America.

Hogarth, R. M., & Makridakis, S. (1981). Forecasting and planning: An evaluation. *Management Science, 27,* 115-138.

House, R. J., & Howell, J. M. (1992). Personality and charismatic leadership. *The Leadership Quarterly, 3,* 81-108.

Illies, J. J., & Reiter-Palmon, R. (2008). Responding destructively in leadership situations: The role of personal values and problem construction. *Journal of Business Ethics, 82,* 251-272.

Karsh, E. & Rautsi, I. (1991). *Saddam Hussein: A political biography.* New York: Grove Press.

Kets de Vries, M. F. R., & Miller, D. (1985). Narcissism and leadership: An object relations perspective. *Human Relations, 38,* 583-601.

Klein, K. J., & House, R. J. (1998). *Further thoughts on fire: Charismatic leadership and levels of analysis.* In F. Dansereau & F. J. Yammarino (Eds.), Leadership: The multiple level approaches (Monographs in Organizational Behavior and Industrial Relations, Vol. 24, Part B, pp. 45-52). Greenwich, CT: JAI Press.

Kuhn, T. S. (1970). *The structure of scientific revolutions.* Chicago, IL: University of Chicago Press.

Licuanan, B. F., Dailey, L. R., & Mumford, M. D. (2007). Idea evaluation: Error in evaluating highly original ideas. *Journal of Creative Behavior, 41,* 1-27.

Ligon, G. S., Hunter, S. T., & Mumford, M. D. (2008). Development of outstanding leadership: A life narrative approach. *The Leadership Quarterly, 19,* 312-334.

Locke, E. A. (1991). The motivation sequence, the motivation hum, and the motivation core. *Organizational Behavior and Human Decision Processes, 50,* 288-299.

Malici, A. (2005). Discord and collaboration between allies: Managing external threats and internal cohesion in Franco-British relations during the 9/11 era. *Journal of Conflict Resolution, 49,* 90-119.

Meredith, M. (1997). *Nelson Mandela: A biography.* New York: St. Martin's Press.

Moghaddam, F. M. (2005). The staircase to terrorism: A psychological exploration. *American Psychologist, 60*(2), 161-169.

Mumford, M. D. (2006). *Pathways to outstanding leadership: A comparative analysis of charismatic, ideological, and pragmatic leadership.* Mahwah, NJ: Erlbaum.

Mumford, M. D., Blair, C. S., Dailey, L., Leritz, L. E., & Osburn, H. K. (2006). Errors in creative thought? Cognitive biases in complex processing activity. *Journal of Creative Behavior, 40,* 75-109.

Mumford, T. V., Campion, M. A., & Morgeson, F. P. (2007). The leadership skills strataplex: Leadership skill requirements across organizational levels. *The Leadership Quarterly, 18,* 154-166.

Mumford, M. D., & Connelly, M. S. (1991). Leaders as creators: Leader performance and problem solving in ill-defined domains. *The Leadership Quarterly, 2,* 289-316.

Mumford, M. D., Dansereau, F., & Yammarino, F. J. (2000). Followers, motivations, and levels of analysis: The case of individualized leadership. *The Leadership Quarterly, 11,* 313-341.

Mumford, M. D., Espejo, J., Hunter, S. T., Bedell-Avers, K. E., Eubanks, D. L., & Connelly, S. (2007). The sources of leader violence: A comparison of ideological and non-ideological leaders. *The Leadership Quarterly, 18,* 217-235.

Mumford, M. D., Friedrich, T. L., Caughron, J. J., & Byrne, C. L. (2007). Leader cognition in real-world settings: How do leaders think about crisis? *The Leadership Quarterly, 18,* 515-543.

Mumford, M. D., Gessner, T. L., Connelly, M. S., O'Connor, J. A., & Clifton, T. C. (1993). Leadership and destructive acts: Individual and situational influences. *The Leadership Quarterly, 4,* 115-147.

O'Connor, J. A., Mumford, M. D., Clifton, T. C., Gessner, T. E., & Connelly, M. S. (1995). Charismatic leaders and destructiveness: An historiometric study. *The Leadership Quarterly, 6,* 529-555.

Reeves, L. M., & Weisberg, R. W. (1994). The role of content and abstract information in analogical transfer. *Psychological Bulletin, 115,* 381-400.

Rivera, J. B. (1994). *Visionary versus crisis-induced charismatic leadership: An experimental test.* Unpublished doctoral dissertation, Texas Tech University, Lubbock.

Runco, M. A. (2002). Creative and critical thought. *Inquiry: Critical Thinking Across Disciplines, 22,* 31-37.

Sandowsky, D. (1995). The charismatic leader as narcissist: Understanding the abuse of power. *Organizational Dynamics, 24*(4), 57-71.

Schütz, A. (1998). Audience perceptions of politicians' self-presentational behaviors concerning their own abilities. *The Journal of Social Psychology, 138,* 173-188.

Shah, A. K., & Oppenheimer, D. M. (2008). Heuristics made easy: An effort-reduction framework. *Psychological Bulletin, 134,* 207-222.

Staub, E. (1999). The roots of evil: Social conditions, culture, personality, and basic human needs. *Personality & Social Psychology Review, 3,* 1790-192.

Sternberg R. J. (2003). A duplex theory of hat: Development and application to terrorism, massacres, and genocide. *Review of General Psychology, 7,* 299-328.

Sternberg, R. J. (2007). A systems model of leadership: WICS. *American Psychologist, 62,* 34-42.

Strange, J. M., & Mumford, M. D. (2002). The origins of vision: Charismatic versus ideological leadership. *The Leadership Quarterly, 13,* 343-377.

Tucker, R. C. (1990). *Stalin in power: The revolution from above 1928-1941.* New York: W. W. Norton.

Uhl-Bien, M., Marion, R., & McKelvey, B. (2007). Complexity leadership theory. Shifting leadership to the knowledge era. *The Leadership Quarterly, 18,* 298-318.

Watkins, P. R. (1983). Decision maker preferences for information in complex decision making: New directions for operations research interventions. *European Journal of Operational Research, 14,* 288-295.

Watkins, M. (2001). Principles of persuasion. *Negotiation Journal, 17,* 115-137.

Williams, R. M., Jr. (1979). Change and stability in values, value systems: A sociological perspective. In M. Rokeach (Ed.), *Understanding Human Values* (pp. 47-70). New York: The Free Press.

Woodman, R. W., Sawyer, J. E., & Griffin, R. W. (1993). Towards a theory of organizational creativity. *Academy of Management Review, 18,* 293-321.

Wright, P. (1974). The harassed decision maker: Time pressures, distractions, and the use of evidence. *Journal of Applied Psychology, 59,* 555-561.

Yukl, G. (2006). *Leadership in organizations* (6th ed.). Upper Saddle River, NJ: Prentice-Hall.

CHAPTER 3

THE ENVIRONMENT OF DESTRUCTIVE LEADERSHIP

Paul W. Mulvey and Art Padilla

In this chapter we focus on the environments of organizations that give rise to destructive leadership. We refer to previously developed frameworks of toxic leadership (Padilla, Hogan, & Kaiser, 2007; Padilla & Mulvey, 2008a). From an environment perspective we use an organization ecology framework, which focuses away from positional leaders and emphasizes the importance of the interplay among leader and followers on the one hand, and contexts on the other. A comprehensive review of the leadership literature demonstrates that a small portion of published articles assess the context of leadership (Porter & McLaughlin, 2006) and an even smaller proportion looks beyond the bounds of the organization. We present propositions to develop more fully an existing model of destructive leadership (Padilla & Mulvey, 2008b). Finally, we discuss the benefits and challenges of such an approach to the study of leadership and suggest avenues for further study and research.

When Leadership Goes Wrong: Destructive Leadership, Mistakes and Ethical Failures, pp. 49–71

INTRODUCTION

This chapter considers organizational contexts of destructive leadership using a comprehensive or organizational ecology approach. While the phrase is somewhat polemical, by "organizational contexts" we mean to include the environments, circumstances, and conditions within which the process of destructive leadership and followership takes place. The chapter adds to a growing research stream focusing on the broader leadership process rather than on leaders exclusively or primarily (see also Mumford et al., 2007; Padilla et al., 2007). We begin with a discussion of the organization ecology and systems perspectives as a framework for a more comprehensive approach. This is followed by an examination of five specific environmental elements: (1) checks and balances (both external and internal to the organization); (2) organizational complexity; (3) instability and dynamism; (4) perceived threat; and (5) cultural values. Given the recent global financial collapse, we devote special attention to the absence of checks and balances, including (a) the external elements of the media, experts and expert field, and government agencies and (b) the internal elements of governance and executive pay structures. We conclude with a discussion of the benefits of a more comprehensive approach to the study of leadership and directions for future inquiries. We make two additional points. First, only by including organizational contexts is a deeper and more sophisticated understanding of leadership processes possible. Second, destructive leadership cannot be understood without a full examination of the entire leadership process, and particularly the institutional and organizational crucibles within which it exists.

Humans are primarily social creatures. They associate and connect with others within the context of societies, institutions, and traditions that have evolved slowly over decades and even centuries. Leadership is a process that involves a leader, a group of followers, and the organizational settings where the leader-follower interactions occur. Most definitions of "leadership" appreciate these relationships (e.g., Burns, 1978; House et. al., 1999; Yukl, 2010). The problem is not that the definitions are very different from one another or that they exclude followers and organizational contexts. The problem appears to be that most quantitative research disregards the comprehensiveness of the definitions: Porter and McLaughlin (2006) estimate that three out of every four empirical articles ignore followers and organizational contexts, focusing instead on leader behaviors and traits. We attempt to address the organizational contexts specifically in the following pages.

The leader-centric emphasis of research seems related to three factors. One is a fascination with leaders, particularly toxic ones associated with destructive results (Burns, 1978). A second one is a popular conception of leadership that looks to the top of organizations and political structures for answers to organizational problems. However, a focus on leaders neglects the environment in which these organizations and social structures exist (Heifetz, 1994; Kellerman, 2007; Meindl, Erhlich, & Dukerich, 1985; Pfeffer, 1977; Pfeffer, 1981; Pfeffer & Salancik, 1978; Salancik & Meindl, 1984). In the related area of organizational behavior (OB), many have suggested that scholars ignore the "O" and emphasize the "B," thus discounting organizational environments and contexts that define behaviors (e.g., Cappelli & Sherer, 1991; Ilgen & Klein, 1988; Mowday & Sutton, 1993; O'Reilly, 1991). A third factor might be more important: simultaneous analysis of leaders, followers, and organizational environments is both difficult and problematic (Meindl, 1995). Nonetheless, leadership research from a broader or systems perspective seems to be on the rise in the literature (e.g., Antonakis, Cianciolo, & Sternberg, 2004; Boal & Hooijberg, 2000; Kelly, Ryan, Altman, & Stelzner, 2000; Padilla et al., 2007; Porter & McLaughlin, 2006).

THE ORGANIZATION ECOLOGY AND SYSTEMS PERSPECTIVES

Organizational ecology borrows from the process of natural selection in biology (Hannan & Freeman, 1977, 1984). The theory focuses on explaining the diversity of organizational forms and the survival and failure of organizations at the population level (Hannan, 2005). Rather than focusing on the leader and organization's ability to adapt or learn to explain the survival or failure of an organization, population ecology examines organizational survival through selection. A key feature explaining resistance to change is that most organizations have structural inertia that hinders adaptation when the environment changes. Within a population of organizations, environmentally incompatible organizations are eventually replaced through competition with organizations better suited to external conditions (Hannan & Freeman, 1977).

Systems theory is a complementary framework that gives greater attention to the environment in which organizations exist. Theorists in this vein include Lewin (1943), Katz and Kahn (1966), Weick (1979), and Senge (1990). Their approaches emphasize feedback loops from and interrelationships with the environment rather than the specific elements of the system. In contrast to organizational ecologists, systems theorists argue that organizations and leaders of those organizations have the ability to adapt and learn, subsequently influencing outcomes.

Unfortunately, neither leadership nor toxic leadership (i.e., leadership situations where leader, followers, and environments combine to produce negative or destructive outcomes for the group or organization (see

Padilla et al., 2007) has been thoroughly explored from ecological or systems perspectives (Wielkiewicz & Stelzner, 2005). In the related area of ethics, Ashforth, Gioia, Robinson, and Trevino (2008) propose that:

> we need a considerably more holistic or dynamic understanding regarding the interplay of environmental, organizational, and individual forces—that is, a more macro view—to help us understand the etiology and evolution of corruption. (p. 673)

In taking a broader, more comprehensive perspective, we assume that leadership is not a person. Leadership exists as a process occurring within a broad social system with followers in an organizational setting and a larger contextual environment. This process leads to consequences, and those consequences or results are either good or bad for the team, organization, or nation. Most leadership situations are neither perfectly good nor perfectly bad (Padilla et al., 2007). Most tend to fall in the middle of a continuum that ranges from clearly destructive on the one hand to mostly positive on the other. Toxic leadership situations leading to destructive outcomes leave the organization worse off relative to its rivals.

We posit that the environment can overwhelm "good" leaders and "good" followers so much so that destructive outcomes can result. Upper echelon theory, as revised, coincides with this perspective. The revision of upper echelon theory, originally proposed by Hambrick and Mason (1984), reconciles the opposing leadership and population ecology perspectives by noting both are possible as the amount of managerial discretion will vary from situation to situation (Hambrick, 2007; Hambrick & Finkelstein, 1987). We concur with this position and expand upon it in discussing the environment of destructive leadership.

The Environment of Destructive Leadership

Examining the notion of toxic leadership, Padilla et al. (2007) noted that four universal environmental factors are important for destructive leadership: absence of checks and balances and institutionalization, instability and dynamism, perceived threat, and cultural values. In this chapter we extend this perspective by exploring these and related factors. We formulate propositions embedding them within a more comprehensive destructive leadership model developed by Padilla and Mulvey (2008a, 2008b). Due to space limitations, we do not discuss in great detail the characteristics and behaviors of followers, or the way in which environments affect followers and vice versa. But clearly susceptible followers are indispensable in the toxic triangle (toxic leaders, susceptible followers, and conducive environments) that leads to destructive outcomes. The propositions that follow are represented in Figure 3.1. We assume that toxic leader and follower behavior mediates the relationship between environmental factors and destructive outcomes for the organization (Padilla et al., 2007; Padilla & Mulvey, 2008a).

(1) CHECKS AND BALANCES

Our general proposition is that weak or ineffective organizational settings and institutions further isolate leaders from outside scrutiny and oversight and encourage toxic leader and follower behavior specifically, and the process of destructive leadership, generally. An important consideration is the extent to which central power is "checked" by controls and influence from other internal and external organizational sources. Managerial discretion in the management literature (Crossland & Hambrick, 2007; Finkelstein & Hambrick, 1990), or the notion of presidentialism from political science (Linz, 1994; Mainwaring & Scully, 1995), concern the degree to which senior managers or government executives are insulated from the supervision and influence of others. It refers to centralization of decision making

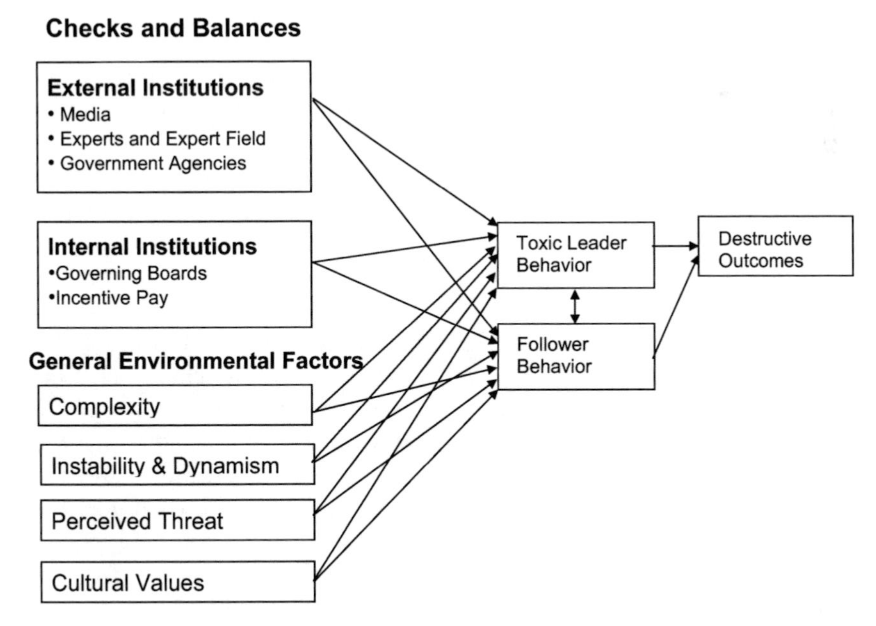

Figure 3.1. Environmental influences on toxic leader and follower behavior and destructive outcomes.

and independence from institutional guidelines. Certain follower characteristics, (e.g., a culture of dependence, poverty, low levels of education) often contribute to or exacerbate tendencies toward centralization of power (Padilla et al., 2007).

Centralized governing structures stand in sharp contrast to organizational environments with empowered followers and with effective institutions that share authority and responsibilities. There is an interesting paradox here: the stronger and more autonomous the central authority, the less empowered and influential the followers and the less effective the organizational controls. Put differently, destructive organizational consequences are mitigated if the leader gives up control and decision autonomy and shares power with followers and organizational processes. Next, we discuss three external checks and balances to the organization: the media and expert field, and government agencies. This is followed by an examination of internal checks and balances. We suggest that factors related to the board's composition and its governing structure will likely influence the emergence of destructive leadership. The backdrop of the financial crisis and related scandals during 2008 in the United States and Europe provide the basis for our discussion of checks and balances.

(1a) External Influences

The Media. The earliest use of the term "fourth estate" in reference to the press or media is found in Thomas Carlyle's (1894) book, *On Heroes and Hero-Worship and the Heroic in History,* the same book that introduced the "Great Man" theory. The notion of the media as the fourth estate (the other "estates," in a more modern interpretation, are the legislative, judicial, and executive branches) rests on the idea that the media's function is to act as a guardian of the public interest and a watchdog of government and industry.

Depending on one's view, this is either an expedient myth promoted by the media industry or an important component of the checks and balances that form part of modern democracies. Authors of the U.S. Constitution apparently believed the press was powerful and independent enough to provide balance to the three branches of government. Freedom of the press (along with freedom of religion and speech) is clearly written into the U.S. Constitution in its First Amendment. Early in their regimes totalitarian rulers will attempt to abolish or significantly limit the freedom of the press as a way to strengthen central power and control. This was the formulaic pattern for Lenin, Mao, Castro, and, more recently in Latin America, with Chavez and Morales (Padilla et al., 2007).

Media such as newspapers, magazines, and television remain popular and fairly reliable sources of information in the West. The print media has held significant power during the last century over public opinion and has indeed served as an important check for misguided, unlawful, and toxic leadership. Many political and organizational scandals have been exposed first in newspapers. For instance, the Watergate scandal in the United States was initially reported in and extensively followed up in the *Washington Post* (Woodward & Bernstein, 1972). Additionally, the Hewlett Packard spying scandal was exposed by investigative reporters from *Newsweek* magazine (Kaplan et al., 2006).

Although there is ample evidence the media still wields significant influence over destructive leaders and on the process of destructive leadership, the industry is in decline. Between 2001 and 2008, daily circulation for newspapers has declined 8.4% and 11.4% in Sunday circulation. Between November 2004 and November 2005, ratings for the nightly news fell 6% and share fell 3%. That is an acceleration of the pace of decline in recent years. It translates into overall viewership on the three commercial nightly newscasts of 27 million viewers, or a decline of some 1.8 million viewers from November 2004. From the start of *CNN* in 1980, nightly news viewership for the Big Three networks has fallen by some 25 million, or 48% (The State of the News Media, 2008). The media also suffers from a loss of reporters, reduced budgets, and decreased column inches committed to the news (The State of the News Media, 2008). Reaching the public has been become much more difficult as potential audiences continue to fragment their attention among radio, television, the Internet, and print media. For example, the radio industry has several new technology platforms including satellite radio, Internet radio, HD radio, podcasts, MP3/iPod listening, and cell phone radio (The State of the New Media, 2008). While over the longer run, other forms of information will surely emerge, in the short run it is difficult to imagine how the coverage of local and state governments will fare in the absence of reporters who are assigned those "beats."

Blogs (a shortening of "Web logs") and other Internet-based sources of information are on the ascendancy. Some coordinated efforts using the Internet have had significant results and have affected the stories covered by the mainstream media. When Verizon tried to censor NARAL's (National Abortion Rights Action League) use of text messaging in 2007, quick action by "Save the Internet" led Verizon to reconsider its position and led to FCC hearings. But these new forms of information cannot yet duplicate, for example, the armies of lifelong correspondents who cover, for instance, the White House or the Asian economies. Some blogs have emerged as reliable information sources in some specialist areas, but they have yet to assume the key characteristics of mainstream news that drive public trust, such as accepted standards, editing, and reliability (Gunter, Campbell, Touri, & Gibson 2009). As Coleman (2005) notes:

> If there are democratic claims to be made for the Internet, their realization is closely linked to the capacity of ordinary people to enter, shape, and govern it to a greater extent than with any previous communication medium. It is as an extension of media freedom that blogging should be taken seriously. (p. 289)

Trends of decline and uncertain influence are disturbing because they might impair efforts to warn about and rein in destructive leadership. In the past, when the media have highlighted aspects of destructive leadership, there has been a salutary effect, at least temporarily, on further destructive leadership. For example, executive turnover in U.S. firms was greater where the *Wall Street Journal* reported fraud or lawsuit than in matched firms where fraud or lawsuits were not reported (Zhang, Bartol, Smith, Pfarrer, & Khanin, 2008). The Enron revelations resulted in well-known U.S. legislative initiatives such as Sarbanes-Oxley, which limit and modify certain organizational and accounting practices. Despite different methods of analyses, another study found that the media significantly influences perceptions about the effectiveness or ineffectiveness of leaders and of leadership when organizational performances are either very good or very bad (Meindl et al., 1995).

However, when the media does not report on experiences of destructive leadership or when it looks the other way, further destructive behaviors by the leader ultimately leading to toxic outcomes may be encouraged. The former Governor of New York, Elliott Spitzer, is a case in point. Strassel (2008) observed that the "press corps acted as an adjunct of Spitzer power, rather than a skeptic of it" (p. A21). The media colluded with Spitzer by not providing the needed level of checks and balances: *Time* magazine had named Spitzer "Crusader of the Year;" *Atlantic Monthly* fulsomely referred to Spitzer as a "rock star;" and the *Washington Post* compared him to Teddy Roosevelt (Strassel, 2008).

Experts and Expert Field. The media often use pundits or experts to comment or translate in simpler terms business, scientific, and political events. The use of expert sources by the media is done for three reasons: to add credibility to news reports; to provide facts and verify findings; and to enhance objectivity. However, research indicates that the public is less trustful of expert sources, at the very same time that the media's influence is more fragmented and waning in importance (Boyce, 2006). Nonetheless, we agree the media remains a powerful "check and balance," even if its expert sources might increasingly be perceived as partisan: a decline in the influence and impact of the media will be associated with greater toxicity.

Proposition 1: A weaker media industry, including the print media and television, as a component of the environment, will be associated with higher levels of toxic leader behaviors.

Government Agencies. The government entities that regulate business activities in the United States include agencies such as the Securities and Exchange Commission (SEC), Federal Deposit Insurance Corporation (FDIC), the Federal Trade Commission (FTC), the Federal Reserve Board (Fed) and its 12 districts, the Office of the Comptroller of the Currency, the Office of Thrift Supervision, and the National Credit Union Administration. At the state level, state regulatory agencies supervise banks in states in which they were chartered. There are three issues regarding these agencies: the nature and speed of changes, the fractured nature of government regulation, and insufficient funding. Technology and product innovation have created pressures for regulators. New financial instruments, such as derivatives and credit default swaps, and increased speed in the movement of financial products within and across national boundaries, have caused serious challenges for regulators and legislators. Many regulators did not appreciate the speed of change and complexity of new products (Siskey & Fournier, 2008). Many of these agencies have pointed to a lack of sufficient funding and authority to accomplish their missions (although conservative critics might argue that government agencies are naturally ineffective and unnecessary).

First, the U.S. financial regulation system is unusually splintered compared to the other G10 countries. Other G10 nations usually have one major regulatory agency whereas the list in the U.S. is long and jurisdiction may be somewhat unclear. The U.S. government is currently seeking solutions to streamline and strengthen its regulatory system (Hitt, 2009). A splintered regulatory system requires significant cooperation among the responsible agencies to coordinate activities and possibly prevent destructive leadership outcomes.

Second, a pattern of understaffed, underfunded, and inept government regulatory government agencies has been evident in several recent financial industry toxic events in the United States. The current state of the financial industry is evocative of the savings and loans scandals of the late 1980s, although the current crisis seems to be on a much larger scale. For example, Seidman (1997) noted in the 1980s and 1990s banking problems were primarily, but not exclusively, the result of unsound real estate lending. The changes introduced in the Tax Reform Act of 1986, the FDIC increasing its insurance coverage to $100,000, and allowing the S&L firms to expand their business practices all contributed to unsound lending. John G. Medlin, Jr., former CEO of Wachovia Corporation, argued:

> Part of the problem back in the 80s was that they had the tremendous inflow of money burning a hole in their pocket and they went out and lent it, unfortunately, not very wisely. (Federal Deposit Insurance Corporation, 1997b, p. 106)

The savings and loan banks, which were either marginally capitalized or insolvent, took on:

> high-risk ventures that ultimately increased losses to the thrift insurance fund, and it is widely believed that ineffective monitoring and supervision, as well as the regulators, inability to close insolvent thrifts due to inadequate funds, permitted them to do so. (Federal Deposit Insurance Corporation, 1997a, p. 439)

When the dot-com bubble burst in 2001, the SEC staff was about 3,000. SEC chief accountant, Lynn Turner, noted that even if the SEC doubled its staff to 6,000, it may not be enough to keep up with the fraud investigations ("Can underfunded," 2002). Even if there were enough regulators for the U.S. government agencies, the current administration is having difficulty filling positions. For example, as of April, 2009 only one of the Treasury's 15 senior-level staff positions had been filled ("Heavy vetting," 2009).

Ineptitude by the SEC might be partly behind the financial fiasco caused by Bernie Madoff's elaborate Ponzi scheme. In his recent testimony to the U.S. House of Representatives Committee on Financial Services, financial investigator Harry Markopolos (2009) illuminated shortcomings of "regulatory structures, procedures, and institutions in place to prevent such crimes and is the subject of this hearing" (p. 1). Markopolos first provided evidence to the SEC's Boston regional office about Madoff almost nine years prior to his testimony in the U.S. Congress. This evidence, Markopolos felt, should have triggered an SEC investigation of Madoff's activities (Markopolos, 2009). During the nine intervening years, Markopolos noted that he feared for his life and that there was an "abject failure by the regulatory agencies we entrust as our watchdog" (p. 1).

Proposition 2: The weaker government regulation is, as a component of the environment, the higher the levels of toxic leader behavior.

Proposition 3: The greater the number of overlapping government agencies, as a component of the environment, the higher the levels toxic leader behavior.

(1b) Internal Influences

Governing Boards. Although performance reviews of corporate boards are on the rise (Lawler & Finegold, 2005), corporate boards are seldom examined in a systematic and effective way (Conger, Finegold, & Lawler, 1998). Lack of oversight by board members leads to poor performance and decisions (Schnatter, 2008). A formal separation of the CEO and chair of the board positions may have an influence on destructive leadership (Padilla & Mulvey, 2008b). Members of boards may lack the independence or are disinclined to take action when faced with destructive leaders or their poor decisions. For example, Persons (2006) found that organizations charged with fraud or a lawsuit were less likely remove the CEO when the CEO also shared the board chairman position. In contrast to the United States, separate CEO and chair positions are now common practice in Europe (i.e., Dahya & Travlos, 2000; Kakabadse, Kakabadse, & Barratt, 2006). A recent study found that the same person shared the CEO and chair roles in 80% of U.S. firms while 90% of U.K. firms divided these roles ("So, are," 2006).

The composition of the board members also seems to have an influence on the likelihood of corporate malfeasance (Beasley, 1996; Mintz, 2006). Several studies have found that firms without fraud have boards with significantly higher percentages of outside members (i.e., those who are not affiliated with the organization) than firms where fraud had occurred (Beasley, 1996; Uzun, Szewczyk, & Varma, 2004). The probability of fraud decreases with greater outside director ownership and longer board member tenure on the board (Beasley, 1996). Additionally, Beasley, Carcello, Hermanson, and Lapides (2000) found that companies committing fraud had weaker governance mechanisms characterized by fewer audit committees, fewer independent audit committees and boards, and fewer audit committee meetings.

Governing boards attempt to influence top management behavior with incentive systems, although these attempts may have unintended consequences. For example, during economic downturns, CEO incentive pay and poor corporate performance increase the likelihood of financial misrepresentation (Agrawal & Chadha, 2005; Harris, 2008; O'Connor, Priem, Coombs, & Gilley, 2006). To counter this toxic leader behavior, the SEC is pursuing legal action against a few of these leaders with a rarely used section of the 2002 Sarbanes-Oxley Act, Section 304. The SEC is trying to prevent corporate leaders from defrauding shareholders while at the same time receiving sizeable incentives and selling stock (Ryan, 2009). Furthermore, although misrepresentation depresses future organizational performance, these negative effects are alleviated by CEO replacement and increased board independence (Harris, 2008). The damage may not be limited, however, to the offending organization. Kang (2008) found that "interlocked" board members of an organization charged with fraudulent behavior (board members sitting on multiple corporate boards) had negative effects on the stock price of the nonfraudulent organization.

Proposition 4: A governance structure that combines the CEO and Chair of the Board positions will be associated with higher levels of toxic leader behavior.

Proposition 5: The greater the proportion of inside board members, the higher levels of toxic leader behavior.

Proposition 6: The greater use of incentive pay during a downturn in corporate performance, the higher levels of toxic leader behavior.

GENERAL ENVIRONMENTAL FACTORS

Moving from the external and internal checks and balances in the environment, we now review general environmental factors. We propose these factors also have an influence on the emergence and duration of destructive leadership. We expand on those factors first proposed by Padilla et al. (2007). They include complexity, instability and dynamism, perceived threat, and cultural values.

Complexity. The complexity of the environment refers to the number and diversity of factors and relevant issues facing an organization (Child, 1972). More complex organizational environments present leaders and top management teams with large amounts of information (Child, 1972), implying greater demands on management to process this often conflicting information (Wiersema & Bantel, 1993). Organizations in newer or fast-cycle industries with greater technological innovation tend to have more complex environments (Castrogiovanni, 2002). Organizations in such circumstances tend to respond with increased differentiation and specialization (Dooley & Van de Ven, 1999; Pfeffer & Salancik, 1978). Fleming and Zyglidopoulos (2008) argue that this environmental complexity also allows unethical behavior to escalate because the added complexity creates lower transparency by greater segmentation of tasks and roles and subsequently greater possibility for destructive leadership to flourish (Baucus & Near, 1991; Fleming & Zyglidopoulos, 2008).

In the most recent financial debacle, Kaufman (2007) maintains that the Federal Reserve and Treasury failed in several regards to keep pace with the complexity in the financial markets. Specifically, they failed in three areas: in developing solutions limiting financial excesses; in staying current with the transformation of the markets; and in failing to understand and price new credit instruments.

Proposition 7: The greater the complexity of the environment, the higher the levels toxic leader behavior.

Instability and Dynamism. Toxic leadership is more likely to emerge in times of instability in the social, organizational, or political environment. During unstable times, leaders are better able to increase their power and control. Several authors argue, for example, that leaders may make fundamental changes in the organization or society to restore order during crises (e.g., Conger & Kanungo, 1987). Also, advances in technology and rapidly changing market conditions reflect environmental dynamism. Dynamism refers to the degree of unpredictability and speed of change in a given industry (Zahra, Priem, & Rasheed, 2005).

Turbulence and dynamism may lead to destructive leadership. Hansen, McDonald, Messier, and Bell (1996) argue that rapid industry growth is associated with a higher probability of managerial fraud. Nielson (2008) and Brass, Butterfield, and Skaggs (1998) propose that organizations competing in rapidly changing, globally-focused environments require the use interorganizational teams, which increases the possibility for unethical behavior. As work and roles become more complicated, fraud may be more difficult to identify.

The relationship between turbulence and fraud is neither simple nor clear, however. One study by Baucus and Near (1991) argues complexity and differentiation cause responsibilities to be diffuse such that no one is in a position to spot or prevent managerial fraud. Firms competing within highly turbulent environments were more likely to commit illegal acts compared to those in moderately turbulent environments (Baucus & Near, 1991). On the other hand, the same study also found that firms competing in less turbulent environments were more likely to commit fraud compared to those in moderately turbulent environments. This supports a curvilinear relationship between turbulence and fraud; too little or too much turbulence seems to be associated with fraud.

The global financial crisis of 2008-2009 has created a substantial amount of instability in global markets. Governments in North American and Europe and Asia have attempted to quell the financial unrest, with varying degrees of success. In doing so, governments are giving their treasuries unprecedented power ("Bailout agreement," 2008).

Proposition 8: Instability and dynamism in the environment will be associated with higher levels of toxic leader behavior.

Perceived Threat. Instability is related to the perception of threat in the organization. Instability is often seen as a threat to both leaders and followers. Some leaders will create and heighten the perception of an external or internal threat in order to gain more power. Several studies have demonstrated that increasing threats to followers will increase followers' support and identification with nonparticipative, charismatic leaders (e.g., Cohen, Solomon, Maxfield, Pyszczynski, & Greenberg, 2004; Solomon, Greenberg, & Pyszczynski, 1991). Furthermore, Jost et al. (2007) found that intolerance of ambiguity or uncertainty and perception of threat predicted political orientation. Low tolerance for ambiguity and perceptions threat both predicted politically conservative views. Regardless of beginning political orientation, people seem to move toward greater conservatism after exposure to significant threat such as the terrorist attacks on 9/11 (Bonanno & Jost, 2006).

Following Padilla et al. (2007), we propose that when the perception of threat or when a culture of dependency exists, followers are more willing to accept assertive, nonparticipative leadership.

Proposition 9: The greater perception of external threat, the more likely followers will accept assertive leadership.

Proposition 10: The greater perception of external threat, the more likely followers will accept nonparticipative leadership.

Proposition 11: Perception of threat will be positively related to instability in the organization.

Cultural values. Cultures comprise the attitudes, experiences, beliefs and values of a social organization. They exist at multiple levels including divisions, organizations, nations, and regions, and have multiple dimensions (House, Hanges, Javidan, Dorfman, & Gupta, 2004). For example, leadership in a U.S. headquartered organization may be relatively egalitarian reflecting the national and company culture, whereas local leadership of the same organization in India or Indonesia may have a more authoritarian leadership style, reflecting those national cultures and traditions. Leadership is deeply influenced by the culture in which it exists (Hofstede, 1991, House et al., 2004).

Destructive leadership may be rationalized by those observing the behavior and the behavior may take on institutional momentum (Anand, Ashforth, & Joshi, 2004; Fleming & Zyglidopoulos, 2008). Rationalizations are defined as mental strategies that justify illegal or immoral behavior to the destructive leader and followers (Anand et al., 2004). On the other hand, leaders and followers may exist in a social cocoon or microculture whose norms and standards for acceptable behavior may be quite different from the rest of the organization and society at large (Anand et al., 2004; Greil & Rudy, 1984).

A combination of cultural and organizational values may be more conducive to toxic leadership. In a collectivistic society or organization, leaders have the potential to have greater influence because they operate in an environment in which followers may think of group, organizational, or societal needs beyond their own self-interests (Luthans, Peterson, & Ibrayeva, 1998). In a study of three nations with a matched samples of 100 CEOs, Crossland and Hambrick (2007) found evidence that the national values of Japan constrained the influence of CEOs in that country compared to CEOs in Germany and the United States. CEOs in Japanese firms had lower levels of executive discretion. The authors concluded this was directly related to the country's very strong values of collectivism and uncertainty avoidance. The finding also supports the view that cultural tendencies toward inclusiveness, consensus, and risk aversion impose inherent limitations on executive discretion in Japan. Cultural influences seem to limit the extent of destructive leadership and this effect may be particularly powerful during an organizational or national crisis.

Power distance, the degree to which followers in a group, organization, or nation expect power to be distributed equally, influences the likelihood of toxic consequences. Those in a high power distance collective expect unequal power distribution; they expect stratification economically, socially, and politically (Javidan, Dorfman, Sully de Luque, & House, 2006). Increased power distance in a group is conducive to toxic leadership because leaders in such setting might not receive much, if any, dissent (Tourish & Pinnington, 2002).

Finally, uncertainty avoidance is the extent to which followers in a group, organization, or nation rely on policies, procedures, and norms to reduce future unpredictability (Hofstede, 1991). With higher the uncertainty avoidance, followers will desire regulation, reliability, organization, laws, social norms, and specific processes to govern behavior and maintain order and predictability (Javidan et al., 2006). Unless the toxic leader controls the rule making process, toxic leader's behavior will be restricted in these environments as rules and laws may prevent and reign in their authority (Crossland & Hambrick, 2007)

In cultures that value lack of dissent, collectivism, lower uncertainty avoidance, and high power distance, individuals may be more likely to support, or not to question or otherwise challenge, destructive leaders (Luthans et al., 1998; Tourish & Pinnington, 2002).

Proposition 12: Lower uncertainty avoidance will be associated with higher levels of toxic leader behavior.

Proposition 13: Collectivism will be associated with higher levels of toxic leader behavior.

Proposition 14: High power distance will be associated with higher levels of toxic leader behavior.

BENEFITS AND FUTURE RESEARCH CHALLENGES.

Benefits. The benefits of focusing more broadly on the situational environment of destructive leadership are several. First, a more holistic view of leadership will be more likely to avoid an attributional bias, called the fundamental attribution error, ascribed to and by leaders (Heider, 1958; Salancik & Meindl, 1984). Meindl et al. (1985) in a series of studies found evidence of this error:

> there is nevertheless a tendency to link leadership not only with variations in company performance, but also with the performance of entire industries, which are undoubtedly affected by factors well beyond the control of any single firm or management. (p. 98)

It is challenging to understand destructive leadership without examining the entire leadership process, including the characteristics of followers and the institutional and organizational contexts within which the leadership processes exist (Osborn, Hunt, & Jauch, 2002). By including institutional and organizational contexts a deeper and more sophisticated understanding of leadership processes is possible. In addition, by examining inter-relationships among leader behaviors and traits on the one hand and follower and organizational contexts on the other, the dynamics of the destructive leadership processes will be illuminated more clearly. More effective remedies to mitigate its effects might be developed as a result. The foregoing discussion, for example, highlights the overarching importance of checks and balances. An absence of appropriate controls on power and managerial discretion seems clearly to be associated with the presence of toxic outcomes.

An interesting "paradox" about the nature destructive leadership flows out of this discussion. Leaders with great power and managerial discretion are, we suggest, more likely to be associated with destructive outcomes. Only by giving up power to followers and by creating more effective checks on their own control and discretion can leaders build organizations less likely to incur in toxicity and destruction. Put differently, leaders who surround themselves with "yes" men and women may be hearing what they want to hear but their organizations might suffer from it.

Future Research Challenges. Despite repeated calls for more holistic research on the leadership process and not just the leader or leader-follower interactions (i.e., Pfeffer, 1977; Porter & McLaughlin, 2006), a general lack of such research indicates it is clearly a difficult and encumbering task. Analysis of leaders, followers, organizational climate and context is challenging for several reasons. First, measuring the environment comprehensively is problematic. Sufficient variation in environmental data is required to analyze meaningfully the relationships with leaders and followers. In many leadership and toxic leadership studies, the environment is assumed to be constant. This is tantamount to taking the partial derivative of a complicated mathematical equation where only one factor is allowed to vary. Yet, there are ways to consider the organizational conditions in a more methodical way: Osborn et al. (2002) provide a review of methods and tactics used to measure the context. Second, given the need to have some variation environmental data and observations, collecting large sample sizes with enough data is also difficult. Finally, longitudinal research is likely needed to clarify how the environment of toxic leadership develops over time in association with leader-follower relationships.

Increased use of case studies, within and across organizational groupings, is one solution. Qualitative approaches to the study of leadership are moderately rare in academic journals, but these studies are often responsible for radical shifts in the ways scholars think about problems. They offer longitudinal perspectives that other approaches routinely miss. Disciplines such as anthropology widely use ethnographic methods, a form of research that focuses on close observation of particular phenomena. Scholars in business, psychology, social work, and history have widely used the case method as a basic scientific investigatory tool for decades. The usefulness of the case approach is its practicality: lectures and theories alone cannot provide the confrontation with real world experiences needed to understand a wide array of situations. Business cases provide detailed information about a particular manager or about conditions and problems in different industries and companies, with each case requiring its own diagnosis and solution. Other cases, such as the famous idiographic study by Gruber (1981) in his analysis of Charles Darwin, take an account of a person or group of persons in a situation (e.g., Conger, 1998; Isabella, 1990; and Roberts & Bradley, 1988).

SUMMARY

By looking at leadership more comprehensively as a process involving leaders, followers, and organizational environments, we suggest that richer and more useful research questions are possible. Broader approaches also suggest remedies to the challenges of toxic leadership that might be missed by focusing on leader traits or behaviors. This chapter presents a number of propositions focusing on environmental issues within which leaders and followers interact. Despite the comprehensiveness of definitions of the term "leadership," quantitative research continues to falter in taking a comprehensive view toward explaining this leadership phenomenon (Porter & McLaughlin, 2006). We suggest here that the current leader-centric research emphasis in both the leadership and organizational behavior literatures is caused by the fascination with leaders and with a popular conception of leadership that looks to the top of organizations and political structures to the neglect of the environment in which these organizations and political structures exist (e.g., Heifetz, 1994; Ilgen & Klein, 1988). It is also certainly related to the challenges of conducting comprehensive studies of the leadership process that encompass leader, followers, and environments over time.

A final note regarding the "paradox" of destructive leadership is useful. Leaders in tight control, with significant power and managerial discretion, are, we suggest, associated with followers who are not empowered to act and to question authority and with organizational environments devoid of meaningful checks and balances. Leaders who surround themselves with "yes" followers are, potentially and paradoxically, planting the seeds for the eventual destruction of their own organizations. There might be a similar linkage here between charisma and weaker, more deferential followers and less effective institutions and organizational environments. The paradox, we think, is worth further thought.

REFERENCES

Agrawal, A., & Chadha, S. (2005). Corporate governance and accounting scandals. *Journal of Law and Economics, 48(2),* 371-406.

Anand, V., Ashforth, B. E., & Joshi, M. (2004). Business as usual: The acceptance and perpetuation of corruption in organizations. *Academy of Management Executive, 18*(1), 39-53.

Antonakis, J., Cianciolo, A. T., & Sternberg, R. J. (2004). *The nature of leadership.* London, England: SAGE.

Ashforth, B. E., Gioia, D. A., Robinson, S. L., & Trevino, L. K. (2008). Re-viewing organizational corruption. *Academy of Management Review, 33*(3), 670-694.

Bailout agreement reached (2008). *Investment Dealers' Digest, 74*(37), 17.

Baucus, M. S., & Near, J. P. (1991). Can illegal corporate behavior be predicted? An event history analysis. *Academy of Management Journal, 34*, 9-36.

Beasley, M. S. (1996). An empirical analysis of the relation between the board of director composition and financial statement fraud. *Accounting Review, 71*, 433–465.

Beasley, M. S., Carcello, J. V., Hermanson, D. R., & Lapides, P. D. (2000). Fraudulent financial reporting: Consideration of industry traits and corporate governance mechanisms. *Accounting Horizons, 14*, 441-454.

Boal, K. B., & Hooijberg, R. (2000). Strategic leadership research: Moving on. *Leadership Quarterly, 11*(4), 515-549.

Bonanno, G. A., & Jost, J. T. (2006) Conservative Shift among High-Exposure Survivors of the September 11th Terrorist Attacks. *Basic & Applied Social Psychology, 28*(4), 311-323.

Brass, D. J., Butterfield, K. D., & Skaggs, B. C. (1998). Relationships and unethical behavior: A social network perspective. *Academy of Management Review 23*(1), 14-31.

Boyce, T. (2006). Journalism and expertise. *Journalism Studies*, 7(6), 889-906.

Burns, J. (1978). *Leadership*. New York: Harper & Row.

Can underfunded SEC enforce new rules? (2002). *Investor Relations Business, 7(9)*, 1-2.

Cappelli, P., & Sherer, P. D. (1991). The missing role of context in OB: the need for a mesolevel approach. *Research in Organizational Behavior, 13*, 55-110.

Carlyle, T. (1894). *On heroes and hero-worship and the heroic in history*. London, England: Chapman & Hall.

Castrogiovanni, G. J. (2002). Organization task environments: Have they changed fundamentally over time? *Journal of Management, 28*(2), 129-150.

Child, J. (1972). Organization structure, environment, and performance: The role of strategic choice. *Sociology, 6*, 1-22.

Cohen, F., Solomon, S., Maxfield, M., Pyszczynski, T., & Greenberg, J. (2004). Fatal attraction: The effects of mortality salience on evaluations of charismatic, task-oriented, and relationship-oriented leaders. *Psychological Science, 15*, 846-851.

Coleman, S. (2005). Blogs and the new politics of listening. *Political Quarterly, 76*(2), 272-280.

Conger, J. A. (1998). Qualitative research as the cornerstone methodology for understanding leadership. *Leadership Quarterly, 9*(1), 107-121.

Conger J. A., Finegold D., & Lawler E. E. (1998). Appraising boardroom performance. *Harvard Business Review, 76*(1), 136-148.

Conger, J., & Kanugo (1987). Toward a behavioral theory of charismatic leadership in organizational settings. *Academy of Management Review, 12*, 637-647.

Crossland, C., & Hambrick, D. C. (2007). How national systems differ in their constraints on corporate executives: A study of CEO effects in three countries. *Strategic Management Journal, 28*(8), 767-789.

Dahya, J., & Travlos, N. G. (2000). Does the one man show pay? Theory and evidence on the dual CEO revisited. *European Financial Management, 6*(1), 85-98.

Dooley, K., & Van de Ven, A. (1999). Explaining complex organizational dynamics, *Organization Science, 10*(3), 358-372.

Federal Deposit Insurance Corporation. (1997a). An examination of the banking crises of the 1980s and early 1990s, Volume I. Retrieved from http://www.fdic.gov/bank/historical/history/421_476.pdf

Federal Deposit Insurance Corporation. (1997b). *Panel 4: The 1980s in retrospect.* Symposium proceedings, Volume II. Retrieved from http://www.fdic.gov/bank/historical/history/vol2/panel4.pdf

Finkelstein, S., & Hambrick, D. C. (1990). Top-management-team tenure and organizational outcomes: The moderating role of managerial discretion. *Administrative Science Quarterly, 35,* 484-503.

Fleming, P., & Zyglidopoulos, S. C. (2008). The escalation of deception in organizations. *Journal of Business Ethics, 81*(4), 837-850.

Greil, A. L., & Rudy, D. R. (1984.) Social cocoons: Encapsulation and identity transformation organizations. *Sociological Inquiry, 54*(3), 260-278.

Gruber, H.E. (1981). *Darwin on man: A psychological study of scientific creativity* (2nd ed.). Chicago, IL: Chicago University Press.

Gunter, B., Campbell, V., Touri, M., & Gibson, R. (2009). Blogs, news and credibility. *Aslib Proceedings: New Information Perspectives, 61*(2), 185-204.

Hambrick, D. C. (2007). Upper echelons theory: An update. *Academy of Management Review, 32,* 334-343.

Hambrick, D. C., & Finkelstein, S. (1987). Managerial discretion: A bridge between polar views of organizational outcomes. *Research in Organizational Behavior, 9,* 369-406.

Hambrick, D. C., & Mason, P. A. (1984). Upper echelons: The organization as a reflection of its top managers. *Academy of Management Review, 9,* 193-206.

Hannan, M. T., & Freeman, J. (1977). The population ecology of organizations. *American Journal of Sociology, 82,* 929-964.

Hannan, M. T., & Freeman, J. (1984). Structural inertia and organizational change. *American Sociological Review, 49,* 149-164.

Hannan, M. T. (2005). Ecologies of organizations: Diversity and identity. *The Journal of Economic Perspectives, 19*(1), 51-70.

Hansen, J. V., McDonald, J. B., Messier, W. F., & Bell, T. B. (1996). A generalized qualitative-response model and the analysis of management fraud. *Management Science, 42,* 1022-1032.

Harris, J. D. (2008). Effects financial misrepresentation: Antecedents and performance. *Business and Society, 47*(3), 390-401.

Heavy vetting. (2009). *New Republic, 240*(5), 1.

Heider, F. (1958). *The psychology of interpersonal relations*. New York: Wiley.

Heifetz, R. (1994). *Leadership without easy answers*. Cambridge, MA: Harvard University Press.

Hitt, G. (2009, February 26). Bank regulation. *Wall Street Journal* (Eastern edition), p. A.2.

Hofstede, G. (1991). *Cultures and organizations: Software of the mind*. New York: McGraw-Hill.

House, R. J., Hanges, P. J., Ruiz-Quintanilla, S. A., Dorfman, P. W., Javidan, M., Dickson, M., & Associates. (1999). Cultural influences on leadership and organizations: Project GLOBE. In W. H. Mobley, M. J. Gessner, & V. Arnold (Eds.), *Advances in global leadership* (pp. 131-233). Stamford, CT: JAI Press.

House, R. J., Hanges, P. W., Javidan, M., Dorfman, P., & Gupta, V. (Eds.). (2004). *Culture, leadership, and organizations: The GLOBE study of 62 societies*, Thousand Oaks, CA: SAGE.

Ilgen, D. R., & Klein, H. J. (1988). Organizational behavior. *Annual Review of Psychology, 40*, 327-351.

Isabella, L. (1990). Evolving interpretations as a change unfolds: How managers construe key organizational events. *Academy of Management Journal, 33*(1), 7-41.

Javidan, M., Dorfman, P. W., de Luque, M. S., & House, R. J. (2006). In the eye of the beholder: Cross cultural lessons in leadership from project GLOBE. *Academy of Management Perspectives, 20*(1), 67-90.

Jost J. T., Napier J. L., Thorisdottir H., Gosling, S. D., Palfai, T. P., & Ostafin, B. O. (2007). Are needs to manage uncertainty and threat associated with political conservatism or ideological extremity? *Personality and Social Psychology Bulletin, 33*(7), 989-1007.

Kang, E. (2008). Director interlocks and spillover effects of reputational penalties from financial reporting fraud. *Academy of Management Journal, 51*(3), 537-555.

Kakabadse, A., Kakabadse, N. K., & Barratt, R. (2006). Chairman and chief executive officer (CEO): That sacred and secret relationship. *Journal of Management Development, 25*(2), 134-150.

Kaplan, D. A., Breslau, K., Stone, B., Joseph, N., McGinn, D., & Gordon, D. (2006). Suspicions and spies in Silicon Valley. *Newsweek, 148*(12), 40-47.

Katz, D., & Kahn, R. L. (1966). *The social psychology of organizations*. New York: Wiley.

Kaufman, H. (2007, November 13). Who's watching the big banks? *Wall Street Journal* (Eastern edition), p. A25.

Kellerman, B. (2007). Followers flex their muscles. *U.S. News and World Report, 143*(18), 78.

Kelly, J. G., Ryan, A. M., Altman, B. E., & Stelzner, S. P. (2000). Understanding and changing social systems. In J. Rappaport & E. Seidman (Eds.), *Handbook of community psychology* (pp. 133-159). New York: Kluwer Academic/Plenum.

Lawler, E. E., & Finegold, P. (2005). Reward practices and performance management system effectiveness *Organizational Dynamics, 32*(4), 396-404.

Lewin K. (1943). Defining the "field at a given time." *Psychological Review, 50*, 292-310.

Linz, J. (1994). *The failure of presidential democracy.* Baltimore: Johns Hopkins University Press.

Luthans, F., Peterson, S. J., & Ibrayeva, E. (1998). The potential for the "dark side" of leadership in post-communist countries. *Journal of World Business, 33*, 185-201.

Mainwaring, S., & Scully, T. (1995). Party systems in Latin America. In S. Mainwaring & T. Scully (Eds.), *Building democratic institutions: Party systems in Latin America* (pp. 1-34). Stanford, CA: Stanford University Press.

Markopolos, H. (2009, February 4). Testimony of Harry Markopolos, CFA, CFE before the U.S. House of Representatives Committee on Financial Services,

Retrieved from http://online.wsj.com/public/resources/documents/MarkopolosTestimony20090203.pdf

Meindl, J. R. (1995).The romance of leadership as a follower-centric theory: A social constructionist approach. *Leadership Quarterly, 6*, 329–341.

Meindl, J. R., Ehrlich, S. B., & Dukerich, J. M. (1985). The romance of leadership. *Administrative Science Quarterly, 30*(1), 78-102.

Mintz, S. M. (2006). A comparison of corporate governance systems in the US, UK and Germany. *Corporate Ownership and Control, 3*(4), 24-34.

Mowday, R.T., & Sutton, R.I. (1993). Organizational behavior: Linking individuals and groups to contexts. *Annual Review of Psychology, 44*, 195-229.

Mumford, M. D., Espejo, J., Hunter, S. T., Bedell, K. E., Eubanks, D. L., & Connelly, S. (2007). The sources of leader violence: A multi-level comparison of ideological and non-ideological leaders. *The Leadership Quarterly, 18*, 217-235.

Nielson, R. P. (2008). Corruption networks and implications for ethical corruption reform. *Journal of Business Ethics, 42*, 125-149.

O'Connor, J., Priem, R., Coombs, J., & Gilley, K. M. (2006). Do CEO stock options prevent or promote fraudulent financial reporting? *Academy of Management Journal, 49*(3), 483-500.

O'Reilly, C. A. (1991). Organizational behavior: where we've been, where we're going. *Annual Review of Psychology, 42*, 427-458

Osborn, R. N, Hunt, J. G., & Jauch, L. R. (2002). Toward a contextual theory of leadership. *The Leadership Quarterly, 13*(6), 797-837.

Padilla, A., Hogan, R., & Kaiser, R. B. (2007). The toxic triangle: Destructive leaders, susceptible followers, and conducive environments. *Leadership Quarterly, 18*(3), 176-194.

Padilla, A., & Mulvey, P. W. (2008a, April). *A theoretical model of destructive leadership.* 2008 Annual Conference for the Society for Industrial and Organizational Psychology (SIOP), San Francisco, California.

Padilla, A., & Mulvey, P. W. (2008b). Leadership toxicity: Sources and remedies. *Organizations and People, 15*(3), 29-39.

Persons, O. S. (2006). The effects of fraud and lawsuit revelation on U.S. executive turnover and compensation, *Journal of Business Ethics, 64(4)*, 405-419.

Pfeffer, J. (1977). The ambiguity of leadership. *Academy of Management Review, 2*, 104-112.

Pfeffer, J. (1981). Management as symbolic action: The creation and maintenance of organizational paradigms. In L. L. Cummings & B. M. Staw (Eds.), *Research in Organizational Behavior* (Vol. 3, pp. 1-52). Greenwich. CT: JAI Press.

Pfeffer, J., & Salancik, G. R. (1978). *The external control of organizations: A resource dependence perspective.* New York: Harper & Row.

Porter, L. W., & McLaughlin, G. B. (2006). Leadership and the organizational context: Like the weather? *The Leadership Quarterly, 17*(6), 559-576.

Roberts, N. C., & Bradley, R. T. (1988). Limits of charisma. In J. A. Conger & R. N. Kanungo (Eds.), *Charismatic leadership: The elusive factor in organizational effectiveness* (pp. 253-275.) San Francisco: Jossey-Bass.

Ryan, R. G. (2009, August 5). The SEC vs. CEO pay. *Wall Street Journal* (Eastern Edition), p. A11.

Salancik, G. R., & Meindl, J. R. (1984). Corporate attributions as strategic illusions of management control. *Administrative Science Quarterly, 29*, 238-254.

Schnatter J. (2008, October 25). Where were the Boards? *Wall Street Journal* (Eastern edition), A11.

Seidman, L. W. (1997, January 16). *The world financial system: Lessons learned and challenges ahead.* Volume II: Symposium Proceedings, Retrieved from http://www.fdic.gov/bank/historical/history/vol2/panel3.pdf

Senge, P. (1990). *The fifth discipline. The art and practice of the learning organization.* New York: Doubleday.

So, are two heads better than one?: Behind the veil of the CEO and chairman relationship. (2006). *Strategic Direction, 22*(11), 19-21.

Siskey, K. & Fournier, E. (2008). How the bailouts should change regulation. *International Financial Law Review, 27*(11), 20-24.

Solomon, S., Greenberg, J., & Pyszczynski, T. (1991). A terror management theory of social behavior: The psychological functions of self-esteem and cultural worldviews. In M. Zanna (Ed.), *Advances in experimental social psychology, 24*, 93-159, Orlando, FL: Academic Press.

The State of the New Media (2008). Retrieved from http://stateofthemedia.org/2008.

Strassel, K. (2008, March 12). Spitzer's media enablers. *Wall Street Journal*, p. A21.

Tourish, D., & Pinnington, A. (2002). Transformational leadership, corporate cultism and the spirituality paradigm: An unholy trinity in the workplace? *Human Relations, 55*(2), 147-172.

Uzun, H., Szewczyk S. H., & Varma R. (2004). Board composition and corporate fraud. *The Financial Analysts Journal, 60*(3), 33-43.

Weick, K. (1979). *The social psychology of organizing* (2nd ed.) New York: McGraw-Hill

Wielkiewicz, R., & Stelzner, S. (2005). An ecological perspective on leadership theory, research, and practice. *Review of General Psychology, 9*(4), 326-341.

Wiersema, M. F., & Bantel, K. A. (1993). Top management team turnover as an adaptation mechanism: The role of the environment. *Strategic Management Journal, 14*(7), 485-504.

Woodward, B., & Bernstein, C. (1972, June 19). GOP security aide among 5 arrested in bugging affair. *The Washington Post*, p. A1.

Yukl, G. A. (2010). *Leadership in organizations* (7th ed.). Englewood Cliffs, NJ: Pearson Education.

Zahra, S. A., Priem, R. L., & Rasheed, A. A. (2005). The antecedents and consequences of top management fraud. *Journal of Management, 31*(6), 803-828.

Zhang, X., K. Bartol, K. G., Smith, M., Pfarrer, D., & Khanin. (2008). CEOs on the edge: Earnings manipulation and stock-based incentive misalignment. *Academy of Management Journal, 51*(2), 241-258.

CHAPTER 4

UNDERSTANDING THE CAUSES OF DESTRUCTIVE LEADERSHIP BEHAVIOR

A Dual-Process Model

Mo Wang, Robert Sinclair, and Marilyn Nicole Deese

Compared to the large amount of studies focused on the outcomes of destructive leadership, antecedents of destructive leadership have received relatively little attention. As such, the current chapter proposes a dual-process model to understand the causes of destructive leadership behavior (DLB). This model conceptualizes DLB as stemming from two psychological processes—a self-regulatory process which suggests the importance of psychological resources and a social cognitive process based on the theory of planned behavior. The model also considers the roles that leaders' traits may play in these two processes. Specifically, we describe the direct and indirect influences of the five factor model, psychological resilience, and so-called "dark side" traits on supervisors' DLBs.

When Leadership Goes Wrong: Destructive Leadership, Mistakes and Ethical Failures, pp. 73–97

While much attention has been given to effective leadership and its implications for employees and organizations, the idea of destructive leadership is relatively new. Destructive leadership behavior (DLB) describes behavior by a leader, supervisor, or manager that violates the legitimate interest of the organization by undermining or sabotaging the organization's goals, tasks, or resources or by affecting subordinates' motivation, well-being, or job satisfaction (Einarsen, Aasland, & Skogstad, 2007). Accordingly, destructive leaders are usually viewed as pursuing selfish goals, controlling and coercing their subordinates, and compromising subordinates' quality of life (Padilla, Hogan, & Kaiser, 2007).

The consequences of DLB have been studied rather extensively. Destructive leaders cause substantial harm to their subordinates as well as the organization as a whole. DLB often precipitates subordinates' deviant or counterproductive behavior (Mitchell & Ambrose, 2007), leading to lower profits and decreased customer satisfaction (Detert, Trevino, Burris, & Andiappan, 2007). Further, hostile leaders often have subordinates who are less committed to their organizations and less satisfied with their jobs (Schaubroeck, Walumbwa, Ganster, & Kepes, 2007). Tepper (2000) found that subordinates who reported higher levels of abuse from their superiors were more likely to leave their jobs, which increased the risk of human capital loss for the organization. Similarly, abusive leadership behaviors have been found to be negatively related to subordinates' organizational citizenship behaviors and affective commitment (Aryee, Chen, Sun, & Debrah, 2007). With outcomes such as these, DLB is clearly harmful to the organization's bottom line, but the detrimental effects do not stop there. Subordinates are also likely to suffer in the wake of DLBs. Schaubroeck and colleagues (2007) found that subordinates with hostile leaders had increased anxiety levels. In addition, subordinates with abusive supervisors are more likely to have more family problems (Hoobler & Brass, 2006; Tepper, 2000) and suffer from psychological distress (Tepper, 2000; Yagil, 2006). Further, employees who have a destructive leader also report higher levels of emotional exhaustion (Grandey, Kern, & Frone, 2007).

Unfortunately, DLB is not only harmful, it is increasingly prevalent. For example, Salin (2005) reported that 8.8% of respondents reported that they had at least occasionally been bullied by their supervisors (an important type of DLB) in the past 12 months, and 1.6% reported that they had been bullied at least weekly. Salin also found that sizable proportions of participants reported being subjected to other types of negative supervisor behaviors at least weekly, such as being ordered to do work clearly below their level of competence (13.7%), having important information withheld from them (7.4%), being given tasks with unreasonable or impossible targets or deadlines (5.3%), and having one's own opinions and views ignored (5.1%). Such findings illustrate the importance of research on understanding causes of destructive leadership.

However, compared to the large amount of studies focused on the outcomes of destructive leadership, antecedents of destructive leadership have received relatively little attention. To date, the existing literature has mostly focused on antecedents of abusive supervision, which resembles destructive leadership but excludes some forms of destructive leadership, such as physical abuse (Tepper, 2000, 2007). This literature has shown that abusive leadership behaviors result from an interaction between the supervisor's experience of injustice and his/her personal characteristics (Aryee et al., 2007; Hoobler & Brass, 2006; Tepper, Duffy, Henle, & Lambert, 2006). These studies assume that abusive supervisors displace their frustration from experiencing injustice onto their subordinates. However, this view is rather narrow, as it largely ignores the role that supervisors' attitudes and norms of their social environment may play as antecedents of DLB. As such, the current chapter proposes a dual-process model (Figure 4.1) to understand the causes of DLBs. This model conceptualizes DLB as stemming from two psychological processes—a self-regulatory process which suggests the importance of psychological resources (e.g., Hobfoll, 2002) and a social cognitive process based on the theory of planned behavior (e.g., Ajzen, 1991). We also consider the roles that leaders' traits may play in these two processes. Specifically, we describe the role of the five factor model, psychological resilience, and so-called "Dark Side" traits, all of which have multiple direct and indirect influences on supervisors' DLBs (see Figure 4.1).

We begin by presenting a behavioral definition of destructive leadership. We then discuss the role of self-regulatory and social cognitive processes in DLB as well as the antecedents that can be uniquely derived from each process. Leader traits that fit to each process are then scrutinized and incorporated as potential antecedents and moderators of these processes. We conclude by highlighting ways to further extend our model for continued theoretical development and improved human resource management practices.

A BROAD BEHAVIORAL DEFINITION OF DESTRUCTIVE LEADERSHIP

Consistent with Einarsen et al. (2007), we conceptualize destructive leadership as intentional or unintentional leaders' behaviors that result in negative outcomes for an organization or its employees. Our approach has at least three important features. First, it highlights the idea that DLBs differ in their primary targets. Some DLBs negatively affect the organization, such as terminating important relationships with other

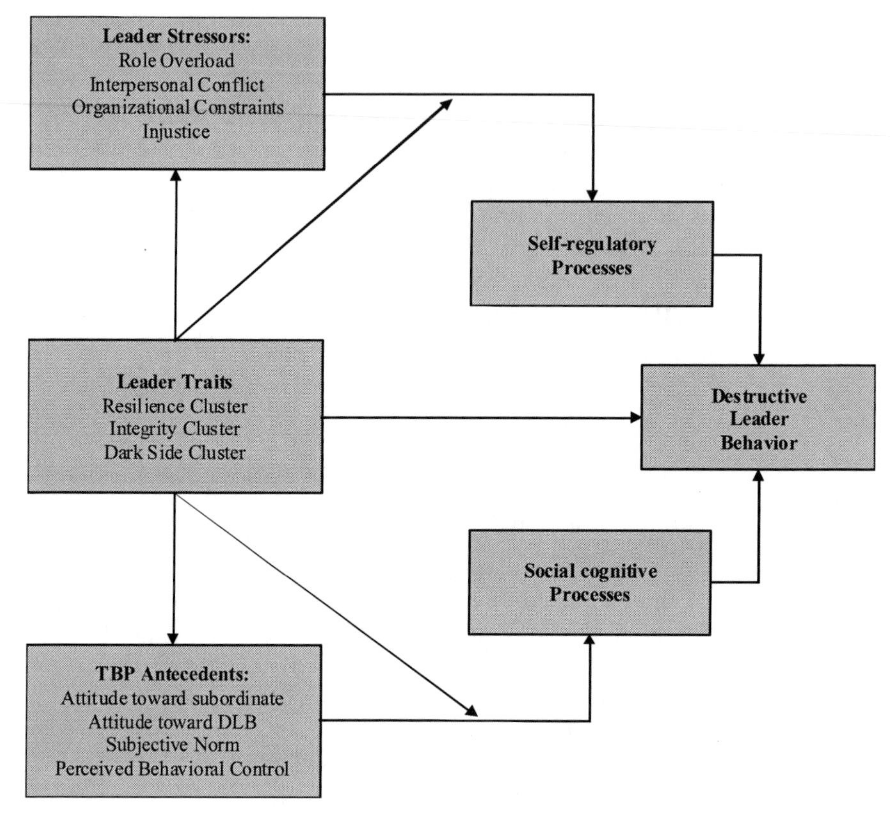

Figure 4.1. The proposed dual-process model of destructive leader behavior.

departments. Other DLBs primarily harm individual employees, such as belittling or physically assaulting subordinates. These different forms of behavior are likely to have different antecedents and consequences. Second, our model assumes that both the content and context of leader behaviors need to be considered to determine whether they are destructive. For example, increasing subordinates' performance goals could be beneficial when subordinates have sufficient resources, but detrimental when subordinates lack the necessary resources to adapt to the higher performance demands. Finally, our definition does not impose an assumption regarding the leader's intention. A leader may be abusive in the midst of an organizational crisis, because he/she loses self-control in the heat of the moment. Such a leader may not have destructive intentions, but his/her behavior may have destructive effects. Thus, the intention to carry out destructive behaviors may not make a difference, as destructive behaviors will result in negative outcomes regardless of the leader's intentions. One important implication of this issue is the need to distinguish intention-based DLBs from those resulting from failed self-regulation.

A DUAL-PROCESS MODEL

The central proposition of our dual process model is that DLB is influenced by two distinct but interrelated psychological processes. The first is a self-regulatory process based on the resource perspective. It mainly accounts for DLBs that are led by a nonintention based process (or as Mitchell & Daniels [2003] called it, a "not-rational" process). The second process is a social cognitive process based on the theory of planned behavior. It mainly accounts for DLBs that are led by an intention based process, which emphasizes the influence of social attitudes and the social context.

Destructive Leadership as Failed Self-Regulation

The central premise of the self-regulatory process is that DLBs could occur when leaders fail to effectively regulate their affective experiences and subsequent behaviors. We draw on the resource perspective to detail the mechanism guiding in this process. According to Hobfoll (2002), resources reflect the total capability an individual has to fulfill his or her centrally valued needs. Wang (2007) suggested that this total capability may include one's physical resources (e.g., muscle strength), financial resources (e.g., income and assets), social resources (e.g., social support), cognitive resources (e.g., intelligence), emotional resources (e.g., mood and affect), and motivational resources (e.g., goal commitment). Hobfoll's (1989) conservation of resources theory suggests that people strive to obtain, retain, protect, and foster valued resources and minimize any threats of resource loss. This conservation process includes two parallel mechanisms, accumulation and protection. The accumulation mechanism refers to people using their resources to regulate their behaviors and actions and exert control over the environment to gain new resources to improve their fulfillment of valued needs. The protection mechanism refers to people withdrawing their resources (e.g., disengaging from the task; setting a lower goal; investing less effort) to protect themselves from resource loss. In particular, individuals are compelled to protect their resources from three possible circumstances, when resources are threatened, when resources are lost, and/or when individuals do not receive the results they expected after investing their resources. In the workplace, threats to resource loss usually take the form of excessive job demands, whereas resource loss involves the energy and efforts expended toward meeting such demands (Brotheridge & Lee, 2002). The achievement of positive resource conservation outcomes largely depends on the extent to which employees can regain the resources they value by investing their resources in meeting these job demands. If the resources gained from working are less than the resources lost from meeting job demands, resource loss may occur and employees may subsequently engage in the protection mechanism. These employees may invest fewer resources in regulating their job-related behaviors and emotions.

Following the resource conservation perspective, we conceptualize the supervisor-subordinate interaction as a process that could result in resource changes for either or both parties. The well-documented beneficial effects of transformational leadership (e.g., Bass, 1998; Judge & Piccolo, 2004) can be cited as support of this conceptualization, because the beneficial mechanism of transformational leadership can be viewed as a resource-generating process for both supervisors and subordinates.

Given our interest in predictors of DLB, we mainly focus on supervisors' resource changes through their interactions with subordinates. In a normal supervisor-subordinate interaction, the supervisor's leadership role involves mentoring, guiding, and motivating subordinates to reach organizational objectives (Vroom & Jago, 2007). These responsibilities certainly demand that supervisors invest resources. Nevertheless, by mentoring subordinates and solving their problems, supervisors may have potential to gain several important resources. For example, cooperation and co-production may foster feelings of social companionship and relatedness (Dormann & Zapf, 2004). Solving subordinates' problems and mentoring them may lead to a sense of competence and accomplishment (Bass, 1998). Further, subordinates expressions of gratitude may increase leaders' feelings of self-esteem. Thus, in a normal supervisor-subordinate interaction, it is not difficult for supervisors to reach a balance between resource loss and resource gain.

However, when supervisors are preoccupied by other demands and their resources have been drained by their efforts to fulfill those demands, they simply may lack additional resources to effectively manage their interactions with their subordinates. This is likely to create an imbalance between investing resources and regaining resources, resulting in a net resource loss for supervisors. This theorizing has received consistent support in the emotional labor literature (Dormann & Zapf, 2004; Grandey, Dickter, & Sin, 2004).

Applying the resource perspective to leadership suggests that demanding situations drain leaders' resources, which undermines their ability to regulate their affective reactions and subsequent behaviors. As such, it is not surprising that resource depletion leads to negative affective reactions such as anger toward social targets, anxiety about performing tasks, and aggressive behaviors (Beal, Weiss, Barros, & MacDermid, 2005). In addition, unsuccessful supervisor-subordinate interactions may also place an accumulating load on supervisors' resources. Previous studies have found that the anger, anxiety, and aggressive thoughts caused by resource loss can last for a long time, making people less efficient in regulating their emotions (McCullough, Bono, & Root, 2007). Over time, these individuals may be more likely to displace aggression on an irrelevant target (Bushman, Bonacci, Pdersen, Vasquez, & Miller, 2005). Therefore, the cumulated negative affect would facilitate aggressive thoughts and behavioral tendencies, which could start the DLBs directed toward other subordinates in motion.

The resource perspective suggests that the antecedents most likely to lead to failed self-regulation are those that tax supervisors' resources. Perhaps the most important of these are work related stressors, as they represent the aspects of the work environment that require resource-invested adaptive responses (Bakker, Demerouti, & Euwema, 2005). We discuss four types of stressors that are particularly relevant to supervisors' work environments. They are role overload, interpersonal conflict, organizational constraints, and supervisors' experience of injustice.

Role overload refers to situations when the job role requires more resources from an employee than he or she has available (Jones, Flynn, & Kelloway, 1995). For example, supervisors often need to be task oriented but at the same time considerate of their subordinates' well-being (Judge, Piccolo, & Ilies, 2004). They also need to assess their employees' performance and provide appropriate feedback and mentoring. These demands often may generate inconsistent demands for the supervisors, such as when supervisors must prioritize short-term deadlines over supporting and mentoring subordinates (e.g., King & King, 1990). Therefore, role overload is likely to drain supervisors' resources and decrease their ability to regulate their emotions and behaviors.

Interpersonal interaction comprises a significant portion of what leaders do. Such social interactions are often a source of satisfaction and personal fulfillment (Nielsen, Jex, & Adams, 2000), but can also lead to interpersonal conflict, defined as negatively charged interactions with others in the workplace (Spector, 1987), ranging from minor momentary disagreements to heated disputes that in extreme cases may escalate to physical violence (O'Leary-Kelly, Griffin, & Glew, 1996). Interpersonal conflict may manifest as a chronic stressor as well as an acute stressor, which taps individual's resources via cognitive processes (e.g., rumination; McCullough et al., 2007) and affective processes (e.g., negative emotions and mood; Spector, 1987), respectively. As such, supervisors who have interpersonal conflict with other people at work are less likely to effectively regulate their negative emotions and behaviors, and in turn, are more likely to exhibit DLBs.

It is well known that organizational conditions do not always facilitate employees' work. In fact, organizational conditions may even constrain employees' efficiency because of unnecessary rules and procedures, a lack of resources, or unclear organizational goals. For supervisors, organizational constraints include unavailable, inadequate, or poor quality information, insufficient budgetary and material support, poor human resource support, and a lack of job-related authority (Peters & O'Conner, 1980). Facing such organizational constraints, it is conceivable that supervisors would have to rely more on their personal resources to meet their job-related demands, which could undermine the resources that they allocate to regulate their emotions and behaviors (Beal et al., 2005).

Finally, literature on workplace aggression suggests injustice as a potential stressor. Experiences of injustice may influence self regulation through several pathways, such as stress (cf. Cropanzano, Goldman, Benson & Lehman, 2005) and frustration (cf. Fox & Spector, 1999). Aryee et al. (2007) characterized the effects of supervisor experiences of injustice as "trickling down" to subordinates. When supervisors experienced more frustration from their own experiences of injustice, they were more likely to engage in abusive supervision. Similarly, Tepper et al. (2006) found that supervisors' experiences of procedural injustice led to increased supervisor depression and subsequently to more frequent reports of abusive supervision from subordinates. Finally, Hoobler and Brass (2006) found that leaders experiences of contract violations, which are likely to create perceptions of injustice, were associated with subordinates' reports of abusive leadership. A self-regulatory framework can account for all of these findings, as depression, frustration, and contract breach all should deplete leaders' resources, making them less able to refrain from DLB.

To summarize, based on the resource perspective, we argue that DLBs occur when leaders fail to effectively regulate their affective experiences and subsequent behaviors. We argue that supervisor job-related stressors are a critical influence on this process, as they are likely to impose extra demands on supervisors' resources. Therefore, the resource perspective provides a non-intentional account of the causes of DLBs and highlights the likelihood of within leader variation in destructive leader behavior.

Destructive Leadership as a Social Cognitive Process

In this section, we draw on the theory of planned behavior to propose a social cognitive process that accounts for intention-based reasons supervisors engage in DLBs. Ajzen and Fishbein (Ajzen, 1991; Ajzen & Fishbein, 1980; Fishbein & Ajzen, 1975) proposed the theory of planned behavior to explain social cognitive influences on peoples' behavior. A central factor in the theory of planned behavior is the individual's intention to perform a given behavior. The term "intention" is defined as a motivational indicator of how hard people are willing to try, or how much effort they are planning to exert, in order to perform the behavior (Ajzen, 1991). The theory of planned behavior argues that any behavior is more likely when individuals have stronger intentions to engage in that behavior. This is because individuals with stronger intentions would be more likely to choose that behavior over other options and to continue investing effort until the behavior is carried out.

DLB could be viewed as an outcome of supervisors intentions to engage in such behavior. But, how are such intentions formed? According to the theory of planned behavior, both individual factors and context-specific factors determine intentions. Specifically, individual's attitudes are the most important individual factors predicting the intention. Attitude refers to "a psychological tendency that is expressed by evaluating a particular entity with some degree of favor or disfavor" (Eagly & Chaiken, 1993, p. 1). In other words, attitude is a latent and relatively enduring construct regarding a distinguishable object (e.g., a person, an organization, social groups, and behaviors) which can be inferred through observable affective, cognitive, and behavioral responses (Eagly & Chaiken, 1993; Manstead, 1996).

The theory of planned behavior framework focuses on two types of attitudes as predictors of behavioral intention, attitude toward the behavior and attitude toward the target. Attitude toward the behavior is the predictor that directly leads to intention. People who hold more favorable attitudes about a behavior should have stronger intentions to perform it (Ajzen, 1991). Attitudes toward the target indirectly lead to behavioral intention through their influence on attitudes toward the behavior (Eagly & Chaiken, 1993; Solinger, van Olffen, & Roe, 2008). This is because attitudes toward the target activate valence-consistent behaviors toward the target in the person's social cognitive network. In such an associative network, attitudes toward targets and valences of the behaviors are linked. The strength of each link is positively related to the similarity between the attitude and the valence (Berkowitz, 1989, 1993). Therefore, if a person holds a positive attitude toward a target, positive behavioral intention toward that target would be activated. Applying these mechanisms to DLB, we contend that supervisors' attitudes toward the particular subordinate and their attitudes toward DLBs should be important antecedents of their intentions to engage in destructive behavior.

The theory of planned behavior also identifies subjective norms as an important predictor of behavioral intention. Subjective norms refer to the perceived social acceptance or pressure to perform or not perform a specific behavior in a specific social context (Ajzen, 1991). Bandura (1969) argued that social norms determine whether particular behaviors will be encouraged or discouraged. Thus, people are more likely to develop behavioral intention when they perceive that a behavior is encouraged or approved by people in their social environment (e.g., Millham, 1974; Rudolph, Caldwell, & Conley, 2005). Therefore, supervisors' perceptions about how much people in their work environment approve of DLBs should predict how likely they will be to engage in DLB. The most important influences on supervisors in this context would most likely be the supervisors' peers and their own immediate supervisors.

Finally, the theory of planned behavior argues that people's control over the particular behavior in the specific social context influence their behavioral intentions. When a particular behavior is not under supervisors' volitional control (e.g., due to the lack of opportunities or resources), they are unlikely to be successful in performing the behavior and as such are unlikely to form strong intentions to engage in the behavior (Ajzen, 1991). Therefore, supervisors' perceived control over their ability to engage in DLBs is another important antecedent to consider in predicting their intention to perform these behaviors.

In sum, the theory of planned behavior suggests that DLBs occur when leaders form the intention to engage in destructive leadership. We argue that the supervisor's attitude toward destructive behaviors, attitude toward the particular subordinate, perceived norms regarding the social approval for DLBs, and perceived control over the behavior in the specific social context are important antecedents of this process. Whereas the self-regulatory process described above suggests that destructive leadership occurs through a nonintentional process stemming from depleted resources, this social cognitive process emphasizes intention—based features of destructive leadership. Further, it should be noted that although we argue supervisors' attitudes, subjective norms, and perceived control over the behavior to be important antecedents of DLBs, previous empirical studies that examined these antecedents in predicting other behaviors often showed that attitudes and perceived control accounted for more variance than subjective norms (Ajzen, 1991). These patterns may suggest that the influence of the social environment on behaviors may be overshadowed by the other antecedents.

The Roles of Leader Traits in the Dual-Process Model

The final portion of our model concerns the effects of leaders' individual differences on their DLB. Although the study of individual differences includes many potentially relevant constructs such as sex (Hershcovis et al., 2007), values (e.g., Illies & Reiter-Palmon, 2008), and moral reasoning (Turner, Barling, Epitropaki, Butcher, & Miller, 2002), personality traits have received the most interest from researchers. Therefore, we will address three questions related to personality and DLB. What do we mean by personality? What kinds of personality traits are likely to be associated with destructive leadership? And, how are personality traits likely to influence DLB? Rather than attempt to provide a comprehensive review of this literature, we will identify three important clusters of personality traits that have at least some conceptual and/or empirical support as likely antecedents of destructive leader behavior. They include integrity traits grounded in the five factor model of personality, resilience traits drawn from individual differences in response to stress, and "dark side" traits based on research on derailed leaders. These models encompass critical streams of personality literature that include both overlapping and distinct constructs and measurement systems.

The Integrity Cluster. The five factor model (FFM) of personality is the most heavily studied model in applied psychology. The FFM stemmed from a lexical research tradition which emphasized natural language as a source of understanding of the structure of personality (Wiggins, 1996). FFM adherents argue that five broad traits capture much of the variation in natural language descriptions—openness to experience, conscientiousness, extraversion, agreeableness, and neuroticism, with each trait being defined by several narrower facets (e.g., McCrae & Costa, 1999). These broad traits and their respective facets may be characterized as a model of biologically-based dispositions rather than as an all-encompassing model of individual variation in personality (cf. McAdams & Pals, 2006).

Some FFM-related research focuses on compound traits (sometimes referred to as syndromes) reflecting combinations of the FFM dimensions. The most relevant of these to destructive leadership is what we refer to as the integrity cluster. Ones and Viswesvaran (2001) summarize a great deal of FFM research suggesting that many forms of negative organizational behavior (e.g., telling lies, drug and alcohol use, maladaptation to stress, and aggressive customer service behaviors) appear to reflect a specific personality combination of conscientiousness, agreeableness, and neuroticism—integrity. Thus, considering the negative nature of DLB, destructive leaders are likely to be low in conscientiousness (e.g., undisciplined, careless, and with a lack of respect for authority), low in agreeableness (distrustful, hostile, and unkind), and high in neuroticism (e.g., impulsive, unstable, and prone to negative emotions). Consistent with this general idea some leadership research has reported that integrity is associated with an increased likelihood of senior leader derailment (e.g., Lombardo, Ruderman, & McCauley, 1988). Further, meta-analyses have confirmed the importance of conscientiousness and agreeableness as predictors of counterproductive behavior (e.g., Salgado, 2002). Finally, many studies have demonstrated specific components of the integrity cluster as predictors of related behavior such as studies linking negative affectivity to aggression (e.g., Fox & Spector, 1999).

The Resilience Cluster. Personality-based resilience concerns relatively stable individual differences in how people respond to potentially stressful events. Resilient leaders are less likely to appraise events as stressful, less likely to have intense negative reactions to stressors, more likely to choose effective coping strategies, and less likely to experience adverse outcomes from stressors. Resilience traits can be described as cognitively-oriented characteristic styles that people have for (a) interpreting demanding events as potentially threatening or potentially rewarding, (b) evaluating their own capacity to respond to demanding events, and (c) constructing positive interpretations of prior experiences. Three frequently-studied traits are psychological capital, core self-evaluations, and hardiness.

Psychological capital (PsyCap) is a relatively new concept from the literature on positive psychology and human strengths. Luthans et al. (2007) describe PsyCap as a composite of four such strengths. They are hope (e.g., believing that one can accomplish his/her goals), optimism (a positive outlook about the future), resilience (the ability to adapt to challenging events) and self-efficacy (the belief that one can successfully complete tasks or goals). Although PsyCap is a relatively new concept, a growing body of research demonstrates that higher levels of PsyCap are associated with higher job satisfaction and better job performance (Luthans, Avolio, Avey, & Norman, 2007).

Core self-evaluations (CSEs) reflect individual differences in self-esteem, generalized self-efficacy, locus of control, and emotional stability (Judge, Locke, & Durham, 1997). As such, CSEs reflect fundamental appraisals of the self, other people, and the world (Judge, Erez, Bono, & Thoresen, 2002). A growing literature shows that CSEs are associated with higher job and life satisfaction and better job performance (cf. Judge & Bono, 2001; Judge, et al., 2002; Judge, Erez, Bono, & Thoresen, 2003; Judge et al., 1997). As with psychological capital, few studies have examined CSEs in relation to stress resilience but a substantial body of empirical literature links each of the constituent parts of CSE to mental health outcomes.

Hardiness consists of three dimensions—commitment, control, and challenge (cf. Maddi, Kahn, & Maddi, 1998; Maddi & Kobasa, 1984). *Commitment* reflects a general tendency to be engaged by and finding meaning and purpose in one's life. *Control* reflects the belief that one is capable of effectively responding to demanding situations in their lives. Finally, *challenge* includes cognitive flexibility and tolerance for ambiguity, which allow people to easily integrate unexpected or otherwise stressful events and to view them as opportunities for personal growth, rather than as threats. Although hardiness has received less attention in the organizational psychology literature than in military and health psychology, many studies link hardiness to health outcomes (e.g., Bartone, Ursano, Wright, & Ingraham, 1989; Florian, Mikulincer, & Taubman, 1995).

According to McAdams and Pals' (2006) taxonomy, PsyCap, CSEs, and hardiness may be viewed as characteristic adaptations—traits reflecting relatively stable ways people learn to adapt to situations in their lives that may be modified through experience. Thus, one critical distinction from the FFM may be the relative stability of such traits. For example, intervention research has suggested the promise of hardiness training (cf. Maddi et al., 1998), and shows that psychological capital can be developed (Luthans, Avey, Avolio, Norman, & Combs, 2008; Luthans, Avey, & Patera, 2008). However, these traits also share a consistent theme that few studies have linked them to DLB, highlighting the need for more attention to their effects.

The Dark Side Cluster. A final area of personality research generating a great deal of interest among scholars interested in dysfunctional leadership concerns the so-called dark side of personality. Leadership scholars have long recognized that an inability to effectively manage interpersonal relationships plays a prominent role in leader derailment (cf. McCall & Lombardo, 1983; Van Velsor & Leslie, 1995). Hogan and Hogan (2001) characterize the dark side traits as dysfunctional aspects of personality that may coexist with desirable social skills, enabling people to make good social impressions, at least in the short term. They also argue that dark side traits are nonlinearly related to performance, with moderate levels being more desirable than either high or low levels and that by their nature, dark side traits are quite difficult to detect in initial social interactions, such as in employment interviews. One thing that makes dark side traits compelling in the study of leadership is that leaders who have them may do quite well in the short term and their shortcomings may be exceedingly difficult to expose. Thus, recent research has been devoted to developing a better understanding of how to select for these traits. Our model concerns their role in how leaders respond to stressful situations as well as the social context of leadership.

Drawing from Horney's (1950) interpersonal model of neuroses, Hogan and Hogan (2001, 2005) described three broad categories of dark side traits potentially associated with destructive leader behavior. All of these traits involve ways people manage interpersonal relationships in order to deal with anxiety. Traits concerning *moving away* from others involve protecting oneself by maintaining distance from others. Leaders who are overly cautious or distrustful of others fit this profile. *Moving toward* others reflects excessive conformity and dependence. Benson and Campbell (2007) suggest that leaders who micromanage fit this profile. Finally, traits comprising *moving against* others involve exploiting others. Leaders who manage through manipulation or intimidation provide a good example of this profile. The empirical literature on this framework and/or on specific traits related to the dark side is small but growing (cf. Khoo & Burch, 2008; Moscoso & Salgado, 2004; Paunonen, Lönnqvist, Verkasalo, Leikas, & Nissinen, 2006; Penney & Spector, 2002; Rosenthal & Pittinsky, 2006). However there are still relatively few applied studies focusing on leaders and very few specifically linking dark side traits to destructive aspects of leadership.

Our model emphasizes several pathways through which leaders' destructive traits are likely to be related to DLB. First, we predict a direct effect of traits on DLB such that, all other things being equal, leaders with low resilience, low integrity, or high levels of dark side traits also are more likely to engage in destructive behavior. Second, some kinds of destructive leaders, by virtue of their characteristic styles, may be more likely to experience more stress as well as more difficulty regulating their responses to stressors. For example, one would expect that leaders with low agreeableness and high neuroticism might experience more interpersonal conflict than their agreeable and emotionally stable counterparts. Similarly, leaders with low levels of resilience might be more prone to sense injustice in their work environment. Third, destructive traits are likely to moderate the relationship between stressors and self-regulatory processes. For example, leaders with lower psychological capital are likely to have fewer resources available for self-regulation and should experience greater resource depletion in response to stressors, suggesting that they should be more likely to experience failures of self-regulation under stress. Fourth, destructive leader traits should be directly related to leaders' perceptions of all of the components of the theory of planned behavior. Specifically, leaders with destructive personalities should have poorer attitudes toward subordinates, be more likely to see destructive behavior as an appropriate response, more likely to perceive subjective norms that favor, or at least less strongly prohibit destructive behavior, and be less likely to feel they can control their behavior. Finally, in addition to shaping how leaders perceive the social context, leaders with destructive personalities should be more likely to act destructively when features of the social context suggest that it is permissible to engage in destructive behavior. For example, while strong social norms might encourage any leader to behave more destructively, it seems likely that certain personality characteristics might strengthen the effects of these norms.

IMPLICATIONS AND FUTURE DIRECTIONS

Looking beyond the specific propositions in our model, we see two broad directions for future destructive leadership research, each of which raises several interesting questions. These include further attention to the potential role of subordinate behavior in eliciting DLBs and greater attention to the feedback loops likely present in the model. The social context model also provides a theoretical framework to both generate hypotheses and understand the potential effects of interventions aimed at lessening the occurrence of DLB.

Subordinates' Influence on Leaders' DLB

Previous leadership research has generally not paid as much attention to the nature of proximal situational influences on DLB—the immediate trigger events that might elicit DLB. One key point of our chapter is that DLB does not occur in a social vacuum—DLB is more likely in some social contexts. One area of research that might advance understanding of the social context of DLB concerns the potential role of follower behavior in eliciting DLB. Padilla et al. (2007) describe two types of followers who contribute to destructive leadership, conformers and colluders. Conformers fear the consequences of failing to comply with the leader's demands whereas colluders essentially support the destructive leader's agenda. We describe a third possibility, that certain kinds of subordinate behaviors are more likely to elicit DLB.

Leader-member exchange (LMX) literature provides a model of the kinds of follower behaviors that may elicit DLB. Several reviews of this literature demonstrate that followers who perceive a higher quality exchange relationship feel obligated to respond with higher levels of effort, commitment, and so forth (cf. Gerstner & Day, 1997; Ilies, Nahrgang, & Moregson, 2007). Liden and Maslyn (1998) described four aspects of a high quality social exchange relationship. They are loyalty, liking, contribution, and professional respect. Behaviors perceived by leaders as reflecting the inverse of each of these dimensions should be particularly likely to elicit DLB. Thus, DLB seems most likely when leaders perceive their subordinates as being disloyal, unlikeable, incompetent (i.e., poor contributors), and/or disrespectful. For example, underqualified subordinates lack the necessary education or skills to meet their job requirements (Khan & Morrow, 1991). Such subordinates will likely require leaders to exert more effort to train them, spend more time monitoring their performance, and expend more resources dealing with job-related problems (e.g., poor product quality, untimely completion of the task, etc.). Our depiction of the self-regulatory process suggests that these demands impose extra loads on supervisors' resources and compromise their ability to regulate negative emotions and behaviors, increasing the likelihood of DLB. Leaders are also more likely to hold negative attitude toward such subordinates, which the social cognitive process suggests will lead to higher DLB intention.

These forms of what might be termed as destructive follower behavior (DFB) have not received as much attention in past research. However, we suggest that DFB has a distinct nomological network from positive follower behavior such as citizenship behavior. Several theoretical perspectives suggest the importance of studying the relationship between DFB and DLB. First, past literature on follower victimization has demonstrated that aggressive followers are likely to elicit aggressive responses from leaders (cf. Aquino & Lamertz, 2004). Second, literature on workplace incivility (Cortina, Magley, Williams, & Langhout, 2001; Pearson & Porath, 2005) suggests that destructive leaders and followers may get locked into a escalating spiral of progressively more negative behavior and progressively more negative in-kind responses. Third, from a leader's perspective, DFB represents a breach of the leader's psychological contract with the follower. While breaches of leaders' contracts have received less attention in literature, the breach literature supports the proposition that leaders experience intense negative reactions to violations of their expectations (cf. Zhao, Wayne, Glibkowski, & Bravo, 2007) and at least some literature suggests the possibility of individual differences in how leaders respond to breaches (cf. Chen, Tsui, & Zhong, 2008).

Future research can study several interesting questions about such behaviors. For example, narcissists are generally likely to make external and hostile attributions about others' behavior, particularly in the face of social rejection (Twenge & Campbell, 2003) and therefore, might be more sensitive to potential indications of subordinate disloyalty. Given that hostile attributions often mediate the aggression response (cf. Bing et al., 2007; Hoobler & Brass, 2006), one might predict that narcissistic leaders might be more likely to have destructive responses to subordinate acts they perceive as indicative of disloyalty.

One interesting direction for DLB research would be to investigate whether different personality traits moderate how destructive leaders perceive these subordinates' acts, as leaders could differ in the forms of negative exchanges that elicit their most intense responses. A leader with a hostile attributional style may be more likely to interpret any particular behavior as indicative of disrespect, whereas leaders with unrealistically high performance expectations may be more prone to see certain behaviors as indicative of incompetence. Finally, social norms likely influence how leaders respond to negative follower behaviors. In organizations that have strong social norms against destructive behavior, leaders might be more prone to respond in ways that are more functional in the long term, such as through provision of developmental feedback, additional training, or even through following normal disciplinary channels rather than taking matters into their own hands.

The Dynamics of DLB

A second interesting direction for future work concerns the nature of feedback loops in the DLB model. In its present incarnation, our model describes a unidirectional causal flow from situational and dispositional characteristics to DLB to outcomes. However, DLB occurs in a dynamic organizational context that warrants further attention and theory development. In particular, DLB may create vicious cycles that may be quite difficult for organizations to interrupt without substantial intervention, such as replacing a destructive leader. Three feedback loops seem most salient—the effects of DLB on other leaders' behavior, on followers' behavior, and on the leader's own behavior.

First, DLB can influence the social norms of other leaders. When more senior and/or well-respected leaders engage in DLB, it not only affects their followers, but likely sends powerful messages to other leaders about the appropriateness of DLB. In effect, DLB may be a form of socially contagious bullying. One of the critical influences on this feedback loop is how the organization responds to a leader's transgressions. Organizations may either implicitly or explicitly accept a leader's destructive behavior, by not punishing a leader who engages in destructive behavior, by rewarding that person for other accomplishments, or even by holding that leader in high esteem for destructive actions that fit a particular leader prototype (e.g., leaders receiving praise for excessively high performance standards for followers). A leader's formal and informal status in the organization probably influences the nature of the organization's response, such that higher status leaders can get away with more DLB and their behavior is likely to have stronger effects on norms as perceived by other leaders. In some cases, these group dynamics may have unpredictable effects on followers. For example, Tucker, Sinclair, and Thomas (2005) found that some group level stressors appeared to have positive effects on soldiers' mental health and/or appeared to attenuate the effects of individual level stressors. They suggested that such stressors might have a galvanizing effect. In effect, people may band together, in the present case, against a destructive leader. Such processes may certainly contribute to political or organizational leaders being forced out of positions of power, but have received little attention in empirical leadership literature in psychology.

Conversely, when destructive leaders experience sanctions, reprimands, and so forth, it likely has positive effects on how other leaders perceive the contextual influences on DLB described in our model. Organizations that respond assertively to such transgressions may create virtuous cycles in which appropriate responses to DLB influence the social context for leaders in terms of how they perceive norms while providing important information about the organization's level of support for employees affected by the leader's actions. Of course, there is considerable entropy in organizations and many proactive responses may be required to stimulate the virtuous cycle, particularly in cases where powerful leaders are less likely to experience the full force of an organization's policies about appropriate behavior.

A second set of dynamic processes concerns the effects of DLB on followers' behavior. Followers who experience DLB may engage in a variety of externalizing and/or internalizing responses. Externalizing responses involve followers' reciprocal responses to DLB. Followers may become less loyal and eventually leave the organization, they may be less respectful toward or develop a dislike for their leader, or they may attempt to lower their contributions and increase their outcomes (by engaging in less effort, more theft, etc.). For example, Tepper, Henle, Lambert, Giacalone, and Duffy (2008) linked abusive supervision to subordinates' organizational deviance. These followers' behaviors may in turn trigger more DLB through either the self-regulatory process or the social cognitive process. On the other hand, victims of DLB may have internalized responses such as lower self-esteem, negative mental health outcomes (Dezsofi, 2008), and even be at greater risk for future mistreatment (Aquino & Lamertz, 2004). Additional support for this idea comes from research describing a cyclical relationship between leader behavior and subordinate well-being (Dierendonck, Haynes, Borrill, & Stride, 2004).

Finally, when leaders engage in DLB it probably affects their own subsequent behavior depending on the outcomes the leader experiences. For example, Padilla et al. (2007) point out that DLB can have positive consequences. Such positive consequences may encourage the leader to engage in subsequent DLB. A cognitive consistency argument (Kelley, 1973) suggests that leaders who engage in DLB are likely to adapt their perceptions of the social context to fit their behavior, thus leading to further DLB. In effect, DLB may become a characteristic adaptation style that leaders learn as an acceptable response to events in their organization.

Taken together, disentangling the potential effects of follower behavior and the social dynamics of leadership represent an ambitious research agenda. However, we want to briefly acknowledge three other potentially fruitful directions for future research. First, although productive and counterproductive forms of leadership may be negatively correlated, at least some research suggests they are empirically distinct (cf. Dezsofi, 2008; Duffy, Ganster, & Pagon, 2002). Thus, most leaders probably engage in at least some positive and some negative behavior. Given that leadership researchers often focus on either positive or negative forms of leadership, but not both, there are many interesting questions remaining about their relative effects on outcomes. Second, we have not addressed differential antecedents across various forms of destructive leadership. It seems likely that both the broad categories of situational influences (e.g., stress, social norms) and specific variables within each category (e.g., various traits) would predict different forms of bad behavior. Integrative models such as ours highlight the need for empirical studies focusing on both individual differences and social influences in relation to multiple forms of destructive leadership. Finally, it would be particularly interesting from a policy development perspective to examine within person differences in both productive and destructive leadership over time. Is destructive leader behavior more or less pliable than constructive behavior? The answer to that question would have important implications for the relative emphasis on practices that emphasize changing leaders' behavior (e.g., training and development) as opposed to leader selection.

CONCLUSION

Empirical studies of positive aspects of leadership number in the thousands. Unfortunately, researchers increasingly recognize the need for similar attention to destructive aspects of leadership. As evidence accumulates about both individual and situational aspects of destructive leadership, researchers will be able to offer increasingly better recommendations for empirically supported practice. Such recommendations might differ dramatically depending on whether DLB is shown to be attributable to characteristics of individual leaders, features of the situational context, or interactions of personal characteristics and situation features. The general concept of a person by environment interaction is almost a truism in the field of psychology. However, the relative lack of attention to the social context of destructive leadership represents a major limiting factor in understanding about how to respond effectively to DLB. Hopefully, our model and other work in this volume represent an important step forward in this understanding.

AUTHOR NOTE

Correspondence regarding this research should be addressed to Mo Wang, Department of Psychology, University of Maryland, College Park, Maryland, 20742. Electronic mail may be sent to mwang@psyc.umd.edu

REFERENCES

Ajzen, I. (1991). The theory of planned behavior. *Organizational Behavior and Human Decision Processes, 50*, 179-211.

Ajzen, I., & Fishbein, M. (1980). *Understanding attitudes and predicting social behavior.* Englewood Cliffs, NJ: Prentice-Hall.

Aquino, K., & Lamertz, K. (2004). A relational model of workplace victimization. *Journal of Applied Psychology, 89*, 1023-1034.

Aryee, S., Chen, Z. X., Sun, L., & Debrah, Y. A. (2007). Antecedents and outcomes of abusive supervision: Test of a trickle-down model. *Journal of Applied Psychology, 92*, 191-201.

Bakker, A. B., Demerouti, E., & Euwema, M. C. (2005). Job resources buffer the impact of job demands on burnout. *Journal of Occupational Health Psychology, 10*, 170-180.

Bandura, A. (1969). *Principles of behavior modification.* New York: Holt, Rinehart & Winston.

Bartone, P. T., Ursano, R. J., Wright, K. M., & Ingraham, L. H. (1989). The impact of a military air disaster on the health of assistance workers: A prospective study. *The Journal of Nervous and Mental Disease, 177*, 317-328.

Bass, B. M. (1998). *Transformational leadership: Industrial, military, and educational impact.* Mahwah, NJ: Erlbaum.

Beal, D. J., Weiss, H. M., Barros, E., & MacDermid, S. M. (2005). An episodic process model of affective influences on performance. *Journal of Applied Psychology, 90*, 1054-1068.

Benson, M. J., & Campbell, J. P. (2007). To be, or not to be, linear: An expanded representation of personality and its relationship to leadership performance. *International Journal of Selection and Assessment, 15*, 232-249.

Berkowitz, L. (1989). Frustration–aggression hypothesis: Examination and reformulation. *Psychological Bulletin, 106*, 79-83.

Berkowitz, L. (1993). *Aggression: Its causes, consequences, and control.* New York: McGraw-Hill.

Bing, M. N., Stewart, S. M., Davison, H. K., Green, P. D., McIntyre, M. D., & James, L. R. (2007). An integrative typology of personality assessment for aggression: Implications for predicting counterproductive workplace behavior. *Journal of Applied Psychology, 92*, 722–744.

Brotheridge, C. M., & Lee, R. T. (2002). Testing a conservation of resources model of the dynamics of emotional labor. *Journal of Occupational Health Psychology, 7,* 57-67.

Bushman, B. J., Bonacci, A. M., Pdersen, W. C., Vasquez, E. A., & Miller, N. (2005). Chewing on it can chew you up: Effects of rumination on triggered displaced aggression. *Journal of Personality and Social Psychology, 88,* 969-983.

Chen, Z. X., Tsui, A. S., & Zhong, L. (2007). Reactions to psychological contract breach: A dual perspective. *Journal of Organizational Behavior, 29,* 527-548.

Cortina, L. M., Magley, V. J., Williams, J. H., & Langhout, R. D. (2001). Incivility in the workplace: Incidence and impact. *Journal of Occupational Health Psychology, 6,* 64-80.

Cropanzano, R., Goldman, B. M., & Benson, L., III. (2005). Organizational justice. In J. Barling, E. K. Kelloway, & M. R. Frone, (Eds.), *Handbook of work stress* (pp. 63-87). Thousand Oaks, CA: SAGE.

Detert, J. R., Trevino, L. K., Burris, E. R., & Andiappan, M. (2007). Managerial modes of influence and counterproductivity in organizations: A longitudinal business-unit-level investigation. *Journal of Applied Psychology, 92,* 993-1005.

Dezsofi, J. A. (2008). *Job stressors, high-quality leadership, and health in U.S. Army Soldiers: The role of counterproductive leadership.* Unpublished master's thesis, Portland State University, Department of Psychology.

Dierendonck, D., Haynes, C., Borrill, C., Stride, C. (2004). Leadership behavior and subordinate well-being. *Journal of Occupational Health Psychology, 9,* 165-175.

Dormann, C., & Zapf, D. (2004). Customer-related social stressors and burnout. *Journal of Occupational Health Psychology, 9,* 61-82.

Duffy, M. K., Ganster, D. G., & Pagon, M. (2002). Social undermining in the workplace. *Academy of Management Journal, 45,* 331-351.

Eagly, A. H., & Chaiken, S. (1993). *The psychology of attitudes.* Fort Worth, TX: Harcourt Brace Jovanovich College.

Einarsen, S., Aasland, M. S., & Skogstad, A. (2007). Destructive leadership behaviour: A definition and conceptual model. *The Leadership Quarterly, 18,* 207-216.

Fishbein, M., & Ajzen, I. (1975). *Belief, attitude, intention, and behavior: An introduction to theory and research.* Reading, MA: Addison-Wesley Pub. Co.

Florian, V., Mikulincer, M., & Taubman, O. (1995). Does hardiness contribute to mental health during a stressful real-life situation? The roles of appraisal and coping. *Journal of Personality and Social Psychology, 68,* 687-695.

Fox, S., & Spector, P. E. (1999). A model of work frustration-aggression *Journal of Organizational Behavior, 20,* 915-931.

Gerstner, C. R., & Day, D. V. (1997). Meta-analytic review of Leader-Member Exchange theory: Correlates and construct issues. *Journal of Applied Psychology, 82,* 827-844.

Grandey, A. A., Dickter, D. N., & Sin, H.-P. (2004). The customer is not always right: Customer aggression and emotion regulation of service employees. *Journal of Organizational Behavior, 25,* 397-418.

Grandey, A. A., Kern, J., & Frone, M. R. (2007). Verbal abuse from outsiders versus insiders: Comparing frequency, impact on emotional exhaustion, and the role of emotional labor. *Journal of Occupational Health Psychology, 12*, 63-79.

Hershcovis, M. S., Turner, N., Barling, J., Arnold, K. A., Dupre', K. E., Inness, M., et al. (2007). Predicting workplace aggression: A meta-analysis. *Journal of Applied Psychology, 92*, 228-238.

Hobfoll, S. E. (1989). Conservation of resources: A new attempt at conceptualizing stress. *American Psychologist, 44*, 513–524.

Hobfoll, S. E. (2002). Social and psychological resources and adaptation. *Review of General Psychology, 6*, 307-324.

Hogan, R., & Hogan, J. (2001). Assessing leadership: A view from the dark side. *International Journal of Selection and Assessment, 9*, 40-51.

Hoobler, J. M., & Brass, D. J. (2006). Abusive supervision and family undermining as displaced aggression. *Journal of Applied Psychology, 91*, 1125-1133.

Horney, K. (1950). *Neuroses and human growth*. New York: Norton.

Ilies, R., Nahrgang, J. D., & Moregson, F. P. (2007). Leader-member exchange and citizenship behaviors: A meta-analysis. *Journal of Applied Psychology, 92*, 269-277.

Illies, J. J., & Reiter-Palmon, R. (2008). Responding destructively in leadership situations: The role of personal values and problem construction. *Journal of Business Ethics, 82*, 251-272.

Jones, B., Flynn, D. M., & Kelloway, E. K. (1995). Perception of support from the organization in relation to work stress, satisfaction, and commmitment. In S. L. Sauter & L. R. Murphy (Eds.), *Organizational risk factors for job stress* (pp. 41-52). Washington, DC: American Psychological Association.

Judge, T. A., & Bono, J. E. (2001). Relationship of core self-evaluations traits—self-esteem, generalized self-efficacy, locus of control, and emotional stability —with job satisfaction and job performance: A meta-analysis. *Journal of Applied Psychology, 86*, 80-92.

Judge, T. A., Erez, A., Bono, J. E., & Thoresen, C. J. (2002). Are measures of self-esteem, neuroticism, locus of control, and generalized self-efficacy indicators of a common core construct. *Journal of Personality and Social Psychology, 83*, 693-710.

Judge, T. A., Erez, A., Bono, J. E., & Thoresen, C. J. (2003). The core self-evaluations scale: Development of a measure. *Personnel Psychology, 56*, 303-331.

Judge, T. A., Locke, E. A., & Durham, C. C. (1997). The dispositional causes of job satisfaction: A core evaluations approach. *Research in Organizational Behavior, 19*, 151-188.

Judge, T. A., & Piccolo, R. F. (2004). Transformational and transactional leadership: A meta-analytic test of their relative validity. *Journal of Applied Psychology, 89*, 755-768.

Judge, T. A., Piccolo, R. F., & Ilies, R. (2004). The forgotten ones? The validity of consideration and initiating structure in leadership research. *Journal of Applied Psychology, 89*, 36-51.

Kelley, H. H. (1973). The processes of causal attribution. *American Psychologist, 28*, 107-128.

Khan, L. J., & Morrow, P. C. (1991). Objective and subjective underemployment relationships to job satisfaction. *Journal of Business Research, 22,* 211-218.

Khoo, H. S., & Burch, G. S. J. (2008). The dark side of leadership personality and transformational leadership: An exploratory study. *Personality and Individual Differences, 44,* 86-97.

King, L. A., & King, D. W. (1990). Role conflict and role ambiguity: A critical assessment of construct validity. *Psychological Bulletin, 107,* 48-64.

Liden, R. C., & Maslen, J. M. (1998). Multidimensionality of leader-member exchange: An empirical assessment through scale development. *Journal of Management, 24,* 43-72.

Lombardo, M. M., Ruderman, M. N., & McCauley, C. D. (1988). Explanations of success and derailment in upper-level mangement positions. *Journal of Business and Psychology, 2,* 199-216.

Luthans, F., Avey, J. B., Avolio, B. J., Norman, S. M., & Combs, G. M. (2008). Psychological capital development: Toward a micro-intervention. *Journal of Organizational Behavior, 27,* 387-393.

Luthans, F., Avey, J. B., & Patera, J. L. (2008). Experimental analysis of a web-based training intervention to develop Positive Psychological Capital. *Academy of Management Learning & Education,* 7, 209-221.

Luthans, F., Avolio, B., Avey, J. B., & Norman, S. M. (2007). Positive psychological capital: Measurement and relationship with performance and satisfaction. *Personnel Psychology, 60,* 541-572.

Maddi, S. R., Kahn, S., & Maddi, K. L. (1998). The effectiveness of hardiness training. *Consulting Psychology Journal: Practice and Research, 50,* 78-86.

Maddi, S. R., & Kobasa, S. C. (1984). *The hardy executive: Health under stress.* Chicago, IL: Dorsey Professional Books.

Manstead, A. S. R. (1996). Attitudes and behaviour. In G. R. Semin & K. Fiedler (Eds.), *Applied social psychology* (pp. 3-29). London: SAGE.

McAdams, D. P., & Pals, J. L. (2006). A new big five: Fundamental principles for an integrative science of personality. *American Psychologist, 61,* 204-217.

McCall, M., & Lombardo, M. (1983). *Off the track: why and how successful executives get derailed.* Technical report, Center for Creative Leadership, Greensboro, NC.

McCrae, R. R., & Costa, P. T. (1999). A five-factor theory of personality. In L. R. Pervin & O. P. John (Eds.), *The handbook of personality* (2nd ed., pp. 139-153). New York: Guilford Press.

McCullough, M. E., Bono, G., & Root, L. M. (2007). Rumination, emotion, and forgiveness: Three longitudinal studies. *Journal of Personality and Social Psychology, 92,* 490-505.

Millham, J. (1974). Two components of need for approval score and their relationship to cheating following success and failure. *Journal of Research in Personality, 8,* 378-392.

Mitchell, M. S., & Ambrose, M. L. (2007). Abusive supervision and workplace deviance and the moderating effects of negative reciprocity beliefs. *Journal of Applied Psychology, 92,* 1159-1168.

Mitchell, T. R., & Daniels, D. (2003). Motivation. In W. C. Borman, D. R. Ilgen, & R. J. Klimoski (Eds.), *Handbook of psychology* (Vol. 12, pp. 225-254). New York: Wiley.

Moscoso, S., & Salgado, J. F. (2004). "Dark Side" personality styles as predictors of task, contextual, and job performance. *International Journal of Selection and Assessment, 12*, 356-362.

Nielsen, I. K., Jex, S. M., & Adams, G. A. (2000). Development and validation of scores on a two-dimensional workplace friendship scale. *Eduactional and Psychological Measurement, 60*, 628-643.

O'Leary-Kelly, A. M., Griffin, R. W., & Glrew, D. J. (1996). Organization-motivated aggression: A research framework. *Academy of Managment Review, 21*, 225-253.

Ones, D. S., & Viswesvaran, C. (2001). Personality at work: Criterion-focused occupational personality scales used in personnel selection. In B. W. Roberts & R. Hogan (Eds.), *Personality psychology in the workplace* (pp. 63-92). Washington DC: APA Books.

Padilla, A., Hogan, R., & Kaiser, R. B. (2007). The toxic triangle: Destructive leaders, susceptible followers, and conducive environments. *The Leadership Quarterly, 18*, 176-194.

Paunonen, S. V., Lönnqvist, J., Verkasalo, M., Leikas, S., & Nissinen, V. (2006). Narcissim and emergent leadership in military cadets. *The Leadership Quarterly, 17*, 475–486.

Pearson, C. M., & Porath, C. L. (2005). On the nature, consequences, and remedies of workplace incivility: No time for "nice"? Think again. *Academy of Management Executive, 19*, 7-18.

Penney, L. J., & Spector, P. E. (2002). Narcissism and counterproductive work behavior: Do bigger egos mean bigger problems? *International Journal of Selection and Assessment, 10*, 126-134.

Peters, L. H., & O'Conner, E. J. (1980). Situational constraints and work outcomes: The influences of a frequently overlooked construct. *Academy of Management Review, 5*, 391-397.

Rosenthal, S. A., & Pittinsky, T. L. (2006). Narcissistic leadership. *The Leadership Quarterly, 17*, 617-633

Rudolph, K. D., Caldwell, M. S., & Conley, C. S. (2005). Need for approval and children's well-being. *Child Development, 76*, 309-323.

Salgado, J. F. (2002). The Big Five personality dimensions and counterproductive behaviors. *International Journal of Selection and Assessment, 10*, 117-125.

Salin, D. (2005). Workplace bullying among business professionals: Prevalence, gender differences and the role of organizational politics. *Perspectives Interdisciplinaires sur le Travail et la Santé, 7*, 3.

Schaubroeck, J., Walumbwa, F. O., Ganster, D. C., & Kepes, S. (2007). Destructive leader traits and the neutralizing influence of an "enriched" job. *The Leadership Quarterly, 18*, 236-251.

Solinger, O. N., van Olffen, W., & Roe, R. A. (2008). Beyond the three-component model of organizational commitment. *Journal of Applied Psychology, 93*, 70-83.

Spector, P. E. (1987). Interactive effects of perceived control and job stressors on affective reactions and health outcomes for clerical workers. *Work & Stress, 1*, 155-162.

Tepper, B. J. (2000). Consequences of abusive supervision. *Academy of Management Journal, 43*, 178-190.

Tepper, B. J. (2007). Abusive supervision in work organizations: Review, synthesis, and research agenda. *Journal of Management, 33*, 261-289.

Tepper, B. J., Duffy, M. K., Henle, C. A., & Lambert, L. S. (2006). Procedural injustice, victim precipitation, and abusive supervision. *Personnel Psychology, 59*, 101-123.

Tepper, B. J., Henle, C. A., Lambert. L S., Giacalone, R. A., Duffy, M. K. (2008). Abusive supervision and subordinates organizational deviance. *Journal of Applied Psychology, 93*, 721-732.

Tucker, J. S., Sinclair, R. R., & Thomas, J. L. (2005). The multilevel effects of occupational stressors on soldiers' well-being, organizational attachment, and readiness. *Journal of Occupational Health Psychology, 10*, 276-299.

Turner, N., Barling, J., Epitropaki, O., Butcher, V., & Miller, C. (2002). Transformational leadership and moral reasoning. *Journal of Applied Psychology, 87*, 304-311.

Twenge, J. M., & Campbell, W. K. (2003). "Isn't it fun to get the respect that we're going to deserve?" Narcissism, social rejection, and aggression. *Personality and Social Psychology Bulletin, 29*, 261-272.

Van Velsor, E., & Leslie, J. B. (1995). Why executives derail: Perspectives across time and cultures. *Academy of Management Executive, 9*, 62-72.

Vroom, V. H., & Jago, A. G. (2007). The role of the situation in leadership. *American Psychologist, 62*, 17-24.

Wang, M. (2007). Profiling retirees in the retirement transition and adjustment process: Examining the longitudinal change patterns of retirees' psychological well-being. *Journal of Applied Psychology, 92*, 455-474.

Wiggins, J. S. (1996). *The five-factor model of personality: Theoretical perspectives*. New York: Guilford Press.

Yagil, D. (2006). The relationship of abusive and supportive workplace supervision to employee burnout and upward influence tactics. *Journal of Emotional Abuse, 6*, 49-65.

Zhao, H., Wayne, S. J., Glibkowski, B. C., & Bravo, J. (2007). The impact of psychological contract breach on work-related outcomes: A meta-analysis. *Personnel Psychology, 60*, 647-680.

CHAPTER 5

IGNORING THE SIGNPOSTS

A Process Perspective of Unethical and Destructive Leadership

Diane J. Chandler and Dail Fields

This chapter examines how salient dimensions of leaders, followers, and organizations interact within organizational processes to enable unethical and destructive leadership behavior. Three questions frame this discussion: (a) how and why did leaders venture down paths of destructive behaviors?, (b) why did these leaders persist in behaviors that most knew or would identify as unethical and destructive?, and (c) why were these behaviors tolerated, and in some instances rewarded, by organizations and followers? This chapter assesses how social-cognitive tendencies operating within organizational processes affect destructive leadership behavior through leadership selection, self-enhancement motives, escalation of commitment, threat-rigidity response, organizational commitment, feedback-seeking behaviors and feedback environment, and pressures for conformity. Six propositions derive from a process model for unethical and destructive leadership.

When Leadership Goes Wrong: Destructive Leadership, Mistakes and Ethical Failures, pp. 99–143

INTRODUCTION

Research in organizational studies has presented alternative conceptualizations of negative, unethical, and destructive leadership, as well as the consequences of these leader behaviors (Einarsen, Aasland, & Skogstad, 2007; Padilla, Hogan, & Kaiser, 2007; Schilling, 2009). Destructive leadership has been defined as repeated behaviors that work against the legitimate interests of an organization and its members including the undermining the organization's goal, resources, and quality of working life (Einarsen et al., 2007). Destructive leadership may involve dominance, coercion, manipulation of others, and selfish leader-focused orientation (Lipman-Blumen, 2005; Padilla et al., 2007). While previous studies have considered leader and follower characteristics that may be associated with the occurrence of destructive leadership, organizations succeed or fail based on the effectiveness and resilience of their processes for strategy and human resource development (Collins, 2001; Pfeffer & Sutton, 2006). As a result, antecedents of destructive leadership must be considered within the contexts of organizational processes. The purpose of this chapter is to examine how certain key variables of leaders, followers, and organizations may interact within organizational processes to enable unethical and destructive leadership.

In a recent qualitative study, Schilling (2009) found that only 25% of the identified variables accounting for negative leadership behaviors were attributable to individual leader characteristics, whereas 75% were attributed to situational variables. Leadership characteristics alone do not fully account for why leaders behave destructively. In most organizational settings, situational variables are strong determinants of employee behaviors. If followers in an organization observe leaders' disregard of honesty, integrity, and ethical behavior, the minimum result may be confusion and an implied directive that such behaviors are an acceptable norm, setting the stage for social pressure to exhibit unethical, negative, and possibly destructive behaviors (Bazerman & Benaji, 2004; Brass, Butterfield, & Skaggs, 1998; Schweitzer & Gibson, 2008). Therefore examining organizational processes and the related outcomes are important for understanding how destructive leadership behavior may arise and be tolerated in organizational settings (Brown & Treviño, 2006a; Manz, Anand, Joshi, & Manz, 2008; Padilla et al., 2007; Schilling, 2009).

In explaining unethical and destructive leadership behavior, researchers have focused primarily on the characteristics of (a) leaders (Benson & Hogan, 2008; Dotlich & Cairo, 2003, Kellerman, 2004; Kets de Vries, 1993, 2006), (b) followers (Lord & Brown, 2004; Offerman, 2004), (c) environmental variables (Schilling, 2009; Zimbardo, 2006, 2007), or (d) a conflux of leader, follower and environmental conditions (Padilla et al.,

2007; Popper, 2001; Rhode, 2006; Vardi & Weitz, 2004). However as we review and observe examples of destructive organizational leaders whose unethical and sometimes malicious behaviors have come to light, we are confronted by three penetrating questions related to why organizations and their members ignore the obvious signposts, the tell-tale signs of unethical and destructive leadership actions:

- How and why did such leaders venture down paths of such destructive behaviors?
- Why did these leaders persist in behaviors that most knew or would identify as unethical and destructive?
- Why were these behaviors tolerated, and in some instances rewarded, by organizations and followers?

The focus of this chapter is to address these three questions by examining how characteristics of leaders, followers, and organizations interact, while highlighting the organizational processes seldom explored in relationship to unethical and destructive leadership. Specifically we examine the effects of cognitive tendencies operating in organizational processes such as (a) self-enhancement motives (Pfeffer & Fong, 2005), (b) escalation of commitment (Street & Street, 2006), (c) threat-rigidity response (Staw, Sandelands, & Dutton, 1981), (d) organizational commitment (Peterson, 2003), (e) feedback-seeking behaviors and the feedback environment (Herold & Parsons, 1985; Janssen & Prins, 2007; Whitaker, Dahling, & Levy, 2007), and (f) pressures for conformity (Zimbardo, 1969, 2006, 2007).

Although unethical leadership behavior may not immediately eventuate in destructive organizational outcomes, the seeds of destruction have been sown despite whether or not unethical behaviors ever come to light, creating a desensitizing effect upon ethical values, standards, and conduct. Therefore, a fundamental premise of this chapter is that unethical leadership behavior is ultimately destructive in nature. Hence, we link the terms unethical and destructive leadership in tandem.

Figure 5.1 presents a model showing the linkages among the major organizational processes analyzed in this chapter.

1. WHY DO LEADERS VENTURE DOWN UNETHICAL AND DESTRUCTIVE PATHS?

In addressing the first of three major questions, we begin by examining the leadership selection process itself involving common selection biases. Some have argued that executive leaders are chosen to address short-term

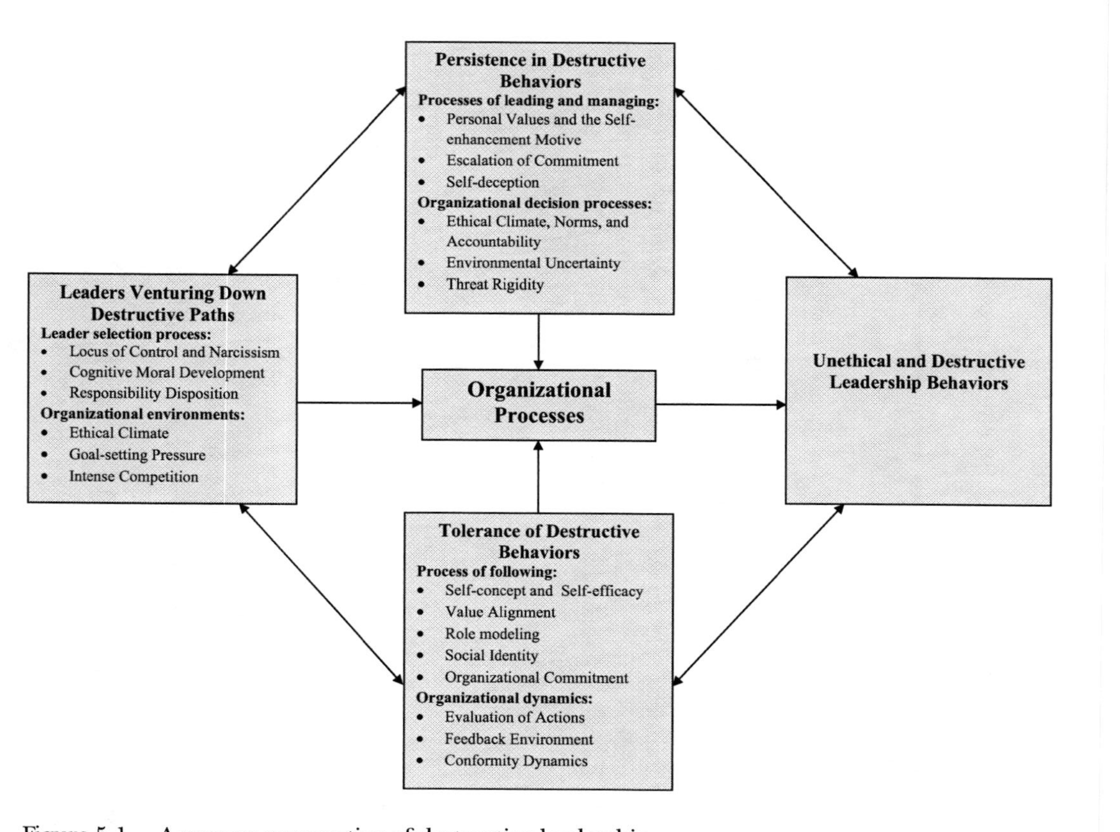

Figure 5.1. A process perspective of destructive leadership.

fixes rather than long-term success (Hogan & Kaiser, 2008), while others pinpoint the lack of systematically applied and valid selection criteria (DeVries, 1992), including demonstrated character and integrity (Treviño, Hartman, & Brown, 2000).

1.1. Oversights in the Leadership Selection Process

The fundamental area of leadership selection is a relevant topic when considering the unethical and destructive behavior of leaders. The effects of the methods by which leaders are selected have not been explored extensively or empirically in the leadership literature (De Cremer & van Dijk, 2008). These methods may be laden with bias. Bias in leadership selection derives from the attraction-selection-attrition (ASA) framework (Schneider, 1987). The ASA process suggests that selection decisions tend to reflect in-group bias based on perceived similarities of candidates to existing occupants of organizational positions of power. This tendency operates, in part, due to a confirmation bias known as the "halo effect," or the perception that positive qualities in one area apply to another (Cooper, 1981; Meindl & Erlich, 1987). Schneider, Goldstein, and Smith (1995) cautioned that leadership selection based exclusively on similarity-attraction may lead to over-homogenization that limits organizational flexibility and performance, producing an in-group bias. However, other empirical results suggested that perceived perceptions of threats or danger may alter the in-group focus to perceived tendencies toward more decisive, directive leaders (Hoyt, Simon, & Reid, 2009). If those making leadership selections tend to view current environmental conditions as threatening, there is an increased likelihood that candidates perceived as more directive and dominant may be preferred. While a dominant personality alone may not signal a tendency toward unethical or destructive behaviors, powerful personalities combined with perceived organizational threats may be a toxic combination (Padilla et al., 2007).

Observing that most executive searches are conducted without a systematic assessment process, Harshman and Harshman (2008) noted, "there seems to be a general feeling among boards and search firm executives that asking top level (Board of Directors, CEO, or president) candidates to participate in an assessment is demeaning and will drive good candidates away" (p. 186). Others advocate the use of formal cognitive and leadership assessments to evaluate leadership skills and technical ability (Hogan, 2006; Hogan, Curphy, & Hogan, 1994; Hogan, Raskin, & Fazzini, 1990). For example in a meta-analysis, Judge, Colbert, and Ilies (2004) found that the relationship between intelligence and leadership effectiveness, although significant, was lower than expected. Perceived intelligence was more strongly associated with leadership than intelligence measured objectively with tests. In addition, consistent with cognitive resource theory, the relationship of intelligence with leadership effectiveness declined significantly when leaders were under greater stress. Therefore, traditional intelligence assessments may not predict how leaders will interact in decision-making situations when under pressure. However as Padilla and Mulvey (2008) observed, most leadership selection measures assess productive job behaviors, not counterproductive ones, creating an imbalanced evaluative procedure.

Although intelligence, personality, world view, and style may be observable, other markers, such as character, integrity, and ethical standards, albeit less observable, remain vitally important to assess. In particular, "dark side" characteristics of leaders, which may underlie unethical and destructive behavior, are difficult to detect through assessments because candidates with strong social skills and a positive self-esteem demeanor may camouflage these characteristics (Hogan et al., 1994). In addition, a candidate may present several attributes that are highly consistent with the key characteristics within implicit leadership models used by the organizational selectors. However, as the "halo effect" suggests, there is a tendency to associate the presence of a few key attributes with the presence of others that may be unrelated. For example in their study of retail store managers, Porr and Fields (2006) found leadership success on an attribute considered important by different observers resulted in vastly different assessments of the same managers. Since most leadership selectors have little experience or expertise in the selection process, the role of their implicit leadership assumptions may be a key determinant in leader selection decisions. Without realizing it, leadership selectors may be unknowingly hiring those with hidden "dark side" characteristics that might later sabotage personal and organizational integrity.

As De Cremer and van Dijk (2008) noted, assigning the label of "leader" can make two possible competing individual motives salient. On one hand, being selected as a leader may motivate a person to model socially responsible behavior; on the other, selection as a leader may trigger feelings of personal entitlement to receive special privileges or rewards. Experimental results have shown that followers are more accepting of appointed leaders taking larger shares of available rewards and that appointed leaders exhibit lower levels of social responsibility than elected leaders (De Cremer & van Dijk, 2008). However, the latter differences disappeared when the appointed leaders demonstrated social responsibility and ethical behavior. Sessa and Kaiser (2000) observed that the likelihood of hiring unethical and destructive leaders may be reduced when selectors consult others, work as a team, add leadership selection criteria such as demonstrated integrity (Padilla & Mulvey, 2008; Singh, 2008), and emphasize expectations for leaders to demonstrate social responsibility (De Cremer & van Dijk, 2008; De Hoogh & Hartog, 2008). Unethical and destructive leadership might well be mitigated with carefully crafted leadership selection criteria and processes.

1.2. Leader Characteristics

As mentioned, certain personal characteristics of candidates for leadership positions can be readily measured with available standardized assessment instruments and procedures. Other attributes of leaders are more difficult to assess because standardized instruments do not readily exist or because organizations are unwilling to put candidates through an arduous assessment process. However, some of these underassessed leader attributes may be critical indicators of attributes that may lead to unethical and destructive leadership. These attributes include LOC, narcissism, degree of cognitive moral development, and responsibility disposition. These specific four characteristics have been selected for inclusion, as they have been found in the literature to impact the decision-making process and contribute to unethical and destructive leadership.

1.2.1. Locus of Control (LOC)

LOC is identified as a personality attribute that describes how individuals perceive their ability to control events and make attributions about causality (Lefcourt, 1966; Phares, 1976; Rotter, 1966). Those with an internal LOC surmise that they are able to influence events and leadership results based on their ability and skill. Those with an external LOC believe that circumstances outside of themselves are the primary causes for events and their leadership behavior. Researchers have found that managers with an internal LOC were more confident in their ability to control events, coped better with challenging situations, but also opted for riskier strategies in order to advance organizational performance (Anderson, 1977; Miller & Toulouse, 1986; Miller, Kets de Vries, & Toulouse, 1982). Treviño and Youngblood (1990) found individuals with greater internal LOC made more ethical decisions. Leaders with more external LOC were more likely to attribute causes to external conditions, possibly leading to their denial of personal responsibility for destructive behaviors and related outcomes. Leaders higher in self-regulation are more likely to control behaviors and decisions and may be less prone to unethical or destructive behaviors (Moss, Dowling, & Callanan, 2009).

Since the essence of self-regulation is a heightened awareness of self and self-responsibility, it seems likely that external LOC and self-regulation are negatively related. Street and Street (2006) found that those with an external LOC were more likely than those with an internal LOC to select unethical options related to decision-making, suggesting less personal self-regulation. While not necessarily leading directly to destructive leadership behaviors, LOC may impact leaders' interactions with others through role-taking within organizational processes. LOC may affect the way that leaders make attributions and interact with others in organizational processes. Frankly, externals may be more likely to cave to external pressures, while internals may resist regulation. Both tendencies could lead to destructive behaviors worth noting in consideration of the way leaders act within organizational processes. While one would expect a difference in LOC related to persistence in achieving ends (i.e., internals have more persistence than externals), studies have found that there is no significant difference between internals and externals related to persistence (Littig & Sanders, 1979; Pittenger, 2002; Starnes & Zinzer, 1983) and that the effects of LOC may be both context-specific and related to self-efficacy, interpersonal control, and sociopolitical control (Paulus & Christie, 1981).

1.2.2. Narcissism

A second pertinent leader characteristic is narcissism, a personality trait often associated with egotism, self-interest, grandiosity, arrogance, and entitlement (Kets de Vries, 2006; Rosenthal & Pittinsky, 2006). With failure rates among senior executives cited as between 50-60% and the selection process seldom assessing personality (Hogan et al., 1994), narcissism becomes an important variable to consider. For example, narcissistic leaders take more credit for their successes, blame others for their failures, are disposed to lapses in judgment and conduct, and may be abusive (Hogan et al., 1990; Kramer, 2003; Rosenthal & Pittinsky, 2006). Although narcissistic leaders may possess the capacity to attract followers (Kohut, 1966; Maccoby, 2003), the weaknesses inherent to this personality trait can lead directly to unethical behavior through influences on leader actions within organizational processes (Kets de Vries & Miller, 1997; Padilla et al., 2007). Narcissistic leaders may pass selection screening because they possess strengths such as the ability to present a vision in a charismatic fashion, inspire others with rhetoric, and thereby persuade others to follow (Maccoby, 2000). With pressures to hire for competitive advantage, executives charged with selecting leaders may focus on these positive characteristics. However, these strengths may camouflage leaders' underlying self-focus, lack of empathy, desire to control others, distaste for collaboration, and an intense desire to win at all costs. Narcissistic leaders' faults may become more pronounced if they succeed and as their personal need for power nears fulfillment (Maccoby, 2003; Rosenthal & Pittinsky, 2006). Characterized by independence, arrogance, and inordinate need for recognition, narcissists risk intentional isolation to protect their perceived superiority and frequently exhibit amorality and/or moral myopia where "the ends justify the means;" and followers are expected to provide blind support (Rhode, 2006; Rosenthal & Pittinsky, 2006).

Narcissism may develop in childhood after not receiving the caring support needed for healthy psycho-social development. Attributed to damage in the formative "mirroring" process between infant and mother where the child is deprived in some way, this reactive narcissism creates a yearning for positive affirmation and individuation in later adult stages (Kohut, 1971; Pines, 1981; Popper, 2001). These feelings of inferiority may manifest in self-protective defense mechanisms leading to overcompensation (Jordan, Spencer, Zanna, Hoshino-Brown, & Correll, 2003; Ziglar-Hill, 2006), self-enhancement (John & Robins, 1994), and a compulsive need for recognition (Morf & Rhodewalt, 2001). These effects of narcissism may manifest in intimidation of others involved in regulatory processes within organizations limiting the ability of these processes to curb unethical and destructive behaviors of leaders.

1.2.3. Cognitive Moral Development (CMD)

Third, leaders' lack of cognitive moral development (CMD) contributes to destructive leadership and decision making (Treviño, 1986, Treviño & Youngblood, 1990; Treviño, Hartman, & Brown, 2000). Kohlberg (1969, 1984) suggested that moral development advances from obedience motives and fear of punishment (stage 1), to reciprocity exchange (stage 2), to deciding issues of right and wrong based on expectations of others (stage 3), to abiding by rules and laws (stage 4), to internalized standards (stage 5), and then to universally held principles of justice and rights (stage 6) (Kohlberg, Levine, & Hewer, 1983). Stages 5 and 6 are associated with adulthood. Cognitive moral development has been shown to predict ethical decision making (Trevino & Youngblood, 1990). Building on previous models (Kohlberg, 1969, 1984; Rest, 1979, 1986; Trevino, 1986), Jones (1991) further argued that ethical decision making is contingent on the moral intensity of the subject issue, defining moral intensity as "the extent of issue-related moral imperative in a situation" (p. 372). Moral intensity involves the magnitude of the consequences of a decision, probability of effect, temporal immediacy, proximity, and concentration of effort. In an empirical study of ethical decision making, Paolillo and Vitell (2002) found that moral intensity accounted for significant portions of the variance in ethical decision making over other variables including job satisfaction and organizational commitment. It appears that tendencies towards unethical and destructive leadership depend not only on the level of leader moral development, but also the interaction of leaders' moral development with the moral intensity of choices they must make as leaders. It is also likely that individual moral development may affect the nature and intensity of interactions among leader and others within organizational dynamics. Leaders with lower levels of moral development may pull off some "wins" in competitive situations that help insulate destructive leadership behaviors from scrutiny and regulation.

1.2.4. Responsibility Disposition

A fourth leader characteristic relates to responsibility disposition. Pearce, Manz, and Sims (2008) suggested that leaders may be differentiated by their personalized, as compared to socialized, power orientation. The key distinction between these types of power orientations can be measured by the leader's responsibility disposition. Leaders with higher levels of socialized need for power tend to have a high responsibility disposition, while leaders with higher personalized need for power tend to have a low responsibility disposition. Mumford, Helton, Decker, Connelly, and Van Doorn (2003) found that individuals whose values stressed contributions to others, as opposed to personal gain, exhibited greater integrity in making decisions. Accordingly, these leaders may restrain use of power and may be less likely to use power for personal gain. Overall, this research suggests that leaders that have greater regard for socialized power may be less likely to engage in unethical and destructive behavior. In contrast, leaders with a greater need for personalized power may be lower in responsibility disposition and utilize power solely for personal gain (Hogan et al., 1994). Such leaders may persuasively stress the importance of personal allegiance to themselves as leaders, as opposed to loyalty to the overall organization. Compared to other characteristics of leaders considered in selection and promotion processes, LOC, narcissism, cognitive moral development, and responsibility disposition are formidable antecedents that affect leader performance in organizational processes and may thus indirectly make it difficult for organizations to regulate or "rein in" destructive leader behaviors.

Proposition 1. Leader selection processes are likely to overlook underlying leader characteristics such as LOC, narcissism, level of moral development, and responsibility disposition which may affect leader actions in organizational processes and limit the effects of regulatory safeguards to curb destructive leadership behaviors.

1.3. Organizational Characteristics and Processes

To address the question as to how and why leaders venture down unethical and destructive paths, we suggest that both internal and external organizational characteristics and processes contribute to creating ripe environments for such behavior (Treviño, 1986). Three factors impacting organizational context include ethical climate, goal setting pressure, and intense competition.

1.3.1. Ethical Climate

We maintain that ethical climate is a factor contributing to unethical and destructive leadership behavior. Schneider's (1975) commonly accepted definition of organizational climate relates to perceptions that "psychologically meaningful molar [environmental] descriptions that people can agree characterize a system's practices and procedures" (p. 474). In other words, organizational climate is fostered by members' shared perceptions related to the organizational practices and procedures within psychological environments (Reicher & Schneider, 1990). Victor and Cullen (1988) proposed that ethical climates vary along two dimensions, namely ethical criteria relating to ethical decisions based on egoism, benevolence, or principle; and the focus of ethical reasoning relating to the scope of ethical decisions. With the ethical dimension of organizational climate impacting job satisfaction and performance (Cullen, Parboteeah, & Victor, 2003), we argue that when ethical climates exhibit weak ethical criteria and the focus of ethical reasoning is minimal, that unethical and destructive behaviors of leaders are more likely.

For example, in their empirical study, Schminke, Ambrose, and Newbaum (2005) examined the impact of leader moral development upon ethical climate. Sampling 269 participants representing 47 firms, they found that moral development of leaders was strongly correlated with an ethical organizational climate. Second, they found that the relationship between leader moral development and ethical climate was stronger in younger versus older organizations in four out of five ethical climate types, which seemed to suggest that leaders' ethical values, as they apply to organizational development, would be less hindered with fewer levels of bureaucratic and/or organizational structure. Third, results affirmed that value congruence between leaders and employees heightened job satisfaction and commitment, while reducing turnover intentions. These findings affirm that leader values and moral development impact followers' shared assumptions (Schein, 1992), which in turn influence the overall ethical climate. An possible outgrowth of organizational climate is goal-setting pressure.

1.3.2. Goal Setting Pressure

When organizational pressures mount for goal accomplishment, the likelihood of unethical and destructive behaviors may likewise increase. After reviewing nearly 400 goal-setting studies, Locke and Latham (1990) found that the vast majority of these studies focused on the beneficial effects of performance due to setting specific, challenging goals. However, a study investigating Lewicki's (1983) model of deception found that those with unmet specific goals were more likely to engage in unethical behavior than individuals attempting to "do their best" (Schweitzer, Ordonnez, & Douma, 2004). Lewicki also found that the relationship between specific goal setting and unethical behavior was particularly strong when people fell just short of reaching established goals. In the process, leaders may employ deception to protect themselves in order to frame their goal achievement in positivistic terms.

Often, self-deception, the paradoxical capacity to deceive oneself regarding the truth in the process of protecting self-image, may involve evasive mechanisms including willful ignorance, systematic ignoring, emotional detachment, self-pretense, and rationalization. A decision to deceive others may be based on decision makers' perceptions of the costs and benefits of this course of action (Schweitzer et al., 2004). In particular, Lewicki (1983) speculated that people underestimate the costs of being deceptive because of self-justification. It appears, then, that the act of goal setting may alter perceptions of the benefits of engaging in unethical behavior. That is, leaders' setting or accepting specific challenging goals may increase their perceptions of the benefits to be gained, in contrast to the costs, in undertaking unethical behaviors (Schweitzer et al., 2004). Likewise, Barsky (2008) argued that performance goals may intercept employees' ethical sensibilities and disengage their internal moral and social controls (Bandura, 1999), by predicting that increasingly more difficult and specific goals increases the likelihood of unethical behavior. Goal setting pressures and goal achievement may contribute to leaders travelling down paths of unethical and destructive behavior.

1.3.3. Intense Competition

Competitive and unstable environments may place high levels of pressure on organizations to retain market share, financial viability, and dominance. When environments are unstable and unpredictable, the lack of previous precedents for how to make ethical organizational decisions causes organizational leaders to rely on their own personal ethical codes to guide behaviors. Organizational instability may result from shortage of resources, escalating costs, downsizing, mergers, and global factors such as economic recession, which are beyond the organization's and leader's control. A 2005 survey of over 1,000 executives and managers in global business found that 70% of the participants indicated that pressure to meet unrealistic business objectives and deadlines was the most prevalent reason leaders cited in explaining unethical behaviors (American Management Association, 2006). Pressure to meet targets within the constraints of time and resource allocation continues to plague organizational life, which provides greater conditions for ethical violations in the pursuit of survival (Webley & Warner, 2008). Given that leaders may venture down paths of unethical and destructive behaviors, the question arises as to why they persist in these behaviors in light of the potential negative outcomes, which could sabotage their credibility and the viability of their respective organizations.

> **Proposition 2.** Organizational characteristics such as the prevailing ethical climate, pressure to set aggressive goals, and intense competition will combine to limit the impact that organizational processes may have on regulating destructive leader behaviors.

2. WHY DO LEADERS PERSIST IN UNETHICAL AND DESTRUCTIVE BEHAVIORS?

Most leaders confront challenges in their leadership roles related to uncertainty, priorities, decision-making, and interpersonal conflicts, which may challenge or reinforce personal value alignment. Whereas in some situations leaders may be confronted with options to behave unethically, self-monitoring may dissuade them from doing so (Bandura, 1997).

In other cases, leaders may persist in unethical and destructive behaviors. This section specifically addresses leader and organizational characteristics/processes in an attempt to explain the reasons for leaders' persistence in unethical and destructive behavior.

2.1. Leader Characteristics

Leadership characteristics are salient variables in explaining unethical and destructive leadership behavior. We focus on characteristics that have received less attention in the research literature including personal values and the self-enhancement motive, escalation of commitment, and self-deception.

2.1.1. Personal Values and the Self-Enhancement Motive

The ethical values of leaders form a cornerstone of decision making, conduct, and ethical leadership (Cameron, 2003; Heath, 2002; Quinn, 2003). As such, leaders' values create internal pressure to behave in a prescribed way, often in an effort to align behaviors with values (Illies & Reiter-Palmon, 2008; Rokeach, 1973). In other words, individual values are predictive of leader behavior. For example, Bass and Steidlmeier (1998) argued that an absence of honesty, fairness, and a disregard for justice may lead to misdirected and potentially destructive leadership behavior. Furthermore, individual leader values strongly influence the behavior of organizational members and the way that organizational values are implemented (Grojean, Resick, Dickson, & Smith, 2004; Meglino & Ravlin, 1998).

Schwartz (1992, 1994) developed and tested a value framework that incorporates 10 values that are related in a circumflex. The Schwartz value types include (a) self-direction, (b) stimulation, (c) hedonism, (d) achievement, (e) power, (f) security, (g) conformity, (h) tradition, (i) benevolence, and (j) universalism. These 10 values can also be aggregated into four major dimensions of self-enhancement, self-transcendence, conservatism, and openness to change. Applying Schwartz's value theory, Illies and Reiter-Palmons (2008) found that participants with dominant self-enhancement values were more destructive in leadership situations than participants with self-transcendence values.

Originating from social psychology (Fiske, 2004) and social identity perspectives (Tajfel & Turner, 1986), self-enhancement theory predicts that persons high in self-enhancement tend to see themselves and their behaviors in the most positive light (Pfeffer & Fong, 2005) and ignore or avoid situations which expose unflattering information (Sedikides & Green, 2000). Sedikides (1993) found the self-enhancement motive as the dominant factor in self-evaluation processes over other variables, and Sedikides, Gaertner, and Toguchi (2003) identified self-enhancement as a universal human motive. Overall, leaders' self-enhancement motives tend to prompt self-serving social judgments (Beauregard & Dunning, 1998) and distort self-assessments (Dunning, Meyerowitz, & Holzberg, 1989). Leaders with strong self-enhancement motives tend to favor others who are similar to themselves by establishing in-groups, which then reinforces social identity with others (Pfeffer & Fong, 2005). This propensity influences followers' desire to enhance their self-image (Yun, Takeuchi, & Liu, 2007) and to discount contrary information (Kunda, 1987). With a natural tendency of followers wanting to associate with "winners," self-enhancing leaders attract allies, followers, and supporters. Many leaders have access to resources, which enable them to act at will and believe they will not encounter interference or serious consequences from organizational processes that might limit behaviors that are headed in destructive directions (Keltner, Gruenfeld, & Anderson, 2003). In summary, leaders may venture down paths of unethical and destructive behaviors as a result of formidable self-enhancement motives, which may override other personal values and professional and social expectancies, thereby fostering unethical and destructive behavior.

2.1.2. Escalation of Commitment

A primary reason that leaders may doggedly persist in unethical and/or destructive behaviors, even if these approaches are not producing anticipated results, is a phenomenon described as escalation of commitment. Identified as "escalation" Staw (1976, 1981) and "entrapment" (Rubin & Brockner, 1975), the term describes the decision to continue a course of action in the face of negative feedback about prior resource allocation, uncertainty surrounding the likelihood of goal attainment, and choice about whether to continue (Brockner 1992). Street, Robertson, and Geiger (1997) argued that exposure to escalation situations increases the likelihood that individuals will select unethical decision-making options. Furthermore, leaders may escalate commitment to failing courses of action to (a) align actions with their belief system (Biyalogorsky, Boulding, & Staelin, 2006), (b) avoid cognitive dissonance (Festinger, 1957), (c) justify or rationalize their behavior (Bobocel & Meyer, 1994; Brockner, 1992), (d) diffuse responsibility and assign blame to others (Whyte, 1991), and (e) heighten prospects of success (Whyte, 1986).

Paradoxically, Whyte, Sakes, and Hook (1997) found a significant positive relationship between a leader's self-efficacy and the tendency to persist in a failing initiative. They concluded, "[T]hose with a high level of skill and a history of selecting courses of action and making them pay off, are most likely to engage in the pursuit of a failing policy" (p. 428). Keil, Depledge, and Rai (2007) found that problem recognition and escalation of commitment were inversely related and that selective perception and illusion of control significantly affected both. Selective perception describes how people cognitively structure problems based on personal experience. Previous experiences may bias the information sought by leaders and create a tendency to disregard contradictory information (Hogarth, 1987). The illusion of control is the tendency to place success probability above objective reality, such as in the case of those with a previous success history or with entrepreneurs (Keil et al., 2007).

When leaders confront problems, the way forward may be unclear. In escalating commitment to a failing course of action, they may engage in unethical behaviors to counter negative feedback from the environment (McCain, 1986). Street and Street (2006) found that the greater the magnitude of the escalation situation (i.e., how large and broad an impact an escalating situation was in terms of increasing monetary values), the greater the likelihood of unethical behavior. Finally, by virtue of their roles, leaders have positional power, defined as the "capacity to alter others' states by providing or withholding resources and administering punishments" (Keltner et al., 2003, p. 267). If leaders feel a reduced sense of power, they may escalate their commitment to prevent perceived failure, off-set an impending negative self-portrayal, or reframe their strategies in pursuit of a course of action to minimize negative effects of perceived failure (Raven, 2001). Therefore, escalation of commitment may contribute to the pursuit of unethical and destructive leadership behavior because leaders may persevere in pursuing goals at any and all costs.

2.1.3. Self-Deception

Bronner (2003) enumerated several decision-making pathologies that may explain leaders' unwillingness to challenge unethical or destructive courses of actions. The pathologies focus on such self-deceptive practices as unrealistic framing of decisions, including the information received about decisions and their related consequences. Self-deception, the paradoxical capacity to deceive oneself regarding the truth in the process of protecting self-image, is a powerful psychological determinant (Tenbrunsel & Messick, 2004). Self-deceivers deny and/or conceal the truth, avoid personal commitment, and display evasive mechanisms including willful ignorance, systematic ignoring, emotional detachment, self-pretense, and rationalization (Fingarette, 2000; Haight, 1980; Martin, 1986).

If leaders fail to seek adequate information, devalue the information sources, and selectively perceive information received, they may cognitively push the moral implications of a decision to the background, allowing them to pursue deviant behaviors, whether consciously or unconsciously (Ludwig & Longenecker, 1993; Tenbrunsel & Messick, 2004). Ironically by ignoring or avoiding moral implications of decisions, self-interested leaders actually can retain self-perceptions that they are ethical leaders. Tenbrusel and Messick described this inductive self-deception process as "ethical numbing," where repeated exposure to ethical dilemmas fosters tolerance for and support of unethical decision-making, removing leaders from ethical scrutiny, and further reinforcing self-deception. Self-deception of leaders, when combined with positional power and personal persuasion, may then lead to the persistence of unethical and destructive practices.

Proposition 3. Leader characteristics such as personal values, self-enhancement motives, self-deception, and tendencies to escalate commitment will affect leader behavior within organizational processes and perpetrate patterns of unethical and destructive leader behavior.

2.2. Organizational Characteristics and Processes

To further address the question as to why leaders persist in unethical and destructive behaviors, three specific organizational dimensions are addressed: ethical climate and norms, environmental uncertainty, and reactions to perceived threats (threat rigidity).

2.2.1. Ethical Climate and Norms

Ethical climate is influenced by organizational history, structures, and practices including the founder's and subsequent leaders' personal values, ethical policies and procedures, legal oversight, decision-making processes, and accountability structures (Dickson, Smith, Grojean, & Ehrhart, 2001; Schein, 1992; Victor & Cullen, 1988). However, the existence of stated ethical organizational policies, such as a code of ethics, does not necessarily inhibit unethical behavior. For example, Webley and Werner (2008) found gaps in organizations' ethics policies and ethical practices. Such gaps may arise if ethics policies are not reflected in strategic goals and operating methods (Webley, 2003). When top organizational leaders do not regularly espouse and demonstrate behaviors consistent with ethical principles, it is likely that lower level managers and leaders may see ethics codes and policies merely as symbolic, but not necessarily normative, which encourages further deterioration of ethical standards.

Consistent with this assertion, Treviño, Weaver, Gibson, and Toffler (1999) surveyed 10,000 employees in six large U.S. corporations, resulting in three relevant findings. First, if employees were aware of relevant ethical and legal issues, they may be more likely to ask the right questions and ultimately do the right thing when faced with an ethical dilemma. An effective ethics/compliance management program encourages employees to look for ethical/legal advice within the company. Second, in cases where employees perceived that an ethics/compliance program was oriented primarily to protecting top management from blame, employees expressed greater tendencies to undertake unethical behaviors, were less committed to the organization, and rarely reported ethical/legal violations to management. Third, top leadership was a key in creating an effective ethical culture where employees perceived that executives take ethics seriously and consider ethics as important as the bottom line. When workers perceived such a climate was present, they were more aware of ethical issues, were less likely to consider unethical behaviors, and more likely to report unethical conduct.

Dickson et al. (2001) proposed that ethical climate proceeds directly from the values and motives of the organizational founders and early organizational leaders. They argued that ethical climate is created

> when organizational founders and subsequent leaders explicitly attend to their own values, determine the values that they wish to instill in organizational members, and make strategic organizational decisions that will facilitate the development of shared perceptions of appropriate ethical behavior. (p. 198)

When environmental conditions are stable and predictable, organizational members generally have been found to follow ethical standards (Dickson et al., 2001). Conversely when the environment is unstable and unpredictable, members confront unfamiliar circumstances, where no precedent informs ethical decision-making. In this case, if ethical values and standards are not well established, leaders' unethical/destructive behavior becomes more likely. Clear accountability structures are one safeguard against leaders' unethical conduct.

Accountability within organizations is established when managers and employees expect that they will be called upon to explain, justify, and defend their behaviors and self-evaluations to one or more others (Lerner & Tetlock, 1999, 2003). In support of this assertion, Sedikides, Herbst, Hardin, and Dardis (2002) and Sedikides and Herbst (2002) found that accountability deters self-enhancement because of evaluation expectancy within organizational/social contexts. Although accountability may assist to safeguard ethical decision making, it is not fool-proof, as the effects of accountability are susceptible to dynamics of given situational contexts

(Tetlock, 1992). Sedikides et al. (2002) concluded that self-enhancement is a controllable bias in response to admonitions for truthfulness, which accountability is designed to foster.

2.2.2. Environmental Uncertainty

Scholars pose various external factors related to the environment in explaining unethical/destructive leadership and corporate corruption. For example, Baucus (1994) identified both pressure, or the urgent corporate demands or constraints upon a firm; and the need, or the lack of adequate resources, as impacting the tendency to "cut corners" within uncertain environments (p. 704). A scarcity of financial and human resources creates what Pfeffer and Salancik (1978) termed resource dependence, whereby firms depend on stakeholders (i.e., customers, suppliers, regulators, the media) to acquire the needed resources to ensure viability. As a result of inadequate resources, leaders may compromise ethical standards to retain a competitive edge. For example, Staw and Szwajkowski (1975) assessed 87 Fortune 500 firms that had violated Federal Trade Commission Laws and found that firms within environments with scarce resources were more likely to violate the law to cope with external demands than those that were not. Similarly many scholars argue that the greater the stakeholder pressures, the more likely a firm will demonstrate corrupt behavior (DeCelles & Pfarrer, 2004; Finney & Lisieur, 1982; Szwajkowski, 1985). Within a culture of competition and environmental uncertainty (Coleman, 1987), unachievable target goals may further compel leaders to compromise ethical standards (DeCelles & Pfarrer, 2004; Kulik, O'Fallon, & Salimath, 2008).

In addition to stakeholder pressures and resource dependence, environmental complexity coalesces with these and other external factors to create further uncertainty and possible unethical and destructive leadership behavior. Fleming and Zyglidopoulous (2008) proposed a model of organizational deception identifying organizational complexity as a moderating variable in what Elliot and Schroth (2002) termed the "fog of complexity," where unethical and destructive behavior is "difficult to control or understand as more activities are conducted out of the boundaries of normal managerial control" (p. 104). Because of environmental complexity, the default systems of leaders may amplify their own skewed cognitive filters and blind spots (McNamera, Luce, & Tompson, 2002) and exacerbate ethical compromise. In summary, competition within uncertain environments highlights the organizational demands that turbulence and change processes incur (Palmer & Wiseman, 1999), which may heighten predictable unethical corporate behavior from a loosening of checks and balances to a lack of regulation (Baucus & Near, 1991).

2.2.3. Threat-Rigidity Response

The threat-rigidity response (Staw et al., 1981) may help explain why leaders choose to persist in unethical and destructive behaviors. A "threat" is typically defined as a negative or adverse situation over which decision makers have little control and in which there is a potential for salient loss (Chattopadhyay, Glick, & Huber, 2001; Dutton & Jackson, 1987). Given competition amid times of environmental uncertainty, turbulence, scarcity of resources, and change, leaders are exposed to conditions outside their control and repertoire that threatens to impede their work. Therefore, they may seek to reduce uncertainty by resorting to behaviors characterized by caution, restriction in information processing, and centralization of control (Chattopadhyay et al., 2001; Harrington, Lemak, & Kendall, 2002; Sitkin & Pablo, 1992). In so doing, leaders may centralize their power, resulting in further rigidity. Staw et al. (1981) argued that threat-rigidity effects, which create psychological stress and anxiety, can either be healthy and functional or maladaptive and dysfunctional. If maladaptive, leaders may respond to threats by engaging in unethical and destructive behaviors to reduce the perceived threats from the environment for self-protection or organizational survival and viability. As a result, legitimate threats to the organization may lead to intergroup conflict, competition for resources, and pressures for uniformity, which augment leadership control and the restriction of information, further enhancing unethical tendencies. Conversely, toxic leaders may use perceived threats for personal advantage as a way to heighten follower dependency and exercise inordinate control (Kellerman, 2004; Lipman-Blumen, 2005).

A different theoretical lens, "prospect theory," has also been applied to threat situations proffering different conclusions. According to prospect theory, people who perceive themselves to be in a negative situation tend to seek risk to better their position (Case & Shane, 1998; Kahneman & Lavallo, 1993; Kahneman & Tversky, 1979). While prospect theory may appear at first to contradict the threat-rigidity thesis, Chattopadhyay et al. (2001) suggested that the risk-seeking response of prospect theory will occur when a threat is perceived as controllable, while the threat-rigidity response will be manifested when a threat is perceived as uncontrollable. Palmer, Danforth, and Clark (1995) found evidence for both prospect theory and threat-rigidity response in a study of hospitals. Poor performing hospitals exhibited some riskier courses of action than superior performing hospitals. However, these risk-taking actions seemed to be embedded in an overall rigid response pattern and may have been viewed within the threatened organizations as a single risky alternative pursued within a general frame of control.

Because the threat-rigidity response is characterized by restricting some types of information flow, increasing emphasis on efficiency, and centralizing decision-making (D'Aveni, 1989), it tends to limit the capability of the organization to adapt to changing conditions and to increase the focus of top management on short-term objectives over longer-term goals. Likewise, perceived resource shortages may lead to reduction of the number of managers, leading to greater concentration of authority and power in the remaining managers. In these cases, perceptions and reactions to perceived organizational threats may prompt leaders' unethical and destructive behavior to protect self-esteem through a self-serving bias (Campbell & Sedikides, 1999) and/or to insure organizational viability at all costs (Chattopadhyay et al., 2001).

Proposition 4. Organizational conditions such as ethical climate, norms, and accountability; environmental uncertainty; and perceived threats to organizational survival will impact organizational processes and reduce limitations on destructive behavior of leaders.

3. WHY ARE UNETHICAL AND/OR DESTRUCTIVE LEADERSHIP BEHAVIORS TOLERATED BY FOLLOWERS AND OTHER ORGANIZATIONAL STAKEHOLDERS?

Although leaders may acknowledge the benefits of ethical leadership reflecting values of corporate social responsibility, honesty, integrity, and believing that "ethics pay" (Rhode, 2006), many violate the trust of stakeholders, not the least of whom are followers, when engaging in unethical and/or destructive leadership behavior. Leader behaviors impacting followers include greed, lying, cheating, intentional deception, theft, extortion, and interpersonal manipulation, to name a few (Bok, 1999; Cruver, 2002; Doris, 2002; Martin, 1986). This section addresses specific follower and organizational characteristics which contribute to followers and stake holders tolerating unethical and potentially destructive leader behaviors.

3.1. Follower Characteristics

In addition to leader and organizational characteristics and processes which impact unethical and destructive leadership behavior, followers likewise have been shown to exert influence on leader behavior (Berg, 1998; Kellerman, 2008; Offerman, 2004; Rost, 1993). As Whicker (1996) argued: "To blame the decline of many institutions and organizations in the United States on bad leadership is to oversimplify the complex relationship between leaders and followers" (p. 51). Followers may play a highly instrumental role in supporting the unethical behavior of leaders by passive or active complicity (Kellerman, 2004; Lipman-Blumen, 2005; Padilla et al., 2007; Vardi & Weitz, 2004). Six specific follower characteristics contribute to the active and/or passive support of the leaders' unethical/destructive behavior. The most salient characteristics related to followers and other organizational stakeholders are (a) self-concept, (b) self-efficacy and LOC, (c) values, (d) role modeling, (e) social identity, and (f) organizational commitment.

3.1.1. Self-Concept

Follower self-concept relates to the ways followers view themselves and their self-worth. Thought to derive from individuals' knowledge of themselves including personality, image of one's physical appearance, persona, and self-schemas, Lord and Brown (2004) defined the self-concept as "the overarching knowledge structure that organizes memory and behavior ... and includes trait-like schemas that organize social and self-perceptions in specific situations" (p. 14). They argued that leaders' behaviors are proximal determinants of followers' self-concept activation. Contributing to the development of the followers' self-concept, the leader-member exchange (LME) process fosters a psychological interaction enabling followers to experience protection and security, achievement and effectiveness, inclusion and belongingness, and commitment and loyalty (Messick, 2005). Graen and Uhl-Bien (1995) described the outcome of this psychological exchange as the formation of in-groups and out-groups, dyadic relationships of contrasting degrees of trust, interaction, and closeness. In-groups comprise the inner circle and can be conformers or colluders in leaders' unethical behavior (Padilla et al., 2007). As such, Lord, Brown, and Freiberg (1999) cited that research has supported several precursors to (LME), namely leaders "liking" followers, follower demographics, and perceived attitudinal similarity (cf. Engle & Lord, 1997). As a result, followers' self-concepts may be strengthened leading to further motivation, self-regulation, and information processes. Since people are motivated to preserve and increase their sense of self-esteem and status, followers will be highly motivated to preserve their self-identity, especially in their relationship to leaders within social contexts (Hogg, 2001; Hogg & Reid, 2001; Shamir, House, & Arthur, 1993).

The self-concept may be reinforced by the roles followers or stakeholders play in relationship to leaders (Brewer & Gardner, 1996). For example, leaders may increase followers' self-esteem through appraisals, performance evaluations, and other positive reinforcements and rewards. If leaders are engaging in the slippery slope of unethical behavior, followers may unwittingly contribute to the process by remaining silent, unwilling to confront superiors about unethical behavior (Kellerman, 2004). If as Berg (1998) suggested the responsibility for the leader-follower relationship resides with the follower and if the underlying leader expectation is an "unchanging request for obedience," then the likelihood of unethical and destructive behaviors being supported by followers will be strengthened (p. 33).

3.1.2. Self-Efficacy and LOC

Followers possess varying degrees of beliefs about their self-efficacy, defined as the freedom and power to act for specific purposes (Bandura, 1986). In certain situations, followers may disengage their own personal agency and self-sanctions related to ethical and moral behavior. This process of ethical/moral disengagement includes a reduction of self-monitoring and judgment, leading to detrimental conduct (Bandura, 1999; Bandura, Barbaranelli, Caprara, & Pastorelli, 1996). In addition to self-efficacy, followers' locus of control (LOC) (e.g., Rotter, 1966, 1990) also contributes to how followers participate in or resist unethical behaviors of leaders. As such, followers with an internal (LOC) may take more initiative to resist or confront the unethical behavior of leaders than those with an external LOC who may be more easily manipulated.

3.1.3. Value Alignment

Value alignment between leaders and followers may likewise impact organizational processes that facilitate or tolerate unethical and/or destructive leader behavior (Bass & Stedlmeier, 1999; Shamir et al., 1993). Lord and Brown (2001, 2004) contended that leader behaviors activate and reinforce values in followers. For example, self-direction, achievement, power, and security (Schwartz, 1992, 1994) may be activated by leader-follower value compatibilities. Value similarity between leaders and followers forges increased follower motivation, commitment, and satisfaction (Jung & Avolio, 2000). Value incongruence may result in followers sublimating their espoused and realized values in the face of leaders' unethical practices. In these cases, the cognitive dissonance experienced by followers may create pressures for reconciliation with a leader that is possible only through tolerance of the leader's incongruent behaviors. Further, it is also possible that followers are selected by leaders because they share similar values that favor unethical behavior (Padilla et al., 2007).

3.1.4. Role Modeling

Another contextual factor in unethical/destructive behavior is role modeling by followers. Followers may model behaviors of their organizational leaders, or peers/counterparts. Advanced by social cognitive theory, role modeling describes a form of observational learning generated from what individuals attend to, retain, produce, and are motivated by when viewing others' capabilities (Bandura, 1986). Generally speaking, people seek role models to whom they can aspire (Bandura, 1997). In examining the impact of three types of role models on the ethical development of leaders (e.g., childhood role models, career mentors, and top managers), Brown and Treviño (2006b) found that having an ethical mentor in one's career was positively related to ethical leadership. Conversely, Bandura et al. (1996) found that role modeling can also include moral disengagement, or the process of selectively disengaging self-sanctions when faced with unethical conduct by a leader. The outcomes of moral disengagement include cognitive rationalization of unethical conduct and consequences, self-justification, and blaming the victim/s. In a setting where moral disengagement is wide-spread, prosocial behavior is undermined, and unethical or destructive behaviors are acceptable.

3.1.5. Social Identity

When followers attract to various organizational settings and roles through the ASA cycle (Schneider, 1987), they engage in a socialization process whereby shared beliefs, attitudes, expectations, and behaviors are interwoven with leaders, inclusive of the organizational vision and culture (Hogg, 2005). In-group association and distinctiveness, based on basic positive self-concepts needs, coalesce into in-group behaviors and prototypes. When followers are socially adept, they may identify more strongly with the organization and desire favored treatment by leaders. In the psychological exchange between followers and leaders, followers glean a sense of vision and direction, protection and security, inclusion and belonging, personal effectiveness, and pride, self-respect, and direction (Messick, 2005). In exchange, followers reciprocate by offering gratitude, loyalty, commitment, sacrifice, and obedience. Therefore when followers and leaders like each other, valuable LMEs benefit both parties (Graen & Uhl-Bien, 1995). As Lord and Brown (2001) observed, since followers desire to nurture positive self-evaluations based on these exchanges, they may be "especially sensitive to the affective feedback from leaders, using it as a basis for constructing a reflected self-identity" (p. 42). Leaders also activate and reinforce follower identity in the modeling of values as they relate to goal achievement (Lord & Brown, 2001), resulting in powerful psychological and emotional attachments (Popper, 2001). Because of this beneficial LME, followers may heighten organizational commitment and, in so doing, may acquiesce to unethical leadership behaviors to maintain their social standing, relational connections, and attachment to the leader (Brass et al., 1998; O'Reilly & Chatman, 1986).

3.1.6. Organizational Commitment

Organizational commitment of followers has been the subject of research related to unethical behavior (Cullinan, Bline, Farrar, & Lowe, 2008; Peterson, 2003; Street, 1995) and is distinctive from escalation of commitment. Organizational commitment is a multidimensional construct involving affective attachment to and identification with the organization (Meyer & Allen, 1991; Mowday, Porter, & Steers, 1982; Porter, Steers, Mowday, & Boulian, 1974). If as O'Reilly and Chatman (1986) argued, that organizational commitment is predicated on followers' psychological attachment and identification with the goals, values, and characteristic of the organization, then we maintain that followers with high levels of organizational commitment may experience cognitive dissonance in the face of leaders' unethical behavior. In order to uphold socially constructed organizational identity, followers therefore may deny problems to avoid the negative intrapersonal residue that the awareness of ethical/destructive behavior brings. In such cases, followers may ignore the leadership infraction, rationalize it away, or react to it through moral agency. Examples include Enron employees who realized something was awry but because of the company reputation were compliant and complacent in the face of telltale signs of leadership malfeasance (Cruver, 2002).

Various antecedents impact organizational commitment including positive factors such as job satisfaction, job security, and employee performance, as well as negative factors including role ambiguity, role conflict, incongruent job-fit alignment, and organizational turnover (Porter et al., 1974). Research examining the relationship between organizational commitment and ethical decision making reveal that followers with higher organizational commitment were less likely to engage in unethical behavior leading to personal gain and harmful organizational outcomes (Tang & Chiu, 2003). Cullinan et al.'s (2008) study involving employees from three companies found similar results, suggesting that followers with higher levels of organizational commitment may have a longer-term orientation, which would overshadow consideration of the short-term personal gains derived from unethical behavior.

When organizations face decline and crisis, five behavioral modes of commitment have been identified: (a) exit, active negative commitment, (b) voice, active positive commitment, (c) loyalty, passive positive commitment, (d) neglect, positive negative commitment, and (e) silence (Bar-Haim, 2007; Hirshman, 1970; Rusbult, Farrell, Rogers, & Mainous, 1988). We suggest that in the face of unethical leadership behavior followers with high levels of organizational commitment, LOC, and a strong belief/value system will be more apt to remain loyal to the organization, retain a sense of voice, and resist unethical/destructive leadership behavior. Or if the pressures to engage in unethical behaviors persist, followers' commitment may decrease and their intention to leave will escalate (Peterson, 2003). Conversely, those who do not have high levels of organizational commitment will be more inclined to make an exit (active negative commitment), become neglectful of their jobs (positive negative commitment), or be more obliging in allowing unethical leadership behavior to continue (silence).

In support of this assertion, Street (1995) predicted that the high levels of organizational commitment and cognitive moral development of followers would increase the likelihood of whistle-blowing. The organizational commitment of followers is an important variable in answering the question related to why leaders persist in behaviors that they knew were unethical and destructive. Factors influencing followers' passive acceptance of, collusion with, or active position against unethical behavior may be impacted by their tenure with the organization and the size of the organization (cf. Dozier & Miceli, 1985). In summary, followers' self-concepts, self-efficacy and LOC, values, role modeling behavior, social identity, and organizational commitment interact with leader characteristics and organizational processes in contributing to the support of leaders' unethical and destructive behavior.

Proposition 5. Characteristics of followers including self-concept, self-efficacy, LOC, value alignment, need for role modeling, social identity, and organizational commitment will combine to inhibit follower willingness to engage organizational processes that would limit destructive leader behaviors.

3.2. Organizational Dynamics

The reason followers and other organizational stakeholders tolerate unethical and destructive leadership behavior relates specifically to conducive environments. Factors previously identified as important antecedents include environmental instability, threat perception, cultural values, lack of checks and balances, and effective structural accountability (Padilla et al., 2007; Sedikides et al., 2002). Our focus includes three additional organizational processes: evaluations of actions, the feedback environment, and conformity dynamics.

3.2.1. Evaluations of Actions

Organizational explanations for actions may affect the willingness of employees to accept unethical leader behaviors and/or engage in unethical behaviors themselves. Schweitzer and Gibson (2008) found that organizational explanations that violate community standards of fairness (i.e., a company taking advantage of its market power) led to higher levels of employee intentions to behave unethically. The opposite effect was found for organizational explanations that were more consistent with community standards of fairness, such as a company passing along materials cost increases. Schweitzer and Gibson also found that employees obtained greater satisfaction and reduced anger from engaging in unethical behavior following perceived violations of fairness by an organization.

Anderson and Bateman (1997) found that cynicism and disillusionment in the workplace led to distrust of leaders' motives, believing that employers might exploit employee contributions and other business relationships. Employee cynicism was predicted by excessively large compensation awards to executives, poor organizational performance, and impending layoffs. Anderson and Bateman found that employee cynicism about an organization predicted their intended lack of compliance with unethical requests from management. Paradoxically, cynicism toward a company and its management may reduce compliance with unethical requests.

3.2.2. Feedback Environment

The feedback environment refers to the contextual aspects of day-to-day supervisor-subordinate and coworker-coworker feedback processes, as opposed to the formal performance appraisal feedback (Steelman, Levy, & Snell, 2004). Feedback within organizational contexts has informational value, which assist leaders and followers meet goals and regulate behavior (Ashford, Blatt, & VandeWalle, 2003; VandeWalle, 2003). The feedback environment may suggest to followers, peers, and other stakeholders the degree of organizational support for feedback to leaders about their behavior. If the feedback environment discourages inquiry related to job performance and personal interaction, we contend that unethical and destructive leadership behavior will be more likely. Key determinants of feedback-seeking behavior relate to the perception of the ego cost of doing so (Ashford & Cummings, 1983), as influenced by goal orientation (Ashford et al., 2003).

For example, Whitaker, Dahling, and Levy (2007) posited that individuals who focused more on learning, as opposed to performance outcomes, were less concerned about the ego cost of seeking feedback. This supports the notion that high power and performance-oriented leaders would likely resist feedback seeking behavior, which could reinforce power disinhibition and unethical behavior. If, as Whitaker et al. suggested, feedback-seeking behavior leads to role clarity, then job performance will likely be a positive outcome. However as Ashford et al. (2003) cautioned, the motives and outcomes for seeking or quenching feedback seeking behavior should be evaluated (i.e., to perform well, defend/enhance leader ego, or enhance impression management), as the cost of isolation from feedback may incur devastating results, as seen in the recent avalanche of corporate scandals.

In a study of 150 subordinate–supervisor dyads across a variety of organizations, Rosen, Levy, and Hall (2006) found that when employees have greater access to information regarding behaviors that are acceptable and desired at work, perceptions of politics are reduced, and work outcomes are enhanced. Feedback environments supporting high levels of informal supervisor and coworker interaction are also associated with higher employee morale, as indicated by job satisfaction and organizational commitment, resulting in higher levels of organizational citizenship. Both positive and negative feedback are both essential for organizational viability, especially as leaders model the feedback-seeking process. As Herold and Parsons (1985) asserted, "negative feedback is not only important but needs to be assessed independently of positive feedback" (p. 304). Thus, we maintain that organizational environments typified by feedback-seeking on all organizational levels will increase job performance and lesson the propensity for unethical and destructive leadership behavior.

3.2.3. Conformity Pressures

Research on situational factors impacting human behavior has revealed the power of context in shaping how people respond in given situations (Bandura, 1999). Conformity in the perpetration of unethical and destructive behavior, particularly as it relates to leaders and followers in specific contexts, has received research attention. In particular, three research initiatives demonstrate the process of de-individuation, dehumanization, and the evil of inaction among participants who were ordinary people. The outcome of these studies, as summarized below, affirms the powerful effect of conformity processes when faced with group pressures to acquiesce to a certain view point or with pressures from authority figures to engage in unethical and/or destructive behavior.

One classic study on conformity to group norms undertaken by social psychologist Solomon Asch (1951, 1955) related to visual perception. Asch predicted that few participants would conform to the majority's obvious incorrect responses related to judging the relative length of lines written on cards. When making solo decisions, participants made correct judgments 99% of the time. However when participants answered as a part of a group, after respondents intentionally gave incorrect answers, they responded incorrectly about 75% of the time. Only 25% of the participants were able to maintain their correct answers, despite the group's differing opinion.

In a second social conformity study known as the 1971 Stanford Prison Experiment (SPE), Zimbardo (2006, 2007; Zimbardo, Maslach, & Haney, 1999) observed that situational context had a powerful effect on the behaviors of students placed in the roles of guards and prisoners in a simulated prison environment. Designed to assess the effects of social distance and pressures for conformity within emerging group norms, some "guards" came to abuse their power by demeaning and degrading the "prisoners," actually fellow students; while others either went through their jobs methodically or were more reluctant to adopt more abusive approaches. However, none of the "good" guards intervened to limit the abusive behaviors of other guards, nor actively complained either to their abusive peers or to the supervisors of the simulation. The psychological and emotional experimental effects on participants were so detrimental that the 14-day experiment was abruptly called off after 6 days.

Zimbardo's (2007) results are of particular interest when considering how pressures for conformity may stifle follower or peer tendencies to speak out against unethical or destructive leadership behaviors. When people are placed in relatively unusual settings where the rules for behaviors and interactions may be ill-defined and not perceived as consistent with previous experiences, a set of dynamic psychological processes may induce people to do evil, which Zimbardo termed "the Lucifer effect." The behaviors adopted by these SPE "emergent leaders" may have provided a kind of sense-giving for other members of the group taking up relatively unfamiliar roles. Indeed, sense-giving, in which information is provided to help organizational members understand themselves, the nature of their work roles, and their relationships with others in the organization is a critical role for organizational leaders (Foldy, Goldman, & Ospina, 2008). However, this sense-giving gone awry by students assigned as guards illustrates the relative power of situations to incrementally introduce 'evil' into the average behaviors of otherwise good people. In more typical organizational situations, it may be similarly easy for persons working without contact with individual customers, constituents, or students to become cognitively caught up in a similar "us/them" perceptual trap. In such a case, Zimbardo's work (1969, 2006, 2007) illustrates the relative ease with which peers and followers alike can become compliant with the expectations and pressures to conform and accept unethical and/or destructive behaviors of leaders.

A third conformity study conducted by Milgram's (1974) on obedience to authority likewise demonstrated that average people will conform to authority even when it could possibly bring harm to others. Asked to apply electric shock as punishment in the process of assisting people improve their memory in the learning process, over two-thirds (67%) of all participants (i.e., teachers) actually applied the highest shock levels of 450 volts at the urging of the authority figure supervising the setting, despite the desperate (but simulated) cries of the learners. The results convincingly demonstrated that one situational variable could cause compliance rates of over 90% of participants and conversely drop to a low of 10%. Situational context proved to be a powerful determiner of behavior, which in this simulated obedience study, surprised even Milgram himself.

All three of these studies affirm that, given specific situational contexts, average people may conform to dysfunctional group norms and disengage morally in supporting destructive conduct when authority figures so dictate and/or they justify their own behavior and minimize personal responsibility (Bandura, 1999; Bandura et al., 1996).

Proposition 6. Organizational characteristics such as prevailing evaluation of actions, the feedback environment, and pressures for conformity will combine to reduce the occurrence and effects of organizational processes designed to limit destructive leader behaviors.

SUMMARY

We set out in this chapter to consider how characteristics of leaders, followers, and organizational settings combine with organizational processes to provide answers to three questions. The questions were: (a) how and why do leaders venture down unethical and destructive paths?, (b) why do leaders persist in unethical and destructive behaviors?, and (c) why are unethical and/or destructive leadership behaviors tolerated by followers and other organizational stakeholders? After considering alternative perspectives related to each question, we believe we have demonstrated that considering the processes within organizations provides a powerful approach for understanding how destructive leadership arises and persists in organizations. Specifically, better understanding of destructive leadership requires consideration of the organizational processes that place people in leadership roles and limit internal regulation, which subsequently enable leaders to continue down paths that are detrimental to the organization and its members. Focusing on the processes that are the essence of how organizations operate enabled us to provide additional perspectives in which to evaluate how and why unethical and destructive leadership behaviors occur and explain why organizational members ignore the obvious signposts these behaviors present.

Within the unique dynamics between leaders, followers, and organizational/situational contexts, the complexity and potential fallout of unethical and destructive leadership resulting in damaged lives and organizational demise cannot be understated. Building upon previous conceptual frameworks (Brown & Treviño, 2006a; Jones, 1991; Padilla et al., 2007), we offered new lenses for viewing unethical and destructive leadership by exploring additional social-cognitive and management processes applied to unethical and destructive leadership, such as the leadership selection process, leaders' escalation of commitment, self-enhancement motives, followers' organizational commitment, and the organizational processes impacted by goal setting pressures, threat rigidity, the feedback environment, and conformity dynamics.

Our analyses suggest that leader characteristics as well as internal and external variables may impact organizational processes limiting the ability of these processes to regulate and safeguard against unethical and destructive leader behaviors. From a practical viewpoint, increased awareness of these possible limitations may help organizations develop and implement watchful approaches to identify and curb destructive and/or unethical leadership behaviors at an early stage. Clearly the more prepared an organization may be to identify and curb such behaviors, the more likely it is that norms for regulations within the organization will be reinforced and have the desired effect.

Directions for Future Research

The propositions presented above provide the primary basis for future research concerning how the interplay of leader, follower, and organizational characteristics within organizational processes may unintentionally facilitate destructive leadership. These propositions are summarized in Table 5.1.

We anticipate that testing proposition 1 may have significant payoff both theoretically and practically, in that the underlying implicit leadership models involved in leadership selection decisions are rarely made known. Consequently, the extent to which such characteristics as cognitive moral development and responsibility dispositions of leadership candidates are considered important attributes and thus are thoroughly

Table 5.1. Propositions for Future Research

Proposition 1. Leader selection processes are likely to overlook underlying leader characteristics such as LOC, narcissism, level of moral development, and responsibility disposition which may affect leader actions in organizational processes and limit the effects of regulatory safeguards to curb destructive leadership behaviors.

Proposition 2. Organizational characteristics such as the prevailing ethical climate, pressure to set aggressive goals, and intense competition will combine to limit the impact that organizational processes may have on regulating destructive leader behaviors.

Proposition 3. Leader characteristics such as personal values, self-enhancement motives, self-deception, and tendencies to escalate commitment will affect leader behavior within organizational processes and perpetrate patterns of destructive leader behaviors.

Proposition 4. Organizational conditions such as ethical climate, norms, and accountability; environmental uncertainty; and perceived threats to organizational survival will impact organizational processes and reduce limitations on destructive leader behaviors.

Proposition 5. Characteristics of followers including self-concept, self-efficacy, LOC, value alignment, need for role modeling, social identity, and organizational commitment will combine to inhibit follower willingness to engage organizational processes that would limit destructive leader behaviors.

Proposition 6. Organizational characteristics such as prevailing explanations for actions, the feedback environment, and pressures for conformity will combine to reduce the occurrence and effects of organizational processes designed to limit destructive leader behaviors.

investigated in the selection process is also unclear. In addition, impression management efforts may be more successful for candidates with personality tendencies that include narcissism. Better understanding of the evaluation criteria used by participants in the selection process will be critical for limiting the acceptance of persons who arrive in leadership roles with tendencies that increase the likelihood of unethical and destructive behaviors.

Examination of the additional five propositions will largely bring to light the effects of both individual and organizational level variables in establishing and implementing norms that serve to regulate leader behaviors and bring leaders back from destructive behavioral patterns. We particularly anticipate that better understanding of the interplay between organizational pressures and the individual characteristics of leaders holds substantial promise. For example, self-enhancement motives of leaders may have limited negative effects until the leader's organization or unit is faced with threats to survival. When faced with perceived threats, these leaders may have increased tendencies toward rigidity in behaviors, limiting information flow and blocking scrutiny of their behaviors.

Besides these propositions, our analyses suggest additional questions requiring further exploration: (a) what additional leadership selection criteria and assessments need to be developed to accurately evaluate "dark side" leader and follower characteristics to assist organizations prevent unethical/destructive leadership (Hogan et al., 1994)?, (b) in what organizational or situational contexts will leaders of proven integrity bow to unethical/destructive leadership behavior?, (c) what do exemplars of ethical organizational climate teach us about how to avoid unethical practices related to structural and accountability processes?, and (d) how might business and corporate ethics training be radically reevaluated and revised to include the most up-to-date research in real-world contexts to foster applied praxis? Insights from such research would have long-range implications in strengthening leaders, followers, and organizational processes in order to effectively address the obvious signposts of unethical and destructive leadership, foster ethical behavior and sustainability at all organizational levels, and promote public trust.

REFERENCES

American Management Association. (2006). *The ethical enterprise: A global study of business ethics (2005–2015)*. New York: Author.

Anderson, C. R. (1977). Locus of control, coping behaviors, and performance in stress settings: A longitudinal study. *Journal of Applied Psychology, 62*(4), 446-451.

Anderson, L. M., & Bateman, T. S. (1997). Cynicism in the workplace: Some causes and effects. *Journal of Organizational Behavior, 18*(5), 449-469.

Asch, S. E. (1951). Studies of independence and conformity: A minority of one against a unanimous majority. *Psychological Monographs, 70*, Whole No 416.

Asch, S. E. (1955, Nov.). *Opinions and social pressure.* Scientific American, *193*, 31-35.

Ashford, S. J., & Cummings, L. L. (1983). Feedback as an individual resource: Personal strategies of creating information. *Organizational Behavior and Human Performance, 32*, 370-398.

Ashford, S. J., Blatt, R., & VandeWalle, D. (2003). Reflections on the looking glass: A review of research on feedback-seeking behavior in organizations. *Journal of Management, 29*(6), 773-799.

Bandura, A. (1986). *Social foundations of thought and action: A social cognitive theory.* Englewood Cliffs, NJ: Prentice Hall.

Bandura, A. (1997). *Self-efficacy: The exercise of control.* New York: W. H. Freeman.

Bandura, A. (1999). Moral disengagement in the perpetration of inhumanities. *Journal of Personality and Social Psychology Review, 3*(3), 193-209.

Bandura, A., Barbaranelli, C., Caprara, G. V., & Pastorelli, C. (1996). Mechanisms of moral disengagement in the exercise of moral agency. *Journal of Personality and Social Psychology, 71*(2), 364-374.

Bar-Haim, A. (2007). Rethinking organizational commitment in relation to perceived organizational power and perceived employment alternatives. *International Journal of Cross Cultural Management,* 7(2), 203-217.

Barsky, A. (2008). Understanding the ethical cost of organizational goal-setting: A review and theory development. *Journal of Business Ethics, 81*(1), 63-81.

Bass, B. M., & Steidlmeier, P. (1999). Ethics, character, and authentic transformational leadership. *The Leadership Quarterly, 10*(2), 181-217.

Baucus, M. S. (1994). Pressure, opportunity and predisposition: A multivariate model of corporate illegality. *Journal of Management, 20*(4), 699-721.

Baucus, M. S., & Near, J. P. (1991). Can illegal corporate behavior be predicted? An event history analysis. *Academy of Management Journal, 34*(1), 9-36.

Bazerman, M. H., & Banaji, M. R. (2004). The social psychology of ordinary unethical behavior. Social Justice Research, *17*(2), 111-115.

Beauregard, K. S., & Dunning D. (1998). Turning up the contrast: Self-enhancement motives prompt egocentric contrast effects in social judgments. *Journal of Personality and Social Psychology, 74*(3), 606-621.

Benson, M. J., & Hogan, R. (2008). How dark side leadership personality destroys trust and degrades organizational effectiveness. *Organizations & People, 15*(3), 10-19.

Berg, D. N. (1998). Resurrecting the muse: Followership in organizations. In E. B. Klein, F. Gabelnick, & P. Herr (Eds.), *The psychodynamics of leadership* (pp. 27-52). Madison, CT: Psychosocial Press.

Biyalogorsky, E., Boulding, W., & Staelin, R. (2006). Stuck in the past: Why managers persist with new product failures. *Journal of Marketing, 70*(2), 108-121.

Bobocel, D. R., & Meyer, J. P. (1994). Escalating commitment to a failing course of action: Separating the roles of choice and justification. *Journal of Applied Psychology, 79*(3), 360-363.

Bok, S. (1999). *Lying: Moral choice in public and private life*. New York: Vintage Books.

Brass, D. J., Butterfield, K. D., & Scaggs, B. C. (1998). Relationships and unethical behavior: A social network perspective. *Academy of Management Review, 23*(1), 14-31.

Brewer, M. B., & Gardner, W. L. (1996). Who is this "we"? Levels of collective identity and self representations. *Journal of Personality and Social Psychology, 71*(1), 83-93.

Brockner, J. (1992). The escalation of commitment to a failing course of action. *Academy of Management Review, 17*(1), 39.

Bronner, R. (2003). Pathologies of decision-making: Causes, forms, and handling. *Management International Review, 43*(1), 85-101.

Brown, M. E., & Treviño, L. K. (2006a). Ethical leadership: A review and future directions. *The Leadership Quarterly, 17*(6), 595-616.

Brown, M. E., & Treviño, L. K. (2006b, August). *Role modeling and ethical leadership*. Paper presented at the 2006 Academy of Management Annual Meeting. Atlanta, GA.

Cameron, K. (2003). Ethics, virtuousness, and constant change. In N. M. Tichy & A. R. McGill (Eds.), *The ethical challenge: How to lead with unyielding integrity* (pp. 185-194). San Francisco: Jossey-Bass.

Campbell, W. K., & Sedikides, C. (1999). Self-threat magnifies the self-serving bias: A meta-analytic integration. *Review of General Psychology, 3*(1), 23-43.

Case, R., & Shane, S. (1998). Fostering risk taking in research and development: The importance of a project's terminal value. *Decision Sciences, 29*(4), 765-783.

Chattopadhyay, P., Glick, W., & Huber, G. (2001). Organizational actions in response to threats and opportunities. *Academy of Management Journal, 44*(5), 937-955.

Coleman, J. W. (1987). Toward an integrated theory of white-collar crime. *American Journal of Sociology, 93*(2), 406-439.

Collins, J. (2001). *Good to Great*. New York: HarperCollins.

Cooper, W. H. (1981). Ubiquitous halo. *Psychological Bulletin, 90*(2), 218-244.

Cruver, B. (2002). *Anatomy of greed: The un-shredded truth from an Enron insider.* New York: Carroll & Graf.

Cullen, J. B., Parboteeach, K. P., & Victor, B. (2003). The effects of ethical climate on organizational commitment: Two-study analysis. *Journal of Business Ethics, 46*(2), 127-141.

Cullinan, C., Bline, D., Farrar, R., & Lowe, D. (2008). Organization-harm vs. organization-gain ethical issues: An exploratory examination of the effects of organizational commitment. *Journal of Business Ethics, 80*(2), 225-235.

D'Aveni, R. A. (1989). The aftermath of organizational decline: A longitudinal study of the strategic and managerial characteristics of declining firms. *Academy of Management Journal, 32*(3), 577-605.

DeCelles, K. A., & Pfarrer, M. D. (2004). Heroes or villains? Corruption and the charismatic leader. *Journal of Leadership & Organizational Studies, 11*(1), 67-77.

De Cremer, D., & van Dijk, E. (2008). Leader-follower effects in resource dilemmas: The roles of leadership selection and social responsibility. *Group Processes & Intergroup Relations, 11*(3), 355-369.

De Hoogh, A. H. B., & Den Hartog, D. N. (2008). Ethical and despotic leadership, relationships with leader's social responsibility, top management team effectiveness and subordinates' optimism: A multi-method study. *The Leadership Quarterly, 19*(3), 297-311.

DeVries, D. L. (1992). Executive selection: Advances but no progress. *Issues & Observations, 12*(4), 1-5.

Dickson, M. W., Smith, D. B., Grojean, M. W., & Ehrhart, M. (2001). An organizational climate regarding ethics: The outcome of leader values and the practices that reflect them. *The Leadership Quarterly, 12*(2), 197-217.

Doris, J. M. (2002). *Lack of character: Personality and moral behavior.* New York: Cambridge University Press.

Dotlich, D. L., & Cairo, P. D. (2003). *Why CEOs fail: The 11 behaviors that can derail our climb to the top and how to manage them.* San Francisco: Jossey-Bass.

Dozier, J. B., & Miceli, M. P. (1985). Potential predictors of whistle-blowing: A prosocial behavior perspective. *Academy of Management Review, 10*(4), 823-836.

Dunning, D., Meyerowitz, J. A., & Holzberg, A. D. (1989). Ambiguity and self-evaluation: The role of idiosyncratic trait definitions in self-serving assessments of ability. *Journal of Personality & Social Psychology, 57*(6), 1082-1090.

Dutton, J., & Jackson, S. (1987). Categorizing strategic issues: Links to organizational action. *Academy of Management Review, 31*(1), 85-105.

Einarsen, S., Aasland, M. S., & Skogstad, A. (2007). Destructive leadership behaviour: A definition and conceptual model. *The Leadership Quarterly, 18*(3), 207-216.

Elliot, A. L., & Schroth, R. J. (2002). *How companies lie: Why Enron is just the tip of the iceberg.* London, England: Nicholas Brealey.

Engle, E. M., & Lord, R. G. (1997). Implicit theories, self-schema, and leader-member exchange. *Academy of Management Journal, 40*(4), 988-1010.

Festinger, L. (1957). *A theory of cognitive dissonance*. Evanston, IL: Row, Peterson.

Fingarette, H. (2000). *Self-deception* (2nd ed.). Berkeley, CA: University of California Press.

Finney, H. C., & Lesieur, H. R. (1982). A contingency theory of organizational crime. In S. B. Bacharach, *Research in the sociology of organizations* (Vol. 1, pp. 255-299). Greenwich, CT: JAI.

Fiske, S. T. (2004). *Social beings: Core motives in social psychology.* New York: Wiley.

Fleming, P., & Zyglidopoulous, S. C. (2008). The escalation of deception in organizations. *Journal of Business Ethics, 81*(4), 837-850.

Foldy, E. G., Goldman, L., & Ospina, S. (2008). Sensegiving and the role of cognitive shifts in the work of leadership. *The Leadership Quarterly, 19*(5), 514-529.

Graen, G. B., & Uhl-Bien, M. (1995). Relationship-based approach to leadership: Development of leader-member exchange (LMX) theory of leadership over 25 years: Applying a multi-level multi-domain approach. *The Leadership Quarterly, 6*(2), 219-247.

Grojean, M. W., Resick, C. J., Dickson, M. W., & Smith, D. B. (2004). Leaders, values, and organizational climate: Examining leadership strategies for establishing an organizational climate regarding ethics. *Journal of Business Ethics, 55*(3), 223-241.

Haight, M. R. (1980). *A study of self-deception*. Atlantic Highlands, NJ: Humanities Press.

Harrington, R., Lemak, D., & Kendall, K. (2002). The threat-rigidity thesis in newly formed teams: An empirical test. *Journal of Business and Management, 8*(2), 127-145.

Harshman, C. L., & Harshman, E. F. (2008). The Gordian knot of ethics: Understanding leadership effectiveness and ethical behavior. *Journal of Business Ethics, 78*(1-2), 175-192.

Heath, E. (2002). *Morality & the market: Ethics & virtue in the conduct of business*. Boston: McGraw Hill.

Herold. C. K., & Parsons, D. M. (1985). Assessing the feedback environment in work organizations: Development of the job feedback survey. *Journal of Applied Psychology, 70*(2), 290-305.

Hirshman, A. O. (1970). *Exit, voice, and loyalty.* Cambridge, MA: Harvard University Press.

Hogan, R. (2006). *Personality and the fate of organizations.* Mahway, NJ: Erlbaum.

Hogan, R., & Kaiser, R. B. (2008). Learning a lesson in executive selection. *Issues & Observations, 27*(6), 22-24.

Hogan, R., Curphy, G. J., & Hogan, J. (1994). What we know about leadership: Effectiveness and personality. *American Psychologist, 49*(6), 493-504.

Hogan, R., Raskin, R., & Fazzini, D. (1990). The dark side of charisma. In K. E. Clark & M. B. Clark (Eds.), *Measures of leadership* (pp. 343-354). West Orange, NJ: Leadership Library of America.

Hogarth, R. M. (1987). *Judgment and choice: The psychology of decision* (2nd ed.) New York: Wiley.

Hogg, M. A. (2001). Social categorization, depersonalization, and group behavior. In M. A. Hogg & R. S. Tindale (Eds.), *Blackwell handbook of social psychology: Group processes* (pp. 56-85). Oxford, England: Blackwell.

Hogg, M. A. (2005). Social identity and leadership. In D. M. Messick & R. M. Kramer (Ed.), *The psychology of leadership: New perspectives and research* (pp. 53-80). Mahwah, NJ: Erlbaum.

Hogg, M. A., & Reid, S. A. (2001). Social identity, leadership, and power. In A. Y. Lee-Chai & J. A. Bargh (Eds.), *The use and abuse of power: Multiple perspectives on the causes of corruption* (pp. 159-180). Philadelphia, PA: Psychology Press.

Hoyt, C. L, Simon, S., & Reid, L. (2009). Choosing the best (wo)man for the job: The effects of mortality salience, sex and gender stereotypes on leader evaluations. *The Leadership Quarterly, 20*(2), 233-246.

Illies, J. J., & Reiter-Palmon, R. (2008). Responding destructively in leadership situations: The role of personal values and problem construction. *Journal of Business Ethics, 82*(1), 251-272.

Janssen, O., & Prins, J. (2007). Goal orientations and the seeking of different types of feedback information. *Journal of Occupational and Organizational Psychology, 80*(2), 235-249.

John, O. P., & Robins, R. W. (1994). Accuracy and bias in self-perception: Individual differences in self-enhancement and the role of narcissism. *Journal of Personality and Social Psychology, 66*(1), 206-219.

Jones, T. M. (1991). Ethical decision making by individuals in organizations: An issue-contingent model. *Academy of Management Review, 16*(2), 366-395.

Jordan, C. H., Spencer, S. J., Zanna, M. P., Hoshimo-Brown, E., & Correll, J. (2003). Secure and defensive high self-esteem. *Journal of Personality and Social Psychology, 85*(5), 969-987.

Judge, T., Colbert, A. E., & Ilies, R. (2004) Intelligence and leadership: A quantitative review and test of theoretical propositions. *Journal of Applied Psychology, 89*(3), 542-552.

Jung, D. I., & Avolio, B. J. (2000). Opening the black box: An experimental investigation of the mediating effects of trust and value congruence on transformational and transactional leadership. *Journal of Organizational Behavior, 21*(8), 949-964.

Kahneman, D., & Lavallo, D. (1993). Timid choices and bold forecasts: A cognitive perspective on risk taking. *Management Science, 39*(1), 17-31.

Kahneman, D., & Tversky, A. (1979). Prospect theory: An analysis of decisions under risk. *Econometrica, 47*(2), 263-291.

Keil, M., Depledge, G., & Rai, A. (2007). Escalation: The role of problem recognition and cognitive bias. *Decision Sciences, 38*(3), 391-421.

Kellerman, B. (2004). *BAD Leadership: What it is, how it happens, why it matters*. Boston: Harvard Business School Press.

Kellerman, B. (2008). *How followers are creating change and changing leaders*. Boston: Harvard School Press.

Keltner, D., Gruenfeld, D. H., & Anderson, C. (2003). Power, approach, and inhibition. *Psychological Review, 110*(2), 265-284.

Kets de Vries, M. F. R. (1993). *Leaders, fools, and impostors: Essays on the psychology of leadership.* San Francisco: Jossey-Bass.

Kets de Vries, M. F. R. (2006). The spirit of despotism: Understanding the tyrant within. *Human Relations, 59*(2), 195-220.

Kets de Vries, M. F. R., & Miller D. (1997). Narcissism and leadership: An object relations perspective. In R. P. Vecchio (Ed.), *Leadership: Understanding the dynamics of power and influence in organizations* (pp. 194-214). Notre Dame, IN: University of Notre Dame Press.

Kohlberg, L. (1969). Stage and sequence: The cognitive-development approach to socialization. In D. A. Goslin (Ed.), *Handbook of socialization theory and research* (pp. 347-480). Chicago: Rand McNally.

Kohlberg, L. (1984). *The psychology of moral development: The nature and validity of moral stages.* San Francisco: Harper & Row.

Kohlberg, L., Levine, C., & Hewer, A. (1983). *Moral stages: A current formulation and a response to critics*. Basil, Switzerland: S. Karger.

Kohut, H. (1966). Forms and transformations of narcissism. *Journal of the American Psychoanalytic Association, 14*, 243-272.

Kohut, H. (1971). *The analysis of the self.* New York: Basic Books.

Kramer, R. M. (2003, October). The harder they fall. *Harvard Business Review, 81*(10), 58-66.

Kulik, B. W., O'Fallon, M. J., & Salimath, M. S. (2008). Do competitive environments lead to the rise and spread of unethical behavior? Parallels from Enron. *Journal of Business Ethics, 83*(4), 703–723.

Kunda, Z. (1987). Motivated inference: Self-serving generation and evaluation of causal theories. *Journal of Personality and Social Psychology, 53*(1), 37-54.

Lefcourt, H. M. (1966). Internal-external control of reinforcement: A review. *Psychological Bulletin, 65*(4), 206-220.

Lerner, J. S., & Tetlock, P. E. (1999). Accounting for the effects of accountability. *Psychological Bulletin, 125*(2), 255-275.

Lerner, J. S., & Tetlock, P. E. (2003). The impact of accountability on cognitive bias: Bridging individual, interpersonal, and institutional approaches to judgment and choice. In S. Schneider & J. Shanteau (Eds.), *Emerging perspectives on judgment and decision making* (pp. 431-457). Cambridge, MA: Cambridge University Press.

Lewicki, R. J. (1983). Lying and deception: A behavioral model. In M. H. Bazerman & R. J. Lewicki (Eds.), *Negotiating in organizations* (pp. 68–90). Beverly Hills, CA: SAGE.

Lipman-Blumen, J. (2005). *The allure of toxic leaders: Why we follow destructive bosses and corrupt politicians—and how we can survive them.* Oxford, England: Oxford University Press.

Littig, L. W., & Sanders, J. A. (1979). Locus of control and persistence: Effects of skill and chance sets on session and post-session indices. *Bulletin of Psychonomic Society, 13*, 387-389.

Locke, E. A., & Latham, G. P. (1990). *A theory of goal setting and task performance.* Englewood Cliffs, NJ: Prentice Hall.

Lord, R. G., & Brown, D. J. (2001). Leadership, values, and subordinate self-concepts. *The Leadership Quarterly, 12*(2), 133-152.

Lord, R. G., & Brown, D. J. (2004). *Leadership processes and follower self-identity.* Mahwah, NJ: Erlbaum.

Lord, R. G. Brown, D. J., Freiberg, S. J. (1999). Understanding the dynamics of leadership: The role of follower self-concepts in the leader/follower relationship. *Organizational Behavior and Human Decision Processes, 78*(3), 167-203.

Ludwig, D. C., & Longenecker, C. O. (1993). The Bathsheba syndrome: The ethical failure of successful leaders. *Journal of Business Ethics, 12*(4), 265-273.

Maccoby, M. (2000). Narcissistic leaders: The incredible pros, the inevitable cons. *Harvard Business Review, 78*(1), 69-77.

Maccoby, M. (2003). *The productive narcissist: The promise and peril of visionary leadership.* New York: Broadway Books.

Manz, C. C., Anand, V., Joshi, M., & Manz, K. P. (2008). Emerging paradoxes in executive leadership: A theoretical interpretation of tensions between corruption and virtuous values. *The Leadership Quarterly, 19*(3), 385-392.

Martin, M. W. (1986). *Self-deception and morality.* Lawrence, KS: University Press of Kansas.

McCain, B. E. (1986). Continuing investment under conditions of failure: A laboratory study of the limits to escalation. *Journal of Applied Psychology, 71*(2), 280-284.

McNamara, G., Luce, R. A., & Tompson, G. H. (2002). Examining the effect of complexity in strategic group knowledge structures on firm performance. *Strategic Management Journal, 23*(2), 153-170.

Meglino, B. M., & Ravlin, E. C. (1998).Individual values in organizations: Concepts, controversies, and research. *Journal of Management, 24*(3), 351-389.

Meindl, J. R., & Ehrlich, S. B. (1987). The Romance of Leadership and the Evaluation of Organizational Performance. *Academy of Management Journal, 30*(1), 91-109.

Messick, D. (2005). On the psychological exchange between leaders and followers. In D. M. Messick & R. M. Kramer (Eds.), *The psychology of leadership: New perspectives and research* (pp. 81-96). Mahwah, NJ: Erlbaum.

Meyer, J. P., & Allen, N. J. (1991). A three-component conceptualization of organizational commitment. *Human Resource Management Review, 1*(1), 61-89.

Milgram, S. (1974). *Obedience to authority.* New York: Harper & Row.

Miller, D., & Toulouse, J. M. (1986). Strategy, structure, CEO personality and performance in small firms. *American Journal of Small Business, 10*(3), 47-62.

Miller, D., Kets de Vries, M. F. R., & Toulouse, J. (1982). Top executive locus of control and its relationship to strategy making, structure, and environment. *Academy of Management Journal, 25*(2), 237-253.

Morf, C. C., & Rhodewalt, F. (2001). Unraveling the paradoxes of narcissism: The dynamic self-regulatory processing model. *Psychological Inquiry, 12*(4), 177-196.

Moss, S. A., Dowling, N., & Callanan, J. (2009). Towards an integrated model of leadership and self regulation. *The Leadership Quarterly, 20*(2), 162-176.

Mowday, R. T., Porter, L. W., & Steers, R. M. (1982). *Employee-organization linkages: The psychology of commitment, absenteeism, and turnover.* New York: Academic Press.

Mumford, M. D., Helton, W. B., Decker, B. P., Connelly, M. S., & Van Doorn, J. R. (2003). Values and beliefs related to ethical decisions. *Teaching Business Ethics, 7*(2), 139-170.

O'Reilly, C. A., & Chatman J. (1986). Organizational commitment and psychological attachment: The effects of compliance, identification, and internalization on prosocial behavior. *Journal of Applied Psychology, 71*(3), 492-499.

Offerman, J. (2004). When followers become toxic. *Harvard Business Review, 82*(1), 54-60.

Padilla, A., & Mulvey, P. (2008). Leadership Toxicity: Sources and remedies. *Organisations & People, 15*(3), 29-39.

Padilla, A., Hogan, R., & Kaiser, R. B. (2007). The toxic triangle: Destructive leaders, susceptible followers, and conducive environments. *The Leadership Quarterly, 18*(3), 176-194.

Palmer, T. B., & Wiseman, R. M. (1999). Decoupling risk taking from income stream uncertainty: A holistic model of risk. *Strategic Management Journal, 20*(11), 1037-1062.

Palmer, T., Danforth, G., & Clark, S. (1995). Strategic responses to poor performance in the health care industry: A test of competing predictions. *Academy of Management Journal, 38*(1), 125-129.

Paolillo, J. G. P., & Vitell, S. J. (2002). An empirical investigation of the influence of selected personal, organizational and moral intensity factors on ethical decision making. *Journal of Business Ethics, 35*(1), 65-74.

Paulus, D., & Christie, I. L. (1981). Spheres of control: An interactionist approach to assessment of perceived control. In H. M. Lefcourt (Ed.), *Research on the locus of control construct* (Vol. 1, pp. 35-45). San Diego, CA: Academic Press.

Pearce, C. L., Manz, C. C., & Sims, H. P., Jr. (2008). The roles of vertical and shared leadership in the enactment of executive corruption: Implications for research and practice. *The Leadership Quarterly, 19*(3), 353-359.

Peterson, D. K. (2003). The relationship between ethical pressure, relativistic moral beliefs and organizational commitment. *Journal of Managerial Psychology, 18*(6), 557-572.

Pfeffer, J., & Fong, C. T. (2005). Building organization theory from first principles: The self-enhancement motive and understanding power and influence. *Organization Science, 16*(4), 372-388.

Pfeffer, J., & Salancik, G. R. (1978). *The external control of organizations*. New York: Harper & Row.

Pfeffer, J., & Sutton, R. (2006). *Hard facts, half truths, and total nonsense: Profiting from evidence-based management*. Boston: Harvard Business School Press.

Phares, E. S. (1976). *Locus of control in personality*. Morristown, NJ: Central Learning Press.

Pines, M. (1981). Reflections on mirroring. *International Review of Psychoanalysis, 11*, 27-42.

Pittenger, D. J. (2002). The two paradigms of persistence. *Genetic, Social, and General Psychology Monographs, 128*(3), 237-268.

Popper, M. (2001). *Hypnotic leadership: Leaders, followers, and the loss of self.* Westport, CT: Praeger.

Porr, D., & Fields, D. (2006). Implicit leadership effects on multi-source ratings for management development. *Journal of Managerial Psychology, 21*(7), 651-668.

Porter, L., Steers, R., Mowday, R., & Boulian, P. (1974). Organizational commitment, job satisfaction and turnover among psychiatric technicians. *Journal of Applied Psychology, 59*(5), 603-609.

Quinn, R. (2003). Ethics and fundamental decisions. In N. M. Tichy & A. R. McGill (Eds.), *The ethical challenge: How to lead with unyielding integrity* (pp. 159-184). San Francisco: Jossey-Bass.

Raven, B. H. (2001). Power/interaction and interpersonal influence: Experimental investigations and case studies. In A. Y. Lee-Chai & J. A. Bargh, *The use and abuse of power: Multiple perspectives on the causes of corruption* (pp. 217-240). Philadelphia, PA: Taylor & Francis.

Rest, J. R. (1979). *Development in judging moral issues*. Minneapolis, MN: University of Minnesota Press.

Rest, J. R. (1986). *Moral development: Advances in research and theory*. New York: Praeger.

Reicher, A. E., & Schneider, B. (1990). Climate and culture: An evolution of constructs. In B. Schneider (Ed.), *Organizational climate and culture* (pp. 5-39). San Francisco: Jossey-Bass.

Rhode, D. L. (2006). Introduction: Where is the leadership in moral leadership? In D. L. Rhode (Ed.), *Moral leadership: The theory and practice of power, judgment, and policy* (pp. 1-53). San Francisco: Jossey-Bass.

Rokeach, M. (1973). *The nature of human values*. New York: The Free Press.

Rosen, C. C., Levy, P. E., & Hall, R. J. (2006). Placing perceptions of politics in the context of the feedback environment, employee attitudes, and job performance. *Journal of Applied Psychology, 91*(1), 211-220.

Rosenthal, S. A., & Pittinsky, T. L. (2006). Narcissistic leadership. *The Leadership Quarterly, 17*(6), 617-633.

Rost, J. C. (1993). *Leadership for the twenty-first century.* Westport, CT: Praeger.

Rotter, J. B. (1966). Generalized expectancies of internal versus external control of reinforcements. *Psychological Monographs, 80* (whole no. 609).

Rotter, J. B. (1990). Internal versus external control of reinforcement: A case history of a variable. *American Psychologist, 45*(4), 489-493.

Rubin, J. Z., & Brockner, J. (1975). Factors affecting entrapment in waiting situations: The Rosencrantz and Guildenstern effect. *Journal of Personality and Social Psychology, 31*, 85-92.

Rusbult, C. E., Farrell, D., Rogers, G., & Mainous, A. G., III. (1988). Impact of exchange variables on exit, voice, loyalty and neglect: An integrative model of responses to declining job satisfaction. *Academy of Management Journal, 1*(3), 599-627.

Schein, E. H. (1992). *Organizational culture and leadership* (2nd ed.). San Francisco: Jossey-Bass.

Schilling, J. (2009) From ineffectiveness to destruction: A qualitative study on the meaning of negative leadership. *Leadership, 5*(1), 102-128.

Schminke, M., Ambrose, M. L., & Neubaum, D. O. (2005). The effect of leader moral development on ethical climate and employee attitudes. *Organizational Behavior and Human Decision Making, 97*(2), 135-151.

Schneider, B. (1975). Organizational climates: An essay. *Personnel Psychology, 28*(4), 447-479.

Schneider, B. (1987). The people make the place. *Personnel Psychology, 40*(3), 437-454.

Schneider, B, Goldstein, H. W., & Smith, D. B. (1995). The ASA framework: An update. *Personnel Psychology, 48*(4), 747-773.

Schwartz, S. H. (1992). Universals in the content and structure of values: Theory and empirical tests in 20 countries. In M. Zanna (Ed.), *Advances in Experimental Social Psychology* (Vol. 25, pp. 1-65). New York: Academic Press.

Schwartz, S. H. (1994). Are there universal aspects in the content and structure of values? *Journal of Social Issues, 50*(4), 19-45.

Schweitzer, M. E. & Gibson, D. E. (2008). Fairness, feelings, and ethical decision-making: Consequences of violating community standards of fairness. *Journal of Business Ethics, 77*(3), 287-301.

Schweitzer, M. E., Ordonney, L., & Douma, B. (2004). Goal-setting as a motivator of unethical behavior. *Academy of Management Review, 47*(3), 422-433.

Sedikides, C. (1993). Assessment, enhancement, and verification determinants of the self-evaluation process. *Journal of Personality and Social Psychology, 65*(2), 317-338.

Sedikides, C., & Green, J. D. (2000). On the self-protective nature of inconsistency negativity management: Using the person memory paradigm to examine self-referent memory. *Journal of Personality & Social Psychology, 79*(6), 906-922.

Sedikides, C., & Herbst, K. (2002). How does accountability reduce self-enhancement?: The role of self-focus. *Revue Internationale De Psychologie Sociale, 15*(3-4), 113-128.

Sedikides, C., Gaertner, L., & Toguchi, Y. (2003). Pancultural self-enhancement. *Journal of Personality and Social Psychology, 84*(1), 60-79.

Sedikides, C., Herbst, K. C., Hardin, D. P., & Dardis, G. J. (2002). Accountability as a deterrent to self-enhancement: The search for mechanisms. *Journal of Personality and Social Psychology, 83*(3), 592-605.

Sessa, V. I., & Kaiser. (2000). *Executive selection*. San Francisco: Jossey-Bass.

Shamir, B., House, R. J., & Arthur, M. B. (1993). The motivational effects of charismatic leadership: A self-concept based theory. *Organization Science, 4*, 1-17.

Singh, J. (2008). Imposters masquerading as leaders: Can the contagion be contained? *Journal of Business Ethics, 82*(3), 733-745.

Sitkin, S. & Pablo, A. (1992). Reconceptualizing the determinants of risk behavior. *Academy of Management Review, 17*(1), 9-39.

Starnes, D. M., & Zinzer, O. (1983). The effect of problem difficulty, locus of control, and sex on task persistence. *The Journal of General Psychology, 108*(2), 249-255.

Staw, B. M. (1976). Knee-deep in the big muddy: A study of escalating commitment to a chosen course of action. *Organizational Behavior and Human Performance, 16*, 27-44.

Staw, B. M. (1981). The escalation of commitment to a course of action. *Academy of Management Review, 6*(4), 577-586.

Staw, B. M., & Szwajkowski, E. (1975). The scarcity munificence component of organizational environments and the commission of illegal acts. *Administrative Science Quarterly, 20*(3), 345-354.

Staw, B., Sandelands, L., & Dutton, J. (1981). Threat-rigidity effects in organizational behavior: A multilevel analysis. *Administrative Science Quarterly, 26*(4), 501-524.

Steelman, L. K., Levy, P. E., & Snell, A. F. (2004). The feedback environment scale (FES): Construct definition, measurement and validation. *Education and Psychological Measurement, 64*, 165-184.

Street, M. (1995). Cognitive moral development and organizational commitment: Two potential predictors of whistle-blowing. *Journal of Applied Business Research, 11*(4), 104-110.

Street, M., & Street, V. (2006). The effects of escalating commitment on ethical decision-making. *Journal of Business Ethics, 64*(4), 343-356.

Street, M. D., Robertson, C., & Geiger, S. W. (1997). Ethical decision making: The effects of escalating commitment. *Journal of Business Ethics, 16*(11), 1153-1161.

Szwajkowski, E. (1985). Organizational illegality: Theoretical integration and illustrative application. *Academy of Management Review, 10*(3), 558-567.

Tajfel, H., & Turner, J. C. (1986). The social identity theory of intergroup behavior. In S. Worchel, & W. G. Austin (Eds.), *Psychology of intergroup behavior* (pp. 7-24). Chicago: Nelson-Hall.

Tang, T. L., & Chiu, R. K. (2003). Income, money, ethics, pay satisfaction, commitment and unethical behavior: Is the love of money the root of evil for Hong Kong employees? *Journal of Business Ethics, 46*(1), 13-30.

Tenbrunsel, A. E., & Messick, D. M. (2004). Ethical fading: The role of self-deception in unethical behavior. *Social Justice Research, 17*(2), 223-236.

Tetlock, P. E. (1992). The impact of accountability on judgment and choice: Toward a social contingency model. In L. Berkowitz (Ed.), *Advances in Experimental Social Psychology* (Vol. 25, pp. 331-376). New York: Academic Press.

Treviño, L. K. (1986). Ethical decision making in organizations: A person-situation interactionist model. *Academy of Management Review, 11*(3), 601-617.

Treviño, L. K., & Youngblood, S. A. (1990). Bad apples in bad barrels: A causal analysis of ethical decision-making behavior. *Journal of Applied Psychology, 75*(4), 378-385.

Treviño, L. K., Hartman, L. P., & Brown, M. (2000). Moral person and moral manager: How executives develop a reputation for ethical leadership. *California Management Review, 42*(2), 128-142.

Treviño, L., Weaver, G., Gibson, D., & Toffler, B. (1999). Managing ethics and legal compliance: What works and what hurts. *California Management Review, 41*(2), 131-151.

VandeWalle, D. (2003). A goal orientation model of feedback-seeking behavior. *Human Resource Management Review, 13*(4), 581-607.

Vardi, Y., & Weitz, E. (2004). *Misbehavior in organizations: Theory, research, and management*. Mahway, NJ: Erlbaum.

Victor, B., & Cullen, J. B. (1988). The organizational bases of ethical work climates. *Administrative Science Quarterly, 33*(1), 101-125.

Webley, S. (2003). *Developing a code of business ethics*. London, England: Institute of Business Ethics.

Webley, S., & Werner, A. (2008). Corporate codes of ethics: Necessary but not sufficient. *Business Ethics, 17*(4), 405-415.

Whitaker, B., Dahling, J., & Levy, P. (2007). The development of a feedback environment and role clarity model of job performance. *Journal of Management, 33*(4), 570-591.

Whicker, M. L. (1996). *Toxic leaders: When organizations go bad*. Westport, CT: Quorum Books.

Whyte, G. (1986). Escalating commitment to a course of action: A reinterpretation. *Academy of Management Review, 11*(2), 311-321.

Whyte, G. (1991). Diffusion of responsibility: Effects on the escalation tendency. *Journal of Applied Psychology, 76*(3), 408-415.

Whyte, G., Saks, A. M., & Hook, S. (1997). When success breeds failure: The role of self efficacy in escalating commitment. *Journal of Organizational Behavior, 18*(5), 415-432.

Yun, S., Takeuchi, R., & Liu, W. (2007). Employee self-enhancement motives and job performance behaviors: investigating the moderating effects of employee role ambiguity and managerial perceptions of employee commitment. *Journal of Applied Psychology, 92*(3), 745-756.

Ziglar-Hill, V. (2006). Discrepancies between implicit and explicit self-esteem: Implications for narcissism and self-esteem instability. *Journal of Personality, 74*(1), 119-143.

Zimbardo, P. (1969). The psychology of evil: A situationist perspective on recruiting good people to engage in anti-social acts. *Research in Social Psychology, 11,* 125-133.

Zimbardo, P. (2006). On the psychology of power: To the person? To the situation, To the system? In D. Rhode (Ed.), *Moral leadership: The theory and practice of power, judgment, and policy* (pp. 129-157). San Francisco: Jossey-Bass.

Zimbardo, P. (2007). *The Lucifer Effect: Understanding how good people turn evil.* New York: Random House.

Zimbardo, P. G., Maslach, C., & Haney, C. (1999). Reflections on the Stanford Prison Experiment: Genesis, transformations, consequences. In T. Blass (Ed.), *Obedience to authority: Current perspectives on the Milgram Paradigm* (pp. 193-237). Mahwah, NJ: Erlbaum.

CHAPTER 6

THE NATURE, PREVALENCE, AND OUTCOMES OF DESTRUCTIVE LEADERSHIP

A Behavioral and Conglomerate Approach

Ståle Einarsen, Anders Skogstad, and Merethe Schanke Aasland

The present article presents a definition and a taxonomy of destructive leadership based on a behavioral approach in opposition to the approach traditionally taken in leadership research where a one-sided emphasis on the personality of these "dark leaders" is the rule. Destructive leadership is then defined as any repeated behaviors that may undermine or sabotage either the organization itself or the subordinates of the leader. Building on these two dimensions, organizational directed behaviors and subordinate directed behaviors, that both may range from being highly pro to highly anti, a model is created that pinpoint four basic forms of destructive leadership; Laissez-faire leadership, Derailed leadership, Tyrannical leadership and Supportive but disloyal leadership. The model further implies that a leader may display both constructive as well as destructive behaviors, as leaders often face the dilemma of siding either with the goals or interests of the organization or with the goals and interests of their subordinates. Hence, the present article argues for a conglomerate perspective on leadership behaviors in order to

When Leadership Goes Wrong: Destructive Leadership, Mistakes and Ethical Failures, pp. 145–171

understand the full nuances in leaders' behaviors, making it difficult to distinguish between pure 'good' and pure "bad" leaders. The latter is also pinpointed by data on the prevalence of destructive leadership presented showing that destructive leadership is quite common in working life, at least in its more passive and less severe forms. Data are then presented showing that all the above mentioned forms of destructive leadership have significant negative relationships with both subordinate and organizational outcomes.

INTRODUCTION

Two important biases exist in leadership research and writings. First of all, leadership research often equates a leader with a good and efficient leader (Kellerman, 2004). Hence, most writings on leadership are based on the implicit assumption that to improve leadership it is sufficient to do more of what is already regarded as positive and productive. Furthermore, one sees leaders as inherently good people that do not need to worry about whether or not they at times may behave badly or commit mistakes. This position is exemplified by all those text-books that ignore the issue of potential bad or unwanted behaviors among leaders. For instance, the very popular and informative book of Yukl (2010) *Leadership in Organizations* does not include the terms "abusive supervision" or "destructive leadership" in its subject index. The same is true for Peter G. Northouse's (2007) book *Leadership: Theory and Practice*.

Second, writings that do exist on destructive forms of leadership have traditionally, explicitly or at least implicitly, equated destructive leadership with a "dark side" of the individual leader's personality. Hence, many studies have tried to identify personality traits in those leaders who fail or who derail from the path of constructive and effective leadership. This tradition of looking for the "evil within" has a long tradition in social psychology; although much evidence talks to the opposite (see Zimbardo, 2004). For instance, the work of Adorno and colleagues gave us the notion of the "authoritarian personality" (Adorno, Frenkel-Brunswik, Levinson, & Sanford, 1950). Later, Kets de Vries (1979) studied destructive leaders with a psychoanalytic perspective, focusing on the so-called "narcissistic" leaders. The concepts of "the dark side of leadership" (Conger, 1990; Hogan, Raskin, & Fazzini, 1990; Howell, 1988) substantiates that not all charismatic leaders focus on the common good of the organization and their followers. Rather, some leaders obviously have their own personal needs and interest at heart. Studies have shown that these leaders are characterized by an exaggerated and dysfunctional need for power, by narcissism, an authoritarian personality, and with a tendency for blaming others when failing themselves (House & Howell,

1992). Later on, concepts such as "toxic leaders" (Lipman-Blumen, 2005) and "crazy bosses" (Bing, 1992), among many others, likewise, have such connotations of personality flaws embedded.

Yet, such a focus on leaders traits in the search for negative aspects of leadership may have some problematic implications, not at least in applied settings. First of all, such a focus may lead to leaders being either seen as "white angels" (the rule) or as "black demons" (the anomaly), while few are seen as what they probably are, namely "grey suites" who portray all kinds of both good and bad behaviors depending on the situation and the systems that govern their everyday life (Skogstad, 2008). One may easily underestimate the risk factors and dilemmas leaders inherently face in their leadership role and within any kind of position of power, organizational structure and culture, appropriately illustrated with the words of Philip G. Zimbardo (2004):

> While a few bad apples might spoil the barrel (filled with good fruit/people), a vinegar barrel will always transform sweet cucumbers into sour pickles—regardless of the best intentions, resilience, and genetic nature of those cucumbers. So does it make more sense to spend our resources on attempts to identify, isolate and destroy a few bad apples or to learn how vinegar works so that we can teach cucumbers how to avoid undesirable vinegar barrels? (p. 47)

The management of destructive leadership then becomes a search for those very few and very bad "apples in the barrel," alienating the issue of bad leader behaviors from most training and development programs. Hence, one may train presumably good leaders to become even better, without an adequate focus on those pitfalls which most leaders probably will encounter sooner or later.

To avoid a one-sided emphasis on personality we will argue that there is a strong need for a firm behavioral approach to the study of destructive leadership. The question of personality traits as antecedents then becomes an empirical and not a definitional issue. Only by a behavioral approach may we enlighten and train leaders in the full range of possible behaviors that they may need and show in the role as a leader; only then may we create fair and safe early-detection systems for destructive leadership; only then may we fully discover the forces within the organization that act to shape such behaviors in the first place; only then may we train employees to be aware of and report safely those instances where one or more leaders behave in ways that they should not, be it in terms of inefficiency, in terms of legal aspects or in terms of ethics.

The present chapter will provide such a behavioral framework for the study of destructive leadership by presenting a definition and a taxonomy of destructive leadership behaviors based on two theoretically derived dimensions found in many theories and models of group dynamics and organizational behaviors. We will also show how a leader may display both constructive as well as destructive behaviors, as leaders often face the dilemma of siding either with the goals or interests of the organization or with the goals and interests of their subordinates, which at times may differ. Hence, the present article will show how we need a conglomerate perspective on leadership behaviors in order to understand the full nuances in leaders' behaviors. A conglomerate perspective on organizational behaviors implies that an actor, in our case a leader, may portray different kinds of behaviors that may occur simultaneously or that may occur in sequence (van de Vliert, Euwema, & Huismans, 1995). A leader may portray behavior that in some respects must be considered constructive while simultaneously may be considered as destructive from another point of view. Alternatively, the leader has a repertoire of behaviors including both destructive and constructive elements. In the following, we will also summarize some results from studies in our ongoing research on the nature, prevalence and outcomes of destructive leadership based on such a behavioral and conglomerate approach, building on the notion that to be able to identify and combat destructive leadership, we need to know what it is in terms of nuanced behavioral descriptions.

The Nature of Destructive Leadership Behaviors

A Definition of Destructive Leadership

Different concepts have been introduced to describe destructive leadership behaviors such as "petty tyranny" (Ashforth, 1994), "abusive supervision" (Tepper, 2000), and "toxic leadership" (Lipman-Blumen, 2005). These concepts describe leaders who behave in a destructive manner towards followers, and may include behaviors such as intimidating followers, belittling or humiliating them in public, or exposing them to aggressive nonverbal gestures (Aryee, Sun, Chen, & Debrah, 2007; Ashforth, 1994; Tepper, 2000). Studies have shown such behaviors to be destructive for the motivation, efficiency and health of followers and thereby possibly also pose a problem for the organization (e.g., Tepper, 2007). Yet, leaders may also behave destructively in a way that primarily effects the organization (Einarsen, Aasland, & Skogstad, 2007; Kellerman, 2004; Lipman-Blumen, 2005; Vredenburgh & Brender, 1998). Concepts proposed in the literature to describe such anti-organizational behaviors include, for example, "flawed leadership" and "impaired managers" (Lubit, 2004). Leaders may, for instance, hamper the execution of tasks, reduce the quality of work performed in the department, reduce the efficiency of subordinates, or more directly act in a way that hamper relationships with customers and clients (Padilla, Hogan, & Kaiser, 2007). The behavior of leaders may undermine or sabotage the organization's goals, tasks, resources, and effectiveness both directly through their own behaviors and through their potential negative effect on the behavior of subordinates. In extreme cases, leaders may in this way also perform illegal acts such as stealing resources from the company. As mentioned above, leaders may have their own best interests at heart more so than the best interest of the company. Hence, there are clearly both a subordinate and an organizational dimension in destructive leadership (see also Einarsen et al., 2007).

In addition, the lack of initiative and the lack of appropriate responses by leaders may also pose a problem. Leaders' passiveness and lack of appropriate leadership, exemplified by laissez-faire leadership (see e.g., Bass & Riggio, 2006) have been shown to be associated with negative consequences for followers and leader effectiveness (Hinkens & Schriesheim, 2008; Judge & Piccolo, 2004; Skogstad, Einarsen, Aasland, Torsheim, & Hetland, 2007). Passive leadership represents a leadership style where the leader has been nominated and still exists physically in the leadership position, but in practice has abdicated from the responsibilities and duties designated to him/her (Lewin, Lippitt, & White, 1939), implying that the leader did not accomplish legitimate expectations from subordinates or from superiors and the owners of the organization (Skogstad et al., 2007). With their concept of "poor leadership," distinguishing between an active and a passive component, Kelloway and colleagues (Kelloway, Sivanathan, Francis, & Barling, 2005) argue that passive leadership is both *distinct from* active leadership and has negative effects *beyond* those attributed to a lack of transformational leadership. Hence, leaders may be experienced as destructive both by doing things they should not be doing and by not doing what they are expected to do.

Building on the notion that leaders may undermine or sabotage both followers and the organization itself, we have earlier proposed the following definition of destructive leadership behavior;

> the systematic and repeated behavior by a leader, supervisor or manager that violate the legitimate interest of the organization by undermining and/or sabotaging the organization's goals, tasks, resources, and effectiveness and/or the motivation, well-being or job satisfaction of subordinates. (Einarsen et al., 2007, p. 208)

The definition emphasizes that destructive behaviors may be directed towards both followers as well as towards the organizations itself, or towards both. Further, to be defined as destructive the behaviors have to be repeated and systematic as opposed to single behaviors such as an isolated outburst of anger. Here we side with Tepper (2000) who defined abusive supervision as "subordinates perceptions of the extent to which supervisors engage in the sustained display of hostile verbal and nonverbal behaviors, excluding physical contact" (p. 178). A single mistake or a single instance of incivility by a leader is not sufficient to evaluate such leadership as destructive. Single mistakes are human and to be expected. Multiple mistakes are also human, but may still pose a serious problem to the organization. Hence, if incivility becomes repeated it represents destructive leadership, irrespectively of its intentions or causes.

An important feature of the proposed definition is that it excludes any reference to "intent" or "motive," thus embracing instances where there is a clear intent to cause harm as well as instances of thoughtlessness or the lack of skills (see also Einarsen et al., 2007). Hence, we employ a strict behavioral definition where underlying constructs such as intent, is of no relevance to the determination of whether or not a destructive behavior has occurred. Intent may only be verified by the focal leader, hence being of little relevance in applied settings and difficult to verify in scientific terms (see also Buss, 1961 for a discussion on intent in interpersonal aggression). Including intent in the definition may only provide the leader with a final saying regarding the nature of the behavior exhibited, as compared to followers' or observers' perceptions of destructive leadership. Furthermore, it really does not matter why a leader acts as he or she does if their behavior is repeated and of a kind that will likely harm either the organization or it's employees. Thus, the main issue is the actual behaviors and their potential consequences, rather than their underlying psychological intentions and motivations.

As compared to Tepper's definition, we broaden the domain of behavior to include all kinds of inadequate or bad leader behaviors, physical as well as verbal, active as well as passive and indirect as well as direct (see also Buss, 1961). Accordingly, destructive leadership consists of any kind of repeated and systematic behavior that undermines or sabotages either the motivation, the well-being or the job satisfaction of followers or the goals, resources or effectiveness of the organizations.

Further, destructive leadership is about that what violates or is in opposition to the *legitimate interest* of the organization (see also Sackett & DeVore, 2001) and their definition of "counterproductive workplace behavior"). The term "legitimate interest" narrows down the range of behaviors to those that may be seen as illegal, immoral, or otherwise counterproductive from an organizational point of view. Yet, by employing the concept of legitimate interest, we restrict what an organization can and cannot expect from it's leaders to what can be considered as legal, reasonable and justifiable within a given cultural context. Hence, the perception of destructive leader behavior will vary between different cultures and societies over time, and even, to some extent, between organizations depending on their legitimate goals within a given society. For example, in times of war, exposing soldiers to a risk of dying can probably not be defined as destructive leadership, while doing so in times of peace probably would. Including this term in the definition also prohibits those leaders who defer from joining an illegal or unethical management culture to be considered destructive even if their behavior is deviant as seen by the company norm. In such cases, a leader refusing to obey such norms would actually represent constructive leadership. Employers as well as employees are obligated to behave in accordance with norms, laws, and agreements that exist in the given culture.

A TAXONOMY OF DESTRUCTIVE LEADERSHIP BEHAVIORS: THE DESTRUCTIVE AND CONSTRUCTIVE LEADERSHIP MODEL

Based on the above definition we have developed a model of leadership behavior that includes both constructive and destructive elements and that incorporates both active behaviors and the lack of appropriate behavior. The model is based on three assumptions, that is; that destructive leadership is about two main classes for behaviors; those mainly directed at subordinates and those mainly directed at the organization (see also Bass, 1990 for a description of such basic dimensions in leadership theory). Second, it is based on the assumption that a leader's behaviors on both dimensions may range from being highly pro to being highly anti, hence departing from most models of leadership which mainly see leadership on dimensions from "low" to "high," from "little" to "much" or from "ineffective" to "effective," for example, as found in *The Managerial Grid* by Blake and Mouton (1985). A range of studies have shown leaders to bully and harass their subordinates, that is, showing a high level of behaviors directed at subordinates but in a manner that are "anti" regarding the motivation and well-being of these subordinates. Similarly, a leader committing fraud is actively managing the organizations assets, but in an "anti" way. Only looking at behaviors on a continuum from "low" to "high," would not necessarily detect the behaviors of such leaders (see Figure 6.1). Third, by cross-cutting the two dimensions we provide four quadrants of leadership with different combinations of destructive and constructive behavior, assuming that leaders are not necessarily either "good" or "bad," but rather may show conglomorated behaviors. According to the logic of the model, a leader may be seen as being constructive on one of the two dimensions (pro), while behaving in breach with the legitimate interest of the organization (anti) on the other dimension, providing a conglomerate perspective on the behaviors of leaders. Again, conglomerate behaviors are different kinds of behaviors that may occur simultaneously or that may occur in sequence (van de Vliert, Euwema, & Huismans, 1995). In addition to a broad category of constructive leadership behaviors where the leaders show a conglomerate of behaviors that are constructive regarding both subordinates as well as the organization, the model contains three basic kinds of destructive leadership where the leader is behaving badly on at least one of the dimensions;

- Tyrannical behavior (pro-organization combined with anti-subordinate behavior),
- Supportive disloyal (pro-subordinate combined with anti-organizational behavior)
- Derailed behavior (anti-subordinate combined with anti-organizational behavior).

In addition, the model contains a category of "laissez-faire" leadership where the leader avoids fulfilling the legitimate expectancies embedded in the role of a leader, hence being passive on both dimensions.

Constructive leadership is about leaders who display pro-organizational as well as pro-subordinate behaviors. The leader then acts in accordance with the legitimate interests of the organization, supporting and working towards the strategy of the organization, while simultaneously motivating

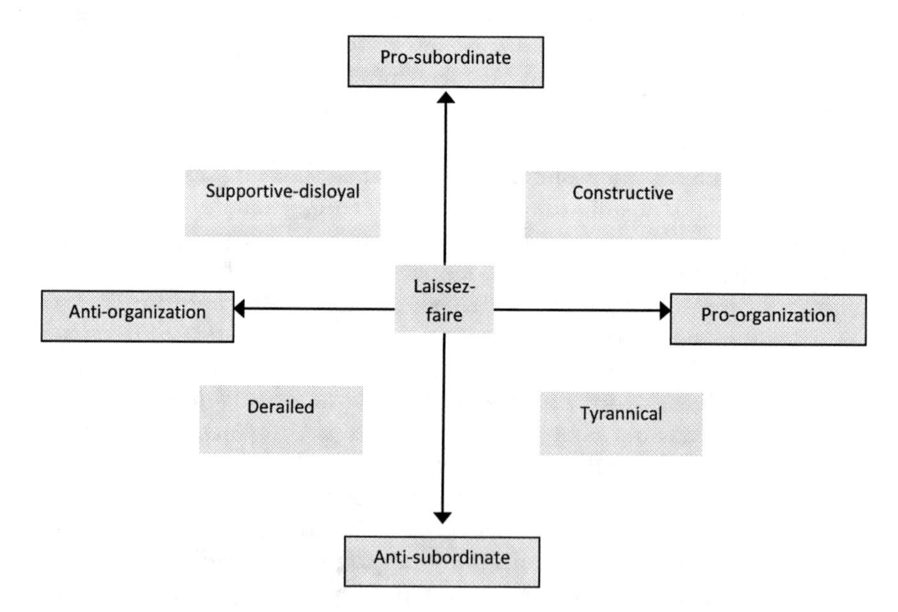

Figure 6.1. The destructive and constructive model of leadership behaviors.

and supporting their followers through considerate behaviors, inspiration and the involvement and participation in decision processes. Hence, constructive leadership reflects both transformational and transactional forms of leadership as described in the "Full Range Leadership Model" (see Bass & Riggio, 2006), and may be seen as a parallel to the "high-high" leader, and what is called "Team Management" in Blake and Mouton's (1985) *The Managerial Grid*. Even though such a broad conceptualization do not do justice to the abundant and varied body of research on constructive forms of leadership (see also Avolio & Gardner, 2005; Bass, 1990), it does pinpoint the main ingredients of all forms of constructive leadership; supporting and motivating subordinates while focusing on the optimal use of organizational resources to achieve legitimate organizational goals. What is the focus of most leadership research is how a leader may accomplish this in the most optimal and effective way.

Tyrannical leadership behavior is manifested when a leader combines pro-organizational and anti-subordinate behaviors. Being pro-organizational, these leaders may behave in accordance with the legitimate goals, tasks, and strategies of the organization. They may even be superior strategists or high performing leaders in terms of technical skills or in terms of task related efficiency. However, they frequently obtain results at the cost of subordinates, not through their willing cooperation (Ashforth, 1994; Einarsen et al., 2007). Being anti-subordinate, tyrannical leaders manipulate, humiliate and intimidate subordinates in order to "get the job done" (e.g., Ashforth, 1994; Kile, 1990; Lombardo & McCall, 1984). Hence, what upper-management may view as an efficient focus on task completion by a leader, may simultaneously be viewed as abusive leadership or even as bullying by subordinates (Einarsen et al., 2007). Leaders who harass their subordinates may nevertheless perform well on other assignments, for example, through specialized skills or competencies (Brodsky, 1976). Leaders who behave destructively towards subordinates may not necessarily be destructive in other interpersonal relationships, be it with customers or business partners or in relation to the upper-management (Skogstad, 1997). Ma, Karri, and Chittipeddi (2004) define this phenomenon as "the paradox of managerial tyranny," arguing that tyrannical leadership may lead to extraordinary performance, even when subordinates suffer, at least in the short run. Yet, abusing subordinates is not in the legitimate interest of the organization, hence defining tyrannical leadership as a certain type of destructive leadership. Tyrannical is then a kind of abusive supervision conducted by a leader who in other respects is taking good care of the organizations by fulfilling its tasks and missions.

Derailed leadership behavior is about portraying both anti-organizational as well as anti-subordinate behaviors. These leaders are anti-subordinate though behaviors such as bullying, humiliation, manipulation and deceiving (see e.g., Ashforth, 1994; Kile, 1990; Lombardo & McCall, 1984), while at the same time conducting anti-organizational behaviors like absenteeism, work withdrawal, shirking, committing fraud, or otherwise by stealing resources (be it financial, time or material resources) from the organization (Einarsen et al., 2007; Lubit, 2004; McCall & Lombardo, 1983). An example would be leaders who use their charismatic qualities for personal gains while exploiting followers as well as their employer (Conger, 1990). Such leader characteristics are also prominent in descriptions of pseudo-transformational leadership as compared to authentic transformational leadership (Bass & Riggio, 2006) and in the concept of narcissistic leadership with characteristics such as arrogance, insatiable need for recognition, anger, lack of empathy, irrationality, and inflexibility (Rosenthal & Pittinsky, 2006). Accordingly, derailed leaders violate the legitimate interest of the organization, both by working against organizational goals and, concurrently, by undermining or sabotaging subordinates. Hence, these leaders may be seen as not only abusive towards subordinates but also towards the organization.

In *Supportive-disloyal leadership behavior* a leader combines pro-subordinate with anti-organizational behaviors. Hence, such leaders may motivate, stimulate and support their subordinates, for example, through inspirational motivation and individualized consideration (Bass & Riggio, 2006). However, these leaders may simultaneously deprive resources from the organization, be it consumption of working hours, material resources or economical resources (Altheide, Adler, Adler, & Altheide, 1978; Ditton, 1977; Einarsen et al., 2007). They may grant their employees more benefits than appropriate and encourage low work ethic or even misconduct. Accordingly, supportive-disloyal leaders direct their subordinates towards inefficiency, or towards other goals than those of the organization, at the same time behaving in a comradely and friendly manner. This leadership style has some features in common with what Blake and Mouton (1985) termed "Country Club Management" as both styles represent an overriding concern with establishing camaraderie with subordinates. Yet, supportive-disloyal leaders are combining this with behaviors that are not in the best and legitimate interest of the organization; theft, fraud, and embezzlement being widespread problems in today's business world even among leaders that are well liked by their subordinates (e.g., the scandals that hit WorldCom and Enron in the first years of the twenty-first century). The intention of the supportive-disloyal leader may not necessarily be to harm the organization; he or she may simply be acting upon a different "vision" or strategy working in support of other values or goals than that of the organization, even believing that he or she acts with the organization's best interest at heart (e.g., narcissistic leadership). By directing and motivating followers to work hard, but in a direction contrary to organizational goals, supportive-disloyal leaders behave contrary to the legitimate interest of the organization.

Yet, destructive forms of leadership are not limited to such active and manifest behaviors as described above. Destructive leadership may also be a function of *passive direct* and *passive indirect* behaviors (see Buss, 1961). Passive and avoiding leadership has frequently been referred to as *laissez-faire leadership*, and as such constituting one of three main types of leadership in the "Full Range Leadership model" (Bass & Riggio, 2006). Bass and Avolio (1990), who are frequently cited in definitions of laissez-faire leadership, describe this type of leadership as

> With Laissez-faire (Avoiding) leadership, there are generally neither transactions nor agreements with followers. Decisions are often delayed; feedback, rewards, and involvement are absent; and there is no attempt to motivate followers or to recognize and satisfy their needs. (p. 20)

Laissez-faire leadership does not merely represent nonbehaviors and nontransactions, as the formal leader position triggers legitimate expectations among both subordinates and superiors, which, when left unfulfilled, may have destructive consequences for subordinates as well as for the organization. Accordingly, metastudies (Bass & Avolio, 1990; Judge & Piccolo, 2004) show that laissez-faire leadership behavior negatively is associated with leader job performance, leader effectiveness and follower satisfaction with the leader. A study by Skogstad and colleagues (2007) showing systematic relationships between laissez-faire leadership behavior and role stress and interpersonal conflict, which in turn predicted bullying at work and distress among subordinates, supports the assumption that *laissez-faire* is a type of leadership which is associated with negative consequences, for subordinates as well as for the organization. Hence, laissez-faire leadership is not a zero-type of leadership. As it is impossible to not communicate (see see Watzlawick, Beavin, & Jackson, 1967) one may also argue that a leader cannot avoid to lead. Doing nothing is also to do something. Hence, by doing nothing a leader would, at least in the long run, run the risk of undermining or sabotaging one's followers or the organization itself.

The Prevalence of Destructive Leadership Behavior

While some researchers claim that destructive or abusive leadership constitutes a low base-rate phenomenon (e.g., Aryee, Sun, Chen, & Debrah, 2007), others believe it to be a substantial problem in many organizations, in terms of both its prevalence and consequences (Burke, 2006;

Hogan, Raskin, & Fazzini, 1990). Yet, in empirical terms we really do not know. Few if any studies have so far investigated the *prevalence* of such destructive leadership in contemporary working life. We will therefore now summarize the results of such a study conducted in a representative sample of the Norwegian work force where the prevalence of the above described forms of destructive leadership were investigated employing subordinate ratings (see Aasland, Skogstad, Notelaers, Nielsen, & Einarsen, 2009). In this study, a representative sample of Norwegian workers were asked, in a paper and pencil questionnaire, to rate the behavior of their immediate supervisor employing four items on each of the four types of destructive leadership described. In addition, six items were included measuring constructive leadership behavior, in which two items measured person-oriented, two task-oriented and two change-oriented leadership behaviors, respectively. These items were scattered among the destructive items to avoid any kind of response style or a "horns effect" where the leader is only seen in negative terms.

The results first of all showed that constructive leadership was by far the most prevalent form of leadership behavior reported by the subordinates, as should be expected. Results also showed that all three kinds of constructive behaviors loaded on the same factor indicating a conglomerate type of constructive leadership where the leader combines task-oriented, subordinate-oriented and change-oriented behaviors. Hence, most leaders behave constructively most of the time.

Second, destructive and constructive behaviors were portrayed quite simultaneously by many leaders as the correlation between constructive leadership and the destructive forms of leadership behavior were modest at best (that is r –.29, ($p < .001$) between constructive leadership and derailed leadership). Hence, many leaders, at least over a period of 6 months showed both constructive and destructive forms of leadership, even if there is a tendency that the best leaders are less destructive than are the second or third best leaders.

Third, experiences of destructive leadership behaviors were very common, at least according to the responses of Norwegian employees. As many as 83.7% in the sample ($N = 2539$) reported exposure to one *or more* of tyrannical, derailed, supportive-disloyal or laissez-faire leadership behavior during the last 6 months. According to an operational criterion focusing on repeated experiences, 33.5% of the respondents reported exposure to at least one destructive leadership behavior "quite often" or "very often or nearly always" during the last 6 months. Based on the same criterion, 21.2% were exposed to one or more instances of laissez-faire leadership behavior, while 11.6% reported one or more instances of supportive-disloyal leadership behavior. Furthermore, the corresponding numbers for derailed leadership behavior was 8.8%, while the prevalence rate of tyrannical leadership behavior was reported to be 3.4%. Hence, exposure to some form of destructive leadership is quite common, with laissez-faire leadership and supportive-disloyal leadership being the most prevalent ones.

The observed prevalence rates in Aasland and colleagues' study (2009) are far higher than those reported in two somewhat comparable studies conducted by Schat and colleagues (Schat et al., 2006) and Hubert and van Veldhoven (2001). Schat and colleagues reported that, during the last 12 months, 13.5% of the respondents were exposed to aggression from their superior, while Hubert and van Veldhoven found an average prevalence rate of about 11%. However, these two studies are only partially comparable with the Norwegian study as they only investigated *one* form of destructive leadership behavior, namely *aggressive* behavior. Consequently, they neither investigated passive forms of destructive leadership nor destructive forms of leadership that may also include constructive elements (cf. popular-disloyal and tyrannical leadership behaviors). Furthermore, these studies did not measure destructive behavior targeting the organization. Hence, there is a need to assess a broader range of destructive leadership behavior, as was the case in the presented study (Aasland et al., 2009), as this will yield a more nuanced picture of prevalence rates. Accordingly, studies including all the four forms of destructive leadership in the presented model (see Figure 6.1) will probably yield considerable higher prevalence rates than measuring a narrower range of behaviors, as in studies on abusive supervision (see Tepper, 2007 for a review) who mainly look at behaviors on the subordinate dimension in the above presented model.

The Occurrence of Conglomerate Destructive Behaviors

In line with a conglomerate perspective of organizational behavior (see Van de Vliert, 1997) different kinds of leadership behavior may occur simultaneously or sequentially, a perspective seldom taken in leadership research. The prevalence rates of the four types of destructive leadership described above are in itself indicators that such conglomerate behaviors exist among many leaders making it more difficult to distinguish between "good" and "bad" leaders. Hence, many leaders are both good and bad. Another indicator of conglomerate behavior is the intercorrelations between the different forms of destructive leadership. The highest intercorrelations were found between tyrannical leadership and derailed leadership (r = .60), reflecting that both forms consist of anti-subordinate behavior (Aasland et al., 2009). Laissez-faire leadership showed a comparable relationship with derailed leadership (r = .54) substantiating that laissez-faire leadership is, indeed, a destructive form of leadership, and that it is highly related to derailed leadership (as illustrated in Figure 6.1).

Accordingly, laissez-faire leadership showed a relatively high positive correlation (r = .38) with tyrannical leadership. However, the relationships between supportive-disloyal leadership and the other forms of destructive leadership were very weak or insignificant in a negative direction, indicating that this type of destructive leadership do not concur together with the three other forms (Aasland et al., 2009). However, the intercorrelation between supportive-disloyal leadership and constructive leadership was reported to be relatively high (r = .35) substantiating the pro-subordinate characteristics of supportive-disloyal leadership. Again, the study showed moderate negative correlations between different forms of destructive leadership behaviors and *constructive* leadership behavior (Aasland et al., 2009). Hence, destructive leadership is not a phenomenon that exists apart from constructive leadership, but is probably an integrated part of the behavioral repertoire of most leaders.

We may draw a similar conclusion from an English study on harassment by managers (Rayner & Cooper, 2003) where, of 72 managers evaluated by subordinates, only 11.1% were exclusively perceived as being a 'tough manager' where all employees reported bullying behaviors from that manager, and correspondingly only 9.7% of the managers were exclusively perceived as "angels" with no reports of bullying behaviors toward any of the included subordinates. The same study showed that about 28% of the managers were evaluated as either "tough managers with supporters," "middlers with victims," or as "angels with victims." Thus, the authors conclude that leadership consists of conglomerate behavior, representing different behavior and different combinations of behavior in relation to different subordinates, who again may react differently (Rayner & Cooper, 2003).

In order to look more closely into such conglomerate destructive behaviors by leaders, Aasland and colleagues (2009) reanalyzed their representative sample of subordinates ratings of their immediate leaders behavior by the use of a latent class cluster analysis (LCC) (Magidson & Vermunt, 2004). LCC was used to classify the respondents into mutually exclusive but homogeneous groups based on similarities in their ratings of their immediate leader, taking both the frequency and the nature of their experiences into account (see also Notelaers, Einarsen, De Witte, & Vermunt, 2006). Based on the probability to report the behaviors of the leaders in a certain way, Aasland and colleagues (2009) could investigate how the subordinates saw their leaders in a more nuanced way than was the case with the operational criterion method. Compared to the latter method, as employed in the results summarized above, this procedure could, first, indentify reports of systematic and repeated but low frequency behaviors, as when a leader shows many different kinds of behaviors infrequently but where these behaviors aggregated to quite an amount of destructive behaviors. Second, this procedure made it possible to investigate if conglomerate behaviors exist regarding destructive leadership where a subordinate describes his or her leader to portray more than one kind of destructive leadership behaviors.

The results showed that six separate clusters of destructive leadership behavior existed. One group of respondents labelled as "no-destructiveness" and consisting of 39% of the respondents in the sample, was characterized by a high conditional probability of answering "never" to any of the items measuring the four kinds of destructive leadership behavior. Hence, these subordinates claim that their immediate supervisor exhibited no systematic destructive behavior what so ever. This would also mean, then, that 60% of all Norwegian employees do perceive such systematic behaviors in their leaders, even in quite a few of the constructive ones. A second group of respondents, labeled "laissez-faire" constituting 19% of the respondents, had an increased conditional probability of reporting exposure to items measuring laissez-faire leadership combined with a low probability to report any kind of tyrannical, derailed or supportive-disloyal leadership behavior. Yet, another group, consisting of 17% was labeled "sometimes laissez-faire and sometimes supportive-disloyal"; reporting that their superiors showed a conglomerate of both these kinds of behavior. Another group of respondents, comprising ten per cent of the respondents, reported exposure to "supportive-disloyal" leadership behavior only, as they had a low probability to report any other kind of destructive behavior in their immediate superior. A fifth group of respondents were labeled "sometimes destructive" as these subordinates faced destructive leadership behavior in a variety of forms, be it laissez-faire, tyrannical or derailed leadership, however on an occasional basis. These comprised 11% of the total sample. Finally, a sixth group of respondents existed that were labelled "highly abusive" as these respondents reported high exposure to both laissez-faire, tyrannical as well as derailed leadership behavior. The latter group comprised 6% of the respondents in the sample.

Hence, the study by Aasland et al. (2009) showed that exposure to destructive leadership is frequent, at least according to subordinates, but that it represents a complex phenomenon where laissez-faire leadership behavior stands out as the most frequent type. Furthermore laissez-faire leadership behavior is reported, all together, in three different forms; a stand-alone phenomenon, in combination with supportive-disloyal leadership behavior, or as part of a conglomerate in which subordinates report exposure to a combination of both tyrannical and derailed leadership behavior, as well as to laissez-faire leadership (Aasland et al., 2009). The latter seems to come in two forms, an infrequent and a highly frequent form. Furthermore, the results of this study indicate that a pure form of tyrannical behavior seldom occur. This may raise the hypothesis that this is a destructive form of leadership that, at least in the long run, more and more may turn into or are being seen as derailed leadership. Probably, tyrannical leadership only leads to good results in the short run, while its destructive potential concerning the motivation and performance of followers only becomes apparent in the long run when it also impairs organizational goal attainment.

Noteworthy is also the fact that supportive-disloyal behaviors occur quite frequently, even as seen by subordinates, again either as a stand a lone phenomenon or in combination with laissez-faire leadership. Hence, the "black demons" seems to be few in numbers at least in Norwegian working life, while "Grey suits" and the "do—nothings" (Skogstad, 2008) are many.

The study by Aasland and colleagues (2009) investigated subordinates' experiences of destructive leadership behavior over a 6-month period. Hence, the exposures may be experienced simultaneously as well as sequentially. Further, over time, laissez-faire leadership behavior may develop into more active forms of destructive leadership in the same way that tyrannical leadership behavior may evolve into derailed leadership behavior (Ma et al., 2004). Thus, the study substantiates our assumption that destructive leadership represents conglomerate behavior with different classes of behavior occurring simultaneously or sequentially. Studying one single class of destructive leader behavior, for example, leader aggression (Hubert & van Veldhoven, 2001; Schat et al., 2006) or abusive supervision (Tepper, 2007) only, may therefore result in a too constricted focus, resulting in a partial picture of a complex phenomenon.

Outcomes of Destructive Leadership Behaviors

Various empirical studies have shown that experiencing a destructive leader may have serious negative effects on the subordinates' well-being. Studies on abusive supervision have been linked with several indicators of psychological distress, including anxiety (Tepper, 2000), depression (Tepper, 2000), diminished self-efficacy (Duffy, Ganster, & Pagon, 2002), somatic health complaints (Duffy et al., 2002; Kile, 1990), burnout (Tepper, 2000; Yagil, 2006), and job strain (Harvey, Stoner, Hochwarter, & Kacmar, 2007). Yet, fewer studies have investigated the effects of conglomerate behaviors or the effects of behaviors that are mainly destructive regarding the organization.

In a study employing the same representative sample of the Norwegian work force as described in the study above, the present authors found a range of relationships between exposure to the destructive forms of leadership presented in the destructive and constructive leadership model and well-being outcomes as reported by subordinates (Einarsen, Aasland, & Skogstad, 2008). In Figure 6.2, we show how the six groups of respondents described above rate their own job satisfaction. A one-way analysis of variance showed a systematic relationship between the exposure of destructive leadership and job satisfaction (F = 51,71, df (5/2107), p < .001). As can be seen in the figure, a clear relationship between the form and severity of the exposure and the reported level of job satisfaction exist. Yet, subordinates exposed to "supportive-disloyal" behaviors (group 2) alone or in combination with laissez-faire behavior (group 3) did not report any different from the group not reporting exposure to destructive leadership behavior (group 1). Yet, those reporting exposure to "sometimes till often laissez-faire" leadership differed significantly from the three first clusters, and significantly and more pronounced reduced level of job satisfaction was revealed by those exposed to the two most severe patterns of destructive leadership (group 5 and 6). The results again substantiate that laissez-faire leadership, at least when reaching a certain threshold, is not only a type of zero-leadership but constitutes a passive form of destructive leadership (see also Skogstad et al., 2007). Yet, a relatively high exposure to destructive leadership behavior represented by high levels of tyrannical, derailed as well laissez-faire leadership was

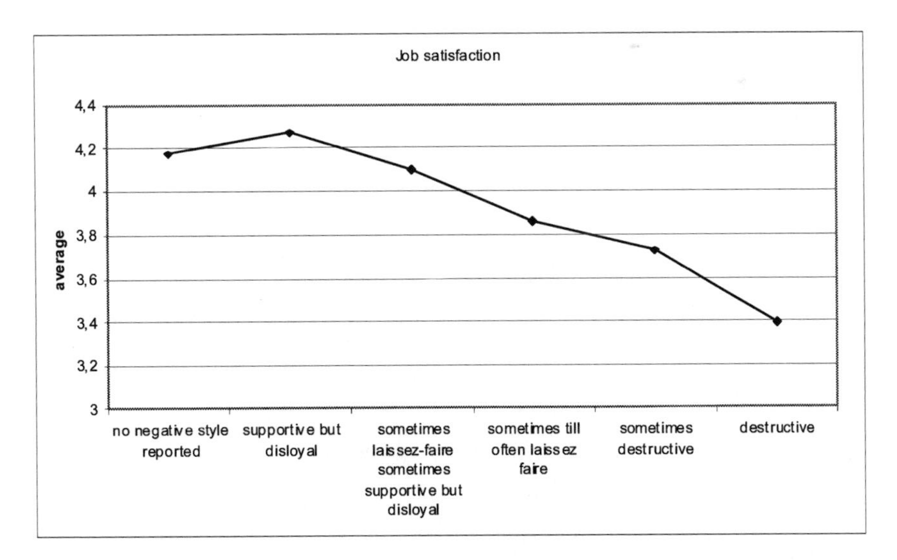

Figure 6.2. Reported job satisfaction in six groups of respondents with different experiences regarding their exposure to destructive leadership behavior by their immediate leader.

clearly associated with the lowest levels of job satisfaction. Accordingly, extant research substantiate that abusive supervision is associated with lowered job satisfaction (Tepper, 2000; Tepper, Duffy, Hoobler, & Ensley, 2004). Likewise, a metastudy (Judge & Piccolo, 2004) shows that laissez-faire leadership is negatively and consistently associated with job satisfaction.

Figure 6.3 also shows how the same respondents report in regard to mental health complaints in the form of reporting symptoms of anxiety and depression. Again, systematic relationship were revealed (F = 48,36, $df(5/2180)$, $p < .001$) (see Figure 6.3), and again the cluster with no exposure to destructive leadership behavior reported the best mental well-being with a low level of mental health complaints and, again, the cluster reporting exposure to supportive-disloyal leadership (cluster 2) did not report different than did those nonexposed. Yet, all other groups (clusters 3 to 6) reported significantly higher levels of health complaints than those nonexposed. Comparable findings have been found among targets of bullying. A study among 199 subordinates who had experienced bullying from one or more of their superiors identified systematic relationships between "tyrannical leadership," but also partly between "supportive-disloyal" and "laissez-faire leadership" behavior, and symptoms of posttraumatic stress (Nielsen, Matthiesen, & Einarsen, 2005). Likewise, in

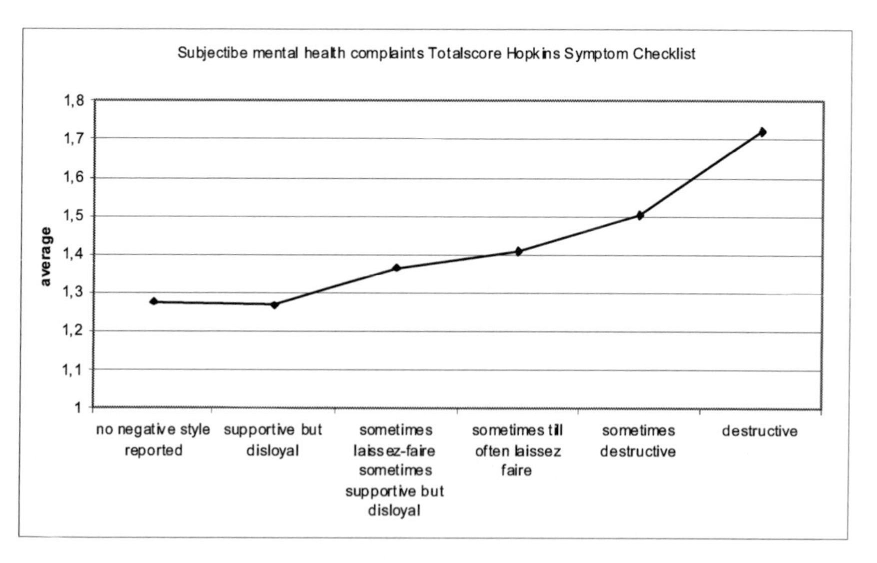

Figure 6.3. Reported mental health complaints in six groups of respondents with different experiences regarding their exposure to destructive leadership behavior by their immediate leader.

an interview-based study of 50 teachers in the United States who had been mistreated by school principals over a long period of time (6 months to 9 years), revealed that the respondents experienced shock, disorientation, humiliation, loneliness, and injured self-esteem (Blase & Blase, 2004). The principals' abuse of teachers was also associated with severe emotional problems, including chronic fear, anxiety, anger, and depression (Blase & Blase, 2004). Passive-avoidant leadership, defined as leaders avoiding their responsibility, and in many cases showing an absence of leadership behaviors, has also been positively associated with exhaustion and cynicism, which are key components in the burnout syndrome (Hetland, Sandal, & Johnsen, 2007; Maslach, Schaufeli, & Leiter, 2001).

In studies of abusive supervision a positive association has also been found with intentions to quit (Tepper, 2000, Tepper, Carr, Breaux, Geider, Hu, & Hua, 2009). Likewise, in a qualitative study among Swedish PhD students who had dropped out of the program, Frischer and Larsson (2000) identified supervisors' laissez-faire behavior to be the main reason for this "drop-out."

Analysis of the representative Norwegian sample (Einarsen et al., 2008) also revealed significant associations between exposure to destructive leadership and intentions to leave the organization within the next 12 months (see Figure 6.4). The patterns of relationships between groups are the same as those reported for job satisfaction and mental health complaints. There were significant differences between those nonexposed (cluster 1) and all other groups except for those reporting "supportive-disloyal" leadership (cluster 2). In line with the proposed model of destructive and constructive leadership behaviors, supportive disloyal leadership behavior does not seem to portray a particular problem for subordinates, at least not in its pure form. Yet, it is worth noticing that it is not associated with positive outcomes. Hence, one may argue that leaders manifesting this type of leadership are seen very differently by their subordinates, probably based on whether or not the subordinates acknowledge the destructive aspects of their behavior on the organizational dimension.

Yet, experiencing systematic supportive but disloyal behavior by ones immediate boss is related to subordinates' report of work-withdrawal (Skogstad, Notelaers, & Einarsen, 2009). In a study employing a second wave of data collection among the same Norwegian representative sample (N = 1452) four groups of subordinates where discovered again employing latent class cluster analysis; no exposure; exposure to some laissez-faire leadership, exposure to supportive but disloyal leadership combined with some laissez-faire, and exposure to both tyrannical, derailed and laissez-fair leadership. This study (see also Figure 6.5) showed that those subordinates that where exposed to supportive but disloyal leadership (in combination with laissez-faire) were related to ele-

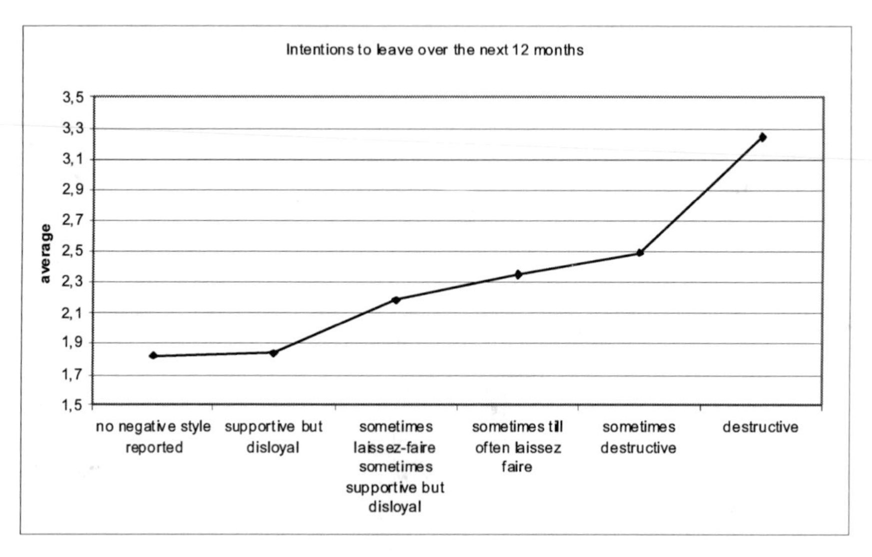

Figure 6.4. Intentions to leave during the next 12 months among 6 groups of respondents with different experiences regarding their exposure to destructive leadership behavior by their immediate leader.

vated levels of work withdrawal in the form of increased absenteeism and tardiness and reduced job input (Skogstad, Notelaers, & Einarsen, 2009).

The level of work withdrawal among those experiencing supportive disloyal leadership was as high as among those employees who reported extensive abuse behaviors in the form of a combination of tyrannical, derailed and Laissez-faire behaviors. Hence, a ripple effect may follow from leaders behaving in an anti-organizational way. It may also be that those exposed to tyrannical and derailed behaviors may perceive threats from their leader resulting in subordinates not daring to withdraw from their work as much as they may want to. In his metastudy Tepper (2007) documented that abusive supervision may result in various resistance behavior by part of the subordinates, such as resisting to behave according to supervisor's requests, as well as to substance abuse. Systematic relationships between abusive supervision and organizational deviance were also found by Tepper and colleagues in a later study (Tepper et al., 2009). In line with these studies, a study by Harris, Kacmar, and Zivnuska (2007) found that abusive supervision was negatively related to self-rated and leader-rated job performance. Hence, it is substantiated that destructive forms of leadership, including those where the target is mainly the organization are associated with reduced subordinate performance or contraproductive behavior. However, it is reason to believe that

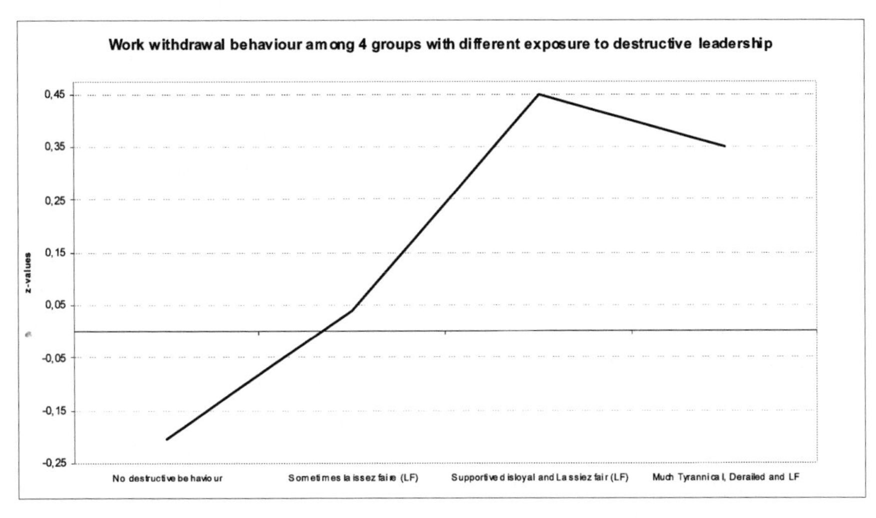

Figure 6.5. Work withdrawal among four groups of employees with different exposure to destructive leadership, employing *z*-scores (Skogstad, Notelaers & Einarsen, 2009).

personality factors among subordinates as well as situational factors may play additional roles in explaining these relationships between destructive forms of leadership and outcomes (see also Tepper, Carr, Breaux, Geider, Hum, & Hua, 2009).

Conclusions and Implications

The present chapter has described the very nature of destructive leadership building on a behavioral and a conglomerate approach. Based on this approach we conclude that destructive leadership behaviors come in many shapes and forms, in both passive and active variants, along two basic dimensions; pro-organizational versus anti-organizational behavior, and, pro-subordinate versus anti-subordinate behavior (see also Aasland, Einarsen, & Skogstad, 2008; Einarsen et al., 2007). Based on our definition of destructive leadership and the following taxonomy of destructive leadership behaviors, we may infer that many leaders portray both constructive as well as destructive behaviors, a claim supported by empirical data from a representative sample of the Norwegian work force (Aasland et al., 2009). Furthermore, this empirical study also showed that destructive leadership behaviors are quite prevalent, at least as seen by subordinates, as only a minority of those surveyed had no observations of such systematic behaviors in their immediate leader. As seen by followers, destructive leadership is quite frequent, at least in passive and less intense forms. Hence, destructive leadership is not to be seen as a 'deviant' phenomenon represented by a few "dark leaders" only, as most leaders may show such behaviors from time to time. Hence, it may be a better characterisation to define leaders in general as "grey suits" characterized by many constructive as well as some destructive behaviors, rather than being either "white angels"' or "black demons" (Skogstad, 2008).

The conclusions drawn above have important theoretical, methodological and applied implications. From a theoretical perspective, the presented destructive and constructive leadership model and the reported empirical findings imply that destructive leadership in the future should be viewed as an integral part of what constitutes leadership behavior in general. Including this "dark" side of leadership in models and theories of leader behaviors has the potential of providing a more accurate and nuanced understanding of the very phenomenon of leadership than what has been typical in the leadership literature so far. Adopting a conglomerate perspective on leadership behavior will also open a range of new avenues for the analysis of leadership behavior, as well as its antecedents and consequences. First, a conglomerate perspective on leadership invites us to investigate how constructive and destructive aspects of leadership are related, and to question how and why such behaviors co-occur. Second, antecedents of both destructive leadership in particular, and leadership in general, should be investigated in a nuanced way where different kinds of leader behaviors may have quite different antecedents. Third, different types of destructive leadership may also have quite different consequences (see also Hershcovis & Barling, 2009), as shown above where supportive disloyal leadership behaviors were not related to subordinate job satisfaction or mental health problems as were more abusive forms of destructive leadership. Yet, at the same time the former showed to be related to counterproductive behaviors among subordinates, making it a rather destructive form of leadership from the perspective of the organization.

From a methodological perspective, the measurement of leadership should clearly cover constructive as well as destructive leader behaviors. In addition, methods of measurement as well as statistical techniques taking a conglomerate perspective on leadership behaviors into consideration should be developed and tested.

Regarding applied implications, organizations should be prepared to investigate and manage cases where employees complain or blow the whistle on alleged leader destructive behaviors. Hence, organizations need policies with preventive as well as restorative elements (see also Einarsen & Hoel, 2008). Organizations must realise that a leader may behave destructively for a number of reasons, including personality factors, a stressful work situation, lack of competence, inherited role expectations, or even the adherence to predominant but "noxious" values in the organizational culture. In line with this, behavior is always a result of a complex interplay between a wide range of internal and external factors. Yet, although scientifically of profound interest, we will argue that the "why" is of less importance than the "how" and "what" when dealing with destructive leadership in real world organizations. While dispositions per definition are difficult to change, behaviors are necessarily not. Training, proper instructions, empirically based feedback, rewards, and sanctions are what may be needed to retain constructive leader behavior and to alter behaviors that are destructive. By taking a behavioral and conglomerate approach as presented above one may avoid the "witch-hunting" of supposedly "dark" leaders, taking a more balanced position where a variety of constructive as well as destructive leader behaviors are considered to be within a "normal" range of leader behaviors, which are changeable, as opposed to an unchangeable "dark" leader.

REFERENCES

Aasland, M. S., Skogstad, A., Notelaers, G., Nielsen, M. B., & Einarsen, S. (2009). The prevalence of destructive leadership behaviour. *British Journal of Management*. DOI: 10.1111/j.1467-8551.2009.00672.x

Adorno, T. W., Frenkel-Brunswick, E., Levenson, D. J., & Sanford, R. N. (1950). *The autortitarian personality*. New York: Harper & Row.

Altheide, D. L., Adler, P. A., Adler, P., & Altheide, D. A. (1978). The social meaning of employee theft. In J. M. Johnson, & J. D. Douglas (Eds.), *Crime at the top: Deviance in business and the professions*. Philadelphia, PA: J. B. Lippincott.

Aryee, S., Chen, Z. X., Sun, L.-Y., & Debrah, Y. A. (2007). Antecedents and outcomes of abusive supervision: Test of a trickle-down model. *Journal of Applied Pscyhology, 92*(1), 191-201.

Ashforth, B. (1994). Petty tyranny in organizations. *Human Relations, 47*, 755-778.

Avolio, B., & Gardner, W. L. (2005). Authentic leadership development. Going to the root of positive forms of leadership. *Leadership Quarterly, 16*, 315-338.

Bass, B. M. (1990). *Bass & Stogdill's Handbook of leadership: Theory, research and managerial applications* (Vol. 3). New York: The Free Press.

Bass, B. M., & Avolio, B. J. (1990). *Transformational leadership development: Manual for the Multifactor Leadership Questionnaire*. Palo Alto, CA: Consulting Psychologists Press.

Bass, B. M., & Riggio, R. E. (2006). *Transformational leadership*. Mahwah, NJ: Erlbaum.

Bing, S. (1992). *Crazy bosses: Spotting them, serving them, surviving them*. New York: Morrow.

Blake, R. R., & Mouton, J. S. (1985). *The Managerial Grid III*. Houston, TX: Gulf.

Blase, J., & Blase, J. (2004). The dark side of school leadership: Implications for administrator preparation. *Leadership and Policy in Schools, 3*(4), 245-273.

Brodsky, C. M. (1976). *The harassed worker*. Lexington, MA: Lexington Books.

Buss, A. H. (1961). *The psychology of aggression*. New York: Wiley.

Burke, R. (2006). Why leaders fail: Exploring the dark side. *Int. Journal of Manpower, 27*, 91-100

Conger, J. A. (1990). The dark side of leadership. *Organizational Dynamics, 19*(2), 44-55.

Ditton, J. (1977). *Part-time crime: An ethnography of fiddeling and pilferage*. London, England: Billings.

Duffy, M. K., Ganster, D., & Pagon, M. (2002). Social undermining in the workplace. *Academy of Management Journal, 45*, 331-351.

Einarsen, S., Aasland, M. S., & Skogstad, A. (2007). Destructive leadership behaviour: A definition and conceptual mode. *The Leadership Quarterly, 18*, 3, 207-216.

Einarsen, S., Aasland, M. S., & Skogstad, A. (2008, April). *The nature, prevalence and consequences of destructive leadership*. Paper presented at SIOP San Francisco, CA.

Einarsen, S., & Hoel, H. (2008). Bullying and mistreatment at work: How managers may prevent and manage such problems. In A. Kinder, R. Hughes, & C. L. Cooper (Eds), *Employee well-being support. A workplace resource* (pp. 161-173). Chichester, England: Wiley.

Frischer, J., & Larsson, K. (2000). Laissez-faire in research education—an inquiry into a Swedish doctoral program. *Higher Education Policy, 13*, 131-155.

Harris, K. J., Kacmar, K. m., & Zivnuska, S. (2007). An investigation of abusive supervision as a predictor of performance and the meaning of work as a moderator of the relationship. *Leadership Quarterly, 18*, 252-263.

Harvey, P., Stoner, J., Hochwarter, W., & Kacmar, C. (2007). Coping with abusive supervision: The neutralizing effects of ingratiation and positive affect on negative employee outcomes. *The Leadership Quarterly, 18*, 264-280.

Hetland, H., Sandal, G. M., & Johnsen, T. B. (2007). Burnout in the Information Technology sector: Does leadership matter? *European Journal of Work and Organizational Psychology, 16*(1), 58-75.

Hershcovis, S., & Barling, J. (2009). Towards a multi-foci approach to workplace aggression: A meta-analytic review of outcomes from different perpetrators. *Journal of Organizational Behaviour.* DOI: 10.1002/job.621

Hinkens, T. R., & Schriesheim, C. A. (2008). An examination of "non-leadership." *Journal of Applied Psychology, 93*, 1234-1248.

Hogan, R., Raskin, R., & Fazzini, D. (1990). The dark side of charisma. In K. E. Clark & M. B. Clark (Eds.), *Measures of leadership*. West Orange, NJ: Leadership Library of America.

House, R. J., & Howell, J. M. (1992). Personality and charismatic leadership. *Leadership Quarterly, 3*, 81-108.

Howell, J. M. (1988). Two faces of charisma: Socialized and personalized leadership in organizations. In J. A. Conger & R. N. Kanungo (Eds.), *Charismatic leadership: The elusive factor in organizational effectiveness*. San Francisco: Jossey-Bass.

Hubert, A. B., & van Veldhoven, M. (2001). Risk sectors for undesirable behaviour and mobbing. *European Journal of Work and Organizational Psychology, 10*, 415-424.

Judge, T. A., & Piccolo, R. F. (2004). Transformational and transactional leadership: A meta-analytic test of their relative validity. *Journal of Applied Psychology, 89*(5), 755-768.

Kellerman, B. (2004). *Bad leadership. What it is, how it happens, why it matters.* Boston: Harvard Business School Press.

Kelloway, E. K., Sivanathan, N., Francis, L., & J. Barling. (2005). Poor leadership. In J. Barling, E. K. Kelloway, & M. R. Frone (Eds.), *Handbook of Work Stress.* Thousand Oaks, CA: SAGE.

Kile, S. M. (1990). *Helsefarlige ledere - og medarbeidere* [Health endangering leaders and employees]. Oslo, Norway: Hjemmets Bokforlag.

Kets de Vries, M. F. R. (1979, July-august). Managers can drive their subordinates mad. *Harvard Business Review,* 125-134.

Lewing, K., Lippitt, R., & White, R. K. (1939). Patterns of aggressive behaviour in experimentally created social climates. *Journal of Social Psychology, 10,* 271-301.

Lipman-Blumen, J. (2005). *The allure of toxic leaders. Why we follow destructive bosses and corrupt politicians—and how we can survive them.* Oxford, England: Oxford University Press.

Lombardo, M. M., & McCall, M. W. (1984). *Coping with an intolerable boss* (Special Report). Greensboro, NC: Center for Creative Leadership.

Lubit, R. (2004, March/April). The tyranny of toxic managers: Applying emotional intelligence to deal with difficult personalities. *Ivey Business Journal,* 1-7.

Ma, H., Karri, R., & Chittipeddi, K. (2004). The paradox of managerial tyranny. *Business Horizons, 4*(4), 33-40.

Magidson, J., & Vermunt, J. K. (2004). Latent class models. In D. Kaplan (Ed.), *The SAGE Handbook of Quantitative Methodology for the Social Sciences.* Thousand Oaks, CA: SAGE.

McCall, M. W. J., & Lombardo, M. M. (1983). *Off the track: Why and how successful executives get derailed* (report No. 21). Greensboro, NC: Center for Creative Leadership.

Maslach, C., Schaufeli, W. B., & Leiter, M. P. (2001). Job burnout. *Annual Review of Psychology, 52,* 397-422.

Nielsen, M. B., Matthiesen, S. B., & Einarsen, S. (2005). Ledelse og personkonflikter: Symptomer på posttraumatisk stress blant ofre for mobbing fra ledere [Leadership and interpersonal conflicts: Symptoms of posttraumatic stress among targets of bullying from supervisors]. *Nordisk Psykologi, 57*(4), 391-415.

Notelaers, G., Einarsen, S., De Witte, H., & Vermunt, J. (2006). Measuring exposure to bullying at work: The validity and advantages of the latent class cluster approach. *Work & Stress, 20*(4), 288-301.

Northouse, P. G. (2007). *Leadership: Theory and practice.* London, England: SAGE.

Padilla, A., Hogan, R., & Kaiser, R. B. (2007). The toxic triangle: Destructive leaders, susceptible followers, and conducive environments. *The Leadership Quarterly, 18,* 176-194.

Rayner, C., & Cooper, C. L. (2003). The black hole in "bullying at work" research. *International Journal of Management and Decision Making, 4*(1), 47-64.

Rosenthal, S. A., & Pittinsky, T. L. (2006). Narcissistic leadership. *The Leadership Quarterly, 17*, 617-633.

Sackett, P. R., & DeVore, C. J. (2001). Counterproductive behaviours at work. In N. Anderson, D. S. Ones, H. K. Sinangil, & C. Viswesvaran (Eds.), *Handbook of Industrial, Work & Organizational Psychology* (Vol. 1, pp. 145-164). London: SAGE.

Schat, A. C. H., Frone, M. R., & Kelloway, E. K. (2006). Prevalence of workplace aggression in the u.s. workforce: Findings from a national study. In E. K. Kelloway, J. Barling, & J. J. Hurrell (Eds.), *Handbook of Workplace Violence* (pp. 47-90). Thousand Oaks, CA: SAGE.

Skogstad, A. (2008, November). *Nuances in destructive leadership. Theoretical and methodological issues.* Paper presented at The Nordic Network meeting on Bullying at the Workplace, Reykjavik, Iceland.

Skogstad, A. (1997). *Effects of leadership behaviour on job satisfaction, health and efficiency.* Doctoral thesis, faculty of psychology. University of Bergen, Norway.

Skogstad, A., Einarsen, S., Torsheim, T., Aasland, M., & Hetland, H. (2007). The destructiveness of Laissez-faire leadership behaviour. *Journal of Occupational Health Psychology, 12*(1), 80–92.

Skogstad, A., Notelaers, G., & Einarsen, S. (2009, May). *Exposure to destructive leadership: Relationships with job satisfaction, work-withdrawal and intentions to leave.* Paper presented at the 14th European Congress of Work and Organizational Psychology, Santiago de Compostela, Spain.

Tepper, B. J. (2000). Consequences of abusive supervision. *Academy of Management Journal, 43*(2), 178-190.

Tepper, B. J. (2007). Abusive supervision in work organization: Review, synthesis, and research agenda. *Journal of Management, 33*(3), 261-281.

Tepper, B. J., Carr, J. C., Breaux, D. M., Geider, S., Hu, C., & Hua, W. (2009). Abusive supervision, intention to quit, and employees' workplace deviance: A power/dependence analysis. *Organizational Behaviour and Human Decision Processes, 109*(2), 156-167.

Tepper, B. J., Duffy, M. K., Hoobler, J., & Ensley, M. D. (2004). Moderators of the relationship between coworkers' organizational citizenship behaviour and fellow employees' attitudes. *Journal of Applied Pscyhology, 89*, 455-465.

Van de Vliert, E. (1997). *Complex interpersonal conflict behaviour: Theoretical frontiers.* Hove, England: Psychology Press.

Vredenburgh, D., & Brender, Y. (1998). The hierarchical abuse of power in work organizations. *Journal of Business Ethics, 17*(12) 1337-1347.

Watzlawick, P., Beavin, J. H., & Jackson, D. D. (1967). *Pragmatics of human communication. A study of interactional patterns, pathologies, and pradoxes.* New York: W. W. Norton.

Yagil, D. (2006). The relationship of abusive and supportive workplace supervision to employee burnout and upward influence tactics. *Journal of Emotional abuse, 6*, 49-65.

Yukl, G. (2010). *Leadership in organizations*. New York: Pearson.

Zimbardo, P. G. (2004). A situationist perspective on the psychology of evil: Understanding how good people are transformed into perpetrators. In A.

Miller (Ed.), *The social psychology of good and evil: Understanding our capacity for kindness and cruelty* (pp. 21-50). New York: Guildford.

Van del Vliert, E., Euwma, M. C., & Huismans, S. E. (1995). Managing conflict with a superior or a subordinate: Effectiveness of a conglomerated perspective. *Journal of Applied Psychology, 80*(2), 271-281.

PART II

ABUSIVE SUPERVISION

CHAPTER 7

MAKING SENSE OF ABUSIVE LEADERSHIP

The Experiences of Young Workers

Gina Grandy and Alison Starratt

We adopt a constructivist grounded theory approach to understand the experience of abusive leadership among a group of 30 young workers. Our findings reveal that abusive behaviors by supervisors serve as sensemaking triggers for young workers. In making sense of these experiences, young workers engage in three processes namely, *Diagnosing Behavior as Bipolar, Constructing as Child* and *Scrutinizing Skills*. We propose that these sensemaking processes serve to moderate the relationships between abusive leadership and individual and organization level outcomes.

INTRODUCTION

Olson, Nelson, and Parayitam (2006) propose a sensemaking (Weick, 1995) framework to better understand and manage aggression in the workplace. They suggest several interruptions (e.g., downsizing, overworking employees, "stretch" goals) that might trigger sensemaking processes and,

When Leadership Goes Wrong: Destructive Leadership, Mistakes and Ethical Failures, pp. 175–202

in turn aggressive workplace behavior. They argue that organizations need to be aware of these triggers and the resulting sensemaking so as to prevent and manage aggression at work. We too believe that a sensemaking lens can help organizations manage the "dark" side of organizational life. Our interest, however, is not on the aggressor, rather the "victim" of workplace abuse, specifically abusive leadership. Through a constructivist grounded theory approach (Charmaz, 2006) and drawing upon interviews with thirty young workers, sensemaking emerges as a critical part of young workers' experiences of abusive leadership. Here we interpret the subordinate's experience of abusive leadership (e.g., yelling, criticism) as a trigger for sensemaking. In this paper, we draw upon Weick's (1995) work on sensemaking to understand how these young workers make sense of their negative occurrences with supervisors at work.

In North America, the overwhelming majority of graduating high school students has held part-time jobs (Greenberger & Steinberg, 1986). Despite their prevalence in the workforce, little research attention has been devoted to young workers' attitudes, behaviors and work-related experiences (Loughlin & Barling, 2001). Young workers should be of great interest in the health and safety literature, due to the high number of accidents involving young workers each year in North America and Europe, as well as the emotional risk they endure (Canadian Centre for Occupational Health and Safety, 2006; European Agency for Safety and Health at Work, 2008). The impact of leadership style upon young workers' behaviors and work-related experiences is an important consideration that requires further research. Kelloway, Mullen, and Francis' (2006) research on leadership and safety indicates that poor leadership, that is, a passive leadership style, contributes negatively to young workers' safety consciousness and perceptions of safety climate. Kelloway et al. contend that other types of poor leadership, those which are more aggressive and punitive in nature (e.g., abusive and unethical), are likely to have even more detrimental effects on safety and other individual and organizational outcomes. Vaez, Ekberg, and LaFlamme (2004) reveal that abusive events at work are unequally frequent in young working people (20 to 34 years old) compared to other populations. They also note that threat and violence occur more often than bullying and sexual harassment. There is still much to learn about abuse in organizations and young workers. We take the occurrence of abuse among young workers as a given and seek to uncover how abusive leadership can serve as a trigger for sensemaking.

We conceptualize abusive leadership as *employees' perceptions of the extent to which supervisors engage in hostile and nonhostile (e.g., unfriendly, intimidating, displeasing, or upsetting) verbal and nonverbal behaviors—excluding physical contact—over an extended period of time. These behaviors may or may not be deliberate actions by the supervisor, but whether deliberate or not, the consequences can be far reaching for the employees, social groups and organizations as a whole.* Our findings reveal that abusive behaviors by supervisors serve as sensemaking triggers for young workers. In making sense of these experiences, young workers engage in three processes namely, *Diagnosing Behavior as Bipolar, Constructing as Child,* and *Scrutinizing Skills*. We propose that these sensemaking processes serve to moderate the relationships between abusive leadership and individual and organization level outcomes.

In exploring how young workers make sense of their experiences of abusive leadership our contribution is twofold. First, abusive leadership is a growing, but understudied phenomenon in organization studies (Tepper, 2007; Tierney & Tepper, 2007). Our qualitative approach builds upon the extant literature and offers a rich account of abusive leadership. Moreover, it extends our knowledge of abusive leadership to the experiences of young workers, something virtually absent in the extant literature. Second, applying a sensemaking framework to understand abusive leadership from the perspectives of the subordinates reveals that sensemaking processes may very well moderate the experience of abusive leadership and its outcomes. Awareness of these processes may facilitate the organization's ability to better manage and respond to abusive leadership in the workplace.

LITERATURE REVIEW

Two important considerations need to be presented before proceeding with the literature review. First, the need for a literature review given our adoption of constructivist grounded theory (Charmaz, 2006) requires explaining. Grounded theorists often debate the appropriateness of an initial literature review when adopting a grounded theory approach (Charmaz, 2006). For our research, it was the initial literature review that led us to the conclusion that we needed to start fresh and look to the *actual* stories of young workers in order to understand their experiences of abusive leadership. As a result, we felt that a constructivist grounded theory approach would be the best means through which to accomplish this. Here we highlight the key extant literature on abusive leadership that led us to the decision to adopt a constructivist grounded theory approach. Second, our decision to draw upon sensemaking (Weick, 1995) to understand the experiences of the young workers did not occur before data collection. It was through an iterative process of data collection and analysis that the sensemaking processes we focus upon in this chapter emerged. Our findings encouraged us to look to the work of Weick and others to aid in how we made sense of the sensemaking of the young workers. For the purposes of theoretically grounding the findings we present in this chapter, in this literature review we also discuss the concept of sensemaking and how abusive behaviors by supervisors serve as a trigger for sensemaking by subordinates.

Abusive Leadership

Tepper (2007) and Tierney and Tepper (2007) draw attention to the important and growing area of research that is focused upon the "dark" side of leadership. To date, Tepper reports that approximately only 20 articles have been written about the topic, but he also notes that it is an area that is receiving considerable attention. Tepper (2000, 2007) has coined it "abusive supervision," but there are numerous terms used to explain and measure abusive leadership. Abusive leadership has been referred to as petty tyranny (Ashforth, 1994, 1997), supervisor aggression (Schat, Desmarais, & Kelloway, 2006), bad leadership (Kellerman, 2004), leader bullying (Ferris, Zinko, Brouer, Buckley, & Harvey, 2007), workplace bullying (Hoel & Cooper, 2001), toxic leadership (Lipman-Bluman, 2005) and destructive leadership (Einarsen, Aasland, & Skogstad, 2007). Table 7.1 provides definitions for the assortment of terms used to describe abusive behavior in the extant literature.

To date, the empirical and conceptual research on abusive leadership reveals a number of antecedents and consequences. In regards to antecedents, both leader (e.g., personality, leader ability, experience, bias for operational work) and situational (e.g., number of subordinates, culture, rivalry of competition, power) considerations have been discussed (Hoobler & Brass, 2006; Schilling, 2008; Tepper, Duffy, Henle, & Lambert, 2006). By most accounts, abusive leadership is subjective in nature. By this we mean that it is the perception of feeling abused as experienced by subordinates that is of interest when studying abusive leadership. Our literature review, however, revealed less agreement on other aspects of abusive leadership and identified areas that require further exploration.

First, the extent to which the abusive behaviors are intended varies across conceptualizations of abusive leadership. Intent does not play a role in Tepper's (2000, 2007) conceptualization of abusive supervision, Keashly's (1998) emotional abuse or Ashforth's (1994, 1997) petty tyranny, but intent does play a role in Schat et al.'s (2006) supervisor aggression and Duffy, Ganster, and Pagon's (2002) social undermining. Second, the nature of abusive behaviors as physical or nonphysical differs. Destructive leadership (Einarsen et al., 2007) includes both physical and verbal actions, and workplace aggression (Baron & Neuman, 1998) includes both

Table 7.1. Terms and Definitions of Abusive Behavior at Work

Construct	*Definition*	*Author(s)*
Abusive Supervision	"Subordinates' perceptions of the extent to which their supervisors engage in the sustained display of hostile verbal and non-verbal behaviors, excluding physical contact."	Tepper, 2000, p. 178.
Bad Leadership	Effective (e.g., the inability to produce the desired change) and unethical (e.g., acting in self interest, failing to distinguish between right and wrong) actions by a manager or individual in a position of formal or informal power.	Kellerman, 2004.
Destructive Leadership	"The systematic and repeated behavior by a leader, supervisor or manager that violates the legitimate interest of the organization by undermining and/or sabotaging the organization's goals, tasks, resources, and effectiveness and/or the motivation, well-being or job satisfaction of subordinates."	Einarsen et al., 2007, p. 208.
Emotional Abuse	"The hostile verbal and non-verbal behaviors that are not explicitly tied to sexual or racial content yet are directed at gaining compliance from others."	Keashly, 1998, p. 85.
Narcissistic Leadership	Individuals possessing formal and informal power who are preoccupied with establishing their adequacy, power, beauty, status, prestige, and superiority. It can be reactive, self-deceptive, or constructive in nature.	Kets de Vries, 2004; Kets de Vries & Miller, 1985.
Negative Leadership	Behaviors by supervisors and managers ranging from ineffective to destructive aspects.	Schilling, 2008.
Leader Bullying	"Represents strategically selected tactics of influence by leaders designed to convey a particular image and place targets in a submissive, powerless position whereby they are more easily influenced and controlled, in order to achieve personal and/or organizational objectives."	Ferris et al., 2007, p. 197.
Perceived Leader Integrity	"Subordinates perceptions of their leaders' integrity in organizational settings" (primarily unethical and ethical interpersonal relations).	Craig & Gustafson, 1998, p. 140.
Petty Tyranny	Managers' use of power and authority oppressively, capriciously, and vindictively.	Ashforth, 1994, 1997.
Supervisor Aggression	Supervisor behavior "that is intended to physically or psychologically harm a worker or workers in a work-related context."	Schat et al., 2006 in Tepper, 2007, p. 264.
Social Undermining	Supervisor "behavior intended to hinder, over time, the ability to establish and maintain positive interpersonal relationships, work-related success, and favorable reputation."	Duffy et al., 2002, p. 332.

Table continues on next page.

Table 7.1. Continued

Construct	*Definition*	*Author(s)*
Toxic Leaders	"Leaders who engage in numerous destructive behaviors and who exhibit certain dysfunctional personal characteristics." The actions of these individuals may or may not be intentional, but result in serious and enduring harm on subordinates and organizations.	Lipman-Bluman, 2005, p. 18.
Workplace Aggression	"Behaviors performed by individuals in order to harm others with whom they work or previous worked."	Baron & Neuman, 1998, p. 446.
Workplace Bullying	When "one or several individuals over a period of time perceive themselves to be on the receiving end of negative actions from one or several persons, in a situation where the target of bullying has difficulty in defending him or herself against these actions."	Hoel & Cooper, 2001, p. 4.

physical and psychological behaviors, while petty tyranny (Ashforth, 1994, 1997) includes only nonphysical behaviors, and emotional abuse (Keashley, 1998) focuses upon abusive interpersonal (verbal and nonverbal) behaviors. Third, there is disagreement about the extent to which behaviors are hostile or not. Tepper argues that abusive supervision entails hostile verbal and nonverbal actions. In his review piece of abusive supervision, Tepper (2007) is critical of Ashforth's work on petty tyranny because Ashforth includes both hostile and nonhostile behaviors in his conceptualization of abusive leadership. Fourth, Tepper (2007) draws attention to the direction of the abuse. He argues that much of the literature around workplace bullying and victimization does not really isolate horizontal abuse in the workplace (e.g., among coworkers) from downward abuse (e.g., supervisor to subordinate) and this makes it difficult to understand the particularities of abusive leadership. Fifth, most of the literature on abusive leadership draws from other areas of research to inform the development of scales to measure abusive leadership (e.g., interpersonal justice, workplace bullying). Furthermore, a lot of the extant research is quantitative in nature leaving little room to evaluate abuse in the words of those who experience it. Keashly (1998, 2001) and Schilling (2008) employ a qualitative approach to better understand abusive leadership. Building upon their work, we argue here that in order to understand the subjective experience of abusive leadership, we need to have richer descriptions from those who actually experience it. Finally, Ashforth (1997) calls for more research on abusive leadership in different demographic groups. With the exception of the research of Dupre, Inness, Connelly, Barling, and Hoption (2006) on workplace aggression as an outcome of abusive supervision and Vaez et al. (2004) on the frequency of abusive events among young working people, there is little research that has explored young workers' experiences of abusive leadership.

As a result of these six conclusions that emerged from our initial literature review on abusive leadership we decided that we needed to look to the actual experiences of young workers in order to understand the nature of abusive leadership as experienced by this demographic group. We felt that a constructivist grounded theory approach would facilitate our ability to start fresh and ground our conclusions in the data we collected, rather than basing our conclusions upon data that has emerged from other areas of research, not specific to young workers.

Sensemaking and Abusive Leadership

In her work on organizational socialization, surprises, and sensemaking, Louis (1980) argues that sensemaking is triggered by surprise events and it involves a thinking process whereby individuals draw upon retrospective accounts to explain the discrepant events or surprises. In organizational life individuals develop or are exposed to scripts that outline appropriate behavior and expected outcomes of that behavior. When the scripts ring true, that is, when expected and actual outcomes align, there is no need for individuals to engage in thinking processes (Louis, 1980). However, when there is a discrepancy between expected outcomes and actual outcomes these surprises trigger a need for explanation. Individuals engage in a process of reflection and engagement with the past to ascribe meaning to the surprises. Meaning is assigned to the discrepant events as an outcome of sensemaking, rather than concurrently as the surprise happens (Weick, 1995). In our research, we propose that an individual's experience of an abusive behavior from a supervisor runs contrary to the individual's expectation of appropriate leader behavior. Individuals become frustrated by the situation that they cannot change and in turn engage in sensemaking processes to explain the experience (Olson et al., 2006). As such, the behavior described by participants in our research as abusive in nature are surprise events that serve as triggers for the individual to engage in a thinking process (or sensemaking) to explain the events and resolve the tension or dissonance that the individual feels.

Similar to most other researchers who study abusive leadership, we understand abusive leadership to be subjective. In this way, it is the *perception of abuse* that is significant enough to warrant negative individual and organizational outcomes. It is for this reason that we believe a sensemaking framework is fitting to better understand the experience of abusive leadership among young workers. As argued by Olson et al. (2006), "it is the perception and the interpretation of the event via the sensemaking process, rather than the event itself" (p. 388) that serves as the trigger. Sensemaking is grounded in perception and therefore provides a useful heuristic for understanding the experience of abusive leadership. The focus shifts from whether or not the abuse is "real" to understanding how individuals perceive it to be abusive, the processes they engage in to explain the surprise event of abusive leadership and how the experience results in a variety of negative outcomes.

Weick (1995) describes sensemaking as "talk about reality as an ongoing accomplishment that takes form when people make retrospective sense of situations in which they find themselves and their creations" (p. 15). Weick describes seven properties of sensemaking including grounded in identity construction, retrospective, enactive of sensible environments, social, ongoing, focused on and by extracted cues and driven by plausibility rather than accuracy. He notes that these properties serve as a rough guideline and in doing this he leaves room so that these seven properties of sensemaking need not be prescriptive of every sensemaking process.

First, sensemaking processes are strongly tied to an individual's desire for coherence in how she understands herself (her self-concept), relative to others in particular contexts. Thus, sensemaking is grounded in identity construction, that is, an individual's need for consistency and clarity in how she (and others) defines herself, relative to others (social context). When consistency is absent or unsettled by an event, then the individual will strive to regain coherence in how she defines herself through sensemaking processes. Second, in attempting to regain order and consistency in identity and overall expectations of outcomes, the individual will draw upon the past to make sense of the present. Sensemaking is retrospective and reflexive in that only after we experience an event can we reflect upon it and make sense of it. Third, sensemaking is concerned with the "activity of making" (Weick, 1995, p. 30). Organizational life and experiences are codetermined by environmental influences and individual actions, that is, in part individuals create their own experiences. Fourth, an appreciation of the social context is critical to sensemaking. Identity construction, enactment and other aspects of sensemaking occur in a social context, whereby relations with others (and context in general) inform our meaning making processes. For example, a part of our self-definition (or identity) is informed by how we see ourselves relative to others. Fifth, sensemaking is an ongoing accomplishment whereby the past, present, and future are inseparable in many ways. Moreover, the past is malleable (Gioia, Corley, & Fabbri, 2002) and meanings can be altered to explain the present dissonance. Emotion plays an important role in this (Weick, 1995). A discrepant event is disruptive and this disruption cues emotions. Should we experience a feeling that seems familiar, that is, a feeling we experienced in the past at some point, we draw upon the past to help make sense of the present experience. The drawing upon, and even reconstruction of the past, occurs because it *feels* the same, not necessarily because *it is* the same (Weick, 1995). Sixth, in explaining discrepant events we extract certain points of reference or cues. These cues are often simple and familiar frames that represent to us a more significant or larger aspect of our experience or knowledge base. And finally, accuracy is not a requirement of sensemaking (Weick, 1995). Perceptions need not be accurate in order for sensemaking to occur. The cues and subsequent meaning making need to plausible, reasonable and memorable. "People see and find sensible those things that they can do something about" (p. 60) and often in the meaning making process individuals distort and filter information from what they deem to be noise so that they are not overwhelmed with data.

For our research, we draw upon sensemaking as a theoretical lens because the experiences of young workers that we encountered could not be completely explained by existing constructs from the abusive leadership literature. Individuals engaged in a process of meaning making to explain the discrepant events they experienced (abusive behaviors from supervisors) so as to relieve the tension they experienced and return to a state of equilibrium.

RESEARCH DESIGN

This study is a part of a larger research project that set out to develop a model of abusive leadership as experienced by young workers (Starratt & Grandy, 2010). The larger study entailed determining a definition of abusive leadership, the behaviors associated with abusive leadership and the individual and organizational outcomes of abusive leadership as experienced by young workers. We adopted a constructivist grounded theory (CGT) (Charmaz, 2006) approach so that a model of abusive leadership could be developed that was grounded in the experiences of young workers, rather than assuming that the experiences of young workers simply reflected the existing literature. We understand CGT to be a flexible methodological strategy that is theory building in nature (Charmaz, 2006). CGT is inductive and it involves an iterative process of data collection and analysis and ongoing comparisons across data (Charmaz, 2006).

True to the exploratory nature of grounded theory and qualitative research, our research revealed unique findings around young workers' efforts to make sense of their experiences of abusive leadership. These struggles of young workers could not be explained by the extant literature on abusive leadership. This triggered us to engage in a more comprehensive literature review to explain our findings. As a result, the research question we present here, that is, to explore how young workers make sense of their negative occurrences with supervisors at work, was emergent in nature.

Methods

Thirty young workers (between the ages of 18-25), who identified themselves as having negative experiences with a supervisor, were interviewed using a semistructured format. We refer to participants using pseudonyms. Most of these individuals (20) were employed in the service industry (e.g., clothing retail, restaurants) in Canada, and others were employed in manufacturing, marketing and academia (e.g., research assistant). Length of employment varied from 3 months to 3 years. Interviews ranged from 25 to 90 minutes and 3 participants were contacted for follow-up discussions. Interviews began by asking participants about their jobs and their experiences at work (Describe your job; What does your job entail?; Describe a typical day of work for you; Describe the organization you work for; What is important in this organization?). If experiences with supervisors did not surface naturally from the discussion, participants were prompted with questions specific to their relations with their supervisors (Describe your supervisor? Describe a typical interaction with your supervisor?).

As is advocated by grounded theorists (Charmaz, 2006; Glaser & Strauss, 1967) data collection and analysis were iterative in nature. Theoretical sampling (Charmaz, 2006) guided data collection. An initial five interviews were conducted and analyzed and a result of this it was determined that experiences from a diverse range of occupations, as well as whenever possible interviewing more than one individual from the same workplace, would lead to a more comprehensive understanding of the phenomenon.

Data Analysis

Data analysis was ongoing as more data was collected; therefore the process of data analysis was not as linear as it might appear from our description. Interviews were transcribed verbatim and data analysis involved a process of line-by-line coding and focused coding (Charmaz, 2006) of each individual transcript first, followed by comparison across transcripts (See Table 7.2 for an initial and focused coding sample). Memo writing (Charmaz, 2006) was a critical component of the data anal-

Table 7.2. Initial and Focused Coding Sample (Trevor)

Data	*Initial Coding*	*Focused Coding*	*Associated Memo*	*Aspect of Abusive Leadership*
What would be your typical interaction with your supervisor?				
Least amount possible. Sometimes she'll come in and talk to you and I just don't look up from prepping. It's what I try to do on the daily, otherwise you're going to get into it....	Distancing Distancing by focusing upon formal task	Distancing	Distancing	Behavior of Abusive Leadership
I just don't care, I'll just do it the way to make her shut up and that's it. That's all I really care about, getting in and out of there with the least amount of headache possible	Complying (avoiding conflict)	Feeling Helpless	Feeling Helpless	Outcome
Say if like the guy who just quit how he asked for three weeks to get this one weekend off which is this weekend that just went by. He had a wedding to go, he asked, he asked, he asked, they said they were going to give it to him off so he just didn't come in. And they'll complain the whole weekend, rag him out, talk shit about him to other people and stuff like that but then when he comes in on Monday they won't really say anything. That's how bipolar, just like short memory they have there too. They always threaten to kick you out and everything else but like if people just don't show up and stuff like that, like there's people who have worked there for a year who show up for like 70% of their shifts.	Talking about other employees behind their backs Rationalizing —medical condition Threatening (firing) Being inconsistent	Talking Behind Employees' Backs Diagnosing Behavior as Medical Condition/ Bipolar Threatening Employees	Talking Behind Employees' Backs Diagnosing as Bipolar Threatening Employees	Behavior of Abusive Leadership Sense making Process Behavior of Abusive Leadership
[*I*] treat it [*work*] like a big joke, which it is. You know, so that's the only way I can brush it off in a way. Even though when I come home at nights, even my girlfriend will be saying that my fuse is a lot shorter when I come [*from work*].	Not taking job seriously (distancing) Affecting outside life	Distancing Affecting Sense of Self	Distancing Affecting Sense of Self	Outcome Outcome

Table 7.3. Partial Memo for Constructing As Child

Constructing Manager as Child
Employees have various "coping" mechanisms for dealing with a bad boss that range from passive to aggressive. One passive coping mechanism is to dismiss the boss' authority by referring to them as children or as possessing childlike qualities. Childish should not be mistaken for cute and innocent, but rather immature and incapable of performing adult tasks and fulfilling adult responsibilities. By distinguishing themselves from the boss as the more mature and grown up person in the relationship, the boss is stripped of credibility. This allows employees to believe that they are above their bosses and in many ways smarter, more capable and more respectable.
"She just like stares at me. It's little things like she'll be over standing next to the sink and she'll have a pot that is too liquidy or something like that and she wants to pour it out but she needs that little thing you put in the sink to stop the little chunks from going down into the drain. And she'll stand there with the pot in her hand, one hand and ask me to come over while I'm putting up a table of fifteen people, to come over and put the thing in for her. So I go over and put the thing in for her and then she puts the pie down and looks at it for a second. She's like "it's upside down." And she's not holding anything and all it is a metal sheet that you have to pick up, flip around, and put back down." —*Trevor.*
"I don't really have much respect for her, so it really has stopped bothering me as much as it used to. Because I just think she's kind of a silly woman. When I don't really have respect for her, I don't really care about what she has to say and I'll kind of obey it to humour her just because she still is technically my boss." —*Jane.*
"And so I was just like, I found it was really immature of her to be giving dirty looks to a seventeen year old when she's twenty-four and a manager." —*Julie.*
"It seems so immature on her part, I felt like I was in middle school. She never directly said anything to the people she had problems with." —*Kelly.*

ysis process (See Table 7.3 for a partial sample memo). These memos (and corresponding focused codes) were revisited and revised throughout the data collection and analysis process. Data collection continued until the point of saturation; when no new themes emerged. In this chapter we focus upon the sensemaking processes that emerged from the stories of young workers, including *Diagnosing Behavior as Bipolar, Constructing as Child* and *Scrutinizing Skills*.

SENSEMAKING PROCESSES

The young workers that we interviewed re-told stories that depicted various hostile and nonhostile verbal and nonverbal supervisor behaviors that occurred over an extended period of time. We categorized these as behaviors of abusive leadership. Table 7.4 provides a description of each of these 10 behaviors. Although individuals were not prompted to specifically describe the "outcomes" per se of these abusive behaviors, individuals did talk about numerous individual (e.g., feeling helpless, feeling stressed, justifying retaliation) and organizational (e.g., employee turnover, creating a destructive culture) outcomes that occurred as a result of being on the receiving end of these behaviors.

Other aspects of the individuals' stories were more difficult to categorize as behaviors or outcomes of the abusive leadership. In some incidents financial incentives (e.g., the pay or the need for the money) and the social relations built at work (e.g., friends at work) served as a means through which an individual could rationalize her decision to continue working at her place of employment. We interpreted these considerations as moderators of abusive leadership and its outcomes. Moreover, individuals struggled to explain the reasons why these experiences of abusive leadership happened. It was as if individuals expected to be treated fairly and with respect in the workplace by their supervisors and when they instead perceived supervisors to be abusive, it triggered a sensemaking process that allowed individuals to rationalize the unexpected behaviors and in turn reduce the dissonance they felt. We propose here that the subordinate's experience of abusive leadership was a surprise event that triggered the sensemaking process of these young workers. It is also important to note that we likely played a role in triggering sensemaking processes. Our asking participants to talk about their experiences at work may have served as a cue to individuals that their experiences of abusive leadership were discrepant events that required sensemaking.

Our findings revealed that individuals struggled to explain the behaviors of their supervisors. Three sensemaking processes were prevalent in the stories, each of which reconstructed the supervisor in a way that called the supervisor's credibility into question. The three sensemaking processes included *Diagnosing as Bipolar, Constructing as Child* and *Scrutinizing Skills*. Through these efforts young workers discredited their supervisors' ability to lead and minimized the supervisors' importance and authority. In turn, we theorize that these sensemaking efforts moderate the effects of the abuse. Successful efforts (more persuasive accounts) to reconstruct the supervisor as unqualified or incompetent affected individual and organizational outcomes of the abuse.

Diagnosing Behavior as Bipolar

Diagnosing behavior as Bipolar involved explaining sudden, extreme changes in mood by the supervisor as a medical condition in order to

Table 7.4. Behaviors of Abusive Leadership as Experienced by Young Workers

Behavior	*Description*	*Behavior*	*Description*
Playing Favorites	Perception that a supervisor views some employees more positively than others and as such provides these favorites with increased freedom, praise, better shifts, etc. Supervisors can use favorites as a means through which to punish an employee that has in some way displeased them. It is perceived to be a deliberate attempt to make one or more employees feel ostracized from the rest of the staff.	Putting Employees Down	Putting an employee down could involve a range of activities including, making a "mean" comment about the employee's personality or putting down the quality of their output. The criticism is not meant to be constructive and is perceived as humiliating, degrading or negative. It is not public in nature (see Public Criticism).
Dealing Dirty Work as Punishment	Perception that a supervisor assigns work to employees that is considered dirty or degrading as punishment (e.g., cleaning the toilets).	Public Criticism	Offering critical comments about an employee or her performance in the presence of others (e.g., customers, co-workers) is similar to putting employees down, however, the public nature of it makes the experience of abuse more severe.
Threatening Employees	Making threats is an act whereby one party warns another party that there will be a specific consequence if a particular action is taken. It is perceived by the individual as stressful and creates a fear-driven environment if bosses are constantly using threats as a means for control.	Unrealistic Expectations	It is perceived to be unacceptable when an employer leads employees to believe that they must do everything that is asked of them—even tasks that are perceived to be unreasonable. From giving employees an hour's notice to come in to work for a shift to punishing employees who cannot fulfill the employer's unrealistic expectations of perfection, sometimes it is impossible for employees to meet their boss' demands.

Blurring the Lines Between Personal and Professional	The perceived lack of professionalism and complaints of personal issues being brought into the workplace. Some employees experienced high discomfort at the disclosure of personal details while others simply had no interest whatsoever in wasting time listening to the stories.	Telling Lies	Whether it is about pay, hours, job description, perks, etc. it is perceived to be inappropriate for someone in a position of authority to "lie" to their subordinates.
Talking Behind Employees' Backs	A supervisor's tendency to discuss issues pertaining to one employee with another employee.	Illegal Practices	Illegal practices encompass any actions that the boss takes at work that are outside legal boundaries. It can be anything from short changing employees on their paycheques to stealing tips from the employees.

rationalize the otherwise unexplainable change in behavior. Bipolar disorder is a psychiatric condition defined as recurrent episodes of significant disturbance in mood. The moods can seem extreme and can occur on a spectrum that ranges from debilitating depression to unbridled mania. Sometimes the feelings of depression and mania can go back and forth quickly within the same day. Numerous young workers used bipolar disorder as a descriptor for their bosses describing the sudden, extreme changes in mood that they witnessed. Describing their supervisor as bipolar also appeared to help the employee to rationalize *why* the manager's moods change suddenly, given that employees were unable to think of any other rational explanation for the drastic shift in mood. Most often there was no obvious trigger for the mood swing or the event that triggered the mood swing was so insignificant that individuals were unable to believe that a "healthy" person would be affected by the event so severely. Employees came to expect the sudden changes and they knew that certain looks or actions were indicative of a bad mood swing.

Trevor and Erica worked at the same restaurant and they described their supervisor's unexplainable, sudden changes in behavior. Trevor labeled her behavior as bipolar and Erica's example served to further illustrate the sudden mood swings and unpredictability of the supervisor. "I don't know, sometimes I wonder if she's bipolar because she'll be really, really nice and then all of a sudden she'll be snapping and screaming at people at the top of her lungs," noted Trevor.

> I was there working and I didn't come cut some desserts right away and she started yelling at me, just pointless yelling. Her husband came in and said the customers were getting uncomfortable because they could hear her and she just didn't care. She just kept yelling at me, saying I'm useless, worthless, that I should be working faster. If it were someone else it would have been done a lot faster and they would have done exactly what she said and she could really find someone else to replace me if she wanted to. And then maybe an hour or so later she comes down singing with a piece of pie saying "happy birthday"... really, "happy birthday to me." —Erica.

Erica also noted that most of the staff felt the same way about the supervisor at Erica and Trevor's place of work. She commented that it was pointless to discuss her feelings with the supervisor and that "you'll sit there and you'll take it just to get the money and possibly vent to someone else. Most of the staff feels the way you do anyway." In this way, coworkers and those in an young worker's personal life become outlets through which to express their frustrations, concerns and confusion.

Other individuals describe how certain times of the day, the amount of time spent in the office or particular topics of conversation in part explained the pattern of their supervisors' unpredictable change of emotions. In trying to manage relations with their supervisors, individuals avoided their supervisors during the "bad" mood swings or asked for favours during the "good" mood swings. Participants, however, were at a loss as to how to predict the mood swings. They simply tried to take note of the changes and adapt accordingly.

> It really depends on his mood, a lot of the time during summer he hasn't been around so much [*and*] he'll be super friendly. He might even be bipolar or something because half the time he'll be the friendliest, nicest guy in the world. If you ask him a question when he's in a good mood, like for example, he was really happy one day so I asked him if I could have a week off in the middle of the summer to go away with my family and he's like "of course we can do that for you." I didn't know but one of his favourites [*favoured employee*] had asked the same and he said they don't give time off in the summer. Everyone was really mad because they couldn't take time off and here I am, just a summer staff, and I get to take time off. Honestly, it's just asking him at the right time. —Lisa

Similar to Erica, Julie implied that social relations with co-workers played a role in how individuals "coped" with the erratic behaviors of the supervisor. Conversing with each other about their experiences provided a platform through which to reduce the sense of isolation and provided clarity to the unexplainable events of abuse.

> The way that we kind of talk about her is she's really bipolar. I'm sure [*other employee*] told you this. She'll go into work and she'll be like super peppy, like "hey what's up? "She'll tell you all about her newest boy toy or what's happening with her personal life, blah blah blah. And then you'll turn around and come back and she'll just be cursing and stomping around with this furious look on her face and you're just like ok. Then she'll start yelling at you for doing something and she'll just punish you for the stupidest little things. —Julie.

Of particular interest to us was that numerous participants actually used the term "bipolar" in their descriptions of their supervisors. It was as if individuals could label "it" a medical condition it would serve as a persuasive rationale for the abusive behavior. In turn, this plausible account would facilitate an individual's ability to explain the otherwise unexplainable and unexpected behaviors of a supervisor at work.

Constructing as Child

Constructing as Child was a sensemaking process that involved dismissing the supervisor's authority by referring to him as a child or as possessing childlike qualities. Supervisors were seen to be immature and incapable of fulfilling adult responsibilities to such an extent that the supervisor was stripped of credibility. Childishness should not be mistaken for cute and innocent, but rather immature and incapable of performing adult tasks and fulfilling adult responsibilities. By constructing themselves as the more mature and "grown-up" person in the relationship, the young worker stripped the supervisor of credibility. This allowed employees to believe that they were superior to their bosses and in many ways more intelligent, capable and respectable.

Jane explained how her supervisor was "mean," but she dismissed her as a "silly woman," thus stripping her boss of credibility. Jane recognized that she had to appear to be receptive in receiving feedback from her supervisor. At the same time, however, in trying to deal with the unexplainable abusive behavior, Jane constructed her supervisor as unimportant, inferior and insignificant. She no longer respected her supervisor so the impact of the abusive behavior was lessened.

> I just kinda take it and go but I don't really have much respect for her. So it really has stopped bothering me as much as it used to. I just think she's kind of a silly woman. When I don't really have respect for her, I don't really care about what she has to say and I'll kind of obey it to humour her just because she still is technically my boss. I really don't get as bothered by it anymore. —Jane

Kelly compared the behavior of her supervisor to that of someone in grade school, where adolescents criticize individuals behind their backs, rather than confronting individuals face-to-face as an adult should. In this way, Kelly constructed her supervisor as an adolescent incapable of taking the responsibility of management seriously. "It seems so immature on her part, I felt like I was in middle school. She never directly said anything to the people she had problems with." In a similar way, Julie dismissed the actions of her supervisor as "immature." Julie also indicated that as the older person in a management position her supervisor should know better. In turn, Julie's implied that her supervisor was really the child of the relationship, incapable of acting like an adult.

> And so I was just like, I found it was really immature of her to be giving dirty looks to a seventeen year old when she's twenty-four and a manager. She was showing the new girl bathing suits and I went up to her and said "oh [*supervisor's name*] I got that bathing suit" and I pointed to this green and blue one. She just turns to me and was like "you got that bathing suit? You better not have taken the last medium!" That was immature and childish almost like "you got the last [*bathing suit*] like blah blah blah." And I was just like, what are you talking about? —Julie

Retrospectively, young workers' stories revealed that they expected their supervisors to act as a "grown-up" should act, that is, responsible, fair and nonemotive. Supervisors should be role models to subordinates whereby supervisors should lead by example, as an adult is expected to do for a child. When supervisors' behaviors did not align with this expectation, the young workers engaged in a process of sensemaking extracting cues to provide clarity on the discrepant events that they experienced. In this way, the young workers stripped the supervisor of credibility (e.g., a childish manager) and this minimized the impact of the abusive behavior.

Scrutinizing Skills

Scrutinizing Skills was a sensemaking process that involved critically assessing the technical or management skills (or lack thereof) of supervisors so as to minimize the significance of the supervisor's role in the organization. Through the stories individuals implied that they expected a manager to possess a certain level of business knowledge and managerial skills. A particular set of skills and knowledge separated the manager from their subordinates, that is, supervisors were more qualified for the manager role. A manager could have excellent business knowledge and little managerial experience and vice versa. Sometimes having one was enough to compensate for lacking the other, but in some cases it led employees to doubt their manager's overall abilities.

Business skills referred to a general knowledge of the industry in which the company operated. Managerial skills, on the other hand, referred to the manager's expertise at running the organization and managing its employees. If a manager possessed neither business nor managerial skills employees questioned the manager's value and competence in that position. In making sense of their experiences of abusive leadership, if employees constructed their supervisor as lacking in business and management skills, it resulted in employees feeling hostile towards the organization for hiring such a person or frustrated in their day-to-day interactions with their boss. In this way, scrutinizing skills could make the effects of the abusive leadership more pronounced. Criticizing a boss' business or managerial skills was also a means for employees to discredit their boss. By downplaying or challenging their supervisors' capabilities, employees minimized their boss' importance and role and the effect of the abusive leadership behavior.

Kelly admitted that her boss had a lot of experience as a waitress (business knowledge), but adamantly denied that her boss was capable of being a manager in the same setting. Her supervisor's overconfidence and superiority made it easier for Kelly to reconstruct her supervisor as incompetent and someone who lacked the required managerial skills for the position. Her supervisor's over confidence served as a cue for Kelly in making sense of her experiences.

> She's been working for 10 years so she's pretty experienced at the whole golf course waitress thing, which she is but she's doesn't know how to handle the manager thing. I think if people complain, she's like "they don't know what they're talking about because I've been in this business for so long." That's kind of the attitude she has. —Kelly

John also scrutinized his supervisor's lack of managerial skills. He noted how he felt the organization should be managed, something his supervisor was incapable of achieving. In this way, John stripped his supervisor of credibility and positioned himself in a superior position in regards to managerial skills.

> I think she's a bad boss in the way that she runs the store. She focuses on some things wrong and other things that aren't very. I just think she should focus more on keeping the staff, keeping a good staff. Like valuing older employees, guys that have been there a long time, better than the way she does. She focuses on the wrong things. Like we don't get raises but she doesn't make any money. But then she won't do promotion to sell, she won't work hard to make more money. So that's why I think she's a bad boss. —John

The Success of Sensemaking

The more persuasive the explanation that individuals constructed the more successful the sensemaking efforts were in moderating the effects of the abusive leadership behaviors. Individuals constructed social groups as a part of this process to make their explanation more believable to them and others. Social groups were a way for employees to feel less isolated in their feelings of anger or dislike of the supervisor. It allowed them to vent their feelings and frustrations about their boss to others who understood them. It was also easier to maintain certain beliefs as a group than it was as an individual.

Vanessa indicated that knowing others were in a similar situation and that they could talk about their experiences with each other, made her feel less alone and reasonable in the feelings she experienced as a result of the abuse. Rebecca, on the other hand, had left the place of employment where she experienced abusive leadership and felt that not sharing her experiences with her coworkers about the abuse made it more difficult. She felt that her coworkers dealt with the abuse better than she did and without the social support or the "me too experience," the effects of the abusive behavior were stronger.

> I just felt so inferior next to him and there was no reason. I think it helped because all the staff were in the same situation. I had twenty great friends from the summer that I worked with so we talked about it a lot or we would go get drunk together and talk about it. Not a good way to deal with it, but whatever. —Vanessa.

> I think it might be [*why she continued to work there*] because I saw everybody else doing it. Just because there are other women forty years old, twenty years older than I am, and they seemed to be handling it relatively well so I felt like I had to as well. I shudder at the thought of going back, but I don't think that will last too much longer. I'm worried for myself if I ever find myself in that position [*again*], but at least I know [*that it is not right*]. — Rebecca

Rebecca's quote indicated that the sensemaking efforts of individuals were not always successful in facilitating the individual's ability to regain a state of equilibrium. The experience of abusive leadership triggered sensemaking partially because the discrepant event so severely affected the individual's sense of self. Rebecca felt that if others could deal with it or were "OK" with the supervisor's behavior then she should be as well. As a result, she felt that something must be wrong with her and who she was as a person. Even after leaving the place of employment, Rebecca was still unable to reconcile the impact that the experiences had upon how she understood herself as an individual.

Travis commented that the impact of the abusive leadership was so profound that it affected how he treated others.

> I got pretty stressed out, and started getting pretty short with other people. I also started acting like he does, pretty much getting pretty pissed at our drivers. At the time, it doesn't bother me, but once I come down I usually feel kind of bad.

He noted that retrospectively he realized that he was not acting as himself, rather mimicking his supervisor's behavior. In effect, his efforts to make sense of the abusive leadership were not successful and as a result, his behavior and self-concept were affected. Only later could he reflect upon the events and realize just how significant the experience had been.

Overall, young workers efforts of sensemaking were more successful when they could identify and share with a group. In many incidents, this lessened the effects upon their self-concept and other individual and organizational outcomes.

DISCUSSION

Based upon our findings we conceptualize abusive leadership as employees' perceptions of the extent to which supervisors engage in hostile and nonhostile verbal and nonverbal behaviors (excluding physical contact) over an extended period of time. Our findings suggest that the experience of abusive leadership can serve as a trigger for sensemaking in young workers. Similar to Olson et al. (2006), who argue that actions such as downsizing and "stretch goals" are violations of employees' psychological contracts, we argue here that the abusive behaviors experienced by young workers are also violations of their psychological contracts. These young workers expect to be treated fairly and with respect by their supervisors and not to be threatened, lied to or publicly criticized. The experience of abusive leadership is a surprise event (Louis, 1980) that the individual strives to explain. These young workers engage in three processes of sensemaking to try and explain their experiences and reduce the dissonance between their expectations and actual experiences.

Plausiblility

Weick (1995) contends in sensemaking individuals produce plausible, rather than accurate accounts of explanation. The three sensemaking processes discussed here were plausible, persuasive and memorable, although not necessarily accurate. Individuals' efforts to explain the erratic mood swings of their supervisors as bipolar disorder were indeed interesting. The young workers produced no medical evidence (e.g., discussion of medical appointments or supervisors talking about a medical disorder) nor did the young workers have any specific medical knowledge of bipolar disorder to accurately diagnose the behavior of their supervisors. Yet, explaining the behavior of their supervisors as a medical condition was certainly persuasive. It drew attention to the severity of the behavior in that if the supervisor was not taking medication or receiving medical attention for such a medical disorder, then he should have been. Moreover, if it was a medical disorder then the young workers' experience of abusive behavior was "real" and more believable to the young worker and those around them, rather than based upon perception alone. We theorize that this sensemaking process, if successful, moderated (lessened) the individual outcomes of the abuse. If a rational, scientific explanation was plausible (in this case a medical disorder), it would be easier to excuse the behavior of the boss and thereby minimize the individual outcomes of the abuse. We expect that negative organizational outcomes, however, would be heightened because over time individuals would be less inclined to follow orders and more likely to avoid their supervisors, thus resulting in counterproductive behaviors.

Stripping the supervisors' of credibility through constructing as child and scrutinizing skills were also persuasive and plausible explanations of the abusive leadership. Society (e.g., schools, churches, families, legal systems) socializes us to believe that "adults" or elders are (or should be) responsible, knowledgeable and in turn regarded with respect. Adults serve as role models to youths. Of course, this is not always an accurate depiction of elders. Our findings indicated that young workers constructed their supervisors as immature, possessing child-like qualities or engaging in adolescent behaviors as a way to explain the experience of abusive leadership. The actions of a supervisor who acted child-like could then be more easily dismissed as foolish, silly and unimportant. As a result, the supervisor as elder did not deserve respect as an elder normally would. If individuals were successful in constructing the supervisor as child, the young worker could rationalize ignoring or being disrespectful to the supervisor. We propose that this sensemaking process also moderated (lessened) the outcomes of the abusive leadership.

In a similar way, those holding a formal position of authority as supervisor or manager were expected to be responsible, as well as possess particular skills and knowledge of how the business operates and how to manage people. If supervisors did not, this was considered unacceptable in the business world. Again, this does not always accurately reflect reality. There are many businesses, business owners and managers that have experienced great success (e.g., profits, career advancement, bonuses) because of luck, connections, or mistreating others. Moreover, Loughlin and Barling (2001) argue that young workers likely enter the working work already feeling betrayed by organizations. Young workers have witnessed the effects of downsizing and forced retirements on their parents. As a result young workers are weary of organizations (and those in management) and are less likely to make the same sacrifices made by their parents (Loughlin & Barling, 2001). In this way, young workers may lack respect for those in management positions regardless of their behavior. It is, however, *reasonable* to expect that managers have adequate skills and knowledge to operate a business and its people. By discrediting the supervisor because they lacked business knowledge or managerial skills the young workers were able to rationalize the abusive leadership. Supervisors were incompetent and this explained the inappropriate behavior in the workplace. Scruntizing skills as a sensemaking process, however, could lessen or increase the effects of the abusive behavior. The perceived incompetence of a supervisor could result in increased hostility and frustration on the part of the young worker, thus making the effects of the abusive leadership more pronounced. On the other hand, a successful effort at discrediting the supervisor could "free" the young worker from feeling that they should respect and obey their supervisor. In this way, the young worker could minimize the significance of the manager and thus reduce the effect of the abusive leadership.

Retrospective and Ongoing

The sensemaking effects of these young workers were both retrospective and ongoing (Weick, 1995). Individuals' experiences of the abusive leadership could only be described and explained after they had experienced it. Moreover, the past played a critical role in how these young workers understood the present. The abusive leadership described here occurred over an extended period of time, not just on one occasion. As the individual experienced feelings of humiliation in the present, it resonated as a familiar frame or memory of a similar feeling in the past. The sensemaking process bridged the past and present (and likely the future). In this way, experiences of abusive leadership from the past were linked to experiences in the present. Parker and Grandy (2009) make a similar argument in their research on leadership and change in a varsity athletic team in Canada. Their participants draw upon past experiences with the organization under a different leader to make their sensemaking processes in the present more believable and persuasive. In this way, the present cannot be understood without consideration of the past.

It is important to acknowledge the ongoing nature of sensemaking as it pertains to the experiences of abusive leadership because of the impact it can have upon the well-being of individuals and organizational performance. If young workers continue to experience abusive leadership they will work harder to make sense of these events. In doing this, some of the individual effects of the abusive leadership may certainly be reduced (e.g., less humiliated). The sensemaking efforts, however, are not without other costs. Young workers will avoid their supervisor, ignore them, or simply comply. These behaviors become habitual over time and the worker may carry these counterproductive behaviors onto relations with other supervisors or to other organizations. This means that the organizational outcomes of abusive leadership will be intensified leading to decreased productivity, increased turnover, and a destructive organizational culture. Moreover, individuals may engage in risky and unhealthy patterns of behavior to cope with the abusive experiences as evidenced in Vanessa story of drinking with coworkers to deal with the experiences. Exposure to abusive leadership over time will likely have a lasting impact upon the young workers. The first experiences of young adults in the working world may impact their attitudes, self-esteem, health and safety, job satisfaction, and job performance throughout their working lives. Kets de Vries (2004) work on narcissistic leadership indicates that past experience influences present and future experiences. This transference means that relationships with past supervisors color relationships with future supervisors. Undoubtedly, this line of thinking rings true for workers of all ages who experience abusive leadership, however, the first experiences in the working world may form the only basis from which young workers can build expectations for their next job and their future career progression. Therefore it becomes even more critical that organizations understand the nature of abusive leadership as experienced by young workers, that is, what it is, how individuals "deal" with abusive leadership, and the possible outcomes so that organizations might prevent it from happening or intervene early in the individual's career.

Identity Construction, Social Context, and Enactment

The young workers in our study exerted significant efforts to make sense of their experiences of abusive leadership, partly because it deeply affected their sense of self. Feelings of helplessness and humiliation unsettled individuals' self-esteem and confidence. It made them question who they were as individuals and how others (supervisors, coworkers, customers) viewed them. In this way, the sensemaking efforts were critical to regaining a level of comfort, consistency and coherence in their identities, in and outside of their occupations. Weick (1995) draws attention to the social aspect (and context in general) of sensemaking. Olson et al. (2006) also contend that social support can serve as a buffer to job dissatisfaction, proactive job search and various unproductive employee behaviors (e.g., absenteeism). In a similar way, Lipman-Bluman (2005) argues that building social bonds is one of the constructive outcomes for followers of toxic leaders. Here we saw how social networks at work (and even at home) were important in the sensemaking process. Communicating with others who shared the same experiences increased the likelihood of successful sensemaking, that is, producing a more believable, plausible explanation. Through interactions with each other, the young workers in part created their environment (enactment). Justifying retaliation (e.g., stealing, leaving work early) was also easier if it was shared with others. Moreover, when strong social networks were absent, as was evident in Rebecca's story, it made the struggle of sensemaking more complex and the effects of the abusive leadership more pronounced.

This emotional aspect of abusive leadership raises questions around the possible differences between experiences of abusive leadership among younger and older workers. Carstensen, Mayr, Pasupathi, and Nesselroade's (2000) research on emotional experience across the adult life span indicates that the frequency of negative emotions declined as an individual aged (up to approximately age 60). This means that a young worker aged 18 is likely to experience more negative emotions than a 34-year old worker. Furthermore, the research reveals that emotional regulation was greater in older adults than in younger adults, that is, older adults have a higher tendency to maintain positive emotional states and maintain the absence of negative emotional states. This may mean that younger workers are more likely than their older counterparts to perceive leadership as abusive and that the experience of abuse may be more severe because younger workers have a lower level of emotional regulation.

CONCLUSIONS

Given the limited, but growing body of research on abusive leadership we hope that organizations start to take the experience of abusive leadership seriously. Our findings reveal, however, that sensemaking processes are critical to understanding the nature of abusive leadership. Our focus upon young workers is also an important contribution of this research. As newcomers to the organizational world, it is critical to ensure a safe, healthy and quality experience of employment (Loughlin & Barling, 2001), otherwise the outcomes can be far reaching over numerous years for many organizations.

We suggest several avenues for future research. First, replicating the study conducted here with a larger sample size would improve the generalizability of the study and thereby increase its persuasiveness. Second, research that directly compares the experiences of abusive leadership among young and older workers would better illuminate the distinctions (if any) between different age categories of workers. This will allow organizations to tailor training to the specific needs of its workers. Third, future research should investigate the antecedents of abusive leadership among young and older workers. The antecedents of abusive leadership as it pertains to young workers' experience may indicate that supervisors' perceptions of young workers are different and therefore lead to increased activity of abusive leadership directed at young workers. Fourth, future research should also investigate the possible links between specific behaviors and outcomes to the sensemaking processes identified in this research. For example, it may be that telling lies is correlated more with diagnosing behavior as bipolar, whereas talking behind employees' back is correlated more with constructing as child.

For practitioners, we also suggest several ways forward. First, we contend that acknowledging bad leadership is as common as good leadership in organizations is a critical step (Kellerman, 2004). We spend more time talking about and training individuals to become good leaders that the presence and nature of bad leadership is overlooked or neglected. Moreover, organizations need to understand that the perception of abuse is enough to warrant negative outcomes. As such, managers need to set aside their own views of what abuse entails and demonstrate greater empathy for those who perceive to experience abusive leadership. Second, organizations need to become familiarize with the various antecedents, behaviors and outcomes of abusive leadership. Based upon this knowledge, sensitivity training should be developed for supervisors so that they understand what is appropriate or not in the context of the workplace. Third, an external confidential hotline, organized through a head or regional office, should be available workers to use. This would provide workers with a mechanism through which to voice their concerns without fear of retaliation by supervisors. Finally, organizations should familiarize newcomers with the norms of the organizations early in their socialization processes. Informing newcomers of behaviors that are appropriate or not, will allow workers to better align their expectations with those of the organization.

REFERENCES

Ashforth, B. (1994). Petty tyranny in organizations. *Human Relations, 47*(7), 755-778.

Ashforth, B. (1997). Petty tyranny in organizations: A preliminary examination of antecedents and consequences. *Canadian Journal of Administrative Sciences, 14*(2), 126-140.

Baron, R. A., & Neuman, J. H. (1998). Workplace aggression—the iceberg beneath the tip of workplace violence: Evidence on its forms, frequency and targets. *Public Administration Quarterly, 21*(4), 446-464.

Canadian Centre for Occupational Health and Safety. (2006). *Young workers zone.* Retrieved May 22, 2007, from http://www.ccohs.ca/youngworkers/

Carstensen, L. L., Mayr, U., Pasupathi, M., & Nesselroade, J. R. (2000). Emotional experience in everyday life across the adult life span. *Journal of Personality and Social Psychology, 70*(4), 644-655.

Charmaz, K. (2006). *Constructing grounded theory: A practical guide through qualitative analysis*. London, England: SAGE.

Craig, S. B., & Gustafson, S. B. (1998). Perceived leader integrity scale: An instrument for assessing employee perceptions of leader integrity. *Leadership Quarterly, 9*(2), 127-145.

Duffy, M. K., Ganster, D. C., & Pagon, M. (2002). Social undermining in the workplace. *Academy of Management Journal, 45*(2), 331-351.

Dupre, K. E., Inness, M., Connelly, C. E., Barling, J., & Hoption, C. (2006). Workplace aggression in teenage part-time employees. *Journal of Applied Psychology, 91*(5), 987-997.

Einarsen, S., Schanke Aasland, M., & Skogstad, A. (2007). Destructive leadership behaviour: A definition and conceptual model. *Leadership Quarterly, 18*(3), 207-216.

European Agency for Safety and Health at Work. (2009). *Young people—introduction*. Retrieved February 25, 2009, from http://osha.europa.eu/en/priority_groups/young_people

Ferris, G. R., Zinko, R., Brouer, R. L., Buckley, R. M., & Harvey, M. G. (2007). Strategic bullying as a supplementary, balanced perspective on destructive leadership. *Leadership Quarterly, 18*(3), 195-206.

Gioia , D. A., Corley, K. G., & Fabbri, T. (2002). Revising the past (while thinking in the future perfect tense). *Journal of Organizational Change Management, 15*(6), 622-634.

Glaser, B. G., & Strauss, A. L. (1967). *Discovery of grounded theory: Strategies for qualitative research*. Chicago, IL: Aldine.

Greenberger, E., & Steinberg, L. (1986). *When teenagers work: The psychological and social costs of adolescent employment.* New York: Basic Books.

Hoobler, J., & Brass, D. (2006). Abusive supervision and family undermining as displaced aggression. *Journal of Applied Psychology, 91*(5), 1125-1133.

Hoel, H., & Cooper, C. L. (2001). Origins of bullying: Theoretical frameworks for explaining workplace bullying. In N. Tehrani (Ed.), *Building a culture of respect: Managing bullying at work* (pp. 3-19). London, England: Taylor & Francis.

Keashly, L. (1998). Emotional abuse in the workplace: Conceptual and empirical issues. *Journal of Emotional Abuse, 1*(1), 85-117.

Keashly, L. (2001). Interpersonal and systematic aspects of emotional abuse at work: The target's perspective. *Violence and Victims, 16*(3), 233-266.

Kellerman, B. (2004). *Bad leadership*. Boston: Harvard Business Review Press.

Kelloway, E. K., Mullen, J., & Francis, L. (2006). Divergent effects of transformational and passive leadership in employee safety. *Journal of Occupational Health Psychology, 11*(1), 76-86.

Kets de Vries, M. (2004). Organizations on the couch: A clinical perspective on organizational dynamics. *European Management Journal, 22*(2), 183-200.

Kets de Vries, M., & Miller, D. (1985). Narcissism and leadership: An object relations perspective. *Human Relations*, 38(6), 583-601.

Lipman-Blumen, J. (2005). *The allure of toxic leaders*. Oxford, England: Oxford University Press.

Loughlin, C., & Barling, J. (2001). Young workers' work values, attitudes, and behaviours. *Journal of Occupational and Organizational Psychology, 74*(4), 543-558.

Louis, M.R. (1980). Surprise and sense making: What newcomers experience in entering unfamiliar organizational settings. *Administrative Science Quarterly, 25*(2), 226-251.

Olson, B. J., Nelson, D. L., & Parayitam, S. (2006). Managing aggression in organizations: What leaders must know. *Leadership & Organization Development Journal, 27*(5), 384-398.

Parker, D., & Grandy, G. (2009). Looking to the past to understand the present: Organizational change in Canadian varsity football. *Qualitative Research in Organizations and Management: An International Journal, 4*(3), 231-254.

Schat, A. C. H., Desmarais, S., & Kelloway, E. K. (2006). *Exposure to workplace aggression from multiple sources: Validation of a measure and test of a model.* Unpublished manuscript, McMaster University, Hamilton, Canada.

Schilling, J. (2008). From ineffectiveness to destruction: A qualitative study on the meaning of negative leadership. *Leadership, 5*(1), 102-128.

Starratt, A., & Grandy, G. (2919). Young workers' experiences of abusive leadership. *Leadership and Organizational Development Journal, 31*(2), 136-158.

Tepper, B. J. (2000). Consequences of abusive supervision. *Academy of Management Journal, 43*(2), 178-190.

Tepper, B. J. (2007). Abusive supervision in work organizations: Review, synthesis and research agenda. *Journal of Management, 33*(3), 261-289.

Tepper, B. J., Duffy, M. K., Henle, C. A., & Lambert, L.S. (2006). Procedural injustice, victim precipitations, and abusive supervision. *Personnel Psychology, 59*(1), 101-123.

Tierney, P., & Tepper, B. (2007). Introduction to the *Leadership Quarterly* special issue: Destructive leadership. *Leadership Quarterly, 18*(3), 171-173.

Vaez, M., Ekberg, K., & LaFlamme, L. (2004). Abusive events at work among young working adults: Magnitude of the problem and its effect on self-rated health. *Relations Industrielles, 59*(3), 569-583.

Weick, K. (1995). *Sensemaking in organizations*. Thousand Oaks, CA: SAGE.

CHAPTER 8

EXPLAINING HOSTILE ACTIONS

Integrating Theories of Abusive Supervision and Conflict Asymmetry

Sonja Rispens, Ellen Giebels, and Karen A. Jehn

In this chapter, we apply a conflict asymmetry theoretical framework and introduce a stage model describing how conflict raised by a subordinate triggers abusive supervision, what hostile actions supervisors are likely to use, and the consequences of these hostile actions for target, supervisor, and other organizational observers. We argue that any type of conflict (task, process, or relationship conflict) raised by the subordinate may trigger hostile actions from the supervisor. Our standpoint is that this happens because of how supervisors perceive and interpret the conflict with their subordinate. To inspire empirical research we suggest some interesting lines of future inquiry and conclude with a discussion of the practical implications of this model.

When Leadership Goes Wrong: Destructive Leadership, Mistakes and Ethical Failures, pp. 203–222

INTRODUCTION

Abusive supervision is a significant social problem: targets of abuse suffer personally (e.g., depression), abusive actions affect the functioning of organizations (e.g., reduced productivity), and abusive supervision may even lead to societal disasters (e.g., shooting incidents, hostage takings). We define abusive supervision as hostile actions perpetrated by hierarchically more powerful supervisors against less powerful targets. These hostile actions range from socially excluding the target to physical assault. Why supervisors may act hostile is still not quite clear, since past research has paid more attention to the consequences of abusive supervision rather than the antecedents (Tepper, 2007). In this chapter, we argue that asymmetrical conflict perceptions between supervisors and subordinates can easily escalate into abusive supervision. Past research on abusive supervision has largely focused on the perspective of the target of abuse (e.g., Aquino & Thau, 2009; Tepper, 2000), therefore, we lack insight into the perspective and motivation of the abusive supervisor (for an exception see Aryee, Chen, Sun, & Debrah, 2007). A few empirical studies suggest that supervisors act in an abusive manner towards subordinates when they perceive injustice or wrongdoing by the organization; and this effect gets stronger when the abusive supervisor also has an adverse personality profile, such as one that reflects affective negativity or general authoritarianism (Aryee et al., 2007; Hoobler & Brass, 2006). In addition, Tepper (2007) suggests in his review article that the research on abusive leadership is rather phenomenon-driven and is in need of theory. In this chapter, we apply a conflict asymmetry theoretic framework (Jehn & Rispens, 2008; Jehn, Rispens, & Thatcher, 2010) to introduce a stage model that describes how conflict with a subordinate triggers abusive supervision, what hostile actions supervisors are likely to use, and the consequences of these hostile actions for target, and other organizational observers.

Definitions of Constructs: What Are We Talking About?

Before introducing our stage model of abusive supervision, we first want to introduce our core constructs. In this paragraph, we define the constructs that are central to our theoretical model. As said before, we define *abusive supervision* as hostile actions perpetrated by a hierarchically powerful supervisor against a less powerful target. A hierarchically powerful supervisor refers to a person who occupies a higher position in the hierarchy than the target. For example, a team supervisor is higher in the organizational hierarchy than a team member. This distinction can also be applied to other (organizational) settings such as a teacher versus a student. A *target* of abusive supervision is an individual who occupies a lower position in the hierarchical ranks (i.e., a subordinate) who, consequently, exhibits less power and who is the focus of hostile actions perpetrated by a supervisor.

Power is defined as the relative ability of an individual to control or influence others (French & Raven, 1959; Keltner, Gruenfeld, & Anderson, 2003; Overbeck & Park, 2001) and in organizational settings the construct of power is closely linked to hierarchical positions. Thus, a team supervisor is better able to control or influence a team member than vice versa, because of the resources (e.g., the possibility of firing a team member) that are available to occupants of higher hierarchical positions.

Hostile actions are behavioral manifestations aimed to hurt another party and to restore what the supervisor believes is damaged (e.g., respect, power). In the case of abusive supervision, these actions are executed by the more powerful supervisors. These hostile actions refer to specific behaviors such as socially excluding, isolating, minimizing, chastising, and punishing the powerless target.

In general, *conflict* is defined as perceived incompatibilities (Boulding, 1962) by the parties involved, and is an inevitable aspect of organizational life. Conflict has been studied in various contexts ranging from the conflict dynamics between married couples (e.g., Gottman & Krokoff, 1989) to managing conflict between nations (e.g., Hopmann, 1996). Interorganizational relationships can also be marked by conflicts (e.g., Pondy, 1969; Putnam & Poole, 1987). Within organizations, conflicts can occur between coworkers or workgroup members (e.g., Amason, 1996; Giebels & Janssen, 2005; Jehn, 1995; Rispens, Greer, & Jehn, 2007), between groups or departments (e.g., Nauta, De Dreu, & Van der Vaart, 2002), or between an employee and supervisor (e.g., Rahim, Antonioni, & Psenicka, 2001). Conflicts usually involve two or more parties, each of which may have different perceptions about the conflict. That is, the conflicting parties can disagree about the level of conflict between them (Jehn et al., 2010) or they can disagree about the type of conflict (cf. Jehn & Rispens, 2008). We explain this concept of *conflict asymmetry* in more detail in the following section.

A CONFLICT ASYMMETRY THEORETIC FRAMEWORK: A STAGE MODEL

Conflicts between supervisors and subordinates may occur for a number of reasons. However, a typical distinction within the conflict research tradition is between task, relationship, and process conflict (e.g., Behfar, Peterson,

Mannix, & Trochim, 2008; Jehn & Bendersky, 2003; Jehn & Mannix, 2001; Jehn & Rispens, 2008). Task conflicts center on the content of the work, whereas relationship conflicts are disputes regarding personality clashes or value differences (Jehn, 1995). Process conflicts are disagreements about logistical and distribution issues such as how task accomplishment should proceed, who's responsible for what, or how things should be delegated (Jehn & Mannix, 2001). An abundance of research has investigated the positive and negative consequences of these three conflict types on outcomes such as performance, satisfaction, turnover intentions, and extra-role behaviors (e.g., De Dreu & Weingart, 2003; Giebels & Janssen, 2005; Greer, Jehn, & Mannix, 2008; Jehn, 1995; Rispens et al., 2007; Rispens, Greer, Jehn, & Thatcher, 2009). However, these past studies have, in general, focused upon conflict among peers.

"Vertical" disputes (i.e., between supervisors and subordinates) have not received as much attention in past research as other facets of conflict. Previous research on conflict in the superior-subordinate context, focused mostly on role conflict (e.g., Schaubroeck, Ganster, Sime, & Ditman, 1993) or on supervisors' conflict management styles (e.g., Rahim & Buntzman, 1989). However, less attention has been given to the process of conflict between supervisors and subordinates and how those conflicts can escalate into abusive behavior. In the first part of the stage model (see Figure 8.1), we argue that *any type of conflict* raised by the subordinate may trigger hostile actions from the supervisor. Our standpoint is that this happens because of how supervisors *perceive and interpret* the conflict with their subordinate.

Stage 1: Conflict as Trigger

When subordinates enter a conflict with their supervisor, there is the chance of escalation. Conflict escalation is defined as an increase of both the intensity of the conflict and the severity of tactics used in pursuing it (Pruitt & Rubin, 1986; Wall & Callister, 1995). One common model within the conflict research tradition about escalation is the aggressor-defender model (Pruitt & Rubin, 1986). In this model the conflicting parties see the other as the aggressor and the self as the victim or the defender. The aggressor, who has a goal that is in conflict with the other party, begins with mild conflict tactics, and moves to stronger ones if the mild tactics do not work. The defender reacts, which fuels the escalation process. In our conflict asymmetry framework of abusive supervision, the aggressor would be the subordinate *as perceived by the supervisor* and the defender would be the supervisor.

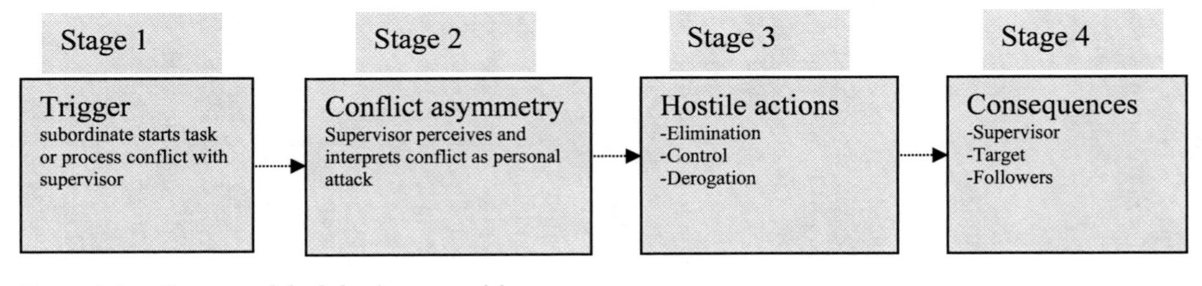

Figure 8.1. Stage model of abusive supervision.

We propose that any type of conflict may trigger abusive supervision (see also Figure 8.1). It may be easier to imagine that when a supervisor dislikes a subordinate (i.e., a relationship conflict) that hostile actions are more likely to occur than when they have a task dispute. However, according to our reasoning, it does not matter whether the conflict is actually about the process, the task, or the relationship; what we argue is that the mere *perception* of the conflict type by the supervisor matters.

Stage 2: Conflict Asymmetry

The most critical aspect of conflict and how it may lead to abusive behavior is the way in which supervisors perceive and interpret the conflict (Olson-Buchanan & Boswell, 2008; Sitkin & Bies, 1993). How people perceive the world is influenced by many individual differences, such as, for example, experience, or, personality. These individual differences affect interests, values, and mental scripts which in turn shape the lens through which people perceive and interpret the world around them, leading them to pay attention to certain stimuli but to ignore others (John & Robbins, 1994). An abundance of research has demonstrated that individuals working together in organizations are often dissimilar in terms of experience, personality, skills, and values (e.g., Pelled, Eisenhardt, & Xin, 1999). It is, therefore, likely that any two people may differ in their perception of the same phenomenon. Indeed, recent conflict research revealed that individual team members may differ dramatically in their perception of the level of conflict within a team (Bono, Boles, Judge, & Lauver, 2002; Jehn & Chatman, 2000; Jehn et al., 2010; Pelled, 1996). That is, where one team member may perceive there is hardly any conflict in the team another may perceive that the team is characterized by high levels of conflict (see also Figure 8.2). Furthermore, it is also possible that conflicting parties differ in their perception of the *content* of the conflict. Whereas one party may be convinced that the issue is task related, the opposing party may perceive the conflict as a personal attack (cf. Jehn & Rispens, 2008; Rispens, 2009; Simons & Peterson, 2000). For example, the subordinate may believe the dispute solely centers on the task whereas the supervisor may perceive the disagreement as a relationship conflict.

A factor that is likely to influence how a conflict between supervisor and subordinate is perceived by the involved parties is, of course, the difference in hierarchical position or power. Social psychological research on social power reveals that those in power differ significantly from those lacking power in terms of cognition, but also in affect and behavior. The majority of studies imply that having power (rather than lacking power) increases abstract thinking, deindividuation of subordinates, reliance on

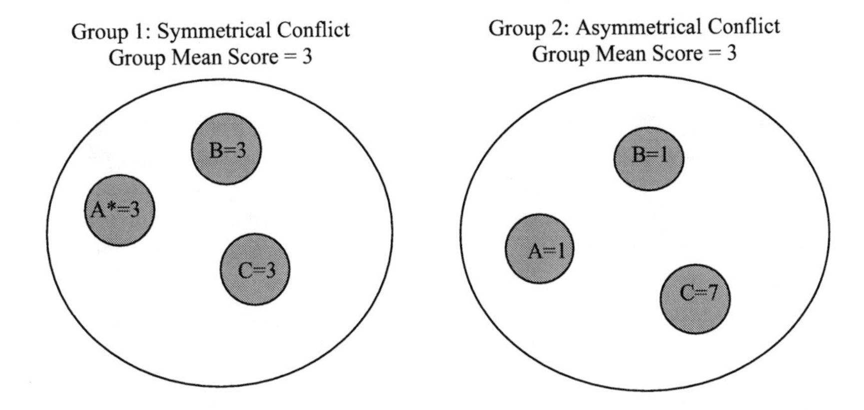

Example survey item: "How much conflict is there in your workgroup?" (Scale 1-7)

* The gray circles indicate members in the group; thus, each group has member A, B, and C.

(Figure adapted from Jehn & Rispens, 2008, p. 268).

Figure 8.2. Examples of conflict asymmetry in workgroups.

heuristics and stereotypes, less perspective taking, and, positive risk perceptions (e.g., Anderson & Galinsky, 2006; Keltner et al., 2003; Smith & Trope, 2006). In addition, numerous studies have shown that those in power display more positive emotions and affect (e.g., Sutton & Davidson, 1997). Regarding actual behavior, empirical research suggests that high power individuals are more willing to take risks (Anderson & Galinsky, 2006) and that individuals with heightened power break social norms more often. For example, Ward and Keltner (as cited in Keltner et al., 2003) found that randomly assigned group supervisors in three-person groups were more likely to grab cookies with no restraint, eat more of them, and chew with their mouths open. To summarize, research on social power has demonstrated that an individual's level of power influences perceptions, cognition, and behavior. We therefore expect that supervisors perceive conflicts with subordinates differently than how subordinates perceive those conflicts, and that supervisors are likely to act differently because of their higher power position.

Only a few studies have investigated conflicts between supervisors and subordinates. One study by Xin and Pelled (2003) investigated whether conflicts between supervisors and subordinates have the same structure and dynamic as conflicts among peers (where there are no power differences). Where previous research consistently confirmed that task and relationship conflict are distinguishable constructs (e.g., Amason, 1996; Jehn, 1995), Xin and Pelled's study suggests that superiors only perceive pure emotional (i.e., relationship) conflicts or mixed conflict (i.e., a combination of relationship and task conflict aspects) with their subordinates. Similarly, a recent study implies that power differences can explain how people perceive a conflict; supervisors are more likely to focus upon the socioemotional side of conflict whereas employees (powerless) are more likely to center upon the instrumental-task aspect of the conflict (Rispens & Giebels, 2009). These empirical findings are, we argue, crucial for understanding the causes of abusive leadership.

Among peers, task conflicts can lead to an increase in performance (e.g., Jehn, 1995) or decision making quality (Amason, 1996). However, based on the scant research on conflicts between supervisors and subordinates, this seems unlikely for vertical task conflicts. No matter if and how the subordinate perceives the conflict with the supervisor (at least partially), supervisors are likely to perceive the conflict as a relationship conflict. There is not necessarily a correspondence between objective events and the interpretation or perception of conflict (cf. Korsgaard, Jeong, Mahony, & Pitariu, 2008). Supervisors may perceive the subordinate as criticizing or challenging them, which may be difficult for supervisors to accept. Supervisors may perceive those criticisms as an insult to their position (Xin & Pelled, 2003) because typically, supervisors are expected to have more knowledge and experience (Tsui, Xin, & Egan, 1995). In addition, supervisors may feel their social standing or reputation is threatened (Fast & Chen, 2009) when a subordinate engages in task or process conflict with them (cf. Xin & Pelled, 2003). Therefore, we propose that supervisors are likely to perceive task or process conflicts as relationship conflicts. Past conflict research has demonstrated the negative consequences of relationship conflict for individual well-being (e.g., De Dreu, Van Dierendonck, & Dijkstra, 2004), performance (e.g., Jehn, 1995), and the relationship quality between the fighting parties (Xin & Pelled, 2003).

In sum, we expect supervisors to perceive any conflict with their subordinate as a personal attack. As a consequence they are likely to feel disrespected and attacked by their subordinate. In addition, relationship conflicts are characterized by heightened feelings of anger (e.g., Jehn, 1997). Supervisors are likely to react according to their feelings of disrespect, anger, and being attacked. Research by Baron, Neuman, and Geddes (1999) shows that individuals who feel attacked by others justify their own acts of aggression against the attackers. When supervisors perceive to be under attack, they are likely to reciprocate in order to get even or to restore the power balance. Several studies have shown that in social interactions individuals reciprocate the other's unpleasant or aggressive behaviors (Burgoon, Le-Poire, & Rosenthal, 1995). This "getting even" will fuel the conflict escalation process in which both the intensity of the conflict and the severity of tactics used in pursuing it are increased (Pruitt & Rubin, 1986; Wall & Callister, 1995). Specifically regarding powerholders (i.e., supervisors), recent research demonstrates that when they feel incompetent in their power role powerholders are more likely to display aggressive behavior (Fast & Chen, 2009). Individuals who have a high power position are more likely to use threats and punishments (De Dreu, Giebels, & Van de Vliert, 1998) which is consistent with the literature on abusive supervision. Thus, in the second stage of the phase model we expect that the supervisor will perceive the conflict as a relationship dispute, even if the subordinate raised an issue related to the task or the work process. In the following section, we will elaborate upon the hostile actions that follow leaders' conflict perceptions.

Stage 3: Hostile Actions

Supervisors who perceive a relationship conflict; that is, they feel personally attacked by the subordinate (regardless the actual conflict types) may decide to engage in hostile actions to establish elimination, control, or, derogation (cf. Berdahl, 2008) (see also Figure 8.1). Elimination refers to a range of hostile actions aimed to get rid of the threat. Elimination can occur on the social level by excluding the subordinate, to segregate the subordinate, or to deny opportunities to the subordinate. For example, a supervisor could decide to not inform the subordinate of important decisions regarding the tasks, not to invite the target to a department meeting, or to ignore the input from a target during a meeting. On the economic level elimination refers to, for example, restriction of financial resources and on the physical level elimination refers to, in the extreme, murder.

Control is another method the supervisor can use (Berdahl, 2008). Supervisors in general have the opportunity to control valued resources or outcomes and they can use this control to bribe or threaten the subordinate to coerce. Control can be executed by social approval or rejection. In addition, it may be exerted with economic coercion (e.g., by hiring "yes men") or to use physical force (e.g., torture or assault).

The third set of hostile actions supervisor may use is to establish derogation (Berdahl, 2008). It involves representing the subordinate as incompetent or immoral with the goal of preventing anyone taking the subordinate seriously. Supervisors can accomplish derogation by applying slander or stereotyping, for instance. Targets may also be sabotaged and even assaulted and humiliated.

Once a target is socially excluded and isolated, it becomes easy, or at least easier, for the supervisor to turn to derogation. We argue that abusive supervisors may slander and/or stereotype the socially excluded target, portraying the target as incompetent and "difficult" to others, in order to find coalition partners, or followers.

In sum, supervisors who perceive to be involved in a relationship conflict with a subordinate have an array of hostile actions to choose from. What remains rather vague in the literature on abusive leadership is what the supervisors may gain or think they may gain from these actions. We will elaborate upon this gap in the literature in the following section, in which we examine the consequences of abusive supervision. We not only pay attention to the supervisory point of view, but we will also consider the consequences for the targets of abusive supervision, and the effect this has on others in the workgroup or department.

Stage 4: The Consequences

Supervisor Outcomes

Recent research seems to suggest that powerful individuals are less capable of empathizing with a less powerful individual and how they think and feel (Galinsky, Magee, Inesi, & Gruenfeld, 2006). These authors conclude that it is a psychological state that makes perspective taking less likely; high-power individuals are less focused on the meaningful psychological experiences of those around them. In case of abusive supervision, we propose that supervisors may not care about what negative psychological effect the hostile behavior has on an individual.

Regarding the behavior of the supervisor, the assumption we make is that abusive supervision is a means to an end (cf. Ferris, Zinko, Brouer, Buckley, & Harvey, 2007; Tepper, 2007) and not necessarily a mere consequence of trait or character (Kellerman, 2004). That is, we believe the ultimate goal of applying hostile actions towards a target by a supervisor is to reestablish the power balance or power hierarchy by harming the target. As we described earlier, supervisors can choose between many hostile actions ranging from socially excluding the target to elimination of the target. In addition, applying hostile actions towards a target may also serve as a way of releasing frustration or to get even with the subordinate. Thus, supervisors may feel relieved or satisfied after displaying hostile actions towards the target. Specifically, when supervisors perceive that they have succeeded and re-established the power balance.

Of course, being abusive may also have negative consequences for supervisors, specifically when those actions get noticed by others. When the abuse is observed by others in organizations where abuse is not condoned, the supervisor may lose her or his job. Nevertheless, although the negative consequences can be severe, the literature on abusive supervision suggests that supervisors are often likely to get away with hostile actions. One way abusive supervisors are able to remain in their position is by gaining coalition partners or followers, which we will discuss in more detail below.

Target Responses

Whereas abusive supervisors try to reestablish the power balance, we argue that abused targets try to gain feelings of control. That is, targets are searching for ways to bring about change (Tjosvold & Wisse, 2009) such that they are no longer targets of the abuse. To establish a heightened sense of control targets can choose between exit, loyalty, or voice (Berdahl, 2008; Hirschman, 1970). An abused target may exit the situation, either physically (e.g., call in sick or quitting their job) or psychologically (i.e., emotional and social withdrawal). Research indeed reports a positive relationship between abusive supervision and absenteeism (Tepper, Duffy, & Shaw, 2001). In addition, reduced commitment and increased intentions to quit are positive correlates with abusive supervision (Duffy, Ganster, & Pagon, 2002; Tepper, 2000), as well as reduced task performance (Harris, Kacmar, & Zivnuska, 2007).

Loyalty refers to a course of action that increases targets' feelings of control by being loyal to and obeying the abusive supervisor. Targets may perceive that being loyal and obeying will stop the hostile actions. Loyalty does not challenge the power status-quo, rather it restores it. And a positive consequence is the performance increase (Ferris et al., 2007; cf. Salin, 2003) which is likely to positively affect the subordinate ("best loyal subordinate" etc.).

Voice challenges the status quo, and is the most risky course of action abused targets may take. Risky in the sense that the abusive supervisor will portray the target as "difficult" or a "troublemaker." Voice is the only way to increase targets' feelings of control while staying in the relationship with the abusive supervisor. In the abusive supervision literature, a lot of attention has been paid recently to what we refer to as displaced voice (i.e., when actions speak rather than words). Empirical studies suggest an association between abusive supervision and organization deviance (e.g., Duffy et al., 2002; Thau, Bennett, Mitchell, & Marrs, 2009). According to Tepper (2000), because targets of abusive supervisors view the organization as partly to blame, they aim their deviance behaviors at the organization. In addition, research by Zellars, Tepper, and Duffy (2002) concluded that victims of abusive supervision restore their sense of control by withholding voluntary citizenship behaviors (e.g., helping a colleague) that would otherwise benefit the organization. Consistent with Frone's (2000) findings, this would suggest that conflict with supervisors affects outcomes of organizational relevance while conflict with coworkers impact those of personal relevance. Another aspect of voice that has not received as much attention as the deviance hypothesis, is employee resistance (for an exception see Tepper et al., 2001), and that targets may actively seek coalition partners to exercise voice.

How targets will react is of course dependent upon if and how they perceive the hostile actions by the supervisor, and what type of hostile actions the abuser employs. For example, being socially excluded can be a process that is not necessarily immediately recognized by the target. Many studies examining the effects of social exclusion manipulated the construct in a laboratory environment (e.g., Van Beest, Van Dijk, & Wilke, 2003) in which social exclusion is almost immediately recognized by the target. However, in the "real organizational world" it is more likely that this process evolves gradually, leading the target to realize it only after it is too late. If the abusive supervisor uses increased control and monitoring, or threatens to withhold a promotion, this may result in increased anxiety, stress and, consequently, the development of burnout by the target.

Consequences for Others: When Observers Become Followers

In addition to the focal actors (the abusive leader and the subordinate target), in most organizations there are often other individuals who initially are observers of the abuse but ultimately get involved. We refer to these individuals as followers. Followers have not been as extensively studied as (abusive) supervisors, yet they play a pivotal role in the spread of hostile actions. Padilla, Hogan, and Kaiser (2007) recently emphasized the role of followers and abusive supervision. These authors distinguish two types of followers that support abusive supervision: conformers and colluders. Conformers support abusive supervisors out of fear whereas colluders actively participate in the hostile actions of supervisors. Padilla et al. argue that conformers are motivated by a prevention focus (Higgins, 1997), that is, to minimize the negative consequences of not complying with the abusive supervisor. Colluders are thought to act with a promotion focus (Higgins, 1997), meaning that they try to personally benefit from going along with the abusive supervisor. Both types of followers support the hostile actions of leaders because of unmet needs and insecurity (conformers) or because of self-promotion (colluders). And, obviously, this affects targets in a negative way for they perceive to be surrounded by nonsupportive coworkers who may even actively engage in the hostile behaviors.

We like to add a third type of followers that Padilla et al. (2007) did not address. We refer to these followers as oblivious. Oblivious followers are those who get manipulated by the abusive supervisor to join in the hostile actions. An example may help to clarify our point here. Often, abusive supervisors will socially exclude the victim. Once the target is isolated, or during the process of isolation, the leader may choose to increase control. For example, the supervisor may decide to overtly increase monitoring the target's work activities and outcomes. Increased monitoring is a signal to co-workers that the target is not performing as he or she should be. Being closely monitored means that target has less opportunity for self-monitoring, which has been found to increase the likelihood of emotional exhaustion (Wharton, 1993), and emotional exhaustion has been found to be related to absenteeism (Deery, Iverson, & Walsh, 2002). More so, close monitoring causes targets to withhold citizenship or extra-role behaviors (Niehoff & Moorman, 1993) which is likely to get noticed by coworkers since citizenship behaviors are often characterized by a strong reciprocity norm (Ng & Van Dyne, 2005). When targets are not adhering to the reciprocity norm (i.e., when coworkers observe that the target is bailing out) this can lead to negative impressions by the coworkers, who, as a result, may decide to ignore the target as a form of punishment for not doing what he or she ought to do (i.e., ostracism; Williams, 1997). Thus, whether intentional or not, abusive supervisors may manipulate followers (i.e., other subordinates) in such a way that the "oblivious" will join in the hostile actions.

CONCLUSION

In this chapter we have introduced a conflict asymmetry framework to study abusive supervision. We have presented a stage model in which subordinates act as a trigger by engaging in a task or process conflict with their supervisor. Based on how the supervisor perceives the conflict, hostile actions are likely to be employed, with various consequences for the target, the supervisor, and the followers. This framework is a first step in what we hope will inspire future research.

Our framework can be broadened and deepened, when the interactive process of abusive supervision is added onto our model. That is, a focus on the roles of both parties which is sorely needed provides theoretical foundations for understanding how the process of abuse unfolds over time. In this chapter, we have suggested that one key aspect of how targets will react to hostile actions is whether or not the target is aware of those actions. When abusive supervisors apply implicit or covert actions such as exclusion, targets do not necessarily immediately recognize these actions

(Stewart, Bing, Davison, Woehr, & McIntyre, 2009). Targets are likely to choose different behavioral reactions depending on the type or felt severity of the abuse (Hoobler & Brass, 2006). Being socially excluded by the abusive leader may trigger different behavior than being verbally abused in front of others.

In addition, we urge researchers to investigate how abusive supervision breeds followers. To be able to understand how this process works empirically, a multilevel and longitudinal research design is necessary. When applying a multilevel design, researchers are also able to include organizational context variables that may moderate the relationship between abusive supervision and the emergence of followers, such as complex change or other forms of uncertainty in the organizational realm. For example, a period of radical organizational change is likely to influence interpersonal interactions and behaviors. During times of downsizing supervisors may perceive that hostile actions are functional or a necessary evil (Margolis & Molinsky, 2008) in determining who stays and who does not. In addition, times of change are characterized by increased feelings of uncertainty, which may make supervisors more sensitive to conflicts with subordinates.

The framework of how asymmetric conflict perceptions can escalate into abusive supervision has several implications for both leaders and organizations. Regarding abusive supervisors, the research seems to suggest that they are less capable to empathize with the perspective of targets (Galinsky et al., 2006). In general, those in power experience less compassion (Van Kleef, Oveis, Van der Löwe, LuoKogan, Goetz, & Keltner, 2008). Supervisors should be made aware of these findings, which we believe is a necessary step in order to diminish the emergence of abusive supervision. Furthermore, as studies on asymmetrical conflict perceptions suggest (Jehn et al., 2010; Xin & Pelled, 2003), supervisors are likely to perceive and interpret conflict triggered by subordinates as a personal attack, regardless of the subordinates' motive. Awareness on the part of supervisors may enhance their use of asking more questions, to regulate their own emotions even more than they may already do, in situations of conflict. It is necessary for supervisors to require more information from the subordinate regarding the conflict. Supervisors should try to inform themselves in those situations, to prevent their own feelings of respect and authority from getting hurt, and also to prevent escalation of the conflict into hostile actions. More so, supervisors need to be aware that fear is not a good motivator. Although employing hostile actions may release supervisors' frustration or anger, in the long run employees do not want to work for or with someone who makes them afraid. Fear is linked to urges to escape (i.e., turnover, absenteeism), and narrows down people's information processing capacity (cf. Fredrickson & Branigan, 2005; Öhman, & Mineka, 2001), which in turn will decrease their performance.

Organizations have to watch out for abusive supervisors. The literature suggests that organizations can prevent abusive supervision by encouraging a culture in which abuse and hostile actions are not tolerated (Tepper, 2007). For example, by developing clear policies on how to act when abusive supervision is observed or by installing a formal third party (e.g., mediator, ombudsperson). Organizations can also play a role in harnessing employees by offering workshops or training on how to deal or cope with abusive supervisors. In addition, employees can be trained in how to engage in or handle a conflict with their supervisor.

The stage model we proposed in this chapter we hope will inspire future research and theorizing on abusive supervision. The negative consequences of abusive supervision for targets, organizations, and the society as a whole, are evident. Which means that researchers should pursue the quest to find ways to empower targets, to inform (potential) abusers, and ultimately, to diminish the negative effects of abusive supervision.

REFERENCES

Amason, A. (1996). Distinguishing the effects of functional and dysfunctional conflict on strategic decision making: Resolving a paradox for the top management teams. *Academy of Management Journal, 39*, 123-148.

Anderson, C., & Galinsky, A. D. (2006). Power, optimism, and risk taking. *European Journal of Social Psychology, 36*, 511-536.

Aquino, K., & Thau, S. (2009). Workplace victimization: Aggression from the target's perspective. *Annual Review of Psychology, 60*, 717-741.

Aryee, S., Chen, Z. X., Sun, L.-Y., & Debrah, Y. A. (2007). Antecedents and outcomes of abusive supervision: Test of a trickle-down model. *Journal of Applied Psychology, 92*, 191-201.

Baron, R. A., Neuman, J. H., & Geddes, D. (1999). Social and personal determinants of workplace aggression: Evidence for the impact of perceived injustice and the type A behavior pattern. *Aggressive Behavior, 25*, 281-296.

Behfar, K., Peterson, R., Mannix, E., & Trochim, W. (2008). The critical role of conflict resolution in teams: A close look at the links between conflict type, conflict management strategies, and team outcomes. *Journal of Applied Psychology, 93*, 170-188.

Berdahl, J. L. (2008). Introduction: Social power in action. *Social Justice Research, 21*, 255-262.

Bono, J. E., Boles, T. L., Judge, T. A., & Lauver, K. J. 2002. The role of personality in task and relationship conflict. *Journal of Personality, 30*, 311-334.

Boulding, K. (1962). *Conflict and defense.* New York: Harper & Row.

Burgoon, J. K., Le-Poire, B. A., & Rosenthal, R. (1995). Effects of preinteraction expectancies and target communication on perceiver reciprocity and compensation in dyadic interaction. *Journal of Experimental Social Psychology, 31*, 287-321.

De Dreu, C. K. W., Giebels, E., & Van de Vliert, E. (1998). Social motives and trust in integrative negotiation: The disruptive effects on punitive capability. *Journal of Applied Psychology, 83*, 408-422.

De Dreu, C. K. W., Van Dierendonck, D., & Dijkstra, M. T. M. (2004). Conflict at work and individual well-being. *International Journal of Conflict Management, 15*, 6-26.

De Dreu, C. K. W., & Weingart, L. R. (2003). Task versus relationship conflict, team performance, and team member satisfaction: A meta-analysis. *Journal of Applied Psychology, 88*, 741-749.

Deery, S., Iverson, R., & Walsh, J. (2002). Work relationships in telephone call centres: Understanding emotional exhaustion and employee withdrawal. *Journal of Management Studies, 39*, 471-496.

Duffy, M. K., Ganster, D., & Pagon, M. (2002). Social undermining in the workplace. *Academy of Management Journal, 45*, 331-351.

Fast, N. J., & Chen, S. (2009). When the boss feels inadequate: Power, incompetence, and aggression. *Psychological Science, 20*, 1406-1413.

Ferris, G. R., Zinko, R., Brouer, R. L., Buckley, M. R., & Harvey, M. G. (2007). Strategic bullying as a supplementary, balanced perspective on destructive leadership. *Leadership Quarterly, 18*, 195-206.

Fredrickson, B. L., & Branigan, C. (2005). Positive emotions broaden the scope of attention and thought-action repertoires. *Cognition and Emotion, 19*, 313-332.

French, J. R. P., & Raven, B. (1959). Bases of Social Power. In D. Carwright (Ed.), *Studies in Social Power* (pp. 150-167). Ann Arbor, MI: Institute of Social Research.

Frone, M. R. (2000). Interpersonal conflict at work and psychological outcomes: testing a model among young workers. *Journal of Occupational Health Psychology, 5*, 246-255.

Galinsky, A. D., Magee, J. C., Inesi, M. E., & Gruenfeld, D. H (2006). Power and perspectives not taken. *Psychological Science, 17*, 1068-1074.

Giebels, E. & Janssen, O. (2005). Conflict stress and reduced wellbeing at work: The buffering effect of third-party help. *European Journal of Work and Organizational Psychology, 14*, 137-155.

Gottman, J. M., & Krokoff, L. J. (1989). Marital interaction and satisfaction—a longitudinal view. *Journal of Consulting and Clinical Psychology, 57*, 47-52.

Greer, L. L., Jehn, K. A., & Mannix, E. A. (2008). Conflict transformation: An exploration of the interrelationships between task, relationship, and process conflict. *Small Group Research, 39*, 278-302.

Harris, K. J., Kacmar, K. M., & Zivnuska, S. (2007). An investigation of abusive supervision as a predictor of performance and the meaning of work as a moderator of the relationship. *Leadership Quarterly, 18*, 252-263.

Higgins, E. T. (1997). Beyond pleasure and pain, *American Psychologist, 52*, 1280-1300.

Hirschman, A. O. (1970). *Exit, voice, and loyalty: responses to decline in firms, organizations, and states*. Cambridge, MA: Harvard University Press.

Hoobler, J. M., & Brass, D. J. (2006). Abusive supervision and family undermining as displaced aggression. *Journal of Applied Psychology, 91*, 1125-1133.

Hopmann, P. T. (1996). *Negotiation process & the resolution of international conflicts.* Columbia, SC: University of South Carolina Press.

Jehn, K. A. (1995). A multimethod examination of the benefits and detriments of intragroup conflict. *Administrative Science Quarterly, 40*, 256-282.

Jehn, K. A. (1997). A qualitative analysis of conflict types and dimensions in organizational groups. *Administrative Science Quarterly, 42*, 530-557.

Jehn, K. A., & Bendersky, C. (2003). Intragroup conflict in organizations: A contingency perspective on the conflict-outcome relationship. *Research in Organizational Behavior, 25*, 187-242.

Jehn, K. A., & Chatman, J.A. (2000). The influence of proportional and perceptual conflict composition on team performance. *The International Journal of Conflict Management, 11*, 56-73.

Jehn, K. A., & Mannix, E. (2001). The dynamic nature of conflict: A longitudinal study of intragroup conflict and group performance. *Academy of Management Journal, 44*, 238-251.

Jehn, K. A., & Rispens, S. (2008). Conflict in workgroups. In C.I. Cooper & J. Barlings (Eds.): *Handbook of Organizational Behavior, : Micro Approaches* (Vol. 1, pp. 262-276). Thousand Oakes, CA: SAGE.

Jehn, K. A., Rispens, S., & Thatcher, S. M. B. (2010). The effects of conflict asymmetry on workgroup and individual outcomes. *Academy of Management Journal, 53*.

John, O. P., & Robbins, R. W. (1994). Accuracy and bias in self-perception: Individual differences in self-enhancement and the role of narcissism. *Journal of Personality and Social Psychology, 66*, 205-219.

Kellerman, B. (2004). *Bad leadership: What it is, how it happens, why it matters.* Boston: Harvard Business School Press.

Keltner, D., Gruenfeld, D. H., & Anderson, C. (2003). Power, approach, and inhibition. *Psychological Review, 110*, 265-284.

Korsgaard, M. A., Jeong, S. S., Mahony, D. M., & Pitariu, A. H. (2008). A multilevel view of intragroup conflict. *Journal of Management, 34*, 1222-1252.

Margolis, J. D., & Molinsky, A. (2008). Navigating the bind of necessary evils: Psychological engagement and the production of interpersonally sensitive behavior. *Academy of Management Journal, 51*, 847-872.

Nauta, A., De Dreu, C. K. W., & Van der Vaart, T. (2002). Social value orientation, organizational goal concerns and interdepartmental problem solving behavior. *Journal of Organizational Behavior, 23*, 199-213.

Ng, K. Y., & Van Dyne, L. (2005). Antecedents and performance consequences of helping behavior in work groups: A multi-level analysis. *Group and Organization Management, 30*, 514-540.

Niehoff, B. P., & Moorman, R. H. (1993). Justice as a mediator of the relationship between methods of monitoring and organizational citizenship behavior. *Academy of Management Journal, 36*, 527-556.

Öhman, A., & Mineka, S. (2001). Fears, phobias, and preparedness: Toward an evolved module of fear and fear learning. *Psychological Review, 108*, 483-522.

Olson-Buchanan, J. B., & Boswell, W. R. (2008). An integrative model of experiencing and responding to mistreatment at work. *Academy of Management Review, 33*, 76-96.

Overbeck, J. R., & Park, B. (2001). When power does not corrupt: Superior individuation processes among powerful perceivers. *Journal of Personality and Social Psychology, 81*, 549-565.

Padilla, A., Hogan, R., & Kaiser, R. B. (2007), The toxic triangle: Destructive leaders, vulnerable followers, and conducive environments. *Leadership Quarterly, 18*, 176-194.

Pelled, L. H. (1996). Relational demography and perceptions of group conflict and performance: A field investigation. *The International Journal of Conflict Management, 7*, 230–246.

Pelled, L. H., Eisenhardt, K. M., & Xin, K. R. (1999). Exploring the black box, An analysis of work group diversity, conflict, and performance. *Administrative Science Quarterly, 44*, 1-28.

Pondy, L. R. (1969). Varieties of organizational conflict. *Administrative Science Quarterly, 14*, 499-506.

Pruitt, D. G., & Rubin, J. Z. (1986). *Social Conflict: Escalation, Stalemate, and Settlement.* New York: Random House.

Putnam, L. L., & Poole, M. S. (1987). Conflict and negotiation. In F. M. Jablin, L. L. Putnam, K. H. Roberts, & L. W. Porter (Eds.), *Handbook of organizational communication: An interdisciplinary perspective* (pp. 549-599). Beverly Hills, CA: SAGE.

Rahim, M. A., & Buntzman, G. F. (1989). Supervisory power bases, styles of handling conflict with subordinates, and subordinate performance and satisfaction. *Journal of Psychology, 123*, 195-210.

Rahim, M. A., Antonioni, D., & Psenicka, C. (2001). A structural equations model of leader power, subordinates' styles of handling conflict, and job performance. *International Journal of Conflict Management, 12*, 191-211.

Rispens, S. (2009). *When conflicts don't escalate: The influence of conflict characteristics on the co-occurrence of task and relationship conflict in teams.* Paper submitted for publication.

Rispens, S., & Giebels, E. (2009, August). *Making sense of he said she said: The influence of power on 3rd parties' conflict perceptions.* Paper presented at the Academy of Management Conference, Chicago, Illinois.

Rispens, S., Greer, L. L., & Jehn, K. A. (2007). It could be worse: A study on the alleviating roles of trust and connectedness in intragroup conflict. *International Journal of Conflict Management, 18*, 325-344.

Rispens, S., Greer, L. L., Jehn, K. A., & Thatcher, S. M. B. (2009). *It's not so bad after all: How relational closeness buffers the effect of relationship conflict on helpful and deviant group behaviors.* Paper submitted for publication.

Salin, D. (2003). Ways of explaining workplace bullying: A review of enabling, motivating and precipitating structures and processes in the work environment. *Human Relations, 56*, 1213-1232.

Schaubroeck, J., Ganster, D. C., Sime, W. E., & Ditman, D. (1993). A field experiment testing supervisory role clarification. *Personnel Psychology, 46*, 1-25.

Simons, T. L., & Peterson, R. S. (2000). Task conflict and relationship conflict in top management teams: The pivotal role of intragroup trust. *Journal of Applied Psychology, 85*, 102-111.

Sitkin, S. B., & Bies, R. J. (1993). Social accounts in conflict situations: Using explanations to manage conflict. *Human Relations, 46*, 349-370.

Smith, P. K., & Trope, Y. (2006). You focus on the forest when you're in charge of the trees: Power priming and abstract information processing. *Journal of Personality and Social Psychology, 90*, 578-596.

Stewart, S. M., Bing, M. N., Davison, H. K., Woehr, D. J., & McIntyre, M. D. (2009). In the eyes of the beholder: A non-self-report measure of workplace deviance. *Journal of Applied Psychology, 94*, 207-215.

Sutton, S. K., & Davidson, R. J. (1997). Prefrontal brain asymmetry: A biological-substrate of the behavioral approach and inhibition systems. *Psychological Science, 8*, 204-120.

Tepper, B. J. (2000). Consequences of abusive supervision. *Academy of Management Journal, 43*, 178-190.

Tepper, B. J. (2007). Abusive supervision in work organizations: Review, synthesis and research agenda. *Journal of Management, 33*, 261-289.

Tepper, B. J., Duffy, M. K., & Shaw, J. D. (2001). Personality moderators of the relationships between abusive supervision and subordinates' resistance. *Journal of Applied Psychology, 86*, 974-983.

Thau, S., Bennett, R. J., Mitchell, M. S., & Marrs, M. B. (2009). How management style moderates the relationship between abusive supervision and workplace deviance: An uncertainty management theory perspective. *Organizational Behavior and Human Decision Processes, 108*, 79-92.

Tjosvold, D., & Wisse, B. (2009). Introduction. In D. Tjosvold & B. Wisse (Eds.), *Power and Interdependence in organizations* (pp. 2–13). Cambridge, MA: Cambridge University Press.

Tsui, A., Xin, K., & Egan, T. D. (1995). Relational demography: The missing link in vertical dyadic linkage. In S. E. Jackson & M. N. Ruderman (Eds.), *Diversity in work teams: Research paradigms for a changing workplace* (pp. 97-129). Washington, DC: American Psychological Association.

Van Beest, I., Van Dijk, E., & Wilke, H. (2003). The excluded player in coalition formation. *Personality and Social Psychology Bulletin, 29*, 237-247.

Van Kleef, G. A., Oveis, C., Van der Löwe, I., LuoKogan, A., Goetz, J., & Keltner, D. (2008). Power, distress, and compassion: Turning a blind eye to the suffering of others. *Psychological Science, 19*, 1315-1322.

Wall, J. A., & Callister, R. R. (1995). Conflict and its management. *Journal of Management, 21*, 515-558.

Wharton, A. S. (1993). The affective consequences of service work: Managing emotions on the job. *Work and Occupations, 20*, 205-232.

Williams, K. D. (1997). Social ostracism. In R. M. Kowalski (Ed.), *Aversive interpersonal behaviors* (pp. 133-170). New York: Plenum Press.

Xin, K. R., & Pelled, L. H. (2003). Supervisor-subordinate conflict and perceptions of leadership behavior: A field study. *Leadership Quarterly, 14*, 25-40.

Zellars, K. L., Tepper, B. J., & Duffy, M. K. (2002). Abusive supervision and subordinates' organizational citizenship behavior. *Journal of Applied Psychology, 87*, 1068-1076.

CHAPTER 9

NEGATIVE EMOTION-POSITIVE OUTCOMES

A Study of Construction Project Managers

Dirk Lindebaum

There is a rich stock of studies indicating how positive and negative leader emotions influence a variety of positive and negative follower outcomes. However, little empirical evidence exists to suggest under what circumstances negative emotions can yield desirable outcomes for individuals operating in a given organizational context. Using a series of semi-structured interviews with construction project managers (n = 19) from the United Kingdom, this study proffers valuable insights into how anger is often enacted to help individuals ensure the progress of projects, be it in negotiations with other parties or affairs on site with operatives.

INTRODUCTION

Emotions are with us, wherever we are, and that surely implicates the workplace as well. We may attempt to leave them at the office entrance

When Leadership Goes Wrong: Destructive Leadership, Mistakes and Ethical Failures, pp. 223–243

upon arrival at work, like the old-fashioned time cards inserted into the attendance recorder, but oftentimes it does not work. Their potent influence on our behavior is simply too prevalent to be neglected—especially at work when we compete for resources and status through interactions with others. Several influential reviews are a testimony to this effect (e.g., Barsade & Gibson, 2007).

Indeed, this potency extends to the realm of leadership as well, a process which tends to be imbued with emotion (George, 2000). One prominent stream of research suggests that positive leader emotion is conducive to achieve beneficial follower outcomes (Bono & Ilies, 2006). In congruence with this, George (1996) contends that "leaders who feel excited, enthusiastic, and energetic themselves are likely to similarly energize their followers," while she also draws attention to the contrary, for "leaders who feel distressed and hostile [are] likely to negatively activate their followers" (p. 84). Empirical evidence for the latter is accumulating, such as Starratt and Grandy's (2008) study on young workers' experiences of abusive leadership or Lewis's (2000) laboratory study on how followers react to negative emotional expression of leaders.

By and large, there appears to be a predominance of studies in the leadership arena that examine *positive* emotion in relation to *positive* outcomes as well as studies that explore *negative* emotion in relation to *negative* outcomes (e.g., Sy, Côté, & Saavedra, 2005). However, this bipolar emphasis does not capture the whole range of emotion surfacing in leader-follower interactions at work; negative emotion, after all, is an inescapable characteristic in the workplace. Depending upon situation and context, negative emotion may not necessarily yield negative outcomes. Indeed, from a functionalist perspective, the notion of a truly negative emotion is more myth than reality.[1] As Frijda (2007) contends, all emotions are potentially adaptive states of action readiness, and Fitness (2008) adds that they "may or may not have destructive consequences" (p. 61).

One important differentiation must be applied here, and that concerns the question for whom the display of negative emotion has positive implications. In this chapter, I am not concerned with the impact of an individual's emotion on certain cognitive decision-making tasks (see George, 2000, for a review), but rather with the behavioral prescriptions attached to a specific type of occupation. As such, my interest rests with the types of negative emotion that help individuals be effective in their job and, therefore, are likely contribute to organizational effectiveness as well. I should point out from the outset that this may introduce conflict; while the use of negative emotion (in this case anger) as a central characteristic of one's role may help one be effective in the job, one pays also a price in terms of physiological costs (Steptoe, Cropley, Griffith, & Kirschbaum, 2000). Hence, being effective in one's job by using anger may mean high stress levels and physiological arousal both for one's self and colleagues. The crucial point to bear in mind here is organizational short-term gain and not the long-term well-being of individuals. It is at this juncture where the chapter comes face to face with the leitmotif of this edited volume, for it recognizes the potentially destructive long-term implications for individuals—both in terms of quality of interpersonal relationships and well-being.

It shall be understood that the dearth of studies investigating the use of negative emotion and its potential benefit for increased leader effectiveness greatly hampers the development of contextual theories, "theories that guide us in identifying specific kinds of work conditions and/or events (physical, social, or economic) associated with specific affective states" (Brief & Weiss, 2002, p. 299). Given these critical voices, Barsade and Gibson (2007) quite legitimately ponder under what circumstances negative emotion can lead to positive organizational outcomes.

Drawing upon the qualitative data component of an ongoing mixed-method investigation into emotional intelligence (EI), transformational leadership, and their implications for performance in construction project management, the purpose of this chapter is to detail the *use of* negative *emotion* (as one component of the EI construct, see Mayer & Salovey, 1997) in relation to subjective leader effectiveness. This subjective perception fits closely with what de Sousa (1987) denotes as *paradigm scenarios*. According to this argument, individuals do not only learn the appropriateness of their emotion and emotional behaviors, but also their significance and power. In this chapter, I do not distinguish between anger that is expressed in a controlled or uncontrolled way, as this would lead me into the domain of the emotion regulation literature. I should note, though, that I use some quotes where individuals had to control their emotion to explicate the use of anger as a function of hierarchical position.

Reverting back to Barsade and Gibson (2007), I apply their critical question to the construction industry, which is typically characterized as one of the most men-dominated and aggressive industries (Fielden, Davidson, Gale, & Davey, 2000; Smithers & Walker, 2000). The role of construction project managers (CPMs) is of intrinsic interest here, for they occupy a central position in the management of the construction process (Harris & McCaffer, 2001), relating to various parties with different social and educational backgrounds, and, perhaps most significantly, different vested interests.

The chapter unfolds along, and touches upon, the following key issues. First, I seek to provide some contextual background as far as the characteristic management style in construction is concerned-and the type of emotion it often entails. Thereafter, I discuss the data and briefly the technical aspects thereof in terms of their collection. In line with this chapter's purpose, I squarely center upon the role of emotion (especially anger) in attaining positive organizational outcomes. As a final step I synthesize these findings with results from previous studies in an attempt to fill in what I believe are important missing pixels in the overall picture of leader effectiveness. As the chapter draws to a close, I hope that the imperative to consider leader effectiveness as a function of context has gained the visibility it undoubtedly deserves.

BACKDROP OF STUDY: EMOTION IN CONSTRUCTION

> The management style of many contracting companies is based upon the street fighting man. Banter and joking, usually at the expense of others, is used for point scoring when things are on a reasonably even keel. If that fails or the *pressure* is great, *verbal abuse* and *shouting* are the weapons to instill *fear* and maintain *power* in the office corridor. (Smyth, 2000, pp. 12-13, italics added for emphasis)

The above quote rather tellingly circumscribes the parameters within which the typical management style in construction tends to fall. It is by far no isolated case, and even more explicit examples are featured elsewhere (e.g., Loosemore & Galea, 2008). In light of the above quote, I adopt Zeelenberg and colleagues' (2008) summary concerning the key aspects of emotion. According to them,

> emotions are acute, they are relatively momentary experiences. This differentiates emotions from moods, that typically last longer, and from other more general affects. Emotions are about something or someone: you are angry with someone; you regret a choice, etc. Emotions typically arise when one evaluates an event or outcome as relevant for one's concerns or preferences. (p. 20)

When Solomon (1993) suggests that emotions signal an individual's engagement with the world, one may reasonably assume, based upon the introductory quote, the ways in which that engagement manifests itself in the context of construction (and how it potentially reflects collective sentiments). Thus, it appears safe to portray construction as an emotionally charged environment. After all, wherever there are fierce competition and adversarial relationships, it is the emotion that renders them as such.

To a significant degree, this adversarial atmosphere is influenced by the men-dominated culture in construction, which has important implications for the nature of power structures in construction organizations. Men, in particular, tend to preserve dominance of the public domain by engaging in goal-directed behavior and politics, as well as dispassionate reason, to engender a productive image about themselves (e.g., Parkin, 1993). Others extends this view by suggesting that emotionality is chiefly defined within a men power structure that values "emotional strength," connoting repression of, and control over, emotions (Domagalski, 1999). Indeed, we know that men, in particular, often avoid engaging with emotional information with great endeavor. In congruence with the above notion of emotional strength, the performance of men in construction tends to be assessed against "a particular stereotype which supports and promotes decisiveness, toughness, self-reliance, resolution and control" (Loosemore & Galea, 2008, p. 126). Behaviors of this type may be a *sine qua non* in surviving as a CPM, especially against the backdrop that construction is consistently characterized by aggressive/authoritative management styles, adversarial relationships, tight profit margins, fierce competition and the imperative to be able to respond to extreme short-term pressures at work (Dainty, Bryman, & Price, 2002; Holt, Love, & Nesan, 2000). Under these conditions, it is germane to probe and better understand what behavioral role choices CPMs opt for in order to succeed. Preliminary research indicates that anger is quite prevalent given the above pressures and demands in construction (Goldenhar, Hecker, Moir, & Rosecrancea, 2003), and that it can be appropriate in some environments (Dainty, Cheng, Moore, 2004). Note that the role of a CPM is one of the most stressful functions in the building process (Djebarni, 1996). High turnover intentions in construction are a testament to this effect (Lingard, 2003).

The quality of interpersonal relationships in construction has been recognized as a central feature in a recent government-commissioned report, which stressed the poor quality of them (e.g., Office of the Deputy Prime Minister, 2004). There is growing consensus among scholars that construction can only improve its performance by developing a better grasp of the interpersonal dynamics of its employees (Dulaimi & Langford, 1999). Still, scholars continue to indicate that construction is by no means a "touchy-feely" industry, and that intimate and comfortable relationships are usually not formed between CPMs and subordinates (Butler & Chinowsky, 2006).

THE DATA

The qualitative data presented here are part of a mixed-method study, as mentioned earlier. Examined within the interpretive tradition (Sandberg, 2005), they have a distinct phenomenological dimension. That is, I was interested in the *lived experiences* of CPMs as far as their use of emotions in the pursuit of effectiveness is concerned. Indeed, such view implies a subjective perspective on leader effectiveness, but it is the meaning that they append to the phenomenon in question (Dey, 1993) that is of interest here, primarily because it so significantly informs their behavior.

The underlying maxim throughout the interviews was to invite individuals to reflect upon and narrate situations that they experienced within the functions as CPMs. To achieve this, scenarios and questions were provided to the CPMs to elaborate upon in any detail they deemed fit. For instance, questions sought to explore whether emotions are important to the job of CPMs and whether they believe that emotions (positive or negative) can assist in solving problems. Accordingly, I denoted the main stream in the data analysis section as "the role of emotions in attaining goals," which is further decomposed into the substreams (1) positive emotion and attitudes as well as (2) anger. The initial responses to these situations were often followed by questions like "why would you act like that?" or "can you explain that further?" to elicit more details. In particular, I detail how a CPM's anger oftentimes serves a strategic role in attaining goals in construction, though it must be reemphasized that this is a subjective assessment on the part of CPMs. Therefore, it shall be understood that the significance of *context* cannot be overemphasized in this analysis.

Sample

As indicated earlier, the focus of this study rests upon CPM. Irrespective of specialization, the project manager "oversees the day to day control of the process conducted on site including liaison with the architect/civil engineer regarding instructions, payments, progress meetings, and commercial dealings with sub-contractors, etc" (Harris & McCaffer, 2001, p. 313). In so doing, CPMs often relate to parties with different education and social backgrounds (i.e., subcontractors and architects), which often have rather distinct vested interests. Consequently, their ability to maneuver through and navigate the intricate web of social interactions has immediate and decisive implications for the success of a project.

The sample of this study is a nonrandom purposive one, and I conducted a total of 19 semistructured interviews with CPMs employed at four different U.K. construction organizations (medium to large in size). All CPMs interviewed were White British men aged between 26 and 62 years. It was stipulated with senior directors that the interviewees must be in charge of the day-to-day running of the construction site. Years of experience ranged between 1 and 35 years. Especially older CPMs attained their positions after having started as craftsmen on site (e.g., joiner), while many younger CPMs completed a university degree prior to embarking upon a career in construction. Note that the CPM ID numbers are followed by their age (*in parenthesis*), so as to highlight any differences in reaction between the younger and older CPMs that potentially exist.

Procedure

Senior directors of the respective organizations provided the contact details of the CPMs, all of whom were unknown to me. Prior to the interviews, the CPMs received a statement detailing the rationale and background information to this study. Duration of interviews amounted to 30-60 minutes on average. Importantly, the study also incorporated what is known as respondent validation (Bryman, 2004), so as to add trustworthiness to the findings. The accounts CPMs produced during the feedback sessions are woven into the chapter, were appropriate, in order to highlight how and why they use negative emotions in the pursuit of goals

The Role of Emotion in Attaining Goals

Positive Emotion and Attitudes

The data indicates a disproportionately low share of incidents where CPMs, based upon their experience, hinted at the use of positive emotion in order to attain desirable organizational goals. However, despite this disproportionate imbalance, the few references to positive emotion are informative. In reflecting upon their use of emotion, CPM 4 (39) and 17 (40) both converged on one common point, as exemplified by the former. In his words, "if you're positive about finding a solution and you can get, invariably you will, but if you go into it thinking you can't resolve it, invariably you won't." Having suggested an almost identical view, the latter extended this point by arguing that "ultimately, that decides which way a project gets steered." Crucially, these statements are more a reflection of typical mindset rather than necessarily behavioral in nature, as discussed prior. From the behavioral perspective of positive emotion, CPM 3 (37) explicitly believed they enable him to achieve whatever he sets out to achieve.

> Put it this way, if I've got a goal and it's gonna happen, and it is, there is no unequivocal way, it is gonna happen, I'll be very direct and very upbeat and very focused and get everyone to buy into what I wanna do. You know, and people generally run along with that.

In reading the above response, a rather uncompromising attitude comes to the fore. He seems to know that his being "direct and upbeat" generally achieves the desired effect, namely, that others are on board. Others complemented this view by referring to how their positive attitude keeps ticking over, even in the face of hardship (CPM 1 (62)).

In traversing the more neutral grounds, there was evidence to suggest that CPMs acknowledged the centrality of emotions in construction project management.

> To make our business work you've got to become a good people person. If you get a grip of those emotions and you get a grip of what makes people tick, yeah? That is the key to a project being a successful one that makes money and everybody's happy or one that loses money and upsets the client. (CPM 17 (40))

His comment is in line with the suggestions made by CPM 2 (32), who further underpinned the central role of emotion in the management of construction projects. To him, emphasis upon emotion is a critical factor that decides the project's success or failure, respectively. More precisely, he argued that:

> I think they're, well, they're one of the key management tools we have, i.e. if you understand emotion you can help manage people as individuals far better than being emotionally detached ... I would say they're key.

What is instantly striking is the reference to emotion as a key management tool, albeit he does not specify what type of emotion he has in mind in the above statement. CPM 15 (34) did not directly refer to the use of positive emotion, suggesting that the time for ill-tempered individuals in construction may be over. Rather, he refers to them by exclusion (i.e., the absence of shouting).

> There's no room in this industry any more for hot-heads and all that screaming and balling.... People who are just sort of like divorced from the whole environment around them.

But this statement does not represent what the majority of CPMs felt about the role of emotion at work. This finds expression in the ensuing section.

Anger

Overall, there was a distinct preponderance of accounts indicating that, when pressure is intense, CPMs tend to be rather short-fused, taking recourse to anger to ensure progress of the project. The account of CPM 8

(55) points to a potent explanation for this. Note that this is a direct contradiction to what CPM 15 (34) stated above.

> I think the kind of people the industry attracts, you know, are the less well-disciplined ... much less well-disciplined ... even within the professions ... I think people do reflect their environment as well.

One may detect, at least in part, an underlying rationale for the above statement in the account revealed by CPM 5 (44). He suggested that, because of its size, the organization he works for is "driven by systems and procedures rather than personalities." He went on to suggest that individuals are not assessed on "emotional things", but instead on "fact and figures." CPM 4 (39) believed that someone who brings openly emotion into workplace will not get very far in construction. Overall, he believed that construction is "not very receptive ... (laughs) as an industry to emotional things really." In aggregate, however, this non-receptiveness to emotion appears to exclude the feelings of anger and frustration. In fact, many CPMs converged on the notion that anger and frustration are the most frequently experienced emotions at work. The degree to which some CPMs have experienced anger is conveyed in what CPM 14 (68) commented on this issue.

> There's times when ... there's been some incidents when I'll feel very upset, very angry, and that will ... affect me when certain things happen ... I think it's probably other people not giving things the same level of importance as I do, so then I feel that they should do, and then therefore I feel ... really the raw emotion is anger really, towards them.

Notable in the above excerpt was his reference to anger as a *raw* emotion, especially when others do not live up to his expectations. In this regard, breaches of health and safety regulations and noncompliance with promises rendered were frequently seen as catalysts giving rise to anger and frustration. For many CPMs, integrity and honesty were highly regarded characteristics.

The preceding quote is also indicative of how intimately emotion and thought are intertwined. In the aforementioned case, anger arose in response to an evaluation where others were considered to not comply with his expectations. Interestingly, some of the CPMs were quick to mention that anger, carefully dosed, was conducive to resolving a problem in their favor. They appeared to employ anger in a deliberate fashion after initial requests to carry out a certain task or highlighting their perspective on a particular issue did not yield desirable results for them. For instance, CPM 1 (62) was explicit in his approach to request a certain task to be executed, stating that he is habitually courteous with other people, but that he "comes down hard on them" if they fail to comply. Object lessons in this respect are proffered by CPM 5 (44) and 2 (32). As with other CPMs, there was a strong sense that they habitually regret using anger to resolve a problem, yet would readily do so because things get done this way. For instance, shouting and bawling was used by CPM 5 (44).

> We get certain contractors ... that are very arrogant, very brash, and they have to be perhaps dealt with a bit more firmly.... You have to meet their over-arrogance about their own performance in a different way really. It's no good being too gentle with them really.... There was a particular contractor that was actually doing brickwork for us, that wasn't really meeting their obligations and the best way to get, you know, them to improve, wasn't really to shout and bawl at them and enter into a row over it. But that's the way it became really.... But probably shouting and bawling isn't one of the most skilled ways, but might be appropriate at certain times.

Albeit admitting that his conduct may not be most appropriate way, he eventually used shouting and bawling in order to resolve the problem. CPM 2 (32) produced a remarkably similar account, though here intentionality is more conspicuous than in the previous quote.

> Not too long ago in a project meeting I had a rather emotional outbreak with the structural engineer, on the basis that they were trying to turn the tables contractually without any justification, and it had been going on for quite a while.... It was drawn to a conclusion with an emotional outburst, I'm afraid. Retrospectively did I regret it? Probably not, actually, because it resolved the matter.... The outburst was a decision that was made by myself, it wasn't emotionally uncontrolled, it was a controlled outburst. It came after a point when something had developed and wasn't moving on and had been discussed for a while ... I saw the outburst as bringing something to a conclusion beyond that of basic contractual discussion.

Noteworthy is his remark "I'm afraid" when reflecting upon the fact that it came to an emotional outburst, which he did *not* regret after all. Others put it more diplomatically, suggesting that they would 'raise their profiles' to lend more visibility to their presentation (CPM 13 (37)). Interestingly, during the feedback sessions, CPM 2 (32) suggested an informative extension to the above, saying that he "is forced by the culture to be tough", for otherwise he would be "run over." As a result, more benevolent or emphatic behaviors (e.g., "let the guys go earlier") would quickly incur him the reputation as being too soft. Therefore, such behaviors were seen as disadvantageous. CPM 18 (32) subscribes to the same notion, saying that on large projects he has to be stricter (and sometimes harsher) with his staff so that they "fly along with the project." Not only has one to be forceful with others occasionally (e.g.,

CPMs 6, 5, and 18), but also one has to appear stressed to be seen as productive (CPM 2 (32)). However, it would be simplistic to suggest that all CPMs felt the "anger" mechanism would always function and retain its influence. Cautionary words were expressed by some CPMs, which was most evident in the account of CPM 18 (32). After an incident on site made him feel very upset and swear at his operatives, he critically evaluated the potential consequences thereof.

> It worked, it had the response I was hoping it would, everybody went out onto site and what hadn't been addressed was actioned straight away, so all in all it worked. I think if that happened often, you know, if you were always speaking to people, swearing at people, eventually it would reach a point where it wouldn't have an effect. So if you use it every once in a while, I think it works.

It follows that, while he got things done after swearing at his operatives, he seemed to understand the limitation of this approach. It is safe to say that the previous example indicates some degree of reflection on his behavioral response to the situation described above. Also, instead of letting the anger roam unfettered without explanation, he believed that emotion attains maximum impact if the display thereof is coupled with an explanation as to why he feels like he did. Still, a predominant approach in the use of emotion was the recourse to anger or aggression toward other individuals or parties. This seemed especially fuelled by the need to attain goals in the fast-track nature of construction. After all, as CPM 19 (*44*) put it, "we've got all to deliver." CPM 12 (53) put it even more affirmatively in the feedback session, maintaining that "if we don't have a profit, we don't have a business. Full stop."

An almost complete absence of critical self-reflection became conspicuous in the interview with CPM 6 (*57*). Indeed, *prima facie* he appeared very aware of who is and how he comes across to others:

> I'm forceful but if I've been given a job to do, I've done it. That's how I am, that's my nature. You won't change me. And the director said that to me, a couple of days ago, he said, "I know you're hard, I don't want to change you, but just relax a bit. Can you come down a little bit?" ... I'm very forceful with people, people listen. When I go out, if one of my managers can't get something done out there, if I go out it gets done. You know, that's how I am.

He appears aware of being forceful with others, because he was told to come down by his director. And yet, he concurrently admits that no one is likely to change him. What cannot be said with certainty is whether he knows how others feel and think about him and cannot be bothered to change, or whether his professed awareness is simply an illusion. That is, a preferred mode of behaving that is internalized to such an extent that a questioning of its appropriateness does not seem necessary. Either way, it is less disputable that others expressed their concern about his forcefulness. This did not seem to affect the success he enjoyed with the projects under his supervision. The excerpt below gives expression to it.

> They're [the clients] happy with me on phase one, they give me phase two, they give me phase three, phase three, they give me section four or they give me this out here, [a project with a] value of a hundred and eighty odd million. (CPM 6 (57))

At the discretion of the client, he was repeatedly awarded a number of phases for a major project. This would seem to suggest that primacy is given to meeting the clients expectations (i.e. "they were happy with him"). True, his forcefulness is addressed as an issue of concern, but he appeared adamant in his attitude that no one can change him and, implicitly, knows that his way of conduct gets results. This view represented an extreme way of conduct, and was indeed not shared by all other CPMs. One, and only one CPM, specifically addressed the argument of conduct in construction. He elaborated the following:

> In this industry you've got to be very, very careful, not just what you say as a CPM, but how you conduct yourself and how you go about your business and how you talk to people. (CPM 3 (37))

It was instructive to see that so many CPMs emphasized the need to control their emotions at work vis-à-vis their admission that anger is relatively frequently used as means of drawing an issue to a conclusion. Many CPMs testified that they definitely had to restrain themselves during project meetings, be it due to an inappropriate or untrue comment or personality clashes. The context of such meetings was seen as an important factor. That is to say, in a meeting with a design team and clients the imperative to control emotion is higher than for a meeting with contractors. Arguing from many years of experience in construction, CPM 3 (37) described the seething feelings and the control thereof as follows:

> You just wanna rip these people in half sometimes, but you've got to bite your lip as well at the same time. So you've got to have a bit of passion about it.

During the interview it was sought to elicit CPMs' responses to situations where they got infuriated by an inappropriate comment by a colleague during a project meeting. It was again CPM 3 (37) who provided a most illuminating statement.

> Let the meeting finish, get them into the room, bollock 'em.... If they've said something that's out of order, ... that frustrated me or annoyed me so much, I would have to let them know where I lie on the subject of what they've done in that meeting. If they've embarrassed me or they've embarrassed the company ... and I've been there, and this has happened in the past, and the best way to deal with it is get that person in the office, shut the door and you can fucking well tell them, (laughs) all right.

As a result, in such situations, several CPMs admitted to have difficulties to regulate their anger. This would manifest itself as being very affirmative, though in most cases not below the level of decency (i.e., not swearing and insulting). In stark contrast, CPM 6 (57) was outspoken about a recent Health and Safety issue he witnessed and resolved on his site.

> I lost it on the subcontractors, and the site manager told them every time they went out they wasn't wearing safety helmets, they wasn't wearing eye protection and they wasn't wearing their gloves. So I went up there with him. I said, "Look, lad, put your helmets on." And this one, "Effing this, and effing that." I wasn't being awkward with him, I just wanted him to put his helmet on. So I lost it with him, didn't I, effing and blinding at me. So I lost it proper. "Get off that scaffold, get off this job now. If you don't get off that scaffold and go I'll have the police here to remove you." So what happened was I lost it with him, and it'd took us ages to get these people on site, this specialist company, and when he walked all of them walked, they were all in one car. So I lost the lot of them (laughs) and we had to start all over again. So, I did lose it then, I do at time to time. If someone's being awkward with me or having a go, I am like that.

What becomes apparent from the above is that the operative's failure to comply with the CPM's request to wear safety equipment triggered an intense response in him. Ultimately, this led to the departure of the entire specialist company, thus impacting on the project's progress (i.e., "we had to start all over again" (CPM (6)). While this situation, as a stand-alone incident, would indeed suggest that his lack of emotional control had detrimental consequences in the short-term for the project, his previous reference to being awarded repeat business worth several million pounds suggests that this obstacle did not prevent him in the past from satisfying the clients. However, some CPMs also understood that expressing anger is a directional issue. That is, they may express it to individual or contractual parties with lower power, but not with their line managers. This selective point is clearly conveyed in the words of CPM 19 (44). To quote:

> You've got to relate to people at their level.... You've gotta tailor your response to the audience that you're with.

Knee-jerk reactions of the kind describes above are incidents some CPMs were eager to avoid, asserting that they are not keen to be associated with them. Circumspection appeared to be of paramount importance for them, for an erratic and nondeliberate response was seen as unprofessional and not conducive. CPM 17 (40) expressed this as follows: "I wouldn't want to give the impression to anybody else in that design team or project team that I knee-jerk." Yet, the above accounts also suggest that such tendency may weaken under the immense pressure permeating construction.

DISCUSSION

In this chapter, I sought to highlight the conditions and circumstances under which the CPMs' use of anger can entail positive implications for them, and by extension, for the organization. In so doing, I addressed a research topic about which little empirical research is available in the extant literature. From the outset, I stressed the demarcation between the role and effects of emotion in individual decision-making tasks, where individuals are less subject to the constraints of their organizational environments, and those situations in which individual decision-making may effectively be impaired as a result of intense emotion (i.e., anger), but where the resultant behavior nevertheless yields desirable outcomes for them and their organization.

The accounts produced by CPMs were contextually rich and proffered an insight into the predominant behaviors they enact in order to succeed in the adverse working environment of construction, even though, as stated above, individual decision-making capacity can be impaired as a result of anger (Lerner & Tiedens, 2006). Rather, it is the short term nature of construction that penetrates the nature of social interaction and renders such a behavioral approach perhaps not publicly desirable, but practically expedient.

Foremost among the findings is that CPMs relatively quickly take recourse to anger to resolve an argument or gridlock in negotiations in their and hence their organization's favor (e.g. CPM 2 (32), 1 (62), and 18 (32)). Note that this pertains to situations involving contractual parties with lower power status (e.g., subcontractors). Recall further that the performance of men in construction is often assessed against criteria such as decisiveness and toughness (Loosemore & Galea, 2008), and that, from the CPMs own perspective, they are not primarily assessed in terms of their emotional skills, but in terms of demanding fact and figures. Several theoretical implications emerge as a result of this study, and they meaningfully inform our understanding of contextual leader effectiveness.

Implications for Theory

To highlight the contextual nature of subjective leader effectiveness discussed in this chapter, it is worth explicating anger in greater detail, especially why it can erupt so readily in the present context. Typically, anger is seen as an adaptive emotion, designed to ensure self-protection in periods of perceived threat or attack (Stanley & Burrows, 2001). These threats may not necessarily be outright lethal, but can be very much symbolic in nature, such as the threatened loss of self-esteem, projected self-image, or status (Stanley & Burrows, 2001). Therefore, on the more symbolic side, anger is often seen as an interference with achievement. Achievement—and, for that matter, progress—is of paramount importance in construction.[2] Note that several CPMs suggested in the feedback sessions that "blowing one's trumpet" (CPM 2 (32)) and showing off one's accomplishments is fairly habitual in construction. CPM 1 (62) put that rather bluntly, stating that his "CV is the best in the company."

It is worth laboring the soil in which the use of anger can be cultivated. On occasion, obstinate and passionate commitment to a particular course of action can turn into a fixation, regardless of consequences (Staw & Ross, 1989), and this can also imply sustaining a consistent image of oneself (Forgas, 1985). That is, in the case of CPMs, being seen as an achiever. Thus, any interference with achievement can be seen as a symbolic threat to losing ones "achiever image."

As mentioned earlier, the assessment of performance is often (1) based upon facts and figures and (2) occurs against particular stereotypes which constitute very specific social presentation needs for CPMs. In order to be seen as an effective CPM, they may have to display anger on occasion, perhaps even against their volition, to raise the visibility of their presentations and to preserve their achiever image. This may be further fuelled by the fast-track nature of construction, fierce competition, and the need to meet extreme short-term pressures of the project (Bryman, Bresnen, Ford, Beardworth, & Keil, 1987; Dainty et al., 2002).

Anger then, may be displayed as a result of three salient factors. First, the fear of losing one's reputation as an achiever seems distinct (i.e., negative reinforcement) and, as a result, the likelihood increases that an individual's behavior will recur to this effect (Arnold, Robertson, & Cooper, 1991). Second, it serves as a vehicle to engender results favorable to CPMs and their organizations, as some CPM explained (e.g., CPM 15 (57)) in the present analysis. Of course, this is a subjective view on leader effectiveness, but one reflected in several CPM accounts. Underlying this is a process whereby the meaning and priorities CPMs attach to the project are conveyed to both subordinates on site and other parties implicated in the construction process (e.g., subcontractors). Third, it is an integral tool for securing and sustaining those social presentation or impression management approaches so idiosyncratic to construction. As such, anger is often acted out through the prescriptions and demands of CPM roles. Thus, anger appears to be embedded in the occupational culture of construction and embraces a strategic function to be successful as a CPM (see also Fineman, 2004). Again, this argument does not indiscriminately apply across CPM interactions with members of staff or other contractual parties. The analysis indicates that operatives on site or subcontractors are more likely to feel the CPMs' anger than, for instance, the client. A bout of anger, for instance, helped CPM 18 (32) to motivate his operatives to execute the instructions they ignored prior.

It is, then, not surprising that anger is sometimes associated with stronger leadership (Bass & Stogdill, 1990). For instance, Tiedens (2001) ascertained in a series of experiments that those expressing anger enjoy higher status conferral and are seen as more competent by others. In addition, Antonakis (2003) seriously doubts whether an emotional outburst is detrimental to leader effectiveness. On the contrary, he posits that emotional outbursts can be conducive if timing and dosage are appropriate, though he also remarks that this only applies "as long as these emotions reflect collective sentiments and moral aspirations (p. 359). However, examples from negotiation studies further demonstrate the positive effects of anger. Van Kleef, De Dreu, and Manstead (2004) found that a negotiator who faces an angry counterpart is more likely to concede than a negotiator who faces a happy counterpart. Akin to the high-pressure environment in construction and the direction of anger downward in power relationships detailed in the textual analysis, van Kleef et al.'s (2004) experimental study occurred under high time pressure and when the negotiator who faced the angry counterpart had lower power. Recall that the analysis suggests that emotional responses have to be tailored to the audience at hand, and that being angry toward a line manager or client is seen as disadvantageous.

Linking the present analysis with the above empirical findings, therefore, distinctly suggests the preeminent role of anger in attaining desirable outcomes in the context of construction. In consideration of such synthesis, the argument that the display of anger suggests lack of emotional regulation and is persistently associated with leader *ineffectiveness*, as maintained by popular as well more scientifically-inclined writers (Goleman, 1998; Prati, Douglas, Ferris, Ammeter, & Buckley, 2003), becomes a rather indefensible position. Instead of regarding anger as *role-violating* behavior (Lewis, 2000), it seems that it is a *role-obligatory* behavior of CPMs, crucially important for leader effectiveness in decisive and defining moments of the project. In effect, it is intimately entwined with the roles CPMs perform within the intricate and fragmented process on project sites. Therefore, Lewis's suggestion that "in a specific organizational context, choosing *appropriate* emotions to express reflects a leader's ability to respond in an effective way" (p. 222, italics for emphasis) appears correct.

We may, on the other hand, not forget to construe the above discussion in light of the earlier reference to the accumulation of physiological costs, both for CPMs themselves and their subordinates. It is widely known that the role of a CPM is one of the most stressful functions in the building process (Djebarni, 1996). High turnover intention in construction may be a testament to this effect (Lingard, 2003).

Thus, despite the significant contribution of this study to our understanding of contextual leadership effectiveness, one unequivocal limitation remains; it does only provide a snapshot account of CPMs' experience in relation to how they use their emotion. As a result, future research would benefit from a longitudinal design, where both CPMs and their subordinates are incorporated as sources of data (e.g., semistructured interviews), so as to be able to evaluate both sides of the story. Such design could be complemented with what is called event-sampling or experience sampling (e.g., Miner, Glomb, & Hulin, 2005), where individuals (both CPMs and team members) record at specified or random times their emotion, mood and behavior. Upon completion of such study, the data could be examined with a view to better understand how the display of certain emotions affects those to whom they are directed as well as those who display it—and any resultant emotion cycles that may result from that interaction (see Hareli & Rafaeli, 2008).

CONCLUSION

Brief and Weiss's (2002) observed that we do not know enough about the specific features of work environments that help produce particular emotion. From there, this study provides scholars and practitioners in the realm of leadership research with instructive evidence to better understand, from the CPMs' own lived experiences, the positive influence of anger in the leadership process and how it fosters desirable outcomes at work. True, scholars have compiled a great deal of evidence demonstrating that feeling and expressing positive affect is crucial to success both in organizations and life (see Barsade & Gibson, 2007, for a review). Nevertheless, especially in conjunction with other empirical findings, this study strongly suggests that positive emotion is one part of the overall formula of leader effectiveness—it appears insufficient to provide an accurate estimate of how leaders can be effective across contexts and situations.

NOTES

1. Therefore, the reference to negative emotion in the title is primarily illustrative to highlight the purpose of this chapter.
2. Any delay in the progress of projects can spell disaster for the organization. Several CPMs concurred that the penalty systems in place for missing targets can spell disaster for a company. For instance, if a project is handed over late by a week, liquidated damages for the additional period can be considerable. The purpose of liquidated damages is to agree in advance what should be paid by the contractor to the client in the event that construction works overrun. One CPM provided the example of £70,000 ($113.000) in liquidated damages per week for a recent project.

ACKNOWLEDGMENTS

I would like to thank Effi Raftopoulou, Catherine Cassell, and the two reviewers for their most insightful comments on an earlier draft of this chapter. This research project has been supported by studentships from Manchester Business School and the Economic Social Research Council (+3), as well as grants from the Statistical Society of Manchester and the Northern Leadership Academy (all United Kingdom).

REFERENCES

Antonakis, J. (2003). Why "Emotional Intelligence" does not predict leadership effectiveness: A comment on Prati, Douglas, Ferris, Ammeter, and Buckley (2003). *International Journal of Organizational Analysis, 11*(4), 355-361.

Arnold, J., Robertson, I. T., & Cooper, C. L. (1991). *Work psychology: Understanding human behaviour in the workplace*. London, England: Pitman.

Barsade, S. G., & Gibson, D. E. (2007). Why does affect matter in organizations? *Academy of Management Perspectives, 21*(1), 36-59.

Bass, B. M., & Stogdill, R. M. (1990). *Bass & Stogdill's handbook of leadership: Theory, research, and managerial applications*. New York: Free Press.

Bono, J. E., & Ilies, R. (2006). Charisma, positive emotions and mood contagion. *Leadership Quarterly, 17*, 317–334.

Brief, A. P., & Weiss, H. M. (2002). Organizational behaviour: Affect in the Workplace. *Annual Review of Psychology, 53*(1), 279-307.

Bryman, A. (2004). *Social research methods* (3 ed.). Oxford, England: Oxford University Press.

Bryman, A., Bresnen, M., Ford, J., Beardworth, A., & Keil, T. (1987). Leader orientation and organisational transcience. *Journal of Occupational Psychology, 60*(1), 15-19.

Butler, C. J., & Chinowsky, P. S. (2006). Emotional intelligence and leadership behavior in construction executives. *Journal of Management in Engineering, 22*(3), 119-125.

Dainty, A. R. J., Bryman, A., & Price, A. D. F. (2002). Empowerment within the UK construction sector. *Leadership & Organization Development Journal, 23*(6), 333-342.

Dainty, A. R. J., Cheng, M. I., & Moore, D. R. (2004). A competency-based performance model for construction project managers. *Construction Management and Economics, 22*(8) 877-886.

De Sousa, R. (1987). The rationality of emotion. Cambridge, MA: MIT Press.

Dey, I. (1993). *Qualitative data analysis: A user-friendly guide for social scientists*. London, England: Routledge.

Djebarni, R. (1996). The impact of stress in site management effectiveness. *Construction Management & Economics, 14*(4), 281-293.

Domagalski, T. A. (1999). Emotion in organizations: Main currents. *Human Relations, 52*(6), 833-852.

Dulaimi, M. F., & Langford, D. (1999). Job behaviour of construction project mangers: Determinants and assessment. *Journal of Construction Engineering and Management, 125,* 256-264.

Fielden, S. L., Davidson, M. J., Gale, A. G., & Davey, C. L. (2000). Women in construction: the untapped resource. *Construction Management & Economics, 18*(1), 113-121.

Fineman, S. (2004). Getting the measure of emotion—and the Cautionary Tale of Emotional Intelligence. *Human Relations, 57*(6), 719-740.

Fitness, J. (2008). Fear and loathing in the workplace. In N. M. Ashkanasy & C. L. Cooper (Eds.), *Research companion to emotion in organizations* (pp. 61-72). Cheltenham, England: Edward Elgar.

Forgas, J. P. (1985). *Interpersonal behaviour: The psychology of social interaction*. Oxford, England: Pergamon Press.

Frijda, N. (2007). *The laws of emotion*. Mahwah, NJ: Erlbaum.

George, J. M. (1996). Group affective tone. In M. West (Ed.), *Handbook of Work Group Psychology.* Sussex, England: Wiley.

George, J. M. (2000). Emotions and leadership: The role of emotional intelligence. *Human Relations, 53*(8), 1027-1055

Goldenhar, L. M., Hecker, S., Moir, S., & Rosecrance J. (2003). The "Goldilocks model" of overtime in construction: not too much, not too little, but just right. *Journal of safety research, 34*(2), 215-226.

Goleman, D. (1998). *Working with emotional Intelligence*. London, England: Bloomsbury.

Hareli, S., & Rafaeli, A. (2008). Emotion cycles: On the social influence of emotion in organizations. *Research in Organizational Behavior, 8,* 35-59.

Harris, F., & McCaffer, R. (2001). Modern construction management. Oxford, England: Blackwell Science.

Holt, G. D., Love, P. E. D., & Nesan, L. J. (2000). Employee empowerment in construction: an implementation model for process improvement. *Team Performance Management: An International Journal, 6*(3/4), 47-51.

Lewis, K. M. (2000). When leaders display emotion: how followers respond to negative emotional expression of male and female leaders. *Journal of Organizational Behavior, 21*(2), 221-234.

Lerner, J. S., & Tiedens L. Z. (2006). Portrait of the angry decision maker: How appraisal tendencies shape anger's influence on cognition. *Journal of Behavioral Decision Making, 19,* 115-137.

Lingard, H. (2003). The impact of individual and job characteristics on "burnout" among civil engineers in Australia and the implications for employee turnover. *Construction Management and Economics, 21*(1), 69-80.

Loosemore, M., & Galea, N. (2008). Genderlect and conflict in the Australian construction industry. *Construction Management and Economics, 26*(2), 125-135.

Loosemore, M., Dainty, A., & Lingard, H. (2003). *Human resource management in construction projects: Strategic and operational approaches*. London, England: Taylor & Francis.

Mayer, J. D., & Salovey, P. (1997). What is emotional intelligence? In P. Salovey & D. Sluyter (Eds.), *Emotional development and emotional intelligence: Implications for educators* (pp. 3-31). New York: Basic Books.

Miner, A. G., Glomb, T. M., & Hulin, C. (2005). Experience sampling mood and its correlates at work. *Journal of Occupational & Organizational Psychology, 78*(2), 171-193.

Naoum, S. G. (2001). *People and organizational management in construction*. London, England: Thomas Telford Books.

Office of the Deputy Prime Minister. (2004). *The Egan Review: Skills for Sustainable communities*. London: Author.

Parkin, W. (1993). The public and the private: Gender, sexuality and emotion. In S. Fineman (Ed.), *Emotion in organizations* (pp. 167-189). London, England: SAGE.

Prati, M., Douglas, C., Ferris, G. R., Ammeter, A. P., & Buckley, M. R. (2003). Emotional intelligence, leadership effectiveness, and team outcomes. *The International Journal of Organizational Analysis, 11*, 21-40.

Sandberg, J. (2005). How do we justify knowledge produced within interpretive approaches? *Organizational Research Methods, 8*(2), 41-68.

Smithers, G. L., & Walker, D. H. T. (2000). The effect of the workplace on motivation and demotivation of construction professionals. *Construction Management & Economics, 18*(7), 833-841.

Smyth, H. (2000). *Marketing and selling construction services*. Oxford, England: Blackwell Science.

Solomon, R. (1993). *The passions: emotions and the meaning of life.* Indianapolis, IN: Hackett.

Stanley, R. O., & Burrows, G. D. (2001). Varieties and functions of human emotion. In R. Payne & C. L. Cooper (Eds.), *Emotions at work: Theory, research, and application for management* (pp. 3-19). Chichester, England: Wiley.

Starratt, A., & Grandy, G. (2008). Young workers' experiences of abusive leadership: A grounded theory approach. *Conference Proceedings of the British Academy of Management (BAM) Conference in Harrogate, 9-11 September.*

Staw, B. M., & Ross, J. (1989). Understanding behavior in escalation situations. *Science, 246*(4927), 216-220.

Steptoe, A., Cropley, M, Griffith, J., & Kirschbaum, C. (2000). Job strain and anger expression predict early morning elevations in salivary cortisol. *Psychosomatic Medicine, 62*, 286-292.

Sy, T., Côté, S., & Saavedra, R. (2005). The contagious leader: Impact of the leader's mood on the mood of group members, group affective tone, and group processes. *Journal of Applied Psychology, 90*(2), 295-305.

Tiedens, L. Z. (2001). Anger and advancement versus sadness and subjugation: The effect of negative emotion expressions on social status conferral. *Journal of Personality and Social Psychology, 80*(1), 86-94.

Toor, S. R., & Ofori, G. (2008). Leadership for future construction industry: Agenda for authentic leadership. *International Journal of Project Management, 26*(6), 620-630.

van Kleef, G. A., De Dreu, C. K. W., & Manstead, A. S. R. (2004). The interpersonal effects of anger and happiness in negotiations: A motivated information processing approach. *Journal of Personality and Social Psychology, 87*(4), 510-528.

Zeelenberg, M., Nelissen, R., M.A., Breugelmans, S., H., & Pieters, R. (2008). On emotion specificity in decision making: Why feeling is for doing. *Judgment and Decision Making, 3*(1), 18-27.

PART III

TOXIC LEADERSHIP, NARCISSISM, AND (UN)ETHICAL LEADERSHIP

CHAPTER 10

THE CORPORATE REFLECTING POOL

Antecedents and Consequences of Narcissism in Executives

Dean B. McFarlin and Paul D. Sweeney

When leadership goes wrong in an organization, it's important to understand why that occurs and what can or should be done about it. As illustrated by the previous chapters, there are many types of bad leadership. In our chapter, we focus on narcissistic leadership. Excessive narcissism is characterized by a profound sense of importance, the pursuit of grandiose fantasies, a preoccupation with attention and an unwillingness or inability to consider the perspective of others, among other things. At the same time, narcissists can be charming and charismatic, at least for a time. We review a growing body of empirical literature has taken this person-based and clinical focus and placed it squarely in a work and interpersonal setting. We begin by exploring the roots of excessive narcissism, including personal and situational antecedents. Next, we assess the state of the art when it comes to research on narcissism, especially in corporate leadership and any impact on employee, company, and firm performance. Finally, we present steps that firms can take to reduce the odds of hiring narcissistic executives as well as

When Leadership Goes Wrong: Destructive Leadership, Mistakes and Ethical Failures, pp. 247–283

minimize the damage caused by narcissists already in leadership ranks. This includes our effort to extend the research into specific actions that can be taken by organizations and individuals alike to deal with narcissism.

INTRODUCTION

Leadership will always be the subject of intense study. Already one of the most researched topics in all of social science, a recent search for leadership-related articles in a popular business research database generated over 80,000 "hits" since 1980. If your interests turn more toward the popular, then you could scan through the roughly 20,000 titles that Barnes and Noble now has for sale on leadership. Clearly, people want to know what makes leaders tick. And many, particularly in the business world, want to become better leaders—someone with the bold visions, strategic insights, and motivational talents that produce corporate as well as personal success.

Indeed, much of the popular literature on leadership has a "how to" or "here's how I did it" quality to it, with advice distilled down into the all-too-familiar sets of "10 laws," "20 principles," or "5 secrets" for successful leadership. These approaches tend to be relentlessly positive, which clearly strikes a chord with many people—apparently even Atilla the Hun was "up tone" about leadership (Roberts, 1990).

Yet an irony is that for many employees their superiors do anything but lead. Many employees feel their bosses are focused on personal agendas, if not personal enrichment—often at the expense of organizational success. This can help explain why large numbers of employees report that they have had a "bad" boss in their career and why the direct supervisor is a pernicious and consistent cause of employee stress and turnover (Hogan, Raskin, & Fazzini, 1990, 1994; McFarlin & Sweeney, 2002). Hogan et al. (1990), for example, estimate that the prevailing rate of leader incompetence approaches 70%!

Why Study Narcissistic Leaders?

Today, some might feel that 70% figure is too low. A global economic crisis is staring us in the face, driven, at least in part, by hubris and greed among executives who apparently didn't know what they were doing. In the process, business leadership has been knocked off its high horse. Look at the numbers. Trust in corporations and in anything CEOs say has dropped precipitously between the end of 2007 and the end of 2008, especially in the United States. According to one recent survey, by December 2008 only 17% of some 4,500 college-educated Americans reported that they trusted corporate CEOs as credible sources of information. Put simply, attitudes toward corporate leadership in the United States are at all time lows, Enron and the dot-com bust of several years ago notwithstanding (Edelman, 2009).

Those earlier scandals also remind us that we've been through this before, with spasms of executive greed, indulgence, and corrosive abuse of power periodically provoking outrage before dying down again (Lipman-Blumen, 2005). Today, the popular press is again full of articles fulminating about the risks to companies and employees of projecting too much charisma, infallibility, dependence, wisdom—you name it—onto senior executives (cf. Schopen, 2009).

Consequently, this is an opportunity to more closely examine bad leadership in corporations—to understand why it occurs, when it occurs, and what can or should be done about it. Of course, there are many types of bad bosses. But we focus in this chapter on narcissistic leadership—a phenomenon that is especially pernicious. Excessive narcissism is characterized by, among other things, disproportionate self-focus, the pursuit of grandiose fantasies, and the need to project power and dominance. This is especially dangerous when combined with the apparent charm and charisma that many narcissistic leaders project—something that attracts followers. But, they are also preoccupied with getting attention and are unwilling or unable to consider the perspectives of others. Their profound sense of importance goes hand in hand with feelings of entitlement. They appear to have high esteem, but it is either a façade or built on a weak foundation. As a result, narcissistic individuals feel vulnerable underneath their positive veneers and are constantly on guard: they dismiss feedback, externalize blame, and can turn aggressively on those who challenge them. Consider the corporate leader who is excessively narcissistic—he or she can literally ride the company off the tracks into oblivion, blaming and abusing employees who offer criticisms or who otherwise get in the way of their flawed visions and overwhelming feelings of entitlement (McFarlin & Sweeney, 2002).

Based on this description, it is tempting to disparage any attention given to narcissistic leaders in business as narrow, misplaced, and nonscientific—better treated by psychotherapists than serious social scientists. We disagree with this view. Of all the types of "bad bosses" we are interested in narcissists for three reasons. First, narcissism is not narrowly confined to a few isolated individuals. Narcissism seems to be common, if not replete, in senior executive ranks—the literature is full of examples of narcissistic leaders in corporations. Indeed, narcissism is more common and more difficult to extinguish than one might expect (McFarlin &

Sweeney, 2002). In one study of a large fortune 500 company, it was estimated that about half of management was inept (Millikin-Davies, 1992, as cited in Hogan et al., 1990). Among the most common complaints was that these managers tyrannized their subordinates and stole their ideas. These behaviors are commonly associated with narcissism in the literature (McFarlin & Sweeney, 2002).

Second, it is important not to underestimate the potential negative impact of narcissism in the executive ranks of today's organizations. While it is true that the behavior of executives is constrained by many factors inside and out of the firm, studies show that senior leaders still have a good deal of latitude for their strategic choices—let alone their treatment of others (Finkelstein, Hambrick, & Cannella, 2009). And latitude attracts narcissistic managers to do what they do best—serve their personal needs for attention and control. Interest in narcissism is not misplaced—if anything, it may be underemphasized.

Third, attention to executive narcissism has grown dramatically among social scientists and the boundaries of our understanding have expanded considerably, especially in the last decade. We know, for example, that it is important to not only understand a narcissistic leader's tendencies and styles, but also the organizational conditions under which narcissism flourishes. Recent work on narcissism reflects individual difference variables as well as contextual factors—research that shares much of the contingency-oriented approach found in the broader literature on leadership, motivation, decision-making and related topics (e.g., Morf & Rhodewalt, 2001).

Chapter Preview

We begin by exploring the roots of excessive narcissism, including both dispositional and situational antecedents. Next, we assess the state of the art when it comes to research on narcissism, especially in corporate leadership. What are the behavioral consequences of narcissism and what impact does it have on employee, company, and firm performance? Finally, we present steps that firms can take to reduce the odds of hiring narcissistic executives as well as minimize the damage caused by any narcissistic leaders already in the workforce. In addressing this last point, we try to extend research into specific actions that can be taken by organizations and individuals dealing with narcissism.

DEFINING NARCISSISM AND ITS ANTECEDENTS

Narcissism is essentially a personality trait—one that, as it increases in intensity, can produce attributes that have negative impacts on others. For narcissistic individuals, life is "an arena" in which they strive for admiration, success, and status. And when narcissistic people engage in reality distortion to protect their overblown self-images, pursue grandiose plans for success, and attack or abuse anyone who dares to challenge them, the results—especially when they hold executive roles—are typically destructive (Campbell, Bush, Brunell, & Shelton, 2005).

The mythical figure Narcissus fell in love with his own beautiful reflection in a pool of water and was unable to stop gazing at his image before wasting away. This extreme example aside, having some level of self-love helps us attend to our own legitimate needs in a variety of areas (Kets de Vries, 1995). Without some level of self-focus, we would not get out of bed in the morning. Indeed, narcissism exists on a continuum—from functional to problematic. Some, such as Kets de Vries and Miller (1985), suggest that there may be thresholds in the continuum of narcissism that could serve as demarcation points defining the "healthy" and "unhealthy" narcissist. The metaphor of a race car captures this idea—up to a point speed wins races. But past a certain point, the driver loses control—too much speed kills. Likewise, executives who can harness or limit their narcissism may achieve positive results, but those who cannot may destroy their companies and wreak havoc with employees in the process.

In this chapter, our focus is on excessive levels of narcissism. Yes, there is arguably a level of hubris that is productive, if not essential, for senior corporate leaders—a "healthy" narcissism that produces confident, bold executives who can inspire based on visions that have been thought through rather than reflect grandiose flights of fancy. These executives have real confidence and have the ability to be empathetic as well as introspective (Kets de Vries, 1995). But an analysis of many ineffective corporate leaders suggests that they have crossed the proverbial line—that their problems were rooted in excessive narcissistic tendencies which produced counterproductive behaviors, a lack of integrity, and ultimately, failure (Allio, 2007; Rosenthal & Pittinsky, 2006).

The roots of narcissism are complex and have been discussed and debated in the clinical psychology literature for decades. Some experts argue that narcissism has a genetic component. Others suggest that parenting styles play a major role in the development of narcissistic adults (Kets de Vries, 1995). For them, narcissism in adulthood is a reaction to parents who were conditional in their affection and approach. Some experts have suggested that parents who were aloof or who offered children excessive praise can foster the development of narcissistic personality traits (Kets de Vries, 1995; Otway & Vignoles, 2006; Vogel, 2006). The broader point is that parenting practices may sow the seeds of self-doubt and rage, with narcissistic tendencies developing to protect the individual from resulting insecurities. These tendencies to pursue grandiose fantasies combined with the need to exert dominance over others, both protects the self and provides an outlet for pent-up rage and hostility toward parents. In turn, these twin needs then become self-fulfilling prophecies which feed and strengthen the inflated self-images held by narcissists (Kets de Vries & Miller, 1985; Morf & Rhodewalt, 2001).

This pattern also acts to strengthen behaviors that keep personal fantasies going (e.g., exhibitionism, excessive impression management and attention-seeking, flawed visions). It also helps maintain the dominance that narcissists often crave by ruthlessly exploiting, manipulating, and raging at those around them, especially when challenged. In this way, they avoid facing their inner demons and craft a façade of infallibility, superiority, and entitled self-importance for the world around them to see and applaud. Indeed, given their closeted insecurities, narcissistic individuals constantly crave adoration because of their inner fragility. Moreover, that fragility prompts obsession with slights, criticism, or negative feedback, real or imagined—anything that may compromise their crafted self-images will be ferociously attacked, further reinforcing dominance needs (see Bogart, Benotsch, & Pavlovic, 2004; Kets de Vries, 1995; Morf & Rhodewalt, 2001; Wallace & Baumeister, 2002).

WHAT WE KNOW ABOUT NARCISSISM IN MANAGEMENT

As we have just noted, the narcissism concept originated in the clinical literature (cf. Otway & Vignoles, 2006), but yet took roots in other, more empirical fields. Narcissism among managers, especially those in the executive suite, has been subject to systematic study for at least 25 years, with Kets de Vries being a leading early example of someone whose work has continued to have an impact (e.g., Kets de Vries & Miller, 1985; Kets de Vries, 1995). And, the study of narcissism has increasing momentum among researchers in the organizational sciences, perhaps in response to recent executive excesses. As a result, our knowledge about the effects of narcissism in the workplace has expanded considerably. In this chapter, we will examine this work, focusing on that which might translate more directly into the workplace and employee relations with management. Specifically, we will discuss research on (a) the characteristics of narcissists, including measurement and identification issues; (b) the consequences of narcissism on the workforce; and (c) the performance of narcissistic managers. In the process, we will also examine some contextual factors (e.g., role of followers, organizational features) that might exacerbate or buffer the negative effects of excessive narcissism. We will finish with a section on dealing with the narcissist and their effects in an organization.

Personal Characteristics of Narcissists

To unambiguously determine the effects of narcissism, we must be able to measure the construct and accurately identify individuals. We turn our attention to this topic first before reviewing research on specific characteristics of narcissists.

Pinpointing Narcissism

Narcissists can be difficult to identify in organizations, especially without extended interaction. Indeed, holding aside the ample negatives of the narcissist that become clearer over repeated interactions (Hogan & Kaiser, 2005; Paulhus, 1998), brief encounters with narcissistic leaders can sometimes be pleasant experiences. After all, narcissism involves projecting a positive view of the self—and people can find such confidence attractive (Campbell, Rudich, & Sdeikides, 2002; John & Robins, 1994; Rhodewalt & Morf, 1995). Plus, narcissism is also linked with extroversion —narcissistic leaders can be exciting, charming, and engaging. They are also said to be bold and decisive—traits many are drawn to (Deluga, 1997; Paulhus, 1998).

As a result, identifying narcissistic leaders can prove challenging, as can convincing others who only view the leader from a narrow or distant perspective. In fact, distant observers may only see the narcissistic leaders' positives and attribute the problems that a close subordinate perceives to the subordinate's own foibles (McFarlin & Sweeney, 2002). Moreover, the positive features many narcissistic leaders possess, at least on the surface, often help them rise to prominent positions (Finkelstein et al., 2009). And, once there, narcissists may rate themselves higher in leader effectiveness as well as receive higher ratings of effectiveness from others (Paulhus, 1998). While this assessment from others may well dissipate over time, especially as narcissistic leaders' weaknesses become more apparent, it underscores why many of us should expect to run into, if not work for, a narcissistic leader at some point in our careers. In short, narcissistic people frequently find their way into senior management positions and are adept at staying there.

Are there Narcissistic Subtypes?

We just noted that many narcissistic people display positive or at least apparently positive behaviors. And given the right circumstances, these attributes and behaviors might be seen as very useful to organizations. This would make it very difficult for organizations to take preventative measures against harmful effects of narcissistic leadership. For example, Khurana (2002) claims that troubled companies tend to look for narcissistic "saviors" to lead their turnaround efforts. In these situations, employees often prefer visible leaders who take bold and decisive action—again characteristic of many narcissistic personalities. Leaders displaying such behavior have been called "productive" narcissists (Maccoby, 2000), or "constructive" narcissists (Kets de Vries & Miller, 1985).[1]

Making distinctions among various "types" of narcissism is appealing, but this notion has not been clearly established empirically. Most contemporary research on narcissism uses a scale to pre-identify individuals and then studies their reactions to or behavior with others. Development and use of the Narcissistic Personality Inventory (NPI) scale, the most commonly used instrument, has brought the study of the concept from solely a clinical disorder to a personality dimension on which individuals are assigned scores (see Emmons, 1984; Raskin & Hall, 1979). Research provides extensive support for the psychometric quality of this scale, including among nonclinical populations (e.g., Corry, Merritt, Mrug, & Pamp, 2008; Emmons, 1984; Emmons, 1987; Raskin & Terry, 1988) and this scale has fostered a great deal of new research, much in the social psychology and organizational science areas.

Nevertheless, this research has essentially sidestepped the issue of narcissistic types, preferring instead to look at (linear) associations of NPI scores with various dependent variables. If Kets de Vries and Miller (1985) and others are correct, then there may be thresholds in the distribution of narcissism scores that could serve as demarcation points defining the "healthy" and "unhealthy" narcissist. But those demarcation points are ambiguous, especially since narcissism has usually been treated as a personality dimension on a continuum. Only a few studies have examined such nonlinear effects and those were generally not supportive of different types of narcissism, much less their differential effects.

Chatterjee and Hambrick (2007), for example, did *not* find nonlinear effects of narcissism in their study of CEO decision making and performance. This is an important finding because the argument that only a subset of narcissists has the unique mix of qualities that make them "productive" or "healthy" was not supported. Instead, their data showed that the full range of narcissism was associated with impacts on their dependent variables. We must be cautious about drawing too many conclusions from Chatterjee and Hambrick's findings—especially since so few studies have tested for nonlinear effects of narcissism. That said, we are aware of only three studies that have tested for "threshold effects" of narcissism—and none have found supportive results (i.e., Chatterjee & Hambrick, 2007; Sedikides, Rudich, Gregg, Kumashiro, & Rusbult, 2004; Zuckerman & O'Laughlin, 2008).

We recommend that future researchers embrace more non-linear tests and do more to address what we feel are definition problems in the narcissism literature. For instance, Rosenthal and Pittinsky (2006) alert us to the fact that it is sometimes hard to know where narcissism begins and ends. Some authors include confidence and assertiveness in their definition of narcissism, while also claiming narcissists can be thoughtful when dealing with others, realistic, and able to laugh at themselves (see Kets de Vries & Miller, 1985; Maccoby, 2000). Yet some might argue that these latter characteristics (e.g., thoughtful, etc.) should *exclude* someone being considered excessively narcissistic (Rosenthal & Pittinsky, 2006).

In fact, we would make that argument ourselves. However, there is little doubt that narcissism is associated with projected confidence and high self-regard—something we will discuss in more detail later. For now, we note that self-esteem—even if that is fragile or unstable—is regularly associated with narcissism. We located over 65 separate studies of this relationship and found a weighted average correlation of .29 between the two constructs.[2] Many of these studies also found that narcissism had an impact on interpersonal reactions and performance after self-esteem was statistically controlled. Likewise the impact of narcissism did not go from good to bad as one might predict from the "distinct type" hypothesis.

In short, while narcissists may have some appealing features such as projecting self-confidence, those features often help them maintain their narcissistic self-views (Morf & Baumeister, 2001). So far there is relatively little evidence of "healthy" and "unhealthy" types of narcissism. It is possible that the set of features they possess could be advantageous in some situations—thereby appearing "healthy."[3] But situations change—sometimes rapidly, with those "healthy" advantages quickly becoming liabilities (Chatterjee & Hambrick, 2007; Paulhus, 1998).

Another empirical approach to identify distinct types of narcissism—possibly including "healthy/unhealthy" or "productive/unproductive"—is to examine the multidimensionality of the construct. Emmons (1984) was among the first to do so using the NPI scale, finding four distinct factors—*entitlement/exploitativeness* (e.g., "I'll never be satisfied until I get all that I deserve"), *leadership/authority* ("I have a natural talent for influencing other people"), *superiority/arrogance* ("I am a born leader") and *self-absorption/admiration* ("I think I am a special person"). These four factors were moderately correlated with one another. Distinctive in the study were the correlations of narcissism with abasement and aggression toward others, dominance and exhibitionism. Scores were also highly correlated with self-monitoring tendencies and social anxiety. The only positive or productive dimensions associated with narcissism were self-esteem and extroversion. Narcissism was also negatively correlated with self-ideal discrepancy. Apparently, narcissists are happy with the way they are and see little room for improvement (see also Emmons, 1987; Raskin & Terry, 1988; Rhodewalt & Morf, 1995). Self-esteem aside, a somewhat negative overall picture of narcissists is painted, without a great deal of upside. All in all, while interesting, the work of Emmons and others on the multidimensionality of narcissism doesn't really provide clear evidence of "types" of narcissistic personalities.

That said, more recent research has provided stronger evidence for a two-factor structure (Corry et al., 2008; Kubarych, Deary, & Austin, 2004). Kubarych et al. found support for the first two factors identified by Emmons (1984, 1987), a finding that was replicated by Corry et al. Both studies found that these factors of Leadership/Authority and Entitlement/Exhibitionism were highly correlated. Each factor was positively associated with extroversion, was negatively correlated with agreeableness, and was unrelated to openness to experience. The Leadership/Authority factor also correlated negatively with neuroticism and positively with conscientiousness ("I work hard to accomplish my goals"). While both factors predicted some positive personality features and revealed some negative ones, the factors acted similarly on these other constructs (see also Brunell, Gentry, Campbell, Hoffman, Kuhnert, & DeMarree, 2008; Judge, LePine, & Rich, 2006; and others).

Once again, this is evidence that increasing levels of narcissism are associated with negative features (e.g., lack of agreeableness) as well as some positive features (e.g., self-esteem, extroversion). But this leaves us with little empirical evidence for two distinct types of narcissism (for an exception, see Rhodwalt & Morf, 1995—where both narcissism factors were highly correlated but produce some different effects).

Some have suggested our inability to detect narcissistic subtypes is limited because most studies focus on "normal" narcissists. In other words, examining more extreme or pathological levels of narcissism would allow possible subtype effects to emerge more clearly. Yet Buss and Chiodo (1991) found that narcissistic acts in the everyday life of students corresponded well to the seven elements used by the DSM-III-R manual to define clinical levels of narcissism. These, in turn, tended to correlate with scores on the NPI scale used in most published research. In short, narcissism may well have adaptive and maladaptive aspects that co-occur and vary in intensity, as any one-dimensional trait might (Rhodewalt & Morf, 1995). Moreover, a given context may determine whether an individual's narcissistic behaviors and tendencies pay dividends or not—at least in the short term. We can also envision specific circumstances where some narcissistic attributes may appear to help (e.g., extroversion when starting a new executive role) and other circumstances where different attributes could prove useful initially (e.g., extreme assertiveness, single-mindedness, and a sense of superiority may help enact change quickly in a crisis).

In essence, we are saying that a different set of narcissistic types may exist. A related possibility is that subtypes are blurred because of the intersection between behavioral tendencies and the situation that narcissists find themselves in. Helpful behaviors in one context might be harmful in another. Moreover, the impact of those behaviors could vary over time—starting out helpful but becoming increasingly toxic, particularly as circumstances change. For now, however, we have relatively little evidence for separate types of narcissists—either because we need more sophisticated research or because the notion of a "healthy" and "unhealthy" narcissist is simply not viable.

Characteristics Associated With Narcissism

As just illustrated, there are plenty of studies addressing the personal characteristics associated with narcissism, with many relying on student samples (see summaries by Rhodewalt & Morf, 1995; Morf & Rhodewalt, 2001). We will not review all of these here, focusing instead on work that can generalize to leaders and followers in organizational settings.

In short, research shows that narcissists think a lot of themselves, a view that's not completely shared by others. And, as noted, narcissism is correlated with self-esteem and extroversion across large number of studies (see Brunell et al., 2008; Rhodewalt & Morf, 1995; others). Narcissists are often socially skilled individuals, especially at initiating relationships, during which others find them entertaining, warm, and interesting during those early (but not later) encounters.

In an interesting study, Paulhus (1998) had subjects interact with others in a group setting for only 20 minutes. Peer ratings of outgoingness, happiness and adjustment—among others—were significantly related to narcissism scores. Apparently, however, narcissists can convey an initial positive impression in even less time. Oltmanns, Friedman, Fiedler, and Turkheimer (2004) took 30 second videos of Air Force recruits' answers to the simple question "what do you like doing?" Later, a set of observers rated the degree of likableness and attractiveness of their personality. Ratings of these "thin slices" slices of behavior were significantly correlated with recruits' narcissism scores.

To convey a positive impression quickly, narcissists rely on their apparent self-confidence (Farwell & Wohlwend-Lloyd, 1998; John & Robins, 1994; Judge et al., 2006), sometimes—particularly in task domains—to the point of being objectively overconfident (Campbell, Goodie, & Foster, 2004; Farwell & Wohlwend-Lloyd, 1998; Gabriel et al., 1994). They are more likely than others to self-nominate and self-promote (Hogan et al., 1990). In conversation and extemporaneous speeches, narcissism is positively correlated with the number of first person pronouns used and negatively related to use of "we" (Raskin & Shaw, 1988). Narcissists view themselves as smart and attractive (Campbell, Rudich, & Sedikides, 2002), more so than others around them do and more than objective measures indicate (Gabriel et al., 1994). Overall, it appears that narcissists rate themselves especially high on "agentic" features (e.g., intellectual pursuits, outgoingness) and are less concerned with their "communal" features such as agreeableness and conscientiousness (Campbell, Rudich, & Sedikides, 2002).

As they approach a variety of tasks, narcissists possess and express very high expectations for success (Farwell & Wohlwend-Lloyd, 1998; Gabriel et al., 1994; Wallace & Baumeister, 2002). This perception is regularly sustained by their reactions to feedback on those tasks—not necessarily the performance level itself. For example, Kernis and Sun (1994) studied how high and low narcissistic subjects reacted to positive and negative feedback about their social skills. The narcissistic respondents gave much more credence and credibility to the positive feedback, but felt negative feedback resulted from a much poorer measure that was produced by a less competent evaluator (see also Smalley & Stake, 1996). Bogart, Benotsch, and Pavlovic (2004) reported that feedback resulting from upward comparisons experienced in everyday life increased hostility among narcissists, but that downward comparisons bolstered their self-esteem and positive affect.

Likewise, Rhodewalt and Morf (1995, Study 1) found that narcissism was associated with internal and enduring aspects about the self after success but not failure. Farwell and Wohlwend-Lloyd (1998) also found that narcissism was correlated positively with internal attributions (ability and effort) for a successful performance, but not with attributions about a partner's performance (see also Campbell, Reeder, Sedikides, & Elliott, 2000; Hartouni, 1992; Ladd, Welsh, Vitulli, Labbe, & Law, 1997; Rhodewalt & Morf, 1998; Rhodewalt, Tragakis, & Finnerty, 2006; and Stucke, 2003, for other attribution studies showing similar effects). These results might explain why narcissists don't seem to adjust their future performance expectations downward after a poor performance, often indicating they are pleased with the way they are and see little room for improvement (Emmons, 1984, 1987; Raskin & Terry, 1988; Rhodewalt & Morf, 1995).

Such chronic self-confidence is often unjustified (Farwell & Wohlwend-Lloyd, 1998; John & Robins, 1994) relative to narcissists' actual performance. And while they try to attribute away negative feedback, they can react to it with more hostility and aggression than those low in narcissism (Kernis & Sun, 1994; McCann & Biaggio, 1989; Rhodewalt & Morf, 1998; Raskin & Novacek, 1989; Stucke, 2003). Likewise, despite their emotional and negative reactions to social rejections (Twenge & Campbell, 2003), narcissists can bounce back to their high-confidence selves, probably by virtue of the self-maintenance processes they chronically engage in (Morf & Rhodewalt, 2001). In short, they can simultaneously fend off potential threats to the self and take personal advantage of opportunities they see for themselves in social situations.

One major casualty from all this defensiveness, self-focus, and unabashed self-enhancement is that the initial positive impressions narcissists generate are often fleeting once people see through them after extended interactions. Earlier, we discussed the Paulhus (1998) study of peer group members' ratings of narcissists—they were generally positive even after just 20 minutes. But Paulhus also found that the rating advantage that narcissists enjoyed in the early, initial meetings, generally deteriorated once these 20 minute interactions were extended to weekly meetings over 2 months. In several cases, the ratings reversed themselves —peers ratings went from agreeable to disagreeable, from happy/adjusted to maladjusted, and from performance-oriented to self-oriented. A second study replicated this pattern and was able to trace these negative trends to bragging, defensiveness, and ability overestimation on the part of narcissists (Paulhus, 1998).

Are we Becoming More Narcissistic?

Of course, rising into senior management takes time. Consequently, a question arises about the relationship between narcissism and age. A related temporal issue to consider is whether we are become more narcissistic over the last decades and subsequent generations—something that may somehow connect to what appears to be an increase in executive scandals and decision-making debacles in recent years. Needless to say, these are very complex issues, as our brief research discussion below will demonstrate.

One position is that narcissism declines as people age (Foster, Campbell, & Twenge, 2003). For instance, Americans are very individualistic (Hofstede, 2001) and some experts suggest that younger Americans have become progressively more self-focused in recent decades (Lasch, 1979; Baumeister, 1987). Indeed, one might expect younger people generally to be more narcissistic since as the years pass and experience is gained with failure, people may generally become other/feedback sensitive. To test this reasoning, Foster et al. (2003) used an internet survey method to collect data from nearly 3,500 participants. Among other items, respondents completed the popular NPI measure described earlier. They found a modest, but significant decline in NPI scores with age—an effect that strengthened when certain controls (e.g., income, gender) were added. Foster et al. (2003) suggested future studies were needed to pinpoint the source of any age effects—such as developmental changes, socialization practices, and birth cohort differences.

In fact, the authors took their own advice in a subsequent study. In that research, they conducted a cross-temporal meta-analysis of narcissism scores from 1979-2006 (Twenge, Konrath, Foster, Campbell, & Bushman, 2008a). All known studies of college students who completed the same narcissism scale across this 27-year period were collected and summarized. In total, 85 different samples comprising over 16,000 participants were located. Twenge et al. (2008a) found that narcissism scores among college students actually rose during this generational period, with scores of the most recent set of students being almost two-thirds above scores among students in 1979-1985.

Critics have suggested, however, that birth cohort or generational effects have not clearly supported the view that a "Generation Me" exists (Trzesniewski, Donnellan, & Robins, 2008a; Trzesniewski, Donnellan, & Robins, 2008b). One objection to the Twenge et al. (2008a) approach is their use of temporal meta-analyses to uncover population-level cohort effects by examining studies relying on small, convenience samples not designed to make such inferences.

Trzesniewski et al. (2008b) addressed is critique empirically. They obtained a large sample of data collected across time from students at University of California (UC) campuses—NPI data was collected in 1988, 1996, and annually from 2002 through 2007 (Raskin & Terry, 1988). Overall, this data set (n = 26,000) was significantly larger than the total number of participants across the 85 samples summarized in Twenge et al. (2008a). Analyses of this larger UC sample found that narcissism levels appeared stable over time. This is important, if for no other reason than it represents a strong test of generational effects. After all, California is the geographic epicenter of the self-esteem movement and should evince a "Generation Me" attitude. The authors also obtained a national probability sample of high school seniors, a study conducted annually since 1976. This study included a measure of self-esteem (Trzesniewski et al., 2008a, 2008b). That data showed no increase in self-esteem scores among those high school seniors (n = 180,000) across a 30-year period (cf. Twenge & Campbell, 2001). Finally, in both data sets, a "self-enhancement" index (difference measures of self-rated intelligence vs. objective/self-report indicators of intelligence) showed no appreciable changes over time.

As a response to the UC results, Twenge, Konrath, Foster, Campbell, and Bushman (2008b) suggested that demographic shifts in California college student populations which occurred after Proposition 209 passed (prohibiting race or ethnicity in admissions decisions)—accounted for the results reported by Trzesniewski et al. (2008a, 2008b). Specifically, they claimed that Proposition 209 led to large increases in Asian populations at the UC campuses starting in 1997 (freshmen were 30% Asian in 1996, increasing to 43% in 2006). This is important because Asian Americans are said to be more self-enfacing and score lower on measures reflecting individualistic views (e.g., self-esteem and presumably narcissism) than other groups. They argued that since these demographic shifts were unique to California, they could mask a broader generational shift toward greater narcissism. To address this possibility, Twenge et al. (2008b) used their 85 study meta-analysis to compare samples collected in California to those from other states. They replicated the finding of no difference in mean narcissism scores in California reported by Trzesniewski et al. (2008a, 2008b), apparently supporting their "Asian influence" hypothesis. Additionally, the remaining non-California studies in their meta-analysis still showed significant annual increases in narcissism.

Our assessment of this controversy favors the Trzesnieski et al. conclusions over Twenge et al. claims for several reasons. First, Twenge et al.'s (2008a, 2008b) data showed the biggest national-level jumps in narcissism *before* 1997 (when the California law took effect), yet little to no increases in California. Second, they report no drop in narcissism scores after 1997 in the California data, something we would expect if Asians entered the sample in large numbers as they suggest (see their Figure 1, p. 920). Both these facts are inconsistent with their explanation. Also, a close look at the admissions data for UC-Davis (the source of Trzesnieski et al. [2008b] data) after the passage of Proposition 209 is informative.[4] Indeed, it is noteworthy that Asian students only increased 1.9% between the years of 2002 and 2007 on the UC-Davis campus. On an average sample size of 4,792 enrolled students, this translates into only 91 more Asian students enrolled in 2007 than did in 2002—the first and last years of UC-Davis data reported by Trzensnieski et al. (2008b).

Moreover, we noted earlier that Twenge et al. (2008b) recalculated their estimates, removing their California data. It would have also been valuable to recalculate their own estimates, adding in the very large California samples of Trzesniewski et al. (2008b). We estimated some of these values and they dramatically reduce the effects reported in Twenge et al. (2008a).[5] Consider the effects reported in light of their dependent variable—the 40 item forced-choice NPI scale. The difference reported by Twenge et al. (2008a) indicates respondent selected only 1.67 more items out of 40 over a 20-year period, itself not an impressive, practical difference. But, the change drops to less than a half an item (.44) when we include the effect of the Trzesniewski (2008b) data, hardly a signature effect of a new generation. Overall, we believe this a compelling finding, especially when taking the size of the Trzesniewski et al. (2008b) sample (approximately 25,000) and its degree of consistency (uniformity in student features, survey administration, etc.) into account.[6]

Overall, our assessment is that there are only some small differences across decades in narcissism. While narcissism might be more common than a casual observer might think, it is not clear whether a pattern of increasing narcissism will characterize the latest generation of those entering the business world. That said, it may be more accurate to say that the corporate world, for whatever reason (e.g., runaway growth in pay and power in the last 30 years), has done more to attract narcissists even if the overall level of narcissism in the population or in specific demographic cohorts, has not changed in any major way. In other words, narcissistic people may have increasingly come to view the business world as an attractive "arena" in which to play out their narcissistic fantasies. Perhaps this could help explain why the ranks of corporate executives seem to have no shortage of excessively narcissistic individuals. Naturally, this is yet another thesis that falls to future research to tease out in more detail.

Performance of Narcissists

One of the most important topics to study in this area is the performance of narcissists, especially given the signals that narcissists send in their interactions with others. If you exude self-confidence and esteem, tell others you think highly of yourself, and make moves to assume leadership positions, you have set a high bar for yourself and drawn a great deal of attention in the process. Of course, attention is what the narcissist wants—they seek out opportunities to display their talents and document their superiority over others (Morf, Weir, & Davidov, 2000; Wallace & Baumeister, 2002).

On balance, it is fair to say that the inflated self-assessments that characterize narcissists are *not* borne out in their performance. For example, earlier we noted that narcissists tend to be overconfident, especially relative to others' views. John and Robbins (1994) studied MBA students' performance in a simulated management committee meeting about employee evaluation and compensation. They found that while narcissism correlated strongly with self-rated performance (presenting the case for a raise), ratings by peers and trained observers not privy to narcissism scores showed no relation with performance on the task. Robins and John (1997) also found that objective measures of quality of performance of an oral argument showed no difference between low and high narcissists, even though the latter group rated themselves much higher than the former. A set of studies by Campbell, Goodie, and Foster (2004) found similar effects. First, narcissism was significantly related to confidence on a general knowledge test, but unrelated to student's actual performance on the test. In study 2, betting and confidence in one's bet was used as a proxy for risk taking behavior. Again, narcissism was associated with overconfidence and this resulted in poorer performance—in this case more lost bets. These effects were largely replicated in a third study—where narcissists' predictions of future performance were based on their expectations rather than on how they actually performed.

And those expectations are quite high indeed. In fact, Gabriel, Critelli, and Ee (1994) found that while narcissism was significantly correlated with self-reported intelligence, no correlation was found with actual performance on an intelligence test. Two other studies also found no impact of narcissism on performance on a cognitive ability task (Paulhus & Williams, 2002) or on a factual judgment task by working MBA students (Ames, Rose, & Anderson, 2006). Yet both studies showed that narcissism was associated with overestimation of actual performance.

A similar pattern of effects, in a different domain and study setting, was observed by Brunell et al. (2008). As noted earlier, these researchers had groups of people work on a task that involved significant interaction. Each group member was given a separate profile of a candidate seeking a job. After some time to read their materials, members began discussing the qualifications of the person they represented, with the goal being to convince the group that their candidate was the best. Brunell et al. found that while narcissism predicted both self and peer-rated leadership, it did not predict successful advocacy of the job candidates; narcissism did not reliably correlate whose candidate was forwarded by the groups.

Judge et al. (2006) examined the relationship between narcissism and task performance among beach patrol officers. They studied several forms of performance and assessed those using supervisor ratings and self ratings. Two performance types were measured—*task* performance was assessed using a multi-item in-role scale (e.g., "adequately completes responsibilities") and *contextual* performance was measured using a popular organizational citizenship scale. This measure looks at the performance of behaviors that are not necessarily part of the job description or evaluation system, but yet are valuable to an organization (e.g., talking up the organization to others; being conscientious with customers, etc.). They found that narcissism was not related to self-reports of contextual behavior but was negatively related to supervisor evaluations. Narcissism was also not related to supervisor ratings of actual performance or to self- ratings. Nor did using two subfactors of the NPI scale predict performance.

While most studies assessing narcissism show either no performance advantage or a negative one, not all do. Raskin (1980) found that narcissism was positively correlated with self-reports of creativity and performance on objective tests of creativity. Likewise, Farwell and Wohlwend-Lloyd (1998) found that narcissistic students were more likely to overestimate current and future course grades than their non-narcissistic peers. They also found that while narcissism and actual course grades were not related in their first study, a positive relation was reported in their second study. Ames and Kammrath (2004) also found that MBA students scoring high in narcissism overestimated their performance on several social judgment tasks, but that narcissism was not correlated with actual performance.

Finally, an interesting study by Wallace and Baumeister (2002) also speaks to this issue. These researchers reasoned that narcissism would either be an impetus or drag on performance, depending on the degree of scrutiny of their output. In particular, they argued that the relation between narcissism and performance would be moderated by the perceived degree of self-enhancement opportunity. In four carefully designed experiments, different manipulations of self-enhancement opportunity and tasks were examined. On tasks where the "glory" had to be shared (i.e., self-enhancement opportunities were reduced), narcissists performed worse than they did when their individual performance stood out. They rose to the challenge and performed best when social comparison information showed the task at hand to be difficult, but did poorly when it was not challenging. Those low in narcissism did not show this differential level of performance—they were not as motivated to seek admiration from others as were the narcissists.

It is important to note, however, that across all of the four studies reported by Wallace and Baumeister (2002) narcissism was not significantly associated with overall performance. The narcissist's good performance in the self-enhancement conditions was offset by their poor performance in the other conditions. Consequently, situational opportunities for recognition drove performance effects.

By extension, one might think that performances observed by superiors (versus subordinates) might activate this concern studied by Wallace and Baumeister (2002). After all, part of the job of a supervisor is to monitor and evaluate their employee's performance and important decisions about organizational resources are involved. Therefore, the opportunity to show off is greater while interacting with supervisors than with subordinates. This issue was indirectly studied by Blair, Hoffman, Helland (2008). These researchers examined the relationship of supervisor and subordinate evaluations of managers in several different performance domains. For each of the practicing managers in their study, Blair et al. (2008) had immediate supervisors and several subordinates complete evaluation forms that asked for ratings of the managers' performance in several different domains, including *conceptual* (judgment, decision making, planning), *interpersonal* (e.g, degree of interpersonal effectiveness, team building, participation), and *integrity* behavior (e.g., "does not misrepresent him/herself for personal gain"). The results showed differences between the two categories of raters. For interpersonal and integrity behaviors (but not conceptual), a correlation was found between narcissism and supervisors' ratings of performance but not between narcissism and subordinates' evaluations.

These findings are consistent with Wallace and Baumeister's hypothesis that the opportunity for recognition or glory sensitizes narcissists to more closely monitor their performance and to "kick it up a notch." In this study, however, while the supervisors did indeed take notice (as apparently intended by the narcissists), they were not duly impressed. In fact, their ratings of performance and integrity were negatively correlated with the managers' degree of narcissism.

One domain of managerial performance that is easily observed and relatively unambiguous in form is the area of sales production. A study by Soyer, Rovenpor, and Kopelman (1999) examined the narcissism—performance link in salespeople. This group was chosen for study for several reasons, all of which might promote better performance among narcissists in that field. For one, narcissists may be attracted in greater numbers to sales in the first place because the job typically has fewer levels of bureaucracy and permits more autonomous actions. Plus, the many visible markers of status and importance (e.g., travel, expense accounts, cars, computers, etc.) should be attractive to the narcissist as would the fact that high performers are often publicly recognized. Finally, their strong extroversion might fit well with the job requirements. In short, a narcissist may have many things in their favor in a sales role.

Soyer et al.'s (1999) results did indeed show that narcissists were satisfied with a job in sales and their narcissism scores were significantly higher than respondents who never had a sales job. Nevertheless, narcissism did not significantly correlate with any of the four measures of sales performance (e.g., average performance to quota, income, etc.). Interestingly, another personality variable, need for achievement, did significantly predict three of the four sales performance measures.

Earlier, we briefly mentioned an interesting study by Chatterjee and Hambrick (2007). This article also speaks to the performance issue, especially among highly visible, practicing leaders of organizations. These researchers conducted a very careful study of the strategic actions and behavior of CEOs in the computer hardware and software industries from 1992 through 2004. Not surprisingly, the response rate of CEOs to requests from researchers is low, even when studying topics of some interest to their business (Cycyota & Harrison, 2006). Getting this group to reply to personality questionnaires is harder still.

Accordingly, Chatterjee and Hambrick (2007) used a clever set of unobtrusive proxies to index the level of narcissism among the CEOs. For example, they obtained press releases and interviews conducted with the CEOs of these firms. The protocols were coded for the relative prominence of the CEO in those publicity pieces as well as the number of first-person singular pronouns stated in those documents. They also obtained the firm's annual reports and coded other indirect indictors of narcissism, such as the prominence of the CEO photograph(s) in those documents. In all, five such measures were calculated, each showing a significant amount of variance. These were summed to create a narcissism index. As a check on the quality of their measure, Chatterjee and Hambrick had security analysts who specialized in the computer industry rate the personality of a subsample of the CEOs. The analysts had covered the industry for an average of 10 years and had interacted with those CEOs in formal, informal, and other settings. The correlation between the analysts' ratings and the unobtrusive narcissism index was .82, adding to the construct validity of their narcissism measure.

After controlling for a number of factors, Chatterjee and Hambrick (2007) looked at the effect of narcissism on several variables including: (a) company performance extremes (e.g., total shareholder returns, TSR and return on assets, ROA); (b) fluctuation of these performance measures across years; and (c) changes in resource deployment (e.g., acquisitions). The findings were interesting and provocative.

First, CEO narcissism was positively associated with the number and size of acquisitions. This is important because researchers have observed that most acquisitions reduce shareholder value (Roll, 1986), with some even turning to the use of executive "hubris" as an explanation for this strategic grandiosity (Hayward & Hambrick, 1997). The Chatterjee and Hambrick (2007) study points to a source of that hubris—narcissism. They also found that fluctuation of firm performance (ROA) was predicted by the CEO's level of narcissism. In other words, those higher in narcissism favored bolder action that would attract attention. Those actions resulted in both big wins and big losses—with wild swings in between.

A final set of analyses showed that CEO narcissism was not related to firm performance—they did not generate better (or worse) performance than those low in narcissism. As Chatterjee and Hambrick (2007) note and we discussed earlier, some have speculated that "productive" narcissism should be more likely to occur in an unstable and dynamic industry because that situation calls for bold strategies (cf. Maccoby, 2007). Accordingly, this study in the software/hardware industry should be considered a strong—but disconfirming—test of the productive narcissist hypothesis. Chatterjee and Hambrick went on to speculate that given their findings, perhaps narcissism may even have a negative effect in less dynamic or stable industries.

In summary, the relation between narcissism and performance in the literature is a lot like narcissists themselves—there is a lot of bluster, some promise, and unreliable success, with only a high self-opinion surviving.

The majority of research shows no positive relation between performance and level of narcissism. The issue of whether there are thresholds or tipping points of degrees of narcissism that might produce better or much better (Maccoby, 2007) performance could be an area of future study. Right now, it is fair to say that despite their expectations and statements to the contrary, narcissists are not better performers; indeed, on some occasions the research shows they are poor performers.

Promise also exists in the area of situational drivers of narcissistic motivation, such as the pressure, visibility, or attention available to the narcissist's performance (Chatterjee & Hambrick, 2007; Wallace & Baumeister, 2002). In the Chatterjee and Hambrick study, however, performance was defined in several ways, including the number and size of acquisitions—a good proxy of visibility and a lighting rod for attention by the financial community. Likewise, in a supplementary analysis, they showed that narcissists were attracted to a challenge (they joined poorly performing companies) and the admiration it would bring if they rose to it. Nevertheless, more direct measures of business visibility and challenge in future studies might provide additional insights and value.

Effects on Others in the Organization

The work by Paulhus (1998) underscores an important component of narcissistic behavior—the impact it has on others in at work. The popular literature concerning business leaders overlaps with the often attractive components of the narcissistic personality. For example, it is often said that confidence is contagious and if so, this is one strong asset of the narcissist. Likewise, a popular conception of leadership is that of a take-charge hero who makes bold decisions quickly and is comfortable on stage—whether in a boardroom or on CNN.

Indeed, it is fair to say that narcissists want to lead others. They often think about power (Raskin, Novacek, & Hogan, 1991) and want to assert their dominance over others (McFarlin & Sweeney, 2002). Moreover, they see themselves as leaders and are often viewed as leaderly as well. For instance, Raskin and Terry (1988) had observer's rate people's performance in leaderless discussion groups. Narcissism was significantly related to observers' ratings of assertiveness, extent of participation in group discussion, exhibitionism, and tendency to criticize others. On the other hand, narcissism was unrelated to both the quality of people's performance as well as their level of cooperativeness.

Along the same lines, Judge et al. (2006) found that narcissism was related to both self and peer ratings of leadership, although the effect was three times as strong for self ratings than for peer ratings. In their second study, however, only self-ratings were positively correlated with leadership behavior; other ratings were negatively related to narcissism. Among military cadets, other researchers found a significant correlation between peer ratings of being a "born leader" and positive aspects of narcissism (high self-ratings) but not negative features of narcissism such as being manipulative (Paunonen, Lonnqvist, Verkasalo, Leikas, & Nissinen, 2006). Finally, Brunell et al. (2008) observed groups involved in simulated managerial decisions. Narcissism was significantly associated with self-ratings and their peers' ratings of leadership. Moreover, the self-ratings of leadership were significantly higher than the ratings of others.[7]

Collectively, these studies show that narcissists can, at the minimum, be seen as leaders or someone with leadership potential—not simply in their own minds, but often in that of others as well. But studies finding significant correlations between leader ratings and narcissism tend to produce those relationships in ad hoc groups that spend little time together. Things might be different in a workplace where extended interactions between employees occur and are expected to continue. Indeed, Judge et al. (2006) found a negative relation between narcissism and confidential leadership ratings provided by superiors in the workplace. Clearly, this latter group has had ample opportunity to observe and form impressions of the narcissist—more than the "thin slices of behavior" that occurred in the other studies.

Interestingly, Paunonen et al. (2006) found leader ratings to be positively related to "egoistic" features of narcissism, but unrelated to more self-centered sides of the construct. These cadets studied by Paunonen et al. had spent nearly six months together in situations where leadership features could be observed. In Brunell et al. (2008), when positive and distinctive individual characteristics were controlled for (e.g., extraversion, agreeableness), others' ratings of leadership were no longer correlated with narcissism. These two studies suggest that the narcissistic tendency to be assertive early in group interactions can mask some seamier attributes of narcissism—attributes that may become clearer over time. All of this underscores the important issue of how much continuing interaction exists when sizing up the impact of narcissists on others in the organization.

That said, it may not take a good deal of interaction with a narcissist to conclude that they are not all they seem to be. We found 12 studies showing that others can quickly identify narcissists and narcissistic behavior. Indeed, the empirical literature shows that people who interact with narcissists—even for short periods of time as in the Brunell et al. study—generally do not share the positive view that narcissists have of themselves, even if they are seen as having some leadership potential. We found at least 19 studies which show a difference between narcissists' self-assessments and those of others about a wide variety of characteristics and behavior. In all cases, narcissists' self-assessments were more positive. Said differently, others have a less than ideal view of narcissists—at least from the narcissist's perspective.

Not surprisingly, this disconnect can prove problematic. For example, in their quest for self-enhancement, narcissists are willing to step over others (Campbell et al., 2000; Gosling, John, Raik, & Robins, 1998; Morf & Rhodewalt, 2001). They may be unrealistic about their level of empathy (Ames & Kammrath, 2004) or oblivious to the perspectives of others because of selfishness (Campbell, Bush, Brunell, & Shelton, 2005; Watson, Grisham, Trotter, & Biderman, 1984). Narcissists tend to assume they are better than others (Campbell, Reeder, Sedikides, & Elliot, 2000; Raskin & Terry, 1988; Paulhus, 1998), may be motivated to demonstrate their superiority (Morf, Weir, & Davidov, 2000), and often fail to acknowledge the positive input of others (Campbell et al., 2000; John & Robins, 1994).

And if narcissists perceive threats to their ego, they respond with aggression toward others (Bushman & Baumeister, 1998). Combine all this with the fact that they commonly brag and otherwise draw attention to themselves (Buss & Chiodo, 1991) and it is easy to see why they upset others in work interactions. Narcissists appear to use relationships with others as an opportunity to feed their need for self-enhancement and, consequently, have trouble in sustaining those relationships (Campbell, 1999; Campbell & Foster, 2002). All in all, a narcissist is the antithesis of "a team player."

Another line of research that speaks to effects of narcissism on others in organizations is work on ethics and counternormative practices by employees. Soyer, Rovenpor, and Kopelman (1999), for instance, asked salespeople and managers questions about their degree of comfort with work behavior that might be questionable (e.g., "A good salesperson is part informant, part con artist," "People will believe most anything if you appear confident and knowledgeable"). Narcissism was significantly correlated with the salespersons' comfort with questionable behavior.

Recently, several additional studies have been conducted, most showing similar effects. Penney and Spector (2002) found that narcissism scores were related to counterproductive work behavior (CWB) such as stealing on the job or doing work incorrectly. They also found that narcissism moderated the relationship between job constraints and CWB. Specifically, when employees experience multiple barriers and frustrations on the job, they were more likely to engage in CWB if they scored high in narcissism.

Likewise, another study found modest correlations between narcissism and a variety of honesty tests (Mumford, Connelly, Helton, Strange, & Osburn, 2001). Similarly, Campbell, Rudich, and Sedikides (2002) found that narcissism scores were negatively related to a scale of self-reported ethical characteristics (e.g., honest, moral, deceptive). Also, Paunonen et al. (2006) found that honesty ratings by peers of military cadets were negatively correlated with a manipulative aspect of narcissism. These findings parallel Brown's (2004) finding that narcissism was related to vengefulness (e.g., "I don't get mad, I get even," and "It's important for me to get back at people who've hurt me"), even after controlling for self-esteem.

Adding to the above findings was a study by Judge et al. (2006) of beach patrol officers and their bosses who were asked about deviant workplace behaviors (e.g., I have taken property from work without permission."). Narcissism was positively and significantly related to supervisors' ratings of employee deviance, but not correlated with self-ratings. Blair, Hoffman, and Helland (2008) also surveyed a set of employed MBA students, as well as their bosses and subordinates. A number of interesting variables were assessed, including narcissism and integrity (e.g., "Does not misrepresent him/herself for person gain"). Their results showed that while supervisor ratings of integrity were negatively correlated with narcissism, this was not true for subordinates.

This finding is noteworthy because narcissists do tend to be viewed by most people, including subordinates, in less than positive ways. Blair et al. (2008) addressed this point and were careful to show that these items were viewed in the same way by both bosses and subordinates; this particular artifact can not explain the results. They did point out that the MBA students themselves chose the subordinate who they wanted to solicit feedback from. Consequently, MBA students could have selected subordinates with whom they had the most affinity. These subordinates may also have been fearful of retribution for poor ratings, even if they were assured confidentiality. Moreover, Blair et al. note that the MBA students' bosses may have viewed them in a more complex or experienced way ("wild-eyed thinker with no detail orientation") than their subordinates. The idea that the observer's vantage point matters in terms of how narcissists are evaluated is an interesting one to explore in future research. On a somewhat related note, a study by Davis, Wester, and King (2008) found that narcissism was predictive of a self-reported tendency to compromise research ethics (e.g., inappropriate authorship; unethical reviewing, etc.) for professors, but not for doctoral students.

A final fascinating study in this area, by Blickle, Schlegel, Fassbender, and Klein (2006), looked at personality correlates of white-collar crime. Not content to examine self-reports of ethical lapses in behavior, these researchers went directly to those who actually committed and were convicted of white collar crimes in Germany. In particular, they sampled from inmates at correctional institutions who were former high-level managers and executives. Each had been convicted of white-collar crimes—these included embezzlement, fraud, tax evasion, and bribery, with the financial damage to their respective firms averaging over $3.5 million. Blickle et al. (2006) also obtained a second, matched set of managers who were currently employed in similar companies with equivalent levels of responsibility. The results showed that narcissism predicted respondent's status (i.e., criminal vs. noncriminal), even after controlling for social desirability. Overall, narcissism is closely related to poor attitudes and behavior concerning ethical practices in organizations.

DEALING WITH MANAGERIAL NARCISSISM

While we obviously know quite a bit about narcissism, it's equally clear that many unanswered questions remain. Indeed, as we have seen, the literature about narcissism presents a murky picture in many respects (e.g., about the different "types" of narcissism and the impact of contextual factors, just to name a few). So there is no doubt that the need for more research exists—perhaps now more than ever in these difficult times where the need for leaders with integrity is acute.

Yet the response we have always received from a "need more research" refrain from people in corporations is this—"we can't wait for all the scientific questions to be resolved, we need help now!" Consequently, in this final section we present action suggestions based on our current, albeit limited, understanding of narcissistic leaders. We break these suggestions into two basic parts: personal and organizational. First, we focus on employees who find themselves—all too frequently—in the position of working for an excessively narcissistic boss or leader. In a nutshell, these personal suggestions will involve raising employee self-awareness and diagnostic skills as well as presenting specific tactics for responding to narcissistic leaders.

After presenting these person-level suggestions, we conclude this chapter by presenting some ideas, policies, and strategies that companies should embrace to keep narcissistic people from running wild through their top management ranks. In essence, companies should take steps to preclude narcissists from getting a foothold and create an environment where it is difficult for narcissists to operate in positions of power.

How Employees Can Deal With Their Narcissistic Leaders

Dealing with Narcissistic Exploitation and Manipulation

A common problem many employees face when working for narcissistic leaders is their tendency to exploit and manipulate to advance or protect themselves. The narcissistic leader may lie, distort or withhold information, engage in blaming, and play any number of psychological games with subordinates. Perhaps the first challenge employees must rise to when it comes to exploitation and manipulation is detecting it in the first place. This is no small task. In essence, employees must determine whether they are actually dealing with a narcissistic boss and, if so, then assess the damage that is being inflicted (e.g., does being blamed for the narcissist's own flaws have negative career implications?).

Next, employees must evaluate their options for responding—which depend on the seriousness of the situation and whether others are experiencing manipulative behavior and are willing to step forward. In any case, options range from short-run avoidance (i.e., staying away from the narcissist as much as possible—impractical over the long term) to filing complaints with higher ups to forming coalitions to resist the narcissistic leader. Regardless, we advocate creating a log of any incidents experienced and maintaining a library of any e-mails or documents received that might attest to the narcissists' manipulative behavior. Naturally, all options have drawbacks. A coalition typically has a better chance of exposing narcissistic malfeasance, but coalitions can be notoriously difficult and time-consuming to build, especially if subordinates are afraid of retribution. Likewise, filing complaints with Human Resources or other senior leaders can expose subordinates to scrutiny and narcissistic revenge. But if employees have strong performance records and can present themselves as being interested in helping the company rather than trashing their boss, written complaints can work (McFarlin & Sweeney, 2002).

Dealing With Narcissistic Tantrums

One of the themes we have touched on throughout this chapter is the narcissist tendency to exert power and dominate others. This can produce explosive temper tantrums and inappropriate rages in narcissistic leaders, especially when they feel they are being threatened or criticized. Typically, being passive or cowering in the face of such tantrums ultimately feels reinforcing to the narcissist (i.e., their explosions "work" to crush opposition). For subordinates, all of the options we have mentioned for dealing with manipulation are also relevant here—as are their respective drawbacks. That said, these suggestions do not directly address how employees should behave when they are on the receiving end of a narcissistic tantrum.

Consequently, we suggest employees try to display strength instead of weakness when facing narcissistic tantrums. For instance, employees should literally stand their ground, maintaining direct eye contact and speak firmly in response to the narcissist. They can also use interruption tactics to disrupt a narcissistic tantrum (e.g., by asking for more information, restating issues, disagreeing, or stating one will leave the interaction unless the narcissist calms down). After the incident passes, subordinates should write down the details and begin a paper trail with the narcissist to create a record. For instance, subordinates can send the narcissist an e-mail to solicit additional information, to officially disagree with the narcissist's points, or to raise concerns about how they were treated. Subordinates also should be ready to escalate their complaints up the line if the narcissistic leader retaliates (McFarlin & Sweeney, 2002).

Dealing With Narcissistic Impression Management

Another insidious problem with narcissistic leaders is that their self-aggrandizing tendencies often result in excessive impression management behavior. This can include a variety of self-promotional behavior, ingratiation with higher-ups, and, what really rankles subordinates, credit-stealing. Like manipulative and exploitative behavior, a key for subordinates with impression management abuse is to be able to recognize it when they see it. In essence, subordinates need to be attuned to impression management tactics and contextual factors that create impression management opportunities. Dealing with credit-stealing is a particular challenge and subordinates should look for ways to communicate their contributions (e.g., via the grapevine or written efforts) to correct the record. Longer term, subordinates may want to put roles, responsibilities, and credit-sharing activities in writing prior to starting on major tasks or projects. This may help blunt any credit-stealing efforts by narcissistic superiors (McFarlin & Sweeney, 2002).

Dealing With Narcissistic Visions

Narcissistic leaders tend to have grandiose self-regard and often see themselves as infallible. And when narcissists occupy the executive suite, personal monument-building and vision-based excesses are common. For instance, narcissists may pursue risky gambits and expensive dreams as a testament to their own superiority (e.g., in the form of over-the-top acquisitions, new business launches, and so on).

Moreover, narcissistic visions tend to encourage rather than discourage dependency. After all, narcissists want adoring and subservient followers—something a lofty and inspiring vision can bolster. Once again, subordinates need to educate themselves about the clues that suggest a corporate vision is the product of narcissistic fantasies. For instance, red flags should go up if the vision being pushed is somehow wrapped up in the leader's reputation, persona, or past achievements. Likewise, if the vision seems overly bold and ignores obvious implementation risks, external factors, or costs, subordinates should be wary. To combat all of this, subordinates should document and investigate their concerns, perhaps with the help of outside experts willing to share their assessment with the rest of the management team (McFarlin & Sweeney, 2002).

Stepping back for a moment, it is important to underscore the role subordinates often play in enabling flawed narcissistic visions—as well as putting up with other narcissistic abuses. As Lipman-Blumen (2005) has pointed out, anxiety, fear, and self-doubt among subordinates create the kind of dependency that many flawed leaders crave. This is what can cause subordinates to suspend disbelief or not question their leaders—no may how crazy their ideas are. Recognizing that their anxieties may encourage the embrace of false visions will help subordinates see things as they really are and embolden them to speak out. And taking the initiative to do so cuts to the core of what good leadership really is. On a broader level, this means followers need to abandon their roles as passive, dependent servants of leaders and become proactive, independent employees who desire stronger leadership skills and take responsibility for the firm. Only in this way will followers learn to "kick their addition" to the lofty, illusory visions that narcissistic leaders often present (Lipman-Blumen, 2005; McFarlin & Sweeney, 2002).

Taking on Narcissistic Leaders: A Positive View of the Process

Before we leave this section, we want to end on a "glass is half full" note. Employees who must combat narcissism in their companies often find it a difficult, dangerous, and depressing chore—where the odds are long and there seems to be little upside (short of leaving the firm). Consequently, it may be helpful for beaten-down subordinates to reframe what they are facing. In other words, we would encourage subordinates to look for what Lipman-Blumen (2005) argues are the "opportunities" in working for a toxic leader like a narcissist. Specifically, working for a narcissist may be an excellent opportunity for subordinates to: (1) exercise leadership themselves, at least on an informal basis, to counteract the leader; (2) learn from a negative role model about how not to behave; (3) become more aware of their own moral superiority, building self-esteem in the process; (4) vent about the leader's excesses and foibles in ways that build espirit de corps across the firm; and (5) learn how to build coalitions to organize and fight back (a theme we have revisited repeatedly in this section).

How Organizations Can Deal With the Challenge of Narcissistic Leaders

We turn our attention in this final section to some steps and strategies that organizations may want to adopt to combat narcissism in their ranks. This process starts, we believe, by adopting hiring practices that will make it harder for narcissists to get inside the firm and cause trouble. Granted, that will always be an imperfect solution. Consequently, we will also discuss things firms can do to bolster their internal defenses against narcissism in the ranks.

Job One: Avoid Hiring Narcissists in the First Place

The bottom line is that many screening techniques used when firms hire managers are tailor-made for narcissists. In other words, interview processes are often tilted toward self-presentation skills. Interviewees who project charm, confidence, assertiveness, and charisma—while taking personal credit for every success and attributing problems elsewhere—often do quite well. And, put simply, schmoozing and pumping themselves up are what narcissistic leaders often do very well indeed. Once exposed, narcissists often have an easy time moving on to the next unsuspecting company, propelled forward by syrupy recommendations designed to offload the narcissist somewhere else as soon as possible.

Fortunately, firms can put hiring practices into place that will minimize the ability of narcissists to avoid detection. First, companies need to embrace a philosophy that looks for the predictors of failure (like narcissism) instead of focusing exclusively on superficial factors that are believed to correlate with leadership success. Moreover, managerial candidates should be asked about how they approached conflict, hardships, or difficult challenges they have encountered on the job, with the interview team focusing on anything in the answers that might reveal narcissistic tendencies. For instance, blaming subordinates, castigating rivals, or attributing success to only personal characteristics may all be worrisome signs. Interviewers should also be trained to be cautious and avoid falling under the charm offensive narcissistic managers may unleash. Finally, the screening process could include personality instruments designed to detect narcissism (McFarlin & Sweeney, 2002).

Adopt Policies That Promote Subordinate Development and Succession Planning

Naturally, the hiring process is not foolproof and firms should assume that some narcissistic individuals will end up on the payroll. And unfortunately, once in management ranks, most narcissistic individuals have little interest in developing their subordinates or planning for succession. After all, doing so would mean creating competent (and threatening) rivals who might push them out of the limelight. The nasty succession battles we often read about in the business press are undoubtedly driven by narcissism in many cases. Narcissistic CEOs want to keep their jobs while undermining potential successors. Likewise, narcissistic successors often covet the CEO role and will do what they can to get it (McFarlin & Sweeney, 2002).

But companies are not helpless. They can enact policies to encourage better succession planning and employee development. Indeed, this arguably should start at the top with the board of directors—something that is especially important when times are tough. And when companies get into trouble, boards of directors sometimes turn to narcissistic, imperial leaders to serve as CEO in the mistaken belief that imposing a "strong will" on the firm will turn things around. Current board practices remain problematic in many cases. For instance, by some estimates, over 60% of CEOs in American corporations are also serving as board chair, putting too much power in one person's hands. To limit cronyism that can provide a free pass for narcissistic executives, especially in difficult times, board director terms should be limited. Moreover, boards should take steps to ensure that strong leadership development and succession plans are implemented and rigorous performance measurements for the CEO are in place (Allio, 2007).

Other recommendations for board-level improvements in succession planning efforts would be to work to ensure that the board is comprised of independent directors not tied to the CEO. An independent board will engender much more confidence in developing and running succession plans for the company. Boards may also want to tie CEO pay to succession planning (i.e., to grade the CEO on well he or she helps identify and develop potential successors).

Develop Cultural Values That Discourage Narcissism

The bottom line is that boards can also play a key role in fostering a corporate culture that values employee development and succession planning (McFarlin & Sweeney, 2002). For example, boards can encourage executives to cultivate cultural values that focus on honesty and integrity. That means creating explicit norms and codes of conduct, with positive behaviors rewarded and negative behaviors punished. Over time, integrity-related values will become institutionalized in the firm, making it less vulnerable to narcissistic excesses (Allio, 2007; see also Appelbaum & Roy-Girard, 2007).

Speaking of which, companies should be creative in their quest to adopt values systems that combat narcissism. And that means looking far and wide for alternative approaches to management. For instance, consider the African management concept of *Ubuntu*. The Ubuntu philosophy is about "connective leadership," with everyone's well-being and humanity in the firm expressed through others. Embracing the communal orientation of many African societies, Ubuntu stresses responsibility—on the part of everyone in the corporate community—to support and nurture all members of that community. At its core, Ubuntu rests on mutuality of purpose and interdependent concern—the essence of the village. Consequently, Ubuntu arguably represents the antithesis of the "me, myself, and I" culture found in many American corporations—a culture that appeals to narcissistic leaders (see Lipman-Blumen, 2005; McFarlin, Coster, & Mogale-Pretorius, 1999; McFarlin & Sweeney, 2002). Perhaps some variant of this approach, Westernized through the corporate family concept, could have some promise.

SUMMARY

The study of narcissism has moved from a focus on clinical classification and analysis to a social/organizational empirical analysis over the last several decades. This shift has provided useful information about the features that characterize the narcissistic personality, the impact of this style on performance, and how they appear and impact others in organizations. We also looked closely at how peers, subordinates and organizations themselves can deal with the challenges presented by narcissistic leadership. More research conducted in functioning organizations is needed and will likely appear over the next decades. Hopefully this work will provide more specific, empirically grounded advice about how to take advantage of or temper this complex narcissistic style of some leaders.

NOTES

1. Another distinction made in the literature is between a covert and an overt narcissist (Wink, 1991). The overt type is said to be characterized by openly expressed power, manipulativeness, and a strong need for admiration. Covert narcissism, on the other hand, reflects defensiveness, hostility toward others and low self-confidence and insecurity. This distinction is unrelated to these other views in that (presumably) both covert and overt narcissism are not a pattern likely to lead to success in most situations.
2. We assembled these studies from the literature here for this review. We would be happy to share this list of studies—as well as others mentioned below—to interested readers.
3. Our reference to a characteristically "healthy" narcissist uses this term from the existing literature and it refers to the impact on organizations rather than physical or mental health per se.
4. We obtained these admissions data from: http://statfinder.ucop.edu/default.aspx. Using overall number of freshman and the number of Asian/Filipino/Pacific Islanders, we simply calculated the percent of "Asian" freshman. While these data include more than Asians, admissions data were not

separated at UC. Regardless, this is a conservative number since we "over-count" Asians, thus deflating the mean NPI score as per Twenge et al.'s (2008b) argument.

5. We used Twenge et al.'s (2008a) equation (p. 883) to calculate mean NPI scores from 1988 (15.62) to 2006 (17.29). This increase represents the endorsement of 1.67 more NPI items (out of 40 total) over these 2 decades. We factored in estimates of these differences using the means reported in Trzesniewski et al (2008b). The study sample sizes are 16,475 versus 25,849, respectively; or what would be 36.3% of the data versus 63.7% if added together. We used these values to weight the means of the two studies in 1988 and 2006 before averaging them. The resulting estimate was an increase in means from 15.58 (1988) to 16.02 (2006)—a new difference of only .44. This is less than ½ item change in the 40 item NPI scale over a nearly 20-year period. Our estimate does not permit a significance test or effect size calculation worth much. Yet, a difference of so little on a 40 item scale does not seem of value practically, especially as it may characterize resulting behavior of the latest generation.
6. Self-enhancement analyses reported in Trzensniewski et al. (2008b) were also contested by Twenge et al. (2008b). They suggested that lack of changes were due to the use of two self-report items included in the large Monitoring the Future (MTF) dataset. This is important—after all, the opportunity to inflate one's self is the playground of narcissists. At the same time, Twenge et al. (2008b) did not comment on a similar lack of changes in the UC-Davis sample that compared objective indicants (SAT and GPA). Also, Twenge acknowledged the lack of self-esteem changes in the large sample MTF (n = 170,000), pointing out that this replicated their earlier results (Twenge & Campbell, 2001) based on a large sample meta-analysis. There, they found no increase in self-esteem over high school, but increases in elementary and college student self-esteem, and suggested that the social forces of high school might mask birth cohort changes. This results in a very complicated set of predictions regarding increases in the self-views of generations, and like Twenge et al. (2008a, 2008b) we believe is very deserving of future research. We believe it is fair to summarize all this work by saying that the there are at least some small differences across decades in narcissism, up and down patterns regarding self-esteem, not just between elementary, high school, and college, but then linear declines as one ages (Twenge & Campbell, 2003). These differences may be as small as less than ½ item endorsement on a 40 item scale, and we are uncertain as to how this might translate into actual, observable behavior. Self-enhancement effects seem stable across generations (even setting aside the MTF data).
7. We conducted these analyses using the means and standard errors provided in the Brunell et al. (2008) studies.

REFERENCES

Allio, R. J. (2007). Bad leaders: How they get that way and what to do about them. *Strategy & Leadership, 35*(3), 12-17.

Ames, D. R., & Kammrath, L. K. (2004). Mind-reading and metacognition: Narcissism, not actual competence, predicts self-estimated ability. *Journal of Nonverbal Behavior, 28,* 187-209.

Ames, D. R., Rose, P., & Anderson, C. P. (2006). The NPI-16 as a short measure of narcissism. *Journal of Research in Personality, 40,* 440-450.

Appelbaum, S. H., & Roy-Girard, D. (2007). Toxins in the workplace: Affect on organizations and employees. *Corporate Governance,* 7(1), 17-28.

Baumeister, R. F. (1987). How the self became a problem: A psychological review of historical research. *Journal of Personality and Social Psychology, 52,* 163-176.

Blair, C. A., Hoffman, B. J., & Helland, K. R. (2008). Narcissism in organizations: A multisource appraisal reflects different perspectives. *Human Performance, 21*(3), 254-276.

Blickle, G., Schlegel, A., Fassbender, P., & Klein, U. (2006). Some personality correlates of business white-collar crime. *Applied Psychology: An International Review, 55,* 220-233.

Bogart, L. M., Benotsch, E. G., & Pavlovic, J. D. (2004). Feeling superior but threatened: The relation of narcissism to social comparison. *Basic and Applied Social Psychology, 26,* 35-44.

Brown, R. P. (2004). Vengeance is mine: Narcissism, vengeance, and the tendency to forgive. *Journal of Research in Personality, 38,* 576-583.

Brunell, A. B., Gentry, W. A., Campbell, W. K., Hoffman, B. J., Kuhnert, K. W., & DeMarree, K. G. (2008). Leader emergence: The case of the narcissistic leader. *Personality and Social Psychology Bulletin, 34,* 1663-1676.

Bushman, B., & Baumesiter, R. F. (1998). Threatened egotism, narcissism, self-esteem, and direct and displaced aggression: Does self-love or self-hate lead to violence? *Journal of Personality and Social Psychology, 75,* 219-229.

Buss, D. M., & Chiodo, L. M. (1991). Narcissistic acts in everyday life. *Journal of Personality, 36,* 543-545.

Campbell, W. K. (1999). Narcissism and romantic attraction. *Journal of Personality and Social Psychology, 77,* 1254-1270.

Campbell, W. K., Bush, C. P., Brunell, A. B., & Shelton, J. (2005). Understanding the social costs of narcissism: The case of the tragedy of the commons. *Personality and Social Psychology Bulletin, 31,* 1358-1368.

Campbell, W. K., Goodie, A. S., & Foster, J. D. (2004). Narcissism, confidence, and risk attitude. *Journal of Behavioral Decision Making, 17,* 297-311.

Campbell, W. K., & Foster, C. A. (2002). Narcissism and commitment in romantic relationships: An investment model analysis. *Personality and Social Psychology Bulletin, 28,* 484-495.

Campbell, W. K., Reeder, G. D., Sedikides, C., & Elliot, A. J. (2000). Narcissism and comparative self-enhancement strategies. *Journal of Research in Personality, 34,* 329-347.

Campbell, W. K., Rudich, E. A., & Sedikides, C. (2002). Narcissism, self-esteem, and the positivity of self-views: Two portraits of self-love. *Personality and Social Psychology Bulletin, 28,* 358-368.

Chatterjee, A., & Hambrick, D. C. (2007). It's all about me: Narcissistic chief executive officers and their effects on company strategy and performance. *Administrative Science Quarterly, 52,* 351-386.

Corry, N., Merritt, R. D., Mrug, S., & Pamp, B. (2008). The factor structure of the narcissistic personality inventory. *Journal of Personality Assessment, 90*(6), 593-600.

Cycyota, C. S., & Harrison, D. A. (2006). What (not) to expect when surveying executives: A meta-analysis of top manager response rates and techniques over time. *Organizational Research Methods, 9,* 133-160.

Davis, M. S., Wester, K. L., & King, B. (2008). Narcissism, entitlement, and questionable research practices in counseling: A pilot study. *Journal of Counseling & Development, 86,* 200-210.

Deluga, R. J. (1997). Relationship among American presidential charismatic leadership, narcissism, and rated performance. *Leadership Quarterly, 8,* 49-65.

Edelman, R. (2009). *2009 Edelman Trust Barometer Executive Summary & Edelman Trust Barometer—Paradise Lost.* Retrieved from www.edelman.com

Emmons, R. A. (1984). Factor analysis and construct validity of the narcissistic personality inventory. *Journal of Personality Assessment, 48,* 291-300.

Emmons, R. A. (1987). Narcissism: theory and measurement. *Journal of Personality and Social Psychology, 52,* 11-17.

Farwell, L., & Wohlwend-Lloyd, R. (1998). Narcissistic processes: Optimistic expectations, favorable self-evaluations, and self-enhancing attributions. *Journal of Personality, 66,* 65-83.

Finkelstein, S., Hambrick, D. C., & Cannella, A. A. (2009). *Strategic leadership: Theory and research on executives, top management teams, and boards.* London, England: Oxford University Press.

Foster, J. D., Campbell, W. K., & Twenge, J. M. (2003). Individual differences in narcissism: Inflated self-views across the lifespan and around the world. *Journal of Research in Personality, 37,* 469-486.

Gabriel, M. T., Critelli, J. W., & Ee, J. S. (1994). Narcissistic illusions in self-evaluations of intelligence and attractiveness. *Journal of Personality, 62,* 143-155.

Gosling, S. D., John, O. P., Craik, K. H., & Robins, R. W. (1998). Do people know how they behave? Self-reported act frequencies compared with on-line codings by observers. *Journal of Personality and Social Psychology, 74,* 1337-1349.

Hartouni, Z. S. (1992). Effects of narcissistic personality organization on causal attributions. *Psychological Reports, 71,* 1339-1346.

Hayward, M., & Hambrick, D. C. (1997). Explaining the premiums paid for large acquisitions: Evidence of CEO hubris. *Administrative Science Quarterly, 42,* 103-107.

Hofstede, G. (2001). *Culture's consequences: Comparing values, behaviors, institutions, and organizations across cultures.* Thousand Oaks, CA: SAGE.

Hogan, R., Curphy, G. J., & Hogan, J. (1994). What we know about leadership effectiveness and personality. *American Psychologist, 49,* 493-504.

Hogan, R., & Kaiser, R. B. (2005). What we know about leadership. *Review of General Psychology, 9,* 169-180.

Hogan, R. Raskin, R., & Fazzini, D. (1990). The dark side of charisma. In K. E. Clark & M. B. Clark (Eds.), *Measures of leadership* (pp. 343-354). West Orange, NJ: Leadership Library of America.

John, O. P., & Robins, R. W. (1994). Accuracy and bias in self-perception: Individual differences in self-enhancement and the role of narcissism. *Journal of Personality and Social Psychology, 66,* 206-219.

Judge, T. A., LePine, J. A., & Rich, B. L. (2006). Loving yourself abundantly: Relationship of the narcissistic personality to self- and other perceptions of workplace deviance, leadership, and task and contextual performance. *Journal of Applied Psychology, 91,* 762-776.

Kernis, M. H., & Chien-Ru, S. (1994). Narcissism and reactions to interpersonal feedback. *Journal of Research in Personality, 28,* 4-13.

Kets de Vries, M. F. R. (1995). *Life and death in the executive fast lane.* San Francisco: Jossey-Bass.

Kets de Vries, M. F. R., & Miller, D. (1985). Narcissism and leadership: An object relations perspective. *Human Relations, 38,* 583-601.

Khurana, R. (2002). *Searching for a corporate savior: The irrational quest for charismatic CEOs.* Princeton, NJ: Princeton University Press.

Kubarych, T. S., Deary, I. J., & Austin, E. J. (2004). The narcissistic personality inventory: Factor structure in a non-clinical sample. *Personality and Individual Differences, 36,* 857-872.

Ladd, E. R., Welsh, M. C., Vitulli, W. F., Labbe, E. E., & Law, J. G. (1997). Narcissism and causal attribution. *Psychological Reports, 80,* 171-178.

Lasch, C. (1979). *The culture of narcissism: American life in an age of diminishing expectations.* New York: Norton.

Lipman-Blumen, J. (2005). *The allure of toxic leaders.* New York: Oxford University Press.

Maccoby, M. (2000, Jan.-Feb.). Narcissistic leaders: The incredible pros, the inevitable cons. *Harvard Business Review,* 92-101.

Maccoby, M. (2007). *Narcissistic leaders: Who succeeds and who fails?* Boston: Harvard Business School Press Books.

McCann, J. T., & Biaggio, M. K. (1989). Narcissistic personality features and self-reported anger. *Psychological Reports, 64,* 55-58.

McFarlin, D. B., Coster, E. A., & Mogale-Pretorius, C. (1999). Management development in South Africa: Moving toward an Africanized framework. *Journal of Management Development, 18,* 63-78.

McFarlin, D. B., & Sweeney, P. D. (2002). *Where egos dare: The untold truth about narcissistic leaders—and how to survive them.* London, England: Kogan Page.

Morf, C. C., & Rhodewalt, F. (2001). Unraveling the paradoxes of narcissism: A systematic self-regulatory processing model. *Psychological Inquiry, 12,* 177-196.

Morf, C. C., Weir, C., & Davidov, M. (2000). Narcissism and intrinsic motivation: The role of goal congruence. *Journal of Experimental Social Psychology, 36,* 424-438.

Mumford, M. D., Connelly, M. S., Helton, W. B., Strange, J. M., & Osburn, H. K. (2001). On the construct validity of integrity tests: Individual and situational factors as predictors of test performance. *International Journal of Selection and assessment, 9,* 240-257.

Oltmanns, T. F., Friedman, J. N. W., Fiedler, E. R., & Turkheimer, E. (2004). Perceptions of people with personality disorders based on thin slices of behavior. *Journal of Research in Personality, 38,* 216-239.

Otway, L. J., & Vignoles, V. L. (2006). Narcissism and childhood recollections: A quantitative test of psychoanalytic predictions. *Personality and Social Psychology Bulletin, 32*(1), 104-116.

Paulhus, D. L. (1998). Interpersonal and intrapsychic adaptiveness of trait self-enhancement: A mixed blessing? *Journal of Personality and Social Psychology, 74,* 1197-1208.

Paulhus, D. L., & Williams, K. M. (2002). The dark triad of personality: Narcissism, Machiavellianism and psychopathy. *Journal of Research in Personality, 36,* 556-563.

Paunonen, S. V., Lonnqvist, J., Verkasalo, M., Leikas, S., & Nissinen, V. (2006). Narcissism and emergent leadership in military cadets. *Leadership Quarterly, 17,* 475-486.

Penny, L. J., & Spector, P. E. (2002). Narcissism and counterproductive work behavior: Do bigger egos mean bigger problems? *International Journal of Selection and Assessment, 10,* 126-134.

Raskin, R. (1980). Narcissism and creativity: Are they related? *Psychological Reports, 46,* 55-60.

Raskin, R., & Hall, C. S. (1979). A narcissistic personality inventory. *Psychological Reports, 45,* 590.

Raskin, R., & Novacek, J. (1989). An MMPI description of the narcissistic personality. *Journal of Personality Assessment, 53,* 66-80.

Raskin, R., & Shaw, R. (1988). Narcissism and the use of personal pronouns. *Journal of Personality, 56,* 393-404.

Raskin, R., & Terry, H. (1988). A principal-components analysis of the narcissistic personality inventory and further evidence of its construct validity. *Journal of Personality and Social Psychology, 54,* 890-902.

Rhodewalt, F., & Morf, C. C. (1995). Self and interpersonal correlates of the Narcissistic Personality Inventory: A review and new findings. *Journal of Research in Personality, 29,* 1-23.

Rhodewalt, F., & Morf, C. C. (1998). On self-aggrandizement and anger: A temporal analysis of narcissism and affective reactions to success and failure. *Journal of Personality and Social Psychology, 74,* 672-685.

Rhodewalt, F., Tragakis, M. W., & Finnerty, J. (2006). Narcissism and self-handicapping: Linking self-aggrandizement to behavior. *Journal of Research in Personality, 40,* 573-597.

Roberts, W. (1990). *Leadership secrets of Atilla the Hun.* New York: Grand Central Publishing.

Robins, R. W., & John, O. P. (1997). Effects of visual perspective and narcissism on self-perception: Is seeing believing? *Psychological Science, 8,* 37-42.

Roll, R. (1986). The hubris hypothesis of corporate takeovers. *Journal of Business, 59,* 197-216.

Rosenthal, S. A., & Pittinsky, T. L. (2006). Narcissistic leadership. *The Leadership Quarterly, 17,* 617-633.

Schopen, F. (2009, January 28). Leadership is about more than charisma. *The Times Online.* Retrieved from http://timesonline.co.uk

Sedikides, C., Rudich, E. A., Gregg, A. P., Kumashiro, M., & Rusbult, C. (2004). Are normal narcissists psychologically healthy?: Self-esteem matters. *Journal of Personality and Social Psychology, 87,* 400-416.

Soyer, R. B., Rovenpor, J. L., & Kopelman, R. E. (1999). Narcissism and achievement motivation as related to three facets of the sales role: Attraction, satisfaction and performance. *Journal of Business and Psychology, 14,* 285-304.

Smalley, R. L., & Stake, J. E. (1996). Evaluating sources of ego-threatening feedback: self-esteem and narcissism effects. *Journal of Personality and Social Psychology, 62,* 1036-1049.

Stucke, T. S. (2003). Who's to blame. Narcissism and self-serving attributions following feedback. *European Journal of Personality, 17,* 465-478.

Trzesniewski, K. H., Donnellan, M. B., & Robins, R. W. (2008a). Is "Generation Me" really more narcissistic than previous generations? *Journal of Personality, 76,* 903-917.

Trzesniewski, K. H., Donnellan, M. B., & Robins, R. W. (2008b). Do today's young people really think they are so extraordinary? An examination of secular trends in narcissism and self-enhancement. *Psychological Science, 19*(2), 181-188.

Twenge, J. M., & Campbell, W. K. (2001). Age and birth cohort differences in self-esteem: A cross-temporal meta-analysis. *Personality and Social Psychology Review, 5,* 321-344.

Twenge, J. M., & Campbell, W. K. (2003). "Isn't it fun to get the respect that we're going to deserve?" Narcissism, social rejection, and aggression. *Personality and Social Psychology Bulletin, 29,* 261-272.

Twenge, J. M., Konrath, S., Foster, J. D., Campbell, W. K., & Bushman, B. J. (2008a). Egos inflating over time: A cross-temporal meta-analysis of the narcissistic personality inventory. *Journal of Personality, 76,* 875-901.

Twenge, J. M., Konrath, S., Foster, J. D., Campbell, W. K., & Bushman, B. J. (2008b). Further evidence of an increase in narcissism among college students. *Journal of Personality, 76,* 919-927.

Vogel, C. (2006, Jan/Feb.). A field guide to narcissism. *Psychology Today,* 68-74.

Wallace, H. M., & Baumeister, R. F. (2002). The performance of narcissists rises and falls with perceived opportunity for glory. *Journal of Personality and Social Psychology, 82,* 819-834.

Watson, P. J., Grisham, S. O., Trotter, M. V., & Biderman, M. D. (1984). Narcissism and empathy: Validity evidence for the Narcissistic Personality Inventory. *Journal of Personality Assessment, 48,* 301-305.

Wink, P. (1991). Two faces of narcissism. *Journal of Personality and Social Psychology, 61,* 590-597.

Zuckerman, M., & O'Loughlin, R. E., (2009). Narcissism and well-being: A longitudinal perspective. *European Journal of Social Psychology, 39,* 957-972.

CHAPTER 11

TANGO IN THE DARK

The Interplay of Leader's and Follower's Level of Self-Construal and its Impact on Ethical Behavior in Organizations

Suzanne van Gils,
Niels van Quaquebeke, and Daan van Knippenberg

In romantic views on leadership, leaders are traditionally held responsible for any kind of ethical misconduct in organizations. We aim to add some nuances to this view with the present chapter. We suggest that people generally regard leadership as ethical when the leader takes the collective into account, while only focusing on own gains is largely regarded as unethical. The degree to which leaders' decisions are directed towards the self versus the collective depends on the leaders' level of self-construal, that is, the way in which they see themselves in relation to others. Looking at leader's ethical decision making through this lens suggests that ethical leadership is open to external influence, in that leaders' self-construal is susceptible to external cues. In particular, followers form an important part of such external cues for a leader's level of self-construal. We thus suggest a mechanism via which followers indirectly influence their leaders' ethical decision making. In sum, we put forward a model in which we show how leaders and followers reciprocally affect each other's level of self-construal and thus ultimately the degree to which ethical behavior is enacted.

When Leadership Goes Wrong: Destructive Leadership, Mistakes and Ethical Failures, pp. 285–303

Recent business scandals have confronted the general public with examples of leaders who displayed highly self-enriching behaviors while their companies were at the verge of bankruptcy. The media attention devoted to these scandals, which ranged from manager's acceptance of outrageous bonuses, or private use of company jets, to redecorations of private apartments at company costs, has generally focused on the contrast between the leader's selfish behavior in these cases and the collective-serving behavior that is generally expected.

Based on these examples we define ethical leadership as leadership behaviors that serve the collective. As this definition allows for the possibility that the leader profits from his or her own collective-serving behavior, it is less strict than some other definitions in the field of organizational science, where ethical leadership typically is defined as altruism vis-à-vis egoism (e.g., Bass & Steidlmeier, 1999; Price, 2005; Turner, Barling, Epitropaki, Butcher, & Milner, 2002). In line with similar definitions of ethical leadership, defining ethical leadership as behavior that serves the collective suggests that whether the behavior is ethical or not depends on the culture and norms of the relevant collective (Brown, Treviño, & Harrison, 2005). Consequently, behavior that is considered group-serving in one collective might not be perceived in the same way by another collective (critical exceptions will be discussed briefly at the end of this chapter).

When do leaders take the collective into account? Extant literature on ethical leadership has mainly focused on characteristics of leaders that predispose them to display a certain level of ethical behavior (De Hoogh & Den Hartog, 2008; Loviscky, Treviño, & Jacobs, 2007). Although some research that extends this view has touched upon the subject of contextual influences on ethical leadership (Brown & Treviño, 2006; Flannery & May, 2000) and some theories even include the influence of role models of ethical leadership through social learning (Brown et al., 2005), ethical leadership is still approached as an intrapersonal rather than an interpersonal phenomenon. This view on ethical leadership, and ethical behavior in a broader sense, contrasts with the idea that ethical behavior depends on others. Specifically, in the media, leadership behavior that does not serve the collective is not only portrayed as selfish, it is also perceived as motivating the subordinates to act in the same way. Thus, ethical behavior by followers is attributed to ethical behavior of the leader. Indeed, the CEOs of for example Citigroup, Ford, or Chrysler, who reduced their salaries to the symbolic amount of $1 in an attempt to help their company survive the financial crisis, were publicly applauded for setting a right example.

In order to take the interpersonal influences on ethical behavior into account, and specifically to illustrate the effects of these influences on ethical leadership, we provide a model that builds on the literature on levels of self-construal, discussing circumstances under which individuals focus on outcomes for the collective rather than their own. This literature suggests that collective-oriented behavior depends on the way in which people conceptualize the relationships between themselves and others, and is driven by an interdependent level of self-construal (Markus & Kitayama, 1991; Trafimow, Triandis, & Goto, 1991). Thus we suggest that the cognitive processes evoking an orientation on the collective are similar for leaders and followers, thereby implying that these processes not only evoke ethical leadership but ethical followership as well. However, extensive elaborations on ethical followership go beyond the scope of this chapter.

In recent decades, research on leadership has increasingly paid attention to the role of the follower in leadership processes. Some of this research discussed the importance of followers' attributions for their perceptions of leadership (Meindl, 1995; Meindl, Ehrlich, & Dukerich, 1985, and see chapter Hansbrough and Schyns, this volume). Others discuss a more active role for the follower, for example through building of mutual trust, and suggest that for organizational success it takes "two to tango" (e.g., Ferrin, Bligh, & Kohles, 2008). In line with this latter approach, we suggest an active role for followers on their leader's ethical and unethical decisions. Taking a self-construal based approach allows for this interpersonal influence of the followers on their leaders, because it suggests not only that leaders can influence their follower's level of self-construal, but also that a leader's ethical decisions might be influenced by their social context, leaving room for the followers to indirectly influence their leader's decisions.

In short, we propose a reciprocal model with an active role for the follower in influencing the leader's behavior. In outlining this model we will elaborate on the effects of different levels of self-construal on leader's ethical behavior. In order to do this, we first provide a short overview of research on ethical leadership and self-construal. Next we will discuss the parallels between these two lines of research and discuss how a self-construal based model of ethical leadership allows for a reciprocal interpersonal perspective on ethical leadership. Subsequently, we will discuss how leaders can influence their follower's behavior through levels of self-construal and conclude with illustrations of how followers can influence their leader's level of self-construal.

ETHICAL LEADERSHIP

The topic of ethical and unethical behavior in organizations has been given a lot of attention in the past decade (Ashkanasy, Windsor, & Treviño, 2006;

Brown & Treviño, 2006; Tenbrunsel & Smith-Crowe, 2008; Treviño, Weaver, & Reynolds, 2006). However, within this expanding field, ethical leadership has received relatively little attention. In the paragraphs below, we will give an overview of the existing literature on ethical leadership. First, we will discuss the traditional view on ethical leadership, then we will continue to discuss recent literature that adds external influences to this view, and last we will introduce an interpersonal perspective on ethical leadership.

The traditional view of ethical leadership contends that ethical decision making depends on an individual's personality. For example, De Hoogh and Den Hartog (2008) focused on leaders' social responsibility to predict ethical leadership. Most of the research investigating the influence of the leader's personality on ethical leadership behaviors builds on Kohlberg's (1981) theory of moral development and suggests that the leader's level of moral development determines the extent to which the leader takes the collective into account (e.g., Loviscky et al., 2007; Treviño & Youngblood, 1990). In his theory, Kohlberg describes six stages of development of people's moral judgment, which can be organized in three levels of sophistication. At the preconventional level, individuals are thought to act from an egoistic perspective, mainly focusing on personal consequences. At the conventional level, individuals' actions are driven by what is right or wrong in relative to their social relationships, and focus on relational outcomes. At the postconventional level, individuals are thought to be driven by universalistic principles of rights and justice, and take into account ideal ethical norms. At this level people take the collective into account when making decisions (Kohlberg, 1981). Although Kohlberg's initial theory defines these levels of moral judgment as being static and suggests an upward progress only, more recent adaptations of the theory suggest that people can alternate between the various levels (Rest, Narvaez, Bebeau, & Thoma, 1999). Overall, this research suggests positive effects of higher levels of cognitive moral development, that is, the stage in which individuals take others into account. For example, research showed that followers rate leaders with a higher level of cognitive moral development as more transformational (Turner et al., 2002).

Nuancing the personality based perspective on ethical leadership, recent research has included the effect of external influences (Ashkanasy et al., 2006; Brown & Treviño, 2006; Treviño & Youngblood, 1990). For example, this research has shown that ethical decision making does not only depend on characteristics of the person or the organization, but is also influenced by the characteristics of the ethical issue itself. Issues that have larger consequences, or are viewed as bad by a larger public, or are more probable, or are closer in time or physical distance, or have a more concentrated effect, are perceived as higher in moral intensity and are therefore more likely to lead to a moral decision (Flannery & May, 2000; Jones, 1991). Other research has shown that the presence of organizational rewards and punishments influences ethical behavior in organizations (Ashkanasy et al., 2006), and that seeing other members of the organization being punished for deviant behavior or rewarded for ethical behavior also increases the extent to which people display ethical behavior (Treviño & Youngblood, 1990).

The research discussed above shows how ethical behavior can be driven by intrapersonal factors. However, it does not provide insights in how ethical behavior can be motivated by other people, and thereby overlooks the dynamics between leaders and followers that can bring out ethical behavior in either person. Although there is some research that suggests that ethical behavior might be influenced by an ethical role model through social learning, (Brown & Treviño, 2006) and even defines ethical leadership as "the demonstration of normatively appropriate conduct through personal actions and interpersonal relationships and the promotion of such conduct to followers through two-way communication, reinforcement and decision making" (Brown et al., 2005, p. 120), this research does not discuss the mutual influences leaders and followers have on each other's ethical behavior that are suggested by this definition, but rather focuses on the leader's influence on the follower only. In this paper we introduce a model that takes an interpersonal perspective on ethical leadership, we first suggest that a leader's motivation to take the collective into account depends on their level of self-construal and second propose that an individual's level of self-construal can be influenced by other people and thus may form the underlying mechanism through which leaders and followers motivate each other's ethical behavior. Before outlining our model, we will first shortly discuss the literature on self-construal.

SELF-CONSTRUAL AND EFFECTS ON BEHAVIOR

Research on levels of self-construal suggests that the extent to which someone is responsive to the needs of the collective depends on the way the person perceives the relationship between him or herself and the collective. The interconnectedness between the self and others arises from basic needs to see oneself in a social context (Baumeister & Leary, 1995), and is one of the defining elements in the way people cognitively represent the self. Research on self-construal suggests that the content and structure of the inner self may differ considerably between persons, depending on their view of the self and the relationship between the self and others (Markus & Kitayama, 1991; Trafimow et al., 1991).

Originating from cross-cultural research, self-construal researchers distinguish between an independent level of self-construal and an interdependent level of self-construal. Individuals with an independent level of self-construal define themselves as autonomous, independent persons and focus on differences between the self and others in interpersonal interactions. They demonstrate lower levels of inclusiveness and higher levels of individualism, that is, they define themselves in terms of "I" instead of "we" and focus on individual outcomes. In contrast, individuals with an interdependent level of self-construal define themselves as part of a larger collective and focus on the relationships between the self and others. They demonstrate higher levels of inclusiveness and higher levels of collectivism, that is, they define themselves in terms of "we" rather than "I". In social interactions, individuals with an interdependent level of self-construal concentrate more on collective level outcomes (Markus & Kitayama, 1991; Triandis, 1989; Turner, Oakes, Haslam, & McGarty, 1994).

The way in which individuals construe their self-concept has consequences for other cognitive activities that relate to the self (Cross, Morris, & Gore, 2002). Specifically, it has been found that those with an interdependent level of self-construal will be more attentive and sensitive to information about others (Markus & Kitayama, 1991), and will categorize information in terms of the collective (Turner et al., 1994). Prior research has shown that higher levels of interdependent self-construal lead people to perceive themselves as more similar to others in social comparisons (Kühnen & Hannover, 2000; Stapel & Koomen, 2001), evaluate relational concepts more positively and have a better memory for relational information (Cross et al., 2002). Furthermore, individuals with an interdependent level of self-construal were found to take less risks when making choices related to social approval than individuals with an independent level of self-construal (Mandel, 2003). Combined, this research shows that an interdependent level of self-construal evokes cognitive processes that make the relationships between self and others more salient and important than an independent level of self-construal.

Thus, extant literature provides evidence that the perception of others and attention paid to them differs depending on one's level of self-construal. Whether someone recognizes the needs of the collective therefore is likely to depend on the person's active level of self-construal. Furthermore, these different perceptions are also likely to elicit different behaviors towards others. We have previously suggested that ethical behavior mainly depends on whether the leader's behavior demonstrates that he or she takes the interest of the collective at heart, and that this focus on the collective depends on an individual's level of self-construal. This suggestion presupposes that a certain level of self-construal evokes behaviors that correspond to it. Insights in how self-construal translates into behavior can be found in various streams of literature, which we will discuss in turn.

First, connectionist theories of cognition suggest that self-construal influences behavior through increasing the salience of behaviors congruent with the person's level of self-construal, that is, independent levels of self-construal activate individualistic behaviors, while interdependent levels of self-construal activate behaviors that benefit others rather than only the self. The frameworks of actions and behaviors that are activated by a certain level of self-construal are supposed to function as a looking glass through which own and other's behavior are generated and interpreted (Lord & Brown, 2001; Lord & Emrich, 2000). Research supporting and extending these theoretical claims suggests that levels of self-construal are related to the cognitive activation of congruent values (Verplanken, Trafimow, Khusid, Holland, & Steentjes, 2009). Independent self-construal has been shown to motivate behavior oriented at the individual through activation of personal values, while interdependent self-construal motivates behavior oriented at the collective, based on activation of social norms (Gardner, Gabriel, & Lee, 1999; Verplanken & Holland, 2002; Verplanken, Walker, Davis, & Jurasek, 2008).

Further evidence for the effect of self-construal on behavior comes from research on social value orientation. This research has focused on orientations toward others that can be used to predict whether individuals will cooperate or compete in interactions. These orientations determine how individuals evaluate outcomes for themselves and others in interdependent situations and distinguishes between collective oriented "pro-social" orientations, or in other words, cooperation, and self oriented "pro-self orientations", that is, competition or individualism (Joireman, Van Lange, Kuhlman, Van Vugt, & Shelley, 1997; Van Lange & Liebrand, 1991). With respect to the influence of self-construal on behavior, this research has found that people with a chronic level of individual self-construal (proself value orientation) will act more cooperatively after activation of collective self-construal (prosocial value orientation) because this activation increases the value assigned to the collective good as opposed to individual gain (De Cremer & Van Vugt, 1999). In the light of the current chapter, this research not only supports the idea that an interdependent level of self-construal leads to collective-oriented behavior, but also suggests that a certain level of self-construal can be primed.

Additional research on self-construal suggests that the effects of the activated level of self-construal can be expanded to situations in which people directly interact with others, and specifically to the extent to which they take the other into account. For example, research has shown that activation of a collective level of self-construal lead participants to mimic the other person more, than when an individual level of self-construal was activated (van Baaren, Maddux, Chartrand, de Bouter, & van Knippenberg, 2003). Furthermore, others have found that people with a collective level of self-construal took the recipients knowledge more into account when answering questions than people with an individual level of self-construal (Haberstroh, Oyserman, Schwarz, Kühnen, & Ji, 2002). Together, these studies show that activation of a collective level of self-construal, as opposed to an individual level of self-construal, can indeed lead to an increased tendency to take others into account or to take the other's perspective.

ETHICAL LEADERSHIP AND SELF-CONSTRUAL—PARALLELS AND EXTENSIONS

Although research on independent and interdependent levels of self-construal has not been connected with ethical leadership earlier, the parallels between these two lines of research suggest that a combination of the two might provide a more dynamic model of ethical leadership that rests on interpersonal processes rather than individual characteristics per se. First, both approaches show that behavior that benefits others is based on a cognitive level that makes people take others into account. Whereas in terms of self-construal this level of cognition is represented by interdependent self-construal (Markus & Kitayama, 1991; Trafimow et al., 1991), in the literature on ethics this cognitive level is based on an individual's cognitive moral development. For example, research has associated individual's levels of cognitive moral development, that is, the extent to which individuals focus on consequences for themselves and others when making decisions, with their level of ethical decision making (Treviño & Youngblood, 1990). Both approaches suppose a hierarchy in which a more inclusive cognitive level leads to increases in ethical decision making. This parallel is illustrated in Figure 11.1.

A second parallel between the literature on ethical leadership as well as the literature on self-construal is the suggestion that collective-oriented behavior by the leader leads to positive effects on the followers (van Knippenberg & Hogg, 2003; van Knippenberg, van Knippenberg, De Cremer, & Hogg, 2004). However, while the literature on ethical leadership suggests that the follower's perception of an ethical leader motivates them to display positive behaviors, it does not discuss how these positive behaviors come about. Based on the literature on self-construal, we provide a model that elucidates the underlying cognitive mechanism by suggesting that these positive behaviors are based on the activation of the follower's level of self-construal.

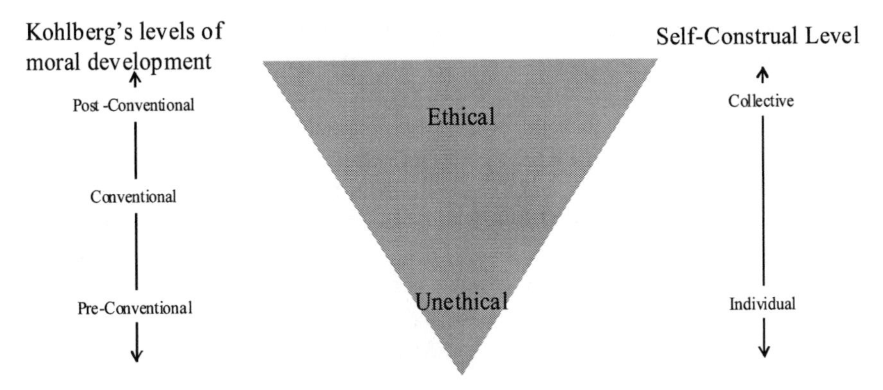

Figure 11.1. Comparison of Kohlberg's levels of moral development and self-construal level.

An important difference between the two lines of research can be found in the proposed antecedents of collective-oriented behavior. As discussed above, in the literature on ethical leadership, collective oriented decision making is supposed to stem from the leader's personality, and specifically the level of moral development. This point of view goes back to Kohlberg's (1981) theory on moral development. Ethical leadership thus rests, according to this literature, on the leader's personality. Consequently, based on this point of view, one would suggest that whether an individual takes the collective into account depends his or her personality and is not dependent on interpersonal influences.

In contrast, taking a social psychological approach to ethical leadership does provide insights in the underlying cognitive structure, and also provides a starting point for a more dynamic view on ethical leadership. The literature on self-construal suggests that the cognitive process underlying collective-oriented decision making, that is, interdependent self-construal, is not a stable personality characteristic, but rather a dynamic cognitive process in which leaders and followers can bring out certain behaviors in each other. In our model, we suggest that activation of a certain level of self-construal in either the leader or the follower depends on the activation of this level by the other party.

The suggestion that levels of self-construal can be activated by another person is supported by various sources. Firstly, theoretical work by Lord and colleagues (1999, 2001) substantiates this claim by suggesting that there are different styles of leadership at different levels of cognitive identity focus (individual-, relational- or group-level), and that through a certain style of leadership, leaders activate a level of self-construal in the follower which corresponds to the displayed style of leadership. The activated level of self-construal is suggested to subsequently influence the follower's goals, self-views and perceptions of the self in the future, that is, possible selves (Lord & Brown, 2001; Lord, Brown, & Freiberg, 1999). Second, experimental manipulations of self-construal provide evidence for the suggestion that one's level of self-construal is context-dependent rather than static, because most experimental manipulations are based on activation of self-construal through cues from the environment, mostly in the form of texts (e.g., Gardner et al., 1999; van Baaren et al., 2003). Finally, empirical research has shown that a leader's display of behavior that serves the collective, for example fairness or self-sacrifice, evokes higher levels of cooperation in followers (De Cremer & van Knippenberg, 2002, 2004, 2005). Moreover, this research has shown that these higher levels of cooperation are driven by a collective level of identification (De Cremer, Tyler, & Ouden, 2005; De Cremer & van Knippenberg, 2005), which can be equated with a collective level of self-construal (van Knippenberg et al., 2004). Together this research demonstrates that a collective level of self-construal can be activated by another person.

Summarizing, we suggest that by extending the literature on ethical leadership with insights from research on self-construal, we can provide a glimpse into the cognitive processes underlying ethical leadership, as well as a more dynamic perspective on the process. As the activation of a certain level of self-construal can be assumed to be similar for leaders and followers, this approach does not only describe how leaders can bring out a collective self-construal and corresponding behaviors in their followers, but also allows for the followers to influence their leader's behavior. In the sections below we will outline our model describing ethical leadership and the influences followers have on their leader's level of self-construal.

ETHICAL LEADERSHIP AND ITS EFFECTS ON FOLLOWERS

In previous sections we have suggested that ethical leaders are those who take the interest of the collective at heart. Indeed, some researchers have demonstrated the extent to which the leader displays behavior that serves the collective is related to the leader's effectiveness, and that this relationship is mediated by the follower's level of identification (van Knippenberg & Hogg, 2003). Based on the research on self-construal cited above we suggest that the leader's level of self-construal influences his or her decisions, with an interdependent level of self-construal leading to more collective-oriented decisions. Recent research provides initial support for this claim by demonstrating that leaders who identify more with the collective (i.e., define themselves as interdependent with the collective), make distributive decisions that are more fair and more representative of the collective interest (Giessner & van Knippenberg, 2008). This influence of the leader's level of self-construal on his or her own behavior is the first step in our model, which is depicted in Figure 11.2.

The leader's level of self-construal does not only affect his or her own behavior, but through this behavior also influences the follower's level of self-construal and subsequent behavior. In this light, research has found that the leader's collective self-construal leads to more identification of the follower with the organization, that is, the follower's collective level of self-construal, and in addition leads to higher levels of job satisfaction for the follower (van Dick, Hirst, Grojean, & Wieseke, 2007). Furthermore, the follower's perception of the leader as having the interest of the collective at heart, measured by follower's indications of the leader's level of moral development, has a positive influence on the follower's attitudes, like job satisfaction, organizational commitment or turnover (Schminke, Ambrose, & Neubaum, 2005).

Research on charismatic leadership demonstrates the effects of the leader's collective level of self-construal, as displayed in direct communication, on the follower's identification with the collective, that is, the follower's level of collective self-construal (Conger, Kanungo, & Menon, 2000; Shamir, House, & Arthur, 1993). In terms of a leader's communication towards followers, research has found that the leader's emphasis on a collective identity, shared values, and inclusive behavior were positively related to followers' identification (Shamir, Zakay, Brainin, & Popper, 2000). In addition, others found that elements in the leader's communication referring to collective missions, beliefs and values (idealized influence) made collective self-construal salient, while elements that referred to employees as unique individuals and emphasized individual differences (individualized consideration) made individual self-construal salient (Paul, Costley, Howell, Dorfman, & Trafimow, 2001). Summarizing, this research shows that the leader's level of self-construal can influence the follower's level of self-construal through his or her behavior.

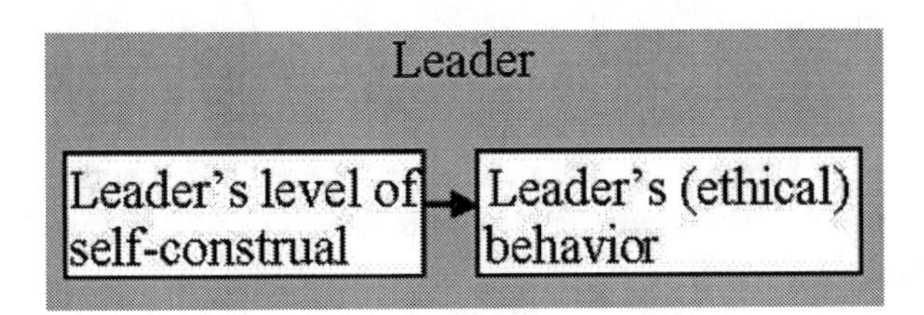

Figure 11.2. First part of the model; The influence of the leader's level of self-construal on the leader's ethical behavior.

Another way in which leaders can influence the follower's level of self-construal is through symbolic behavior. This is supported by research on leader self-sacrifice (e.g., Choi & Mai-Dalton, 1999; De Cremer & van Knippenberg, 2005; van Knippenberg & van Knippenberg, 2005), which demonstrated that the leader can bring out a collective self-construal in followers by displaying a collective self-construal themselves. Specifically, by sacrificing personal gains for the benefit of the team, the leader communicates commitment to the group's goals and care for the interest of the group members (Conger & Kanungo, 1987; Shamir et al., 1993; van Knippenberg & Hogg, 2003). This kind of self-sacrificing behavior has a positive influence on the followers, and has been found to contribute substantially to leadership effectiveness because followers see self-sacrificing leaders as more legitimate and therefore they become motivated to reciprocate the leader's efforts (Choi & Mai-Dalton, 1999). In addition, self-sacrificing leaders have been found to elicit higher levels of performance in followers than self-benefitting leaders (van Knippenberg & van Knippenberg, 2005). More specific research has shown that leader self-sacrifice brings out more cooperation in a public good dilemma, and that this process is mediated by a higher sense of belonging to the group or a collective level of identification (De Cremer & van Knippenberg, 2002, 2005).

FOLLOWER'S INFLUENCE ON LEADER

Although in the above we have mainly discussed the effects of the level of self-construal on the leader's ethical behavior, we suggest that the activation of self-construal is context dependent and thus does not depend only on the leader, but on the followers as well. We argue for a fully reciprocal model of ethical leadership, describing how leaders and followers have a reciprocal influence on each other's level of self-construal and thus influence the extent to which their behavior is ethical (see Figure 11.3).

Initial evidence that activating a different level of self-construal in leaders brings out more collective-oriented behaviors can be found in social psychological research that demonstrates that activation of the collective level of self-construal can evoke a more prosocial use of power (Chen, Lee-Chai, & Bargh, 2001). In addition, research has found that a collective level of self-construal, makes people act more benevolently and generously towards their dyadic partners, than does an individual level of self-construal (Howard, Gardner, & Thompson, 2007). This shows that if the followers activate a collective level of self-construal in their leaders, they will be the recipients of more collectively oriented behaviors, that is, ethical leadership behaviors.

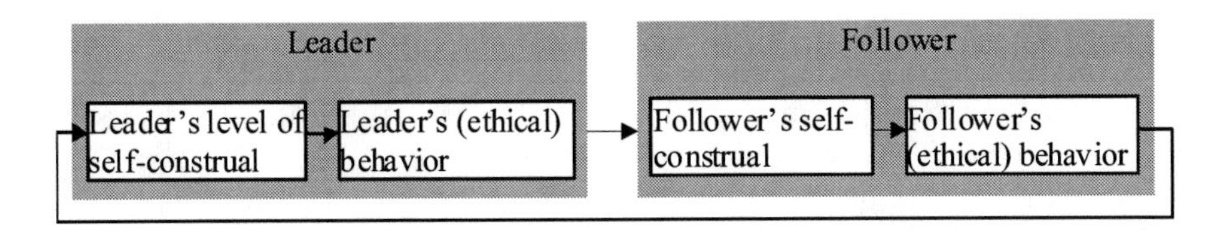

Figure 11.3. Full reciprocal model, illustrating the interplay between leader's and followers' level of self-construal on their ethical behavior.

The question remains how followers can influence their leader's self-construal. As the leader's level of self-construal depends on the (social) context and followers make up a large part of the social context, we suggest that the followers' level of self-construal forms a boundary condition for their leader's behavior. In support of this, theoretical work by Lord and colleagues (1999, 2001) suggests that followers influence their leader because the followers' level of self-construal makes them most susceptible to leadership behaviors that are congruent with this level and therefore leaders will be most effective when acting at that specific level (Lord & Brown, 2001; Lord et al., 1999). In addition to this passive influence of followers on their leaders, we suggest a more active role for the followers in influencing their leader's level of self-construal and hence the leader's behavior. They may do this in a direct way, by expressing a certain level of self-construal when communicating to their leaders. For example, in reporting accomplishments to the leader, followers can either focus on their own individual input in the process ("I"), or focus more on the outcomes for the collective that result from the accomplished task ("we"). Through communicating their level of self-construal in this way, followers may activate a corresponding level of self-construal in the leader. A second way in which followers can activate their leader's self-construal is indirectly through symbolic behavior. Similar to the findings of the effects of leader self-sacrifice and supported by research on prorelationship behavior (e.g., Wieselquist, Rusbult, Foster, & Agnew, 1999), collective-serving acts from the side of the follower communicates the importance assigned to the collective by the follower. These symbolic behaviors may in turn prime the leader's level of self-construal and motivate the leader to display collective-oriented behaviors.

SUMMARY AND IMPLICATIONS FOR ETHICAL LEADERSHIP

Summarizing, we suggest that the conduct of ethical leadership depends on the level of self-construal of the leader. Leadership behaviors that are focused on the collective will activate a corresponding level of self-construal in the followers, which will in turn lead to collectively focused behaviors from the side of the followers. However, the followers are not merely passive recipients of the leader's influence, but influence the leader as well through their own level of self-construal. This process is similar to the leader's influence on the follower. Altogether we suggest a reciprocal model, depicting ethical leadership as a dynamic process in which leaders and followers influence each other's level of self-construal and thereby motivating each other to display behaviors that take the collective into account.

A critical note should be made with regard to our definition of ethical leadership as leadership that takes the collective into account. Although we can assume that the norms in most collectives are acceptable for the society at large, there are some collectives that will advocate norms that are far removed from this. Examples of such groups include religious sects, corrupt organizational groups like the employees of Enron or collectives with fascist beliefs like the Nazis. For these exceptional cases, leader behavior that is in line with the views of the collective cannot be called ethical in any way. In fact, in these cases collective-serving behavior would only lead to increases in unethical behavior (den Nieuwenboer & Kaptein, 2008). It is also possible that the collective norm in certain groups is based on individualism, in which case the leader would serve the collective best by advocating an individual level of self-construal. These rare cases form exceptions to the model proposed in this chapter.

An extension of our model can be found in the fact that leaders usually lead a team of followers instead of one specific individual, and hence are subjected to a range of different influences from different followers. We expect that the more homogeneous the followers' levels of self-construal is, the stronger the salience of the level of self-construal will be in the leader's mind. In the context of leader's influence on followers, Lord and Brown (2001) suggest that in order for the leader to influence the follower's activation of specific values, the leader has to activate a coherent pattern of values. In line with this, we suggest that coherence in the values and levels of self-construal of the followers will lead to stronger activation of that level of self-construal in the leader.

Recognizing the value of different approaches to ethical leadership and ethical decision making, another extension of our model could stem from combinations with research on the influence of personality factors (De Hoogh & Den Hartog, 2008) or external organizational influences to explain why leaders can be motivated to take the collective into account, such as group pressure or financial dependence (cf. Ashkanasy et al., 2006; Tenbrunsel, 1998; Treviño & Youngblood, 1990). Although these factors are not integrated in the current model, interactions between these intrapersonal or external factors and the factors in our model could be regarded as possible extensions. For example, it may be expected that both leaders and followers are more susceptible to primes of the level of self-construal that corresponds to their level of cognitive moral development. In addition, research has suggested that individuals with a higher level of cognitive moral development are less susceptible to external influences (Brown & Treviño, 2006). In line with this, it might be more difficult to activate an individual level of self-construal in people with a higher level of cognitive moral development, and easier to activate a collective level of self-construal in people with a lower level of cognitive moral development. Finally, we can expect additive effects of the leader's level of self-construal and the organization's reward structure when these two match.

A last extension could be found in moderators of our model. Given the differences in power, we might expect that the leader's influence on the followers is stronger than vice versa. The strength of the follower's influence on their leader, however, might be influenced by the extent to which the leader depends on the followers. An important factor in this respect might be leader group prototypicality. Research in the context of leader group prototypicality shows that leaders are more effective and are given more leeway when they are perceived as prototypical (Platow & van Knippenberg, 2001; van Knippenberg & Hogg, 2003). Similarly, the leader's latitude to perform certain behaviors depends on the followers. Research has suggested that leaders who are perceived as deserving to be in the leadership position, are allowed greater latitude to disagree with the group judgments (Hollander, 1992) and could influence the group more. Thus, we can predict that leaders who are perceived as being more prototypical, will have a stronger influence on the followers, while leaders who are less prototypical might be influenced by the followers more. Specifying this suggestion, we can expect the effects of leader prototypicality to be even stronger if the leader is prototypical in domains related to ethics, for example, if the organization has clear ethical norms and the leader is seen to embody these norms, than if the leader is prototypical in other domains, for example, if the leader has an educational background that is considered ideal for the group. In addition to this, the extent to which the followers influence their leader may also depend on the followers' persistence in trying to exert this influence. This persistence may not only depend on the leader's prototypicality, but also on the leader's openness to influence as well as the follower's perception of their own role.

Concluding, in this chapter we have outlined the importance of a collective level of self-construal as a basis for the leader's ethical behavior. Furthermore, we have illustrated that this level of self-construal does not depend on the leader's personality, but is based on a reciprocal process in which leaders and followers influence each other's level of self-construal and in this way influence each other's level of ethical behavior. Through outlining this process we hope to have demonstrated that it takes two to tango, even when it is dark.

REFERENCES

Ashkanasy, N. M., Windsor, C. A., & Treviño, L. K. (2006). Bad apples in bad barrels revisited: Cognitive moral development, just world beliefs, rewards, and ethical decision making. *Business Ethics Quarterly, 16*, 449-473.

Bass, B. M., & Steidlmeier, P. (1999). Ethics, character, and authentic transformational leadership behavior. *Leadership Quarterly, 10*, 181-217.

Baumeister, R. F., & Leary, M. R. (1995). The need to belong: Desire for interpersonal attachments as a fundamental human motivation. *Psychological Bulletin, 117*, 497-529.

Brown, M. E., & Treviño, L. K. (2006). Ethical leadership: A review and future directions. *Leadership Quarterly, 17*, 595-616.

Brown, M. E., Treviño, L. K., & Harrison, D. A. (2005). Ethical leadership: A social learning perspective for construct development and testing. *Organizational Behavior and Human Decision Processes, 97*, 117-134.

Chen, S., Lee-Chai, A. Y., & Bargh, J. A. (2001). Relationship orientation as a moderator of the effects of social power. *Journal of Personality and Social Psychology, 80*, 173-187.

Choi, Y., & Mai-Dalton, R. R. (1999). The model of followers' responses to self-sacrificial leadership: An empirical test. *Leadership Quarterly, 10*, 397-421.

Conger, J. A., & Kanungo, R. N. (1987). Toward a behavioral theory of charismatic leadership in organizational settings. *Academy of Management Review, 12*, 637-647.

Conger, J. A., Kanungo, R. N., & Menon, S. T. (2000). Charismatic leadership and follower effects. *Journal of Organizational Behavior, 21*, 747-767.

Cross, S. E., Morris, M. L., & Gore, J. S. (2002). Thinking about oneself and others: The relational-interdependent self-construal and social cognition. *Journal of Personality and Social Psychology, 82*, 399-418.

De Cremer, D., Tyler, T. R., & Ouden, N. (2005). Managing cooperation via procedural fairness: The mediating influence of self-other merging. *Journal of Economic Psychology, 26*, 393-406.

De Cremer, D., & van Knippenberg, D. (2002). How do leaders promote cooperation? The effects of charisma and procedural fairness. *Journal of Applied Psychology, 87*, 858-866.

De Cremer, D., & van Knippenberg, D. (2004). Leader self-sacrifice and leadership effectiveness: The moderating role of leader self-confidence. *Organizational Behavior and Human Decision Processes, 95*, 140-155.

De Cremer, D., & van Knippenberg, D. (2005). Cooperation as a function of leader self-sacrifice, trust, and identification. *Leadership and Organization Development Journal, 26*, 355-370.

De Cremer, D., & Van Vugt, M. (1999). Social identification effects in social dilemmas: A transformation of motives. *European Journal of Social Psychology, 29*, 871-893.

De Hoogh, A. H. B., & Den Hartog, D. N. (2008). Ethical and despotic leadership, relationships with leader's social responsibility, top management team effectiveness and subordinates' optimism: A multi-method study. *Leadership Quarterly, 19*, 297-311.

den Nieuwenboer, N. A., & Kaptein, M. (2008). Spiraling down into corruption: A dynamic analysis of the social identity processes that cause corruption in organizations to grow. *Journal of Business Ethics, 83*, 133-146.

Ferrin, D. L., Bligh, M. C., & Kohles, J. C. (2008). It takes two to tango: An interdependence analysis of the spiraling of perceived trustworthiness and cooperation in interpersonal and intergroup relationships. *Organizational Behavior and Human Decision Processes, 107*, 161-178.

Flannery, B. L., & May, D. R. (2000). Environmental ethical decision making in the U.S. metal-finishing industry. *Academy of Management Journal, 43*, 642-662.

Gardner, W. L., Gabriel, S., & Lee, A. Y. (1999). "I" value freedom, but "we" value relationships: Self-construal priming mirrors cultural differences in judgment. *Psychological Science, 10*, 321-326.

Giessner, S. R., & van Knippenberg, D. (2008, June). *When does a leader show fair behavior? Influences of group prototypicality and the social context.* Paper presented at the 15th general meeting of the European Association of Experimental Social Psychologists.

Haberstroh, S., Oyserman, D., Schwarz, N., Kühnen, U., & Ji, L. (2002). Is the interdependent self more sensitive to question context than the independent self? Self-construal and the observation of conversational norms. *Journal of Experimental Social Psychology, 38*, 323-329.

Hollander, E. P. (1992). The essential interdependence of leadership and followership. *Current Directions in Psychological Science, 1*, 71-75.

Howard, E. S., Gardner, W. L., & Thompson, L. (2007). The role of the self-concept and the social context in determining the behavior of power holders: Self-construal in intergroup versus dyadic dispute resolution negotiations. *Journal of Personality and Social Psychology, 93*, 614-631.

Joireman, J. A., Van Lange, P. A. M., Kuhlman, D. M., Van Vugt, M., & Shelley, G. P. (1997). An interdependence analysis of commuting decisions. *European Journal of Social Psychology, 27*, 441-463.

Jones, T. M. (1991). Ethical decision making by individuals in organizations: An issue-contingent model. *Academy of Management Review, 16*, 366-395.

Kohlberg, L. (1981). *Essays on moral development: The philosophy of moral development* (Vol. I). San Francisco: Harper & Row.

Kühnen, U., & Hannover, B. (2000). Assimilation and contrast in social comparisons as a consequence of self-construal activation. *European Journal of Social Psychology, 30*, 799-811.

Lord, R. G., & Brown, D. J. (2001). Leadership, values, and subordinate self-concepts. *Leadership Quarterly, 12*, 133-152.

Lord, R. G., Brown, D. J., & Freiberg, S. J. (1999). Understanding the dynamics of leadership: The role of follower self-concepts in the leader/follower relationship. *Organizational Behavior and Human Decision Processes, 78*, 167-203.

Lord, R. G., & Emrich, C. G. (2000). Thinking outside the box by looking inside the box: Extending the cognitive revolution in leadership research. *Leadership Quarterly, 11*, 551-579.

Loviscky, G. E., Treviño, L. K., & Jacobs, R. R. (2007). Assessing managers' ethical decision-making: An objective measure of managerial moral judgment. *Journal of Business Ethics, 73*, 263-285.

Mandel, N. (2003). Shifting selves and decision making: The effects of self-construal priming on consumer risk-taking. *Journal of Consumer Research, 30*, 30-40.

Markus, H. R., & Kitayama, S. (1991). Culture and the self: Implications for cognition, emotion, and motivation. *Psychological Review, 98*, 224-253.

Meindl, J. R. (1995). The romance of leadership as a follower-centric theory: A social constructionist approach. *Leadership Quarterly, 6*, 329-341.

Meindl, J. R., Ehrlich, S. B., & Dukerich, J. M. (1985). The romance of leadership. *Administrative Science Quarterly, 30*, 78-102.

Paul, J., Costley, D. L., Howell, J. P., Dorfman, P. W., & Trafimow, D. (2001). The effects of charismatic leadership on followers' self-concept accessibility. *Journal of Applied Social Psychology, 31*, 1821-1842.

Platow, M. J., & van Knippenberg, D. (2001). A social identity analysis of leadership endorsement: The effects of leader ingroup prototypicality and distributive intergroup fairness. *Personality and Social Psychology Bulletin, 27*, 1508-1519.

Price, T. L. (2005). *Understanding ethical failures in leadership*. New York: Cambridge University Press.

Rest, J., Narvaez, D., Bebeau, M. J., & Thoma, S. J. (1999). *Postconventional moral thinking: A neo-kohlbergian approach*. Mahwah, NJ: Erlbaum.

Schminke, M., Ambrose, M. L., & Neubaum, D. O. (2005). The effect of leader moral development on ethical climate and employee attitudes. *Organizational Behavior and Human Decision Processes, 97*, 135-151.

Shamir, B., House, R. J., & Arthur, M. B. (1993). The motivational effects of charismatic leadership: A self-concept based theory. *Organization Science, 4*, 577-594.

Shamir, B., Zakay, E., Brainin, E., & Popper, M. (2000). Leadership and social identification in military units: Direct and indirect relationships. *Journal of Applied Social Psychology, 30*, 612-640.

Stapel, D. A., & Koomen, W. (2001). I, we, and the effects of others on me: How self-construal level moderates social comparison effects. *Journal of Personality and Social Psychology, 80*, 766-781.

Tenbrunsel, A. E. (1998). Misrepresentation and expectations of misrepresentation in an ethical dilemma: The role of incentives and temptation. *Academy of Management Journal, 41*, 330-339.

Tenbrunsel, A. E., & Smith-Crowe, K. (2008). Chapter 13: Ethical decision making: Where we've been and where we're going. *Academy of Management Annals, 2*, 545-607.

Trafimow, D., Triandis, H. C., & Goto, S. G. (1991). Some tests of the distinction between the private self and the collective self. *Journal of Personality and Social Psychology, 60*, 649-655.

Treviño, L. K., Weaver, G. R., & Reynolds, S. J. (2006). Behavioral ethics in organizations: A review. *Journal of Management, 32*, 951-990.

Treviño, L. K., & Youngblood, S. A. (1990). Bad apples in bad barrels: A causal analysis of ethical decision-making behavior. *Journal of Applied Psychology, 75*, 378-385.

Triandis, H. C. (1989). The self and social behavior in differing cultural contexts. *Psychological Review, 96*, 506-520.

Turner, J. C., Oakes, P. J., Haslam, S. A., & McGarty, C. (1994). Self and collective: Cognition and social context. *Personality and Social Psychology Bulletin, 20*, 454-463.

Turner, N., Barling, J., Epitropaki, O., Butcher, V., & Milner, C. (2002). Transformational leadership and moral reasoning. *Journal of Applied Psychology, 87*, 304-311.

van Baaren, R. B., Maddux, W. W., Chartrand, T. L., de Bouter, C., & van Knippenberg, A. (2003). It takes two to mimic: Behavioral consequences of self-construals. *Journal of Personality and Social Psychology, 84*, 1093-1102.

van Dick, R., Hirst, G., Grojean, M. W., & Wieseke, J. (2007). Relationships between leader and follower organizational identification and implications for follower attitudes and behaviour. *Journal of Occupational and Organizational Psychology, 80*, 133-150.

van Knippenberg, B., & van Knippenberg, D. (2005). Leader self-sacrifice and leadership effectiveness: The moderating role of leader prototypicality. *Journal of Applied Psychology, 90*, 25-37.

van Knippenberg, D., & Hogg, M. A. (2003). A social identity model of leadership effectiveness in organizations. In R. M. Kramer & B. M. Staw (Eds.), *Research in organizational behavior* (Vol. 25, pp. 243-295). Amsterdam: Elsevier.

van Knippenberg, D., van Knippenberg, B., De Cremer, D., & Hogg, M. A. (2004). Leadership, self, and identity: A review and research agenda. *Leadership Quarterly, 15*, 825-856.

Van Lange, P. A. M., & Liebrand, W. B. G. (1991). Social value orientation and intelligence: A test of the goal prescribes rationality principle. *European Journal of Social Psychology, 21*, 273-292.

Verplanken, B., & Holland, R. W. (2002). Motivated decision making: Effects of activation and self-centrality of values on choices and behavior. *Journal of Personality and Social Psychology, 82*, 434-447.

Verplanken, B., Trafimow, D., Khusid, I. K., Holland, R. W., & Steentjes, G. M. (2009). Different selves, different values: Effects of self-construals on value activation and use. *European Journal of Social Psychology, 39*, 909-919.

Verplanken, B., Walker, I., Davis, A., & Jurasek, M. (2008). Context change and travel mode choice: Combining the habit discontinuity and self-activation hypotheses. *Journal of Environmental Psychology, 28*, 121-127.

Wieselquist, J., Rusbult, C. E., Foster, C. A., & Agnew, C. R. (1999). Commitment, pro-relationship behavior, and trust in close relationships. *Journal of Personality and Social Psychology, 77*, 942-966.

CHAPTER 12

LEADERSHIP CORRUPTION

Influence Factors, Process, and Prevention

Jenny S. Wesche, Daniel May, Claudia Peus, and Dieter Frey

Corruption among organization leaders has not yet received much attention in psychological theory and research, despite its prevalence and obvious negative consequences. In this contribution, we take a first step to bridge this gap by examining leadership corruption from multiple angles. Based upon a review of corruption-related literature, we argue that leadership corruption results from an interplay of several antecedents on the micro- (i.e., individual), meso- (i.e., organizational) and macro- (i.e., extra-organizational) level. These include personality characteristics of leaders, the ethical infrastructure of organizations as well as aspects of the societal framework. We continue by combining these factors in a model of learned leadership corruption that accounts for the process by which leaders turn to corruption. The centrepiece of the model is a cost-benefit evaluation of corrupt acts performed by the leader. We assume that individual level influences mainly determine the perception of potential costs of corruption. Organizational and extra-organizational influences on the other hand provide situational cues by which leaders judge both costs and benefits of corrupt deeds. Provided that benefits clearly outweigh costs, we suggest that the probability of leadership corruption will be high. In the last part of our contribution, we discuss potential ways to cut down on leadership corruption by means of personnel selection and adjustments to organizational and legal frameworks.

When Leadership Goes Wrong: Destructive Leadership, Mistakes and Ethical Failures, pp. 305–353

INTRODUCTION

In this contribution, we will explore leadership corruption as one particularly harmful case of "leadership gone wrong." Corruption, that is, the misuse of an organizational position or authority for personal, subunit and/or organizational gain (Ashforth & Anand, 2003), like no other form of wrongdoing in organizational context jolts society. It not only results in financial losses (directly through bribery and embezzlement, or indirectly through distortion of fair market structures and competition etc.). Corruption also causes physical harm to employees (e.g., through unsafe working conditions), customers (e.g., through defective or hazardous consumer goods) and the environment (e.g., through illegal environmental pollution by radiation, waste or emissions or depletion of resources) (cf. McKendall & Wagner, 1997; Szwajkowski, 1985). Because of the manifold consequences of corruption, it is impossible to quantify its costs. Bribes for example are not exclusively monetary and the monetary ones are by their very nature not publicly recorded. The indirect financial consequences like harm to competitors and fair market structures are also hard to quantify. Likewise, the nonfinancial consequences such as injuries or even casualties of employees or customers or environmental damage are not quantifiable in dollar value (Transparency International, 2008).

A more intangible consequence of corruption that is stressed by many researchers (e.g., Ashforth, Gioia, Robinson, & Trevino, 2008; Szwajkowski, 1985) is its detrimental effect on faith and trust in businesses, institutions and society in general. System trust rests on what Luhmann (1979) calls a "presentational" base (i.e., being a representative of the system). In our modern society, people frequently have to interact with individuals they do not personally know, thus a base for interpersonal trust is oftentimes not given. Still they engage in the interaction, as they trust in the system of which the interaction partner is a representative (Lewis & Weigert, 1985). Take the tax office as an example: you may never have seen or even spoken to the clerk at your tax office before, yet you will file your tax return, in the firm belief that the system "tax office" is trustworthy. In modern society, system trust is indispensable (e.g., Parsons, 1951), as without trust in the reliability, effectiveness and legitimacy of laws, currencies, public institutions and business organizations society would disintegrate into "chaos and paralyzing fear" (Luhmann, 1979). Corruption seriously damages system trust and thus endangers functioning of society in general. Therefore we regard the topic of corruption, in particular leadership corruption, and its prevention to be of critical importance for society in general.

This contribution focuses on corrupt leaders, exploring in-depth preconditions and influence factors for leadership corruption. We set our focus on leaders for three main reasons: First, leaders' spheres of responsibility and scopes of authority exceed the ones of regular employees. Thus, the detrimental effect of leaders' corrupt downfalls are far more devastating. Second, leaders have an important indirect influence on organizations' employees through role modeling and shaping the organizational culture (e.g., Schein, 1985, 1990). The higher up in the organizational hierarchy, the stronger the impact of leader behavior. But also lower level leaders function as multipliers, transporting the organization's values down the hierarchy (cf. Litzky, Eddleston, & Kidder, 2006). Third, through their approval or disapproval, leaders have a direct influence on their subordinates' behavior. Leaders ignoring, condoning, authorizing or even reinforcing and rewarding corrupt behavior have been argued to play a critical role in employees' engagement in corruption (Ashforth & Anand, 2003; Ashforth et al., 2008; Litzky et al., 2006; Manz, Anand, Joshi, & Manz, 2008; Pearce, Manz, & Sims, 2008). Taken together, leaders have a great potential to influence the ethicality of organizational performance and the trust in- and outsiders bestow upon the organization concerned.

Answering Ashforth et al.'s call (2008), we set out to explore the phenomenon of corrupt leadership from different perspectives, illuminating influence factors from the micro-, meso- and macro-level. This is crucial to understanding the phenomenon as individuals' actions do not happen in a vacuum but are influenced by the framework provided. Our first section, dealing with the *micro-perspective* on corrupt leadership, focuses on the "bad-apple-question." Here individual predispositions for corrupt behavior will be discussed. In the *meso-level* section we explore group and organizational influences on corrupt leadership behavior, the "bad-barrel-question." To complete the review of influence factors, we focus on extra-organizational factors in our *macro-level* section – following the metaphor, this would correspond to a "bad-barrel-cellar." Having reviewed the influences on leaders' behavior on the micro-, meso- and macro-level, we combine these in a model of learned leadership corruption, analyzing how the different influence factors interact to make a leader fall for corruption the first time and eventually to become twisted in sustained corruption. Building on the model and the discussed influence factors, we complete our contribution with recommendations for preventing and ending corrupt leadership in organizations.

DEFINITION OF CORRUPTION AND LEADERSHIP CORRUPTION

Research in the field of corruption draws from literatures of several disciplines and incorporates aspects from various other concepts in the realm of wrongdoing in organizational context, including organizational misconduct (e.g., Harris & Bromiley, 2007), organizational crime (e.g., Palmer & Maher, 2006), corporate crime (e.g., Palmer & Maher, 2006), corporate illegality (e.g., McKendall & Wagner, 1997), white-collar crime (e.g., Coleman, 1987; Sutherland, 1940), counterproductive work behavior (Sackett & DeVore, 2002) or workplace deviance (Robinson & Bennett, 1995).

Moreover, definitions of corruption abound in the literature. The most general definition of corruption is "the abuse of public power for private benefit" (Rodriguez, Uhlenbruck, & Eden, 2005, p. 383). Very similar, Jain (2001) defines corruption as "acts in which the power of public office is used for personal gain in a manner that contravenes the rules of the game" (p. 73). Sherman (1980, p. 480) augments these definitions by explicitly referring to the private gain of all agents involved in the corrupt act. While the three mentioned definitions refer to corruption in public offices only, organizational scientists transferred these definitions to the more general organizational context. Aguilera and Vadera (2008) define the construct of organizational corruption "as the crime that is committed by the use of authority within organizations for personal gain" (p. 433) while Ashforth and Anand (2003) extend the notion of "gain" by defining organizational corruption as the "misuse of authority for personal, subunit, and/or organizational gain" (p. 2). We regard this latter specification of gain as the most differentiated as well as most inclusive one. Regarding the norms being perpetrated by corruption, the presented definitions refer to legal norms (Aguilera & Vadera, 2008; Sherman, 1980) as well as societal norms (Ashforth & Anand, 2003). We decided to include both in our definition, as despite a major overlap, there are issues that are not illegal but regarded as immoral by most parts of society and vice versa, acts that are forbidden by law, but regarded as a bagatelles by most parts of society. Moreover, we conceptualize corruption as an intentional perpetration (cf. Ashforth et al., 2008), focusing more on the behavior itself than the outcome. This delimitation—which is in concordance with definitions of other concepts of wrongdoing in organizational context (e.g., the definition of counterproductive work behavior by Sackett & DeVore, 2002)—allows more precise hypotheses about potential antecedents and thus means for prevention. As a synthesis of these various definitions, we thus define corruption as *the intentional perpetration by one or more member(s) of an organization—through willful commission or omission in the course of the respective organizational role(s)—that violates legal or societal norms for personal, sub-unit and/or organizational gain*.

According to Ashforth and colleagues (2008), corruption is a meta term, that subsumes various forms of corrupt behavior: like fraud, bribery, graft, embezzlement, and nepotism/cronyism. We acknowledge that these different forms of corruption are likely to occur in different situations (e.g., industries, positions) and are possibly influenced by different specific antecedents. Nevertheless, we think it is important to consider the different forms of corruption in a unifying model, as an "atomization of corruption concepts" hinders a deep-structured and cause-seeking understanding of the problem (Ashforth et al., 2008). We therefore aim to provide a synergistic and integrative model of corruption, assenting to the prevailing perception, that the whole of corruption may be greater than the sum of its parts (e.g., Ashforth et al., 2008).

As stated above, this chapter focuses especially on the problem of *corrupt leaders* and analyzes the factors that contribute to the development of corrupt leadership. According to the above presented general definition, we define corrupt leadership *as the intentional perpetration by a leader of an organization—through wilful commission or omission in the course of his/her organizational role—that violates legal or societal norms for personal, subunit and/or organizational gain*.

1. INDIVIDUAL FACTORS INFLUENCING CORRUPT BEHAVIOR

Looking at the phenomenon of organizational corruption from the micro-level perspective means attributing its occurrence to the deeds of single individuals or small groups within the organization. For observers and those concerned, this may be the most evident and most appealing way to look at the antecedents of corruption in organizations (Ashforth et al., 2008), as the micro-level view promises the advantage of clear responsibilities and quick solutions to overcome corruption—simply by eliminating the bad apple(s) (i.e., the corrupt individuals or groups) from the otherwise healthy barrel (i.e., the organization). It thus allows for the re-establishment of system trust without extensive changes to the system itself (for an example of the individual-centred focus on corruption see Box 1).

We believe that the micro-level perspective is a valuable piece of the jigsaw puzzle to understand corruption. Individuals confronted with the same circumstances (e.g., corruption-conducive situations) do not act identically, as they bring their unique personality as well as their personal ethics into the situation. Accordingly, one individual might take advantage of an opportunity to commit corruption, another might not do so. In trying to answer the question how to know which apples are bad, we will tap into differential and personality psychology and give an overview of personality traits and personal ethics aspects that may influence an individual's propensity to engage in corruption.

Box 1. Example of Person-Centered Focus of Corruption

The prosecution of many of the corporate scandals shaking Germany recently has clearly focused on the micro-level perspective. A prominent example is the case of Peter Hartz, former Chief Human Resource Officer with Volkswagen AG. Hartz, once renowned for advising the German chancellor Gerhard Schröder on reforms of the German job market, was accused in 2006 to have tried to influence top-ranking members of the company's workers' council by providing them with cash and other perks out of company coffers. Although suspicions accompanied the case whether these violations of company policies and law weren't rather system-inherent with Volkswagen than the solitary acts of the former top-manager and a few others (e.g., Edmondson, 2007; Landler, 2008), prosecution and media coverage concentrated mostly on the "rotten apple" Peter Hartz. The case illustrates quite well that the bad apple-view might be in the interest of the organizations involved, by taking away attention from organizational causes of corrupt behavior (cf. Jansen & von Glinow, 1985).

1.1. Personality Traits

According to Guilford (1959), an individual's personality is defined by a distinctive configuration of traits. These personality traits shape our behavior as "enduring patterns of perceiving, relating to, and thinking about the environment and oneself that are exhibited in a wide range of social and personal contexts" (American Psychiatric Association, 1994, p. 630). Literature in the domain of (un-)ethical workplace behaviors addresses a variety of personality constructs as influence factors, ranging from broad personality traits like the Big Five to more narrowly defined concepts like Machiavellianism or self-control.

1.1.1. Broad Personality Traits

Personality research consistently shows that there are five broad factors defining human personality, well known as the "Big Five" (e.g., Costa & McCrae, 1992a, 1992b; Goldberg, 1990; McCrae & Costa, 1987; McCrae & John, 1992). These factors are neuroticism (or, named after the opposite end of the scale, emotional stability), extraversion, openness to experience, agreeableness and conscientiousness.

Looking for links between these traits and corruption, it is instructive to consult research on counterproductive or deviant workplace behaviors (e.g., theft, misuse of company information, acceptance of kickbacks) and (managerial) integrity (cf. Connelly & Ones, 2008). As research indicates, conscientiousness and agreeableness (Berry, Ones, & Sackett, 2007; Salgado, 2002), as well as emotional stability (Berry et al., 2007) are negatively related to counterproductive workplace behaviors and positively related to integrity test scores (Hogan & Brinkmeyer, 1997; Wanek, Sackett, & Ones, 2003). It appears reasonable to expect similar relationships between these three personality traits and corruption in general. However, with regard to *leadership* corruption, these results have to be interpreted with care. Firstly, the samples found in the studies and meta-analyses are not recruited from populations with leadership or management responsibilities. Moreover, meta-analytic results indicate that emotional stability and conscientiousness are both positively correlated to leadership emergence and leadership effectiveness (Judge, Bono, Ilies, & Gerhardt, 2002), which gives us reason to believe that low scores on these constructs may be a potential drawback in the race for leadership positions. Interestingly, Blickle, Schlegel, Fassbender, and Klein (2006) were able to show that in white-collar criminals, levels of conscientiousness were even higher than in a comparison group of white-collar managers.[1] The authors conclude that above-average degrees of conscientiousness are generally needed to reach leadership positions, while an especially high degree of conscientiousness may result in extraordinary technical proficiency. The latter could in turn lower the fear of being detected and thus raise the propensity to engage in criminal acts (Blickle et al., 2006).

For agreeableness, things look different. While it is positively related to leadership effectiveness, it is not correlated to leader emergence (Judge et al., 2002). As low agreeableness scores go along with a tendency towards self-centeredness and low concern for others (Costa & McCrae, 1992b; Digman, 1990), it may give individuals a tough edge that fosters career development. On the other hand, it may also raise the propensity to act egocentrically and against established norms if it suits one's own goals. Results from a study by Terpstra, Rozell, and Robinson (1993) support this line of thought. They found that high interpersonal competitiveness —a concept associated with the low end of the agreeableness scale (cf. Costa & McCrae, 1992b)—leads to a greater propensity to engage in unethical behavior. It thus appears that agreeableness is the most promising among the classical Big Five factors in explaining leadership corruption on the micro-level.

Another personality trait worth considering in the context of broad personality factors is honesty-humility. This trait has been proposed by Ashton and colleagues (2004) as an extension to and reinterpretation of the original Big Five factors. Honesty-humility is described as an individual's degree of trustworthiness, modesty, lack of greed, and lack of slyness (Ashton et al., 2004). Individuals high on honesty-humility have a lower tendency to behave unethically or counterproductively and have higher integrity ratings than low-scorers (Ashton & Lee, 2008; Lee, Ashton, & de Vries, 2005; Lee, Ashton, Morrison, Cordery, & Dunlop, 2008). Individuals high on honesty-humility may thus be expected to have a lower propensity to engage in corrupt behaviors.

1.1.2. Narrow Personality Traits

Regarding more specific personality traits Machiavellianism, locus of control and self-control are the most relevant ones regarding corruption and leadership corruption in particular.

Machiavellianism describes the degree to which a person is emotionally detached in interactions with others, lacks moral concern and is willing to manipulate others to promote his or her own interests (Christie & Geis, 1970). Individuals high on Machiavellianism were found to be more likely to report intentions of unethical behavior than low scorers (Hegarty & Sims, 1978, 1979; Jones & Kavanagh, 1996). Again, it may be assumed that moderate values of Machiavellianism may even be helpful in certain business environments to advance one's own career to a leadership position, as results by Shultz (1993) indicate.

Locus of control refers to an individual's generalized expectancies about control over life (Rotter, 1966). While people with an external locus of control tend to attribute life events to fate or luck, "internals" see life as determined by their own actions. It could be shown that leaders with an internal locus of control score higher on managerial integrity (Baehr, Jones, & Nerad, 1993) and that internals are more likely to make ethical decisions than externals (Terpstra et al., 1993; Trevino & Youngblood, 1990).

Another personality concept relevant to corruption is self-control, defined as "the tendency to avoid acts whose long-term costs exceed momentary advantages" (Hirschi & Gottfredson, 1994, p. 4). People low on self-control tend to look for short-term gratification and are characterized by high impulsivity, activity and risk-affinity, while showing low concern for others (Hirschi & Gottfredson, 1987). Thus, a leader low in self-control might engage in corruption because he or she focuses on the immediate satisfaction of his or her personal needs, but does not see or heed the more distal negative consequences for him-/herself or the company. The concept of self-control as it is presented here has been introduced by Gottfredson and Hirschi (1990) in their general theory of crime. This theory proposes that self-control is the single most important personality trait explaining all kinds of criminal behavior, including white-collar crime (Gottfredson & Hirschi, 1990; Hirschi & Gottfredson, 1987). While the theory (and its applicability to white-collar crime) has raised considerable concerns and critiques (Benson & Moore, 1992; G. E. Reed & Yeager, 1996; Simpson & Piquero, 2002; Steffensmeier, 1989), there is evidence that lack of self-control is indeed a predictor of counterproductive work behaviors (Bechtoldt, Welk, Hartig, & Zapf, 2007; Marcus & Schuler, 2004) and white-collar crime (Blickle et al., 2006). Trevino (1986) has proposed a concept similar to self-control under the name of "ego strength" in her model of ethical decision making, where it is supposed to moderate the relationship between cognitive moral development and ethical behavior. Individuals high on ego-strength are expected to resist impulses and follow their convictions (Trevino, 1986). It may thus be expected that in order to translate ethical reasoning into ethical action, a sufficient level of ego-strength (or self-control) has to be given.

1.1.3. Different Perspectives on the Links Between Personality and Corruption

In trying to answer the question whether there is something like a "corrupt personality," we have identified a set of traits that may be considered individual antecedents to leadership corruption in particular: lack of agreeableness and honesty-humility, high Machiavellianism, external locus of control and low self-control. Although results are not specific to the field of leadership corruption, it seems reasonable to expect that they likewise apply. As mentioned before some of the traits described (e.g., Machiavellianism) might even be helpful in climbing the career ladder.

Our review so far has mostly drawn upon literature on counterproductive and deviant workplace behaviors as well as on the complementary concept of integrity. These constructs however implicitly refer to corruption at the expense of the organization, as they comprise acts that violate the interests and norms of the organizations involved. Thus, our reasoning about personality traits has to be interpreted according to this premise as well. Changing our focus to corruption that ostensibly benefits the organization (or one of its subunits) the proposed relations between these traits and corruption may have to be re-evaluated. Leaders who commit acts of corruption believing that it is to the best for their organization may be highly conscientious, agreeable, have an internal locus of control and so on.[2] Determinants of their propensity to commit corrupt acts may be found elsewhere. In the next section we will therefore discuss another set of potential personal antecedents of leadership corruption: moral standards and ethics.

1.2. Moral Standards and Personal Ethics

Moral standards and personal ethics[3] refer to the overarching principles that guide individuals' behavior in ethical decision situations: What are a person's beliefs about what is right and what is wrong? What ethical decision rules does a person apply? What importance does a person attach to such considerations? It is obvious that these questions are at least as important to explaining an individual's propensity to engage in corruption as is his or her personality structure.

We will address the topic here by referring to three aspects of an individual's ethical principles: *individual moral philosophies*, *cognitive moral development*, and *moral identity*.

1.2.1. Individual Moral Philosophies

Looking for individual differences in moral judgments, Forsyth (1980, 1992) highlights the importance of *individual moral philosophies* or *ethical ideologies* for guiding ethical behavior. These ethical ideologies can be grouped along two basic factors: relativism and idealism. While relativism describes the degree to which one adheres to universal moral principles, idealism captures the degree to which one is willing to accept harm to others in the pursuit of a greater good. Crossing of the two dimensions results in four distinct ethical ideologies called *subjectivism*, *situationism*, *exceptionism* and *absolutism* (see Table 12.1)

Given that following universal moral principles pertains to societal norms and laws that condemn corruption, one can expect that individuals low on relativism will be the most averse to corruption of any kind. This will apply more to absolutism than to exceptionism, as the latter allows for the violation of moral rules if that contributes to a greater good. Highly relativistic individuals may be expected to be more susceptible to corruption, as they rather follow individually held principles that may not be consistent with societal norms and laws. Situationists may be more scrupulous than subjectivists though, as they wish to avoid harm to others. Partial support for the above reasoning comes from research by Henle, Giacalone, and Jurkiewicz (2005), who found that relativism and idealism interact in the prediction of organizational deviance. For highly relativistic participants, high idealism was negatively related to deviance, while low idealism was positively related. Surprisingly, no relations to deviance were found when relativism was low. This latter result may be explained

Table 12.1. Taxonomy of Ethical Ideologies

	High Relativism	*Low Relativism*
	Situationism	*Absolutism*
High idealism	Rejection of universal moral principles, low tolerance to harm in pursuit of a greater good	Adherence to universal moral principles, low tolerance to harm in pursuit of a greater good
	Subjectivism	*Exceptionism*
Low idealism	Rejection of universal moral principles, high tolerance to harm in pursuit of a greater good	Adherence to universal moral principles, high tolerance to harm in pursuit of a greater good

Adapted from Forsyth (1980, 1992).

by the lack of situational moderators tested in the particular study. Only when situational cues (e.g., organizational justice perceptions) tempt deviant behavior, low relativism should have a negative relation to actual deviance (Henle et al., 2005).

Another approach illuminating personal moral philosophies is the analysis of individual predispositions towards two traditional frameworks of ethical reasoning: utilitarianism and formalism (Brady & Wheeler, 1996). While utilitarian ethics judges the morality of an act by its consequences for other people, formalism goes by the degree to which an act follows generally accepted rules or other formal features (Brady & Wheeler, 1996). As research indicates, utilitarian and formal ethics shape moral awareness: while utilitarists identified the moral content of an issue only by the harm caused, formalists identified moral issues both by harm and the violation of norms (Reynolds, 2006). Applying these results to the occurrence of corruption, one might assume that utilitarists will be more prone to engaging in corrupt acts than formalists, as the former may not perceive their deeds as morally objectionable as long as "only" norms are violated but no actual harm is done to others.

1.2.2. Cognitive Moral Development

Trevino (1986) has proposed cognitive moral development as a key influence factor for ethical decision making. The concept of cognitive moral development, introduced by Kohlberg (1969), describes how moral reasoning evolves from middle childhood to adulthood by becoming ever more complex and elaborate. Development is theorized to progress over three consecutive levels of moral reasoning (preconventional, conventional, and principled).

Individuals at the *preconventional level* of cognitive moral development will follow rules and moral standards only if it serves their immediate self-interest, be it through avoidance of punishment or striving for reward. Thus, ethical behavior depends on whether it is adequately incentivized for these people. Individuals at the *conventional level* will accept rules and norms as given by relevant reference groups (i.e., family or employer) or society in general. Obeying to the rules is seen as an obligation towards these groups. When confronted with ethical decision situations, individuals on the conventional level will tend to refer to outside sources to guide their behavior. Finally, individuals who reach the *principled level* of cognitive moral development obtain greater autonomy from rules and norms set by outside influences. Instead, they will align their behavior to more universal principles of justice and rights and will uphold them even against external pressure. These individuals will refer to their own inner ethical framework when confronted with ethical decisions (cf. Trevino, 1986).

Not every individual will reach the highest stage of cognitive moral development. The majority of adults is expected to operate on the conventional level, while only less than 20% of (American) adults are expected to reach the principled level (Rest, Narvaez, Bebeau, & Thoma as cited in Trevino, Weaver, & Reynolds, 2006). Transferring this result to the organizational setting, the majority of leaders may be expected to function on the conventional level as well. As they will refer to outside sources for guidance in ethical decision making, these leaders will be especially susceptible to contextual influences like superiors, peers and formal or informal organizational norms (Trevino et al., 2006), but also to pressures from shareholders and competitors. Provided that these contextual influences do not explicitly condemn corruption, leaders at the conventional level of moral reasoning may be more prone to engaging in corrupt behaviors. Indeed, level of cognitive moral development was found to be linked to ethical behavior: Individuals on higher levels were less likely to choose unethical courses of action (Trevino & Youngblood, 1990).

Through their disposition to accord with norms set by outside sources, leaders on the conventional level should also be vulnerable to "groupthink" (Janis, 1982), a mode of thinking that is characterized by a strong tendency to reach unanimity in groups at the expense of decision quality. One of the symptoms of groupthink is the "unquestioned belief in the group's inherent morality, inclining the members to ignore the ethical or moral consequences of their decisions" (Janis, 1982, p. 174). Thus, through treacherous reinforcement processes within their peer group, leaders may come to conclusions that seem justifiable within the given frame of the group, but may be unacceptable when compared to universal moral standards.

Another disturbing finding on cognitive moral development is brought up by Trevino and colleagues (2006). Summarizing a number of studies (e.g., Elm & Nichols, 1993; Ponemon, 1990, 1992), they point out that older and more experienced managers show lower levels of moral reasoning than do their younger and less experienced counterparts. This is especially disturbing, because older and more experienced managers are usually found in higher ranks of organizations than their younger colleagues and thus have larger scopes of authority and responsibility at their disposal. Yet, it is unclear whether this effect is due to selection or socialization processes (cf. Trevino et al., 2006). Moreover, managers' moral reasoning was found to be on lower levels when concerning work-related issues as compared to nonwork issues (Weber, 1990; Weber & Wasieleski, 2001). In the context of organizational corruption, these findings again highlight the necessity for an ethical organizational framework of norms and processes that may guide the ethical behavior of leaders on lower levels of cognitive moral development.

1.2.3. Moral Identity

A final issue regarding personal ethics that we would like to address is moral identity. This concept roots in self-concept and social identity theories (e.g., Tajfel & Turner, 1979, 1986; Turner & Oakes, 1986) and is defined as "a self-conception organized around a set of moral traits" (Aquino & Reed, 2002, p. 1424). The importance an individual gives to his or her moral identity describes the priority that he or she gives to ethical considerations in different situations and the motivation to act according to these considerations (see Aquino & Reed, 2002; Reed & Aquino, 2003; Trevino et al., 2006 for an overview of identity-based moral motivation).

Studies suggest that self-importance of moral identity predicts ethical behavioral intentions and behavior (Aquino & Reed, 2002; A. I. Reed & Aquino, 2003; Reynolds & Ceranic, 2007). Moreover, individuals with greater self-importance of moral identity show stronger alignment of their behaviors with their ethical predispositions under certain conditions (Reynolds & Ceranic, 2007).

These findings have important implications for corruption as well. Even if leaders do in principle have an ethical framework that speaks against the engagement in corrupt acts, it might not be activated in ethical decision situations, either because moral identity is not central to their self-concept or moral identity is not salient in the particular context. The salience of moral identity may be triggered by installing proper frameworks of norms and rules in organizations.

1.2.4. Conclusion

In the preceding paragraphs, we have discussed personal moral philosophies, cognitive moral development and moral identity as elements of an individual's overarching ethical principles. These factors interact with the more basic personality traits described before (agreeableness, honesty-humility, Machiavellianism, locus of control and self-control) and influence how individuals make ethical decisions, such as the decision to engage in corruption. Our review suggests that an ethical ideology high in relativism and low in idealism, a lack of maturity in cognitive moral development and a lack of centrality of moral considerations in an individual's self-concept may result in a greater likelihood to engage in corrupt acts. Especially with regard to the latter two influences, setting proper boundaries through organizational policies and a living code of ethics may help to prevent corruption.

ORGANIZATIONAL FACTORS INFLUENCING CORRUPT BEHAVIOR

Looking at the organization, the "ethical infrastructure" (Tenbrunsel, Smith-Crowe, & Umphress, 2003) can be differentiated into formal and informal systems: Formal systems are those documented, standardized and visible to anyone inside or outside the organization; conversely, informal systems are indirect signals regarding appropriate conduct that are not verified through formal documents, but rather "felt" by organization members (Falkenberg & Herremans, 1995; Tenbrunsel et al., 2003; Trevino, Butterfield, & McCabe, 1998). Taken together, both formal and informal systems shape the culture and climate of an organization.

In the following sections we will address these organizational factors by combining the psychological perspective on organizational influences (e.g., organizational climate and culture, Trevino, 1990; Victor & Cullen, 1988) with the economics perspective on organizational influences (agency theory, Eisenhardt, 1989) to discuss incentives and opportunities for (un-)ethical behavior provided by the organizational infrastructure.

2.1. Ethical Climate and Culture

The relationship between organizational climate and culture has been object of some discussion in the scholarly literature (e.g., Denison, 1996; James et al., 2008). We will not engage in this discussion here[4] and treat the concepts as two different, yet closely related ways to look at the internal social psychological environment of organizations (Denison, 1996). More specifically, we are interested in those aspects of the two constructs that influence ethical behavior in organizations: ethical climate and ethical culture.

Ethical climate has been defined as "the prevailing perceptions of typical organizational practices and procedures that have ethical content" consisting of "perceived prescriptions, proscriptions and permissions regarding moral obligations in organizations" (Victor & Cullen, 1988, p. 101). Thereby, ethical climate is not necessarily identical with what is deemed ethical according to societal norms or laws, but rather refers to what is perceived as ethical within the organization or its subunits, which may or may not be in line with the societal perspective (Dickson, Smith, Grojean, & Ehrhart, 2001).

Ethical culture on the other hand describes a set of formal and informal control systems in the organization whose interplay either fosters ethical or unethical behavior (Trevino, 1990; Trevino et al., 1998).

2.1.1. Influences of Ethical Climate and Culture

Research provides some support for the notion that *ethical climates* influence ethical behavior in the workplace. Climates that emphasize the importance of following organizational, legal and professional rules, as well as climates that foster respect and caring for others within the organization can be helpful to prevent the occurrence of unethical or corrupt behaviors in the workplace. In contrast, ethical climates that emphasize self-interest seem to be conducive to the development of unethical behavior (Peterson, 2002; Trevino et al., 1998; Wimbush, Shepard, & Markham, 1997).

Research on the effect of *ethical cultures* on ethical behavior in organizations is scarce, but available results are similar to those regarding ethical climates: It seems that cultures emphasizing and actively promoting ethics beyond the mere establishment of a written ethics code foster awareness of ethical issues and ethical behavior (Caldwell & Moberg, 2007; Nill & Schibrowsky, 2005; Trevino et al., 1998).

As ethical climates and cultures are rather general organizational phenomena, it seems reasonable to expect that they will pertain to all kinds of unethical behaviors, corruption being one of them. As leaders are organization members as well, they too will be susceptible to the influences of climate and culture. However, leaders themselves may be important creators of ethical organizational climates and cultures.

2.1.2. Leaders Shaping Ethical Climate and Culture

Dickson, Smith, Grojean, and Ehrhart (2001) claim that the most important factor in shaping *organizational climate* is leader behavior. They propose that leaders and especially founders of organizations influence climate in multiple ways, for example through role modeling, by means of punishment and reward, by defining the organization form and framework, and by providing justification for (un-)ethical acts (Dickson et al., 2001; Grojean, Resick, Dickson, & Smith, 2004). This is quite similar to theorizing by Schein (1985, 1990), who identified five mechanisms through which leaders shape *organizational culture*: (1) allocation of attention, (2) reaction to crisis, (3) role modeling, (4) allocation of rewards and (5) criteria and procedures for selection, promotion and dismissal. The "falling dominoes effect," describing subordinates emulating the behavior they experience from their leaders, could be demonstrated for both positive forms of leadership (e.g., transformational leadership, Bass, Waldman, Avolio, & Bebb, 1987) and negative forms (e.g., aversive leadership, Pearce & Sims, 2002).

Little research has so far directly addressed the links between leader behavior and ethical climates and cultures. In two case studies, Sims and Brinkmann (2002, 2003) employed Schein's (1985) model to analyze how leaders through their effect on corporate culture promoted the collapse of the Salomon Brothers investment bank (Sims & Brinkmann, 2002) and Enron (Sims & Brinkmann, 2003). In both cases, leader behavior contributed to corporate cultures where ethical considerations were uncommon and even unwanted (e.g., by paying attention solely to the bottom line, by reacting to crisis with dishonesty or denial) which in turn lead to the big scandals causing the ruin of the two companies. Applying these results to corruption, leaders may—by means of influencing climates and cultures—either promote or prevent the occurrence of corruption in their scope of authority.

Organizational climates and cultures constitute the organization members' combined perception of and reaction to the organization's formal and informal infrastructure. In the next section, we will address the topic of ethical infrastructure underlying organizational climate and culture and its potential links to corruption in greater detail.

2.2. Ethical Infrastructure Underlying Organizational Culture and Climate

Before discussing the single elements of the ethical infrastructure underlying organizational climate and culture (see Figure 12.1), we want to draw attention to the crucial condition of congruence between the various elements. Falkenberg and Herremans (1995) as well as Tenbrunsel et al. (2003) state that incongruence between the formal and informal ethical infrastructure develops when ethical values prescribed by the formal system (e.g., ethics recorded in corporate ethics statements) become undermined by the informal system (e.g., unethical behavior of superiors spread via informal communication; rumors about people being fired for not taking all means possible to reach the bottom-line, etc.). According to Falkenberg and Herremans counternorms (i.e., accepted organizational practices that are contrary to prevailing ethics standards) develop with incongruent systems and create situations of ambiguous priorities.

In organizations where officials tolerate or even intentionally induce incongruence between formal and informal norms, the formal ethical infrastructure becomes degraded to mere "window-dressing". Sims and Brinkmann (2003) illustrate the problem of "instrumentalization" of business ethics for mere façade purposes, describing the situation at Enron. Enron had business ethics tools like ethics codes and ethics officer, in place, yet the actually practiced culture was the "ultimate contradiction" to the ethical façade. As mentioned above, Sims and Brinkmann demonstrated that Enron's leaders undermined the ethics statements they set up in numerous ways and instances and eventually took them ad absurdum, while preserving the façade of a highly ethical organization to the public.

Empirical evidence on corporate ethics statements supports the case study evidence on the critical importance of concordance between "words and deeds" (Sims & Brinkmann, 2003): Numerous studies show that the mere existence of ethics statements in organizations has little impact on actual ethical behavior, like the prevention of corruption (Boo & Koh, 2001; Kaptein & Schwartz, 2008; Schwartz, 2004; Webley & Werner, 2008). What seems to be crucial is that ethics statements are supported by organizational officials and are actually practiced in the organizational culture. Only the combination of codes with procedures signaling organizational support for them seems to yield positive effects. Valentine and Johnson (2005) found positive effects of reviewing ethics codes during employee orientation. Conversely, Urbany (2005) found that undermined ethics statements are without effect and moreover even evoke cynicism among principled followers.

2.3. Formal Infrastructure

A suitable model to explore the formal organizational infrastructure that influences employees' behavior is agency theory (e.g., Eisenhardt, 1989). It postulates that an agent (i.e., a person that accepted an obligation to act on behalf of his or her principal) will act opportunistically (i.e., in his/her own interest, here: corrupt), if there is inadequate *monitoring* or if *incentives* are not appropriately designed to align principal's (here: owner/shareholder of an organization) and agent's (here: manager/leader) objectives (Davis, Payne, & McMahan, 2007). According to agency theory, the conflict of interest between principals and agents is due to differences in risk aversion and time horizon for profit maximization:

Ethical Infrastructure Within Organizations

Formal Infrastructure	Informal Infrastructure
• **Opportunity**	• **Control**
– centralization of power	– Informal surveillance
– fog of complexity	– Informal sanctioning
• **Motivation**	– active followership
– compensation & reward system	– informal communication
– job promotion & retention	
• **Control**	
– supervisors	
– Board of Directors	
– Ethics/Compliance Office	

Figure 12.1. Ethical infrastructure within organizations.

Principals[5] wish the organization to provide a steady income from dividends and sustainability of the organization, while agents seek to maximize their income during their employment time (cf. Bilimoria, 1995). Thus, managers' time horizon for profit maximization should be shorter and the risks they are willing to take to bring about short-term profits are supposedly higher than those of respective owners and shareholders.

The primary corruption prohibiting mechanisms postulated by agency theory, monitoring and incentive alignment, are concordant with the proposition held by various corruption researchers that opportunity, motivation and a lack of control must be given in order for corruption to occur (Baucus, 1994; McKendall, DeMarr, & Jones-Rikkers, 2002; McKendall & Wagner, 1997). These three factors are postulated to interact to permit corruption, that is, neither of them is sufficient on its own, but all three are necessary prerequisites.

2.3.1. Opportunity

Aguilera and Vadera (2008) state that opportunity for corrupt behavior is given when individuals can engage in such behavior and expect, with reasonable confidence, to avoid detection and/or punishment. In more general terms, McKendall and Wagner (1997) define opportunity as "the presence of a favorable combination of circumstances that makes a possible course of action feasible" (p. 626). Various organizational characteristics can bring about opportunities for corrupt behavior (e.g., access to sensible data or valuable goods, Lange, 2008); Here we will exemplarily discuss centralization of power and complexity as two of the most important organizationally provided opportunities.

Centralization of power as a corruption facilitating organizational characteristic (e.g., de Graaf & Huberts, 2008; Pearce et al., 2008) is especially relevant to leader positions. According to Pearce and colleagues, "centralization of power can plant the seeds of corruption" (p. 357), and these seeds will be unleashed to grow in conjunction with a lack of control and a motivation to take advantage of the situation. De Graaf and Huberts showed in their analysis of several corruption cases that the circumstance of organizational officials having complete autonomy of decision on matters of great importance is linked to corruption. Especially if the matters to decide on are of distinguished relevance for an external party, bribery is likely to occur. But also other forms of corruption, like embezzlement or fraud will possibly occur if an individual's decisions pass unseen and unchallenged.

The other corruption facilitating organizational characteristic we want to stress here is complexity. *organizational complexity* reduces facility of inspection and transparency and thus can provide "hiding places" for corrupt acts when control mechanisms do not reach into the last corners

(Fleming & Zyglidopoulos, 2008). Here again, the interactional nature of the problem of corruption comes into play: It is not organizational size or diversity per se that reduces transparency, thus enabling corruption to pass unseen, but the combination of complex structures with insufficient control mechanisms. Complexity might be either "naturally" given by the organization, for example, through rapid growth and diversification, or purposely built in to create "hiding places" for corrupt acts (see Box 2).

2.3.2. Motivation

Within the meso-perspective that focuses on organizational factors, "motivation" does not refer to individual motives or motivations, but rather to incentives, whose attainment might pose a motivation, irrespective of individual differences. Generally, organizationally provided incentives relate to financial benefits or status. Aligning the agent's interests with the principal's interests through appropriately designed incentives in order to foster desired behavior is one of the core propositions of agency theory (Davis et al., 2007). Conversely, ill-designed incentive schemes can elicit opportunistic, in this case, corrupt behavior. We again want to highlight the interactive nature of this model: Ill-designed incentives only unfold their corruption-conducive effect if opportunities to attain them in a corrupt way plus a lack of control are provided.

The basis of every organizational incentive system (e.g., promotion and compensation procedures) is some kind of performance evaluation, that—with regard to preventing corruption—needs to take into account not only whether goals are achieved but also how. Ashforth and colleagues (2008) highlight the devastating effects of leaders setting (unrealistic) per-

Box 2. Example of Purposely Created Complexity to Hide Corruption

Sims and Brinkmann (2003) give an example of purposely created complexity in their analysis of the Enron case: In order to keep information from the public and debts off the Enron balance sheets, officials were building up a "deceiving web of partnerships" with "special purpose vehicles." Enron crafted relationships that looked (legally) like partnerships, although they were (in practice) subsidiaries (Sims & Brinkmann, 2003). The fabricated "fog of complexity" (Elliot & Schroth, 2002) contributed its share to confusion by multiplying the deceits many times, implicating other parts of the organization (or of the web of partnerships) as they absorbed the contaminated information. For instance, shady financial statements from one subsidiary were incorporated into the overall group statement, or used for forecasts in the strategic planning unit of other dependent subsidiaries, rendering these ones also flawed (Fleming & Zyglidopoulos, 2008). After the implosion of Enron's deceiving financial system, even attorneys could not properly entangle the interwoven systems (Fleming & Zyglidopoulos, 2008), "making the case that Enron was fundamentally a fraud—and it didn't matter if this particular accounting move, or that one, was technically legal" (McLean & Elkind, 2003, p. 414).

formance goals and modeling or condoning the corrupt means used to achieve them by their subordinates—for example Schweitzer, Ordónez, and Douma (2004) found that goal setting can motivate unethical behavior, when people fall short of their goals.

In the following, we will focus on the two most salient incentives in organizations, compensation and promotion. Schein's (1985) mechanism "allocation of rewards" by which leaders shape organizational cultures highlights exactly these two issues: By rewarding the behavior of employees with bonus payments or promotions, leaders signal what is necessary to succeed in the organization, what is prized and expected.[6]

Employment Preservation and Promotion

A person's status in an organization is largely dependent on his or her post. Kulik, O'Fallon, and Salimath (2008) argue that if there is high competition over scarce resources (e.g., posts and promotions), competitors tend to adopt the attitudes and behaviors of the "winner" after each competitive interaction. If now the winner of the competition used corrupt means to win and this gets rewarded instead of detected and punished, "losers" will play by the winner's rules in the next competitive interaction. This can result in a "spiral of pressure" (den Nieuwenboer & Kaptein, 2008): the contagious effect of organization members imitating their seemingly successful colleagues' corrupt behavior when striving to meet performance goals and trapping the ones having already committed performance-driven corruption in an ever increasing pressure to commit more and more corruption to protect their status and reputation. Structural aids to promote an internally competitive environment within an organization, like "stacking policy" or forced ranking systems (i.e., ranking employees from best to worst on a bell curve to determine pay, promotion and dismissal) that for example Ford, General Electric, Microsoft, and Enron (have) use(d) (Abelson, 2001), may thus result in organization-wide corruption (Kulik et al., 2008).

Yet, not only attaining positive outcomes (e.g., promotions) functions as an incentive, also avoiding negative outcomes (e.g., dismissal) might present a strong incentive. Especially leader positions are associated with high social status but also with high salary and many material and immaterial privileges. However, leader positions are also tied to high expectations, for example, fostering firm or unit performance. If superiors' or shareholders' expectations are not met, leaders are in danger of becoming dismissed. Thus, leaders might feel tempted to commit corruption to live up to superiors' or shareholders' expectations, in order to preserve their posts (Denis, Hanouna, & Sarin, 2006).

Compensation and Reward Systems

Compensation systems usually include salary-based and outcomes-based components in varying composition, dependent on the amount of risk/responsibility associated with the agents post (Davis et al., 2007). Since the 1990s a tremendous increase in outcomes-based shares of executive compensation has taken place (e.g., Denis et al., 2006; Murphy, 1999) and several types of outcomes-based compensation have evolved, like stock options, stock grants, or profit-sharing plans. Incentive alignment through outcomes-based compensation is intended to ensure that agents (i.e., employees or managers) have a stake in achieving the outcomes the principal seeks (e.g., Davis et al., 2007; Denis et al., 2006; Eisenhardt, 1989; Lange, 2008). Thus, it is in the agent's personal interest to avoid corrupt acts that harm the organization and its outcomes (e.g. committing embezzlement). However, as Lange points out, other forms of corruption, that are ostensibly conducted "on behalf" of the organization, such as intentional financial misstatements, are ironically encouraged by means of incentive alignment, as agents thus have a stake in bolstering organizational performance.[7] Accordingly, research on the influence of compensation on corruption focuses for the most part on the relationship between financial fraud and equity-based compensation (e.g., stock options and stock grants), a special form of outcomes-based compensation.

Equity-based compensation as a means of incentive alignment between principal and agent has been harshly criticized. Especially stock options have been challenged, because they provide holders with "the potential for unlimited gains, while limiting downside risk" (Donoher, Reed, & Storrud-Barnes, 2007). Harris and Bromiley (2007) explain this position by stating that stock options present a strong incentive to take any means possible to make the market price of shares rise above the strike price, as (1) otherwise the options have no value and (2) the options do include no downside risk, so option holders (unlike stock owners) have nothing to loose if their actions misfire but a lot to gain. Another issue that puts the assumption of goal alignment into question and concerns stock options as well as stock grants, is that most executives sell their shares right after the vesting period in order to realize the financial gain (Ofek & Yermack, 2000) and thus do not (at least not by means of holding shares) built up a long-term commitment regarding sustainable growth as owners do. This is of special concern as individuals can only benefit from financial fraud to the extent that they can exercise options and sell stock before the fraud is reversed or revealed (Johnson, Ryan, & Tian, 2009). Supporting this concern Beneish (1999) found that managers of firms found guilty of earnings overstatements actually sold their holdings and exercised their options in the period when earnings were overstated at inflated prices, that is, before the fraud was detected, made public, and shares fell in price.

Taking into account these aspects, a connection between equity-based compensation and financial misstatement can be assumed. Empirical evidence is mostly supportive, finding an increased likelihood of financial misstatements with an increasing share of equity-based pay in general (e.g., Burns & Kedia, 2006; Denis et al., 2006; Donoher et al., 2007; Harris & Bromiley, 2007; O'Connor, Priem, Coombs, & Gilley, 2006)—only one study found no relationship between the two (Erickson, Hanlon, & Maydew, 2006).

Recent studies provide more differentiated analyses regarding the effects of the various instruments in the area of equity-based pay (vested vs. unvested stock options, restricted vs. unrestricted stock holdings, etc.): Johnson, Ryan, and Tian (2005, 2009) differentiate between restricted and unrestricted stock holdings and vested and unvested options and find a significant effect on financial fraud for unrestricted stock holdings but not for the other three. Similarly, Burns and Kedia (2006) differentiate between the various elements of stock compensation and find that the sensitivity of stock option portfolio to changes in stock price is positively related to financial fraud, while the sensitivities of other components of compensation (i.e., restricted stock, long-term incentive payouts, etc.) have no significant impact. Taken together, two major critical points of equity-based compensation emerge with regard to corruption: (1) Unrestrictedness: too short vesting periods of stock options and grants to encourage an interest in long-term sustainability (Beneish, 1999; Johnson et al., 2009; Ofek & Yermack, 2000) (2) Imperfect interest alignment: limited downside risk but unlimited opportunity to profit from upside trends of stock options (e.g., Donoher et al., 2007; Harris & Bromiley, 2007).

2.3.3. Lack of Control

Increasing control is most often the means of choice to counteract corruption. This reflects the underlying assumption that "in the aggregate, unconstrained behavior will result in corrupt behavior" (Lange, 2008, p. 714). As a reaction to the corporate scandals of the 1990s and 2000s, legislators recommended and prescribed tightened control functions to be built into organizations (U.S. Federal Sentencing Guidelines, 1991; Sarbanes Oxley Act, 2002). We will discuss Boards of Directors, Audit Committees, and Ethics Offices as the main control bodies in organizations with regard to leadership corruption.

Board of Directors

Boards of directors' (BoD) responsibility is to oversee the management of an organization representing shareholders' interests. The role and composition of BoDs differs between countries: In the United States and the United Kingdom BoDs are composed of outside directors as well as executive directors, who are involved in the day-to-day management of the firm while in Germany and the Netherlands, a separation between the management and the BoD exists; managers are not allowed to function simultaneously as directors of the same company (Beetsma, Peters, & Rebers, 2000). Zahra, Priem, and Rasheed (2005, 2007) caution against BoDs serving just as "rubber stamps"[8] for managerial decisions, when BoDs are dominated by management, for example, when BoDs are appointed and chaired by the CEO.

Various aspects have been discussed in the literature that may render BoDs ineffective. The first critical aspect is *board composition and CEO duality*: While the role of boards of directors is to control the activities of top management, the two institutions are oftentimes not clearly separated. As mentioned above, there are countries in which parts of the seats in BoDs are commonly occupied by members of the top management itself and moreover the BoD is in many cases chaired by the CEO him-/herself (i.e., CEO duality). This has been criticized by many researchers (e.g., Fama & Jensen, 1983; Jensen, 1993; Pearce et al., 2008; Zahra & Pearce, 1989; Zahra et al., 2007), as BoDs dominated by outside directors, can more independently monitor and discipline managerial behavior and separation of the positions of BoD chair and CEO ensures checks and balances and prevents a concentration of corporate powers. Empirical evidence mostly supports the proposition that BoDs dominated by management in such ways are related to increased probability of corruption (Beasley, 1996; Dechow, Sloan, & Sweeney, 1996), only Kesner, Victor, and Lamont

Box 3. Example of Ineffective Board of Directors Oversight

The second interim report of Dick Thornburgh, bankruptcy court examiner with the WoldCom case illustrates the detrimental effect of BoDs being degraded to mere "rubber stamps" for managerial decision making: "*WorldCom was dominated by Messrs. Ebbers and Sullivan [the former Chief Executive Officer and the former Chief Financial Officer of WorldCom, respectively], with virtually no checks or restraints placed on their actions by the Board of Directors or other Management. Significantly, although many present or former officers and Directors of WorldCom told us they had misgivings regarding decisions or actions by Mr. Ebbers or Mr. Sullivan during the relevant period, there is no evidence that these officers and Directors made any attempts to curb, stop or challenge the conduct by Mr. Ebbers or Mr. Sullivan that they deemed questionable or inappropriate. Instead, it appears that the company's officers and Directors went along with Mr. Ebbers and Mr. Sullivan, even under circumstances that suggested corporate actions were at best imprudent, and at worst inappropriate and fraudulent. [...] WorldCom Management provided the company's Directors with extremely limited information regarding many acquisition transactions. Several multibillion dollar acquisitions were approved by the Board of Directors following discussions that lasted for 30 minutes or less and without the Directors receiving a single piece of paper regarding the terms or implications of the transactions*" (Kirkpatrick & Lockhart, 2003, p. 7).

(1986) find no relationship. Another problem is the one of *interlocking directorates*: Often top management teams serve on each other's BoDs, creating the danger of collusion or reciprocal favors (e.g., mutually turning a blind eye on fraud) (Pearce et al., 2008). Another critical aspect is *interest alignment between CEO and BoD*: Zahra et al. (2007) suggest, that directors' (restricted) stock options or ownership would ensure that they properly conduct their supervisory duty, as they would have a vested interest in the company's (long-term) performance. Yet, empirical evidence is indefinite: While Beasly (1996) finds a negative relationship between the level of ownership of the firm's common stock held by outside directors and financial statement fraud, O'Connor and colleagues (2006) found an adverse effect, namely that the positive relation between CEO stock options and fraudulent financial reporting was moderated by board of directors stock options: the effect of CEO stock options on fraudulent reporting increased when BoD members also held stock options. This might be interpreted as BoD being more inclined to turn a blind eye on managerial financial fraud, if they likewise benefit from it through their own stock options or holdings.

Audit Committees

Auditing the financial statements of an organization is one of the duties of BoDs. Yet, BoDs usually delegate this responsibility to an audit committee, to ensure higher quality monitoring by providing more detailed knowledge and understanding of the financial information (Beasley, 1996; DeZoort, Hermanson, Archambeault, & Reed, 2002). When audit committees were voluntarily employed, the presence of an audit committee could be interpreted as particular diligence that BoDs gave to their financial monitoring. Yet, empirical evidence on the fraud reducing effect of audit committees was mixed: While Beasley (1996) found no significant effect of the presence of an audit committee on the likelihood of financial fraud, Dechow and colleagues (1996) found that firms manipulating earnings were less likely to have an audit committee.

Yet, under current regulations listed firms must have an audit committee; thus it is important to employ specific measures of audit committee effectiveness (Abbott, Park, & Parker, 2000). Characteristics of audit committees being found to relate negatively to financial fraud and corporate crime are higher meeting frequencies and higher outsider representation on the committee (i.e., higher independence from management) (Abbott et al., 2000; Beasley, Carcello, Hermanson, & Lapides, 2000; Schnatterly, 2003).

Ethics/Compliance Offices and Officers

The main responsibility of ethics officers (EOs) is to improve the organization's ethical performance by overseeing ethical conduct of all employees (Hoffman, Neill, & Stovall, 2008; Izraeli & BarNir, 1998; Smith, 2003), via creating and maintaining the organization's guiding values, principles, and business practices (Morf, Schumacher, & Vitell, 1999). This involves advising management and employees on ethical questions, developing codes of ethics, preparing ethics training programs to foster ethics education and awareness, evaluating and monitoring compliance with the codes, investigating alleged violations of ethics or law and taking remedial action in case of inappropriate behavior by members of the organization (Hoffman et al., 2008; Izraeli & BarNir, 1998; Morf et al., 1999; Smith, 2003).

Although the first corporate ethics office was established as early as 1985 with General Dynamics and many companies followed that example, being incited by legislation (Morf et al., 1999),[9] there is very scarce empirical research on the effectiveness of ethics offices. The only evidence available seems to be somewhat discouraging: Smith (2003) cites a survey by Arthur Andersen that found ethics offices having little impact on reducing unethical actions.

One explanation for the inefficiency of EOs might lie in a lack of independence from management, which Hoffman et al. (2008) and Izraeli and BarNir (1998) advocate to be a necessary condition for EO efficiency. In order to fulfil their functions appropriately, EOs must operate under conditions where they can monitor and report on the ethical aspects of all decision-makers without the pressures of an inherent conflict of interest existing in their employment relationship. In other words, EOs must be able to monitor and critique management decision making without the fear of retaliation, including losing their jobs and possibly their careers. (An example of ineffective ethics office work is given in Box 4.) Yet, both Hoffman et al. (2008) and Morf et al. (1999) find that most EOs rather report to management than to BoD or specialized committees.

2.4. Informal Infrastructure

According to Trevino et al. (1998), the informal ethical system consists of peer behavior and norms. Tenbrunsel et al. (2003) list three forms of the informal ethical infrastructure that communicate and enforce these norms and behaviors: informal communication systems, informal surveillance systems and informal sanctioning systems. Classified according to the schema of the formal infrastructure (opportunity *x* motivation *x* lack of control), these three would fall under "control." As formal control sys-

Box 4. Example of Ineffective Ethics Office Work

An example of ineffective ethics office work is the case of Tom Hooker, Director of Compliance at Strong Capital Management (SCM), who failed to implement measures to monitor and prohibit corrupt actions (e.g., personally trading certain funds to the detriment of fund shareholders) committed by the company's chairman and Chief Investment Officer, Richard Strong. Although Hooker reported Strong's corrupt activities to SCM's in-house counsel (who at that time was also the company's Chief Compliance Officer) neither Hooker nor the counsel took prohibitive action. Warnings directed at Strong did not stop him from engaging in corruption, leading to Strong, Hooker and others involved being sentenced to paying fines (Hoffman et al., 2008; Security and Exchange Commission, 2004). Reasons for Hooker's passiveness can only be speculated on: As Hooker did not personally benefit from the illegal trading activities of Strong, other than financial reasons must have played a role. Lacking formal authority and strong dependence on the chairman might be possible explanations.

tems cannot fully monitor employees' behavior, employees controlling each other can be a powerful supplemental control source (Clapham & Cooper, 2005; Trevino & Victor, 1992).

Informal communication pertains to unofficial messages that convey the ethical norms within an organization. These unofficial messages are communicated in informal hallway conversations, informal trainings (i.e., colleagues showing newcomers the ropes) and organizational myths, sagas and stories (Tenbrunsel et al., 2003; Trevino, 1990). *Informal surveillance* describes monitoring and detection of unethical behavior carried out among colleagues in personal relationships (Tenbrunsel et al., 2003). Informal surveillance does not automatically lead to whistle-blowing to higher authorities. Yet, empirical evidence on peer-reporting show, that directly approaching the perpetrator in lieu of officially reporting is more likely for wrongdoings perceived as unintentional than for ones perceived as intentional (King, 2001), the latter being the case with corruption. *Informal sanctioning* takes the form of group pressure to behave in an ethical manner. Organization members may threaten the perpetrator to punish him or her with isolation from group activities, ostracism and even physical harm (Tenbrunsel et al., 2003). Another way organization members can exert pressure on perpetrators is threatening him or her with whistle-blowing[10] to higher authorities.

Over the last years governments and companies came to realize that informal surveillance and especially whistle-blowing is extremely important for curbing corruption and other counterproductive work behaviors, and therefore devised ways to support it by formal structures like whistle-blowing facilities or ethical ombudsmen or officers, and so forth

(Barnett, Cochran, & Taylor, 1993; Dworkin & Near, 1987, 1997; Hassink, de Vries, & Bollen, 2007; Miceli & Near, 1989; Miceli, Rehg, Near, & Ryan, 1999; Near & Miceli, 2008).

Active, Ethical Followership and Upward Leadership

While the above mentioned mechanisms of informal communication, surveillance and sanctioning work primarily laterally (i.e., among organization members on the same hierarchical level), in order to control leadership corruption oftentimes upward mechanisms are needed. Researchers advocate active, ethical followership (Perreault, 1997) and upward (Uhl-Bien & Carsten, 2007) and shared leadership (Pearce et al., 2008) as safeguards against leadership corruption. Unfortunately, no empirical evidence regarding the effect of active, ethical follower behavior on leadership corruption exists yet. Still we think, that active and ethical followers, who think independently and critically can present a hurdle for leaders pursuing their corrupt plans.

2.5. Conclusion

Taken together, it is apparent that a myriad of organizational factors influences whether leaders engage in corrupt behavior or not. Organizational cultures and climates affect individual members' behavior but are vice versa influenced by individual actions taken. The formal and informal ethical infrastructure, providing opportunities, motivations but also control might be deemed the most direct influences on corruption. However, singular organizational factors, like having ethics codes, might be of little impact if they are not in congruence with and supported by the remaining organizational factors. Examples of these critical organizational factors are appropriate ethical cultures and climates, performance evaluations that reward and condemn ethical and corrupt behavior respectively, vigilant organization members and effective accessory control bodies.

3. EXTRA-ORGANIZATIONAL FACTORS

The next higher level of analysis is the macro-perspective, shedding light on extra-organizational influence factors, here being industry, societal and national characteristics. Although research regarding the macro-perspective on corruption is still in a nascent stage, propositions worthwhile considering have been put forward and will be outlined here.

3.1. Industry Level Influences on Corruption

While Ashforth and colleagues (2008) point out that corruption afflicts all kinds of organizations and industries (i.e., for-profit, not-for-profit, governmental and even religious organizations), there might be differences in the general susceptibility to corruption but also in the prevalence of the different forms of corruption according to the nature of industry and business of organizations. Regarding general susceptibility, Ashforth and colleagues (2008) suggest that recently deregulated industries (i.e., industries where former governmental control and regulation has been removed, for example, the telecommunication industry) may be particularly susceptible to corruption, because competition among firms of the respective industry increases, while external controls, that regulated the market before, no longer exist.

There might also be differences regarding the prevalence of different forms of corruption in different industries. For instance bribery (individual officials) might be particularly prevalent in governmental organizations, where individuals grant licenses and award contracts (e.g., municipal administration) or execute laws (e.g., police officers). Another example would be financial misstatements, which should naturally occur most often in for-profit organizations that are listed on the stock exchange.

Two models regarding industry influences on corruption have been postulated: Baucus (1994) proposed in her model of corporate illegality that firms operating in an industry characterized by intense competition, heterogeneity (e.g., having to deal with conflicting demands from diverse interaction partners) and scarce resources will be prone to behaving illegally as a response to pressure. Conversely, she argued that firms operating in an industry characterized by turbulence (e.g., emerging industries), munificence (plentiful resources) and low intensity of rivalry among firms will be tempted to engage in illegality because of the opportunity to do so. Finally, she proposes that firms operating in mature industries with high levels of illegal activity will engage in illegality due to conditions of predisposition.

Zahra et al. (2005, 2007) propose a set of industry factors influencing corruption that partly overlaps with the one proposed by Baucus (1994): (1) *industry histories, cultures and norms* (i.e., long histories of corrupt leaders, norms of ruthless competition, and so forth, leading to higher tolerance for leader corruption); (2) *industry's expectation regarding payback periods, investment time horizons and return rates* (i.e., influencing expectations of analysts and investors, creating pressures for leaders to fulfil expectations); (3) *industry concentration* (increasing the possibility of collusion through both increased pressure and opportunity); (4) *environmental hostility* (i.e., unfavorable competitive conditions through low or declining demand, low profit margins, high rate of organizational failures, etc.); (5) *environmental dynamism* (i.e., rapid technological advances, market changes, etc.) and (6) *environmental heterogeneity* (i.e., complex and diverse markets, customers, competitors, etc.). Zahra et al. (2005, 2007) propose that high values on these factors contribute to the probability of corruption, as they either increase performance pressures or opportunities for corruption. Yet, except for findings on some single factors, both models hitherto lack empirical evidence.

3.2. Societal and National Factors

Corruption has severe consequences for society in general as it disturbs system trust. As we can witness in times of financial crisis, trust in and among institutions is vital for the functioning of our financial system, the market and society in general (Leonhardt, 2008). Yet, the relationship between corruption and society is not unidirectional: Politicians, lobbyists, legislators and jurisdiction create the framework in which organizations and their members operate. Moreover society influences individuals' behavior by socially accepting or ostracizing behaviors.

Discussing societal influences on corruption, Hofstede's (1983) cultural value dimensions should be taken into account. Several researchers found significant positive associations between Hofstede's cultural value dimensions "collectivism," "power distance," "uncertainty avoidance" and "masculinity" and Transparency International's Corruption Perception Index (e.g., Getz & Volkema, 2001; Husted, 1999; Sanyal, 2005), highlighting the effect that cultural values have on individuals perceiving and engaging in corruption.

Moreover, national legislation plays an important role: The U.S.-American Sarbanes-Oxley Act (also known as SOX, 2002) is probably the most renowned and inclusive act regarding corruption, in particular financial fraud. Among several mandates and requirements it includes standards for auditors, requires CEOs to assume personal responsibility for financial statements, enhances financial reporting requirements, increases penalties for fraud and white-collar crime and establishes government bodies that oversee financial accounting of public companies. Other nations followed, introducing similar legislations like the J-SOX (Japan, passed 2008) and the EURO-SOX (Europe, to be passed). To our knowledge no evaluations of the SOX's effectiveness in reducing corruption exist yet, but we argue that it presents a step in the right direction if the act is not only written down but also enforced.

Important additional control functions are taken over by nongovernmental organizations (NGOs) like Transparency International. These institutions monitor business and governmental organizations with respect to unethical behavior, assist individuals and organizations in combating corruption, conduct research and most important make the information accessible to the public.

3.3. Conclusion

In summary, various propositions regarding the influence of extra-organizational factors on corruption have been put forward, awaiting (further) empirical evidence. The measures taken on national and international levels to combat corruption by governments and NGOs need to be evaluated regarding their impact on the incidence of corruption.

4. THE PROCESS OF TURNING CORRUPT

Up to this point, we have presented and discussed a number of potential micro-, meso- and macro-level antecedents of corruption. In the next step, we will outline how these factors interact in the development of leadership corruption (see Figure 12.2). We propose that at the core of the process of turning corrupt, there is a cost-benefit evaluation by the potential perpetrator(s). In other words, when a leader is confronted with a situation that allows for ethical or corrupt ways of action, he or she will weigh potential advantages against potential drawbacks of these courses of action and their probability of occurrence (Szwajkowski, 1985).

Both costs and benefits have material, social and psychological aspects. *Material costs* resulting from corruption may (among others) be incurred in form of unemployment, and a lowered probability of reemployment as well as in form of legal prosecution and fines. *Social costs* may take the form of societal ostracism and the destruction of professional or even private relationships. Finally, *psychological costs* may come up in form of feelings of guilt, shame, fear or stress, which are not necessarily contingent on detection. The psychological strain on perpetrators may however be attenuated by processes of moral disengagement and rationalization (cf. Ashforth & Anand, 2003).

Turning to the "positive" side, bonus payments, bribes or ill-gotten contracts etc. can be considered *material benefits* from corruption. The psychological valence someone assigns to a material benefit is influenced by individual factors: for highly career-oriented individuals the prospect of a higher post might be more seductive than a singular financial gain. *Social benefits* may result from the respect and admiration of colleagues and followers, who falsely attribute financial or managerial successes achieved by

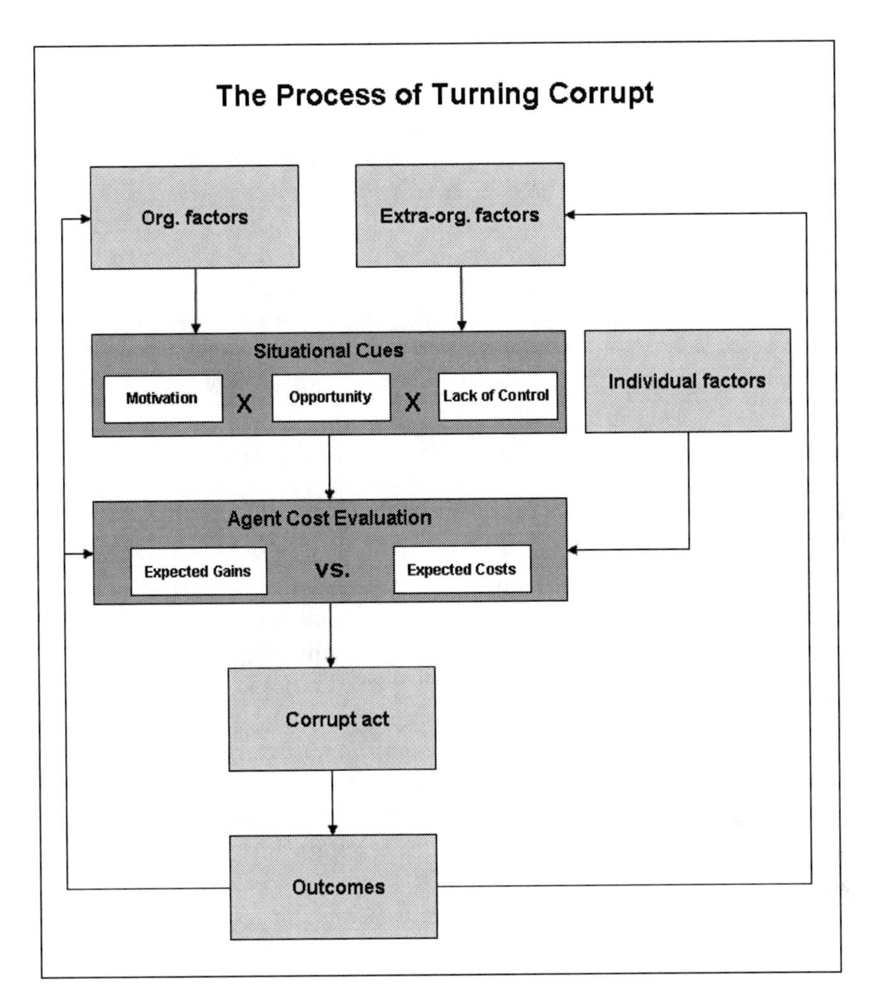

Figure 12.2. The process of turning corrupt.

corrupt means to the leader's proficiency. Additionally, if one gets away with corrupt acts, this may result in feelings of power or invulnerability, presenting *psychological benefits* of corruption.

The evaluation of costs and benefits takes place against the backdrop of opportunity and motivation to engage in corruption as well as control provided by the situation. These three determinants are influenced by organizational and extra-organizational factors. As mentioned earlier, *opportunities* to engage in corruption, like centralization of power or organizational complexity, depend on organizational structure; yet extra-organizational factors, like regulations and legislation may reduce them.

Motivation is mainly provided by the organization as well, through promotion or compensation systems. But also here, extra-organizational factors exert their influence. For example, market appreciation of the organization's stock may affect the magnitude of incentive that stock options or ownership present to the holder. Finally, the amount of *control* is largely determined by the organization itself, yet legislation sets the boundaries, for example, by prescribing the composition of BoDs, requiring audit committees or allowing sentencing attenuation if certain infrastructures are in place. Organizational control functions are either formal (e.g., BoDs, audit committees) or informal (e.g., vigilant ethical followers or peers). Extra-organizational control is provided by government bodies that for example oversee financial accounting or by state attorneys and nongovernmental associations like Transparency International.

Control particularly influences expected material and social costs, which depend on the product of the probability of detection and the sanctions the leader has to face in case of detection (Denis et al., 2006). The *probability of detection* is based on the individual's perception of effectiveness of control functions in and outside the organization. *Material sanctions* are largely determined by company policy and the legal framework. But as mentioned before, there may also be costs resulting from *social sanctions* like societal ostracism in case of detection. If opportunity, motivation and lack of control are simultaneously present to a reasonable extent, the stage is set to get individuals thinking about corruption.

Individual level factors have an important moderating influence on the cost-benefit evaluation. In particular, we assume that personality traits and personal ethics will determine the amount of psychological costs associated with a corrupt act, thus influencing the cost-benefit ratio. To give an example, leaders scoring high on honesty-humility would probably anticipate massive psychological costs when behaving corruptly, as doing so would violate central self-concepts associated with this personality disposition (e.g., being honest, trustworthy, straightforward). Scoring low on relativism or following formalistic ethics would have a similar effect, as violating personally held moral principles should come at a high personal price. Even when situational cues are present, these individuals would probably refrain from engaging in corrupt acts.

Leaders low in agreeableness, high in Machiavellianism or with an external locus of control may on the other hand have a "discount" on psychological costs, as they would be less responsive to negative consequences of their corrupt acts to others. Likewise, leaders low on idealism or following utilitarian ethics should be willing to accept harm to others under certain circumstances, thus incurring lower psychological costs in form of guilt or shame.

The degree of self-control should determine how much risk a leader is willing to take when engaging in corrupt acts. As individuals low on self-control look for immediate satisfaction of their needs, they would probably be willing to accept considerable (potential) sanctions and a relatively high risk of detection, as long as the realized benefits serve their immediate interests.

Stage of cognitive moral development should influence leaders' sensitivity to situational cues. As individuals on the preconventional level are primarily guided by self-interest, they will have the greatest propensity to engage in corruption when the situation allows for it and when benefits are attractive. On the conventional level, leaders will look for positive or negative examples among their peers when interpreting situational cues. Leaders on the principled level of cognitive moral development should be the most "immune" to situational allures, as they will be guided by moral principles that transcend the situation.

Finally, moral identity salience should determine the "signal strength" of ethical considerations when confronted with situations that allow for corruption. When salience is high, individual moral philosophies and cognitive moral development should have a greater impact on the interpretation of situational cues and thus on the cost-benefit evaluation.

The results of a committed corrupt act will in turn influence the cost-benefit evaluations of future acts. Depending on whether the corrupt act has been detected and if so whether the perpetrator has been punished for committing it, this feedback loop will either reinforce the individual in committing corruption or discourage the individual from committing further corrupt acts.

In case of detection and punishment of corruption, the above mentioned expected costs will turn into real adversities and be incurred on the perpetrator. The organization might dismiss the perpetrator and do so without the gratuities common for leaders on "normal" termination of contract. Furthermore, the perpetrator will probably become object of legal prosecution by his or her former employer or public authorities. Litigation might drag the wrongdoing to the public, damaging his or her reputation and hamper future employment. Beyond these more material adversities, the perpetrator has to face the above mentioned psychosocial costs: Friends and colleagues might turn away from him or her, expressing their disappointment and contributing to the perpetrator's feelings of guilt and shame. Having suffered these adversities, and provided that they pose a sufficiently harsh punishment, the perpetrator should refrain from further acts of corruption (and in fact might not get the chance to try again). Depending on the range and impact of the corrupt act, organizations and public authorities may even see the necessity to strengthen corruption prevention through stricter control, be it in form of changes to the organization's structure and policies or through more elaborate and daunting anticorruption legislation.

If the perpetrator gets away with the corrupt act and does not get punished although the act has been detected, things look quite different. The feedback loop changes expectancy values in the cost-benefit evaluation, lowering expected costs and maybe even increasing expected gains (through more audacious acts of corruption, e.g., requesting higher bribes, misstating larger sums, etc.). Obtaining the incentive without being reprimanded for the means to achieve it, might signal to the perpetrator (but also to witnessing colleagues) that the behavior is acceptable, even desired by the organization. If colleagues concur that corrupt behavior does not violate the norm, psychosocial costs likewise are not to be feared. If they do not concur, the perpetrator might face ostracism from his or her colleagues, as he or she violated the norms and for example damaged the professional reputation (e.g., through bribery) or "won" a competition by unfair means (e.g., when colleagues competed for a promotion) and so forth. Psychological costs like fear of detection or strain of permanent self-discipline in order to conceal the act do not occur in this scenario, as the corrupt act is openly tolerated. The feedback loop here may also influence organizational and extra-organizational factors, rendering corruption more socially acceptable in organizational as well as industry cultures.

Finally, if the corrupt act passes without detection, things will work out quite similarly to the "detection without punishment" scenario. However, as the norm violation does not surface, there is no immediate threat of collegial ostracism. In fact, the perpetrator might even find him- or herself to be respected and admired for his or her apparently extraordinary performance. The only possible costs the perpetrator incurs here are the psychological ones, including feelings of guilt and fear of detection requesting constant self-discipline. Analogous to the last scenario, the feedback-loop will influence the cost-benefit evaluation in the direction of encouraging further corruption, through lowering expected costs and maybe even increasing expected gains.

5. WAYS TO CURB CORRUPTION

Having discussed the influence factors for corruption and leadership corruption in particular and outlining their interplay, the important question remains by which means organizations can stop ongoing and prevent future corruption by their leaders.

Regarding *individual factors'* contribution to corruption, it appears that adequate selection of employees and leaders in particular is the measure of choice. Testing potential leaders on integrity (Ones, Viswesvaran, &

Schmidt, 1993), honesty-humility (Lee et al., 2005; Lee et al., 2008), Machiavellianism (Hegarty & Sims, 1978; Jones & Kavanagh, 1996) and cognitive moral development (Kohlberg, 1969; Trevino & Youngblood, 1990) seems to be most appropriate. The Big Five traits and personal moral philosophies on the other hand appear to be too broad constructs to recommend them for specifically selecting "corruption-free apples," as they are connected to many other corruption-unrelated outcomes as well.

Apart from the selection process, measures raising leaders' awareness of moral issues may be helpful to address the individual contribution to corruption. This may be accomplished through specialized trainings or mandatory independent analysis of the ethicality of certain management decisions. Moral reasoning needs to be emphasized by organizational climate and culture, allowing for moral identity to become salient in ethical decision situations. This of cause is a circular process, as leaders themselves shape organizational climate and culture through their actions.

Regarding *organizational factors* our recommendations require more than one intervention: As a first step we recommend a self-critical and honest assessment of the ethical infrastructure of the organization. Ethicality of and congruence between all the systems and elements involved should be assessed. Simultaneously, attention should be paid to the more intangible psychological factors, like climates and cultures. These provide a good starting point as they capture organization members' perception of ethical conduct in organizational life. With regard to the formal ethical infrastructure, assessors should look out for tempting opportunities created through job or organization design, ill-designed incentive schemes, and ineffective control bodies.

Opportunities need to be closed or at least secured through checks and balances. As general ways to reduce opportunities and temptations to commit corruption Lange (2008) stresses restriction of access to sensitive data or valuable materials through passwords, locks, or registered check-ins. Yet, it is probably impossible to close down all opportunities for corruption while maintaining an efficient workflow; the more it is important to be aware of existing opportunities to encounter them with appropriate control mechanisms, thus to increase the expected probability of detection of wrongdoings.

Motivations, be they financial incentives, promotions or other status-relevant issues, need to reward performance under the condition of ethical conduct and not solely bottom-line performance regardless of the means used to achieve it. Especially with regard to the contagious effect of organization members emulating succeeding colleagues, performance evaluations and the incentives based thereupon should be examined carefully so that they do not reward unethical behavior. Moreover, executive compensation in form of (unrestricted) stock options should be reconsidered: It should be debated whether the exorbitant sums resulting from annual CEO compensation packages—in the past years frequently reaching triple digit million dollar sums, due to the "bull market"—are proportionate and expedient or whether the prospect of such huge sums might rather present too great a temptation for managers to withstand.

Control bodies (e.g., BoDs, Audit Committees, or EOs) must be endowed with sufficient capacity and resources, de facto authority and most importantly independence from management (i.e., not being appointed by and in the case of BoDs not being chaired by the CEO). Furthermore, control bodies should be free of conflicting interests (e.g., through interlocking directorates or financial interest alignment with management) in order to be able to fulfil their control functions. Moreover, all members of control bodies should be held legally accountable for proper conduct of the organizations under their control. With regard to EOs, we consent with Hoffman et al. (2008), recommending that EOs should be accountable directly to the BoD rather than to company management; BoDs should decide on hiring, dismissal and compensation level of the individual EO. EOs should rather be seen as "agents of the board, rather than employees of management" (Hoffman et al., 2008, p. 89). Ensuring effective control bodies should further raise the expected probability of detection of corrupt actions.

Finally, the *informal system* should also be assessed with regard to its ethicality: behavioral norms should be discussed and evaluated among organization members in order to detect potential counternorms. Moreover ethical and vigilant members should be encouraged to speak up and voice their concerns. They should be protected from retaliation, taken seriously in their concerns and should find responsiveness in management or the ethics office. The belief that nothing could be done to rectify the situation, is one of the most frequently reported reasons for refraining from whistle-blowing. (Near & Miceli, 2008; Near, Rehg, Van Scotter, & Miceli, 2004). Accordingly, expectations that reporting the wrongdoing would result in change (Masser & Brown, 1996) and responsiveness of management to employee-voiced concerns (Barnett et al., 1993) have been found to be positively associated with whistle-blowing and internal disclosures. We want to give a few additional thoughts on means to encourage whistle-blowing (see Box 5), as we regard it a valuable warning and control system.

Turning to the *extra-organizational factors* one important factor arises that seems to apply both to organizations as to society and legislation in general: The commitment to combating corruption must not be mere lip-service or window-dressing but an honest and serious undertaking! Legislations like the U.S. SOX and its followers (J-SOX, EURO-SOX)

Box 5. Measures to Support Whistle-Blowing

Fear of retaliation seems to be one of the most obstructive factors to whistle-blowing (e.g., Masser & Brown, 1996). Therefore legislators have introduced several acts to protect whistle-blowers from retaliation (in the United States, e.g., for private sector employees: Sarbanes-Oxley Act, 2002; for federal sector employees: Whistleblower Protection Act, 1989, 1994). Yet, empirical results (all cited studies here do not include the Sarbanes-Oxley Act) are mixed: While some studies (Dworkin & Near, 1987, 1997) found that legal protections neither reduced the incidence of retaliation nor increased the incidence of whistle-blowing, others (Miceli & Near, 1989; Miceli et al., 1999) find that the rate of perceived wrongdoing declined while the proportion of those reporting wrongdoing to authorities increased. Still, the number of identified whistle-blowers reporting to be retaliated against did not decrease.

The effect for companies introducing whistle-blowing policies and respective procedures looks more promising: Barnett, Cochran, and Taylor (1993) found a significant increase in the internal disclosures and significant decrease in external disclosures after implementation of policies (e.g., stating responsibility for reporting wrongdoing in codes of ethics, guaranteeing protection, etc.) and procedures (instaling appropriate communication channels and formal investigation procedures). Various studies point to the whistle-blowing supporting effect of including respective statutes in the ethics codes. Trevino and Victor (1992) found that codes of conduct encouraging whistleblowers created a social context that increased the likelihood of peer-reporting. Similarly, in their meta-analysis Mesmer-Magnus and Viswesvaran (2005) found a positive relationship between organizational climate for whistle-blowing and both intentions to and actual whistle-blowing. Generally, means to increase social acceptability of whistle-blowing in organizational and society in general seems to be effective in encouraging employees to report wrongdoing.

present a step in the right direction, provided that these laws are also enforced.

Sanctions of material and immaterial nature for corrupt behavior need to be increased to a level that frightens off potential perpetrators from engaging in it. It is necessary to increase the costs to be expected in case of being caught with corruption, such that it becomes "unaffordable." Regarding national and international legislation this means serious fines and sentences for organizations and perpetrators, but also barring perpetrators from their profession as allotted in the U.S. SOX (2002) appears to be an appropriate penalty for serious corrupt misconduct. International collaboration in combating corruption is of vital importance to prevent "corruption havens." International endeavors like the Anti-bribery Convention by the OECD (Organization for Economic Co-operation and Development) ratified currently by 38 countries present a step in the right direction.

Moreover, society should provide immaterial sanctions by no longer resignedly accepting that corruption and corrupt individuals distort the market and the financial, social and legal system. Openly expressed societal ostracism of corruption and corrupt perpetrators further increases the costs to be incurred on caught perpetrators. Media coverage and information of the public through institutions like Transparency International might form the basis for it.

Drawing a conclusion from our review, model and the given recommendations, we regard corruption and leadership corruption a serious albeit not inevitable or insurmountable problem for organizations and society. Though corrupt leadership has long been and still is a serious problem in all kinds of organizations everywhere in the world, we believe that it is one that can be significantly reduced when the right measures are taken.

NOTES

1. It should be mentioned that this result is at odds with an earlier study by Collins and Schmidt (1993). They found that white-collar criminals actually score lower on conscientiousness than managers from a white-collar comparison group. However, we believe Collins and Schmidt's (1993) study suffers from interpretational flaws: personality was assessed using the California Psychological Inventory (CPI, Gough, 1987). Results were reinterpreted post-hoc in terms of the Big Five, based on descriptive similarities of Big Five's conscientiousness and the CPI constructs socialization, responsibility and tolerance. As empirical results show however, only responsibility is substantially and positively related to conscientiousness (McCrae, Costa, & Piedmont, 1993). Collins and Schmidt's (1993) interpretation of their results in terms of conscientiousness thus seems debatable.
2. Of cause, corruption for personal, sub-unit and organizational benefit are not mutually exclusive: it is well possible that corrupt leaders simultaneously try to maximize one of the benefits while intentionally or unintentionally creating benefits on the others as well. Manipulating stock prices of the employing company for example will not only raise personal benefits from stock options but might (at least on a short-term perspective) also raise the reputation and power of the company itself.
3. We will use the terms "moral" and "ethical" interchangeably in the remainder of this chapter.
4. Acknowledging that both concepts result from different research traditions and that differing views exist (cf. Denison, 1996; James et al., 2008), we will follow Schein's (1990) notion that climate is a manifestation of the underlying organizational culture.
5. We acknowledge that in listed companies agent duality exists. In listed companies different "classes" of shareholders exist: long-term investors (with similar interests as owners in unlisted companies) vs. short-term investors (e.g., private equity firms, hedge funds, etc.). Davis et al. (2007) highlight, that agent duality "may contribute to principal-agent alignment problems and mixed allegiances". While both groups of principals (short- and long-term investors) seek to maximize returns on investments, their methods to achieve such returns may be at odds: While long-term investors

are interested in sustainability and pay-offs from dividends (Bilimoria, 1995), short-term investors prefer risky decisions to bring about quick changes in stock appreciation, that they might benefit from, when selling their shares. Agent duality thus poses the difficult task of balancing and satisfying the shareholders interests, having allegiances to both groups of investors. In this contribution, we will focus on the owners (in unlisted companies) or long-term investors (in listed companies) when referring to principals for the purpose of conciseness.

6. We acknowledge that other forms of incentives like resource allocation, praise, immaterial privileges etc. are also relevant in guiding organization members behavior, yet we believe that the corruption-conducive mechanism as described by Schein (1985) basically works likewise regardless of the specific kind of reward or incentive to be allocated.
7. We acknowledge that there might exist ingenious incentive alignment schemes that take into account sustainable long-term development of organizational outcomes and thus do not elicit the above mentioned unintended effect.
8. Institutions serving as "rubber stamps" are institutions with *de jure* considerable formal power but little *de facto* power, that is, an institution that rarely disagrees with more powerful organs. For an example see Box 3.
9. The Federal Sentencing Guidelines (1991) encouraged organizations to establish internal controls to help prevent, detect, and report criminal behavior and offered reduced fines and sentences if a company had in place personnel and controls to prevent, investigate, and punish wrongdoing.
10. Lateral control attempts (i.e., disclosing perceived wrongdoing of a person of the same status) are usually termed peer-reporting (Trevino & Victor, 1992; Victor, Trevino, & Shapiro, 1993), while upward control attempts (disclosing perceived wrongdoing of the organization or senior officials) are usually termed whistle-blowing (e.g., Miceli & Near, 1985, 1988; Near & Miceli, 1985). For the purpose of simplicity, we will subsume both under the term whistle-blowing. Furthermore, we do not differentiate between organizationally authorized and unauthorized whistle-blowing, which according to MacNab et al. (2007) should be termed reporting and whistle-blowing respectively.

REFERENCES

Abbott, L. J., Park, Y., & Parker, S. (2000). The effects of audit committee activity and independence on corporate fraud. *Managerial Finance, 26*, 55-68.

Abelson, R. (2001, March 19). Companies turn to grades, and employees go to court [Electronic Version]. *The New York Times*. Retrieved November 20, 2009 from http://www.nytimes.com/2001/03/19/business/19GRAD .htmlhttp://www.nytimes.com/2001/03/19/business/19GRAD.html

Aguilera, R., & Vadera, A. (2008). The dark side of authority: Antecedents, mechanisms, and outcomes of organizational corruption. *Journal of Business Ethics, 77*, 431-449.

American Psychiatric Association. (1994). *Diagnostic and Statistical Manual of Mental Disorders* (4th ed.). Washington, DC: Author.

Aquino, K., & Reed, A. I. (2002). The self-importance of moral identity. *Journal of Personality and Social Psychology, 83*, 1423-1440.

Ashforth, B. E., & Anand, V. (2003). The normalization of corruption in organizations. *Research in Organizational Behavior, 25*, 1-52.

Ashforth, B. E., Gioia, D. A., Robinson, S. L., & Trevino, L. K. (2008). Re-viewing organizational corruption. *Academy of Management Review, 33*, 670-684.

Ashton, M. C., & Lee, K. (2008). The prediction of Honesty-Humility-related criteria by the HEXACO and Five-Factor Models of personality. *Journal of Research in Personality, 42*, 1216-1228.

Ashton, M. C., Lee, K., Perugini, M., Szarota, P., de Vries, R. E., Di Blas, L., et al. (2004). A six-factor structure of personality-descriptive adjectives: Solutions from psycholexical studies in seven languages. *Journal of Personality and Social Psychology, 86*, 356-366.

Baehr, M. E., Jones, J. W., & Nerad, A. J. (1993). Psychological correlates of business ethics orientation in executives. *Journal of Business and Psychology, 7*, 291-308.

Barnett, T., Cochran, D. S., & Taylor, G. S. (1993). The internal disclosure policies of private-sector employers: An initial look at their relationship to employee whistleblowing. *Journal of Business Ethics, 12*, 127-136.

Bass, B. M., Waldman, D. A., Avolio, B. J., & Bebb, M. (1987). Transformational leadership and the falling dominoes effect. *Group & Organization Management, 12*, 73-87.

Baucus, M. S. (1994). Pressure, opportunity and predisposition: A multivariate model of corporate illegality. *Journal of Management, 20*, 699-721.

Beasley, M. S. (1996). An empirical analysis of the relation between the board of director composition and financial statement fraud. *Accounting Review, 71*, 443-465.

Beasley, M. S., Carcello, J. V., Hermanson, D. R., & Lapides, P. D. (2000). Fraudulent financial reporting: Consideration of industry traits and corporate governance mechanisms. *Accounting Horizons, 14*, 441-454.

Bechtoldt, M. N., Welk, C., Hartig, J., & Zapf, D. (2007). Main and moderating effects of self-control, organizational justice, and emotional labour on counterproductive behaviour at work. *European Journal of Work and Organizational Psychology, 16*, 479-500.

Beetsma, R., Peters, H., & Rebers, E. (2000). When to fire bad managers: The role of collusion between management and board of directors. *Journal of Economic Behavior & Organization, 42*, 427-444.

Beneish, M. D. (1999). Incentives and penalties related to earnings overstatements that violate GAAP. *Accounting Review, 74*, 425-457.

Benson, M. L., & Moore, E. (1992). Are white-collar and common offenders the same? An empirical and theoretical critique of a recently proposed general theory of crime. *Journal of Research in Crime and Delinquency, 29*, 251-272.

Berry, C. M., Ones, D. S., & Sackett, P. R. (2007). Interpersonal deviance, organizational deviance, and their common correlates: A review and meta-analysis. *Journal of Applied Psychology, 92*, 410-424.

Bilimoria, D. (1995). Corporate control, crime, and compensation: An empirical examination of large corporations. *Human Relations, 48*, 891-908.

Blickle, G., Schlegel, A., Fassbender, P., & Klein, U. (2006). Some personality correlates of business white-collar crime. *Applied Psychology: An International Review, 55*, 220-233.

Boo, E. H. Y., & Koh, H. C. (2001). The influence of organizational and code-supporting variables on the effectiveness of a code of ethics. *Teaching Business Ethics, 5*, 357-373.

Brady, F. N., & Wheeler, G. E. (1996). Am empirical study of ethical predispositions. *Journal of Business Ethics, 15*, 927-940.

Burns, N., & Kedia, S. (2006). The impact of performance-based compensation on misreporting. *Journal of Financial Economics, 79*, 35-67.

Caldwell, D., & Moberg, D. (2007). An exploratory investigation of the effect of ethical culture in activating moral imagination. *Journal of Business Ethics, 73*, 193-204.

Christie, R., & Geis, E. L. (1970). *Studies in Machiavellianism*. New York: Academic Press.

Clapham, S., & Cooper, R. (2005). Factors of employees' effective voice in corporate governance. *Journal of Management and Governance, 9*, 287-313.

Coleman, J. W. (1987). Toward an integrated theory of white-collar crime. *American Journal of Sociology, 93*, 406-439.

Collins, J. M., & Schmidt, F. L. (1993). Personality, integrity, and white collar crime: A construct validity study. *Personnel Psychology, 46*, 295-311.

Connelly, B. S., & Ones, D. S. (2008). The personality of corruption: A national-level analysis. *Cross-Cultural Research, 42*, 353-385.

Costa, P. T., & McCrae, R. R. (1992a). Four ways five factors are basic. *Personality and Individual Differences, 13*, 653-665.

Costa, P. T., & McCrae, R. R. (1992b). *NEO PI-R: Professional Manual*. Odessa: Psychological Assessment Resources.

Davis, J., Payne, G. T., & McMahan, G. (2007). A few bad apples? Scandalous behavior of mutual fund managers. *Journal of Business Ethics, 76*, 319-334.

de Graaf, G., & Huberts, L. W. J. C. (2008). Portraying the nature of corruption using an explorative case study design. *Public Administration Review, 68*, 640-653.

Dechow, P. M., Sloan, R. G., & Sweeney, A. P. (1996). Causes and consequences of earnings manipulation: An analysis of firms subject to enforcement actions by the SEC. *Contemporary Accounting Research, 13*, 1-36.

den Nieuwenboer, N. A., & Kaptein, M. (2008). Spiraling down into corruption: A dynamic analysis of the social identity processes that cause corruption in organizations to grow. *Journal of Business Ethics, 83*, 133-146.

Denis, D. J., Hanouna, P., & Sarin, A. (2006). Is there a dark side to incentive compensation? *Journal of Corporate Finance, 12*, 467-488.

Denison, D. R. (1996). What is the difference between organizational culture and organizational climate? A native's point of view on a decade of paradigm wars. *Academy of Management Review, 21*, 619-654.

DeZoort, F. T., Hermanson, D. R., Archambeault, D. S., & Reed, S. A. (2002). Audit committee effectiveness: A synthesis of the empirical audit committee literature. *Journal of Accounting Literature, 21*, 38-75.

Dickson, M. W., Smith, D., Grojean, M. W., & Ehrhart, M. (2001). An organizational climate regarding ethics: The outcome of leader values and the practices that reflect them. *Leadership Quarterly, 12*, 197-217.

Digman, J. M. (1990). Personality structure: Emergence of the Five-Factor Model. *Annual Review of Psychology, 41*, 417-440.

Donoher, W. J., Reed, R., & Storrud-Barnes, S. F. (2007). Incentive alignment, control, and the issue of misleading financial disclosures. *Journal of Management, 33*, 547-569.

Dworkin, T. M., & Near, J. P. (1987). Whistleblowing statutes: Are they working? *American Business Law Journal, 25*, 241-264.

Dworkin, T. M., & Near, J. P. (1997). A better statutory approach to whistle-blowing. *Business Ethics Quarterly, 7*, 1-16.

Edmondson, G. (2007, January 24). VW's scandal: The buck stops here? [Electronic Version]. *BusinessWeek*. Retrieved February 15, 2009 from http://www.businessweek.com/globalbiz/content/jan2007/gb20070124_023187.htm

Eisenhardt, K. M. (1989). Agency theory: An assessment and review. *Academy of Management Review, 14*, 57-74.

Elliot, A. L., & Schroth, R. J. (2002). *How Companies Lie: Why Enron is Just the Tip of the Iceberg*. London: Nicholas Brealey.

Elm, D. R., & Nichols, M. L. (1993). An investigation of the moral reasoning of managers. *Journal of Business Ethics, 12*, 817-833.

Erickson, M., Hanlon, M., & Maydew, E. L. (2006). Is there a link between executive equity incentives and accounting fraud? *Journal of Accounting Research, 44*, 113-143.

Falkenberg, L., & Herremans, I. (1995). Ethical behaviours in organizations: Directed by the formal or informal systems? *Journal of Business Ethics, 14*, 133-143.

Fama, E. F., & Jensen, M. C. (1983). Separation of ownership and control. *Journal of Law and Economics, 26*, 301-325.

Fleming, P., & Zyglidopoulos, S. C. (2008). The escalation of deception in organizations. *Journal of Business Ethics, 81*, 837-850.

Forsyth, D. R. (1980). A taxonomy of ethical ideologies. *Journal of Personality and Social Psychology, 39*(1), 175-184.

Forsyth, D. R. (1992). Judging the morality of business practices: The influence of personal moral philosophies. *Journal of Business Ethics, 11*, 461-470.

Getz, K. A., & Volkema, R. J. (2001). Culture, perceived corruption, and economics: A model of predictors and outcomes. *Business & Society, 40*, 7-30.

Goldberg, L. R. (1990). An alternative "description of personality": The Big-Five factor structure. *Journal of Personality & Social Psychology, 59*(6), 1216-1229.

Gottfredson, M. R., & Hirschi, T. (1990). *A General Theory of Crime*. Stanford: Stanford University Press.

Gough, H. G. (1987). *The California Psychological Inventory Administrator's Guide*. Palo Alto: Consulting Psychologists Press.

Grojean, M., Resick, C., Dickson, M., & Smith, D. (2004). Leaders, values, and organizational climate: Examining leadership strategies for establishing an organizational climate regarding ethics. *Journal of Business Ethics, 55*, 223-241.

Guilford, J. P. (1959). *Personality*. New York: McGraw-Hill.

Harris, J., & Bromiley, P. (2007). Incentives to cheat: The influence of executive compensation and firm performance on financial misrepresentation. *Organization Science, 18*, 350-367.

Hassink, H., de Vries, M., & Bollen, L. (2007). A content analysis of whistleblowing policies of leading European companies. *Journal of Business Ethics, 75*, 25-44.

Hegarty, W. H., & Sims, H. P. (1978). Some determinants of unethical decision behavior: An experiment. *Journal of Applied Psychology, 63*, 451-457.

Hegarty, W. H., & Sims, H. P. (1979). Organizational philosophy, policies, and objectives related to unethical decision behavior: A laboratory experiment. *Journal of Applied Psychology, 64*, 331-338.

Henle, C. A., Giacalone, R. A., & Jurkiewicz, C. L. (2005). The role of ethical ideology in workplace deviance. *Journal of Business Ethics, 56*, 219-230.

Hirschi, T., & Gottfredson, M. R. (1987). Causes of white-collar crime. *Criminology, 25*, 949-974.

Hirschi, T., & Gottfredson, M. R. (1994). The generality of deviance. In T. Hirschi & M. R. Gottfredson (Eds.), *The generality of deviance* (pp. 1-22). New Brunswick, NJ: Transaction.

Hoffman, W., Neill, J., & Stovall, O. (2008). An investigation of ethics officer independence. *Journal of Business Ethics, 78*, 87-95.

Hofstede, G. (1983). The cultural relativity of organizational practices and theories. *Journal of International Business Studies, 14*, 75-89.

Hogan, J., & Brinkmeyer, K. (1997). Bridging the gap between overt and personality-based integrity tests. *Personnel Psychology, 50*, 587-599.

Husted, B. W. (1999). Wealth, culture, and corruption. *Journal of International Business Studies, 30*, 339-359.

Izraeli, D., & BarNir, A. (1998). Promoting ethics through ethics officers: A proposed profile and an application. *Journal of Business Ethics, 17*, 1189-1196.

Jain, A. K. (2001). Corruption: A review. *Journal of Economic Surveys, 15*, 71-121.

James, L. R., Choi, C. C., Ko, C.-H. E., McNeil, P. K., Minton, M. K., Wright, M. A., et al. (2008). Organizational and psychological climate: A review of theory and research. *European Journal of Work and Organizational Psychology, 17*, 5-32.

Janis, I. L. (1982). *Groupthink: Psychological Studies of Policy Decisions and Fiascoes*. Boston: Houghton Mifflin.

Jansen, E., & von Glinow, M. A. (1985). Ethical ambivalence and organizational reward systems. *Academy of Management Review, 10*, 814-822.

Jensen, M. C. (1993). The modern industrial revolution, exit, and the failure of internal control systems. *Journal of Finance, 48*, 831-880.

Johnson, S. A., Ryan, H. E., Jr., & Tian, Y. S. (2005). *Executive Compensation and Corporate Fraud.* Unpublished working paper, Louisiana State University.

Johnson, S. A., Ryan, H. E., Jr., & Tian, Y. S. (2009). Managerial incentives and corporate fraud: The sources of incentives matter. *Review of Finance, 13*, 115-145.

Jones, G. E., & Kavanagh, M. J. (1996). An experimental examination of the effects of individual and situational factors on unethical behavioral intentions in the workplace. *Journal of Business Ethics, 15*, 511-523.

Judge, T. A., Bono, J. E., Ilies, R., & Gerhardt, M. W. (2002). Personality and leadership: A qualitative and quantitative review. *Journal of Applied Psychology, 87*, 765-780.

Kaptein, M., & Schwartz, M. (2008). The effectiveness of business codes: A critical examination of existing studies and the development of an integrated research model. *Journal of Business Ethics, 77*, 111-127.

Kesner, I. F., Victor, B., & Lamont, B. T. (1986). Board composition and the commission of illegal acts: An investigation of Fortune 500 companies. *Academy of Management Journal, 29*, 789-799.

King, G. (2001). Perceptions of intentional wrongdoing and peer reporting behavior among registered nurses. *Journal of Business Ethics, 34*, 1-13.

Kirkpatrick, & Lockhart. (2003). WorldCom, Inc., Case No. 02-15533 (AJG), Second interim report. Southern District of New York: United States Bankruptcy Court.

Kohlberg, L. (1969). Stage and sequence: The cognitive-developmental approach to socialization. In D. A. Goslin (Ed.), *Handbook of Socialization Theory and Research* (pp. 347-480). Chicago: Rand McNally.

Kulik, B., O'Fallon, M., & Salimath, M. (2008). Do competitive environments lead to the rise and spread of unethical behavior? Parallels from Enron. *Journal of Business Ethics, 83*, 703-723.

Landler, M. (2008, January 16). Volkswagen corruption trial includes seamy testimony [Electronic Version]. *The New York Times*. Retrieved November 20, 2009 from http://www.nytimes.com/2008/01/16/business/16bribe.html

Lange, D. (2008). A multidimensional conceptualization of organizational corruption control. *Academy of Management Review, 33*, 710-729.

Lee, K., Ashton, M. C., & de Vries, R. E. (2005). Predicting workplace delinquency and integrity with the HEXACO and Five-Factor models of personality structure. *Human Performance, 18*, 179-197.

Lee, K., Ashton, M. C., Morrison, D. L., Cordery, J., & Dunlop, P. D. (2008). Predicting integrity with the HEXACO personality model: Use of self- and observer reports. *Journal of Occupational and Organizational Psychology, 81*(1), 147-167.

Leonhardt, D. (2008, September 30). Lesson from a crisis: When trust vanishes, worry [Electronic Version]. *The New York Times*. Retrieved November 20, 2009 from http://www.nytimes.com/2008/10/01/business/economy /01leonhardt.html

Lewis, J. D., & Weigert, A. (1985). Trust as a social reality. *Social Forces, 63*, 967-985.

Litzky, B. E., Eddleston, K. A., & Kidder, D. L. (2006). The good, the bad, and the misguided: How managers inadvertently encourage deviant behaviors. *Academy Of Management Perspectives, 20*, 91-103.

Luhmann, N. (1979). *Trust and Power: Two Works by Niklas Luhmann* (G. Poggi, Trans.) (2nd ed.). New York: Wiley.

MacNab, B., Brislin, R., Worthley, R., Galperin, B. L., Jenner, S., Lituchy, T. R., et al. (2007). Culture and ethics management: Whistle-blowing and internal reporting within a NAFTA country context. *International Journal of Cross Cultural Management, 7*, 5-28.

Manz, C. C., Anand, V., Joshi, M., & Manz, K. P. (2008). Emerging paradoxes in executive leadership: A theoretical interpretation of the tensions between corruption and virtuous values. *The Leadership Quarterly, 19*, 385-392.

Marcus, B., & Schuler, H. (2004). Antecedents of counterproductive behavior at work: A general perspective. *Journal of Applied Psychology, 89*, 647-660.

Masser, B., & Brown, R. (1996). "When would you do it?" An investigation into the effects of retaliation, seriousness of malpractice and occupation on willingness to blow the whistle. *Journal of Community and Applied Social Psychology, 6*(2), 127-130.

McCrae, R. R., & Costa, P. T. (1987). Validation of the Five-Factor model of personality across instruments and observers. *Journal of Personality and Social Psychology, 52*, 81-90.

McCrae, R. R., Costa, P. T., & Piedmont, R. L. (1993). Folk concepts, natural language, and psychological constructs: The California Psychological Inventory and the five-factor model. *Journal of Personality, 61*, 1-26.

McCrae, R. R., & John, O. P. (1992). An introduction to the Five-Factor model and its applications. *Journal of Personality, 60*, 175-215.

McKendall, M. A., DeMarr, B., & Jones-Rikkers, C. (2002). Ethical compliance programs and corporate illegality: Testing the assumptions of the Corporate Sentencing Guidelines. *Journal of Business Ethics, 37*, 367-383.

McKendall, M. A., & Wagner, J. A., III. (1997). Motive, opportunity, choice, and corporate illegality. *Organization Science, 8*, 624-647.

McLean, B., & Elkind, P. (2003). *The Smartest Guys in the Room: The Amazing Rise and Scandalous Fall of Enron*. New York: Penguin Books.

Mesmer-Magnus, J., & Viswesvaran, C. (2005). Whistleblowing in organizations: An examination of correlates of whistleblowing intentions, actions, and retaliation. *Journal of Business Ethics, 62*, 277-297.

Miceli, M. P., & Near, J. P. (1989). The incidence of wrongdoing, whistle-blowing, and retaliation: Results of a naturally occurring field experiment. *Employee Responsibilities and Rights Journal, 2*, 91-108.

Miceli, M. P., Rehg, M., Near, J. P., & Ryan, K. C. (1999). Can laws protect whistle-blowers? Results of a naturally occurring field experiment. *Work and Occupations, 26*, 129-151.

Morf, D. A., Schumacher, M. G., & Vitell, S. J. (1999). A survey of ethics officers in large organizations. *Journal of Business Ethics, 20*, 265-271.

Murphy, K. J. (1999). Executive compensation. In O. Ashenfelter & D. Card (Eds.), *Handbook of Labor Economics* (Vol. 3b, pp. 2485-2563). North Holland: Elsevier Science.

Near, J. P., & Miceli, M. P. (2008). Wrongdoing, whistle-blowing, and retaliation in the U.S. government: What have researchers learned from the Merit Systems Protection Board (MSPB) survey results? *Review of Public Personnel Administration, 28*, 263-281.

Near, J. P., Rehg, M. T., Van Scotter, J. R., & Miceli, M. P. (2004). Does type of wrongdoing affect the whistle-blowing process? *Business Ethics Quarterly, 14*, 219-242.

Nill, A., & Schibrowsky, J. A. (2005). The impact of corporate culture, the reward system, and perceived moral intensity on marketing students' ethical decision making. *Journal of Marketing Education, 27*, 68-80.

O'Connor, J. J. P., Priem, R. L., Coombs, J. E., & Gilley, K. M. (2006). Do CEO Stock options prevent or promote fraudulent financial reporting? *Academy of Management Journal, 49*, 483-500.

Ofek, E., & Yermack, D. (2000). Taking stock: Equity-based compensation and the evolution of managerial ownership. *Journal of Finance, 55*, 1367-1384.

Ones, D. S., Viswesvaran, C., & Schmidt, F. L. (1993). Comprehensive meta-analysis of integrity test validities: Findings and implications for personnel selection and theories of job performance. *Journal of Applied Psychology, 78*, 679-703.

Palmer, D., & Maher, M. W. (2006). Developing the process model of collective corruption. *Journal of Management Inquiry, 15*, 363-370.

Parsons, T. (1951). *The Social System*. London: Routledge & Kegan Paul.

Pearce, C. L., Manz, C. C., & Sims jr., H. P. (2008). The roles of vertical and shared leadership in the enactment of executive corruption: Implications for research and practice. *The Leadership Quarterly, 19*, 353-359.

Pearce, C. L., & Sims jr., H. P. (2002). Vertical versus shared leadership as predictors of the effectiveness of change management teams: An examination of aversive, directive, transactional, transformational, and empowering leader behaviors. *Group Dynamics: Theory, Research, & Practice, 6*, 172-197.

Perreault, G. (1997). Ethical followers: A link to ethical leadership. *Journal of Leadership and Organizational Studies, 4*, 78-89.

Peterson, D. K. (2002). Deviant workplace behavior and the organization's ethical climate. *Journal of Business and Psychology, 17*, 47-61.

Ponemon, L. (1990). Ethical judgments in accounting: A cognitive-developmental perspective. *Critical Perspectives on Accounting, 1*, 191-215.

Ponemon, L. (1992). Ethical reasoning and selection-socialization in accounting. *Accounting, Organizations, and Society, 17*, 239-258.

Reed, A. I., & Aquino, K. (2003). Moral identity and the expanding circle of moral regard toward out-groups. *Journal of Personality and Social Psychology, 84*, 1270-1286.

Reed, G. E., & Yeager, P. C. (1996). Organizational offending and neoclassical criminology: challenging the reach of a general theory of crime. *Criminology, 34*, 357-382.

Reynolds, S. J. (2006). Moral awareness and ethical predispositions: Investigating the role of individual differences in the recognition of moral issues. *Journal of Applied Psychology, 91*, 233-243.

Reynolds, S. J., & Ceranic, T. L. (2007). The effects of moral judgment and moral identity on moral behavior: An empirical examination of the moral individual. *Journal of Applied Psychology, 92*, 1610-1624.

Robinson, S. L., & Bennett, R. J. (1995). A typology of deviant workplace behaviors: A multidimensional scaling study. *Academy of Management Journal, 38*, 555-572.

Rodriguez, P., Uhlenbruck, K., & Eden, L. (2005). Government corruption and the entry strategies of multinationals. *Academy of Management Review, 30*, 383-396.

Rotter, J. B. (1966). Generalized expectancies for internal vs. external control of reinforcement. *Psychological Monographs: General and Applied, 80*, 1-28.

Sackett, P. R., & DeVore, C. J. (2002). Counterproductive behaviors at work. In N. Anderson, D. S. Ones, H. K. Sinangil & V. Viswesvaran (Eds.), *Handbook of Industrial, Work and Organizational Psychology* (Vol. 1, pp. 145-164). London: Sage.

Salgado, J. F. (2002). The Big Five personality dimensions and counterproductive behaviors. *International Journal of Selection and Assessment, 10*, 117-125.

Sanyal, R. (2005). Determinants of bribery in international business: The cultural and economic factors. *Journal of Business Ethics, 59*, 139-145.

Schein, E. H. (1985). *Organizational Culture and Leadership: A Dynamic View* (1. ed.). San Francisco: Jossey-Bass Publishers.

Schein, E. H. (1990). Organizational culture. *American Psychologist, 45*, 109-119.

Schnatterly, K. (2003). Increasing firm value through detection and prevention of white-collar crime. *Strategic Management Journal, 24*, 587-614.

Schwartz, M. S. (2004). Effective corporate codes of ethics: Perceptions of code users. *Journal of Business Ethics, 55*, 321-341.

Schweitzer, M. E., Ordónez, L., & Douma, B. (2004). Goal setting as a motivator of unethical behavior. *Academy of Management Journal, 47*, 422-432.

Security and Exchange Commision. (2004). United States of America against Strong Capital Management, Inc., Strong Investor Services, Inc., Strong Investments, Inc., Richard S. Strong, Thomas A. Hooker, Jr. and Anthony J. D'Amato [Electronic Version]. Retrieved November 20, 2009 from http://www.sec.gov/litigation/admin/34-49741.htm

Sherman, L. W. (1980). Three models of organizational corruption in agencies of social control. *Social Problems, 27*, 478-491.

Shultz, C. J. (1993). Situational and dispositional predictors of performance: A test of the hypothesized Machiavellianism x structure interaction among sales persons. *Journal of Applied Social Psychology, 23*, 478-498.

Simpson, S. S., & Piquero, N. L. (2002). Low self-control, organizational theory, and corporate crime. *Law & Society Review, 36*, 509-547.

Sims, R. R., & Brinkmann, J. (2002). Leaders as moral role models: The case of John Gutfreund at Salomon Brothers. *Journal of Business Ethics, 35*, 327-339.

Sims, R. R., & Brinkmann, J. (2003). Enron ethics (or: Culture matters more than codes). *Journal of Business Ethics, 45*, 243-256.

Smith, R. W. (2003). Corporate ethics officers and government ethics administrators: Comparing apples with oranges or a lesson to be learned? *Administration Society, 34*, 632-652.

Steffensmeier, D. (1989). On the causes of "white-collar" crime: An assessment of Hirschi and Gottfredson's claims. *Criminology, 27*, 345-358.

Sutherland, E. H. (1940). White-collar criminality. *American Sociological Review, 5*, 2-10.

Szwajkowski, E. (1985). Organizational illegality: Theoretical integration and illustrative application. *Academy of Management Review, 10*, 558-567.

Tajfel, H., & Turner, J. C. (1979). An integrative theory of intergroup conflict. In W. G. Austin & S. Worchel (Eds.), *The social psychology of intergroup relations* (pp. 33-47). Monterey, CA: Brooks-Cole.

Tajfel, H., & Turner, J. C. (1986). The social identity theory of intergroup behavior. In S. Worchel & W. G. Austin (Eds.), *Psychology of Intergroup Relations* (pp. 7-24). Chicago: Nelson Hall.

Tenbrunsel, A. E., Smith-Crowe, K., & Umphress, E. E. (2003). Building houses on rocks: The role of the ethical infrastructure in organizations. *Social Justice Research, 16*, 285-307.

Terpstra, D. E., Rozell, E. J., & Robinson, R. K. (1993). The influence of personality and demographic variables on ethical decisions related to insider trading. *Journal of Psychology: Interdisciplinary and Applied, 127*, 375-389.

Transparency International, e. V. (2008). *Corruption Perceptions Index*. Berlin: Transparency International.

Trevino, L. K. (1986). Ethical decision making in organizations: A person-situation interactionist model. *Academy of Management Review, 11*, 601-617.

Trevino, L. K. (1990). A cultural perspective on changing and developing organizational ethics. *Research in Organizational Change and Development, 4*, 195-230.

Trevino, L. K., Butterfield, K. D., & McCabe, D. L. (1998). The ethical context in organizations: Influences on employee attitudes and behaviors. *Business Ethics Quarterly, 8*, 447-476.

Trevino, L. K., & Victor, B. (1992). Peer reporting of unethical behavior: A social context perspective. *Academy of Management Journal, 35*, 38-64.

Trevino, L. K., Weaver, G. R., & Reynolds, S. J. (2006). Behavioral ethics in organizations: A review. *Journal of Management, 32*, 951-990.

Trevino, L. K., & Youngblood, S. A. (1990). Bad apples in bad barrels: A causal analysis of ethical decision-making behavior. *Journal of Applied Psychology, 75*, 378-385.

Turner, J. C., & Oakes, P. J. (1986). The significance of the social identity concept for social psychology with reference to individualism, interactionism, and social influence. *British Journal of Social Psychology, 25*, 237-252.

Uhl-Bien, M., & Carsten, M. K. (2007). Being ethical when the boss is not. *Organizational Dynamics, 36*, 187-201.

United States Sentencing Commission. (1991). *Federal Sentencing Guidelines manual.* Washington, DC: U.S. Government Printing Office.

United States Public Laws. (2002). The Sarbanes-Oxley Act of 2002, Public Law 107-204 (H. R. 3763). Washington, DC: U.S. Government Printing Office.

Urbany, J. (2005). Inspiration and cynicism in values statements. *Journal of Business Ethics, 62*, 169-182.

Valentine, S., & Johnson, A. (2005). Codes of ethics, orientation programs, and the perceived importance of employee incorruptibility. *Journal of Business Ethics, 61*, 45-53.

Victor, B., & Cullen, J. B. (1988). The organizational bases of ethical work climates. *Administrative Science Quarterly, 33*, 101-125.

Wanek, J. E., Sackett, P. R., & Ones, D. S. (2003). Towards an understanding of integrity test similarities and differences: An item-level analysis of seven tests. *Personnel Psychology, 56*, 873-894.

Weber, J. (1990). Managers' moral reasoning: Assessing their responses to three moral dilemmas. *Human Relations, 43*, 687-702.

Weber, J., & Wasieleski, D. (2001). Investigating influences on managers' moral reasoning. *Business & Society, 40*, 79-110.

Webley, S., & Werner, A. (2008). Corporate codes of ethics: necessary but not sufficient. *Business Ethics: A European Review, 17*, 405-415.

Wimbush, J. C., Shepard, J. M., & Markham, S. E. (1997). An empirical examination of the relationship between ethical climate and ethical behavior from multiple levels of analysis. *Journal of Business Ethics, 16*, 1705-1716.

Zahra, S. A., & Pearce, J. A., II. (1989). Boards of directors and corporate financial performance: A review and integrative model. *Journal of Management, 15*, 291-334.

Zahra, S. A., Priem, R. L., & Rasheed, A. A. (2005). The antecedents and consequences of top management fraud. *Journal of Management, 31*, 803-828.

Zahra, S. A., Priem, R. L., & Rasheed, A. A. (2007). Understanding the causes and effects of top management fraud. *Organizational Dynamics, 36*, 122-139.

PART IV

LEADER ERRORS AND FAILURE

CHAPTER 13

LEADERS' PERSONAL EXPERIENCE AND RESPONSE TO FAILURE

A Theoretical Framework and Initial Test

Kathleen Boies, Melanie Ann Robinson, and Maria Carolina Saffie Robertson

Learning from failure has long been recognized as essential to leadership development. The purpose of this chapter is to present a theoretical framework of leaders' personal experience of failure and an initial test. In this framework, we specify antecedents of leaders' perception of the impact of failure. The impact is then hypothesized to determine the personal consequences and the type of responses that leaders adopt when facing failure. The theoretical framework was tested using qualitative data from 16 educational leaders. This initial test indicates that the framework is promising and may serve as a useful basis for future research.

When Leadership Goes Wrong: Destructive Leadership, Mistakes and Ethical Failures, pp. 357–382

"I think failure is large. It can be a very large word. It can be many things."

"A failure would be if we did not push hard enough for something to work."

"Failure is when it is not working and it can't go on without me."[1]

The study of failure in leadership has largely focused on analyzing the causes of large-scale business failures and ethical scandals based on analyses of CEOs' and top managers' actions (e.g., Finkelstein, 2003; Sonnenfeld & Ward, 2007). In this chapter, we take a different look at failure in leadership and focus more closely on leaders' personal experience of a broad range of failure (to use Wilkinson & Mellahi's, 2005, words, we focus on failures as opposed to Failure). Rather than focusing on why leaders fail or make mistakes, we focus on the aftermath of these events and examine leaders' responses to the failure, as well as the impact of these events on leaders themselves.

In studying the lives and careers of great leaders, one quickly realizes that failure as much as success has influenced their development. It is therefore important to conceptualize failure and understand how leaders react to these experiences. Though learning from failure has long been recognized as a critical aspect in leadership development (e.g., Daudelin, 1996), failure has rarely been studied empirically or been the subject of theory building in that context. The purpose of this chapter is to present a theoretical framework of leaders' personal experience of failure.

Leadership presents a unique context in which to study the impact of failures and mistakes. Leaders are often the engineers of their own situations: for example, they are, more often than others, the instigators of projects and are therefore more likely to have been the initiator of the failed project. Furthermore, they are most often in the best position to change the course of the project when failure occurs. Thus, leaders have latitude that offers an interesting and informative perspective on failure and its impact. In addition, leaders have power over others' failure (e.g., they can decide to fund or not someone else's project or to promote a subordinate or not; Boss & Sims, 2008). Thus, the study of failure in leadership presents an intriguing perspective that is worth developing.

Although several different areas have studied the impact of failure and mistakes on people (e.g., clinical psychology, education, management), and many theories have been put forth that can help explain the influence of failure and mistakes (e.g., attribution theory, trust theories, stress theories), there is little literature specifically focusing on the study of leaders' experience of failure. Thus, this chapter makes a contribution to the existing body of literature by proposing a theoretical framework for understanding leaders' personal experience of failure, and presenting the results of an initial test of some of the propositions derived from the model.

This chapter contributes to a nascent literature on failure in leadership, which takes advantage of the full range of leadership behaviors and experiences (positive and negative) to arrive at a deeper understanding of the leadership process. It answers a call for more research and theoretical development on the topic of failure in the leadership process (e.g., Hunter, Bedell-Avers, & Mumford, 2007). The exploration of leaders' personal experience of failure also has practical implications for leader development, as well as coaching and mentoring, which will be explored in the discussion.

This chapter is organized as follows. We first define failure based on the extant literature. We then integrate the literature on leadership, feedback, goal setting, attribution, affect, and personality into a theoretical framework and generate propositions. An initial test of some of these propositions is then presented, using qualitative data collected from educational leaders about their own experience of failure. Finally, we discuss practical and theoretical implications of the model and initial findings and outline directions for future research.

FAILURE DEFINED

We define failure as the non attainment of initial goals. Our definition is consistent with Cannon and Edmondson (2001) who define failure as "deviation from expected and desired results" (p. 162). This definition is also close to Zhao and Olivera's (2006) definition of error as individuals' decisions and behaviors that (1) result in an undesirable gap between an expected and real state and (2) may lead to actual or potential negative consequences for organizational functioning that could have been avoided" (p. 1013). Zhao and Olivera, however, distinguish errors from failure, as we do. According to them, failures do not carry the assumption that they could have been avoided (which is also consistent with Cannon & Edmondson, 2001). Furthermore, they assert that failure may result from an accumulation of errors (see also Wilkinson & Mellahi, 2005). Their illustrations of errors also help distinguish it from failure. For example, a pharmacist making a mistake in filling a prescription would be considered an error, but not necessarily a failure. Our definition of failure, therefore, entails the notion of nonattainment of goals in a large piece of work, or project. Though there is a distinction between errors and failures, we draw from the error literature in order to derive some of our propositions as these two areas are intimately linked.

In developing our theoretical framework, we also rely on the feedback intervention literature and, in particular, Kluger and DeNisi's (1996) feedback intervention theory. Failure represents a form of feedback that sends a signal to leaders that their behavior or actions need to be adjusted in order to avoid further failure (see, e.g., Deng, Bligh, & Kohles, 2010, for a similar argument with regards to errors). In other words, leaders who see the consequence of their actions receive information as to whether or not they were successful, which can then feed into subsequent actions and decisions. Both failure and success, therefore, might represent a form of feedback.

Overview of the Theoretical Framework

The theoretical framework is articulated around a central construct, leaders' perceived impact of failure. We propose that three categories of variables will determine leaders' perception of the impact of failure on themselves: determination of goals (self-initiated, other initiated but accepted, and imposed by others), individual differences (conscientiousness, learning orientation, performance orientation, and need for achievement), and leaders' perceived cause of failure (external vs. internal attributions). Leaders' perceived impact of failure, in turn, will determine their responses to failure. Leaders will have to make decisions concerning the project, which we refer to as "response to the goal." The failure will also have personal consequences; these are labeled "personal consequences for the leader." Finally, we propose that the experience of failure will trigger a learning process that will influence subsequent initiatives. The framework appears in Figure 13.1. We now turn to a more detailed explanation of the theoretical propositions, starting with a central construct in the framework, namely, perceived impact of failure.

Perceived Impact of Failure

Cannon and Edmondson (2001) classified the impact of failure into three different categories: major, minor and interpersonal. The classification of failure into minor or major is intimately linked to the context and also depends on the interpretation of the people involved in the failure experience (Cannon & Edmondson, 2001, 2005). For example, a major failure for a doctor can mean the death of a patient, whereas a major failure for a chef can be running out of a key ingredient in the middle of the dinner service. Similarly, minor failures can be described as a lack of

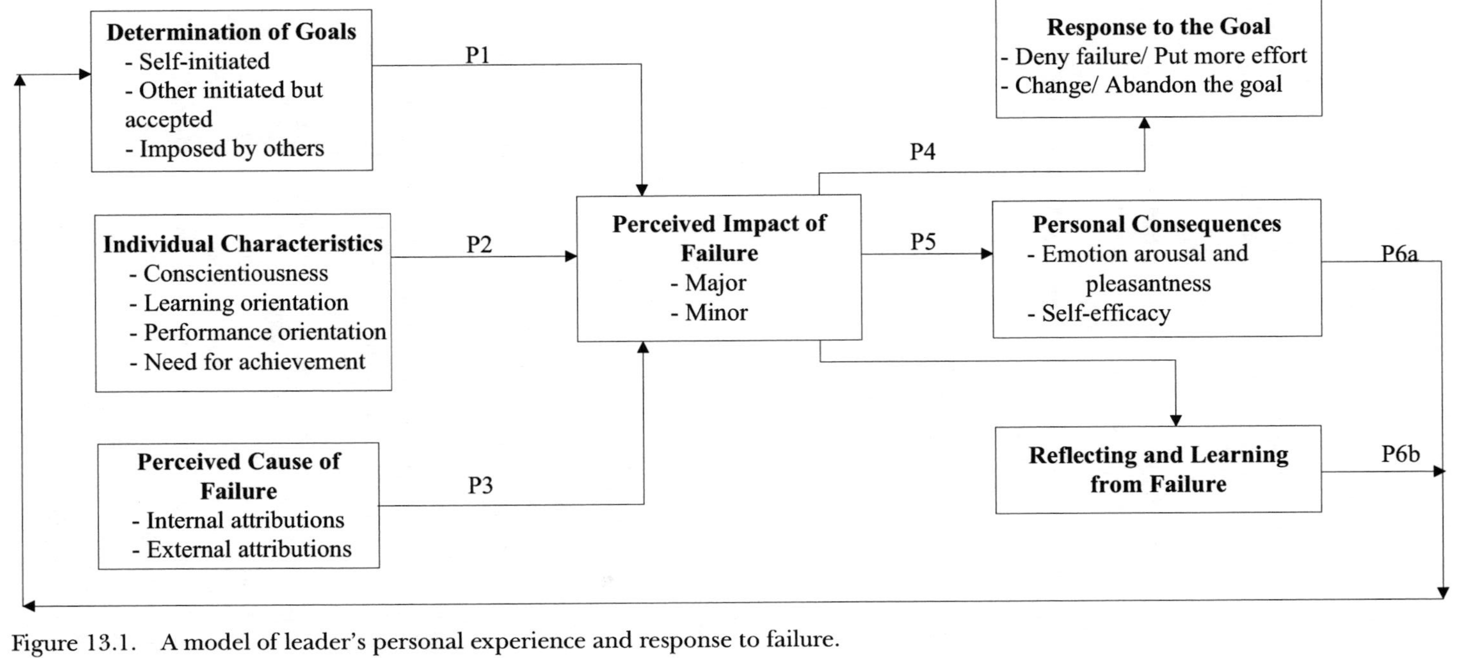

Figure 13.1. A model of leader's personal experience and response to failure.

communication or misunderstanding in one context, and technical problems in another. Interpersonal failure, on the other hand, is defined as those instances in which there is interpersonal conflict and the parties involved persist with their views and opinions, stopping solutions from developing and blocking the progress (Cannon & Edmondson, 2001). Given that this chapter focuses on leaders' reactions to failures at an individual level, and on the impact of failure on leaders themselves, we chose to focus on the two categories of failure impact proposed by Cannon and Edmondson that do not necessarily involve a dyad. Thus, we refer only to major and minor impact of failure and excluded interpersonal failure.

Leaders' perceived impact of failure may be influenced by several antecedents. First, we propose that it will depend on who initiated the project (i.e., who determined goals). Second, it may be influenced by individual characteristics (i.e., conscientiousness, learning orientation, performance orientation, and need for achievement). Finally, it may be influenced by causal attributions. We now turn to antecedents of leaders' perceived impact of failure.

Antecedents of Perceived Impact of Failure

Determination of Goals

Some evidence suggests that different types of goals may determine, to an extent, leaders' perception of the impact of failure. For example, Giessner and van Knippenberg (2008) establish a distinction between maximal and minimal goals. Maximal goals are goals that are ideal, whereas minimal goals are goals that must be reached. They suggest that failure to reach maximal goals should have less severe consequences than failure to reach minimal goals. In other words, depending on the goal, failure to reach it will have more or less severe consequences.

Goals are the cornerstone of Kluger and DeNisi's (1996) feedback intervention theory. Indeed, a first assumption of their theory is that people regulate their behavior by comparing the feedback they receive to a goal (i.e., the feedback-standard gap). An outcome which exceeds the goal would represent positive feedback, whereas an outcome that falls short of the goal would be negative. Thus, feedback interventions provide information about one's performance that may be positive or negative. However, in the case of failure, we consider that the information on one's behavior is negative (i.e., the outcome falls short of reaching the standard). A second assumption of the feedback intervention theory is that goals (or standards) are organized in a hierarchy, according to their closeness to the self—the higher the goal, the closer it is to the self. Kluger and DeNisi suggest that the success of a feedback intervention depends on the goal within this hierarchy. More specifically, a feedback intervention would likely be more successful if it were targeted at a goal at the lower level of the hierarchy, but might fail when aiming towards a goal at the higher levels of the hierarchy. In other words, when feedback interventions attempt to modify behaviors or actions that are closer to the self, they are likely to fail and lead to detrimental effects, because feedback aimed at one's self-concept may be met with defense mechanisms.

Extrapolating the hierarchy proposed by Kluger and DeNisi (1996) to the context of leadership failure, it is proposed that the impact of the failure experience will vary according to the closeness of a project's goal to the self. We assume that the more involvement a leader had in setting a goal, the closer it is to the self. In other words, the higher the level of personal involvement and commitment to a goal or task, the more impact the failure might have for the leader.

Like Kluger and DeNisi (1996), our proposed hierarchy has three levels. At the top of the hierarchy, we find goals that are closest to the self. Thus, the highest level of commitment to the goal in the case of failure might be goals that are self-initiated. Here, the goals involve, or are closely related to, the definition of the self (Kluger & DeNisi, 1996). Therefore, we may expect that the leader will perceive the impact of the failure as major when self-initiated goals are not successful because these goals are closer to their self-concept and failure to reach these goals might be perceived as having more severe consequences.

Proposition 1a. When the goal is self-initiated, the impact of failure is more likely to be perceived as major than minor.

In the midsection of the proposed hierarchy of goals, we include goals that are initiated by others but accepted by the leader. Given that this level corresponds to the middle of the hierarchy of goals, we assume that the higher level would then prevail. That is, goals that are other initiated but accepted by the leader may become relatively close to the self. Therefore, it is expected that the impact of failure will be major if leaders fail at reaching a goal that was initiated by others but accepted.

Proposition 1b. When the goal is initiated by others and accepted by the leader, the impact of failure is more likely to be perceived as major than minor.

The lowest level of the proposed hierarchy is represented by goals that are imposed on the leader. This level is the furthest from the self. Since these goals are far away from the definition and concept of self, it is expected that failure at reaching these goals will have a minor impact for the leader.

Proposition 1c. When the goal is imposed, the impact of failure is more likely to be perceived as minor than major.

Individual Characteristics

Although a large number of individual characteristics could be related to the degree of impact that failure has on a leader, for the purpose of this chapter, the focus has been placed on those characteristics that could have a more significant and consistent influence on the extent to which leaders are affected by failure. In particular, we center on four different individual characteristics and their relationship with the impact of failure. These individual characteristics are: conscientiousness, learning orientation, performance orientation, and need for achievement.

Although according to Barrick and Mount (1991) there is some variability regarding the definition of conscientiousness, they describe a conscientious person as being dependable, organized, hard-working, responsible and persevering. In a meta-analysis, Barrick and Mount found a stable relationship between conscientiousness and all four performance criteria, which included productivity data, turnover/tenure, status change, and salary. They also commented that conscientiousness is an accurate predictor of self-discipline and goal orientation. Furthermore, Stewart, Carson, and Cardy (1996) found a significant relationship between conscientiousness and self-direction, defined as "behavior that demonstrates internal control" (p. 144). This means that conscientious employees are able to supervise themselves, without the need for external control or supervision (Stewart et al., 1996).

Gully, Payne, Koles, and Whiteman (2002) argued that highly conscientious individuals want to avoid making mistakes. In fact, they found that for individuals with high levels of conscientiousness, error avoidance was related to higher levels of self-efficacy than encouragement to experiment (which may lead to failure). These results suggest that highly conscientious individuals avoid making mistakes, because failure is incompatible with their self-perception of conscientiousness. When conscientious leaders do fail, the impact of that failure is likely to be perceived as major.

Proposition 2a. Highly conscientious leaders are more likely to perceive the impact of failure as major than minor.

Also called mastery, or task goal, learning orientation has been referred to as preference for knowledge and skill acquisition (as opposed to a focus on outcomes) (Grant & Dweck, 2003). People with high learning orientation tend to view goals as opportunities to gain understanding and to grow (Grant & Dweck, 2003). Research on learning orientation has mainly been developed with samples composed of children (Elliott & Dweck, 1988). As Elliott and Dweck discussed, researchers have noticed a pattern of reactions towards failure in children with high learning orientation. These children do not focus on the failure itself, but tend to look for solutions to the problem, which increases their positive affect and improves performance (Elliott & Dweck, 1988). Similarly, in a study conducted with resident physicians, Stern, Katz-Navon, and Naveh (2008) found a relationship between learning orientation and error making. Specifically, they found that fostering learning orientation in residents decreased the number of medical errors they made. Since individuals with a learning orientation tend to view failure as an opportunity to learn and grow (Elliott & Dweck, 1988), we expect that leaders with this personal characteristic will perceive the impact of failure in relation to themselves as minor.

Proposition 2b. Leaders with high learning orientation are more likely to perceive the impact of failure as minor than major.

Performance orientation has also been called ego-involved or ability goals by researchers (Grant & Dweck, 2003). Individuals with performance orientation tend to focus on demonstrating one's ability or avoid showing a lack of ability (Grant & Dweck, 2003). Thus, contrary to learning orientation, the focus is more on outcomes than process. People with high performance orientation tend to show helplessness and debilitation when they fail, displaying negative affect and decreasing their performance (Elliott & Dweck, 1988).

Rybowiak, Garst, Frese, and Batinic (1999) commented that errors cannot be completely eradicated from any process. Performance orientation fosters the implementation of control systems to avoid mistakes or failures, but because failure cannot be eliminated, what is really being developed is a negative approach towards mistakes and failure (Rybowiak et al., 1999). This approach creates an attitude of denial towards failure that makes it very difficult to prevent or even solve errors and mistakes when they do occur (Rybowiak et al., 1999). These results suggest that leaders with a performance orientation will perceive the impact of failure as major.

Proposition 2c. Leaders with high performance orientation are more likely to perceive the impact of failure as major than minor.

Need for achievement was first coined by David McClelland to describe individuals who have a desire for reaching significant accomplishments, who seek challenges such as mastering new skills and who have a high need for independence (McClelland & Boyatzis, 1982). As McClelland and Boyatzis commented, people with a high need for achievement tend to focus on being successful and doing well in all projects on which they embark. Therefore, people with a high need for achievement may not be prepared to deal with failure and/or solve situations where there has been a mistake or a failure, because they expect to succeed. To them, any failure may be perceived as major.

Proposition 2d. Leaders with a high need for achievement are more likely to perceive the impact of failure as major than minor.

Perceived Cause of Failure

As discussed by Schyns and Hansbrough (2008), people attribute the cause of failure to factors that might not be in fact the real cause of those mistakes or failures. The attribution of causes of failure is determined by a number of factors, including leadership-related factors and characteristics of mistakes (Schyns & Hansbrough, 2008). In other words, leaders will determine the cause of failure by relying on their own perception, which may or may not be accurate. A common way to conceptualize attributions is in terms of two dimensions: failure may be attributed to either internal or external causes.

Attribution of causes, both internal and external, could have an influence on the perceived impact of failure by leaders. External causes correspond to those factors that are out of the leader's reach, and that have a significant influence on the failure of the project or goal. Some of these external causes include the organizational culture and the lack of support/commitment of followers. According to Hareli and Hess (2008), when the cause of failure is attributed to external factors, the impact on emotions such as guilt, hurt feelings, anger, and shame is marginal. On the other hand, internal causes refer to all of those factors that can be controlled by the leader and that have a direct influence on the failure of a goal or task. Internal causes include, but are not restricted to, lack of competence, inability to use the appropriate resources, and misjudgment of the situation. Hareli and Hess note that failure is particularly hurtful when it is believed to be due to personal characteristics. When people attribute failure to internal causes, they tend to devalue themselves.

In a study conducted with undergraduate students, Holschuh, Nist, and Olenjnik (2001) found that the attribution of causes not only influenced the adoption of future goals, but that it also had an impact on the emotional reactions experienced by students who failed. It is therefore suggested that there will be a relationship between attribution of causes and the perceived impact of failure. When the leader believes that the failure is due to external factors, then the perceived impact of failure will be minor. On the other hand, when the leader attributes the failure to internal causes, the perceived impact for the leader will be major.

Proposition 3a. When the cause of failure is believed to be external, the perceived impact of failure is more likely to be perceived as minor than major.

Proposition 3b. When the cause of failure is believed to be internal, the perceived impact of failure is more likely to be perceived as major than minor.

Response to the Goal

When failure has occurred, leaders are in a unique position to react to it. Not only will they have a personal reaction to the failure, but it will also be their responsibility to make decisions regarding the project, which they could continue, change, or interrupt. Kluger and DeNisi (1996) define four types of responses to feedback interventions, which can translate into four types of responses to failure: increasing efforts to attain the project's goal, changing the goal of the project, abandoning the project altogether, or denying the failure. Leaders' reaction may in part be determined by the severity of the consequences of the failure (i.e., its impact).

According to goal setting theory, people are motivated to attain a goal (Locke & Latham, 1990). Therefore, the natural response in the face of adversity, according to goal setting theory, should be to increase effort in order to reach the goal and bring the project to term. This, according to Kluger and DeNisi (1996), will occur only to the extent that there is a relatively high likelihood of success (i.e., the goal is clear, there is commitment towards the project, and there is belief in the likelihood of success). This suggests that increasing efforts in the face of failure is more likely to occur when the impact of failure is minor, and therefore reversible. Kluger and DeNisi also assert that people may reject the negative feedback that they receive on their performance. In other words, leaders may refuse to see or accept the failure, which will lead to responses such as rationalization. This is more likely to occur in the case of minor failures, because when failures are major, it would be more difficult for the leader to avoid and/or deny the situation altogether.

This relates to Staw and colleagues' (e.g., Staw, 1976) notion of commitment to a failing course of action. Staw and Ross (1978) posited that one would continue to commit to a policy in the face of adversity if there were a possibility to recover the losses. These propositions were subsequently tested and supported in an experiment. Specifically, Staw and Ross found that when the failure was attributed to endogenous causes (which referred to causes that the subject may have foreseen prior to making the decision; according to our definition, this may be perceived as major failure) one was less likely to commit more resources to a decision than when the failure was considered to be minor.

Proposition 4a. When the perceived impact of failure is minor, leaders will deny failure and/or put more effort and resources into the project.

When the perceived impact of failure is major, leaders' responses to the goal will be different. According to Kluger and DeNisi (1996), when the gap between the performance and the standard is very wide, a likely response might be to abandon the goal or lower the standard (i.e., change the goal). This suggests that when the failure is perceived as major, leaders are more likely to abandon the project altogether and cut their losses. Alternatively, leaders might choose to change the objectives of the project.

Proposition 4b. When the perceived impact of failure is major, leaders will respond by changing or abandoning the goal.

Personal Consequences for the Leader

In addition to dealing directly with the goals of the project, leaders faced with failure will also experience personal turmoil that may be reflected in the experience of negative emotions and a loss of self-efficacy. Once again, there is some evidence in the literature, albeit indirect, to suggest that the severity of the impact of the failure will partly determine the personal consequences for the leader. For example, Nummenmaa and Niemi (2004) found that failure on social perception skills tests (as opposed to other types of tests such as cognitive tasks, which may be considered further removed from the self and therefore less impactful) led to the strongest affective reactions.

Scholars have proposed different taxonomies of emotions. One that is particularly useful for the purpose of the present chapter is the two-dimensional model outlined by Russell (1980). According to this taxonomy, emotions can be represented by a circumplex composed of two orthogonal dimensions. The first dimension refers to pleasantness, whereby emotions can range from pleasant to unpleasant. The second dimension refers to arousal—emotions, in addition to being pleasant or unpleasant, also present different degrees of activation. For example, sadness is an unpleasant and low arousal emotion, whereas anger is an unpleasant and high activation emotion (Feldman, Barrett, & Russell, 1998; Russell, 1980).

Generally speaking, negative (unpleasant) emotions are triggered by negative events, such as failure (e.g., Taylor, 1991). Kluger and DeNisi (1996) assert that feedback interventions will influence both emotion pleasantness and arousal. That is, negative feedback would be expected to lead to unpleasant emotions, whereas the opposite would be expected for positive feedback. Moreover, the further the feedback intervention is from the goal (i.e., the greater the feedback-standard gap), the more emotional arousal one should experience. Failure may be considered negative feedback on one's performance. Furthermore, major failure would be expected to be associated with wider feedback-standard gaps, in Kluger and DeNisi's terms, than would minor failures. Thus, failures that are perceived as major would be associated with negative emotions higher in arousal than failures perceived to be minor.

Proposition 5a. When the perceived impact of failure is major, leaders will experience negative emotions that are higher in arousal than when the perceived impact of failure is minor.

In addition to experiencing negative emotions, leaders facing failure may also experience a decrease in self-efficacy. Self-efficacy is defined as a belief in one's capacity to be successful at a given task (Bandura, 1997). It is generally considered to be task-specific.

One specific self-efficacy construct that applies more readily to the leadership context is leadership self-efficacy. This construct is especially relevant for understanding leaders' personal experience of failure because, as Paglis and Green (2002) pointed out, this construct is particularly important in understanding leaders' desire to engage in new initiatives and therefore to take risks. Leadership self-efficacy relates to leaders' belief in their capacity to successfully perform leadership-related tasks, such as setting directions, securing followers' commitment, and overcoming hurdles associated with change (Paglis & Green, 2002). More specifically, Hannah, Avolio, Luthans, and Harms (2008) define leadership self-efficacy as "leaders' beliefs in their perceived capabilities to organize the positive psychological capabilities, motivation, means, collective resources, and courses of action required to attain effective, sustainable performance across their various leadership roles, demands, and contexts" (p. 670).

Evidence from three different sources suggests that leadership self-efficacy will be negatively influenced by failures. First, many studies have shown the positive link between success and self-efficacy (Bandura, 1997). Second, studies have also shown a link between failure and self-efficacy (e.g., Smith, Kass, Rotunda, & Schneider, 2006). Bandura also suggests that failure at certain tasks which, adopting our framework, might be considered major, will influence self-efficacy more severely than failure of minor impact. Finally, success has been positively related to leadership self-efficacy. For example, Paglis and Green (2002) found that leadership self-efficacy (more specifically, the dimension of setting directions) was positively related to prior success. Other studies have also found that leadership self-efficacy was positively related to prior performance (see Hannah et al., 2008, for a review). Thus, a logical extension would be that failure at leading a project may lead to a decrease in leadership self-efficacy.

Proposition 5b. When the perceived impact of failure is major, leaders will experience a greater decrease in their leadership self-efficacy than when the failure is minor.

Feedback Loop

When leaders have failed and have subsequently experienced negative emotions and a faltering of their self-efficacy, it is likely to have a negative influence on future initiatives. Indeed, it has been shown that self-efficacy affects goal setting, motivation, and other related concepts such as persistence in the face of adversity (Bandura, 1997; Jacobs, Prentice-Dunn, & Rogers, 1984; Locke & Latham, 2002; Wood & Bandura, 1989). Specifically, empirical evidence has linked leadership self-efficacy to goal difficulty (Kane & Tremble, 2000; Locke & Latham, 2002; Spieker & Hinsz, 2004) and to attempts to take on leadership roles (McCormick, Tanguma, & López-Forment, 2002). Thus, we might expect that the experience of failure for leaders, particularly when the impact is major, will subsequently influence negatively their desire to take risks by initiating new projects and setting difficult goals in the future. This is evidenced by an experiment by Whyte, Saks, and Hook (1997) who showed that participants in the low self-efficacy condition were less likely than those in the high self-efficacy and control conditions to invest a lot into the project and take more chance with respect to attempting to rescue the project.

Proposition 6a. The negative impact of failure on leaders' self-efficacy and emotions will subsequently influence, by lowering, their desire to initiate projects and to set difficult goals for projects.

Failures represent opportunities for learning. However, evidence indicates that learning from failure will occur only to the extent that one is reflective about it (e.g., Hughes, Ginnett, & Curphy, 2006). For example, Boss and Sims (2008) proposed a model of failure in which they speculate that failure will lead to a decrease in self-efficacy and, subsequently, to recovery, to the extent that one practices emotional regulation and self-leadership (both behavioral and cognitive). Daudelin (1996) defines reflection as the process of thinking about an experience by evaluating its meaning and developing inferences. Learning refers to deriving meaning from past experience which then guides future actions. Though not all failures are learning experiences, they are likely to stand out quite strongly in the minds of the leaders, particularly if the failure was perceived as major given that highly emotional events tend to be recalled better than neutral events (Thompson, 1985). If leaders engage in reflection following a failure, this might set in motion a process of learning and hence buffer, at least to an extent, the potentially negative impact of failure on subsequent initiatives.

Proposition 6b. Failures that have a major impact will be more likely to trigger a process of reflection and learning for the leader than failures with minor impact. This, in turn, may buffer the negative impact of failure on subsequent initiatives.

To investigate the relationships proposed in the model, an exploratory study was conducted using data collected from interviews. Interviewees were asked to recall and describe a failed initiative. The interview transcripts were coded and analyzed. In the following sections, the methodology and findings of the study are discussed.

METHODS

Sample and Procedure

The sample was composed of 18 educational leaders who were principals of elementary schools in a large Canadian city. There were 14 women and 4 men; their average age was 48 years old (*SD* = 8.6). They had on average 4.4 years of experience as principals (SD = 4.6). Among the 18 schools, 2 were private schools, and the remainder of the schools were public, belonging to 2 different school boards. Most principals chose to conduct their interviews in English (N = 14); four principals chose to respond in French.

All principals took part in a semistructured interview. For the purpose of this study, principals were asked to "Describe one situation in which you attempted to implement a new project and that failed. Why did it fail? How did you deal with it? What was the outcome?" Some were also asked to define failure in their job. Based on their responses, two principals were removed from the sample because their answers to the question did not correspond to our definition of failure (one only mentioned projects that had succeeded, and the other one mentioned failure that was more interpersonal in nature). The final sample was therefore composed of 16 principals.

Coding

To develop the coding scheme, the interview transcripts were examined to determine which variables from the model were present in the data and develop coding categories for each of them. Four variables could be extracted from the interview data (determination of goals, perceived cause of failure, perceived impact of the failure, and response to the goal). These variables were defined in the introduction. The categories for each variable were developed based on theory and analysis of the interview data.

Based on the analysis of the interview data, one category was added to the coding scheme. For the variable *response to the goal,* the category "consults with others" was added, reflecting the leader's discussions and meetings with others involved in reaching the goal. The categories for the variables *attribution of causes* and *response to the goal* were not mutually exclusive, thus it was possible to code for multiple attributions or responses to the goal in the same interview. Illustrative quotes for each category are presented in Table 13.1.

Two practice interviews (not included in subsequent analyses) were coded independently by two of the authors. They then met to discuss their results. When disagreement occurred in the coding, the authors discussed the point in question until agreement was reached on how it should be coded. Based on these discussions, inter-rater agreement was judged to be acceptable. The sixteen interviews that were part of the sample were then independently coded by these two authors. The overall agreement was 82%. All disagreements were discussed and a consensus was reached in all cases.

Table 13.1. Illustrative Quotes for Each Category of the Coding Scheme

Variable	*Category*	*Illustrative Quote*
Perceived cause of failure	Internal	"It is certainly my fault"
	External	"And I think the reason why is because [others] thought it was too elaborate"
Perceived impact of failure	Minor	"I don't look at it as a failure. I see it more as it is limited ... it is an ongoing process"
	Major	"So that to me that was a major failure"
Response to the goal	Change the goal	"We continued with it, but we did something different..."
	Consult with others	"and so I told them well I am open for your suggestions ... you come up with your ideas"
	Stop the project	"We are not having it for this year"
	Continue with the project	"I've not given up"
	Rationalize the results	"It's not really a failure it is just my perception on how to go about getting to the end and [others] have a different way"

Following Dutton, Ashford, O'Neill, and Lawrence (2001), categories were retained only if they were mentioned in at least 10% of the interviews (i.e., 2 interviews). In addition, although in one instance the perceived impact of failure was both major (prior to making a change to the project) and minor (after the change), we decided to focus exclusively on the impact prior to the change. Perceived impact of failure, therefore, had mutually exclusive categories.

The results were tabulated using frequency tables to assess patterns that emerged from the data. Several interesting patterns emerged and are discussed below.

RESULTS AND DISCUSSION

Determination of Goals and Impact of Failure

Although determination of goals was coded in each interview, there was very little variability in the data for this variable as 87.5% of the projects were coded as being self-initiated (1 initiative was coded as unclear and 1 was coded as initiated by others). As a result, and following Dutton et al.

(2001), only one category was retained for this variable (self-initiated goal). Therefore it was not possible to assess Propositions 1a and 1b, nor any patterns related to determination of goals in subsequent analyses. This variable was therefore removed from further analyses.

Perceived Cause of Failure and Impact of Failure

Several interesting patterns emerged based on the attributions made by the leader when describing the failed initiative. A summary of the results is presented in Table 13.2.

An interesting observation is that leaders who made internal attributions also made external attributions each time (i.e., in this sample, leaders never attributed the cause of their failure to internal factors only). One possible explanation for this finding may be that the leader buffers the effects of internal attributions for failure by also attributing the failure to external causes. Leaders also made internal attributions slightly more often in situations where the perceived impact of the failure was major ($N = 3$) than minor ($N = 2$).

Several interesting observations may also be made when the attributions for failure were directed solely toward external factors. As can be ascertained from Table 13.2, when attributions were made *solely* to external factors, the perceived impact of the failure was much more likely to be minor ($N = 10$) than major ($N = 1$). For example, a participant attributes the failure of her project to external factors, "I think the program itself, for this staff, is not appropriate," and perceives the failure as having a minor impact, "I don't mind that kind of thing but in the true sense of the program it is a kind of failure." This pattern supports Proposition 3a, which stated that the perceived impact of failure will be minor when the causes for the failure are deemed external to the leader.

With respect to the overall sample, when the perceived impact of the failure was major ($N = 4$), the leader generally made both internal and external attributions for the failure (in three cases out of four). For example, this participant evaluates the impact of the failure as major, "I failed miserably quite frankly" and makes both internal "Some of it had to do with the fact that I could not find ownership of it. I tried to [do] stuff myself but I can't do that. It is not consistent enough" and external attributions "I need to find the person who was willing to get on board.... You have to see who's available. I say no one's available."

This finding is interesting in two respects. First, it suggests that internal attributions are often made for major failures. One explanation for this finding might be that leaders feel a greater sense of personal responsibility for failures perceived to be very significant, and thus are more likely to

Table 13.2. Summary of Results

Attributions	*Impact*	*Response to the Goal*				
		CH	*CONS*	*STOP*	*CONT*	*RAT*
Internal (*N* = 5)*	Major (*N* = 3)	2	0	1	2	0
	Minor (*N* = 2)	1	1	1	0	1
	Total (*N* = 5)	3	1	2	2	1
Only External (*N* = 11)	Major (*N* = 1)	1	1	0	0	0
	Minor (*N* = 10)	5	3	2	2	3
	Total (*N* = 11)	6	4	2	2	3
All (*N* = 16)						
Int (*N* = 3), Ext (*N* = 4)	Major (*N* = 4)	3	1	1	2	0
Int (*N* = 2), Ext (*N*=12)	Minor (*N* = 12)	6	4	3	2	4
Int (*N* =5), Ext (*N* = 16)	Total (*N* = 16)	9	5	4	4	4

Note: Responses to goals were not mutually exclusive categories. CH = Change the goal, CONS = Consult, STOP = Stop the project, CONT = Continue with the project, RAT = Rationalize the results, Int = Internal attributions, Ext = External attributions.
* In all cases in which internal attributions were made, external attributions were also made. There were no interviews in which internal attributions alone were made.

attribute the failure to personal or internal reasons. Second, it suggests that in addition to attributing major failures to internal factors, leaders also often attribute major failures to external factors.

There are several possible explanations for this finding. One explanation may be that the goals undertaken in major failures may be larger and more complex, requiring more resources to succeed. As there are more aspects related to the completion of the project, there are more causes to which the failure can be attributed. Another possible reason, as discussed in the preceding section, may be that attributions made by the leader to external factors (when internal attributions are also made) act as buffers for the leader's internal attributions for failure. Thus, the focus for the failure is not solely on personal reasons but also on factors beyond the leader's immediate control. This may lessen the personal impact of the failure for the leader. Overall, this finding provides some support for Proposition 3b, such that the perceived impact of failure is more likely to be major when internal attributions are made for the failure.

Impact of Failure and Response to the Goal

When the perceived impact of the failure was minor, the most frequent response was to change the goal (*N* = 6; e.g., "But it's a mini-failure because I transformed it into another project for this year"[2]). This does not contradict Proposition 4a, which states that leaders will increase their effort toward a goal when the perceived failure is minor. That is, leaders tended to not give up on the project, thus increasing their effort toward goal attainment when the perceived impact of the failure was minor. On the other hand, an interesting finding from the results of the overall sample suggests that when the perceived impact of the goal was major, the most frequent response to the goal was also to change the goal (N = 3, which was also paired with the response to continue the project in two interviews). For example, one participant states, "well, it was a disaster" and goes on to say that her response was to change the goal and continue with the project, "we continued with it, but we did something different."

This finding may be explained by the notion of escalation of commitment (Staw, 1976). Leaders who undertake a project, who perceive the failure to be major and who attribute some of the reasons for this failure to the self, may be more likely to modify and continue with the project because of their commitment to it. Staw found in an experiment that people who felt personal responsibility for failures were most likely to engage in escalation with regard to a course of action. This escalation of commitment in the face of courses of action that were on the road to failure was primarily explained by the need to justify one's actions. Brockner (1992) presents a review of several alternative and complementary explanations for the escalation of commitment phenomenon and concurs that the self-justification explanation explains a significant amount of variance in the decision to escalate. With respect to the finding from the current study, the leaders were responsible for the implementation of the failed initiative and perceived the outcome of the initiative to be a major failure, thus escalation of commitment may provide an interesting explanation for the pattern of responses to the goal noted above.

These patterns provide partial support for Proposition 4b, such that leaders, faced with failed initiatives where the perceived impact of the failure is major, will tend to work toward changing the goal (and continue with the modified goal).

Limitations

As in all studies, several limitations must be acknowledged. First, the qualitative analysis presented in support of the model only presents a limited test of the propositions and is best seen as an aid to theoretical development. The sample was small and the results may be context- and sample-specific. Second, it was not possible to assess all the variables from the proposed model with the data. Third, some variables had limited variability (e.g., determination of goal) and thus could not be used in the analyses. Finally, the results are based on analyses of retrospective accounts of failure by the leaders themselves, and are thus subject to different biases related to recall.

Theoretical Implications and Future Directions

Despite these limitations, the patterns identified from the qualitative analysis provide initial support for many of the propositions. The analysis also suggests that the process of attributions may not be as straightforward as originally suggested in the propositions. Indeed, an interesting observation was that leaders never made only internal attributions. This may be unique to this particular context, but is worth exploring in greater depth. It would suggest the following proposition:

Proposition 3c: When making internal attributions about the cause of failure, leaders will also make external attributions.

Future field research might collect data on all of the variables included in the framework. For example, future studies could collect data on a variety of goals (self-initiated, other initiated but accepted, or imposed) to assess the relationships between these types of goals and perceived impact of failure, how individual characteristics (conscientiousness, learning orientation, performance orientation, and need for achievement) affect perceived impact of failure, and how this in turn can affect a leader's affective response to the failure. Future research may also explore in greater depth the relationship between the perceived impact of failure, leaders' attributions for failure, and responses to failed initiatives. Finally, future research should explore potential moderator variables that could allow more specific predictions with regards to the relation between impact and responses to goals.

The proposed model would benefit from both experimental and field studies to test the proposed relationships. Future studies may examine the personal impact of failure for leaders at different levels of the organizational hierarchy to determine whether the relationships hold for leaders at different levels of the organization (e.g., CEOs, top executives, managers, team leaders). Another interesting avenue for future research may be to investigate the proposed relationships for both formal and informal leaders in organizations. For example, do informal leaders have the same "license to fail" (to borrow the words of Giessner & van Knippenberg, 2008) as do formal leaders? Finally, it would be interesting to examine in greater depth the process by which one's previous experience with failure impacts one's reactions to subsequent initiatives. Such a feedback process is captured in the current model. This examination would require longitudinal studies of leaders' personal experience with success and failure.

Practical Implications

Though leaders can learn from failure through self-reflection, this learning may be enhanced or guided by significant others, such as a boss, a peer, an executive coach and/or a mentor. The latter two might be in the best position to do so, as they have a responsibility to help their protégé, in this case leaders, face failure and learn from these experiences. Cannon and Edmondson (2001) found that coaching and direction predicted shared beliefs about failure in teams. In sum, mentors and executive coaches may be a positive force which helps promote learning from failure and the adoption of a learning orientation by leaders, and which in turn contributes to the development of these leaders.

Another interesting implication of this model relates to the mentoring relationship. Research has identified individual characteristics that facilitate the creation of a mentoring relationship. Singh, Ragins, and Tharenou (2009) found evidence to support the "Rising Star" hypothesis: Individuals on track for promotions, with higher expectations of advancement and who are proactive towards their career are more likely to have a mentor. Furthermore, according to Allen (2004), mentors tend to seek individuals who have a willingness to learn to become their protégé. These findings suggest that individuals who are open to learning from their mistakes and approach failure in a proactive and constructive way may have more opportunities to be mentored. Considering that the literature has shown that mentoring has important and positive consequences for the protégé which include greater career involvement, income, promotions, job and career satisfaction, and career commitment, as well as better self-perceptions, and lower psychological stress and strain, substance abuse, and work-family conflict (Allen, Eby, & Lentz, 2006; Eby, Allen, Evans, Ng, & DuBois, 2008), learning from failure could be a critical characteristic that mentors seek in individuals before establishing the mentoring relationship.

CONCLUSION

The purpose of this chapter was to explore leaders' personal experience of failure and explain their responses to failure. To do so, we outlined a theoretical framework articulated around the impact of failure, and proposed antecedents that might explain leaders' perceived impact of failure. We then hypothesized that the perceived impact of failure might determine leaders' response towards the goal of the project, their affective reaction and their belief in their likelihood of successfully leading change in the future. The theoretical propositions were tested in an exploratory, qualitative, study with educational leaders. This initial test was supportive of the proposed model and therefore indicates that this framework might serve as a useful basis to further understand the process of failure in leadership. This research might have important implications for leaders as well as their coaches and mentors, who must guide their protégé through the difficult path of learning—and recovery—from failure.

ACKNOWLEDGMENTS

We would like to thank Linda Dyer, Gina Grandy, and Tracy Hecht for their comments on earlier versions of this chapter. Special thanks also to Isabelle Goulet, Pavan Ojha, Eugénie Pascal, and Majlinda Zhegu, for their assistance with data processing. This research was supported by a grant from the Social Sciences and Humanities Research Council of Canada awarded to the first author. All three authors contributed equally to this manuscript.

NOTES

1. These quotes are answers that some of our participants provided to the question "How do you define failure in your position?"
2. Original quote in French.

REFERENCES

Allen, T. D. (2004). Protégé selection by mentors: Contributing individual and organizational factors. *Journal of Vocational Behavior, 65*(3), 469-483.

Allen, T. D., Eby, L. T., & Lentz, E. (2006). Mentorship behaviors and mentorship quality associated with formal mentoring programs: Closing the gap between research and practice. *Journal of Applied Psychology, 91*(3), 567-578.

Bandura, A. (1997). *Self-efficacy: The exercise of control*. New York: Freeman.

Barrick, M. R., & Mount, M. K. (1991). The Big Five personality dimensions and job performance: A meta-analysis. *Personnel Psychology, 44*(1), 1-26.

Boss, A. D., & Sims, H. P., Jr. (2008). Everyone fails! Using emotion regulation and self-leadership for recovery. *Journal of Managerial Psychology, 23*(2), 135-150.

Brockner, J. (1992). The escalation of commitment to a failing course of action: Toward theoretical progress. *Academy of Management Review, 17*(1), 39-61.

Cannon, M. D., & Edmondson, A. C. (2001). Confronting failure: Antecedents and consequences of shared beliefs about failure in organizational work groups. *Journal of Organizational Behavior, 22*(2), 161-177.

Cannon, M. D., & Edmondson, A. C. (2005). Failing to learn and learning to fail (intelligently): How great organizations put failure to work to innovate and improve. *Long Range Planning: International Journal of Strategic Management, 38*(3), 299-319.

Daudelin, M. W. (1996). Learning from experience through reflection. *Organizational Dynamics, 24*(3), 36-48.

Deng, B.-H., Bligh, M. C., & Kohles, J. C. (2010). To err is human, to lead is divine? The role of leaders in learning from workplace mistakes. In B. Schyns & T. Hansbrough (Eds.), *When leadership goes wrong: Destructive leadership, mistakes and ethical failures*. Charlotte, NC: Information Age.

Dutton, J. E., Ashford, S. J., O'Neill, R. M., & Lawrence, K. A. (2001). Moves that matter: Issue selling and organizational change. *Academy of Management Journal, 44*(4), 716-736.

Eby, L. T., Allen, T. D., Evans, S. C., Ng, T., & DuBois, D. L. (2008). Does mentoring matter? A multidisciplinary meta-analysis comparing mentored and non-mentored individuals. *Journal of Vocational Behavior, 72*(2), 254-267.

Elliott, E. S., & Dweck, C. S. (1988). Goals: An approach to motivation and achievement. *Journal of Personality and Social Psychology, 54*(1), 5-12.

Feldman Barrett, L., & Russell, J. A. (1998). Independence and bipolarity in the structure of current affect. *Journal of Personality and Social Psychology, 74*(4), 967-984.

Finkelstein, S. (2003). *Why smart executives fail and what you can learn from their mistakes*. New York: Penguin.

Giessner, S. R., & van Knippenberg, D. (2008). "License to fail": Goal definition, leader group prototypicality, and perceptions of leadership effectiveness after leader failure. *Organizational Behavior and Human Decision Processes, 105*(1), 14-35.

Grant, H., & Dweck, C. S. (2003). Clarifying achievement goals and their impact. *Journal of Personality and Social Psychology, 85*(3), 541-553.

Gully, S. M., Payne, S. C., Koles, K. L. K., & Whiteman, J.-A. K. (2002). The impact of error training and individual differences on training outcomes: An attribute-treatment interaction perspective. *Journal of Applied Psychology, 87*(1), 143-155.

Hannah, S. T., Avolio, B. J., Luthans, F., & Harms, P. D. (2008). Leadership efficacy: Review and future directions. *Leadership Quarterly, 19*(6), 669-692.

Hareli, S., & Hess, U. (2008). The role of causal attribution in hurt feelings and related social emotions elicited in reaction to other's feedback about failure. *Cognition & Emotion, 22*(5), 862-880.

Holschuh, J. P., Nist, S. L., & Olenjnik, S. (2001). Attributions to failure: The effects of effort, ability, and learning strategy use on perceptions of future goals and emotional responses. *Reading Psychology, 22*(3), 153-173.

Hughes, R. L., Ginnett, R. C., & Curphy, G. J. (2006). *Leadership: Enhancing the lessons of experience* (5th ed.). Boston: McGraw-Hill.

Hunter, S. T., Bedell-Avers, K. E., & Mumford, M. D. (2007). The typical leadership study: Assumptions, implications, and potential remedies. *Leadership Quarterly, 18*(5), 435-446.

Jacobs, B., Prentice-Dunn, S., & Rogers, R. W. (1984). Understanding persistence: An interface of control theory and self-efficacy theory. *Basic and Applied Social Psychology, 5*(4), 333-347.

Kane, T. D., & Tremble, T. R. (2000). Transformational leadership effects at different levels of the army. *Military Psychology, 12*(2), 137-160.

Kluger, A. N., & DeNisi, A. (1996). Effects of feedback intervention on performance: A historical review, a meta-analysis, and a preliminary feedback intervention theory. *Psychological Bulletin, 119*(2), 254-284.

Locke, E. A., & Latham, G. P. (1990). *A theory of goal setting and task performance*. Englewood Cliffs, NJ: Prentice Hall.

Locke, E. A., & Latham, G. P. (2002). Building a practically useful theory of goal setting and task motivation: A 35-year odyssey. *American Psychologist, 57*(9), 705-717.

McClelland, D. C., & Boyatzis, R. E. (1982). Leadership motive pattern and long-term success in management. *Journal of Applied Psychology, 67*(6), 737-743.

McCormick, M. J., Tanguma, J., & López-Forment, A. S. (2002). Extending self-efficacy theory to leadership: A review and empirical test. *Journal of Leadership Education, 1*(2), 34-49.

Nummenmaa, L., & Niemi, P. (2004). Inducing affective states with success-failure manipulations: A meta-analysis. *Emotion, 4*(2), 207-214.

Paglis, L. L., & Green, S. G. (2002). Leadership self-efficacy and managers' motivation for leading change. *Journal of Organizational Behavior, 23*(2), 215-235.

Russell, J. A. (1980). A circumplex model of affect. *Journal of Personality and Social Psychology, 39*(6), 1161-1178.

Rybowiak, V., Garst, H., Frese, M., & Batinic, B. (1999). Error Orientation Questionnaire (EOQ): Reliability, validity, and different language equivalence. *Journal of Organizational Behavior, 20*(4), 527-547.

Schyns, B., & Hansbrough, T. (2008). Why the brewery ran out of beer: The attribution of mistakes in a leadership context. *Social Psychology, 39*(3), 197-203.

Singh, R., Ragins, B. R., & Tharenou, P. (2009). Who gets a mentor? A longitudinal assessment of the rising star hypothesis. *Journal of Vocational Behavior, 74*(1), 11-17.

Smith, S. A., Kass, S. J., Rotunda, R. J., & Schneider, S. K. (2006). If at first you don't succeed: Effects of failure on general and task-specific self-efficacy and performance. *North American Journal of Psychology, 8*(1), 171-182.

Sonnenfeld, J., & Ward, A. (2007). Firing back: How great leaders rebound after career disasters. *Organizational Dynamics, 37*(1), 1-20.

Spieker, C. J., & Hinsz, V. B. (2004). Repeated success and failure influences on self-efficacy and personal goals. *Social Behavior and Personality, 32*(2), 191-198.

Staw, B. M. (1976). Knee-deep in the Big Muddy: A study of escalating commitment to a chosen course of action. *Organizational Behavior & Human Performance, 16*(1), 27-44.

Staw, B. M., & Ross, J. (1978). Commitment to a policy decision: A multi-theoretical perspective. *Administrative Science Quarterly, 23*(1), 40-64.

Stern, Z., Katz-Navon, T., & Naveh, E. (2008). The influence of situational learning orientation, autonomy, and voice on error making: The case of resident physicians. *Management Science, 54*(9), 1553-1564.

Stewart, G. L., Carson, K. P., & Cardy, R. L. (1996). The joint effects of conscientiousness and self-leadership training on employee self-directed behavior in a service setting. *Personnel Psychology, 49*(1), 143-164.

Taylor, S. E. (1991). Asymmetrical effects of positive and negative events: The mobilization-minimization hypothesis. *Psychological Bulletin, 110*(1), 67-85.

Thompson, C. P. (1985). Memory for unique personal events: Effects of pleasantness. *Motivation and Emotion, 9*(3), 277-289.

Whyte, G., Saks, A. M., & Hook, S. (1997). When success breeds failure: The role of self-efficacy in escalating commitment to a losing course of action. *Journal of Organizational Behavior, 18*(5), 415-432.

Wilkinson, A., & Mellahi, K. (2005). Organizational failure: Introduction to the special issue. *Long Range Planning: International Journal of Strategic Management, 38*(3), 233-238.

Wood, R., & Bandura, A. (1989). Impact of conceptions of ability on self-regulatory mechanisms and complex decision making. *Journal of Personality and Social Psychology, 56*(3), 407-415.

Zhao, B., & Olivera, F. (2006). Error reporting in organizations. *Academy of Management Review, 31*(4), 1012-1030.

CHAPTER 14

THE PARADOXICAL ROLE OF MORAL REASONING IN ETHICAL FAILURES IN LEADERSHIP

Terry L. Price

This chapter argues that leaders can fail in their ethical obligations even when they act for the good of others. The fact that a leader's action is in the interests of people other than herself does not guarantee that she has a sufficient moral justification for her behavior. Leaders confront a multitude of other-regarding considerations. What have followers consented to? How important are the group goals that the leader is trying to achieve? Does a leader owe more to group members than she owes to outsiders because of her position within the group? What action would serve the greater good? Answers to these questions are morally relevant to what a leader ought to do, and the leader who brings such other-regarding considerations to bear on her decision making is certainly engaged in moral reasoning. The paradox this chapter seeks to illuminate, however, is that a leader's commitment to these ethical considerations can actually contribute to unethical leadership. Other-regarding considerations will sometimes compete with standard expectations of morality that apply more generally to everyone—what we might call "the moral rules." Leaders are therefore in a special position to justify rule breaking in the name of their concern for people other than

When Leadership Goes Wrong: Destructive Leadership, Mistakes and Ethical Failures, pp. 383–403

themselves. The main claim of this chapter is that such appeals to other-regarding justifications play an important role in the explanation of ethical failures in leadership. Contrary to what we might expect, a view of leadership ethics that makes concern for others determinative of morality is actually part of the problem it is meant to solve.

INTRODUCTION

Moral reasoning involves identifying the features of a situation that matter morally and drawing on these features to determine how one should act. This basic process of purposely and systematically using moral reasons in decision making is generally something to be encouraged. Indeed, we expect that people's actions will be guided by moral reasons, and we criticize them—both the people and their actions—when morality is not given its due. This expectation fully applies to leaders. First, it is commonplace to suggest that leaders must be held to a higher standard than that to which we hold everyone else. They are role models for others, and they represent not only themselves but also an office, a people, or even a set of ideals. Second, the complexity of the organizations they lead, as well as the intractability of the problems they seek to address, means that their decision making must incorporate multiple factors. As a consequence, there is great room for error. Third, leadership often demands innovation and originality. In fact, Ed Hollander (1964, 1978, 2009) persuasively argues that deviation is central to the way we understand and practice leadership. It is little wonder, then, that ethics holds a central place in both leadership development and scholarship (Ciulla, 2004a). Educators and scholars go to great lengths to make sure leaders are in a position to bring relevant ethical considerations to bear on their decision-making processes.

The everyday assessments we make of leadership behavior tend to assume a clear-cut distinction between moral reasoning and nonmoral reasoning. In its simplest form, this assumption holds that moral reasoning gives weight to the goals and interests of others, whereas nonmoral reasoning carries out its calculations on the basis of the actor's goals and interests. Accordingly, the paradigm of the immoral person is someone who is unmoved by the effects his actions have on others. Perhaps he simply does not care about morality, or he cares only about himself. Kohlberg's (1981, pp. 17-18) theory of moral development supports this distinction by putting the particularistic concerns of self-interest at the lowest stage—what he calls the "preconventional" stage and the universal concerns of broader humanity at the highest stage what he calls the "postconventional" stage. This basic distinction also characterizes the dominant view in the leadership literature, where ethical failures in leadership are explained in terms of a stark contrast between egoism and altruism (Avolio & Locke, 2002; Bass & Steidlmeier, 1999). When a leader behaves unethically, laypeople and scholars alike conclude that he let his ambition, greed, or narcissism get the best of him. Had only the leader controlled his self-interested desires and put the good of others first, he would not have made an ethical mistake.

Ethics is more complicated than this simple distinction suggests, and leadership ethics is more complicated still (Price, 2008). For one thing, in all theories in philosophical ethics, self-interest potentially counts as a good moral reason. The theory of ethical egoism holds that it is the only moral reason, and virtue theory—as developed by the ancient Greeks—denies that there is any opposition between what is good for others and what is good for the individual. Both theories emphasize the ways in which self-interest is tied to the interests of other people, especially to the interests of friends, relatives, or community members (Aristotle, 1985; Rand, 1999). Even moral theories committed to the view that self-interest and morality frequently come apart give some moral weight to self-interest. For example, utilitarianism, which holds that we ought to maximize overall utility, maintains that each person must also consider the effects that his actions will have on his own happiness. Although we are not justified in privileging our own interests, morality requires that we give them equal weight in our utility calculations. Kantian ethics also makes room for our own goals and interests in moral reasoning. According to Kant (1964), we have duties to ourselves—such as the duty to develop our capacities as rational agents—in addition to our duties to others. In fact, some of our duties to others—such as the duty to help people in need—are derived from the fact that we have our own projects, which require the help of others (pp. 90-91). So, on none of these moral views does the fact that an action is in our own interests disqualify it as a good moral reason for acting.

More important for the purposes of this chapter, leaders can fail to fulfill their ethical obligations even when they act for the good of others. The fact that a leader's action is in the interests of people other than herself does not guarantee that she has a sufficient moral justification for her behavior. Many of the distinct complications of leadership ethics derive from a central reality of leadership. The reality is that leaders confront a multitude of other-regarding considerations. What have followers consented to? How important are the group goals that the leader is trying to achieve? Does a leader owe more to group members than she owes to outsiders because of her position within the group? What action would serve the greater good? Answers to these questions are morally relevant to what a leader ought to do, and the leader who brings such other-regarding considerations to bear on her decision making is certainly engaged in moral reasoning. Yet none of these considerations can cover all of morality by itself. At the very least, each consideration must be weighed and balanced against the others. The selfless leader who takes advantage of outsiders to secure the interests of followers has not given morality its due. Nor has the altruistic leader who shirks his special obligations to followers out of a concern for what he takes to be the greater good. There is more to morality than advocates of altruism would have us believe.

Indeed—and this is the paradox my chapter seeks to illuminate—a commitment to what are normally considered ethical considerations can actually contribute to unethical leadership. Other-regarding considerations will sometimes compete with standard expectations of morality that apply more generally to everyone—what we might call "the moral rules." Here, in particular, I have in mind moral rules that tell us not to engage in certain behaviors. For example, we expect people to abide by the prohibition on lying. What, then, is a leader to do when doing what is best for the group requires dishonesty—either with respect to followers or to people outside the group? The leader who uses deception in this case need not be motivated by self-interest—the most obvious source of immorality. Can we simply assume, then, that the other-regarding nature of the considerations that drive her decision to lie gets her off the moral hook? Unfortunately, endorsing this assumption gives her too much leeway. A leader can justify pretty much anything she wants to do in the name of concern for people other than herself. The main claim of my contribution to this volume is that such appeals to other-regarding justifications play an important role in the explanation of ethical failures in leadership. Contrary to what we might expect, a view of leadership ethics that makes concern for others determinative of morality is actually part of the problem it is meant to solve.

To set up this line of argument, the first main section of this chapter describes an exercise that I use when working with future and current leaders. The responses in this exercise suggest that people break the moral rules not only out of self-interest but also out of a concern for others. When their behavior is based on other-regarding considerations, as opposed to self-regarding considerations, rule breakers are in a better position to conclude that they are justified in their actions. How is it possible to believe that one is justified in doing something that is generally prohibited by the moral rules? The second section of this chapter analyzes our moral grammar to show the complexity of moral reasoning behind this belief. Moral demands tell us both what actions are prohibited or required by morality and to whom these prohibitions and requirements apply. So a leader can recognize that morality generally prohibits a particular action yet fail to see that this prohibition applies to him (Price, 2006).

This distinction makes it possible for a leader to use other-regarding considerations as moral reasons in his justification for breaking the moral rules. The third main section of the chapter creates a typology of ethical failures in leadership by connecting these justifications with the operative ethical theories. Chief among the ethical theories that allow leaders to use other-regarding considerations to justify rule breaking are consent theory, moral pragmatism, moral idealism, and communal ethics.

An Exercise in Moral Psychology

Leaders are in a position to do things that other people are not able to do. They often have expertise, authority, and resources that set them apart from others. We give them this kind of power—or allow them to exercise it—so that they can do what is necessary to achieve our collective goals. A secondary consequence, however, is that leaders can also do what we do not want them to do. For example, they can use their power to pursue personal projects and advance more narrow interests. Moreover, though their behavior can seem very public to us, we are often unable to know whether they are taking advantage of the position to serve their own good. Leaders are often able to use public relations and other means to make only positive, other-regarding behavior known to us. However, just because this kind of behavior is available to us, it does not necessarily mean that we have a good, representative sample of how our leaders act (Nisbett & Ross, 1980). Successful leaders can control what we see and what we do not see (Ludwig & Longenecker, 1993). Some of their actions—indeed, many of their actions—will be invisible to us, and it is the behavior that we do not see that we have the most reason to worry about. What are they doing when no one is looking? This worry may explain the recent resurgence in work on leader authenticity (Avolio & Gardner, 2005). We want our leaders to remain true to positive, other-regarding values across contexts—not only when someone is watching them.

I have elsewhere used the notion of invisibility as a metaphor for thinking about leadership ethics (Price, 2006, 2008). The roots of this metaphor are in Plato's (1992) story of the "Ring of Gyges" (pp. 35-36 [359d-360b]). In this tale, the shepherd Gyges discovers a ring that will make him invisible. Gyges uses the ring to satisfy his deepest desires for sex, violence, and domination. It is not a pretty story. We learn of Gyges' seduction of the queen, his murder of the king, and his ascension to ruler of the kingdom. The point of this tale, which is told and endorsed not by Plato but by the character Glaucon, is that we should expect no more and no less from anyone who has the kind of power Gyges has. According to

Glaucon, everyone would behave just as Gyges did. Glaucon's thesis is particularly troubling in leadership contexts because leaders have extraordinary power to do good or evil. They are in a position to use their many "rings" either to advance our interests or to satisfy their own desires.

When I teach this story to ethics students, student leaders, and professionals, I ask them to participate in an exercise that mimics the situation in which Gyges finds himself. To encourage participants in the exercise to examine their own moral psychology, I ask them to write down what they would do if they had the ring of Gyges. I tell them that I will read the answers aloud to the group but that I will keep responses anonymous to reflect the condition of invisibility. The question we try to answer in the resulting discussion is whether current and future leaders will be inclined to behave morally or immorally when they have the perfect opportunity to pursue their own selfish desires.

Two categories of responses are predictable. The first kind of response confirms Glaucon's point. Some participants in the exercise make it clear that the only thing that prevents them from behaving immorally is the fear of getting caught. Let us call them *egoistic responders*. Take away the disincentives to immoral behavior, and they would have a hedonistic field day. Typical responses along these lines include invasions of privacy, robbery, and acts of violence. The invasions of privacy range from listening in to see what others are saying to engaging in sexual voyeurism. Participants regularly write that they would rob a clothing store or bank, and some claim that they would go so far as to commit murder.

A second kind of response, however, denies Glaucon's point. Some participants in the exercise—though, in general, relatively fewer—say that they would not use the ring for any immoral purposes. Let us call them *principled responders*. Pointing to the potentially corrupting influence of their newfound power, many claim that they would destroy the ring. Here their reasoning denies the widely held view that human nature is already corrupt and that the ring simply gives people a chance to act on motivations that reflect their true nature. So too does a variation on this response. Some people claim that their behavior would not change upon finding the ring because self-interest is not what motivates them to act morally in the first place. This reaction to the exercise reflects the belief that morality is both instrumentally *and* intrinsically valuable—the Socratic view to which Glaucon's story is meant to be a response. People who hold this belief see some actions as wrong in themselves. Accordingly, it makes no difference to them that they could use the ring to get away with immorality. Unfortunately, affirmations of the intrinsic value of morality are always clearly in the minority.

This summary of the two basic responses to the exercise gives us reason to think that there may be something to Glaucon's argument. Although it is probably false that everyone would behave immorally if given the chance, it seems that many people would. Still, there is more to the moral psychology behind people's reactions to the exercise than their predictable responses would suggest. If we look very closely at the descriptions of their behavior, it appears that something besides self-interest affects the thinking of some people who would use the ring to do things that we typically find to be immoral. This is not to say that no one would use the ring to feed his basest desires and enrich himself. Some people's predictions about their own behavior can be understood only in terms of selfishness. However, the genuine egoist is generally not that much more common than the person who believes that actions can be wrong in themselves. The most interesting response—and one that is always at least as prevalent as that of egoistic and principled responders—implies that if people had the chance, they would violate moral prohibitions for what they think are good *moral* reasons. In other words, the ring gives them an opportunity to act in ways that they think can be justified by morality.

People often respond to the exercise by claiming that they would use the ring to do good for others. Let us call them *altruistic responders*. In many cases, the good they aim to do is for humanity at large—*the greater good*. Examples include ending poverty or fighting terrorism. Sometimes the means to the ends are made explicit. Advocates of the "Robin Hood" response claim that they would steal from the rich to give to the poor, thereby reflecting the view that a redistribution of resources is necessary to address poverty. Others claim that they would assassinate leaders such as Osama bin Laden. In effect, they would be willing to kill a human being to achieve their good ends.

Yet, even when the means are not made explicit, we can assume that these beneficent ring-holders must be committed to adopting means that we ordinarily believe to be immoral. Using the ring is itself an act of deception and raises serious moral questions about the ring-holders' views of themselves and their place in the moral community. The fact that people believe they need to use extraordinary means to be successful implies that they cannot achieve their ends under their present constraints. They need to go outside current rules and expectations to get the job done. In other words, rule breaking is necessary. In their minds, getting the job done justifies doing something that we think is ordinarily prohibited by morality and, moreover, doing it in a way that makes their behavior immune from the feedback and criticism of others. The ring creates moral free agents, so to speak. Contrary to what some might suggest (Wolfe, 2001), those who have the ring are not free from morality altogether. Instead, they are free to act on morality as they see it.

In other cases, when people admit that they would invade the privacy of others or carry out acts of theft, they claim that it would be for the good of their group, not humanity more generally. Their favored group can be quite large—as in the case of a nation state. In these cases, it is sometimes difficult to tell whether the commitment is ultimately to a particular group's good or to something higher and more inclusive. For example, when a person says that she would spy on other governments for the United States, is that because she favors her own side in global politics or because she wants the world to benefit from her country's ideals? In other words, patriotism can be a manifestation of the in-group bias, or it can be the expression of a person's commitment to values that she thinks ought to apply everyone, regardless of political membership (Simmons, 2007, p. 47).

But it is often clear that the good at which people aim is much less grand, and this fact also comes out in people's responses to the exercise. When the favored group is small—for example, the immediate family—the partiality of the responses is quite easy to recognize. Some people claim that they would use the ring of Gyges to steal resources that would secure a financial future for family members. Behind this response is the idea that society is a competition for scarce resources, less between individuals than between groups. As group members—especially as leaders of groups—people take on special obligations to do what is necessary to advance the interests of other members. Achieving *group goals* may justify using the ring to do what they otherwise should not do—indeed, what they would not be willing to do for themselves.

One important difference between leaders and the character of Gyges is that leaders are ordinarily the intentional recipients of power. We give them the rings; leaders do not find them. Of course, people can become leaders because of unexpected circumstances. But the acquisition of power hardly compares to accidentally finding a magical ring. Indeed, the collective purpose of leadership is part of the explanation of why leaders get the idea that they can do things that the rest of us would not be justified in doing. Our *consent* to the inequalities associated with leadership implies that we expect them to use their power to achieve the ends at which we aim (Hollander, 1964, 1978, 2009). According to this argument, goal achievement does not itself serve as the normative foundation of leadership. Desired consequences explain why we give our leaders behavioral leeway and allow them to deviate from common expectations. Unlike the greater good argument or the group goals argument, then, this understanding of behavioral justification in leadership is only indirectly consequentialist. Because we think that leaders can help us achieve our ends, we consent to their exercise of power (Hobbes, 1991; Locke, 1988).

Morality is therefore a characteristic feature of many reasons people give in response to the "Ring of Gyges" exercise. For example, as compared to the source of Gyges' naked expression of self-interest, consent is a well-respected moral notion. More than that, it is central to thinking about leadership in a democratic society, where consent necessarily serves as the primary grounds for justifying leadership behavior. The consent-based understanding of leadership behavior thus contrasts with egoistic accounts. So too do other explanations leaders might give for using their "rings." Sometimes breaking the moral rules is a means to achieving the greater good. Other times, taking advantage of special powers is necessary given the circumstances in which leaders find themselves. In still other cases, strict conformity to the rules would be inconsistent with discharging special obligations to group members. The language of the greater good, necessity, and special obligations—like the language of consent—is indicative of moral reasoning, and in all of these cases, moral considerations are seriously in play.

It is the ubiquity of these other-regarding considerations that complicates people's reactions to the exercise, just as it complicates leadership ethics. Behavioral options go well beyond the false dichotomy of acting in self-interest or doing the action that is right for its own sake. The wide array of moral considerations creates an ethically murky middle ground between selfishness and conformity. From the perspective of this position, what is ordinarily impermissible can seem the right thing to do in the circumstances precisely because it is consistent with altruism. Nowhere is this truer than in the context of leadership, where the means to collective achievement do not always fit easily in the categories of self-interest or morality. As Michael Walzer (1973) puts it, too much of either self-serving pragmatism or moral principle undermines leader effectiveness. It is for the good of others that leaders must be willing to do what has to be done. Based on their responses, participants in the Gyges exercise would seem to agree.

A Primer in Moral Grammar

In our daily lives, most of us are quite familiar with this ethical middle ground and with how it serves as the site for justification. Although people readily admit that lying is wrong, they sometimes—or, according to psychologists, very often—engage in it (Kornet, 1997). In some cases, of course, the explanation is that lying promotes self-interest. But, in other cases, genuine moral reasoning sits behind a decision to engage in deception. For example, lying may be necessary to protect a person's feelings or to maintain a friend's trust: "That dress looks good on you" or "No, she's not having an affair." In extreme cases, it can be necessary to save lives—as when the Nazis are on your doorstep and Jews are hiding inside, or when intentionally giving false information to a terrorist would prevent a future attack. These "altruistic lies," as Immanuel Kant (1996) calls them, are between the pursuit of self-interest and a commitment to principle. We can endorse the principle that prohibits lying, acknowledging that it would be wrong for us to deviate from it to serve self-interest, while at the same time recognizing that there are some exceptions to the principle. John Stuart Mill (1979) expresses this perspective on the prohibition against deception: "Yet that even this rule, sacred as it is, admits of possible exceptions is acknowledged by all moralists" (pp. 22-23).

This kind of subtlety in moral reasoning capitalizes on an important distinction between the *content* of a moral rule and the *scope* of a moral rule (Price, 2006). The content identifies actions that are generally prohibited or required by morality. With respect to the moral rule against deception, its content gives us the standard prohibition on lying. It tells us that lying is morally problematic. The scope of the rule, however, refers to the application of the prohibition to particular people. Most obviously, questions about the scope of moral rules ask who is *bound* by a particular principle. Ordinarily, we see ourselves as within the scope of the rules and fully bound by principles such as the prohibition on lying. Accordingly, there is a clear consistency between scope and content in the corresponding moral grammar:

I **should not lie**.

Here, the italicized part of the sentence identifies the actor falling within the scope of the rule, and the bolded part notes the rule's content. Who should not do what? Together, they indicate that there is a prohibition on lying and that this prohibition applies to me and my behavior.

Because of features of the situation or because of our role responsibilities, we sometimes question whether we are indeed bound by a moral rule. President Clinton might have asked, for example, whether it was wrong *for him* to deny his affair with Monica Lewinsky in the particular circumstances in which he found himself. In this kind of case, the content and scope of the moral rule seemingly pull apart, and the separation is reflected in our moral grammar.

I **should not lie**?

Setting the italicized part of the sentence off from the bolded part symbolizes our dual moral concerns. The distinction between questions about the content of a moral rule and questions about its scope makes it possible for people to accept both that lying is wrong and that it is sometimes permissible for them to engage in it. They can recognize a rule's content and—at the same time—question its scope in their specific circumstances. So, what we ordinarily assume to be a single, straightforward query ("What should I do?") raises at least two moral questions. One question is about the kinds of things that generally should or should not be done. A second, equally important question is about whether I—as an individual actor—ought to conform my behavior to the general requirement or prohibition. The second question can also arise at the group level and generate a similarly exceptionalist answer: "As a general rule, nations should be prohibited from having nuclear weapons, but we should be allowed to have this capability."

Content questions and scope questions can differ radically in their complexity. With respect to content questions, the goal is to establish what actions are generally morally wrong. These questions are typically easier to answer than are questions about the scope of moral rules. Acts of deception, betrayal, domination, coercion, violence, and the like, rightly sound a moral warning for most of us. In fact, it is difficult to imagine how someone might sincerely claim ignorance of the morally problematic nature of these behaviors. Yet the warning sound merely tells us that we are in morally dangerous territory. It can remain an open question as to whether—in our particular circumstances—we should enter this territory. Scope questions can be especially complicated, and they may have greater impact on people's actual behavior than questions about the content of moral rules. As we have seen, understanding how a principle applies to a person in particular circumstances is hardly straightforward. This contrast in complexity explains how a person who understands fundamental aspects of morality may nevertheless be ignorant of what he ought to do. Learning the content of morality gets him only part way to making a moral decision. He still has to determine whether the moral rules apply to him in his particular circumstances.

A third question for moral reasoning can be equally difficult to answer. This question also concerns the scope of moral rules, but it asks who is *protected* by morality. We can represent this question with the following moral grammar:

I **should not lie** *to them?*

Aspects of the scope of morality are represented by the two italicized parts of the sentence, and—again—the rule's content is in bold. Combining all three, we can ask, "Who should not do what to whom?" The first italicized placeholder indicates the scope question described above. Is the actor bound by the moral rule? An additional scope question—the question of who is protected by the prohibition against deception—is represented by the italicized placeholder at the end of the sentence. This second kind of scope question draws our attention to the fact that morality is—to some extent at least—a social phenomenon. We conduct our moral lives in groups, and we sometimes see group membership as the source of morality. As a result, we can come to believe that people outside our groups are not fully protected by morality. In extreme cases, such as that exemplified by the treatment of Jews by the Nazis, victims can be denied membership in the human community. For example, "[A]ttempts to think them out of the human race meant Jews were humiliated in countless ways which reflected this loss of moral standing" (Glover, 2000, p. 340).

A leader might also think that it is wrong to torture fellow citizens but deny that "enemy combatants" are subject to the same protections. We should resist the temptation to interpret such a leader's treatment of outsiders as a denial of the claim that he is bound by the relevant principle: "The prohibition on torture does not apply to me." Characterizing his moral psychology this way—namely, in terms of the first question about the scope of the prohibition on torture—ignores what looks to be a real distinction between different kinds of scope questions. The leader's reasoning in this case does not deny that morality binds him and his actions—for example, with respect to his behavior toward *us*. The claim is rather that some people—*other* people—are beyond the scope of morality's protections. We have heard President George W. Bush say, for example, that only military personnel can be legitimate prisoners of war (POWs). Ultimately, the question is about *their* classification. They—not he or we—are outside of morality.

Only in the most extreme cases would we expect an individual to think either that he is completely above morality or that others are completely beneath it. First, people generally believe that they are bound by morality, as well as by the particular rule they claim to be justified in breaking. The rule breaker need not claim that as a "god among men," he is completely free of morality's dictates. Nor is it necessary for him to believe that the rule never applies to him. He is not Nietzsche's *übermensch* or Aristotle's "man … preeminent in virtue," neither of whom can be expected to live by our rules (Aristotle, 1981, p. 215; Nietzsche, 1967). More recognizable in everyday life is the leader whose position, circumstances, or goals put him outside the scope of morality "just for this once," as Kant (1964) would put it. "Of course morality applies to me, and of course I should normally follow this rule," the leader might tell himself, "but in this case I am justified in doing what morality ordinarily prohibits" (p. 91). The justification thus appeals not to overblown assumptions about his basic moral status or to a general rejection of a moral principle but, rather, to particular features that characterize his predicament. What are these features? As we have seen, they are the distinctive ethical features of the relationship between leaders and followers—namely, consent, necessity, special obligations, and the greater good. To what actions have followers consented? What behaviors are necessary to achieve group goals? What is the nature of the leader's special obligations to the group? What serves the greater good?

Second, we ordinarily believe that others are protected by morality and that even outsiders are due some of these protections. For example, it would be very odd to find someone who holds that just anyone could be justifiably enslaved. Historically, people have found slavery to be morally problematic, usually restricting it to Barbarians or to people perceived as different from themselves in virtue of their race or other characteristics that the slaveholding group finds morally relevant. In fact, if slaveholders believed anyone could be justifiably enslaved, we could infer that they do not fully understand morality—one central tenet of which is the prohibition on slavery. But people generally understand the content of the moral rules. When it comes to beliefs about slavery, our mistakes have been about the scope of prohibition against it. Group members are protected by the prohibition, whereas outsiders are immune to this kind of protection.

Not even people who are committed to sharp distinctions between themselves and nongroup members defend the claim that they can do whatever they want to "lesser" beings. For example, those who would advocate using sexual humiliation to get sensitive information from a terrorist might well reject using it to entertain the guards. We place similar restrictions on the treatment of nonhuman animals. On the one hand, many people eat animals and, by doing so, support a system of factory farming that causes great pain and distress to fellow sentient beings. It is doubtful that meat-eaters would be willing to inflict this kind of suffering on group members. On the other hand, many of these same people support laws against animal cruelty. So, causing pain to animals is believed to be justified for some pleasures and interests but not for others. Taste and nutrition ostensibly count as good reasons, whereas as pleasure associated with domination and sadism count as bad reasons.

People use moral reasoning, then, not to decide whether they are universally bound by morality or whether others are universally protected by its scope. The predicament in which they find themselves is one in which they must determine *when* they are bound by a particular moral rule or principle, as well as *the extent to which* others are protected by a rule or principle. In leadership contexts, such determinations will often depend on both the perceived importance of the *consequences* of goal achievement and the leader's commitment to *partiality*. Consequentialist reasoning makes it possible for a leader to use group goals or the greater good to support the idea that he is not bound by morality in particular circumstances. Ordinarily, we expect him to abide by the rule in question, and he probably has this general expectation of himself. But it is also true that we expect our leaders to achieve group goals, which is why we permit periodic deviations from the rules. Aristotle (1981) is right that there is no godlike leader—a leader we allow to do what he wants to do whenever he wants to do it (pp. 215-216). Still, we will sometimes want even mere mortals to break the rules when doing so is conducive to the achievement of our goals. We allow the deviations because we think our goals are important—either for their own sake or for the sake of something else.

Examples from the early days of the Obama administration illustrate the conflict between goal achievement and conformity to the rules. Given the near disastrous state of the U.S. economy at the time, Timothy Geithner was nominated and approved as Secretary of the Treasury—despite his failure to pay all of his taxes and despite Obama's insistence from the beginning of his campaign that there are not "two sets of standards, one for powerful people and one for ordinary folks who are working every day and paying their taxes" (Sherling, 2009). Goal achievement was pretty clearly behind the deviation. Although Geithner fell short of the standard and, thus, was a potentially problematic nominee, Obama had to begin fixing the economy. Geithner was *the* person to help him do it.

Tom Daschle, who also owed back taxes, did not fare so well as the nominee to become Secretary of Health and Human Services. After Daschle pulled out of the process, President Obama was quick to take full responsibility for the mistake. But Obama's response went beyond his mea culpa. He continued by explaining the failure in terms of his promises of healthcare reform. Obama was clearly loath to lose someone who was both an accomplished politician and an expert in healthcare. As the President put it in a CBS News interview, he was "very eager to make sure that we could deliver on a commitment that I have to deliver healthcare for the American people" (Obama, 2009). In other words, Obama had high hopes for Daschle and what he could do not only for the administration but also for all of us. Moreover, what it was believed Daschle could do is precisely what Obama had promised would be done. Against the backdrop of Obama's promise, the importance of the expected consequences blinded the new president to concerns of principle and ultimately contributed to his admitted failing.

Whereas consequentialist considerations drive leaders' mistakes about whether they are bound by moral rules, it is their commitments to partiality that warp their beliefs about the extent to which outsiders are protected by these rules. Some leaders make clear their willingness to privilege the values of their own society and the welfare of its members. Indeed they may see social, political, or economic life as a conflict between incommensurable visions of the good. According to the most extreme version of this view, group members count for more—and are most deserving of the protections of morality—just because they are Americans or Christians or members of the same racial or ethnic group. Other leaders profess a more cosmopolitan vision of society. According to this view, we are all members of a common humanity and, therefore, equally deserving of morality's protections. However, even the most cosmopolitan leaders would be hard pressed to count the interests of outsiders as being equal to the interests of members of the group they represent. For one thing, what group would support a leader who openly avows an equal commitment to the interests of nongroup members? Notice too that followers are much less concerned about losses by outsiders—whether in a war or in the marketplace—than they are about their own losses. Followers react this way even when the losses are felt by innocent third-parties. Because followers react this way, leaders often do as well. There are great pressures on leaders to put the interests of group members first. Partiality, we might say, is endemic to leadership.

A Typology of Ethical Failures in Leadership

We can use the distinction between the content of a moral rule and the scope of a rule to develop a psychologically rich account of ethical failures in leadership. Let us first return, however, to the motivational foundations of less complicated accounts. In the introduction of this chapter, I noted that the standard explanation of leader immorality points to nonmoral considerations having to do with self-interest. According to this explanation, leaders know the right thing to do but choose—out of self-interest—not to do it. For these leaders, nonmoral considerations trump moral considerations that privilege the good of others—except, of course, when acting for the good of others serves the leader's self-interest. Although their behavior can look moral, motivations of self-interest are the ones they actually act on. We saw this kind of *descriptive egoism*, for example, in a subset of responses to the Gyges exercise.

Perhaps some leaders give no real weight to moral considerations because they see themselves as being completely outside of the scope of morality. In these cases, leaders mistakenly judge that they are universally exempt from moral requirements. Leaders committed to *amoralism* thus engage primarily in nonmoral reasoning. Their conclusions about the scope of moral principles—namely, that they are universally beyond the reach of such principles—allow them to guide their behavior largely by nonmoral considerations. Moral considerations play a role in the amoralist leader's reasoning only insofar as he needs to adjust his behavior in recognition of the fact that other people take these considerations seriously. Morality does not really matter to him, though peoples' perceptions of it might. Given that other people care about morality, even amoral leaders must sometimes rely instrumentally on moral considerations. In this respect, they are like leaders who sometimes do the right thing out of self-interest.

However, nonmoral considerations that drive the behavior of egoist or amoralist leaders are only part of the story. In fact, I would suggest that they are only a small part of the story. There are many other kinds of moral mistakes to which leaders are susceptible, and these mistakes involve quintessential moral reasoning (Price, 2008). A typology of moral mistakes by leaders, as well as the nature of the considerations behind their ethically questionable behavior, is displayed in Table 14.1. First, a leader can engage in morally wrong conduct because he is truly mistaken about the *content* of moral rules. Sometimes his society is essentially to blame. If his society holds the wrong values, he is more likely to be misguided as well. Basic findings in anthropology teach us that the practice of morality is *culturally relative*, even if what morality objectively requires is not relative (Rachels, 1986). In other words, what people *take to be* the content of moral rules can vary from culture to culture. While we readily see the possibility of moral error in societies other than our own, we sometimes fail to recognize that we are hardly immune to mistakes about the content of moral rules in our own societies.

We can also be mistaken at the individual level. In fact, Western traditions of individualism lend themselves to an approach to morality bordering on *personal relativism*. Behaviors that were once considered wrong—for example, premarital sex and drug use—are increasingly matters of personal identity and choice. In a free society, there is a sense in which the content of moral rules is up for grabs. Precisely because whole societies can be wrong about morality, the vulnerability of cultural standards to individual critique is a very good thing. But it can be dangerous when morality comes to vary from person to person, making it possible for the leader to say that, according to him, his behavior was not wrong at all. President Clinton's conduct in the Monica Lewinsky scandal may serve as the best recent example of this phenomenon. Here I have in mind not Clinton's private conduct, which he admitted was wrong, but his public conduct. It is far from clear that he grasped the wrongness of the lengths to which he went to protect himself from political opponents (Clinton, 2004).

Second, several moral theories provide resources to support a leader's belief that he is not *bound* by moral rules in a particular case. As noted in the introduction of this paper, *ethical egoism* holds the right action is the action that promotes self-interest. Ethical egoism thus differs from descriptive egoism in that the former view tells us what we ought to do,

Table 14.1. A Typology of Ethical Failures in Leadership

Theory Behind the Mistake	*Type of Mistake*	*Language of the Explanation or Justification*	*Predominant Type of Reasoning*
Descriptive egoism	About the importance of morality as compared to self-interest	"I knew I should not break the rule, but I saw it as in my self-interest to do so."	Nonmoral
Amoralism	About whether the leader is bound by morality	"I am universally beyond the scope of morality."	Nonmoral
Cultural relativism	About the content of moral rules	"I live by a different set of moral requirements. These requirements are determined by my society."	Moral
Personal relativism	About the content of moral rules	"I live by a different set of moral requirements. These requirements are determined by my own beliefs about morality."	Moral
Ethical egoism	About whether the leader is bound by moral rules	"Moral requirements do not apply to me when they conflict with my self-interest."	Moral
Virtue theory	About whether the leader is bound by moral rules	"Moral requirements do not apply to me when they conflict with the dictates of my practical wisdom."	Moral
Consent theory	About whether the leader is bound by moral rules	"Moral requirements do not apply to me when I have the permission of followers to break the rules."	Moral
Moral pragmatism	About whether the leaders is bound by moral rules	"Moral requirements do not apply to me when group goals make it necessary to deviate from them."	Moral

Table continues on next page.

Table 14.1. Continued

Theory Behind the Mistake	*Type of Mistake*	*Language of the Explanation or Justification*	*Predominant Type of Reasoning*
Moral idealism	About whether the leader is bound by moral rules	"Moral requirements do not apply to me when they impede my pursuit of the greater good."	Moral
Communal ethics	About whether outsiders are protected by moral rules	"Moral requirements serve the interests of group members, not the interests of outsiders."	Moral

not what people in fact do. According to ethical egoism, moral requirements do not apply to leaders when these requirements conflict with the dictates of self-interest. Similarly, *virtue theory* makes room for a leader to stray from the rules when his "practical wisdom" about what should be done in the circumstances calls for deviation rather than compliance (Aristotle, 1985). Theorists in this tradition believe that virtue is a state of being that cannot be encapsulated in a list of rules (Annas, 2004). In *consent theory*, which was also earlier discussed, it is the permission of followers that justifies rule-breaking behavior by leaders. Followers allow leaders to exercise some discretion—John Locke (1988) called it "prerogative" (p. 375)—to go around the rules when doing so is for the good of the group. In contrast, *moral pragmatism* bases justification for rule breaking not on agreement but on the importance of group goals. Here, in situations in which group goals necessitate rule-breaking behavior, leaders are beyond the scope of the moral requirement represented by the rule. Finally, *moral idealism* denies the moral pragmatist's claim that particular group goals are sufficient for justification. According to advocates of this view, only universal ends such as liberty or equality have the moral weight to justify breaking the rules (Burns, 1978).

Third, some approaches to morality generate mistakes about who is *protected* by morality. Advocates of *communal ethics* often draw hard and fast lines with regard to who counts as an insider and who counts as an outsider. Relying on this view of moral membership, leaders sometimes claim that nongroup members are beyond the scope of moral protections. We see this error in the great breadth of acceptable targets for Islamist terrorism. Simply being a Westerner can be sufficient to put a person at risk for attack. Unfortunately, we also see this kind of mistake in the thinking of many proponents of extreme forms of American patriotism. People inclined to paint all Muslims with one brush may be reluctant to give innocents the moral protection they deserve. Advocates of communal ethics are also susceptible to being wrong about the extent to which their own group members are protected by moral rules. In other words, beliefs about inequality in moral status *between* different communities are often paired with beliefs about inequality in moral status *within* a community. The Taliban leader who enforces strict limitations on the education of girls or perpetuates the practice of honor killings is mistaken about the extent to which girls and women are protected by morality. Here, of course, the explanation of the leader's beliefs will also appeal to the socioreligious context in which he exercises leadership.

This typology of ethical failures in leadership shows the complexity of the psychological sources of leader immorality. It also shows that simply distinguishing between ethics and effectiveness (Ciulla, 1995; Gardner, 1990; O'Toole, 1996) does not allow us easily to sort reasons for action into moral and nonmoral considerations. For one thing, leaders have an ethical obligation to be effective (Ciulla, 2004b). The main point of this chapter is that leaders can fail ethically precisely because they are acting on *moral reasons* that are consistent with—indeed, supportive of—leader effectiveness. In these cases, leaders are doing what followers expect them to do, achieving group goals, nurturing special relationships within the group, and working in the common good. As the typology suggests, the reasoning behind many categories of ethical failures in leadership focuses squarely on the goals and interests of followers and, thus, engages these other-regarding considerations. Hence the paradoxical role of moral reasoning in ethical failures in leadership. Appealing to genuine moral considerations such as consent, necessity, special obligations, and the greater good can actually contribute to leader immorality.

My conclusion is that characteristic problems of leadership ethics are within ethics itself. The ethical struggle leaders confront in their day-to-day lives is less between nonmoral and moral considerations or between self and other than it is between other-regarding considerations and moral rules. This means that we cannot solve problems of immoral leadership by simply telling leaders that they ought to be ethical or that they should put the good of others ahead of self-interest. Other-regarding considerations often get us into a moral argument, but they take us only so far. Solving these problems requires that scholars and practitioners look more critically at moral justification. The opportunities for appealing to other-regarding considerations in leadership are many, and I am inclined to think that, more often than not, these attempts at moral justification constitute a threat to the moral rules. We have long known that there must be moral limits to the pursuit of self-interest. Leadership ethics must now determine the moral limits of the consequentialism and partiality that characterize the *ethical* relationship between leaders and followers. Although consequentialism and partiality are central to this relationship, they can also be the ethical undoing of a leader.

REFERENCES

Annas, J. (2004, November). Being virtuous and doing the right thing. *Proceedings and Addresses of the American Philosophical Association, 78,* 61-75.

Aristotle. (1981). *The politics* (T. A. Sinclair, Trans.). New York: Penguin Books.

Aristotle. (1985). *Nicomachean ethics* (T. Irwin, Trans.). Indianapolis, IN: Hackett.

Avolio, B. J., & Gardner, W. L. (2005). Authentic leadership development: Getting to the root of positive forms of leadership. *Leadership Quarterly, 16,* 315-338.

Avolio, B. J., & Locke, E. E. (2002). Contrasting different philosophies of leader motivation: Altruism versus egoism. *Leadership Quarterly, 13,* 169-171.

Bass, B. M., & Steidlmeier, P. (1999). Ethics, character, and authentic transformational leadership behavior. *Leadership Quarterly, 10,* 181-217.

Burns, J. M. (1978). *Leadership*. New York: Harper & Row.

Clinton, B. (2004). *My life*. New York: Alfred Knopf.

Ciulla, J. B. (1995). Leadership ethics: Mapping the territory. *Business Ethics Quarterly, 5,* 5-24.

Ciulla, J. B. (Ed.). (2004a). *Ethics, the heart of leadership* (2nd ed.). Westport, CT: Praeger.

Ciulla, J. B. (2004b). Ethics and leadership effectiveness. In J. Antonakis, A. T. Cianciolo, & R. J. Sternberg (Eds.), *The nature of leadership* (pp. 302-327). Thousand Oaks, CA: SAGE.

Gardner, J. W. (1990). *On leadership*. New York: Free Press.

Glover, J. (2000). *Humanity: A moral history of the twentieth century*. New Haven, CT: Yale University Press.

Hobbes, T. (1991). *Leviathan* (R. Tuck, Ed.). Cambridge, MA: Cambridge University Press.

Hollander, E. P. (1964). *Leaders, groups, and influence*. New York: Oxford University Press.

Hollander, E. P. (1978). *Leadership dynamics: A practical guide to effective relationships*. New York: Free Press.

Hollander, E. P. (2009). *Inclusive leadership: The essential leader-follower relationship*. New York: Routledge.

Kant, I. (1964). *Groundwork of the metaphysics of morals* (H. J. Paton, Trans.). New York: Harper & Row.

Kant, I. (1996). *Practical philosophy* (M. J. Gregor, Trans.). Cambridge, MA: Cambridge University Press.

Kohlberg, L. (1981). *Essays on moral development: The philosophy of moral development* (Vol. 1). San Francisco: Harper & Row.

Kornet, A. (1997, May-June). The truth about lying: Deception is rampant – and sometimes we tell the biggest lies to those we love the most. *Psychology Today, 3,* 52-57.

Locke, J. (1988). *Two treatises of government* (P. Laslett, Ed.). Cambridge, MA: Cambridge University Press.

Ludwig, D. C., & Longenecker, C. O. (1993). The Bathsheba syndrome: The ethical failure of successful leaders. *Journal of Business Ethics, 12,* 265-273.

Mill, J. S. (1979). *Utilitarianism* (G. Sher, Ed.). Indianapolis, IN: Hackett.

Nietzsche, F. (1967). *On the genealogy of morals and ecce homo* (W. Kaufman, Ed. and Trans.). New York: Random House.

Nisbett, R., & Ross, L. (1980). *Human inference: Strategies and shortcomings of social judgment.* Englewood Cliffs, NJ: Prentice-Hall.

Obama, B. (Writer). (2009, February 4). *Morning edition* [Radio broadcast episode]. In Madhulika Sikka (Producer), Morning Edition. Washington, DC: National Public Radio.

O'Toole, J. (1996). *Leading change: The argument for values-based leadership.* New York: Ballantine Books.

Plato. (1992). *Republic* (G. M. A. Gruge, Trans.). Indianapolis, IL: Hackett.

Price, T. L. (2006). *Understanding ethical failures in leadership.* New York: Cambridge University Press.

Price, T. L. (2008). *Leadership ethics: An introduction.* New York: Cambridge University Press.

Rachels, J. (1986). *The elements of moral philosophy.* New York: Random House.

Rand, A. (1999). The ethics of emergencies. In J. Feinberg & R. Shafer-Landau (Eds.), *Reason and responsibility: Readings in some basic problems of philosophy* (10th ed., pp. 533-537). Belmont, CA: Wadsworth.

Sherling, E. (Executive Producer). (2009, February 3). *The situation room* [Television broadcast]. Atlanta, GA: CNN.

Simmons, J. A. (2007). Patriotic leadership. In T. L. Price & J. T. Wren (Eds.), *The values of presidential leadership* (pp. 35-55). New York: Palgrave Macmillan.

Walzer, M. (1973). Political action: The problem of dirty hands. *Philosophy and Public Affairs, 2,* 160-180.

Wolfe, A. (2001). *Moral freedom.* New York: W. W. Norton.

CHAPTER 15

UNDERSTANDING THE ANTECEDENTS OF UNINTENTIONAL LEADER ERRORS

A Multilevel Perspective

Samuel T. Hunter, Brian W. Tate, Jessica L. Dzieweczynski, and Lily Cushenbery

Negative forms of leadership have recently become a popular topic of study, yet most of the attention has focused on intentionally committed behaviors. To address other forms of negative leadership, the present review will discuss the nature and antecedents of leader errors. We propose an error taxonomy based on Fleishman, Mumford, Zaccaro, Levin, Korotkin, and Hein's (1991) behavioral framework and explore the antecedents of these errors at leader, group, and organization levels of analysis. The review has implications for practice by highlighting factors that should be controlled in order to reduce the frequency of errors. Finally, the review will discuss how leader errors should be incorporated into empirical research and the antecedents and outcomes of errors upon which future research should focus. For practitioners and researchers alike, the review will enhance the understanding of what errors are and why they occur.

When Leadership Goes Wrong: Destructive Leadership, Mistakes and Ethical Failures, pp. 405–443

"The only man who never makes a mistake is the man who never does anything."

—Theodore Roosevelt (1858-1919)

There is general consensus among leadership researchers that highly effective leadership is a relatively rare phenomenon. DeVries and Kaiser (2003), for example, stated that half of all managers may qualify as incompetent. Focusing on subordinate perceptions, this number may be even greater; Hogan and Kaiser (2005) cite statistics showing that 65% to 75% of workers from the general population consider their boss to be the worst part of their job. Such figures emphasize the point that, although transformational, ethical, and authentic leaders may be ideal, they are difficult to find.

There is, however, some disconnection between the frequency with which negative leadership occurs and the amount of research that has been devoted to truly understanding the antecedents, nature, and outcomes of negative leadership. Until relatively recently, leadership research has tended to consider negative leadership as simply an absence of positive leadership (Ashforth, 1994). Recent research on topics such as abusive supervision (Tepper, 2000), supervisor undermining (Duffy, Ganster, & Pagon, 2002), petty tyranny (Ashforth, 1987), destructive leadership (Padilla, Hogan, & Kaiser, 2007), and negative leadership (Tate & Jacobs, 2009), however, demonstrate that many manifestations of negative leadership reflect behaviors that are unique from positive behaviors. For example, trying too hard to please others, administering punishments awkwardly and inconsistently, and failing to address important issues (or ignoring critical information while doing so) represent more than a failure to engage in positive behaviors. In fact, Einarsen, Aasland, and Skogstad (2007) distinguished four types of leadership based on whether leadership is positive or negative for subordinates and/or the organization.

In addition to the evidence underscoring the uniqueness of negative leadership relative to positive leadership, there is some research suggesting that negative leadership can have consequences at least as great in magnitude as positive leadership. For example, a meta-analysis conducted by Podsakoff, Bommer, Podsakoff, and MacKenzie (2006) assessed effect sizes associated with leader contingent/noncontingent reward and punishment behavior and found the strongest effect sizes with the most negative form of behaviors, noncontingent punishment. Given the significant relationships between leadership and individual, group, and organizational outcomes, Podsakoff et al.'s study suggests that negative leadership may have even greater consequences than some forms of positive leadership. Thus, the uniqueness and seriousness of negative leadership mean that future research should work toward developing an understanding of its different forms.

As a useful means of categorizing types of negative leadership, researchers have suggested a distinction between behaviors committed intentionally and unintentionally (Kellerman, 2004). The distinction is useful as intentional and unintentional behaviors are likely to differ, not only in terms of their specific manifestations, but also in terms of their antecedents and outcomes. By reviewing research relevant to leader errors and proposing types and antecedents of errors, the present chapter will focus on the *unintentional* forms of negative leadership. Focusing on leader errors, specifically, will enhance not only focus of the chapter, but will also prevent the chapter from becoming unwieldy by reviewing research on all types of negative leadership.

THE IMPORTANCE OF CONSIDERING LEADER ERRORS

Before defining leader errors and discussing important antecedents, we will first discuss the importance of understanding leader error antecedents. Evidence of the negative impacts of leader errors is readily available and, in many cases, highly visible. Case studies of Three-Mile Island, for example, reveal a number of management errors occurring in the early stages of the disaster—errors that might have been avoided under more careful leadership. A widely cited example of leader error is also seen in reports on the Challenger space shuttle explosion (Violanti, 2006). Despite having evidence for likely equipment and material failure (e.g., O-rings), team leaders either chose to disregard warnings or failed to receive such warnings resulting in a launch that proved disastrous (Reason, 1990).

One need not only focus on large-scale disasters to witness the impact of leader errors. In his review of three organizations and the leaders within them, Nutt (2004) illustrated just how impactful leader errors can be to business. An overzealous CEO at Quaker foods, for example, let his prior successes drive strategic decision making, resulting in an acquisition of a product-line (Snapple) that was incongruent with the strategic plan and culture of the organization. The end result was an initial 10% loss in Quaker foods and a 1.4 billion loss in the eventual sale of Snapple. The overzealous CEO also "stepped-down" from his position shortly thereafter. Along these lines Ross and Staw (1993) explored sunk cost errors displayed by leaders at the Shoreham Nuclear power plant. The project began as a sizeable 75 million dollar development and ballooned to over 5 billion U.S. dollars. Most notably, the power plant was never completed as leaders continued to sink funds into the clearly failing effort. One final example, discussed at length by Finkelstein (2003), involves Motorola's decision to ignore data about the cell phone consumers' desire to switch from analog to digital technology. Despite having clear information about this change, leaders at Motorola continued down an internal forecasting path. The outcome of these decisions was nearly a 30% drop in market share, resulting in a number of organizational layoffs and restructuring.

Such examples illustrate the highly visible and salient negative results of leader errors. What must also be realized, however, is that errors can have a number of positive outcomes as well (van Dyck, Frese, Baer, & Sonnentag, 2005; Sitkin, 1996). These positive outcomes include learning (Dormann & Frese, 1994), resilience and increased creativity and innovation. Witness, for example, Spencer Silver's failed attempt at developing high-strength glue—a 3M product that eventually became the Post-it note (Fry, 1987). Serendipity emerging vis-à-vis leadership efforts is also nicely illustrated in a historical yet relevant consideration of the events leading up to Columbus's voyages across the Atlantic. Planning a trip to the Indies, Columbus made several errors including incorrectly calculating distances in Italian miles rather than the Arabic mile metric used in original calculations (Morison, 1942). More critically, when experts questioned his plans and calculations Columbus disregarded their comments and set forth on a journey for which he and his crew were ill prepared. One final planning error committed by Columbus, an error central to his discovery of North America, was that the trip to the Indies was comprised of open sea rather than the sizable landmass many now call home. Simply stated, Columbus serendipitously ran into North America due to a planning error.

Returning to the twenty-first century, a final example is witnessed in the actions of Jim McCann, CEO of a widely popular and profitable flower delivery chain. In the early 1980s, McCann decided to buy an organization he knew was struggling based largely on its name: 1-800-flowers. What he failed to do, however, was investigate just how bad things were for the organization before he purchased it. To his surprise, the newly acquired company was over seven million dollars in debt, a debt he assumed in the buyout of the company. McCann (1998) referred to this as his biggest professional mistake, noting "When I was examining the company in 1983 I didn't know how to do due diligence; what I did was more like due negligence" (p. 15). What is noteworthy about McCann's story is how profitable he made the company in spite of—or as some might say—because of this error. After the purchase McCann told his employees "Look, we've made a mistake. Now to pay off our debts, we'll just have to expand our plans, play on a bigger stage, and be successful sooner" (p. 15). In 2007, the reported net revenues of 1-800-flowers were 912 million dollars, up nearly 17% from 2006 and certainly up a sizeable amount from the original seven million dollar debt.

For research, describing the nature and antecedents of leader errors has implications for furthering the understanding of negative forms of leadership. We hope that the present discussion of leader errors can both stimulate research on the topic and provide direction for that research. Because there is limited research directly related to the study of leader errors, there has been little guidance as to how to begin to study the phenomenon. Thus, we hope that not only will the present chapter enhance our understanding of the errors leaders make but will also provide groundwork for future research in a critical area. Before reviewing potential antecedents of leader errors across multiple levels of analysis, we will first turn to the task of defining leader error.

LEADER ERRORS DEFINED

Previous Definitions

The investigation of human error is a highly active research area, including input from cognitive psychology, human factors, military research, medical research, and organizational behavior. Not surprisingly, errors have been defined in a number of ways by a wide array of researchers. Examination of these definitions reveals several common themes among them. First, an error must have been avoidable; that is, if an action was a result of wholly extraneous events it cannot be considered an error on the part of the leader (Reason, 1990; Senders & Moray, 1991). Second, an error may come in the form of an action *or inaction*. Thus, failing to take appropriate action may be considered an error. Third, errors result in unintended or unpredicted events, events that were not part of the original goal or plan of action (Zapf, Isic, Bechtoldt, & Blau, 2003). Most often, these outcomes are undesired, but, at times, these outcomes can be serendipitous and/or positive. Fourth and finally, errors are domain specific, making it necessary to develop unique error taxonomies for varying professions, contexts, or domains (Senders & Moray, 1991).

Proposed Definition

Drawing from the error literature, we define a leader error as occurring when: *An avoidable action (or inaction) is chosen by a leader which results in an initial outcome outside of the leader's original intent, goal, or prediction.* There are four points relevant to the proposed definition. First, the definition applies to leaders working toward leadership-relevant goals. Thus, for example, leaders operating in a purely laissez-faire fashion would not be committing errors of inaction because the leaders lack intended end-states or goals associated with leadership. Leaders who *purposefully* choose inaction as a means of achieving a goal or outcome, however, are subject to the definition of error should that inaction result in an outcome outside the leader's original intent. Second and along related lines, our definition applies to those leaders whose goals are formed for the good of the group (e.g., socialized leaders) as opposed to leaders with more self-serving intentions (e.g., personalized leaders). The actions of personalized leaders are more characteristic of deviance, abuse, coercion, and/or other forms destructive leadership (e.g., House & Howell, 1992; Mumford, Espejo, Hunter, Bedell, Eubanks, & Connelly, 2007; Padilla et al., 2007). Third, the proposed definition requires consideration of the *initial* outcomes of a leader's decision(s). Although some mistakes "work out in the end" we have chosen to define error based on proximal rather than distal outcomes of decisions. Distal outcomes are often influenced by a number of extraneous factors outside of the leader's control and are less relevant for deciding if an error has occurred and the variables that contributed to its occurrence. Fourth and finally, the definition stands as an initial starting point for understanding leader errors and their antecedents. Researchers such as Senders and Moray (1991) have noted the need to specify error types within various research domains for substantive gains to be made in the understanding of error. Accordingly, to more accurately define leader error it will be necessary to consider the specific types of errors committed by leaders, a task that first requires a careful consideration of the behaviors that comprise leadership.

Leader Behaviors as a Precursor to Understanding Leader Error

The study of leader behavior is just as rich, if not more so, than the study of error. In fact, there are at least 65 differing classification systems for leader behaviors (Fleishman et al., 1991). Notable models include the two factor approach emerging from the Ohio State and Michigan studies (Likert, 1961, 1967; Stogdill, 1974) as well as the expanded three-factor versions offered by Yukl and colleagues (Yukl, 2007; Yukl, Gordon, & Tabor, 2002). The two and three factor approaches have been criticized for focusing on those behaviors most salient to subordinates rather than essential for performance (e.g., Hunter, Bedell-Avers, & Mumford, 2007). In an attempt to synthesize the vast array of behavioral categorizations and provide a more comprehensive taxonomy of behaviors, Fleishman et al. (1991) reviewed over 65 differing classification schemes of leader behaviors, resulting in the most complete taxonomy of leadership available. The result of their effort is a four-factor model comprised of: (1) information search and structuring, (2) information use in problem solving, (3) managing personnel resources, and (4) managing material resources. These factors and their application to leader errors are presented in Table 15.1.

Table 15.1. Proposed Leader Error Taxonomy

Broad Leader Behavior Category	*Specific Leader Behavior Category*	*Sample Leader Behaviors*	*Sample Leader Errors*
Information Search and Structuring			Errors in Gathering and Structuring Information
	Acquiring Information	Calling clients to determine emerging and future needs	Failing to contact a client that has an important need or urgent request
	Organizing and Evaluating Information	Rank-ordering jobs/tasks to be completed using critical strategic data	Making incorrect rank-order when developing completion lists; placing important tasks too low on the completion list
	Feedback and Control	Monitoring fiscal changes after implementing a new training program in an effort to assess the program's effectiveness	Monitoring inappropriate criteria; choosing not to examine performance changes resulting from implementing training program
Information Use in Problem Solving			Errors in Using Information
	Identifying Needs Requirements	Examining safety reports for new incidents of workplace accidents	Disregarding safety reports; failing to reference prior reports to determine the emergence of trends
	Planning and Coordinating	Developing a strategic plan for the development of a new product line	Failing to consider key constraints in strategic plan; basing plan on incorrect or outdated information
	Communicating Information	Sending e-mails to key employees to inform them of a new product's success	Message written by leader is unclear; messages are sent too often and lose significance; messages are sent to employees that are unrelated to the project
Managing Personnel Resources			Errors in Managing People

Table continues on next page.

Table 15.1. Continued

Broad Leader Behavior Category	*Specific Leader Behavior Category*	*Sample Leader Behaviors*	*Sample Leader Errors*
	Obtaining and Allocating Personnel Resources	Assigning employee to an important task they are well-suited and trained for	Assigning an employee to a task they are unprepared for; hiring employees with unnecessary or redundant skill sets
	Developing Personnel Resources	Sending an employee to a training program that develops a skill necessary for their job	Sending an employee to training that is unnecessary; failing to train employees on skills critical to their success
	Motivating Personnel Resources	Rewarding employees for the completion of a difficult task	Providing employees with rewards they do not value; failing to recognize important successes and efforts
	Utilizing and Monitoring Personnel Resources	Preparing timely and specific performance appraisal reports that emphasize key behaviors	Being excessively critical or hurtful during performance appraisals; making assessments personal rather than behavioral
Managing Material Resources			Errors in Managing Tasks and Things
	Obtaining and Allocating Material Resources	Requesting appropriate funds for new office equipment	Purchasing new office equipment when old equipment functions adequately and other financial needs are pressing
	Maintaining Material Resources	Developing a maintenance program to regularly service machinery to prevent accidents and breakdowns	Waiting until machinery breaks down to repair it; allowing machinery to operate when it is unsafe
	Utilizing and Monitoring Material Resources	Developing reasonable supplies lists and logs where employees record core usage	Failing to track fundamental supply usage; requiring employees to excessively document usage

Note: Columns 1 and 2 represent labels taken from Fleishman et al. (1991).

The Fleishman et al. (1991) model was chosen as our framework to examine leader errors for several reasons. First, the model explicitly describes the relationships *among* leader behaviors. Whereas other behavioral models seem to suggest that leaders engage in one behavior instead of another, the Fleishman et al. model specifically acknowledges that behaviors are interdependent. This is particularly critical in understanding leader errors as they rarely occur in isolation and are typically part of a broader system of mistakes (Reason, 1990; Senders & Moray, 1991). Second, as alluded to above, the model put forth by Fleishman et al. encompasses both the two and three-factor approaches as well as adding behaviors less frequently witnessed by subordinates (e.g., planning, gathering information). The addition of these less-investigated behaviors is especially important for understanding leader errors as mistakes are frequently associated with decision-making when using limited information (e.g., Violanti, 2006). Third, the model is well-regarded in the leadership literature and has been used as a framework in recent theoretical discussions including a multilevel consideration of leader trust (Burke, Sims, Lazzara, & Salas, 2007), providing some evidence of its applicability in investigating new and emerging leadership phenomena. Fourth, because of its emphasis on behavior, the model stands as a particularly useful framework for considering phenomena such as leader errors. More specifically, the behavioral focus may be viewed as more neutral relative to some models of leadership (e.g., vision-based), which often emphasize the positive aspects of leadership such as inspirational motivation or intellectual stimulation. We acknowledge, however, that the use of the Fleishman et al. (1991) model represents *one* perspective of leadership and the use of other leadership taxonomies would likely produce differing perspectives on error.

Proposed Error Taxonomy

Having considered previous error definitions, taxonomies of leader behavior, and offering our own definition of leader error we turn now to the proposed leader error taxonomy presented in Table 15.1. Using the Fleishman et al. (1991) framework, we suggest four broad types of leader error: (1) errors in gathering and structuring information, (2) errors in using information, (3) errors in managing people and (4) errors in managing tasks and resources. The framework highlights the interdependence of behaviors and provides a unique process-based perspective of leader-error. These relationships are illustrated in Figure 15.1 and the discerning reader might observe one notable addition to the model: an inclusion of a feedback loop from errors in managing people to errors in gathering information. This relationship will be discussed further in later

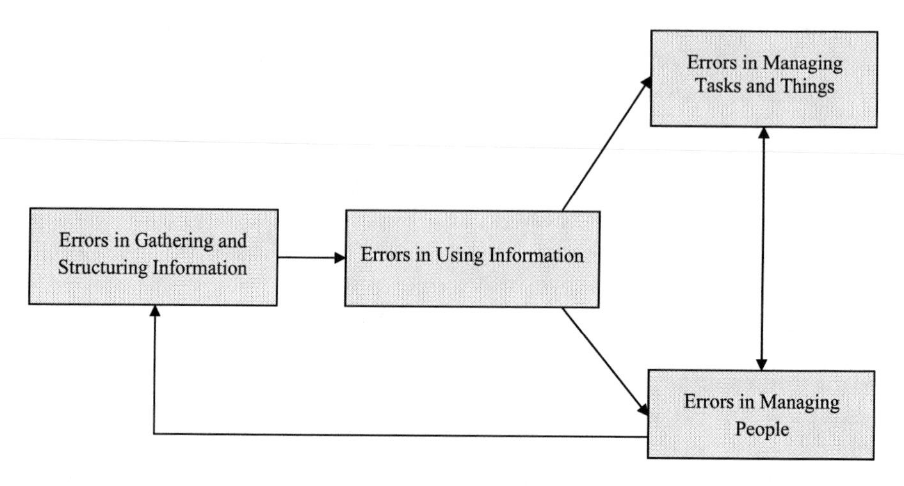

Figure 15.1. Interrelationships among error types.

sections as we examine the critical role of the subordinate in reducing the frequency and negative impact of leader error.

A MULTILEVEL FRAMEWORK FOR EXAMINING LEADER ERROR

With leader errors defined, the question becomes: Why do they occur? The answer, not surprisingly, is complex. Consider, for example, Coca-Cola's decision in 1985 to pursue an alternative product labeled "New Coke," an event widely cited as *the* classic marketing mistake (Oliver, 1986; Rickard, 1995). The events surrounding this decision provide illustration of the complexity involved in leader error. The CEO of the company Robert Goizueta had just come off the success of Diet Coke and was committed to continual change within the company. Goizueta also claimed to have the support of his predecessor, partially insulating himself from potential criticism from others within the company. When feedback regarding the public's initial negative reaction to the new product was received, several members of Goizueta's management team discounted the feedback and the company continued on with the release of the new product. The result was a substantial loss in sales as well as a backlash unrivaled by any other new product introduction. New Coke was boycotted and protested, and the company was sued. In the end, company leaders reinstituted the previous product, termed "Coke Classic," to much fanfare and, ultimately, renewed financial success.

The example illustrates the complex, multilevel nature of error antecedents. Typically, leader errors are not simply a result of flaws in ego but a constellation of factors from multiple levels of analysis. The need for multilevel consideration and investigation has been called for in both management research in general (Hitt, Beamish, Jackson, & Matheiu, 2008) as well as, more specifically, in leadership research (Yammarino, Dionne, Chun, & Dansereau, 2005). These calls appear justified, as the benefits of multilevel investigation are well documented. For example, Hitt, Beamish, Jackson, and Matheiu (2008) provide an excellent discussion on the interplay that occurs among phenomena at multiple levels of analysis. The researchers suggest that understanding the complex nature of organizational phenomena requires a multilevel approach. Taken a step further, some researchers have found paradoxes across levels of analysis. In their review of innovation antecedents, Mumford and Hunter (2005) discovered that what is necessary at one level of analysis may differ, or even conflict, with requirements at other levels. Thus, it appears that a multilevel consideration not only provides a more complete picture of a given phenomenon, but may also reveal relationships that discussions of a more narrow focus may have missed. The present chapter will explore potential error antecedents at the individual, group, and organization levels as well as the interactive effects of these antecedents both within and across levels. We begin at the bottom, the leader level.

Leader Level

At the leader level, we have grouped our discussion into six main categories: (1) dispositions and individual differences, (2) cognitive biases, (3) experience and expertise, (4) stress and fatigue, (5) affect and emotion, and (6) nature of the task.

Individual differences. Although the study of individual differences and leadership has been rich (cf. Lord, DeVader, & Alliger, 1986; Kirkpatrick & Lock, 1991), there has been relatively little work done on negative leader behaviors and leader errors, specifically. What little research that does exist, however, suggests that cognitive closure is an important predictor of leader error. Kruglanski (1989) defined cognitive closure as, "the desire for a definite answer on some topic, any answer as opposed to confusion and ambiguity" (p. 14). Kruglanski and colleagues have shown individuals high in need for closure to use less extensive information searches, especially as those individuals' initial confidence in a decision is high (Bar-Joseph & Kruglanksi, 2003; Kruglanksi, 1989). Thus, it appears that a high need for closure, when combined with strong initial confidence, is likely to be related to continuing commitment errors, errors likely emerging in the managing tasks and materials category of the proposed error framework. Not surprisingly, overconfidence alone has been shown to lead to decrements in financial performance reports of 500 Forbes' CEOs (Malmendier & Tate, 2005) as well as in qualitative examinations of leader error (Finkelstein, 2003; Kilburg, 2006). As it stands, in its own right, overconfidence is a noteworthy individual-level antecedent of leader error, particularly with regard to errors in managing tasks and resources. Specifically, it seems that overconfident leaders may fail to appropriately allocate resources to areas that need them.

Cognitive biases. There are a number of cognitive biases likely to affect the commission of errors. One of the more heavily researched has been termed the fundamental attribution error (Jones, 1979; Nisbett & Ross, 1980; Ross, 1977), which refers to individuals' tendency to attribute negative events to the attributes and personalities of others rather than external or situational causes (Tetlock, 1985). Applied to leadership specifically, Repenning and Sterman (2002) argued that managers are likely to blame subordinates for poor performance rather than the broader organizational system, which is more likely to be the cause of the performance.

Another cognitive bias is termed base-rate neglect or the base-rate fallacy (Bar-Hillel, 1980; Koehler, 1996), which occurs when decision makers ignore or discount previous information and instead rely on less-relevant information. Making the decision to assign a subordinate to an important client based on a recent sales call rather than several years of poor performance serves as an example of base-rate neglect. Along related lines is the general observation that individuals will often see what they want to see (Edmondson, 1996; Norman, 1980). A leader reviewing performance reports, for example, may perceive what he or she expects to see rather than the information actually presented to them.

Although other biases exist (e.g., trade-off aversion) these should suffice to illustrate a basic point: leaders are not wholly rational, calculating machines. Rather they are humans with flaws and biases, biases that are likely to result in misattributions about why things go wrong or right. We argue that these biases are most likely to result in errors managing people, errors such as assigning the wrong person for the task, failing to recognize the efforts of a subordinate, or misattributing poor performance to a subordinate resulting in unnecessary punishment or reprimand.

Expertise and experience. Folk wisdom contends that novices are more likely to make errors than those with more expertise. In fact, there is a sizable amount of support for the general relationship between expertise and performance (Ericsson, Krampe, & Tesch-Römer, 1993; Ericsson & Lehman, 1996). With regard to errors specifically, inexperience is often cited as a primary cause of error in the healthcare industry (e.g., Lesar, Briceland, Delcoure, Parmalee, Masta-Gronic, & Pohl, 1990; Weingart, Wilson, Gibbard, & Harrison, 2000; Wu, Folkman, McPhee, & Lo, 1991).

Thus, expertise would seem to be negatively related to leader errors; however, the expert/error relationship is more complex than it might appear on the surface. Experts can become locked into modes of thinking and rely on previous experience when fresh insight is required. Reason (1990) refers to this phenomenon as the "strong but wrong routine" (p. 57), and there is evidence in support of this argument. For example, Mumford and colleagues demonstrated that information incongruent with an individual's conceptualization of a given context is often discarded, leading to an increase in errors (Blair & Mumford, 2007; Dailey & Mumford, 2006; Licuanan, Dailey, & Mumford, 2007; Mumford, Blair, Dailey, Leritz, & Osborn, 2006). Also, a histriometric analysis of leaders by Bedell-Avers (2008) found outstanding leaders to commit fewer observed errors during their rise to power than at the pinnacle of their power.

Further complicating the issue is evidence that leaders who have experienced prior errors may be more likely to commit future errors, or at least continue on a path of failure. Termed the sunk-cost effect (Staw, 1976), the phenomenon refers to the tendency to continue with an endeavor once an investment of money, resources, effort, or time has been made. In their examination of sunk-cost errors associated with the opening of a power plant, Ross and Staw (1993) describe a number of forces at individual, project, organizational, and social levels that led to decisions to continue with the project, despite abundant evidence that it was a losing endeavor. Such research on sunk-cost errors suggests that experience with early failure on a project does not necessarily lead to reductions in future errors. We argue that errors committed early on in a project may result in errors in managing tasks and resources in the future, as leaders attempt to salvage a project and avoid failure.

Stress and Fatigue. A leader's job is demanding, both mentally and physically (Yukl, 2007). The impact of fatigue on errors is well documented. Most research on the topic has been conducted in medical and military samples. With regard to medical research, there is overwhelming evidence that fatigue is associated with the commission of errors (Gander, Merry, Millar, & Weller, 2000; Jha, Duncan, & Bates, 2001; Kohn, Corrigan, & Donaldson, 2000; Krueger, 1994; Leape, 1994). Similar findings have also been observed in military research. Neri, Shappell, and DeJohn (1992), for example, examined the performance of pilots in a simulated operation under varying levels of fatigue and work operations and found a positive relationship between fatigue and errors. The authors concluded that as fatigue increased, pilots became more willing to engage in risky behaviors if they believed the behaviors would reduce the total time of an operation. Fatigue has also been used to explain numerous safety-related accidents, including those at high-risk facilities such as nuclear power plants (e.g., Baker, Olson, & Morriseau, 1994).

In addition to the general relationship between errors and fatigue, there is some indication that fatigue impacts different types of errors in unique ways. For example, van der Linden, Frese, and Meijman (2003) examined the impact of fatigue on executive functioning (e.g., planning) as well as more automatic tasks such as memory. The researchers found that although automatic tasks were unaffected by fatigue, executive tasks, such as planning, were strongly affected. Thus, fatigue may be a more relevant predictor of certain types of errors than others. In particular, weary leaders engaging in new or novel tasks, tasks for which an automatic response is unavailable, may be more likely to commit errors in making assignments and basic planning decisions. On the other hand, more routine tasks, to which learned responses can be applied, may be relatively unaffected by fatigue.

Affect and Emotion. A review of the study of affect and decision making reveals notable debate among researchers as to whether positive or negative affect leads to more effective decisions (Barsade & Gibson, 2007). A handful of researchers including Martin, Ward, Achee, and Wyer (1993) have suggested that negative affect provides cues to an individual that something is wrong and that more effortful processing is required, resulting in more accurate decision making, a contention that has been supported by a handful of studies (e.g., Mackie & Worth, 1989; Melton, 1995; Kaufman & Vosburg, 1997). On the other hand, there is a sizable literature suggesting that positive affect is related to effective decision making. Largely driven by the work of Isen and colleagues (e.g., Isen, 2001; Isen & Labroo, 2003) several studies have found positive mood to improve decision-making (e.g., Estrada, Isen, & Young, 1997; Staw & Barsade, 1993). A recent meta-analysis by Lyubomirsky, King, and Diener (2005), as well as a comprehensive review (Barsade & Gibson, 2007), has supported this contention. Thus, in the aggregate it appears that negative emotions are more likely to result in leader errors.

Although existing research suggests that there is utility in viewing emotions broadly as either negative or positive, there is likely increased utility in examining the discrete emotions (Raghunathan & Pham, 1999). Anger, in particular, seems to be a potentially significant predictor of leader error. Studies have shown individuals high in anger to behave indiscriminately punitively towards others (e.g., Goldberg, Lerner, & Tetlock, 1999; Lerner, Goldberg, & Tetlock, 1998). In addition, anger has also been linked to overconfidence about the likelihood of task success (Fischhoff, Gonzalez, Lerner, & Small, 2005; Lerner & Keltner, 2005).

In summary, at a broad level, negative affect seems likely to result in leader errors through the use of restricted information searches. With regard to discrete emotions, anger has emerged as being most likely to have an impact on leader error, particularly with regard to errors in managing people. Leaders who are angry may lash out and alienate subordinates in their workgroup, hampering current and future lines of communication. The impact of anger on other types of error such as planning, moreover, should not be discounted, given anger's association with overconfidence. It should be borne in mind that anger may, ultimately, be useful in that it can send signals of dissatisfaction, enhance subordinate motivation or confer power status (Tiedens, 2001). However, recall that the proposed definition of error includes actions chosen that result in outcomes beyond the leader's original intent—purposefully using anger would not be considered an error. Moreover, although positive outcomes may occur (e.g., enhanced motivation) if they were not intended an error would still have occurred.

Nature of the task. The nature of a task can have a notable impact on a leader's actions. To illustrate, consider a leader evaluating the originality of a given product or process. Typically, the value of a product or process is assessed by comparing it to known commodities, including similar products or processes that have been profitable. With highly original ideas, however, there is an inherent lack of comparison groups and, consequently, nothing to tell a leader whether an idea is truly worth pursuing. Errors in evaluating product originality have been examined in a series of studies by Mumford and colleagues. Licuanan, Dailey, and Mumford (2007) found individuals participating in a leadership task to make more errors in evaluating employees' ideas if the idea was highly original than with less original ideas. Similarly, Blair and Mumford (2007) found individuals to make more errors in making decisions about ideas to pursue in an organizational setting as idea originality and time pressure for a decision increased.

In addition to the novelty of a situation, complexity is also likely to be related to leader errors. Leaders are often confronted by high-complexity, ambiguous, and ill-defined problems (Ackoff, 1974; Mason & Mitroff, 1981; Ungson, Braunstein, & Hall, 1981). In response to such problems, as Dearborn and Simon (1958) observed, leaders will typically choose to attend to the aspects of problems that are most pertinent to them and, in doing so, may employ selective perception. Tetlock (1992) offered a similar explanation of decision making in complex conditions, suggesting that leaders make decisions that are the most easily justified to others. Thus, leaders facing complex problems are unlikely to gather all of the information required to make the most well-informed decision possible and will commit errors in gathering and structuring information.

In summary, the investigation of the antecedents of leader error at the individual level reveals a number of noteworthy trends involving the effects of need for closure, expertise, fatigue, affect, and task characteristics on leader errors, which are presented in propositional format in Table 15.2. In addition to the main effect trends highlighted by Table 15.2, there are likely to be interactions among variables at the individual level. In particular, several variables are likely to produce compounding effects on leader errors. High need for closure, specifically, is more likely to result in interpersonal and task-related errors among fatigued leaders than among non-fatigued leaders. Along similar lines, fatigue may also interact with expertise. For example, fatigue, negative affect, and problem complexity may increase the susceptibility of individuals to sunk-cost effects. However, leaders with greater expertise may function better and be less likely to commit sunk-cost errors under such adverse conditions than those with less expertise. Thus, expertise may counteract the negative effects of some individual difference and task characteristics.

Table 15.2. Summary of Propositions Flowing From Leader-Level Antecedents

Proposition 1	Individual differences that limit or reduce the information gathered and received by the leader (e.g., high need for closure, overconfidence) will result in a greater propensity for leader error.
Proposition 2	Leader fatigue will result in a greater propensity for leader error.
Proposition 3	Leaders engaging in highly complex tasks will commit a greater number of errors.
Proposition 4	Leader errors occurring early in the project may increase the likelihood of errors occurring later in a project (i.e., sunk-cost effects).
Proposition 6	At the macro emotion level, negative emotions will result in a greater number of leader errors.
Proposition 7	At the discrete emotion level, leader anger in particular, will lead to an increased propensity for leader error.
Proposition 8	Expertise will limit the occurrence of errors in contexts the leader is familiar with—however, in novel contexts expertise will lead to an increase in leader errors.
Proposition 9	Fatigue will have a compounding effect on error propensity when paired with individual differences typically associated with error occurrence (e.g., need for closure, overconfidence).
Proposition 10	When leaders are engaged in novel or unfamiliar tasks, fatigue will have a stronger impact on leaders with domain-relevant expertise as they will be more likely to apply inaccurate heuristics resulting in an increased propensity for error.

Group Level

Leaders operate within broader social systems, typically organized around clusters or groups of individuals. Accordingly, the social dynamics occurring within these systems are critical to understanding the types of errors leaders might commit. Our discussion on group level antecedents that are likely to have an impact on leader errors includes: (1) team climate, (2) groupthink, (3) personalized charismatic relationships, and finally (4) group level stress. We begin with a discussion on team climate.

Team climate. As noted previously, for a leader to make informed decisions, he/she must have requisite information at hand (Henningsen, Henningsen, Jakobsen, & Borton, 2004). This requires, minimally, a context or climate where group members are aware of what information they should gather and present to the leader (Pinto & Prescott, 1988). West and colleagues (Anderson & West, 1998; West, 2002) describe the importance of goal clarity, termed "vision" in high-functioning, innovative teams. More directly stated, in order for subordinates to gather the appropriate and correct information requested by the leader, the group must have a clear idea of what they should provide to the leader. West and colleagues also discussed the importance of participative safety in teams. Participative safety is described as a team environment where members feel comfortable sharing original ideas and solutions in a non-judgmental atmosphere (West, 1990; West, 2002). The concept of participative safety suggests that as group members feel comfortable with the leader and other group members, they will be more likely to share important information which would include information about their personal needs, requirements, and fears (e.g., Fiedler, 1964; Hersey & Blanchard, 1969). Consequently, leaders of groups with high participative safety will be better informed about decisions—particularly with regard to managing subordinates. Conversely, a threatening environment characterized by distrust, resentment, judgment, and critical assessment is likely to result in reduced communication and discussion of information, and, thereby, greater frequency of leader errors.

Groupthink. Originally coined by Janis (1972), groupthink refers to the factors that arise during group work that insulate a group and diminish its capacity to make effective decisions. Instead of undergoing a thorough decision-making process, groups that suffer from groupthink make decisions prematurely and without careful consideration of additional and alternative information. Although many have criticized the model on various grounds, such as the extent to which it is empirically testable (e.g., Longley & Pruitt, 1980; Moorhead & Montanari, 1986), some researchers have found at least partial support for the theoretical framework (e.g., Henningsen, Henningson, & Eden, 2006; Park, 2000). Esser (1998) provided a review of empirical research on groupthink and concluded that the greatest contribution of the groupthink model may be its heuristic value and much more work remains to be done on the model. Although providing conclusive commentary on the groupthink model is beyond the scope of this discussion, we agree with Esser in that while the specific elements of groupthink are debatable, the underlying message has value. That is, groups who are excessively cohesive and insulated are likely to influence leader decisions in such a way that they will increase the likelihood of errors in using information as well as managing tasks and things.

Personalized charismatic relationships. A phenomenon related to groupthink is the formation of unquestioning, unchallenging relationships with a leader. Howell and Shamir (2005) proposed a follower-based model of leadership, hypothesizing that followers may form either socialized or personalized charismatic relationships with leaders. Personalized charismatic relationships exist when subordinates have low self-concept clarity and high relational identity or, put another way, are largely defined by their relationships to individuals in positions of influence and power. Groups of subordinates characterized by personalized relationships with their leaders are unlikely to question or challenge the leaders. Without some form of accountability, a leader may be susceptible to the individual-level biases noted earlier (e.g., fundamental attribution bias). Thus, we would expect leaders to make errors related to using information as well as managing tasks and things in groups characterized by personalized charismatic relationships.

Group Stress. Leaders are not the only ones affected by stress. Groups too can experience a sense of shared stress (Driskell & Salas, 1991). Staw, Sandelands, and Dutton (1981) claimed that under conditions of stress or crisis, decision making becomes more centralized. Termed the centralization-of-authority hypothesis, researchers contend that under conditions of stress, subordinates defer to a leader more often and that leaders become less likely to seek input from subordinates. Although supported by some research (e.g., Helmreich, 1979), others have challenged this hypothesis based on conflicting evidence (Lanzetta, 1955; Torrance, 1967). Thus, Driskell and Salas (1991) offered a revised version of the model suggesting that although subordinates may defer to a leader in stressful conditions, the receptiveness of leaders to subordinates' input may not change under such conditions. With regard to leader errors, although the receptiveness of leaders to others' input may not vary by group stress, the information that leaders receive may be less in volume and quality in stressful situations, a factor that should lead to greater error frequency.

In summary, group level factors appear to have notable influences on leader error, particularly errors in gathering and structuring information. Given the review of group level factors, it seems safe to conclude that groups whose members lack clarity regarding their assignments and duties, are overly cohesive, simultaneously experience high levels of stress, and lack a system of checks and balances are likely to gather more irrelevant information and suppress relevant information. Thus, leaders may miss opportunities for making effective decisions or continue to make mistakes. Regardless of the outcomes of group-level variables, the review of these variables emphasizes the critical role that subordinates play in reducing the frequency of leader errors.

Organization Level

Leaders and groups operate in a broader context; the organization. Thus, in turning to the organization level, it is clear that a number of structural and bureaucratic factors likely influence the errors leaders make. In addition, there are a number of organizational level variables that are more socially-based, such as culture, that have been shown to have a significant influence on leader error. We begin with a consideration of the structural elements followed by discussions on error management culture, and organizational time pressure.

Table 15.3. Summary of Propositions Flowing From Group-Level Antecedents

Proposition 1	Groups that lack structure and direction are more likely to provide the leader with unnecessary information resulting in increased decision-making complexity and ultimately, a greater propensity for leader error.
Proposition 2	Groups that lack participative safety (climate) will be less willing to share information as well as challenge/question decisions put forth by the leader resulting in a greater propensity for leader error.
Proposition 3	Excessive cohesion, groupthink, or personalized charismatic relationships will decrease the information provided to the leader as well as the questioning of leader decision making resulting an increased propensity for leader error.
Proposition 4	Excessive cohesion, groupthink, or personalized charismatic relationships will result in group insularity and a reduction of external influence thereby increasing the potential for leader error.
Proposition 5	Excessive cohesion, groupthink, or personalized charismatic relationships will have a compounding effect under conditions of group stress, resulting in a self-affirming cycle of decision making and ultimately a greater propensity for leader error.

Communication and organization structure. Error avoidance is dependent on having adequate information at hand to formulate appropriate decisions (Henningsen et al., 2004). At the organization level, this involves communicating requisite and relevant knowledge to decision makers. Unfortunately, some aspects of organizational structure can hinder effective communication. For example, Jablin (1982) found subordinates to perceive lower levels of open communication with their supervisors as organizational size increases, possibly because leaders have to communicate with more individuals as size increases, thereby reducing the personalized nature of communication. Reliance on electronic forms of communication likely exacerbates this trend (Pickering & King, 1995). Research has shown a negative relationship between distance between individuals and measures of communication quality, such as information sharing (e.g., Van den Bulte & Moenart, 1998). Dispersion of organizational members makes it difficult for leaders to both obtain the information necessary to make effective decisions but also to coordinate efforts once decisions have been made (Cummings, 2008), a point illustrated by Warkentin and Beranek's (1999) study of collocated and virtual teams. The authors found a significantly greater number of difficulties in project management (e.g., keeping on schedule, staying on budget) in virtual teams than in collocated teams.

Error management culture. At times, the question is not whether errors will occur but rather how to manage them once they do occur. A number of researchers have proposed that how an organization views and responds to error can have a substantial impact on organizational performance. Edmondson (1996), for example, found that teams with members who feel more comfortable sharing their errors are more likely to learn from those errors and to perform better than teams without such a climate. Extending this observation to the organizational level, van Dyck, Frese, Baer, and Sonnentag (2005) suggested that an organizational culture that facilitates communication about errors, sharing of error knowledge, helping in situations characterized by error, engagement in quick error detection, and careful analysis of errors leads higher levels of organizational goal achievement, survivability and return on assets. In support of this claim, in a sample of German and Dutch organizations, the researchers found error management culture to account for a sizable amount of variance in firm performance above and beyond that accounted for by prior firm performance. Thus, it appears that organizations that manage errors effectively are likely to see improvements in performance. With respect to leader errors, then, we propose that leaders in organizations characterized by an effective error management culture are more likely to learn from prior mistakes, thereby reducing the negative impact of errors as well as the occurrence of future errors.

Time pressure. Given that leaders must consistently make decisions in time-pressed conditions, it is not surprising that a substantial amount of literature has been dedicated to the topic. A seminal investigation of time-pressure on decision making was conducted by Wright (1974) who presented participants with five attributions about 30 cars and asked them to make judgments about the likelihood of buying each car after graduation. Participants were placed in one of three conditions of time pressure. The results of the study revealed that participants in the high time pressure condition focused more on negative attributes when making decisions about the cars, as Wright theorized, in an attempt to avoid making a mistake. Edland and Svenson (1993) reviewed Wright's and subsequent studies on time pressure and decision making and concluded that under conditions of time pressure, individuals become more selective in their information searches, focus on more negative attributes when making decisions, make more errors (i.e., decreased decision accuracy), and may get locked into decisions and fail to consider viable alternatives. Edland and Svenson also discussed conflicting evidence regarding the relationships between time pressure and risk-taking behavior, though findings generally suggest a negative relationship. For example, Ben Zur and Breznitz (1981) found that under conditions of high time pressure, people tend to make less risky decisions. This finding suggests that, regarding creativity in particular, time pressure may limit the exploration of alternative, original solutions to organizational problems and in turn, reduce organizational creativity.

Not only might time pressure impact errors made in decision making, specifically resource allocation, it appears that time pressure might also impact interpersonal errors or errors in managing people. For example, De Dreu (2003) examined time pressure and negotiations in two experimental studies. In the first study, De Dreu found that participants in the high time pressure condition used more stereotyping and heuristic judgments when interacting with a confederate negotiator. In study two, participants were paired with another same-sex participant and asked to engage in a negotiation task. Results indicated that under conditions of high time pressure, participants used less persuasive arguments, offered fewer joint outcomes, and were less likely to revise their initial decisions. In sum, it appears that high time pressure is likely to result in truncated information gathering efforts and in turn, increased errors in allocating resources and managing work tasks. Moreover, organizations characterized by high time pressure are likely to motivate leaders to avoid risky behavior and may, in turn, limit organizational innovation. Finally, time-pressure may also lead to interpersonal errors with subordinates or other organizational stakeholders, particularly in negotiation situations where both sides are attempting to arrive at an effective solution.

In sum, organizational factors can affect leader errors in a number of ways (Table 15.4). First, organizational structure can have notable influence on the amount and nature of information received by a leader, thereby reducing their capacity to make informed decisions. Similarly, organizational environments characterized by high time pressure are also likely to limit the amount of information as well as the processing time required for high-level problem solving. These factors reiterate the general conclusion that errors are simply an element of leadership life. Fortunately, some of the recent work on error management culture suggests that even when errors occur, a work environment that allows for learning and innovation may help leaders cope with the complex and demanding nature of their tasks.

Multilevel Effects

Having considered the main effects and intralevel interactions occurring within each level of analysis, we turn now to a more direct consideration of cross-level influences that may have noteworthy impacts on leader errors. This consideration reveals three general types of cross-level effects: (1) leader/group, (2) leader/organization and (3) group/organization. These interactions are presented in propositional format in Table 15.5. We begin our discussion with individual and group-level interactions.

As noted in our discussion of leader-level antecedents, there are several dispositional variables that may increase the likelihood of errors, variables that often limit or truncate the amount and types information considered by a leader (e.g., need for closure, overconfidence). When these leader dispositions are paired with phenomena at the group-level, such as groupthink (Janis, 1972), a leader may be left with even less relevant information with which to make decisions. In our discussion, we also noted the role of group-stress in decision making. Specifically, it seems that

Table 15.4. Summary of Propositions Flowing From Organization Level Antecedents

Proposition 1	Dispersed communication configuration (e.g., virtual teams) will negatively impact the structure and organization of information presented to the leader, resulting in an increased propensity for leader errors.
Proposition 2	Organizations with strong error management culture will reduce the number and negative impact of errors committed by the leader.
Proposition 3	Organizations characterized by high time-pressure will increase the likelihood of errors committed by the leader.

Table 15.5. Cross-Level Effects Emerging From Multilevel Consideration of Leader Error Antecedents

Proposition 1	Leader dispositions that limit the information received by the leader (e.g., need for closure) will have stronger effects on leader error when paired with group level phenomena such as groupthink.
Proposition 2	Leaders who consistently engage in rushed decision making will be serve as role-models for subordinates creating a culture that is permissive such behavior and as a result, lead to an increased propensity leader error.
Proposition 3	Leaders who frequently commit errors in managing people will create a group culture that is opposed to sharing information with the leader, resulting in increased an increased propensity for leader error.
Proposition 4	When groups under stress defer to the leader, checks and balances on decision making may be reduced resulting in a greater opportunity for errors—opportunities that may be tempered by leadership that accurately structures and manages the gathering of appropriate information.
Proposition 5	Groups who are passionate about their task may compensate when a leader commits and error by putting forth greater effort resulting in increased performance for the group.
Proposition 6	For leaders with domain expertise engaging in new or novel tasks, time-pressure at the organizational level will result in an increased propensity for error.
Proposition 7	Time-pressure at the organizational level will result in increased stress and fatigue for the leader, increasing the likelihood for leader error.
Proposition 8	Leaders working on complex tasks are more likely to commit errors in organizations characterized by dispersed communication structures (e.g., virtual communication).
Proposition 9	Organizations characterized by high time-pressure will make it difficult for leaders to provide structure and feedback to subordinates resulting in high levels of superfluous information being presented to the leader and ultimately reductions in the quality of decision making (i.e., an increase in error).
Proposition 10	Groups characterized by excessive cohesion will make it difficult to develop a culture that learns from previous errors or take advantage of serendipitous outcomes emerging from error.

groups will forgo their own views and defer to the leader under times of stress. Thus, due to decreased checks and balances in such situations, errors may increase for that leader. This increase may be nullified, however, if the leader is able to adequately gather, structure, and manage appropriate information. That is, deferring to a leader is not necessarily a bad thing as long as the leader does not become isolated. Finally, we have noted that leaders who lack skill in reading, regulating, and managing emotions may be prone to errors in managing people. Going further, these types of social errors are likely to alienate subordinates and may create a culture of opposition. These effects may prove particularly problematic to leaders if, within the group, subordinates share information about their own dyadic leader/subordinate interactions resulting in the emergence of normative (i.e., group-level) culture or climate phenomena.

Before moving on, it should be noted that some group-level phenomena may actually result in increased performance after the occurrence of a leader error. Specifically, groups that are passionate about the work they do may work even harder to compensate for an error. Termed "social compensation" (Karau & Williams, 1997; Williams & Karau, 1991), this effect has been observed in cases in which employees "pick up the slack" for co-workers who they believe to have low ability. Thus, in a leadership setting, it seems reasonable to suggest that if a leader commits an error, team members may actually increase their effort to make up for that error, but only if they truly care about their work.

Supplementing the group/leader-level interactions, it appears organizational antecedents may also interact with leader-level influences. For example, although expertise is often viewed as a means of reducing error, our review suggests that new or novel contexts may produce a positive relationship between expertise and error. Moreover, organizational variables such as time-pressure may compound those effects such that experts placed in novel, time-pressured organizational contexts may be more likely to commit errors relative to novices or near-novices. Experts operating in contexts familiar to them, however, are much more likely to adequately manage time pressure via their use of more efficient mental models are less likely to commit errors as a result. Along similar lines, as organizational contexts become more time-pressured, stress and fatigue are likely to emerge as by-products. Fatigue is likely to increase the emergence of cognitive biases (e.g., attribution errors, base-rate fallacy) as leaders have fewer cognitive resources to dedicate toward careful analysis. Finally, it appears that leaders working on highly complex leadership tasks within a dispersed organizational environment (e.g., virtual teams; flex-time) or with very large groups are likely to have greater difficulty than those leaders operating on less complex leadership tasks. More specifically, within dispersed environments or very large groups, sharing information and building relationships may prove particularly difficult and for complex tasks, errors are likely to increase.

Finally, there are likely to be a number of cross-level effects occurring between group-level and organization-level factors that are relevant to our discussion. First, organizations characterized by high levels of time-pressure may make it particularly difficult for leaders to provide structure, feedback, and guidance to subordinates. As a result, groups may present the leader with unnecessary and superfluous information hampering the leader's capacity to make informed decisions. Along similar lines, groups characterized by social phenomena such as excessive cohesion may make it uniquely challenging to develop an organizational culture that successfully manages error due to group insularity and a lack of willingness to share lessons about previous mistakes or failures.

In summary, the above discussion on cross-level effects reveals that leader errors are not only caused by antecedents at various levels of analysis but that these antecedents may also interact with each other in ways that are likely to exacerbate or reduce the occurrence and reoccurrence of leader error. More specifically, the above review of cross-level effects highlights the importance of realizing that errors committed by the leader are not isolated, single-level events. For example, leaders who make interpersonal errors with one subordinate may also, via normative structures, have an impact on group culture resulting in an even greater propensity for future errors. Moreover, organizational antecedents may also interact with leader antecedents, making some aspects of leadership, such as expertise, beneficial to error reduction in some contexts but a potential cause of errors in other contexts. Finally, it should be noted that group and organizational antecedents are not independent of each other and may produce unique cross-level effects as well. For example, although some organizational phenomena such as a culture of error management are desirable for error reduction, the development of such a culture may prove particularly difficult in the presence of some group-level phenomena (e.g., lack of a participative safety culture, groupthink).

DISCUSSION

The present discussion of leader errors reveals several broad trends that contribute to our understanding of error. First, our review suggests that leader errors are the result of multilevel influences. Stated more directly, variables operating at individual, group, and organizational levels contribute substantially to error occurrence. Moreover, the research investigating these variables suggests that these multilevel antecedents are likely to interact with each other to impact the commission of errors. Second, it is clear that error antecedents are characterized by a *complex* pattern of relationships. The extent to which error antecedents derive from and interact across multiple sources and levels highlights the difficulty of avoiding making errors. As mentioned in the introduction to this chapter, people in leadership positions often have to make difficult decisions. Given the difficulty of controlling for all of the causes of errors, the frequency of errors may not be surprising.

Third, the present effort highlights the criticality of considering unique error types in the investigation of leader error. Our review suggested that some antecedents may evidence their impact on specific types of errors and not on errors more globally. An advantage of using the Fleishman et al. (1991) framework is that it allows for the identification of unique types of errors, which, in turn, makes proposing unique antecedent-error relationships possible. Thus, the review shows that (a) unique types of errors exist and (b) the error types may have unique relationships with antecedents.

A final contribution of the present effort is the recognition that leader errors and their causes are best viewed as a dynamic sequence of events. The leadership behavior framework used in the present effort (Fleishman et al., 1991) was chosen precisely for this reason and is helpful in illustrating these interdependent relationships. For example, errors in gathering information are likely to result in errors in developing plans and allocating resources. Further, as subordinates become frustrated from poor assignments or lack of resources, they may reduce their interactions with the leader thereby limiting the information derived from subordinates. This cycle of errors, however, does not have to occur and can be altered through things like social compensation. That is, subordinates who witness the mistakes of a leader may work harder to compensate for that leader and the group may ultimately perform better than (or at least equivalent to) what its performance prior to the error. In short, though errors are interdependent, the commission of one's errors does not always result in a downward spiral of mistakes.

Conclusions Regarding Error Antecedents

Turning now to the antecedent variables specifically, we note several key themes. The first is the role of time in leader errors. Specifically, as timeframes become truncated, due to either pressure from the organization or from a leader him or herself (e.g., as a result of high need for closure), leaders are likely to seek less information. The tendency to seek less information is likely to result in errors in gathering information and, in turn, errors in decision-making and resource allocation. As noted earlier, due to the interdependence of errors, mistakes in one area are likely to have a notable impact on other areas of leadership functioning.

A second theme among antecedents may best be labeled as "locked modes of thinking" on the part of leaders. As leaders become stressed, fatigued, or experience a high degree of negative affect they turn to what they know best and will both abbreviate information searches as well as reduce the number of concepts used when generating solutions and making decisions. Moreover, it seems reasonable to suggest that leaders will be more susceptible to cognitive biases such as attribution bias or base-rate bias under these conditions. This trend is exacerbated when group members become so cohesive that they guard themselves from external sources of information (Howell & Shamir, 2005). The result of this causal amalgamation is filtered, confirmatory information presented to a leader, which perpetuates the error cycle.

A third set of observations emerging from the review of error antecedents is related to leader experience and expertise. Although expertise is typically viewed as a desirable quality in leaders, it appears to present a unique and interesting pattern of results with regard to leader errors. Expertise can help to filter and organize the potentially overwhelming array of information presented to leaders that operate in complex, high-pressure, turbulent environments. Along with expertise, however, comes the tendency for experts to shape and view a problem in such a way as to make it consistent with their personal mental models (Doerner & Schaub, 1990; Hogarth & Makridakis, 1981). Novel problems or situations may present challenges to leaders with high levels of expertise (Mumford, Blair, Dailey, Leritz, & Osborn, 2006) if the problems cannot be solved by decisions that have worked for leaders in the past. Thus, in some situations, leaders with high expertise may have a tendency to try to "fit a square peg in a round hole" and may be more likely to commit errors than leaders with less expertise.

The antecedent themes discussed above speak to a fourth trend emerging from the present effort: the role of the subordinate in preventing the occurrence and limiting the negative impact of leader errors. Recent research has highlighted the reciprocal impact of subordinates' actions on leaders' performance (e.g., Howell & Shamir, 2005; Yukl & Van Fleet, 1992). Subordinates seem to play a large role in helping leaders to avoid errors by actions such as relaying important information to leaders of which the leaders were previously unaware. Leaders who understand the importance of their subordinates are likely to create a work environment that welcomes input and information exchange, provide subordinates with enough structure that they know what information to gather, and listen to subordinate input. A histriometric review of leader errors by Bedell-Avers et al. (2008) showed errors in managing people to have a greater negative impact on leader performance than other types of errors, such as in planning and problem solving. Thus, it appears that leaders should pay special attention to fostering effective working relationships with others, a task substantially easier in an organizational culture that supports the communication and management of error (Edmondson, 1996; van Dyck, Frese, Baer, & Sonnentag, 2005).

Finally, the review of error antecedents highlights the reality that errors are an unavoidable part of leadership. The best way to minimize the impact of errors may be to focus on avoiding mistakes that will cripple a system as a whole rather than to attempt to avoid making any error. Attempts at the latter may not only prove to be impossible, but there is evidence that subordinates are likely to perceive behaviors such as trying to please everyone, which a leader may attempt to do in order to prevent making errors in managing people, negatively (Tate & Jacobs, 2009). The challenge, then, for leaders is to understand which errors are simply unavoidable by-products of organizational life, and which may be disastrous to the system.

Theoretical Implications

The first stage in formal theory development is the identification of key variables (Fleishman & Quaintance, 1984) and it is our hope that the present effort is an important step in this direction. Through our efforts we feel that the groundwork is laid to explore emerging trends and develop expanded theoretical frameworks on the study of error.

The analysis of errors, specifically, also contributes to future theory development by expanding our conceptualization of what researchers view as key or critical leadership actions. That is, by considering "darker" leader behaviors such as errors we can move towards a more *comprehensive* view of leadership. Although we know a great deal about the positive aspects of leadership, the "heroic leadership bias" (Yukl, 1999) has left us in many ways with an incomplete perspective of leadership. Thus, by expanding our framework to include more negative behaviors such as error we can make substantive and incremental gains in our knowledge of leadership.

Practical Implications

From a more practical standpoint, this review provides some insight into what leaders might do to avoid committing serious errors. The first recommendation is that leaders should be aware of the impact that affect, fatigue, and stress can have on decision making; the reduction of each is likely to limit errors committed by leaders. Further, being aware of one's dispositional propensity for error might also help limit the negative impacts of error. Leaders informed that they are high in the trait *need for closure*, for example, may make a more conscious effort to extend information searches when making key decisions. Similar advice may hold true for being aware of likely cognitive biases and their impact on error.

As suggested throughout the chapter, we propose that a key factor in reducing leader error is the subordinate. Leaders often keep a close cadre of subordinates or key lieutenants with whom they seek personal council (Mumford et al., 2006). In addition to serving as sources for information gathering, these subordinates also provide guidance on using that information during the decision-making process. Thus, these subordinates, in particular, may play vital roles in limiting errors associated with more stable trait-like individual differences as well as cognitive biases—antecedents that are inherently difficult to alter and change. Key lieutenants can also facilitate errors, however, through mechanisms such as groupthink or their own dispositions, emotional states, and cognitive biases. Thus, it appears essential that leaders surround themselves with multiple individuals they can trust to provide honest input and with whom they have an effective working relationship.

In addition, it seems to be particularly beneficial for a leader to help develop a strong culture of error management, that is, a working environment that allows individuals to learn from errors as well as to turn mistakes into opportunities for innovation. Such a culture would help offset the challenges faced by working in environments that might increase the propensity for error. Thus, we recommend that organizational leaders aid in the facilitation of an environment where risk is acceptable and learning is viewed as an essential part of organizational functioning.

Finally, along these lines leaders must make conscious efforts to prioritize which errors threaten system and organizational viability and which are better viewed as a byproduct of acceptable risk. The capacity to recognize how errors impact the broader system highlights the importance of forecasting and planning skills (Mumford, Bedell, & Hunter, 2008) as well as developing effective interpersonal relationships with subordinates that encourage the exchange of positive and negative information. Moreover, this observation also speaks to the importance of active engagement in error management. Leaders must realize that errors are a part of their roles and must attempt to explicitly manage errors (Helmreich, 2000; Reason, 1990). Managing errors means dissecting mistakes to learn their causes and outcomes and taking steps to repair damaged relationships with subordinates or other organizational stakeholders (Giessner & van Knippenberg, 2008; Kim, Ferrin, Cooper, & Dirks, 2004).

In sum, the present effort suggests that leaders can limit the occurrence and impact of error via the following recommendations: (1) be cognizant of personal dispositions that might influence propensity toward error, (2) get enough rest and do not discount the importance of physical health on decision making, (3) surround oneself with competent subordinates that are willing to discuss and challenge ideas, (4) be open to feedback from subordinates and be willing to listen to dissent, (5) if errors occur, actively engage in an analysis of the causes without placing unnecessary or harmful blame, (6) repair relationships if they have been damaged by an error to ensure those lines of communication remain open in the future, (7) role-model appropriate responses to errors to help establish a broader culture that learns from and capitalizes on opportunities emerging from error and (8) focus on taking calculated risks and sound decision making rather than seeking to avoid the ultimately unavoidable errors that are simply a part of leadership.

Leader Errors in Future Research

Regarding methodological choices for the study of errors, it appears critical to apply a balanced and varied approach. Although this is generally true for the study of most psychological and social phenomena, the study of leadership—negative leadership in particular—has been hampered by an overemphasis on homogeneous methodology (Hunter et al., 2007). Moreover, given the complexity associated with leader errors, a combination of methods, including qualitative, quantitative, laboratory, and field studies will be necessary to fully understand both why they occur as well as the short and long-term consequences of their committal. For example, because the nature of errors are often tied to the context in which they occur, qualitative studies can provide insight into the processes and outcomes of errors from the perspectives of leaders, subordinates, and, if relevant, actors outside of the organization and stakeholders. Laboratory studies, however, should be useful for isolating the specific antecedents and outcomes of leader errors. Finally, longitudinal studies are likely to greatly contribute to our understanding of leader errors by speaking to the extent to which different types of errors are interdependent and likely to be repeated over time.

Turning to specific avenues for future research, we will now discuss topics related to the outcomes of errors. One potentially interesting topic in particularly is that of how to recover from or manage the consequences of errors. The ability to successfully do so can help to successfully mitigate the potentially negative outcomes of errors. Existing research suggests that recovery depends on the type of error (Kim, Ferrin, Cooper, & Dirks, 2004), a leader's previous history with errors (Maxham & Netemeyer, 2002), context (Hunt, Boal, & Dodge, 1999), and whether the outcome of an error was positive or negative (Cushenbery, Thoroughgood, & Hunter, 2009). Because of the difficulty of avoiding errors, as we have already discussed, an equally important tactic may be effectively controlling the consequences of errors. Thus, we believe that knowing how to respond to errors should be of notable utility to people in leadership positions.

Limitations

Although the present effort makes a number of important contributions to the study of leader errors, there are a number of limitations that should be borne in mind. First, although we made a strong attempt to examine the most critical leader error antecedents, our list of error antecedents is by no means exhaustive. We felt that such a list would have been unwieldy, limiting the practical impact of the manuscript (Klein, Tosi, & Cannella, 1999; Yammarino & Dansereau, 2009). As such, some variables were necessarily omitted from discussion including several personality variables that, although discussed in qualitative analyses of leader errors (e.g., Finkelstein, 2003), have not been fully researched in quantitative fashion. They stand as notable exclusions from the present effort and certainly warrant investigation in future endeavors.

Second, it must be noted that Fleishman et al.'s (1991) taxonomy emphasizes a problem solving approach to leader behavior. Although we believe the framework is well suited for the present discussion of leader errors, it is certainly possible that other behavior models would yield a slightly different collection of error antecedents. Thus, some caution is warranted when applying the findings of this effort to all forms of leadership.

Third, the use of a multilevel framework is largely heuristic, as many constructs (e.g., climate, nature of leadership task) operate at multiple levels of analysis—the decision to discuss them at any given level was based largely on where they have been most prominently investigated. These choices for discussion, however, should not be taken to suggest that their effects at other levels of analysis are unimportant. Finally, a nontrivial portion of the research reviewed employed survey based methodology and as such, some degree of caution is warranted when interpreting the causality of the purported error antecedents.

Summary

In summary, we believe the present effort makes a number of unique contributions to the understanding of leader error. By offering a definition, taxonomy, and exploring the core antecedents of leader error, we believe a more complete picture of why leaders commit errors is gained. It is also clear from this effort that leaders make mistakes for a variety of complex reasons, reasons that are driven by individual, group, and organization factors. Finally, we have offered some general advice for leaders seeking to reduce the negative impact of error. It is our hope that this review serves as the impetus for future empirical and theoretical work on a topic in strong need of research exploration.

ACKNOWLEDGEMENTS

We would like to thank Katrina Bedell-Avers, Christian Thoroughgood, and Joshua Fairchild for their contributions to the present effort. We would also like to thank Michelle Bligh and Dirk Lidenbaum for their helpful suggestions on earlier drafts of this manuscript. Substantial portions of this chapter are based on the original work by Hunter, Tate, Dzieweczynski, and Bedell-Avers titled "Leaders Make Mistakes: A Multilevel Consideration of Why" published in *The Leadership Quarterly.*

REFERENCES

Ackoff, R. L. (1974). *Redesigning the future*. New York: Wiley.

Anderson, N., & West, M. A. (1998). Measuring climate for work group innovation: Development and validation of the team climate inventory. *Journal of Organizational Behavior, 19*, 235-258.

Ashforth, B. E. (1987, August). *Organizations and the petty tyrant: An exploratory study.* Paper presented at the annual meeting of the Academy of Management, New Orleans, Louisiana.

Ashforth, B. (1994). Petty tyranny in organizations. *Human Relations, 47*, 755-778.

Baker, K., Olson, J., & Morisseau, D. (1994). Work practices, fatigue, and nuclear power plant safety performance. *Human Factors, 36*, 244-257.

Bar-Hillel, M. (1980). The base-rate fallacy in probability judgments. *Acta Psychologica, 44*, 211-233.

Bar-Joseph, U., & Kruglanski, A. W. (2003). Intelligence failure and need for cognitive closure: On the psychology of the Yom Kippur surprise. *Political Psychology, 24*, 75-99.

Barsade, S., & Gibson, D. (2007). Why does affect matter in organizations? *Academy of Management Perspectives, 21*, 26-59.

Bedell-Avers, K. E., (2008). *Leader errors: An examination of the implications.* Doctoral dissertation, University of Oklahoma. (Dissertation Abstracts International, AAT 3307950).

Ben Zur, H., & Breznitz, S. J. (1981). The effect of time pressure on risky choice behavior. *Acta Psychologica, 47*, 89-104.

Blair, C. S., & Mumford, M. D. (2007). Errors in idea evaluation: Preference for the unoriginal? *Journal of Creative Behavior, 41*, 196-222.

Burke, S., Sims, D., Lazzara, E., & Salas, E. (2007). Trust in leadership: A multilevel review and integration. *Leadership Quarterly, 18*, 606-632.

Cummings, J. (2008). Leading groups from a distance: How to mitigate consequences of geographic dispersion. In S. Weisband (Ed.), *Leadership at a dis-*

tance: Research in technologically-supported work (pp. 33-50). Mahwah, NJ: Erlbaum.

Cushenbery, L., Thoroughgood, C., & Hunter, S. T. (2009, April). *Impact of leader error on subordinate trust: An experimental investigation.* Paper presented at the Society for Industrial/Organizational Psychology Conference, New Orleans, LA.

Dailey, L. & Mumford, M. D. (2006). Evaluative aspects of creative thought: Errors in appraising the implications of new ideas. *Creativity Research Journal, 18,* 385-390.

De Dreu, C. K. W. (2003). Time pressure and closing of the mind in negotiation. *Organizational Behavior and Human Decision Processes, 91,* 280-295.

Dearborn, D. & Simon, H. (1958). Selective perception: A note on the departmental identifications of executives. *Sociometry, 21,* 140-144.

DeVries, D. L., & Kaiser, R. B. (2003). Going sour in the suite. In S. Steckler, D. Sethi, & R. K. Prescot (coordinators), *Maximizing executive effectiveness.* Workshop presented by the Human Resources Planning Society, Miami, FL.

Doerner, D., & Schaub, H. (1990). Errors in planning and decision making and the nature of human information processing. *Applied Psychology: An International Review, 43,* 433-453.

Dormann, T., & Frese, M. (1994). Error training: Replication and the function of exploratory behavior. *International Journal of Human-Computer Interaction, 6,* 365-372.

Driskell, J. E., & Salas, E. (1991). Group decision-making under stress. *Journal of Applied Psychology, 76,* 473-478.

Duffy, M. K., Ganster, D., & Pagon, M. (2002). Social undermining in the workplace. *Academy of Management Journal, 45,* 331-351.

Edland, A., & Svenson, O. (1993). Judgment and decision making under time pressure. In O. Svenson & J. Maule (Eds.), *Time pressure and stress in human judgment and decision making* (pp. 27-40), New York: Plenum.

Edmondson, A. C. (1996). Learning from mistakes is easier said than done: Group and organizational influences on the detection and correction of human error. *Journal of Applied Behavioral Science, 32,* 5-28.

Einarsen, S., Aasland, M. S., & Skogstad, A. (2007). Destructive leadership behaviour: A definition and conceptual model. *Leadership Quarterly, 18,* 207-216.

Ericsson, K. A., & Lehmann, A. C. (1996). Expert and exceptional performance: Evidence of maximal adaptation to task constraints. *Annual Review of Psychology, 47,* 273-305.

Ericsson, K. A., Krampe, R. T., & Tesch-Römer, C. (1993). The role of deliberate practice in the acquisition of expert performance. *Psychological Review, 100,* 363-406.

Esser, J. K. (1998). Alive and well after 25 years: A review of groupthink research. *Organizational Behavior & Human Decision Processes, 73,* 116-141.

Estrada, C. A., Isen, A. M. & Young, M. J. (1997). Positive affect facilitates integration of information and decreases anchoring in reasoning among physicians. *Organizational Behavior and Human Decision Processes, 72,* 117-135.

Fiedler, F. E. (1964). A contingency model of leadership effectiveness. In L. Berkowitz (Ed.), *Advances in experimental social psychology* (Vol. 1, pp. 149-190). New York: Academic Press.

Finkelstein, S. (2003). *Why smart executives fail and what you can learn from their mistakes*. New York: Portfolio.

Fischhoff, B., Gonzalez, R. M., Lerner, J. S., & Small, D. A. (2005). Evolving judgments of terror risks: foresight, hindsight, and emotion. *Journal of Experimental Psychology: Applied, 11*, 124-139.

Fleishman, E. A., Mumford, M., Zaccaro, S. J., Levin, K., Korotkin, A. L., & Hein, M. B. (1991). Taxonomic efforts in the description of leader behavior: A synthesis and functional interpretation. *Leadership Quarterly, 2*, 245-287.

Fleishman, E. A. & Quaintance, M. K. (1984). *Taxonomies of human performance: The description of human tasks*. San Diego, CA: Academic Press.

Fry, A. (1987). The Post-it-Note: An intrapreneurial success. *SAM Advanced Management Journal, 3*, 4-9.

Gander, P. H., Merry, A., Miller, M. M., & Weller, J. (2000). Hours of work and fatigue-related error: A survey of New Zealand Anesthetists. *Anaesth Intensive Care, 28*, 178-183.

Giessner, S. R. & van Knippenberg, D. (2008). "License to Fail": Goal definition, leader group prototypicality, and perceptions of leadership effectiveness after leader failure. *Organizational Behavior and Human Decision Processes, 105*, 14-35.

Goldberg, J. H., Lerner, J. S., & Tetlock, P. E. (1999). Rage and reason: the psychology of the intuitive prosecutor. *European Journal of Social Psychology, 57*, 781-795.

Helmreich, R. (1979). Big brother ... or Ferdinand the bull? *PsycCRITIQUES, 24*, 410-411.

Helmreich, R. L. (2000). On error management: lessons from aviation. *Quality & Safety in Health Care, 320*, 781-795.

Henningsen, D. D., Henningsen M. L. M. & Eden, J. (2006). Examining the symptoms of groupthink and retrospective sensemaking. *Small Group Research, 37*, 36-64.

Henningsen, D. D., Henningsen, M. L. M., Jakobsen, L. & Borton, I. (2004). It's good to be leader: The influence of randomly and systematically selected leaders on decision-making groups. *Group Dynamics: Theory, Research and Practice, 8*, 62-76.

Hersey, P., & Blanchard, K. (1969). *Management in organizational behavior: Utilizing human resources*. Englewood Cliffs, NJ: Prentice Hall.

Hitt, M. A., Beamish, P. W., Jackson, S. E., & Mathieu, J. E. (2008). Building theoretical and empirical bridges across levels. *Academy of Management Journal, 50*, 1385-1399.

Hogan, R. & Kaiser, R. B. (2005). What we know about leadership. *Review of General Psychology, 9*, 169-180.

Hogarth, R. M., & Makridakis, S. (1981). Forecasting and planning: An evaluation. *Management Science, 27*, 115-138.

House, R. J. & Howell, J. M. (1992). Personality and charismatic leadership. *Leadership Quarterly, 3*, 81-108.

Howell, J. M. & Shamir, B. (2005). The role of followers in the charismatic leadership process: Relationships and their consequences. *Academy of Management Review, 30,* 96-112.

Hunt, J. G., Boal, K. B., & Dodge, G. E. (1999). The effects of visionary and crisis-responsive charisma on followers: An experimental examination of two kinds of charismatic leadership. *Leadership Quarterly, 10,* 423-448.

Hunter, S., Bedell-Avers, K. & Mumford, M. (2007). The typical leadership study: Assumptions, implications, and potential remedies. *Leadership Quarterly, 18,* 435-446.

Isen, A. M. (2001). An influence of positive affect on decision making in complex situations: Theoretical issues with practical implications. *Journal of Consumer Psychology, 11,* 75-86.

Isen, A. M., & Labroo, A. A. (2003). Some ways in which positive affect facilitates decision making and judgment. In S. L. Schneider & J. Shantrau (Eds.), *Emerging perspectives on judgment and decision research* (pp. 365-393). New York: Cambridge University Press.

Jablin, F. M. (1982). Formal structural characteristics of organizations and superior-subordinate communication. *Human Communication Research, 8,* 338-347.

Janis, I. (1972). *Groupthink.* New York: Houghton Mifflin.

Jha, A. K., Duncan, B. W., & Bates, D. W (2001). Fatigue, sleepiness, and medical errors. In Shojania K. G., Duncan B. W., McDonald K. M., & Wachter R. M. (Eds.), *Making healthcare safer: A critical analysis of patient safety practices* (pp. 523-537). Rockville, MD: Agency for Healthcare Research and Quality Evidence Report.

Jones, E. (1979). The rocky road from acts to dispositions. *American Psychology, 34,* 107-117.

Kaufmann, G., & Vosburg, S. K. (1997). "Paradoxical" mood effects on creative problem-solving. *Cognition and Emotion, 11,* 151-170.

Karau, S. J., & Williams, K. D. (1997). The effects of group cohesiveness on social loafing and social compensation. *Group Dynamics: Theory, Research, and Practice, 1,* 156-168.

Kellerman, B. (2004). *Bad leadership: What it is, how it happens, why it matters.* Boston: Harvard Business School Press.

Kilburg, R. (2006). *Executive wisdom: Coaching and the emergence of virtuous leaders.* Washington, DC: American Psychological Association.

Kim, P. H., Ferrin, D. L., Cooper, C. D., & Dirks, K. T. (2004). Removing the shadow of suspicion: The effects of apology versus denial for repairing ability versus integrity based trust violations. *Journal of Applied Psychology, 89,* 104-118.

Kirkpatrick, S. A., & Locke, E. A. (1991). Leadership: Do traits matter. *The Academy of Management Executive, 5,* 48-60.

Klein, K. J., Tosi, H., & Cannella, A. A. (1999). Multilevel theory building: Benefits, barriers, and new developments. *Academy of Management Review, 24,* 243-248.

Koehler, J. J. (1996). The base rate fallacy reconsidered: descriptive, normative, and methodological challenges. *Behavioral & Brain Sciences, 19,* 1-53.

Kohn, L., Corrigan, J. & Donaldson, M. (2000). *To Err is Human: Building a safer health system.* Washington, DC: The National Academies Press.

Krueger G. P. (1994). Fatigue, performance, and medical error. In Bogner, MS, (Ed.), *Human error in medicine hillsdale* (pp. 311-26). Mahwah, NJ: Erlbaum.

Kruglanski, A. W. (1989). The psychology of being "right": The problem of accuracy in social perception and cognition. *Psychological Bulletin, 106,* 395-409.

Lanzetta, J. T. (1955). Group behavior under stress. *Human Relations, 8,* 29-52.

Leape, L.L. (1994). Error in medicine. *JAMA, 282,* 1851-1857.

Lerner, J. S., & Keltner, D. (2001). Fear, anger, & risk. *Journal of Personality and Social Psychology, 81,* 146-159.

Lerner, J. S., Goldberg, J. H., & Tetlock, P. E. (1998). Sober second thought: the effects of accountability, anger, and authoritarianism on attributions of responsibility. *Personality and Social Psychology Bulletin, 24,* 563-574.

Lesar, T. S., Briceland, L. L., Delcoure, K., Parmalee, C., Masta-Gornic, V., & Pohl, H. (1990). Medication prescribing errors in a teaching hospital. *JAMA, 263,* 2329-2334.

Licuanan, B. F., Dailey, L. R., & Mumford, M. D. (2007). Idea evaluation: Error in evaluating highly original ideas. *Journal of Creative Behavior, 41,* 1-27.

Likert, R. (1961). *New patterns of management.* New York: McGraw-Hill.

Likert, R. (1967). *The human organization: Its management and value.* New York: McGraw-Hill.

Longley, J., & Pruitt, D. G. (1980). Groupthink: A critique of Janis's theory. In L. Wheeler (Ed.), *Review of personality and social psychology* (Vol 1, pp. 74-93). Beverly Hills, CA: SAGE.

Lord, R. G., Devader, C. L., & Alliger, G. M. (1986). A meta-analysis of the relationship between personality traits and leadership perceptions: An application of validity generalization procedures. *Journal of Applied Psychology, 71,* 402-410.

Lyubomirsky, S., King, L., & Diener, E. (2005). The benefits of frequent positive affect: Does happiness lead to success. *Psychological Bulletin, 131,* 803-855.

Mackie, D. M., & Worth, L. T. (1989). Processing deficits and the mediation of positive affect in persuasion. *Journal of Personality and Social Psychology, 57,* 27-40.

Malmendier, U., & Tate, G., (2005). CEO overconfidence and corporate investment. *The Journal of Finance, 60,* 2661-2684.

Martin, L. L., Ward, D. W., Achee, J. W., & Wyer, R. S., Jr. (1993). Mood as input: People have to interpret the motivational implications of their moods. *Journal of Personality and Social Psychology, 64,* 317-326.

Mason, R., & Mitroff, I. (1981). *Challenging strategic planning assumptions.* New York: Wiley.

Maxham, J. G., & Netemeyer, R. G. (2002). A longitudinal study of complaining customers' evaluation of multiple service failures and recovery efforts. *Journal of Marketing, 66,* 55-71.

McCann, J. (1998). *Stop and sell the roses: Lessons from business & life.* New York: Ballentine Books.

Melton, R. J. (1995). The role of positive affect in syllogism performance. *Personality & Social Psychology Bulletin, 21,* 788-794.

Moorhead, G., & Montanari, J. R. (1986). An empirical investigation of the groupthink phenomenon. *Human Relations, 39,* 399-410.

Morison, S. E. (1942). *Admiral of the Ocean Sea: A life of Christopher Columbus*. Boston: Little, Brown.

Mumford, M. D., Bedell, K. E., & Hunter, S. T. (2008). Planning for innovation: A multi-level perspective. In M. D. Mumford, S. T. Hunter, & K. E. Bedell (Eds.), *Research in Multi-level Issues: Vol. VII*. Oxford, England: Elsevier.

Mumford, M. D., Blair, C., Dailey, L. R., Leritz, L. E., & Osborn, H. K. (2006). Errors in creative thought? Cognitive biases in a computer processing activity. *Journal of Creative Behavior, 40,* 75-109.

Mumford, M. D., Espejo, J., Hunter, S. T., Bedell, K. E., Eubanks, D. L., & Connelly, S. (2007). The sources of leader violence: A multi-level comparison of ideological and non-ideological leaders. *The Leadership Quarterly, 18, 217-235.*

Mumford, M. D., & Hunter, S. T. (2005). Innovation in organizations: A multi-level perspective on creativity. In F. J. Yammarino & F. Dansereau (Eds.), *Research in multi-level issues* (Vol. IV, pp. 11- 74). Oxford, England: Elsevier.

Neri, D., Shappell, S., & DeJohn, C. (1992). Simulated sustained flight operations and performance, part 1: Effects of fatigue. *Military Psychology, 4,* 137-155.

Nisbett, R. E., & Ross, L. (1980). *Human inference: Strategies and shortcomings of social judgment.* Englewood Cliffs, NJ: Prentice-Hall.

Norman, D. A. (1980). *Errors in human performance. Technical Report*. La Jolla: University of San Diego, Center for Human Information Processing.

Nutt, P. C. (2004). Expanding the search for alternatives during strategic decision-making. *Academy of Management Executive, 18,* 13-28.

Oliver, T. (1986). *The real Coke, the real story.* New York: Penguin.

Padilla, A., Hogan, R., & Kaiser, R. B. (2007). The toxic triangle: Destructive leaders, susceptible followers, and conducive environments. *Leadership Quarterly, 18,* 176-194.

Park, W. W. (2000). A comprehensive empirical investigation of the relationships among variables of the groupthink model. *Journal of Organizational Behavior, 21,* 873-887.

Pickering, J. M., & King, J. L. (1995). Hardwiring weak ties: Interorganizational computer-mediated communication, occupational communities, and organizational change. *Organization Science, 6,* 479-486.

Pinto, J. K., & Prescott, J. E. (1988). Variations in critical success factors over the stages in the project life cycle. *Journal of Management, 14,* 5-18.

Podsakoff, P. M., Bommer, W. H., Podsakoff, N. P., & MacKenzie, S. B. (2006).Relationships between leader reward and punishment behavior and subordinate attitudes, perceptions, and behaviors: A meta-analytic review of existing and new research. *Organizational Behavior and Human Decision Processes, 99,* 113-142.

Raghunathan, R., & Pham. M. T. (1999). All negative moods are not equal: Motivational influences of anxiety and sadness on decision making. *Organizational Behavior and Human Decision Processes, 79,* 56-77.

Reason, J. (1990). *Human error.* Cambridge, MA: Cambridge University Press.

Repenning, N. P., & Sterman, J. D. (2002). Capability traps and self-confirming attribution errors in the dynamics of process improvement. *Administrative Science Quarterly, 47,* 265-295.

Rickard, L. (1995). Remembering new Coke. *Advertising Age, 66,* 6.

Ross, J., & Staw, B. M. (1993). Organizational escalation and exit: Lessons from the Shoreham nuclear power plant. *Academy of Management Journal, 36,* 701-732.

Ross, L. (1977). The intuitive psychologist and his shortcomings. In L. Berkowitz (Ed.), *Advances in experimental social psychology* (Vol. 10, pp. 173-220). New York: Academic.

Senders, J., & Moray, N. P. (1991) *Human error: Cause, prediction, and reduction. Series in applied psychology.* Mahwah, NJ: Erlbaum.

Sitkin, S. B. (1996). *Learning through failure: The strategy of small losses*. London: SAGE.

Staw, B. M. (1976). Knee-deep in the big muddy: A study of escalating commitment to a chosen course of action. *Organizational Behavior and Human Performance, 16,* 27-44.

Staw, B. M., & Barsade, S. G. (1993). Affect and managerial performance: A test of the sadder-but-wiser vs. happier-and-smarter hypotheses. *Administrative Science Quarterly, 38,* 304-331.

Staw, B. M., Sandelands, L. E., & Dutton, J. E. (1981). Threat-rigidity effects in organizational behavior: A multilevel analysis. *Administrative Science Quarterly, 26,* 501-524.

Stogdill, R. M. (1974). *Handbook of leadership: A survey of the literature*. New York: Free Press.

Tate, B. W. & Jacobs, R. R. (2009, April). *Bad to the bone: Empirically defining and measuring negative leadership.* Paper presented at the 24th annual meeting of the Society for Industrial and Organizational Psychology, New Orleans, LA.

Tetlock, P. E. (1985). Accountability: A social check on the fundamental attribution error. *Social Psychology Quarterly, 48,* 227-236.

Tetlock, P. E. (1992). The impact of accountability on judgment and choice: Toward a social contingency model. In M. Zanna (Ed.), *Advances in experimental social psychology* (pp. 331-377). New York: Academic Press.

Tepper, B. J. (2000). Consequences of abusive supervision. *Academy of Management Journal, 43,* 178-190.

Tiedens, L. Z. (2001). Anger and advancement versus sadness and subjugation: The effect of negative emotion expressions on social status conferral. *Journal of Personality and Social Psychology, 80,* 86-94.

Torrance, E. P. (1967). A theory of leadership and interpersonal behavior under stress. In L. Petrullo & B. M. Bass (Eds.), *Leadership and interpersonal behavior* (pp. 100-117). New York: Holt.

Ungson, G. R., Braunstein, D. N., & Hall, P. D. (1981). Managerial Information Processing: A Research Review. *Administrative Science Quarterly, 26,* 116-134.

Van den Bulte, C., & Moenart, R. K. (1998). The effects of R&D team co-location on communication patterns among R&D, marketing, and manufacturing. *Management Science, 44,* 1-18.

Van der Linden, D., Frese, M., & Meijman, T. F. (2003). Mental fatigue and the control of cognitive processes: Effects on perserveration and planning. *Acta Psychologica, 113,* 45-65

Van Dyck, C., Frese, M., Baer, M., & Sonnentag, S. (2005). Organizational error management culture and its impact on performance. *The Journal of Applied Psychology, 90,* 1228-1240.

Violanti, M. (2006). Case Study 15: Should We Stop Using the Letter C? Three Key Players Respond to the February 1, 2003, Columbia Shuttle Events. In S. May (Ed.), *Case studies in organizational communication: Ethical perspectives and practices* (Vol. 402, pp. 253-264). Thousand Oaks, CA: SAGE.

Warkentin, M. E., & Beranek, P. M. (1999). Training to improve virtual team communication. *Information Systems Journal, 9,* 271-289.

Weingart, S. N., Wilson, R. M., Gibberd, R. W., & Harrison, B. (2000). Epidemiology of medical error. *British Medical Journal, 320,* 774-777.

West, M. A. (1990). The social psychology of innovation in groups. In M. A. West, & J. L. Farr (Eds.), *Innovation and creativity at work: Psychological and organisational strategies.* Chichester, England: Wiley.

West, M. A. (2002). Sparkling fountains or stagnant ponds: An integrative model of creativity and innovation implementation within groups. *Applied Psychology: An International Review, 51,* 355-386.

Williams, K. D., & Karau, S. J. (1991). Social loafing and social compensation: The effects of expectations of co-worker performance. *Journal of Personality and Social Psychology, 61,* 570-581.

Wright, P. L. (1974). The harassed decision maker: Time pressure, distractions, and the use of evidence. *Journal of Applied Psychology, 59,* 555-561.

Wu, A. W., Folkman, S., McPhee, S. J., & Lo, B. (1991). Do house officers learn from their mistakes? *JAMA, 265,* 2089-2094.

Yammarino, F. J., & Dansereau, F. (2009). A new kind of OB. In F. J. Yammarino, & F. Dansereau (Eds.), *Research in Multilevel Issues, Vol 9.* Oxford, England: Elsevier.

Yammarino, F. J., Dionne, S. D., Chun, J. U., & Dansereau, F. (2005). Leadership and levels of analysis: A state-of-the-science review. *Leadership Quarterly, 16,* 879-919.

Yukl, G. (1999). An evaluation of conceptual weaknesses in transformational and charismatic leadership theories. *Leadership Quarterly, 10,* 285-305.

Yukl, G. (2007). *Leadership in organizations.* Upper Saddle River, NJ: Prentice-Hall.

Yukl, G., Gordon, A., & Taber, T. (2002). A Hierarchical Taxonomy of Leadership Behavior: Integrating a Half Century of Behavior Research. *Journal of Leadership & Organizational Studies, 9,* 15.

Yukl, G., & Van Fleet, D. D. (1992), Theory and research on leadership in organization. In M. D. Dunnette, & L. M. Hough (Eds.), *Handbook of Industrial and Organizational Psychology* (2nd ed.). Palo Alto, CA: Consulting Psychologists Press.

Zapf, D., Isic, A., Bechtoldt, M., & Blau, P. (2003). What is typical for call centre jobs? Job characteristics and service interactions in different call centers. *European Journal of Work and Organizational Psychology, 12,* 311-340.

CHAPTER 16

TO ERR IS HUMAN, TO LEAD IS DIVINE?

The Role of Leaders in Learning From Workplace Mistakes

Bi-Hong Deng, Michelle C. Bligh, and Jeffrey C. Kohles

Fostering organizational learning has become an increasingly important focus of leadership in complex, uncertain, and rapidly changing environments. Research comparing learning from success versus failure outcomes has emphasized the value of learning from mistakes as potentially triggering higher-level transformative learning. We explore the conceptual relationship between different types of leadership (i.e., authentic, transformational, transactional, laissez-faire, and aversive leadership) and their potential impact on learning from mistakes. In particular, we suggest that the relationship between perceived leadership style and employee error learning is importantly influenced by the employee's mindset (fixed or growth). We present a theoretical model and testable propositions concerning (1) how leaders influence error learning in the workplace, (2) how different types of employees experience, cope, and learn from their errors, and (3) the implications of the impact of leadership style on employee error learning.

When Leadership Goes Wrong: Destructive Leadership, Mistakes and Ethical Failures, pp. 445–475

"The illiterate of the 21st century will not be those who cannot read and write, but those who cannot learn, unlearn, and relearn."

—Alvin Toffler

"He that never changes his opinions, never corrects his mistakes, and will never be wiser on the morrow than he is today."

—Tryon Edwards

Workplace mistakes are inevitable occurrences that organizations strive to minimize. However, organizations often do not have a "blame-free" approach or offer a safe environment for learning. Researchers at SHL Group report that nearly 72% of mistakes made by U.K. employees and 68% of mistakes made by U.S. employees are never reported to managers, and the projected costs of managing poor performers (e.g., hours spent redoing or correcting employee mistakes) can amount to $23 billion in U.K. and $105 billion in U.S. annually (Gale, Litle, & Maynard, 2004; Iziren, 2005; Karsh, 2004; Pomeroy, 2004; SHL Group, 2004). In a recent survey, over 90% of U.S. doctors agreed that physicians should report impaired or incompetent colleagues and significant medical errors to hospital authorities—but in practice, 45% admitted they have failed to report such colleagues and 46% failed to report a serious medical error of which they had direct personal knowledge (Campbell et al., 2007). In addition to concerns over hospitals falsifying records to cover up medical errors (Moore, Lesser, & Smith, 2009; Perez-Pena, 2004), estimates suggest that anywhere from 25,000 to 98,000 deaths per year result from preventable medical errors (Brennan, 2000; Institute of Medicine, 1999).

Although it is relatively hard to document the prevalence of unreported errors and accurately estimate the financial costs of workplace mistakes, the management of errors is nevertheless a common concern of most businesses. Aside from economic costs, errors in organizations can also damage the company's image and decrease customer satisfaction, trust, and loyalty. Errors can also be a source of psychological stress and job dissatisfaction in employees, and may lead to turnover, cause physical injury or even result in death. With such an impact on bottom line performance and employee well-being, managing and dealing with workplace mistakes is clearly worthy of additional attention and investigation. Business mistakes are often hidden from view for many reasons, including "protection of competitive information, protection of employees and management, [and] potential legal exposure" (Mittelstaedt, 2005, pp. 5-6). The taboo of failure is a barrier not only to individual learning, but also stunts a rich area of potential learning in organizations. Fostering increased organizational learning is a major concern as global business shifts to a more knowledge-based economy, and leaders can play a critical role in helping to role model and facilitate learning from mistakes and failures.

Leaders can also do exactly the opposite. Specifically, leaders can use coercive techniques to blame, punish or even ostracize employees who did something "unthinkable": make a mistake. In the context of employee and organizational learning, this is what happens when "leadership goes wrong." As the title of our chapter highlights, "to err is human," and leaders are far from divine or omnipotent forces as the romance of leadership perspective reminds us (Bligh & Schyns, 2007; Meindl, 1995). Leading for learning is not a simple leader-centered process, in which omnipotent leaders notice mistakes, know the right answer, and guide subordinates in finding the correct path on their own in the spirit of supporting the learning process. In reality, leading for learning is more accurately a bidirectional influence process in which leaders and followers acknowledge, process, and react to errors in ways that facilitate successful outcomes and promote learning.

In addition, we do not mean to imply that leaders are never warranted in taking serious action in response to mistakes with dire consequences (e.g., endangerment of public health). However, we hope this chapter will help leaders be cognizant of the tone they set for learning (or not) through their responses to employee errors. In other words, it is important to acknowledge that from a position of authority, leaders' attitudes and behaviors can affect whether employees learn from their mistakes and openly share that learning with others, or hide blunders that may compound into losses of millions of dollars.

Although there is an abundance of literature on leadership and performance outcomes, relatively little empirical research has been done on the impact of leadership on learning outcomes, particularly in the realm of error learning. This gap is surprising given increasing demands for innovation and growth. As Drucker (1996) noted, knowledge workers "by virtue of their position or their knowledge ... make decisions in the normal course of their work that have significant impact on the performance and results of the whole [organization]" (p. 8). Therefore, the current chapter seeks to establish a better understanding of how leaders can actively facilitate and promote error learning in organizations.

A review of the literature also reveals relatively separate bodies of knowledge regarding learning from errors and leadership style. Given that people will have developed certain learning styles, behaviors, and beliefs before they ever set foot in the workplace, an examination of how an employee's mindset (i.e., one's beliefs about whether capabilities are inherited and limited versus learned and malleable) affects learning in the workplace is an important area of inquiry. Specifically, we seek to explore two primary questions. First, how do different leadership styles influence employee learning from errors? Second, does the employee characteristic of fixed or growth mindset impact the relationship between employees' perceptions of their leader and their learning from workplace errors?

In order to explore these questions, we first review the definition of errors before turning to how different leadership styles (i.e., authentic, transformational, transactional, laissez-faire, and aversive) may impact employees' responses to workplace errors. We subsequently explore how an employee's psychological mindset impacts error learning, and present a theoretical model of the interrelationships between leadership style, employee mindset, and error learning. We conclude with some of the implications and research directions stemming from this theoretical approach.

DEFINING ERRORS, MISTAKES, AND FAILURES

Although they are often used interchangeably, researchers have distinguished *errors* or *mistakes* from *failures* and *violations*. Errors are defined as the unintended deviation or nonattainment of a goal, which is potentially avoidable (van Dyck, Frese, Baer, & Sonnentag, 2005; Zhao & Olivera, 2006). Zhao and Olivera define errors as an "individual's decisions and behaviors that (1) result in an undesirable gap between an expected or real state and (2) may lead to actual or potential negative consequences for organizational functioning that could have been avoided" (p. 1013). Failure, in contrast, is the negative or undesired *outcome*, which may or may not be a possible consequence of errors (Cannon & Edmondson, 2001; Zhao & Olivera, 2006). For example, an error does not necessarily result in failure if corrective actions are taken in time to avoid negative consequences. Furthermore, failure might be caused by chance or external factors other than human errors. Failure may also be expected and unavoidable, such as in experimentation where certain trials will fail and others yield success (Cannon & Edmondson, 2001; Lee, Edmondson, Thomke, & Worline, 2004; Zhao & Olivera, 2006). Errors are also distinct from violations or employee misconduct (Vaughan, 1999; Zhao & Olivera, 2006). Violations refer to acts that are deliberate deviations from organizational practices, whereas errors by definition are rarely deliberate (van Dyck et al., 2005; Zhao & Olivera, 2006).

In addition to these distinctions among errors, failures, and violations, previous researchers have developed different categories of errors. Table 16.1 presents three different approaches to the definition and organization of error types. All three approaches conceptualize an error as (1) a *deviation or nonattainment of an expected goal* that is (2) *unintended* and (3)

Table 16.1. Categories of Error Type

Error Type (Riemer, 1976)	Description of errors Emphasize the source contributing to the error
Miscalculations	Human error resulting from **individual** perception, interpretation, understanding, or judgment.
Hold-ups	Mistakes occurring from blockages or breakdowns in the communication network of **an organization** (a condition Riemer terms "social disorganization") that leads to distortions, misinterpretations, and misunderstandings.
Circumstantial errors	Human errors resulting from the immediate and prevailing **circumstances surrounding a task or work event**. For example, circumstantial errors may arise from communicated expectations to the worker that is clear and explicit, yet conflicting or contradictory.
Error Type (Zhao & Olivera, 2006)	**Description of errors Focus on the action of the error itself**
Slips	Actions that are **not carried out as planned** either due to an internal or external distraction, even though the intentions are appropriate for accomplishing the desired goal.
Rule-based mistakes	Mistakes that occur when **well-known rules or procedures are inappropriately or incorrectly applied** in familiar, or so presumed, conditions. Here, the actions are carried out as planned, but the plan is inappropriate for the desired goals.
Knowledge-based mistakes	Mistakes that occur when people are **not able to properly analyze a problem or recognize the relations among its elements** (e.g., faulty logic in causality, incomplete mental models)
Error Type (Crandall, 2007)	**Description of errors At three levels in which it impacts one's life experiences**
Level One: Failures in what we do	Error learning is primarily **surface-level** related to improvement of **knowledge and skills in what we do**.
Level Two: Failures in who we are	Error learning at this level requires individuals to take a **critical look at their own abilities, emotions, and personality, to face the hard truth of who we are**. Here, mistakes focus on the **underlying flaws in one's personal traits, abilities, and emotions** is often manifested in the decisions and actions we take.
Level Three: Failures in who we want to be	Error learning is most difficult and rare at this stage as one examines failures that **violate one's own value systems and the core principles of who we want to be**. These mistakes impinge on our fundamental values and beliefs.

potentially avoidable (Crandall, 2007; Riemer, 1976; Zhao & Olivera, 2006). As illustrated in Table 16.1, there may be differences in the distribution and frequency of the error types that are likely to occur, depending on the work environment and the nature of the task (Riemer, 1976; Zhao & Olivera, 2006). For our purposes, however, variances in error types are not a primary focus, and we use the terms "error," "mistake" and "failure" interchangeably to refer to unintended, potentially avoidable deviations from work-related goals. And although some failures may not be a result of human errors as defined earlier, references to the term '"failure" in this chapter will only encompass failure outcomes specifically related to human errors.

Given these definitions, the value of learning from errors is that they "represent a form of negative feedback (i.e., one has not achieved a goal) and, as such, present the individual with valuable information about how to alter one's course of action to ultimately achieve a goal" (van Dyck et al., 2005, p. 1229). In conceptualizing single-loop and double-loop learning in organizations, Argyris and Schön's (1978) definition of learning revolves around the detection and correction of error. Taking a broader, process-oriented model from Kolb's (1984) experiential learning cycle, learning is defined as the "process whereby knowledge is created through the transformation of experience" (p. 41). Generally the first stage of learning begins with "concrete experience" where a learner actively experiences an activity or event. The second stage involves "reflective observation" when the learner consciously observes and reflects back on that experience. When the learner begins building or conceptualizing a theory or model of what he or she had observed in that experience, this third stage is called "abstract conceptualization." In the final fourth stage of "active experimentation," the learner will plan and engage in testing their hypothesized theory for another upcoming future event or experience. Applying Argyris and Schön's learning objective to Kolb's process of learning, we can define the process of *learning from mistakes* as the identification, analysis, and transformation of an error experience (i.e., a deviation or nonattainment of an expected goal) into knowledge. In addition, the resulting knowledge must be utilized to correct current or future actions, in order to improve the likelihood of achieving successful outcomes.

As a part of the daily work effort, employees will inevitably commit errors, and in some cases will do so on a routine basis (Hughes, 1951; Riemer, 1976). Although mistakes and failures are a common theme across all occupations, in some professions work and routines are organized around the potential for mistakes or mistake-producing situations (Light, 1972; Riemer, 1976). In other words, rituals and systems are developed in occupations with unavoidable risks, such as medicine or construction work, and following those organizational practices or routines allows professionals to take certain risks at work by protecting them from blame in failure cases (Hughes, 1951). In light of the central role that error-management plays in these occupations, leader-follower processes that facilitate learning from errors can play a critical role in individual and organizational successes.

The Role of Leadership: Learning From Mistakes

Commonly, in positive psychology as well as everyday practice, people tend to promote or focus on strengths, valuing successes over failures. This human nature to identify oneself with success is best captured in the old adage, "Success has many fathers, but failure is an orphan." Overcoming this natural tendency to divorce oneself from any connection or responsibility for mistakes is an aspect of leadership and organizational learning that can potentially yield high returns. Yukl (2006) defines leadership as "the process of influencing others to understand and agree about what needs to be done and how to do it, and the process of facilitating individual and collective efforts to accomplish shared objectives" (p. 8). This definition highlights the influence process leaders have over both individuals and the collective, and how leaders set the tone for desired behaviors ("how to do it") and goals ("what needs to be done") within their organization. This definition implies that leaders not only have an impact on employee goals and performance, but also on their learning behaviors and in instilling a culture of exploration and experimentation within the organization as a whole.

Some researchers argue that a different level and type of learning occur from experiencing failure (Cope, 2003; Foil & Lyles, 1985; Mezirow, 1990). Although long-term success is the desired goal for most actions, leaders can potentially help to neutralize the negative connotations and reactions to failures that often inhibit learning from these experiences, especially when these "negative" events hold opportunities for transformative learning. In other words, when an employee's attempt does not achieve the desired outcome, leaders can play a critical role in helping to ensure that the experiential process yields beneficial information for achieving success in the employee's next attempt.

More specifically, there is evidence that certain learning events facilitate higher levels of learning than others. Significant and critical learning events tend to be non-linear and discontinuous, whereas routinized and habitual activities result in gradual, incremental learning seen in lower-level instrumental learning (Cope, 2003). Thus, leaders and followers must recognize that discontinuous learning events, such as opportunities, crises, or breakdowns in the organizational functioning, can become a critical stimulus for higher-level learning such as transformational learning (Cope, 2003). These crises provide the necessary "shocks" and "jolts" required for "unlearning and new higher-level learning and readaption to take place" (Foil & Lyles, 1985, p. 808).

In increasingly ambiguous and uncertain environments, leaders and managers are beginning to move away from more traditional and sometimes retributive ways of dealing with mistakes, and instead recognize that learning from past mistakes is a crucial aspect of their experience base (see Hunter, Tate, Dzieweczynski, & Cushenbery, this volume). For example, error analysis can have positive effects on one's knowledge and experience by providing a mechanism for reducing uncertainty, increasing variety and creativity in approaches, and expanding the search for new opportunities (McGrath, 1999, p. 15). Mistakes can also stimulate both leaders and followers to choose new actions and explore new possibilities as a coping or learning strategy for reducing uncertainty (Politis, 2005). Van Dyck et al. (2005) noted a number of potential positive long-term consequences of error management, including learning, innovation, and resilience. While this is not to say that mistakes should be valued over successes, this research suggests that today's organizations need to simultaneously reduce and manage mistakes while maximizing success and error learning.

The personal lessons formulated from these past successes and failures also influence one's decision-making processes. Individuals often follow a basic two-path strategy when making decisions: exploitation or exploration (March, 1991; Minniti & Bygrave, 2001; Politis, 2005). In the first strategy, the individual opts to *exploit* their preexisting knowledge by choosing actions that replicate or closely resemble ones they have taken before. When exploiting what is already known through "refinement, routine, and implementation of knowledge," this strategy builds on expertise and creates "reliability in experience, which means that stable behavior becomes the dominant state of the learner" (Politis, 2005, p. 408). In contrast, the second strategy consists of choosing new actions and *exploring* options different from those previously taken. Exploration is about "creating variety in an experience resulting in that change in behavior becomes the dominant state" (p. 408). Leaders and followers who favor exploring new possibilities are more likely to learn from variation, experimentation, discovery, and innovation.

Given this framework, it is easy to see how exploiting rather than exploring strategies can become the favored paths for both individuals and organizations (Politis, 2005). The repetition of known behavior patterns that have been successful in the past quickly becomes automatic and even unconscious, and in a stable environment this exploitive learning strategy can be very effective. However, the rapid rate of change in today's organizations characterized by global economies, financial crises, technological revolutions, and consumer and workforce diversity increasingly requires a more explorative learning strategy. As Mittelstaedt (2005) points out, "successful past experience is a powerful force and is difficult to ignore ... failure to recognize that a situation requires actions not in your past experience is often fatal" (p. 34). Levinthal and March (1993) warn of the "temporal myopia" of learning, where leaders and followers fail to recognize that the conditions have changed, and their past successes and learned skills may turn into an impediment and a liability in the new environment.

The Role of Leadership Style in Employee Learning

In overcoming this "temporal myopia" and facilitating learning in oneself and others, some leadership styles may be more effective than others. In this review, we focus specifically on the impact of authentic, transformational, transactional, laissez-faire, and aversive leadership styles on employee error learning. In essence, we posit that Avolio and Bass's (1991) full range leadership theory (FRLT) can be expanded from three dimensions (transformational, transactional, and laissez-faire) to incorporate aversive styles of leadership, as well as more developmental styles such as authentic leadership. Viewing leadership on this extended continuum, the more positive and transformative styles of authentic and transformational leaders are more likely to encourage workplace learning than transactional leadership styles. Moving along the continuum, nontransactional laissez-faire leadership is less likely to foster or sustain employee error learning. Finally, towards the negative end of the leadership continuum, aversive leadership styles are likely to actively discourage and even prevent employee error learning. In the following sections, we will briefly review each style, with an emphasis on exploring how different leadership styles influence learning from errors in the workplace.

Luthans and Avolio (2003) defined authentic leadership as the "process that draws from both positive psychological capacities and a highly developed organizational context, which results in both greater self-awareness and self-regulated positive behaviors on the part of leaders and associates, fostering positive self-development" (p. 243). The characteristics of an authentic leader include: confident, hopeful, optimistic, resilient, transparent, moral/ethical, future-oriented, true to oneself, self-awareness, highly perceptive of others' values, perspectives, and capabilities, awareness of the context in which they operate, self-regulated, positive role model, and gives priority to developing associates (Avolio & Gardner, 2005; Avolio, Gardner, Walumbwa, Luthans, & May, 2004; Luthans & Avolio, 2003).

Thus, the essence of this leadership theory is authenticity and the commitment to cultivate the development of others, suggesting that many of the strengths of this leadership style are realized *through* facilitating employee learning. In positive psychology, authenticity involves both "owning one's personal experiences" and "acting in accord with the true self" (Luthans & Avolio, 2003, p. 242). Authenticity is conceptualized as a state of being that demonstrates a high level of coherence with one's self. This requires accurate *self-awareness*, or clarity of one's own self-concept, and *self-regulation*, the ability to recognize, monitor, and accordingly adjust one's own behavior (Luthans & Avolio, 2003). The influence process of authentic leadership works through positive modeling of the leader's genuine belief in the development of oneself and others (Hannah, 2007). While one might argue that accurate self-awareness is not necessarily a requirement for role modeling learning (e.g., in the case of coaches or therapists), leaders who have egregiously inaccurate self-awareness or poor self-regulation would likely make poor learning role models, as their own learning processes may be severely flawed.

Several of the characteristics of authentic leadership are particularly relevant to facilitating error learning, including an orientation toward doing what is right for followers and the organization, believing that each individual has something positive to contribute, and continually working at self-development (Luthans & Avolio, 2003, pp. 248-249). In many ways, authentic leadership may involve error learning almost by definition, as it includes being cognizant of one's own limitations as a leader, openly discussing those limitations with followers, and allowing one's views to be questioned by others. In addition, authentic leadership involves the belief that developing associates over time has equal importance to task accomplishment, which may often necessitate allowing employees to make mistakes and explore what can be learned from those mistakes. By being attuned to contextual complexity and exploring multiple perspectives of an ambiguous situation or dilemma to seek alternative solutions, authentic leaders are more likely to view errors and mistakes within a broader context and as potentially useful information rather than as justifications for punishment or reprimands. In addition, "authenticity can be raised to the collective level" (Hannah, 2007, p. 105; see also Avolio et al., 2004; Luthans & Avolio, 2003); that is, authentic leaders can shape a "culture of authenticity" through their relationships with organizational members, followers who internalize the leader's values and strive to emulate them, subsequently diffusing those shared values throughout the organization.

Burns (1978) originally described two other leadership styles in the FRLT, transformational and transactional leadership. Whereas contingent reward transactional leaders lead through social exchange (e.g., exchanging financial rewards for productivity), transformational leaders stimulate and inspire followers to achieve both extraordinary outcomes as well as developing themselves as leaders. Bass (1985) describes transformational leadership as motivating followers to do more than the expected by raising followers' levels of consciousness about the importance and value of the group's goals, motivating the followers to transcend their own self-interest for the sake of the collective group, and inspiring followers to aspire to higher-order needs. As a result, followers tend to "feel trust, admiration, loyalty, and respect toward the leader, and they are motivated to do more than they originally intended to do" (Yukl, 2006, p. 262). As Daniels (2007) explains: "the power of internalization is that it is transformational, not transactional. Transactions are temporary. A transformation lasts forever. In such circumstances, human beings are capable of achieving wonderful things" (p. 87).

Transformational and transactional leadership are different but not mutually exclusive (Yukl, 2006). Although transformational leadership focuses more on motivating and transforming followers, an effective leader may also utilize the behaviors of transactional leadership. A transactional leader exchanges valued rewards contingent upon a follower's display of desired behaviors (Burns, 1978). Such a leader would clarify a "right way" to do things, but in a manner that maintains dependence on the leader, rather than empowering the follower as a transformational leader would (Lowe & Kroeck, 1996). Bass (1985) characterizes transactional leaders as those who tend to operate with the status quo of the system or culture, are generally risk avoidant, concerned with constraints and efficiency, and those who use management-by-exception techniques to maintain control through processes and incentives. Although transactional leaders may be effective in getting followers to comply with requests or accomplish tasks, they do not challenge or motivate followers to achieve higher objectives as in the case of transformational leadership. In addition, their tendency to operate within the status quo, general risk avoidance, and emphasis on efficiency and control suggest that transactional leadership is often less effective in role modeling and actively encouraging error learning in employees than transformational leadership.

Laissez-faire leadership is typified by a passive indifference to both the task and followers—thus often termed a form of "non-leadership" (Northouse, 2007; Skogstad, Einarsen, Torsheim, Aasland, & Hetland, 2007). This type of "hands-off" leader would typically ignore problems and follower's needs, abandon responsibility, fail to provide feedback, and avoid necessary decisions or critical issues. Skogstad et al. notes that laissez-faire leadership style is "not only a lack of presence ... but it implies not meeting the legitimate expectations of the subordinates and/or superiors concerned...and may be experienced by subordinates as systematic neglect and ignorance" (pp. 81-87). Thus, laissez-faire leadership behaviors are unlikely to actively facilitate employee error learning, either through role modeling, feedback, or other types of follower development activities.

Finally, as the current volume highlights, recent branches of research have given attention to more negative and even destructive forms of leadership such as pseudo-transformational leaders (Price, 2003), toxic leaders (Lipman-Blumen, 2006), destructive leaders (Einarsen, Aasland, & Skogstad, 2007), and aversive leadership (Pearce & Sims, 2002). In other words, these approaches focus on what happens when leadership goes wrong. Aversive leadership refers to one such negative form of leadership that relies on coercive power (e.g., intimidation, threats) and utilizes harsh forms of discipline (e.g., reprimand, punishment) (Bligh, Kohles, Justin, Pearce, & Stovall, 2007; Pearce & Sims, 2002). Research indicates that exposure to supervisory bullying may have a direct effect on negative emotions, cognitive distraction, and lack of concentration (Skogstad et al., 2007). Therefore, an aversive leadership style may actively discourage employee error learning, both by directly punishing employees for workplace errors, as well as fostering negative emotions and cognitive anguish that indirectly dissuade employees from taking future risks or responsibility for errors.

When visualizing this extended continuum of leadership, it may be helpful to view the different leadership theories as building upon, subsuming, or even overlapping with adjacent styles, rather than as distinctly separate. For example, in reality it is common for many transformational leaders to exhibit transactional behaviors such as contingent rewards and active management-by-exception, and recent research has argued that more pattern-oriented analyses are needed to reflect that the best leaders may be *both* transactional and transformational (O'Shea, Foti, & Hauenstein, 2009). However, it might be less common for transactional leaders to demonstrate transformational behaviors such as inspirational motivation. Some studies have also shown that the factor of passive management-by-exception is significantly correlated with laissez-faire leadership, even though it has been conceptualized as a component of transactional leadership (Antonakis, Avolio, & Sivasubramaniam, 2003). Therefore, the constellation of behaviors attributed to each leadership style in reality may be more fluid than as commonly conceptualized. For example, O'Shea et al. (2009) found that optimally effective leaders used a combination of transformational and contingent reward (e.g., exchange-based transactional leadership) behaviors, coupled with low levels of passive management-by-exception behavior (e.g., remaining uninvolved until problems emerge). Based on these findings, it may be beneficial to examine how pattern-level behavioral dimensions relate to learning in addition to how the broader leadership styles (i.e., transactional, transformational) correlate to learning outcomes.

Linking Leadership Style and Employee Learning

In exploring pattern-level behavioral dimensions related to employee learning outcomes, Ellinger, Watkins, and Bostrom (1999) examined how managers' beliefs and behaviors regarding their role as facilitators of learning contributed to learning outcomes in their organization. The belief that a manager's role is to facilitate learning and development—helping employees to grow and develop—was considered not only a priority, but an essential part of the managerial role. By recognizing deficiencies, discrepancies or perceived gaps, political issues, and developmental opportunities, leaders utilized these occasions to stretch and build the capabilities of their employees.

Ellinger et al. (1999) report two behavioral sets that managers used to *empower employees* (i.e., encouraging personal responsibility and accountability in employees) and *facilitate learning* (i.e., offering guidance and support that encourages learning and development through reaching new levels of understanding and new perspectives). Empowering employees involves holding back by not providing the answers and giving the employees a chance to learn for themselves, framing questions to help employees think through issues rather than giving them the answers, transferring ownership to employees (including ownership of both errors and successes), and being a resource and helping to remove obstacles. Facilitative behaviors include creating and promoting a learning environment, broadening employees' perspectives to see things in new ways, shifting employees' perspectives using illustrative analogies, scenarios, and examples, setting and communicating expectations with a view of the big picture, talking through and working out problems collaboratively, soliciting and providing feedback to employees, and engaging others to facilitate learning.

In general, we note that authentic and transformational leadership styles overlap a great deal with such empowering and facilitative behaviors as described in Ellinger et al.'s (1999) study, and therefore seem likely to foster the most employee error learning. However, transactional leadership has little overlap with any of these behaviors, with the exception of possibly acting as a resource, removing obstacles, and talking through problems, because transactional leadership also involves constant monitoring, concerns with efficiency, and specifying correct behaviors or approaches to accomplishing work. Finally, laissez-faire and aversive leadership styles generally do not display these empowering or facilitative behaviors that in Ellinger et al.'s findings are critical for promoting employee learning.

In another qualitative study, Mulqueen (2005) explored the impact of specific leadership behaviors on learning from failure. This study found that leaders attempt to teach other organizational members to learn from mistakes through three broad behavioral themes that characterize what we might term "learning leadership": (1) acting with an internal locus of control, (2) modeling behaviors for others, and (3) institutionalizing learning processes.

Acting with an internal locus of control involved leaders maintaining a positive focus by visualizing success in light of their own errors or that of employees, portraying a positive and optimistic mood, and highlighting the positives in these potentially negative situations. In addition, learning leaders focused on solutions by framing mistakes as problems to be solved rather than opportunities for blame, shame, or finding fault, and took personal responsibility for situations within their own control, including admitting errors in public when necessary. Finally, behaviors such as seeking an accurate self-image of oneself as a leader, avoiding taking issues personally, keeping promises in their dealings with others, and treating others with respect irrespective of the egregiousness of the error or mistake were other salient characteristics of leaders who promoted error learning.

Modeling behaviors included supporting employees by talking, listening, and being present for employees in the aftermath of mistakes, attending to complexity and learning by recognizing variation and potentially multiple levels of meaning in error situations, and tolerating errors by providing employees with learning opportunities such as noncritical tasks in which they can fail without major negative consequences (as opposed to micromanaging or simply doing the task for them). Taking risks themselves, and sharing failure stories (sometimes using humor) when those risks did not always end favorably, were also emphasized. Leaders who talk about their own failures and how they recovered from them help employees understand that errors are inevitable and not always fatal to either performance outcomes or career successes.

Finally, Mulqueen (2005) found that successful learning leaders *institutionalize a learning process*, often using a learning and performance cycle where leaders and followers jointly set goals and expectations, and leaders monitor performance, provide feedback and coaching, and then assess, evaluate, and reward performance. Making reflection a part of each work activity, conducting learning discussions such as "postmortems" or "lessons learned" where a completed project or deal is dissected for learning opportunities, and providing room to fail for employees to feel safe in learning, innovating, and experimenting were also identified as crucial leader behaviors in promoting error learning.

Some other studies linking leadership behaviors and employee error learning outcomes support the following factors in facilitating learning, which also align with the behavioral themes of learning-oriented leadership in Ellinger et al. (1999) and Mulqueen's (2005) studies: positive feedback, support, acceptance, respect, creating psychological safety (Bagian, 2005; Bryans, 2007; Carmack, 2008; Edmondson, 1999, 2003; Fischer et al., 2006; Gaddis, Connelly, & Mumford, 2004; Rivard, 2006); fairness (Bagian, 2005; Bryans, 2007); allowing team ownership or self-management, holding back to give or share responsibility and allow opportunity to correct error (Bryans, 2007; Edmondson, 1999; Rivard, 2006); communicating clear directions and a motivating rationale for change (Cannon & Edmondson, 2001; Edmondson, 2003; Rivard, 2006); focusing on solutions by defining overall goal and getting employee buy-in and accountability (Bagian, 2005; Rivard, 2006); soliciting and valuing feedback from team members (Edmondson, 1999, 2003; Nembhard & Edmondson, 2006); creating transparency in processes and policies (Bagian, 2005; Carmack, 2008; Fischer et al., 2006); identifying and removing obstacles (Bagian, 2005; Rivard, 2006); being a resource and providing necessary tools (Bagian, 2005; Edmondson, 1999); being visibly involved and taking responsibility (Bagian, 2005; Rivard, 2006); taking followers through and working things out together (Carmack, 2008); being coaching-oriented (Cannon & Edmondson, 2001; Edmondson, 1999, 2003); role modeling (Rivard, 2006); conducting learning discussions, reviewing and debriefing incidents (Fischer et al., 2006; Rivard, 2006); evaluating implemented solutions to assess improvement (Bagian, 2005; Rivard, 2006); sharing narratives of personal experiences and public apologies (Carmack, 2008; Fischer et al., 2006); listening and using illustrations, examples, and inquiry (Rivard, 2006); and taking shame and blame out of errors and positively transforming them into opportunities for learning (Carmack, 2008; Edmondson, 1999; Rivard, 2006).

Taken together, this review of the literature and prior empirical work suggests a number of areas of overlap between leadership that promotes learning and the five leadership styles outlined above. Table 16.2 summarizes how the different leadership theories (i.e., authentic, transformational, transactional, laissez-faire, and aversive) correspond to the various empirical findings of leadership behaviors that have been linked to employee error learning. Based on preliminary empirical findings that have outlined observed leadership behaviors associated with error learning in the workplace, the proposed leadership behaviors have been reorganized into these general categories across studies: (1) core values or beliefs, (2) problem solving, (3) empowering others, (4) institutionalizing learning processes, (5) broadening awareness, (6) creating psychological safety, (7) managing error, and (8) communicating and teaching. In hopes of fostering future research that empirically examines these linkages, we offer the following propositions that sum up the expected relationships outlined in Table 16.2. Given the broad profiles of the leadership styles described above, we have made inferences about behaviors that may correspond to aspects of employee learning; these inferences are offered tentatively in order to stimulate empirical research in this area.

Proposition 1: Authentic and transformational leadership will foster more employee learning from workplace mistakes than transactional leadership.

Proposition 2: Transactional leadership will foster more employee learning from workplace mistakes than laissez-faire leadership.

Proposition 3: Laissez-faire leadership will foster more employee learning from workplace mistakes than aversive leadership.

Proposition 4: Aversive leadership will actively inhibit employee learning from workplace mistakes.

Individual Factors in Learning From Errors: Fixed Versus Growth Mindsets

In the prior sections, we have focused on the potential role of various leadership styles in facilitating and discouraging employee error learning. However, as Manning (2007) points out, "humans are not 'blank slates' to be written upon, but must unlearn old thinking or behavior patterns before they can really learn" (p. 5). Although there is an abundance of literature on the various individual factors that influence general learning, such as self-efficacy and motivation, the next section will discuss the evidence for how one's basic assumptions of growth and change (i.e., fixed versus growth mindset) shape an employee's perceptions of failure, which in turn may either serve to enhance or inhibit learning behaviors.

Dweck's (2000) theory of mindsets has important implications for how employees perceive and cope with mistakes. The "fixed" mindset (also termed entity theory or helpless pattern of behavior) assumes that ability is inherent, and that people are born with a limited capacity for ability.

Table 16.2. Proposed Relationship of Leadership Styles to Employee Error Learning[a]

Theme[b]	*Source*	*Leadership Behaviors*	*Au*	*Trf*	*Trn*	*Lf*	*Av*
Core value/belief	Ellinger et al., 1999	Believes essential role of leader is to facilitate learning and develop employees	+	+	x	–	–
Problem solving	Mulqueen, 2005	Maintaining a positive focus	+	+	/	–	–
	Bagian, 2005; Mulqueen, 2005; Rivard, 2006	Focusing on the solution	+	+	/	–	–
	Carmack, 2008; Ellinger et al., 1999;	Talking through and working out problems together	+	+	/	–	–
	Bagian, 2005; Edmondson, 1999; Ellinger et al., 1999; Rivard, 2006	Being a resource and removing obstacles; proactive	+	+	/	–	–
Empowering others	Bagian, 2005; Edmondson, 1999; Ellinger et al., 1999; Rivard, 2006	Transferring ownership to employees; getting buy-in; accountability	+	+	–	x	x
	Bryans, 2007; Ellinger et al., 1999; Rivard, 2006	Holding back and allowing employee to learn on their own	+	/	–	/	–
Institutionalize learning processes	Mulqueen, 2005	Using a learning and performance cycle	/	/	/	x	–
	Bagian, 2005; Fischer et al., 2006; Mulqueen, 2005; Rivard, 2006	Conducting learning discussions; reviewing & debriefing incidents; assess & evaluate implemented solutions	/	/	/	x	–
	Mulqueen, 2005	Institutionalizing reflection	/	/	x	x	–
Broaden awareness	Mulqueen, 2005	Building self-awareness	+	/	x	x	–

Table continues on next page.

Table 16.2. Proposed Relationship of Leadership Styles to Employee Error Learning[a] Continued

Theme[b]	*Source*	*Leadership Behaviors*	*Au*	*Trf*	*Trn*	*Lf*	*Av*
	Mulqueen, 2005	Attending to complexity and learning	+	/	x	x	–
	Ellinger et al., 1999	Broadening or shifting perspectives; helping to see things in a new or different viewpoint	+	+	x	x	x
	Mulqueen, 2005	Does not take things personally	+	/	/	x	–
Creating psychological safety	Mulqueen, 2005	Keeping promises	+	+	+	x	–
	Edmondson, 1999, 2003; Mulqueen, 2005	Treating others with respect, minimizing concerns about power relations	+	+	/	x	–
	Bagian, 2005; Bryans, 2007; Carmack, 2008; Fischer et al., 2006	Creating transparency of processes/policies; fairness	+	+	+	x	x
	Bagian, 2005; Bryans, 2007; Carmack, 2008; Fischer et al., 2006; Gaddis et al., 2004; Mulqueen, 2005; Rivard, 2006	Support (e.g., acceptance, consideration, positive feedback)	+	+	x	x	–
	Mulqueen, 2005	Using humor	/	/	x	x	–
Managing error	Mulqueen, 2005	Taking risks	/	+	x	x	–
	Bagian, 2005; Mulqueen, 2005; Rivard, 2006	Taking personal responsibility; visibly involved	+	/	/	–	–
	Carmack, 2008; Fischer et al., 2006; Mulqueen, 2005	Admitting failure in public; Sharing failure stories	+	/	x	x	–
	Carmack, 2008; Edmondson, 1999; Mulqueen, 2005; Rivard, 2006	No shaming, blaming, or criticizing	+	/	/	x	–

Table continues on next page.

Table 16.2. Continued

Theme[b]	*Source*	*Leadership Behaviors*	*Au*	*Trf*	*Trn*	*Lf*	*Av*
	Mulqueen, 2005	Tolerating failures; Providing room to fail	+	/	x	x	–
Communicating and teaching	Cannon & Edmondson, 2001; Edmondson, 1999, 2003; Mulqueen, 2005; Rivard, 2006	Leading by example; role modeling; coaching-oriented	+	+	x	x	–
	Mulqueen, 2005; Rivard, 2006	Observing and listening	+	+	+	x	–
	Ellinger et al., 1999; Rivard, 2006	Question framing; inquiry	+	+	x	x	–
	Ellinger et al., 1999; Rivard, 2006	Using illustrative analogies, scenarios, and examples	+	+	x	x	x
	Bagian, 2005; Cannon & Edmondson, 2001; Edmondson, 2003; Ellinger et al., 1999; Rivard, 2006	Setting and communicating expectations with view of big picture; communicating clear directions and motivating rationale for change	+	+	/	x	–
	Edmondson, 1999, 2003; Ellinger et al., 1999; Nembhard & Edmondson, 2006	Soliciting informational feedback; leader inclusiveness	+	+	x	x	–
	Ellinger et al., 1999; Rivard, 2006	Providing informational feedback	+	+	x	x	–

[a] The five leadership styles are: Au = Authentic, Trf = Transformational, Trn = Transactional, Lf = Laissez-faire, and Av = Aversive. The symbols represent the following relationships: "+" = leadership style includes or reflects that behavior, "/" = leadership style might include that behavior, "x" = leadership style does not include that behavior, "–" = leadership style *contradicts* that behavior.

[b] Findings from the empirical studies of leadership behaviors linked to employee learning have been reorganized into different thematic categories for ease of comparison across studies.

Employees with fixed mindsets internalize mistakes as failure, and instead of coping they tend to subsequently avoid challenging tasks and cover up mistakes. In contrast, the "growth" mindset (also termed incremental theory or mastery-oriented pattern of behavior) assumes ability is malleable and can be improved with effort or practice. This assumption leads employees with growth mindsets to view mistakes as learning experiences for personal or professional growth. As a consequence, they welcome challenging tasks and acknowledge and learn from mistakes and failures to improve future performance and increase self-awareness.

Dweck (2000) argues that a person's mindset affects their goal orientation, their perception of failures or setbacks, their emotional reactions, and the coping mechanisms they use to handle challenges. We briefly review each of these factors in relation to error learning.

Goal-orientation. Human behaviors are goal-oriented. In any task, the performance goal is often different from the learning goal (Dweck, 2000). Performance goals are concerned with gaining positive judgments of one's competence and avoiding negative ones, and often involve testing or measuring an employee's intelligence and competence. A follower with a fixed mindset: (1) believes that he or she has a finite level of intelligence or ability, and is likely concerned about protecting the image of one's "inherent" talent; (2) feels an urgency to prove themselves to others: and (3) avoids 'looking dumb' by playing it safe and avoiding situations that might entail risks or mistakes (Dweck, 2000). However, learning goals are concerned with increasing one's competence through learning new skills, mastering novel tasks, or understanding new things. Because employees of the growth mindset believe that there is always room for improvement and learning is a priority, they are more concerned with getting accurate and constructive feedback and stretching themselves than protecting their self-image (Dweck, 2000).

Perceptions of failure. Failure and effort are also perceived differently by the two groups. When one's talent has a fixed limit and performance is interpreted as a test of one's ability, failure seems permanent because no remedial action is available. Effort becomes a negative experience that reduces an employee's belief in his or her own "innate ability" and is perceived as an indication that performance is not up to par. Additional risks and efforts are only likely to reveal inadequacies. In contrast, when one believes that change and growth are possible, then failure outcomes are not final, and there are multiple paths and opportunities for eventual success (Dweck, 2006). Employees with growth mindsets do not let a negative experience or outcome define them; rather, it becomes a source of knowledge and learning. Therefore, effort is positively perceived as a natural part of the learning process.

Emotional reactions. Because failure represents a threat to one's self-identity, fixed mindset employees express stress, frustration, and negative emotions when they encounter challenges or setbacks. Zhao, Dweck, and Mueller's (1998) study examined how depressed students compare to non-depressed students with different mindsets in their reactions to vignettes describing failure. The responses of fixed mindset students looked like those of depressed students, suggesting that an event need not even be a real failure to evoke depression-like thoughts, feelings, and plans. In these students, simply provoking the idea of a major failure "brought forth spontaneous reports of harsh self-judgments, extreme negative feelings, and a desire to escape rather than persist" (Dweck, 2000, p. 46). However, the responses of growth mindset individuals differed significantly, as these students were more likely to focus on new strategies and how increased effort might be applied in the future (Zhao et al., 1998).

Coping mechanisms. Finally, when intelligence and ability are viewed as static, then options for coping with new challenges are limited for employees with fixed mindsets. In a study of how seventh graders would respond to an academic failure, students with a growth mindset reported increased effort or new strategies in the future, while those with fixed mindsets reported studying less and even considered cheating (Dweck, 2006). Because fixed mindset students believe they simply do not have the requisite ability or intelligence, negative outcomes mean resorting to other means of boosting performance outcomes. Dweck notes that as children progress in school and life, they are confronted with more challenges, more complexity, and more choices. In school and in the workplace, the fixed mindset individual may plateau early and not realize his or her full potential, while the growth mindset individual continually learns and grows to achieve new outcomes and higher levels of achievement.

What is particularly interesting about mindsets is that they may serve as a critical intervention point for learning and change. Although the fixed versus growth mindset is often described as a dichotomy, some research suggests that people more accurately fall along a continuum. For example, Dweck (2006) demonstrated that mindsets can be changed and can be temporarily induced. Therefore, the mindset variable has direct impact on how individuals react to and learn from mistakes, and may possibly moderate how other factors, such as leadership styles, impact error learning.

The moderating effects of an employee's mindset on the relationship between perceptions of their manager's leadership style and their error learning can perhaps be explained by the attribution theory of Weiner and colleagues (Jones et al., 1972; Weiner, 1985; Weiner, Nierenberg, & Goldstein, 1976). Attribution theory (Weiner et al., 1976) explains how a person's interpretation of events (i.e., perceptions and attributions of causes to success or failure outcomes) can impact their thinking and behavior (e.g., determine the amount of effort the person will spend on the activity in the future). Attributions are categorized into three causal dimensions: (1) *locus of control* – whether the cause of outcome is internal or external to the individual, (2) *stability*—how stable or transient is the cause over time, and (3) *controllability*—whether causes can or cannot be influenced by the individual.

If we map Dweck's (2000) description of the two mindsets along Weiner's et al. (1976) three causal dimensions of attributions, we might expect differences in interpreting failure outcomes due to factors of ability, effort, and task difficulty. For example, people with fixed mindsets (belief that ability is inherent and therefore change is severely limited or predetermined) would likely view one's ability to be a relatively internal and *stable* factor over which one *lacks much direct control*; whereas people with the growth mindset (belief that ability is malleable and can improve with effort) would more likely view one's ability as an internal factor over which one *can exercise direct control* through the use of effort or practice, which in turn determines the stability of the ability—that is, *how much one practices an ability will determine how much that ability changes or remains stable over time*. Even though effort may be viewed by both as an internal factor, the fixed mindset individual is most likely to view effort as being *stable* over time (i.e., effort is useless because ability has a predetermined limit) whereas growth mindset individuals will see the *instability* of effort as a leverage point (i.e., amount of effort should be adjusted to meet the difficulty of the task at hand). The external factor of task difficulty can be perceived as *stable* and *largely beyond the control* of the fixed mindset individual (i.e., sees challenges as barriers that cannot be overcome), while the growth mindset individual sees the difficulty of a task to be *unstable* and *within their control* because they anticipate that it can significantly change over time by increasing their effort to learn and master the task.

Application of Weiner's attribution theory helps explain why growth mindset individuals would exert more effort to learn in the face of challenges, while fixed mindset individuals are less likely to exert effort and more quick to find blame or excuses for failure. Figure 16.1 poses a model for how Weiner's attribution theory takes place as a part of Kolb's (1984) experiential learning cycle, where (1) a learner's attributions made during the abstract conceptualization stage will impact (2) what they do in the active experimentation stage, that will (3) distinguish the two different experiences and approaches taken by fixed mindset employees versus growth mindset employees.

Given the characteristics and attribution tendencies of the two mindsets, we would expect the buffering and resilient behaviors of employees with growth mindsets to counter the negative influences of more passive and destructive leadership styles (e.g., laissez-faire, aversive) while those

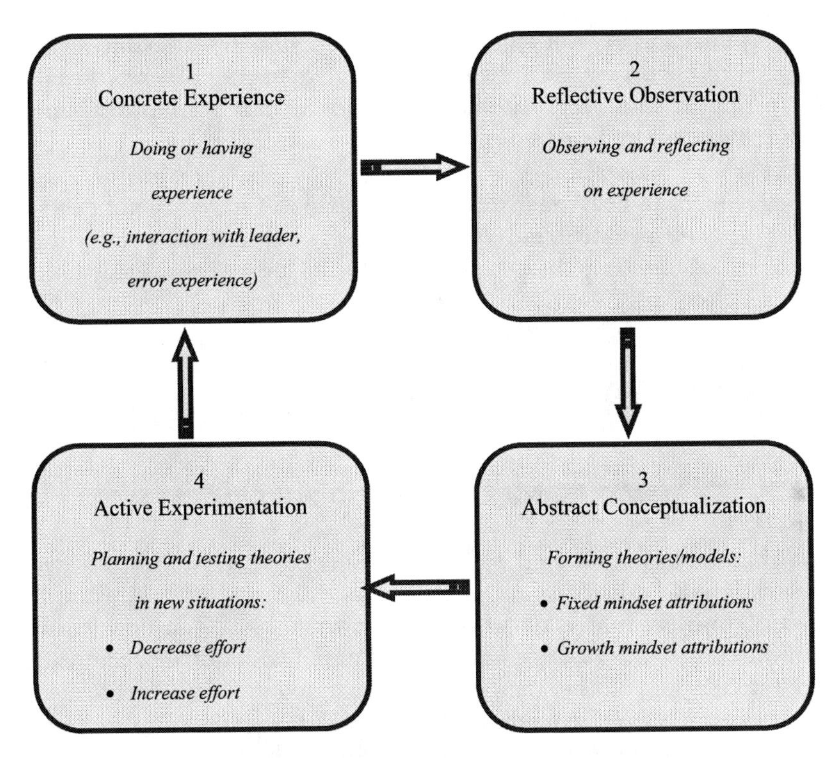

Figure 16.1. Model of learning based on experiential learning cycle and attribution theory.

with fixed mindsets will be less likely to learn from workplace errors, particularly when faced with aversive leadership styles. Also, under the influence of positive leadership (e.g., authentic, transformational), it is likely that employees with fixed mindsets will be less likely to learn from workplace errors than those with growth mindsets.

Proposition 5: Employees with fixed mindsets will be less likely to learn from workplace mistakes than employees with growth mindsets.

Proposition 6: Employee mindset will moderate the relationship between leadership style and employee error learning, such that:

Proposition 6a. Leadership style will be more predictive of error learning in employees with a fixed mindset than in employees with a growth mindset.

Proposition 6b. Authentic and transformational leadership styles will have a significantly greater positive impact on error learning in employees with a fixed mindset than transactional and laissez-faire leadership styles.

Proposition 6c. Aversive leadership style will have a significantly greater negative impact on error learning in employees with a fixed mindset than transactional and laissez-faire leadership styles.

A summative model of the expected relationships between the constructs is visually shown in Figure 16.2.

LEVERAGING ERRORS AND SUCCESSES

This chapter has attempted to build a conceptual relationship between three different bodies of literature: leadership, learning, and workplace errors. Empirical studies on workplace errors, focusing on how learning from different types of errors can be facilitated with appropriate leadership styles and other moderating variables (e.g., gender, job characteristics, team dynamics) is a critical next step in this line of research. For example, researchers have already laid the groundwork for understanding team-level learning, and have examined how context, culture, and other organizational characteristics influence whether or not teams learn from errors and failures (e.g., Bauer & Mulder, 2007; Cannon & Edmondson, 2001; Edmondson, 1999, 2003, 2004; Fischer et al., 2006; Hoff, Pohl, & Bartfield, 2004, 2005, 2006; Leape, 1994; Tjosvold, Yu, & Hui, 2004). The malleable and inducible nature of mindsets also poses interesting interventions for promoting learning in both leaders and followers. By identifying the leadership styles or behaviors that best facilitate learning in organizations, as well as those that do not, this area of research has immense potential in providing practical value for leaders confronted with different types of employee responses to errors, suggesting alternate ways leaders can modify their styles accordingly.

The performance of knowledge workers has become the cornerstone of many organizations' capacity to survive and thrive as the world continues to shift from the industrial to the information age, from the production of products to knowledge and service, and from national to global economies (Schwandt & Marquardt, 2000). Many organizations have recognized that they can only expand in today's fast-paced global environment if they institutionalize organizational learning (Schwandt & Marquardt, 2000). As leaders create, embed, and transmit culture within the organization,

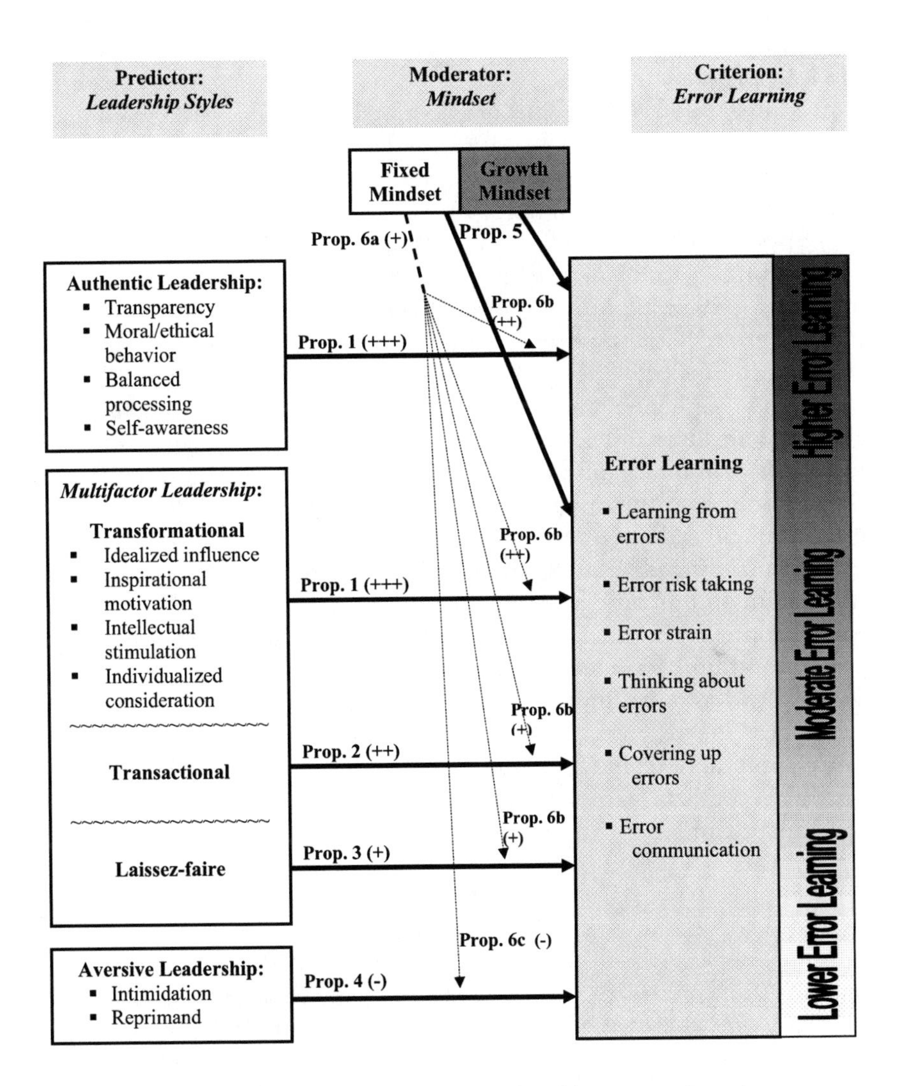

Figure 16.2. Model of leadership styles' relationship to error learning moderated by mindset.

this culture serves to reinforce or constrain certain behaviors even without the direct presence of the leader (Schein, 2004). As opposed to leaders who handle errors and mistakes in punitive or destructive ways, leaders who can create and sustain a culture of learning are key to implementing this strategy. Developing a true culture of learning should include an orientation that explicitly values as well as develops a system for managing and learning from mistakes.

As Mittelstaedt (2006) points out, although mistakes are often committed by individuals, the big costly blunders are usually "team efforts" (p. 12). In other words, large-scale failures are often the result of compounded mistakes that go ignored or are overlooked or even encouraged by the system as a whole (Cannon & Edmondson, 2005; Riemer, 1976). Leaders who lead for *learning* as the *primary* task of their followers, and view the specified job function itself as secondary, can create a culture of learning from both successes and failures. If authenticity can truly be raised to the collective level (Hannah, 2007, p. 105; Luthans & Avolio, 2003), then authentic transformational leaders can help to shape and transform a culture of learning through cultivating relationships with followers who will internalize, emulate, and help to propagate those shared values throughout the organization. A culture that continually learns will also continually adapt to an ever-changing environment. This chapter has attempted to provide a preliminary map for exploring this rapidly evolving terrain, and provide concrete directions for research into how best to lead in contexts where errors and mistakes are an inevitable part of the human condition. As Peter Drucker (as cited in Pearce, 2010, p. 35) noted, "knowledge has to be improved, challenged, and increased constantly, or it vanishes." As we increasingly move into the knowledge era, draconian punishment and blame must give way to leaders and followers who together recognize, learn from, and leverage mistakes in order to continually explore and grow.

REFERENCES

Antonakis, J., Avolio, B. J., & Sivasubramaniam, N. (2003). Context and leadership: An examination of the nine-factor full-range leadership theory using the Multifactor Leadership Questionnaire. *Leadership Quarterly, 14*, 261-295.

Argyris, C., & Schön, D. (1978). *Organizational learning: A theory of action perspective.* Reading, MA: Addison Wesley.

Avolio, B. J., & Bass, B. M. (1991). *The full range leadership development programs: Basic and advanced manuals*. Binghamton, NY: Bass, Avolio & Associates.

Avolio, B. J., & Gardner, W. L. (2005). Authentic leadership development: Getting to the root of positive forms of leadership. *Leadership Quarterly, 16*, 315-338.

Avolio, B. J., Gardner, W. L., Walumbwa, F. O., Luthans, F., & May, D. R. (2004). Unlocking the mask: A look at the process by which authentic leaders impact follower attitudes and behaviors. *Leadership Quarterly, 15*, 801-823.

Bagian, J. P. (2005). Patient safety: What is really at issue? *Frontiers of Health Services Management, 22*, 3-16.

Bass, B. M. (1985). *Leadership and performance beyond expectations*. New York, NY: The Free Press.

Bauer, J., & Mulder, R. H. (2007). Modelling learning from errors in daily work. *Learning in Health and Social Care, 6*, 121-133.

Bligh, M. C., Kohles, J. C., Justin, J. E., Pearce, C. L, & Stovall, J. (2007). When the romance is over: Follower perspectives of aversive leadership. *Applied Psychology: An International Review, 56*, 528-557.

Bligh, M. C., & Schyns, B. (2007). Leading question: The romance lives on: Contemporary issues surrounding the romance of leadership. *Leadership, 3*, 343-360.

Brennan, T. A. (2000). The Institute of Medicine report on medical errors—could it do harm? *New England Journal of Medicine, 342*, 1123-1125.

Bryans, P. (2007). The gendered nature of workplace mistakes. In D. Mctavish & K. Miller (Eds.), *Women in leadership and management* (pp. 109-124). Northampton, MA: Edward Elga.

Burns, J. M. (1978). *Leadership*. New York: Harper & Row.

Campbell, E. G., Regan, S., Gruen, R. L., Ferris, T. G., Rao, S. R., Cleary, P. D., et al. (2007). Professionalism in medicine: Results of a national survey of physicians. *Annals of Internal Medicine, 147*, 795-802.

Cannon, M. D., & Edmondson, A. C. (2001). Confronting failure: Antecedents and consequences of shared beliefs about failure of organizational work groups. *Journal of Organizational Behavior, 22*, 161-177.

Cannon, M. D., & Edmondson, A. C. (2005). Failing to learn and learning to fail (intelligently): How great organizations put failure to work to innovate and improve. *Long Range Planning, 38*, 299-319.

Carmack, H. J. (2008). *How to say I'm sorry: A study of the Veterans Administration Hospital Association's Apology and Disclosure Program*. Unpublished doctoral dissertation, Ohio University, Ohio.

Cope, J. (2003). Entrepreneurial learning and critical reflection: Discontinuous events as triggers for "higher-level" learning. *Management Learning, 34*, 429-450.

Crandall, D. (2007). Learning from failure. In D. Crandall (Ed.), *Leadership lessons from West Point* (pp. 16-31). Hoboken, NJ: Wiley.

Daniels, C. (2007). Developing organizational values in others. In D. Crandall (Ed.), *Leadership lessons from West Point* (pp. 62-87). Hoboken, NJ: Wiley.

Drucker, P. F. (1996). *The effective executive*. New York: HarperCollins.

Dweck, C. S. (2000). *Self-theories: Their role in motivation, personality, and development*. Philadelphia, PA: Psychology Press.

Dweck, C. S. (2006). *Mindset: The new psychology of success*. New York: Ballantine Books.

Edmondson, A. (1999). Psychological safety and learning behavior in work teams. *Administrative Science Quarterly, 44*, 350-383.

Edmondson, A. C. (2003). Speaking up in the operating room: How team leaders promote learning in interdisciplinary action teams. *Journal of Management Studies, 40*, 1419-1452.

Edmondson, A. C. (2004). Learning from mistakes is easier said than done: Group and organizational influences on the detection and correction of human error. *Journal of Applied Behavioral Science, 40*, 66-90.

Einarsen, S., Aasland, M. S., & Skogstad, A. (2007). Destructive leadership behavior: A definition and conceptual model. *Leadership Quarterly, 18*, 207-216.

Ellinger, A. D., Watkins, K. E., & Bostrom, R. P. (1999). Managers as facilitators of learning in learning organizations. *Human Resource Development Quarterly, 10*, 105-125.

Fischer, M. A., Mazor, K. M., Baril, J., Alper, E., DeMarco, D., & Pugnaire, M. (2006). Learning from mistakes: Factors that influence how students and residents learn from medical errors. *Journal of General Internal Medicine, 21*, 419-423.

Foil, C. M., & Lyles, M. A. (1985). Organizational learning. *Academy of Management Review, 10*, 803-813.

Gaddis, B., Connelly, S., & Mumford, M. D. (2004). Failure feedback as an affective event: Influences of leader affect on subordinate attitudes and performance. *Leadership Quarterly, 15*, 663-686.

Gale, C., Litle, J., & Maynard, B. (2004, June 21). US companies lose $105 billion to poor people performance; Across the seven economies surveyed the figure equates to $153 billion. *Business Wire*, p. 1.

Hannah, S. T. (2007). The authentic high-impact leader. In D. Crandall (Ed.), *Leadership lessons from West Point* (pp. 88-106). Hoboken, NJ: Wiley.

Hoff, T. J., Pohl, H., & Bartfield, J. (2004). Creating a learning environment to produce competent residents: The roles of culture and context. *Academic Medicine, 79*, 532-539.

Hoff, T. J., Pohl, H., & Bartfield, J. (2005, February). Creating learning cultures in medicine around mistakes for residents: Considering both type of error and error context. In K. Henriksen, J. B. Battles, E. S. Marks, & D. I. Lewin (Eds.), *Advances in patient safety: From research to implementation* (Vol. 3), Implementation Issues. AHRQ Publication No. 05-0021-3, Rockville, MD: Agency for Healthcare Research and Policy.

Hoff, T. J., Pohl, H., & Bartfield, J. (2006). Teaching but not learning: How medical residency programs handle errors. *Journal of Organizational Behavior, 27*, 869-896.

Hughes, E. (1951). Mistakes at work. *The Canadian Journal of Economics and Political Science, 17*, 320-327.

Institute of Medicine. (1999). *To err is human: Building a safer health system.* Washington, DC: National Academy Press.

Iziren, A. (2005, April 3). Ten million pounds cost of secrets and lies. *Mail on Sunday*, p. 29.

Jones, E. E., Kanouse, D. E., Kelley, H. H., Nisbett, R. E., Valins, S., & Weiner, B. (Eds.). (1972). *Attribution: Perceiving the causes of behavior.* Morristown, NJ: General Learning Press.

Karsh, L. (2004, December 1). The hidden costs of poor people management. *Inc.com*. Retrieved October 1, 2009, from http://www.inc.com/articles/2004/12/karsh.html#

Kolb, D. A. (1984). *Experiential learning: Experience as the source of learning and development.* Princeton, NJ: Prentice-Hall.

Leape, L. L. (1994). Error in medicine. *Journal of the American Medical Association, 272*, 1851-1857.

Lee, F., Edmondson, A. C., Thomke, S., & Worline, M. (2004). The mixed effects of inconsistency on experimentation in organizations. *Organization Science, 15*, 310-326.

Levinthal, D. A., & March, J. G. (1993). The myopia of learning. *Strategic Management Journal, 14*, 95-112.

Light, D. W. (1972). Psychiatry and suicide: The management of a mistake. *American Journal of Sociology, 77*, 821-838.

Lipman-Blumen, J. (2006). *The allure of toxic leaders*. New York: Oxford University Press.

Lowe, K. B., & Kroeck, K. G. (1996). Effectiveness correlates of transformational and transactional leadership: A meta-analytic review of the MLQ literature. *Leadership Quarterly, 7*, 385-425.

Luthans, F., & Avolio, B. (2003). Authentic leadership development. In K. S. Cameron, J. E. Dutton, & R. E. Quinn (Eds.), *Positive organisational scholarship: Foundations of a new discipline* (pp. 241-259). San Francisco: Berrett-Koehler.

Manning, T. T. (2007). Learn to unlearn: Five key belief patterns that sabotage leadership effectiveness. *Academic Reader, 23*, 4-8.

March, J. G. (1991). Exploration and exploitation in organizational learning. *Organization Science, 2*, 71-87.

McGrath, R. G. (1999). Falling forward: Real options reasoning and entrepreneurial failure. *Academy of Management Review, 24*, 13-30.

Meindl, J. R. (1995). The romance of leadership as a follower-centric theory: A social constructionist approach. *The Leadership Quarterly, 6*, 329-341.

Mezirow, J. (1990). How critical reflection triggers transformative learning. In J. Mezirow & Associates (Eds.) *Fostering critical reflection in adulthood: A guide to transformative and emancipatory learning.* San Francisco: Jossey-Bass.

Minniti, M., & Bygrave, W. (2001). A dynamic model of entrepreneurial learning. *Entrepreneurship Theory and Practice, 25*, 465-499.

Mittelstaedt, R. E., Jr. (2005). *Will your next mistake be fatal? Avoiding the chain of mistakes that can destroy.* Upper Saddle River, NJ: Pearson Education.

Mittelstaedt, R. E., Jr. (2006). Will your next mistake be fatal? Creating a culture that learns from its mistakes. *Leadership Excellence, 23*, 12.

Moore, T., Lesser, B., & Smith, G. B. (2009, July 26). Shocking secrets, mistakes, and death: Faked records and fatal blunders at city-run medical centers. *New York Daily News*, p. 6.

Mulqueen, C. (2005). *Learning through failure: A descriptive analysis of leader behavior.* Unpublished doctoral dissertation, University of New Mexico, New Mexico.

Nembhard, I. M., & Edmondson, A. C. (2006). Making it safe: The effects of leader inclusiveness and professional status on psychological safety and improvement efforts in health care teams. *Journal of Organizational Behavior, 27*, 941-966.

Northouse, P. G. (2007). *Leadership: Theory and practice.* Thousand Oaks, CA: SAGE.

O'Shea, P. G., Foti, R. J., & Hauenstein, N. M. (2009). Are the best leaders both transformational and transactional? A pattern-oriented analysis. *Leadership, 5*, 237-259.

Pearce, C. L. (2010). Leading knowledge workers: Beyond the era of command and control. In C. L. Pearce, J. A. Maciariello, & H. Yamawaki (Eds.), *The Drucker difference* (pp. 35-45). New York: McGraw Hill.

Pearce, C. L., & Sims, H. P. (2002). Vertical versus shared leadership as predictors of the effectiveness of change management teams: An examination of aversive, directive, transactional, transformational, and empowering leaders behaviors. *Group Dynamics Theory, Research, and Practice, 6*, 172-197.

Perez-Pena, R. (2004, September 29). Law to rein in hospital errors is widely abused, audit finds. *The New York Times*, p. 1.

Politis, D. (2005). The process of entrepreneurial learning: A conceptual framework. *Entrepreneurial Theory & Practice, 29*, 399-424.

Pomeroy, A. (2004, August). Cost of poor people management is high. *HR Magazine, 49*, 18.

Price, T. L. (2003). The ethics of authentic transformational leadership. *Leadership Quarterly, 14*, 67-81.

Riemer, J. W. (1976). "Mistakes at work": The social organization of error in building construction work. *Social Problems, 23*, 255-267.

Rivard, P. E. (2006). *Change agency and a culture of patient safety at Veterans Administration hospitals.* Unpublished doctoral dissertation, Boston College, Massachusetts.

Schein, E. H. (2004). *Organizational culture and leadership.* San Francisco: Jossey-Bass.

Schwandt, D., & Marquardt, M. J. (2000). *Organizational Learning: From world-class theories to global best practices.* Boca Raton, FL: St. Lucie Press.

SHL Group, PLC. (2004, July). *Getting the edge in the new people economy.* Retrieved November 11, 2008, from http://www.shl.com/edge

Skogstad, A., Einarsen, S., Torsheim, T., Aasland, M. S., & Hetland, H. (2007). The destructiveness of laissez-faire leadership behavior. *Journal of Occupational Health Psychology, 12*, 80-92.

Tjosvold, D., Yu, Z., & Hui, C. (2004). Team learning from mistakes: The contribution of cooperative goals and problem-solving. *Journal of Management Studies, 41*, 1223-1245.

van Dyck, C., Frese, M., Baer, M., & Sonnentag, S. (2005). Organizational error management culture and its impact on performance: A two-study replication. *Journal of Applied Psychology, 90*, 1228-1240.

Vaughan, D. (1999). The dark side of organizations: Mistake, misconduct, and disaster. *Annual Review of Sociology, 25*, 271-305.

Weiner, B. (1985). An attribution theory of motivation and emotion. *Psychological Review, 92*, 548-573.

Weiner, B., Nierenberg, R., & Goldstein, M. (1976). Social learning (locus of control) versus attributional (causal stability) interpretations of expectancy of success. *Journal of Personality, 44*, 52-68.

Yukl, G. (2006). *Leadership in organizations* (6th ed.). Princeton, NJ: Prentice-Hall.

Zhao, W., Dweck, C. S., & Mueller, C. (1998). *Implicit theories and depression-like responses to failure.* Unpublished manuscript, Columbia University, New York.

Zhao, B., & Olivera, F. (2006). Error reporting in organizations. *Academy of Management Review, 31*, 1012-1030.

PART V

ATTRIBUTIONAL PROCESSES

CHAPTER 17

ACADEMIC LEADERSHIP

The Effect of Leader-Follower Incongruence and Cognitive Processes on Perceptions of Leader Adversity

Beata Pawlowska, Susanne Braun, Claudia Peus, and Dieter Frey

This chapter focuses on non-deliberate leader behaviors that can result in adverse leadership perception. Specifically, the first section of this chapter illustrates several unique aspects of the academic context and academic leadership which, in our view, predispose academic leaders to destructive appraisal. Subsequently, we address the influence of situational factors on followers' destructive appraisal of leader behavior. Next, we identify three cognitive processes that may guide adverse leadership perception: the attribution process, the process of prototype matching and the process of transference. The subsequent empirical part of our chapter presents the results of our qualitative analysis which further illustrate the role of those previously introduced processes in adverse leadership perception. Subsequently, we present a conceptual model of adverse leadership perception and apply its assumptions explicitly to the academic context.

When Leadership Goes Wrong: Destructive Leadership, Mistakes and Ethical Failures, pp. 479–512

Finally, the concluding section of this chapter shifts the attention from theoretical descriptions to practical implications.

INTRODUCTION

While intentionally destructive leadership has received a reasonable amount of theoretical and some empirical attention (e.g., Illies & Reiter-Palmon, 2008; Padilla, Hogan, & Keiser, 2007), a theoretical insight and empirical research investigating factors that contribute to destructive appraisal of not deliberately harmful leader behavior are largely lacking. In fact, the majority of leadership research tends to focus on leader behaviors that are more or less effective for organizations (Schilling, 2009). This line of research often assumes that ineffective and counter productive leadership (i.e., destructive leadership) is evidenced by the absence of effective leader behaviors (Ashforth, 1994; Bryman, 2007). However, research investigating destructive aspects of leadership (Ashforth, 1994; Einarsen, Aasland, & Skogstard, 2007; Tepper, 2000) and cognitive leadership research (Epitropaki & Martin, 2004; Lord, Brown, Harvey, & Hall, 2001; Ritter & Lord, 2007) suggest that ineffective leadership is: (a) not limited to the absence of effective behaviors, (b) not limited to intentional behaviors, (c) influenced by experience with significant others and, (d) often misevaluated due to cognitive biases, implicit assumptions and environmental constraints. Consequently, an interesting question that should be posed with respect to leadership is "not so much what leaders should do, but [...] what they should avoid doing" (Bryman, 2007, p. 707). In other words, shifting the focus from effectiveness to ineffectiveness, with simultaneous attention to rendering processes that label a leader as adverse, might be more crucial for the understanding of leadership. Thus, this chapter focuses on nondeliberate leader behaviors that can result in destructive outcomes in a specific context of academia. Specifically, we examine factors that lead followers to construct negative images of their leader resulting in adverse leadership perception. However, though this chapter integrates prior research with findings from a qualitative study we conducted in the academic context, we believe that our exploratory analysis sheds some light on the aspects of leadership in similar organizational contexts that normally lie unexamined in every day interactions and therefore, result in adverse leadership perception. Finally, this chapter does not differentiate between specific types of academic leaders (e.g. a dean, a department chair) or specific types of leadership (e.g. administrative leadership). Although these types of differences are an interesting topic in itself, they are not the focus of this chapter. Rather, we refer to leadership in general terms as an influence relationship between leaders and followers (Yukl, 1998) and focus specifically on situational and cognitive factors that influence everyday leader-follower interactions that may result in adverse leadership perception.

We define adverse leadership as a repeated and nondeliberate leader behavior that violates a follower's beliefs about appropriate leader conduct by: (a) engaging in behaviors that run counter to a follower's expectations (e.g., endorsing the value of achievement over and above the value of compassion) or (b) failing all together to exhibit the requested behavior (e.g., not endorsing the value of compassion at all). The likely effects of adverse leadership may cause reversible or irreversible changes in a follower's perception of leader behavior, including expectation of mistreatment. Consequently, unlike other definitions of destructive leadership (cf. Bligh, Kohles, Pearce, Justin, & Stoval, 2007; Einarsen et al., 2007), our definition of adverse leadership does *not* include the intent to harm an individual or to sabotage the organization, nor does it reflect a leader's deliberate violation of universally accepted values or moral standards. Rather, it points out the potential for the attribution of adversity in the absence of explicit leader intent to cause harm, providing that the followers are repeatedly exposed to a leader's behavior that violates their expectations. Therefore, adverse leadership perception is based on subjective inferences made by a follower about a leader's behavior. However, we argue that the detrimental effects of adverse leadership perception might be no less damaging to the individual or to the organization than are those described by scholars investigating intentionally destructive forms of leadership (e.g. Kelloway, Mullen, & Francis, 2006; Tepper, 2000). We hope that our exploratory investigation will stimulate leadership research in this very direction.

ADVERSE LEADERSHIP PERCEPTION: OUTLINING THE PURPOSE

The central argument of this chapter is that destructive appraisal (i.e., a harsh and damaging assessment of a leader's behavior), which leads to adverse leadership perception, is independent of a leader's intent to cause harm. Moreover, we propose that situational factors and cognitive processes guide this destructive appraisal of leader behavior. Therefore, this chapter explores: (a) the possibility that leaders in certain contexts might be predisposed to this destructive appraisal, (b) the role of transgressions in leader-follower relationships (c) the role of situational factors and their contribution to adverse leadership perception, (d) the role of cognitive processes and their contribution to adverse leadership perception and (e) the ways in which leaders can constructively manage others' perceptions of their behavior. Subsequently, this chapter consists of five main sections.

The first section of this chapter illustrates several unique aspects of the academic context and academic leadership which, in our view, predispose academic leaders to destructive appraisal. Subsequently, we address the influence of situational factors on the followers' destructive appraisal of leader behavior. Specifically, we address leader-follower incongruence (i.e., a miss-match between a leader and a follower with respect to the meaning of values and role expectations) and its relationship to the follower's perception of harm (i.e., transgression). Next, we identify three cognitive processes that may guide adverse leadership perception: the attribution process, the process of prototype matching and the process of transference.

The subsequent empirical part of our chapter presents the results of our qualitative analysis, which illustrates the role of previously introduced processes in adverse leadership perception. Subsequently, we present a conceptual model of adverse leadership perception and apply its assumptions explicitly to the academic context.

Finally, the concluding section of this chapter shifts the attention from theoretical descriptions to practical implications. We discuss the role of academic human resource programs in leadership development and their influence on the prevention of adverse leadership. For instance, we provide suggestions regarding how increased self-awareness, self-reflection, value clarity (Engle & Lord, 1997; Fisher-Yoshida, 2003) and conflict management (De Dreu, Evers, Beersma, Kluver, & Nauta, 2001; Pruitt & Rubin, 1986; Rahim, 2002) can reverse and/or prevent the emergence of adverse leadership perception.

ADVERSE LEADERSHIP PERCEPTION: CONTRIBUTING FACTORS

Are Academic Leaders Predisposed to Destructive Appraisals?

In our opinion three aspects of academia predispose academic leaders to destructive appraisals: the unique nature of leading academic followers, the romanticized notion of academia, and the lack of preparation for the role of a leader.

Leading Academic Followers

The nature of academic leadership is different from that of corporate leadership (Martin, Trigwell, Prosser, & Ramsden, 2003; Mintzberg, 1998). Subsequently, various authors (Bryman, 2007; Raelin, 1995) suggest that traditional leadership theory and practice might not be useful for leading intrinsically motivated academic followers who struggle for professional autonomy and where relationship well-being and self-esteem are derived from fulfilling one's role obligations (Peus, Weisweiler, & Pawlowska, 2008). Thus, as suggested by Raelin (1995), academic leadership is different from leadership in usual organizational settings because the leadership of academics is more a "management of autonomy." In other words, the fundamental problem in leading academics is the maintenance of control while at the same time preserving faculties' cherished autonomy. This paradoxical feature of academic culture (i.e., autonomy vs. dependence dilemma) is one of the key differences that separate academic leadership from other organizational settings. In fact, Askling and Stensaker (2002) characterize universities as "complex and paradox organizations" in which "change ... seems to become the norm rather than the exception" (p. 122). For instance, ongoing political reforms, increasing number of programs, or a continuously increasing number of students place academia in constant need of adjustment. Therefore, their advice for academic leaders is to try to turn complexity into meaning through transparency and sense making. Consistent with this assumption, Mumford (2006) argued that leaders must help followers make sense of the situation by clarifying goals and pathways to goal attainment.

Romancing Academia

Making sense of the situation might be particularly difficult for academic followers. This is because academia is propelled by, and expected to deliver the ideal. The inherent prerogative of being an academic is the necessity to constantly exemplify and deliver excellence in all manners of conduct and, most of all, to benefit the society. For example, academic leaders are expected to create an environment where respect, right to self-expression, nurturance of self-confidence and self-worth guide the process of individual and professional development while, at the same time, they have to safeguard academic freedom of subordinates (Karran, 2007, 2009a, 2009b). These expectations rest on the socially constructed belief that an academic environment shapes the knowledge and the moral nature of human beings. Subsequently, it serves as an ideal standard of behavior for the entire society. Leaders, as a vital part of this environment, also emerge as examples of the ideal. Thus, leadership is a socially constructed reality that bears on the analysis of the organizational environment (Meindl, Ehrlich, & Dukerich, 1985) and vice-versa. That is, organizations are also socially constructed realities that bear on the analysis of leaders. In short, society has developed romanticized and heroic views not only of leader but also of certain professions, academia being one of them. Subsequently, the difference between ideal and real facets of leadership might be greater in academia than in other organizational contexts (Peus, Pawlowska, & Wesche, 2009) and therefore, academic leaders might be predisposed to destructive appraisals (i.e., a harsh and damaging assessment of leader behavior). In fact, ideal value standards can backfire and inadvertently cause employee bitterness and disillusionment: despite the good intentions of leaders (Cha & Edmondson, 2006). That is, an academic leader's behavior deemed by a follower to be as self-benefiting might be assessed as a form of a transgression (i.e., an offence) which in turn, will lead to an attribution of illegitimacy. Putting it differently, academic followers might have a propensity to judge their leaders' behavior too rigorously.

Ad Hoc Leadership

A majority of professors are elevated into a leadership position without adequate training for this role (Long, Allison, & McGinnis, 1993; MacKenzie, McShane, & Wilcox, 2007). A heavy workload exacerbates this often frustrating experience (Bolton, 1996). This confluence of excessive workload, environmental pressures and a lack of preparation for a leadership role might result in a number of deficiencies. For instance, academic leaders' inability to focus on social or relational aspects of academic leadership for which they simply might lack the cognitive resources (Engle & Lord, 1997), might seriously jeopardize leader-follower relationships, which in turn, might have a negative impact on various organizational outcomes. For example, Gardner (2008) observed that currently a disparate experience (e.g., lack of affiliation, alienation) of PhD students contributes to alarming attrition rates.

SITUATIONAL FACTORS: HOW LEADER-FOLLOWER INCONGRUENCE CONTRIBUTES TO THE PERCEPTION OF TRANSGRESSION

There are two key factors that, in our opinion, may contribute to destructive appraisal and, in turn, to adverse leadership perception: leader-follower value incongruence and incongruent role expectations. Specifically, both incongruent values and incongruent role expectations can potentially contribute to the perception that a transgression has been committed and, thereby, give rise to an adverse leadership perception. That is, leader-follower value incongruence and incongruent role expectations are two mechanisms by which good intentions and valid role expectations can backfire.

Value Incongruence

Human values are defined as shared regulatory or proscriptive beliefs about ideal conducts of behavior and end-states of existence that are triggered by object and situation (Rokeach, 1980). They are a vital component of the self-concept (Lydon, 1996), essential to the experience of meaning (Cha & Edmondson, 2006), tied to the affective system (Feather, 1996) and shared by many cultures (Feather, 1996; Fontaine, Poortinga, Delbeke, & Schwartz, 2008).

Schwartz's (1992; Schwartz & Bilsky, 1990) influential theory of the structure of human values suggests 10 universal value types. Those values are considered to be universal because they are recognized in a majority of cultures around the world. For instance, Schwartz (1994) reported that ten universal value types are recognized by 70% of world cultures. Each value is defined by the motivational goal it serves. Values with congruent motivational goals relate positively to one another (e.g., power and achievement). Values with motivational goals that are incongruent relate negatively to one another (e.g., autonomy and dependence). Recently, Schwartz (2006), as reported by Fontaine et al. (2008), proposed a two-dimensional value structure; a person-focused value dimension and a social-focused value dimension. The first dimension regulates the expression of personal characteristics and interests (i.e., person-focused, for example, autonomy, achievement, and power). The second dimension regulates relations with others and the effects on them (i.e., social-focused, for example, benevolence, tradition, security). This sharp distinction between person-focused values and social-focused values may be a key factor contributing to leader-follower conflict in organizations and particularly in academia. For instance, as we indicated above, academia, as an ideal-driven organization, openly endorses socially-focused values (e.g., devoting oneself to the scholarship of teaching, conducting research for the betterment of the society) over and above person-focused values (e.g., conducting research for self benefit, striving for personal power). This, in turn, may have a detrimental effect on the assessment of leader behavior. In fact, Cha and Edmondson (2006) provided initial evidence of the impact that idealized organizational contexts have on leader effectiveness. Specifically, their research showed that when a leader, in order to promote equality within an organization, endorsed a value of unpretentiousness, his purchase of a new property in a prominent neighbourhood was interpreted as a violation (i.e., a transgression). Thus, the authors suggest that the good intentions of this leader resulted in the attribution of hypocrisy. In short, leader-follower value-incongruence (i.e., a miss-match between intended and interpreted meaning of a value) rendered the leader as illegitimate. Interestingly, this process might be exacerbated by the fact that leaders who act in a way congruent with personal values (i.e., self-concordance) believe in their effectiveness and thus, do *not* question their own behaviors (Illies & Reiter-Palmon, 2008). In short, leaders who act in congruence with their personal values are satisfied with what they do, they feel good about what they do and thus, they do not question their own actions. However, this "self-indulgence" may divert their attention from, perhaps more important aspect of effectiveness, namely, the leader-follower value congruence. Subsequently, despite their satisfaction, good intentions and personal well-being leaders may be perceived as adverse. In short, if in the process of benefiting others, leaders do not conjure their values with the values of others, good intentions will backfire. Interestingly, another way in which honest intentions can backfire is the miss-match in the appraisal of relational merit. In other words, incongruent role expectations can also backfire.

Role Expectations Incongruence

Leaders and followers differ in their role expectations of each other. Leaders expect followers to be capable and competent (Day & Crain, 1992; Dockery & Steiner, 1990; Kim & Organ, 1982), whereas followers tend to be more concerned about their interpersonal interactions with their leaders (Dockery & Steiner, 1990; Maslyn & Uhl-Bien, 2001). Thus, subordinates tend to assess leaders' behavior based on implicit leadership theories. In contrast, supervisors tend to assess their subordinates based on implicit performance theories (Dansereau, Yammarino, & Markham, 1995; Engle & Lord, 1997; Epitropaki & Martin, 2004). To that effect, Huang, Wright, Chiu, and Wang (2008) found that the productivity of the group was the primary concern of leaders; however, followers were more likely to place importance on the interpersonal aspects of their relationships with the leaders. In addition, Ehrhart's and Klein's (2001) study showed that about 50% of participants preferred the relationship-oriented leader and only 20% chose the task-oriented leader. The above research suggests that leaders' predominant achievement focus (i.e., task-orientation) might preclude them from forming adequate leader-follower relationships. This, in turn, may result in an unfavorable evaluation of a leader's behavior because achievement-centered behavior violates the follower's expectations regarding the "good" leader behavior. That is, a leader who focuses strictly on achievement might create an imbalance in the leader-follower relationship by creating an image of a task-oriented and not a relationship-oriented leader. However, it is important to notice, that the motivation behind the leader's achievement focus might be beneficial to the follower. Unfortunately, the beneficial aspect of leader's achievement focus might be unnoticed by followers if it is the predominant ingredient in the leader-follower relationship. Subsequently, it might be viewed as an aspect that primarily benefits the leader and thus, as a transgression.

Transgressions and Relationship Trust

Research consistently shows that transgressions can lead to loss of trust, increased negative affect, and negative exchange (Dirks, Lewicki, & Zaaher, 2009). When the transgression occurs, individuals form judgements about the transgressor's future behavior. In such a case, positive expectations are replaced by negative perceptions. Consequently, individuals become unwilling to expose themselves to further vulnerability (Lewicki, McAllister, & Bies, 1998). Therefore, they are unwilling to trust and interact with the transgressor (Dirks & Ferrin, 2001). People also experience negative emotions (e.g., disappointment, frustration, anger, and outrage) following a transgression (Barclay, Skarlicki, & Pugh, 2005). Finally, transgressions result in a decline in cooperation (Bottom, Gibson, Daniels, & Murnighan, 2002). Dirks et al. (2009) suggested that all three factors (i.e., trust, affect and exchange) jointly comprise the domains of relationship damage and repair.

Importantly, Lewicki et al. (1998) argued that as a relationship becomes multifaceted (i.e., operates around different content areas or domains) it can simultaneously involve trust and distrust. This argument relies on the notion that individuals can segment relationships and, thus, allow for the possibility that the complex relationship can, at the same time, be positive in some facets and negative in others. For example, an academic follower may interact with a leader in several facets, including teaching and research, and might trust the leader as a research collaborator, but not as a teacher. Moreover, transgressions may call into question the integrity (i.e., values) (Kim, Ferrin, Cooper, & Dirks, 2004; Sitkin & Roth, 1993) of an individual. More importantly, inferences regarding leader integrity have a significant facility to spill over into other aspects of the relationship (Dirks et al., 2009). This tendency occurs when individuals believe that transgression about integrity is both diagnostic and informative about one's character in a way that transcends situations (Reeder & Brewer, 1979). That is, if followers notice a leader behaving dishonestly in one aspect of a relationship they might assume that this leader will behave dishonestly in all aspects of a relationship. Subsequently, they will expect to be mistreated. Therefore, integrity transgressions produce greater levels of negative affect than other forms of negative behavior. In contrast, transgressions of competence are likely to be task specific, because individuals are less inclined to generalize skills or abilities across other relationship facets (Tranfinow, Bromgard, Finlay, & Ketelaar, 2005). For instance, academic followers are apt to recognize that a lack of competence in teaching is not diagnostic of a leader's analytical competence.

In sum, the above reviewed research suggests that transgressions involving values are regarded as indicative of a leader's character. Moreover, they tend to be generalized because stereotypes are informative about one's character in a way that transcends situations. This tendency of transgressions to spill over to other aspects of leader-follower relationship can be explained by attribution processes. Therefore, followers' cognitions might be the key processes that drive adverse leadership perception.

COGNITIVE FACTORS: WHAT TYPE OF COGNITIVE PROCESSES DRIVE ADVERSE LEADERSHIP PERCEPTION?

The Attribution Process

The attribution of an act to the disposition of the actor (e.g., the attribution of a transgression to a leader's disposition) or to the situation in which the act occurred is highly functional for self-regulation. It enables the observer to determine whether the actor is likely to behave in the same way again (Higgins, 2000). Thus, it enables an individual to evaluate and make sense of a particular situation.

Actor-observer asymmetry is a specific causal attribution process that reflects a "pervasive tendency for actors to attribute their actions to situational requirements, whereas observers tend to attribute the same actions to stable personal dispositions" (Jones & Nisbett, 1972, p. 80). That is, negative and unexpected outcomes, such as unexpected failure, or when prior expectancies are disconfirmed, appear especially to promote causal attributions (Weiner, 1985). In other words, individuals have a tendency to explain their own behavior with situational causes and the behavior of the other person with dispositional causes when they evaluate negative information (e.g., a transgression), but not when they evaluate positive information.

Schyns and Hansbrough (2008) applied those findings to leader-follower relationship. They outlined a model of the attribution of mistakes to leaders. They argued that the processes leading from the occurrence of a mistake to the causal attribution to the leader or the situation is influenced by two factors: (a) the followers' tendency to romanticize leaders and (b) the match between the followers' prototypical image of a leader and their actual leader. Moreover, they noted that the characteristics of mistakes are important in this process. For example, the seriousness of the mistake, the knowledge about the mistake and finally, the consequences of the mistake all play a role in the attribution process. Importantly, they note that the violation of implicit leadership theories by making serious mistakes with known consequences increases the likelihood of attributing mistakes to the leader. That is, the incongruence between followers' implicit leadership theories and actual leader behavior may contribute to the attribution process. We concur with the authors and suggest that leader-follower incongruence contributes to adverse leadership attribution. Moreover, we suggest that followers will not attempt to maintain the romantic view of a leader and thus, will not disregard the prototype inconsistent information when they feel that their leader repeatedly mistreats them. We believe that, instead, this prototype inconsistent information will lead to an adverse perception precisely because it runs counter to the followers' expectations of what a good leader is expected to do. Therefore, a leader who consistently does not fit the leader prototype due to a perceived transgression will be classified as an adverse leader. This is because, as noted by Schyns and Hansbrough (2008) and others (e.g., Malle, Knobe, & Nelson, 2007) in the attribution process it is the negative information that may be especially indicative of the leaders' enduring characteristics. This, in turn, suggests that prototype matching (Lord & Maher, 1991) is another key process that may guide adverse leader perception.

The Process of Prototype Matching

A cognitive approach to leadership is not a new phenomenon in scientific literature. Indeed, leadership literature has long recognized that perceivers rely extensively on default value, an automatic process (Engle & Lord, 1997; Lord & Emrich, 2001; Meindl, 1995; Smith & Zarate, 1992) to activate the cognitive structures that are used in evaluating a leader (Eden & Leviatan, 1975). However, this type of research is seldom applied to the academic context. Importantly, it suggests that followers cognitively compare actual leaders to a leader prototype without a conscious effort. That comparison forms leadership perceptions (Lord, Foti, & De Vader, 1984). Therefore, the perception of a leader is determined by the extent to which the leader's actual characteristics and the leader prototype match (Maurer & Lord, 1991). If a leader behaves contradictory to prototype-based expectations, the result might be an adverse perception. However, though implicit leadership theory stresses that simple prototype matching is the key mental process guiding leader perceptions (Lord &

Maher, 1991), others propose that cognitive processing is more complex (e.g., Chen, 2001; Smith & Zarate, 1992). For example, research shows that the process of prototype matching is highly malleable (Giessner, van Knippenberg, & Sleebos, 2009). This suggests that additional information (e.g. an experience with significant others) is used to help decide whether behavior fits in the prototype category (Chen, 2001). A process of transference is assumed to provide such additional information.

Transference and the Role of Experience

As reported by Ritter and Lord (2007) transference theory suggests that categorization is influenced by both the features of the individual and by experience with significant others. The process of transference utilizes a mental structure developed in a previous relationship, which, in turn, automatically guides cognitive and emotional processes in newly formed relationships. This suggests that transference uses causal theories gained from experience with recent exemplars that are used to classify and subsequently judge new individuals. That is, a mental representation developed in previous relationships with significant others survives over time and serves as a guide in the judgement of new individuals. What differentiates the process of transference from simple prototype matching is the fact that transference implies the activation of affect and treatment expectations, both of which are not present in general prototype matching (Ritter & Lord, 2007). Researchers assume that this process takes place instead of (or in addition to) simple prototype matching (Andersen & Chen, 2002; Smith & Zarate, 1992) whereby the newly activated information is combined with the initial perception (Smith & Zarate, 1992).

Though transference is well established in the literature on self-identity (Andersen & Chen, 2002), Ritter and Lord's (2007) study is the first that applied this concept to the leadership domain. They demonstrated that leader characteristics (and associated underlying attributions) are, indeed, subject to transfer from old to new, similar leaders. Importantly, treatment expectations of justice and abuse also transfer from old to new, similar leaders. That is, without even knowing the new leader, followers with previously abusive leaders expect and prepare to be abused by their new leader. This implies that the effects of transgressions might be long lasting and that they contribute to expectations regarding future treatment. Crucially, Ritter and Lord's (2007) study suggests that transference is behavior specific and not context specific, therefore, the same effects can be expected in an academic context. It also points out how detrimental and long lasting mistreatments received from an abusive leader can be. For instance, previous research shows that an experience of injustice is related to lowered job satisfaction, commitment, trust, cooperation, task performance, and to increased withdrawal, anger, and desire for retribution (Colquitt, Conlon, Wesson, Porter, & Ng, 2001; Kohari & Lord, 2007). Moreover, a process of self-fulfilling prophecy (Merton, 1948) might exacerbate this mistreatment affinity and eliminate the role of perceptual change over time. A follower who expects to be mistreated will react and behave accordingly, and ultimately make decisions that hamper his or her work performance (Bies, 1987; Kramer & Brewer, 1984; Kramer & Messick, 1998; Orbell, Dawes, & Schwartz-Shea, 1994). Thus, the interaction of abuse expectations, and experienced affect (Gray, 2001) would elicit behavioral and affective cycles that re-enact prior leadership relations when new leaders are encountered (Ritter & Lord, 2007). Subsequently, a knowledge structure of relational schema might be permanently tainted by a negative experience, resulting in an aversive pattern, which, if unchecked, will persist over time in a self-fulfilling sequence (Cha & Edmondson, 2006). This is an important observation because knowledge structures of relational schemas are crucial aspects of human cognition. They serve as role-expectations and evaluative standards (Baldwin, 1992; Baldwin & Baccus, 2003; Lord et al., 2001; Lord & Emrich, 2001; Lord & Maher, 1991; Ritter & Lord, 2007). Role expectations, in turn, affect preferences for a particular leader or a particular follower type. Both leaders and followers employ them consciously or unconsciously in order to assess the quality of their relationship (Baldwin & Baccus, 2003; Kenney, Blascovich, & Shaver, 1994). However, if leaders' knowledge structures are different from followers' knowledge structures, a misevaluation of a relationship is likely to occur (Gerstner & Day, 1997; Huang et al., 2008) resulting in adverse leadership perception.

In sum, situational factors, characteristics of a context and cognitive processes all contribute to destructive attributions and therefore, to adverse leadership perception. The following empirical section illustrates our theoretically derived assumptions regarding adverse leadership perception in academia.

EMPIRICAL FINDINGS

In this empirical section of the chapter, we present data collected from group discussions with full professors, assistant professors and doctoral students from a German university who participated in leadership and teamwork development courses. It is important to note that the status of German PhD students is very different from the status of PhD students in other countries. Specifically, German PhD students are mainly employees who report to a professor. Therefore, their relationship with a professor is very much that of a follower and a leader and not a student and a professor.

For the purpose of data collection, full and assistant professors (78 male, 30 female) were instructed to talk about their academic leadership challenges. Doctoral students (29 male, 27 female) discussed their adverse experiences with academic leaders, as well as their expectations regarding effective leadership in academia. All of the discussions were captured in the form of written protocols. Data analysis of discussion protocols was based on grounded theory (Glaser & Strauss, 1967; Linehan & Walsh, 2000) and Mayring's (2007) recommendations for analysis of qualitative data. In the first step, we divided all of the protocol statements into two basic categories: (a) person-oriented challenges and (b) relationship-oriented challenges.

In a subsequent analysis, we explored discussion protocols for additional recurring themes. In this process, we isolated instances of incongruence (role and value) and dispositional attributions. We were also able to identify a few instances where prototype matching and transference might have accounted for adverse leadership perceptions. Finally, we noticed that followers, despite their apparent dissatisfaction with their leaders' behavior, seldom raised their concerns with their leaders. On the other hand, leaders attempted to raise their concerns with their subordinates but experienced discomfort in this process. In other words, issue clarification appeared to be challenging for both leaders and followers. We will illustrate each of these reoccurring themes next.

Role Incongruence: Achievement Orientation Versus Relationship Orientation

In general, the majority of followers in our study felt that their leaders' interests are mostly performance-focused. For instance, many doctoral students reported problems in the creation of an open, collaborative work atmosphere because they believed their leaders overemphasized competition between followers. Since competition is often a hallmark of achievement oriented organizations (Yauch & Wright, 2007), those comments imply that academic leaders with whom those followers interacted might have been predominantly performance-focused. In addition, many doctoral students stated that motivational aspects and general support were often lacking, in particular, with respect to their individual development. Academic followers appear to expect their leaders to be more caring, attentive, motivating and supportive. They expected their leader to show them the way toward success, and to help them make sense of an already stressful situation. In contrast to what some leaders appeared to endorse, most doctoral students were less competitive. In short, numerous doctoral students felt that their leaders paid little attention to relational aspects of the leader-follower interaction. Subsequently, they viewed their leaders as inattentive, competitive and adverse. Paradoxically, as the leaders in our study indicated, they were concerned with the career of their subordinates. In fact, leaders perceived their focus on productivity as an aid to the followers' career. Thus, despite good intentions, leaders were often perceived as adverse. Regrettably, many academic followers in our study judged their leaders' performance-focus as self-serving and thought of it not as a sign of benevolence (i.e., consideration), but as a need for achievement (i.e., power). This might be explained by the fact that academic leaders did not clarify with their followers that their performance focus was, in part, related to follower's career development. Finally, it must be taken into account that in many cases academic followers were certain of the accuracy of their judgement (i.e., self-concordance) and thus, did not attempt to explore for alternative explanations of their leader's behavior.

Value Incongruence: Autonomy Versus Dependence

The majority of academic followers in our analysis stated that they wanted to participate in the decision processes (e.g., prioritization of research projects) and wanted to be able to work autonomously. This is consistent with "the management of autonomy" view of academia to which we referred earlier. Consequently, these academic followers expected the value of autonomy to be honoured by their professors. However, they felt that some academic leaders endorsed dependence instead of autonomy. As a result, a number of academic followers felt that their leaders were overly controlling. This, in turn, resulted in a continuous need for feedback, which also posed a difficulty. Numerous doctoral students reported that receiving timely feedback was a real problem. Not only did many of their professors lack the time for a lengthy feedback session but, in addition, many students complained that without such feedback they could not proceed with their project. In short, in a considerable number of cases, leader-follower value incongruence elicited frustration, dissatisfaction and ultimately resulted in an adverse perception.

Importantly, as pointed out by the majority of participating leaders, the need for supervision (e.g. responsibility for the quality of a final product) often interfered with the wish of letting doctoral students work autonomously. Most professors felt restricted by time pressure and other leadership functions, which called for a high level of organization and thus, a certain level of control. For instance, academic leaders were often challenged with meeting the diverse, sometimes contradictory requirements associated with their own position (e.g., scientific and administrative tasks, dealing with stress and time pressure). Finally, some professors stated that they were willing to integrate their followers' views into decision processes and to delegate some responsibility to them. However, some leaders suggested that if they included their students in the decision process, this often resulted in a loss of respect in the eyes of their colleagues who ended up not taking them seriously enough. In short, our data suggests that many followers might not take into consideration the various management tasks that their professors need to fulfil everyday, including the responsibility for the quality of final projects. Thus, expectedly, they might attribute their adverse experiences to the leader's negative dispositions (e.g., control) and not to their leader's positive dispositions (e.g., responsibility) or situational constraints (e.g., meeting the diverse requirements associated with leadership position). This, in turn, might result in adverse perception.

Transference and Prototype Matching

One of our participating leaders described an interesting example illustrating the role of prototype matching and transference in leader-follower relationships. He described a problem he had encountered when taking over the position of department head. A colleague who had moved to a different university had previously held this position for years. When he began his new duties, he noticed that the previous leader had enforced a strong hierarchy within the department he took over. He, on the other hand, wanted to implement an open, hierarchy free atmosphere. However, to his surprise, a number of his subordinates voiced concerns related to the proposed changes, which resulted in numerous conflicts. Some of them felt rather uncomfortable with the "new rules of the game", did not work autonomously, and consistently sought his approval. They viewed the new leader, at least at the beginning, as illegitimate. Indeed, the leader in question reported that his subordinates felt that he wanted to implement a hierarchy free atmosphere in order to avoid his leadership responsibilities. It is reasonable to assume that in this instance, the characteristics of the past leader emerged as a leader prototype. Moreover, we suspect that mental structures developed in the past relationship guided the followers' judgments about the new relationship (i.e., transference). Subsequently, the leaders' behavior was interpreted as a form of transgression and attributed to the leader's negative disposition (i.e. a lack of competence). This, in turn, resulted in disenchantment (i.e. doubt in his abilities) and a perception of the leader as adverse. Several followers also drew a comparison between their current and past leader. Not surprisingly, the quality and effectiveness of their present leader varied depending on how they judged their past leader (i.e., being better or worse than the present one). We have not encountered an instance where a past relationship with a leader set a standard for a mistreatment expectation in a current leader-follower relationship.

Issue Clarification

A lack of clarification—the ability to understand each other's motivations—might be the key problem which leads to disenchantment and dissatisfaction in leader-follower relationships. Seeking clarification can lead to reattribution of behavior to appropriate causes. This, we assume, could prompt a self-reflection phase. Subsequently, in the future, an individual might monitor his/her leadership perceptions (cf. recommendation section). However, though mutual clarification of common frustrations is necessary, this might be a difficult process. For instance, in our study, numerous leaders reported that they felt uncomfortable when addressing issues that might hurt the followers' feelings. One of the reasons given was the possibility that such a situation might have created a larger than present conflict. This suggests that many issues that should have been addressed remained unresolved. Moreover, as noted by Cha and Edmondson (2006), once negative attributions are made, further causal analysis might be limited, suggesting limited potential for self-correction.

In conclusion, the analysis of adverse leadership experiences in academia supports our assumptions regarding a possible developmental path behind adverse leadership perception. In addition, our results suggest and further support earlier finding, which imply that value and role incongruence, prototype matching, transference, and attribution bias contribute to this process.

A CONCEPTUAL MODEL OF ADVERSE LEADERSHIP PERCEPTION IN ACADEMIA

This section presents a model of adverse leadership perception (see Figure 17.1) with a specific focus on academic leaders. We believe that this model illustrates the self-reinforcing process of adverse leadership perception and contributes to our understanding of: (a) determinants of adverse leadership perception, and (b) factors that may exacerbate or hinder this process.

Initially, once an academic is categorized as the leader, the activated leader prototype causes followers to retrieve, attend to and encode this

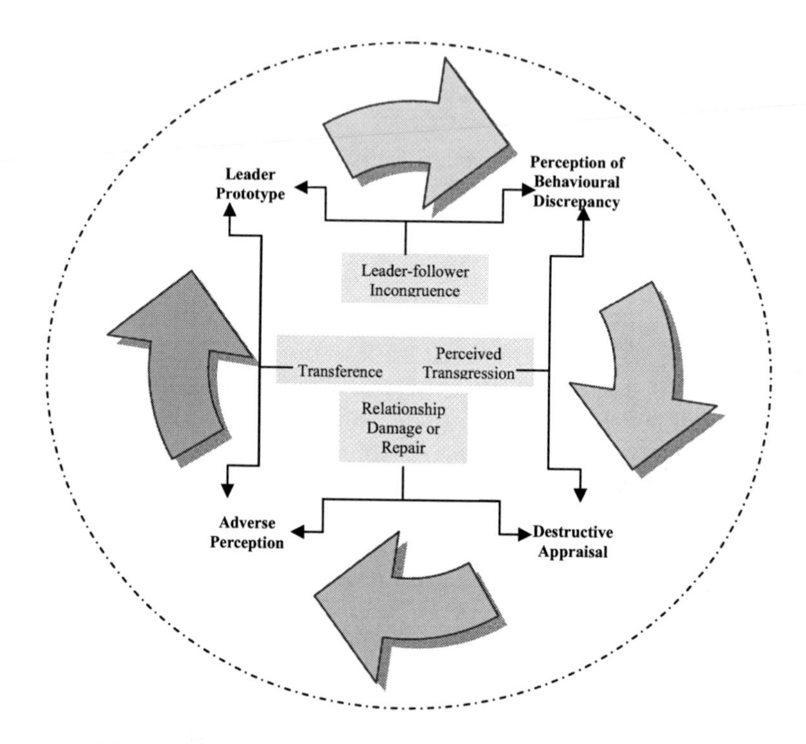

Note: The model emphasizes the self-reinforcing nature of adverse leadership perception elicited by behavioral and cognitive cycles that re-enact impaired leader-follower relations unless attempts toward relationship repair are made.

Figure 17.1. A conceptual model of adverse leadership perception.

ideal consistent information. In this process, the leader's attributes and/or behaviors are compared to prototypical leader characteristics (Phillips & Lord, 1982) and/or previously encountered leader characteristics (Ritter & Lord, 2007). Thus, previously encoded information about a leader's attributes and/or behaviors is transferred onto the image of a new leader. Thus, the evaluation of an academic leader's effectiveness is not based on actual traits and behaviors but, rather, it is a result of the observers' subjective realities (Lord, 1985). Subsequently, role expectations are formed.

Situations where an academic leader's behaviors and values are perceived as contrary (i.e., incongruent) to the activated leader prototype and therefore, follower expectations, are particularly likely to result in the follower's dissatisfaction and the perception of behavioral discrepancy. This is because the inference made by a follower will suggest that a leader is adversative to the "good academic leader" prototype (Mayer,

Davis, & Schoorman, 1995; Simons, 2002). Thus, once a leader's behavior is coded as a prototype breach, observers tend to attribute that action to leader dispositions and to distrust the leader. This happens for several reasons.

First, dispositional inferences are simpler to make than nondispositional ones because academic leaders are directly visible whereas situational constraints, which may legitimately drive a leader's behavior, are invisible (Gilbert & Malone, 1995). Second, academic followers bolster their self-esteem by attributing their leaders' failures to their dispositions, while viewing their own failures as unrelated to their dispositions (Ross & Fletcher, 1985). Moreover, people, including academic followers, tend to blame human agency for harmful events because it allows them to maintain a sense of control. Therefore, attributions caused by transgressions are blame-oriented attributions. Subsequent feelings of threat might restrict the followers' cognitive processing (Janes & Olsen, 2000; Weick, 1995), reduce awareness of important additional information about an academic leader's behavior (Edmondson, 1999; Cha & Edmondson, 2006) making it difficult to stop the destructive appraisal of leader behavior. Feelings of anger, resentment, bitterness, and even outrage that emanate from the perception that one has been betrayed or mistreated (Morrison & Robinson, 1997), may contribute greatly to this process. In fact, academic followers might attribute multiple actions exhibited by an academic leader to a deliberate violation of organizational and relational values in this pattern and thus, feel continuously betrayed and mistreated. Moreover, followers who are repeatedly exposed to a leader's failures (i.e., are disappointed with a leader's behavior) may over time change their perception of leader group prototypicality (Giessner et al., 2009). Subsequently, this new perception might be transferred directly onto the leader's prototype. In this way, a self-reinforcing cycle of adverse leadership perception is set in motion. Paradoxically, this entire process does not originate in the academic leaders' destructive intentions, but in the follower's subjective inferences about leader behavior. However, this process may result in destructive outcomes such as low job performance (Staw & Barsade, 1993), absenteeism (Pelled & Xin, 1999), and low helpfulness (George, 1991). Therefore, it is vital for academic leaders to be aware of this destructive process and to know how it can be prevented or reversed. To that effect, the following section provides some practical suggestions regarding leader's constructive management of others' perceptions of their behavior.

RECOMMENDATIONS: IMPROVING LEADERSHIP IN ACADEMIA

As we noted above, an academic context might be especially vulnerable to contra productive outcomes because academic leaders are seldom prepared for their leadership duties. Consequently, this final part of the chapter focuses on systematic leadership development in academia. We will provide some practical recommendations as to how academic leaders can effectively deal with leader-follower challenges through: (a) self-awareness and reflection, and (b) by integrating conflict management behavior. We suggest that these factors may prevent and/or reverse the development of adverse leadership perception.

Systematic Leadership Development in Academia

In a business context, leadership development has been met with increased interest and attention in recent years (Brungardt, 1996; Day, 2000; Rost, 1993). In this context, leadership is seen as a source for competitive advantage, the so-called "organizational capability—the firm's ability to manage people to gain competitive advantage" (Ulrich & Lake, 1991, p. 77). In business, leadership development takes different forms, for example, 360 degree feedback (Alimo-Metcalfe, 1998), critical reflection (Densten & Gray, 2001), problem-based teaching (Mumford, Zaccaro, Harding, Jacobs, & Fleishman, 2000), or executive coaching (Feldman & Lankau, 2005). However, in the academic context, leaders cope with a lack of systematic development when faced with leadership challenges (Bryman, 2007). This is quite unfortunate given that academic excellence depends not only on researchers' scientific knowledge and skills, but also on their ability to motivate and lead their staff effectively (cf. Frey, Peus, & Jonas, 2004; Peus & Frey, 2009). For instance, the principle-based model of leadership (Frey, 1998), introduced next, can be used as a guiding framework for systematic leadership development in academia that may reverse and/or prevent adverse leadership perception.

Basic Principles for Academic Leadership

The principle-based model of leadership (Frey, 1998; Peus & Frey, 2009) integrates different models of leadership and enables leaders to meet their followers' needs. By integrating the following eight basic principles, academic leaders can improve their abilities in promoting innovation and academic excellence.

- *Principle 1* "Providing meaning and vision"

Leaders should clearly explain the reasons why specific goals are worth pursuing. Followers who understand the reasons why they are supposed to engage their efforts in pursuit of particular goals will actively connect their goals with those of a team. In addition, followers who experience their job as meaningful feel more willing to contribute new ideas and engage themselves for the goals of the team.

- *Principle 2 "Providing transparency through information and communication"*

A leader who provides information to his/her followers that reaches beyond their specific task (e.g., future goals of the department), enables them to be proactive and act responsibly. Through this extended dialogue, new ideas as well as challenges and problems can be addressed before conflicts arise.

- *Principle 3 "Participation and autonomy"*

By giving opportunities for participation and autonomous action to their followers, leaders fulfil a fundamental human need. When followers are encouraged to integrate their opinion and ideas, they experience appreciation and independence.

- *Principle 4 "Ensuring procedural justice"*

Especially in the case of limited resources, when the leader cannot distribute outcomes equally, the underlying rules for decision-making should be explained clearly to ensure the followers' understanding and feeling of justice.

- *Principle 5 "Giving constructive feedback"*

Praising followers is a very important motivator for their performance. However, the provision of constructive criticism is also a crucial factor for success. Constructive feedback should follow the guideline "tough on the issue, soft on the person". In addition, followers should be encouraged to criticize their leaders.

- *Principle 6 "Stimulating by goal-setting"*

Leaders should implement a participative process in order to agree which goals should be pursued. In addition, the goals need to be challenging, specific and measurable. This process ensures that everyone is aware of evaluative standards. In short, the inspiring vision for the entire unit must be broken down into specific goals for every individual.

- *Principle 7 "Fostering personal growth"*

A leader who fosters his/her followers' personal growth takes into account their individual needs for development. The followers' skills, talents, and interests have to be considered in this process. This individualized consideration will result in higher satisfaction and performance.

- *Principle 8 "Serving as a role model"*

A leader's function as a role model is not limited to his/her expertise. It includes his/her characteristics such as personal integrity.

In addition to the basic principles of leadership, a leader has to be aware of the impact that his/her beliefs, values, and actions have on his/her followers. In fact, a leader's self-awareness and value clarity are key, not only for the implementation of these basic leadership principles, but also for the effective fulfilment of leadership roles in general (Tekleab, Sims, Yun, Tesluk, & Cox, 2008). As indicated by our model, attempts toward leader-follower relationship repair (through, for example, self-reflection) might be particularly useful for the prevention of adverse leadership perception. This technique is also useful in the prevention or handling of conflict situations. A leader's ability to self-reflect can influence the outcome and the leader-follower relationship (Tekleab et al., 2008). Therefore, in the next part of the chapter, we describe how academic leadership can profit from heightened self-awareness and value clarity.

Leader Self-Awareness and Value Clarity

This section focuses on answering two questions: (a) How aware are leaders of their underlying values, their behavior, and of their impact on followers? (b) What is the relationship between self-awareness and leadership effectiveness?

A growing body of theory and research highlights the influence of self-awareness and reflection on leader development. Managerial self-awareness is conceptualized as the degree of similarity between the leader's self-description and his/her followers' ratings of the leadership behavior (Church, 1997).

A particularly important area for self-reflection and clarification are leadership values. It is possible that leaders and followers engaged in thoughtful dialogue about the values aimed at reducing differences in understanding of their meaning and implications (e.g., Isaacs, 1992; Schein, 1985), can eliminate the problems associated with value incongruence. At the same time, conflict may exist between such value clarity and its meaningfulness. Specifically, employees may be less connected to organizational values if leaders restrict the meanings they attach to them (Cha & Edmondson, 2006). If leaders present compelling reasons for their actions and highlight ways in which the organization is living up to its values, and then ask for help identifying issues or concerns they might be missing (e.g., Argyris, 1993; Edmondson, Bohmer, & Pisano, 2001), they might reduce their employees' tendency to attribute negative events to their leader's dispositions. This view is consistent with research showing that communication about an actor's situational constraints and realistic expectations about how most people would act in his or her situation may reduce the likelihood of a correspondent dispositional attribution (Gilbert & Malone, 1995).

How is the process of critical self-reflection activated? According to Densten and Gray (2001) critical reflection can be characterized by a "deeper, more intense, and more probing form of reflection" (p. 119). Self-reflection makes the questioning of basic assumptions and practices necessary. Such a level of self-reflection can be reached in individual coaching sessions. The role of a coach is to confront leaders with challenging and unfamiliar experiences. However, even more important are the leader's attitudes, which influence how far he/she profits from the confrontation with the uncommon situation. Yost, Sentner, and Forlenza-Bailey (2000) suggest that the influence of self-reflection is fostered by: *open-mindedness* (i.e., the will to give attention to alternative views and to question common assumptions), *responsibility* (i.e., the desire to actively search for truth and to challenge upcoming problems), and wholeheartedness (i.e. the attitude to overcome uncertainty and to critically evaluate oneself, organizations, and society). In addition, Daudelin (1996) views day-to-day challenges in leadership as a "rich source of learning" (p. 36) which require a set of tools to help leaders use reflection as a way of learning. The process of reflection is subdivided into four stages: (1) an articulation, (2) an analysis of the problem, (3) the formulation and testing of a tentative theory to explain the problem, and (4) a decision and/or an action. A very powerful tool for learning by reflection is asking questions, which vary according to the above-mentioned stages of reflection (e.g., what? why? how? and what else?, Daudelin, 1996).

As evidenced in this chapter, especially challenging for effective leadership are leader-follower conflict situations resulting from different expectations or values. We discuss this issue in the next section. We also provide some suggestions regarding how to integrate followers' perspectives into this process.

Leadership Conflict Management: Dominating Versus Integrating

This section takes a closer look at leaders' conflict behavior and its impact on the leader-follower interaction. Specifically, we illustrate how leaders' integration of self-oriented and other-oriented interests can contribute to successful conflict management and effective leadership.

Although in many cases promoting the welfare of employees may be consistent with organizational performance (Cha, 2004), situations exist in which leaders may need to decide between the two values (achievement vs. relationship). Leader-follower conflict is a good example for this kind of situation. The tension in achievement versus relationship conflict situations may increase the chance that a given leader's actions will be seen as inconsistent with a follower's value set. As a result, leaders who promote achievement-oriented values may be at increased risk for adverse attributions. To reduce the risk of adverse attribution, leaders may need to explicitly acknowledge and cope with the above tension (Evans, 2000), for example, by drawing followers' attention to the possibility of conflicts between caring for and supporting followers on the one hand and sustaining performance standards on the other.

Based on Pruitt and Rubin's (1986) dual concern theory, Rahim (2002) introduced five conflict management styles: avoiding, obliging, dominating, integrating, and compromising. These five basic conflict management styles are distributed along two opposing dimensions: a person's concern for the self and a person's concern for the interests of others. We will briefly describe each of these conflict management styles.

- *Avoiding* (i.e., a low concern for the self and for others)

A leader with an avoiding conflict management style fails to satisfy his own needs, as well as the needs of followers (e.g., by sidestepping in important decisions). This conflict management style is likely to have negative consequences (e.g., follower frustration or withdrawal).

- *Obliging* (i.e., a low concern for the self and high concern for others)

An obliging conflict management style is characterized by a low concern for the self and a high concern for the needs of others (e.g., by playing down differences). This conflict management style is likely to have negative consequences for the leader in situations where selfish interests motivate the actions of the follower.

- *Compromising* (i.e., an intermediate concern for the self and for others)

A leader with a compromising conflict management style is likely to negotiate with his followers the conditions that may benefit both parties. The compromise is often achieved because both parties agree to give up some of their initial requests. Thus, this conflict management style offers a helpful, though sometimes temporary, solution. However, compromising conflict management style is not appropriate in situations where highly complex and important issues are at stake.

- *Dominating* (i.e., a low concern for others and a high concern for the self)
  Leaders who practice this conflict management style tend to focus on their own interests and are likely to force their will on others. A leader who practices this style is likely to ignore the followers' needs, instill fear and provoke followers' objections and negative reactions (e.g. reactance or distrust).
- *Integrating* (i.e., a high concern for the self and for others)
  An integrating conflict management style represents an appropriate problem solving behavior (e.g., discussing different viewpoints, searching for and analyzing several alternatives). It usually demands a high effort and is time consuming. However, it offers a real possibility to find satisfactory solutions benefiting both parties.

It is important to point out that there are situational causes which might make the application of dominating management style necessary. Leaders can make use of this style when a quick decision is needed, an unfavorable decision is inevitable, or even assertive actions of subordinates have to be overcome (Rahim, 2002). However, to prevent followers from causal attributions of the dominating behavior to the person of the leader, leaders must raise their followers' understanding of the situational constraints and/or requirements. For example, our data analysis indicates that PhD students interpret a perceived lack of supervision as a sign of their leader's inconsideration without taking into consideration an array of factors that may interfere with professorial supervisory duties (e.g., administrative tasks, steering committees, holding regular lectures). In order to rectify this situation both leaders and followers should engage in an open discussion regarding their duties and expectations. Subsequently, both sides can adapt their expectations to a reasonable standard. Moreover, open feedback and interpersonal exchange between the leader and the follower about individual constrains can prevent negative attributions and outcomes. However, in situations with less constraints and more time leeway, an integrating conflict management style (i.e., high concern for self and others) provides the opportunity to analyze the underlying problems and subsequently to derive possible solutions to a conflict that take into account various perspectives. This integration of perspectives fosters followers' commitment to a solution, which is often crucial to the successful implementation of new structures. This style was found to be most appropriate for managing leader-follower social conflict (Pruitt & Carnevale, 1993). Therefore, it might be particularly useful to academic leaders. In sum, it seems very useful for academic leaders to:

1. attend professional and systematic leadership development programs, in particular, those that address issues such as transparency, procedural justice or constructive feedback.
2. clarify their values through self-reflection and transparent communication, as well as actual value congruent leadership behavior.
3. take into account their followers' perspective, in particular their expectations, needs and personal goals.
4. adapt their own conflict management behavior to situational conditions, while simultaneously explaining these constrains to their followers.
5. place a greater focus on relational aspects of leadership.

CONCLUSION

Napoleon Hill said that, "What the mind of man can conceive and believe it can achieve." However, what if the conceived is not the result of a consciously cognizing mind but a result of confluence between the thought and factors primarily outside the conscious mind? This question motivated most of this chapter. Specifically, we have argued throughout this work that the human mind has a tendency to drift toward subjective assessments rather than toward objective judgements of behavior. Applying this argument to the area of academic leadership, we have illustrated unintended negative consequences of academic leadership. Moreover, we identified factors which contribute to adverse leadership perception (cf. Table 17.1). Our theoretical model integrated findings from prior research with a qualitative analysis of discussions we led with academic leaders and academic followers. It suggests that prototype matching, leader-follower incongruence (i.e., values and expectations) and transgression all contribute to destructive attribution bias. Subsequently, followers feel mistreated, which increases the risk of adverse leadership perception and thereby leads to negative outcomes. Moreover, idealized organizational contexts might provide to be a particularily fruitful ground for this process to emerge. Therefore, new approaches are particularly necessary in the "idealized" area of academic leadership because: (a) traditional leadership theory and practice might not be suitable to this specific context and (b) this type of research is simply lacking. Accordingly, this chapter attempted to shift the focus of academic research to that very direction and thus, shed specific light on mechanisms through which academic leaders might be exposed to negative sense making which affects both the leaders' and followers' experience at work and has negative consequences on numerous organizational outcomes (e.g., attrition, retention, reputation). This is why we endorsed an idea that the ability to monitor and understand one's own cognitive processes is crucial for effective functioning of both academic leaders and academic followers. For example, human resource initiatives (e.g., self-awareness, self-reflection, conflict management training), in combination with basic principles or leadership (e.g., providing meaning, transparency, and communication), might aid and/or prevent adverse leadership perception. As implied throughout this chapter, such training would facilitate efficiency, satisfaction and well-being and prevent attrition, stress and conflict (cf. Table 17.1).

Finally, academia, as a pinnacle of future hopes, a place of discovery, innovation and progress often is, as it continuously should be, an example where original training breaks new ground in employee development. Unfortunately, leadership development is rarely one of them. Perhaps for academia truly to be able to flourish, academics and policymakers should learn to prosper from the wealth of leadership literature.

Table 17.1. Factors That Contribute to and Prevent Adverse Leadership Perception

Contributing Factors	*Preventive Factors*
–Environmental factors: –Complexity/ autonomy vs. dependence –Idealization/ romanticism –Lack of systematic leadership development Situational factors: –Leader-follower incongruence: values and expectations –Perceived transgressions *Cognitive factors:* –Destructive appraisal –Prototype matching –Transference of negative experiences	–Self-awareness, value clarity and self-reflection –Integration of self and others' interests into conflict management –A careful application of basic leadership principles, for example, o Vision and meaning o Transparency o Participation o Role modeling –Stronger focus on interpersonal aspects of leader-follower relationship –Implementation of systematic leadership development

REFERENCES

Alimo-Metcalfe, B. (1998). 360 degree feedback and leadership development. *International Journal of Selection and Assessment, 6*, 35-44.

Andersen, S. M., & Chen, S. (2002). The relational self: An interpersonal social-cognitive theory. *Psychological Bulletin, 109*, 619-645.

Argyris, C. (1993). *Knowledge for action: A guide to overcoming barriers to organizational change.* San Francisco: Jossey-Bass.

Ashforth, B. (1994). Petty tyranny in organizations. *Human Relations, 47*, 755-778.

Askling, B., & Stensaker, B. (2002). Academic leadership: Prescriptions, practices and paradoxes. *Tertiary Education and Management, 8*, 113-125.

Baldwin, M. W. (1992). Relational schemas and the processing of social information. *Psychological Bulletin, 112*, 461-484.

Baldwin, M. W., & Baccus, J. R. (2003). An expectancy value approach to self-esteem. In S. J. Spencer, S. Fein, M. P. Zanna, & J. M. Olson (Eds.), *The Ontario Symposium: Motivated social perception* (Vol. 9, pp. 171–194). Mahwah, NJ: Erlbaum.

Barclay, L., Skarlicki, D. P., & Pugh, S. D. (2005). Exploring the role of emotions in injustice perceptions and retaliation. *Journal of Applied Psychology, 90*, 629-643.

Bies, R. J. (1987). The predicament of injustice. In L. L. Cummings & B. M. Shaw (Eds.), *Research in organizational behavior* (pp. 289-310). Greenwich, CT: JAI Press.

Bligh, M. C., Kohles, J. C., Pearce, C. L., Justin, J. E., & Stovall, J. F. (2007). When the romance is over: Follower perspectives of aversive leadership. *Applied Psychology: An International Review, 56*, 528-557.

Bolton, A. (1996). The leadership challenge in universities: The case of business schools. *Higher Education, 31*, 491-506.

Bottom, W. P., Gibson, K., Daniels, S., & Murnighan, J. K. (2002). When talk is not cheap: Substantive penance and expressions of intent in rebuilding cooperation. *Organization Science, 13*, 497-513.

Brungardt, C. (1996). The making of leaders: A review of the research in leadership development and education. *Journal of Leadership Studies, 3*, 81-95.

Bryman, A. (2007). Effective leadership in higher education: A literature review. *Studies in Higher Education, 32*, 693-710.

Cha, S. E. (2004). *Walking the talk: Leadership, ambiguity, and perceived commitment to organizational values.* Unpublished doctoral dissertation, Harvard University.

Cha, S. E., & Edmondson, A. C. (2006). When values backfire: Leadership, attribution, and disenchantment in a values-driven organization. *Leadership Quarterly, 17*, 57-78.

Chen, S. (2001). The role of theories in mental representations and their use in social perception: A theory-based approach to significant-other representations and transference. In G. B. Moskowitz (Ed.), *Cognitive social psychology: The Princeton Symposium on the legacy and future of social cognition* (pp. 125-142). Hillsdale, NJ: Erlbaum.

Church, A. H. (1997). Managerial self-awareness in high-performing individuals in organizations. *Journal of Applied Psychology, 82*, 281-292.

Colquitt, J. A., Conlon, D. E., Wesson, M. J., Porter, O. L. H., & Ng, K. Y. (2001). Justice at the millennium: A meta-analytic review of 25 years of organizational justice research. *Journal of Applied Psychology, 86*, 425-445.

Dansereau, F., Yammarino, F. J., & Markham, S. E. (1995). Leadership: The multiple level approaches. *Leadership Quarterly, 6*, 97-109.

Daudelin, M. W. (1996). Learning from experience through reflection. *Organizational Dynamics, 1*, 36-48.

Day, D. V. (2000). Leadership development: A review in context. *Leadership Quarterly, 11*, 581-613.

Day, D. V., & Crain, E. C. (1992). The role of affect and ability in initial exchange quality perceptions. *Group and Organization Management, 17*, 380-397.

De Dreu, C. K., Evers, A., Beersma, B., Kluwer, E. S., & Nauta, A. (2001). A theory-based measure of conflict management strategies in the workplace. *Journal of Organizational Behavior, 22*, 645-668.

Densten, I. L., & Gray, J. H. (2001). Leadership development and reflection: what is the connection? *International Journal of Educational Management, 15*, 119-124.

Dirks, K. T., & Ferrin, D. L. (2001). The role of trust in organizational settings. *Organization Science, 12*, 450-467.

Dirks, K. T., Lewicki, R. J., & Zaheer, A. (2009). Repairing relationships within and between organizations: building a conceptual foundation. *Academy of Management Review, 34*, 68-84.

Dockery, T. M., & Steiner, D. D. (1990). The role of the initial interaction in leader-member exchange. *Group and Organization Studies, 15*, 395-413.

Eden, D., & Leviatan, U. (1975). Implicit leadership theory as a determinant of the factor structure underlying supervisory behavior scales. *Journal of Applied Psychology, 60*, 736-741.

Edmondson, A. (1999). Psychological safety and learning behavior in work teams. *Administrative Science Quarterly, 44*, 350-383.

Edmondson, A. C., Bohmer, R. M., & Pisano, G. P. (2001). Disrupted routines: Team learning and new technology implementation in hospitals. *Administrative Science Quarterly, 46*, 685-716.

Ehrhart, M. G., & Klein, K.J. (2001). Predicting followers' preferences for charismatic leadership: the influence of follower values and personality. *Leadership Quarterly, 12*, 153-179.

Einarsen, S., Aasland, M. S., & Skogstad, A. (2007). Destructive leadership behaviour: A definition and conceptual model. *Leadership Quarterly, 18*, 207-216.

Engle, E. M., & Lord, R. G. (1997). Implicit theories, self-schemas, and leader-member exchange. *Academy of Management Journal, 40*, 988-1010.

Epitropaki, O., & Martin, R. (2004). Implicit leadership theories in applied settings: Factor structure, generalizability, and stability over time. *Journal of Applied Psychology, 89*, 293-310.

Evans, P. A. L. (2000). The dualistic leader: Thriving on paradox. In S. Chowdhury (Ed.), *Management 21C: Someday we'll all manage this way* (pp. 66-82). London: Financial Times Management.

Feather, N. T. (1996). Values, deservingness, and attitudes toward high achievers: Research on tall poppies. In C. Seligman, J. M. Olson, & M. P. Zanna (Eds.),

The Ontario symposium: The psychology of values (Vol. 8, pp. 215-251). Mahwah, NJ: Erlbaum.

Feldman, D. C., & Lankau, M. J. (2005). Executive Coaching: A review and agenda for future research. *Journal of Management, 31*, 829-848.

Fisher-Yoshida, B. (2003). Self-awareness and the co-construction of conflict. *Human Systems, 14*, 3-22.

Fontaine, R. J., Poortinga, Y. H., Delbeke, L., & Schwartz, S. H. (2008). Structural equivalence of the values domain across cultures: Distinguishing sampling fluctuations from meaningful variation. *Journal of Cross-Cultural Psychology, 39*, 345-365.

Frey, D. (1998). Center of Excellence – ein Weg zu Spitzenleistungen [Center of excellence – a way to top-level performance]. In P. Weber (Ed.), *Leistungsorientiertes Management: Leistung steigern statt Kosten senken* (pp. 199-203). Frankfurt, Germany: Campus.

Frey, D., Peus, C., & Jonas, E. (2004). Soziale Organisationen als Centers of Excellence mit Menschenwürde - Zur Professionalisierung der Mitarbeiter- und Unternehmensführung [Social organizations as centers of excellence with human dignity—Professionalization of leadership and business management]. In B. Maelicke (Ed.), *Personal als Erfolgsfaktor in der Sozialwirtschaft* (pp. 27-52). Baden-Baden: Nomos.

Gardner, S. K. (2008). Fitting the mold of graduate school: A qualitative study of socialization in doctoral education. *Innovative Higher Education, 33*, 125-138.

George, J. M. (1991). State or trait: Effects of positive mood on prosocial behaviors at work. *Journal of Applied Psychology, 76*, 299-307.

Gerstner, C. R., & Day, D. V. (1997). Meta-analytic review of leader-member exchange theory: Correlates and construct issues. *Journal of Applied Psychology, 82*, 827-844.

Giessner, S. R., van Knippenberg, D., & Sleebos, E. (2009). License to Fail? How leader group prototypicality moderates the effects of leader performance on perceptions of leader effectiveness. *Leadership Quarterly, 20*, 434-451.

Gilbert, D. T., & Malone, P. S. (1995). The correspondence bias. *Psychological Bulletin, 117*, 21-30.

Glaser, B. G., & Strauss, A. L. (1967). *The discovery of grounded theory: Strategies for qualitative research.* San Francisco: University of California Press; New York: Aldinede Gruyter.

Gray, J. R. (2001). Emotional modulation of cognitive control: Approach-withdrawal states double-dissociate spatial from verbal two-back task performance. *Journal of Experimental Psychology: General, 130*, 436-452.

Higgins, E. T. (2000). Social cognition: Learning about what matters in the social world. *European Journal of Social Psychology, 30*, 3-39.

Huang, X., Wright, R. P., Chiu, W. C. K., & Wang, C. (2008). Relational schemas as sources of evaluation and misevaluation of leader–member exchanges: Some initial evidence. *Leadership Quarterly, 19*, 266-282.

Illies, J. J., & Reiter-Palmon, R. (2008). Responding destructively in leadership situations: The role of personal values and problem construction. *Journal of Business Ethics, 82*, 251-272.

Isaacs, W. N. (1992). *The perils of shared ideals.* PhD thesis, Oxford University.

Janes, L. M., & Olsen, J. M. (2000). Jeer pressures: The behavioral effects of observing ridicule of others. *Personality and Social Psychology Bulletin, 26*, 474-485.

Jones, E. E., & Nisbett, R. E. (1972). The actor and the observer: Divergent perceptions of the causes of behavior. In E. E. Jones, D. E. Kanouse, H. H. Kelley, R. E. Nisbett, S. Valins & B. Weiner (Eds.), *Attribution: Perceiving the causes of behavior* (pp. 79-94). Morristown, NJ: General Learning Press.

Karran, T. (2007). Academic freedom in Europe: A preliminary comparative analysis. *Higher Education Policy, 20*, 289-313.

Karran, T. (2009a). Academic freedom in Europe: Reviewing UNESCO's recommendation. *British Journal of Educational Studies, 57*, 191-215.

Karran, T. (2009b). Academic freedom in Europe: Time for a Magna Charta? *Higher Education Policy, 22*, 163-189.

Kelloway, E. K., Mullen, J., & Francis, L. (2006). Divergent effects of transformational and passive leadership on employee safety. *Journal of Occupational Health Psychology, 11*, 76-86.

Kenney, R. A., Blascovich, J., & Shaver, P. R. (1994). Implicit leadership theories: Prototypes for new leaders. *Basic and Applied Social Psychology, 15*, 409-430.

Kim, P. H., Ferrin, D. L., Cooper, C. D., & Dirks, K. T. (2004). Removing the shadow of suspicion: The effects of apology vs. denial for repairing ability vs. integrity-based trust violations. *Journal of Applied Psychology, 89*, 104-118.

Kim, K. I., & Organ, D. W. (1982). Determinants of leader-subordinate exchange relationships. *Group and Organization Studies, 7*, 77-89.

Kohari, N. E., & Lord, R. G. (2007). Consequences of interactional (in)justice: A look at leader behaviors and follower perceptions. In D. De Cremer (Ed.), *Advances in the psychology of justice and affect* (pp. 233-260). Charlotte, NC: Information Age Publishing.

Kramer, R. M., & Brewer, M. B. (1984). Effects of group identity on resource use in a simulated commons dilemma. *Journal of Personality and Social Psychology, 46*, 1044-1057.

Kramer, R. M., & Messick, D. M. (1998). Getting by with a little help from our enemies. In C. Sedikides, J. Schopler, & C. A. Insko (Eds.), *Intergroup cognition and intergroup behavior* (pp. 219-230). Mahwah, NJ: Erlbaum.

Lewicki, R. J., McAllister, D. J., & Bies, R. J. (1998). Trust and distrust: New relationships and realities. *Academy of Management Review, 23*, 438-458.

Linehan, M., & Walsh, J. S. (2000). Work-family conflict and the senior female international manager. *British Journal of Management, 11*, 49-58.

Long, J. S., Allison, P. D., & McGinnis, R., (1993). Rank advancement in academic careers: Sex differences and the effects of productivity. *American Sociological Review, 58*, 703-722.

Lord, R. G. (1985). Accuracy in behavioral measurement: An alternative definition based on raters' cognitive schema and signal detection theory. *Journal of Applied Psychology, 70*, 66-71.

Lord, R. G., Brown, D. J., Harvey, J. L., & Hall, R. J. (2001). Contextual constraints on prototype generation and their multilevel consequences for leadership perceptions. *Leadership Quarterly, 12*, 311-338.

Lord, R. G., & Emrich, C. G. (2001). Thinking outside the box by looking inside the box: Extending the cognitive revolution in leadership research. *Leadership Quarterly, 11*, 551-579.

Lord, R. G., Foti, R., & De Vader, C. (1984). A test of leadership categorization theory: Internal structure, information processing, and leadership perceptions. *Organizational Behavior and Human Performance, 34*, 343-378.

Lord, R. G., & Maher, K. J. (1991). *Leadership and information processing: Linking perceptions and performance*. Boston: Routledge.

Lydon, J. (1996). Toward a theory of commitment. In C. Seligman, J. M. Olson, & M. P. Zanna (Eds.), *The Ontario symposium: The psychology of values* (Vol. 8, pp. 215-251). Mahwah, NJ: Erlbaum.

MacKenzie, H., McShane, K., & Wilcox, S. (2007). Challenging performative fabrication: Seeking authenticity in academic development practice. *International Journal for Academic Development, 12*, 45-54.

Malle, B. F., Knobe, J. M., & Nelson, S. E. (2007). Actor-observer asymmetries in explanations of behavior: New answers to an old question. *Journal of Personality and Social Psychology, 93*, 491-514.

Martin. E., Trigwell, K., Prosser, M., & Ramsden, P. (2003) Variation in the experience of leadership of teaching in higher education. *Studies in Higher Education, 28*, 247-59.

Maslyn, J. M., & Uhl-Bien, M. (2001). Leader-member exchange and its dimensions: Effects of self-effort and other's effort on relationship quality. *Journal of Applied Psychology, 86*, 697-708.

Maurer, T. J., & Lord, R. G. (1991). An exploration of cognitive demands in group interaction as a moderator of information processing variables in perceptions of leadership. *Journal of Applied Social Psychology, 21*, 821-839.

Mayer, R. C., Davis, J. H., & Schoorman, F. D. (1995). An integration model of organizational trust. *Academy of Management Review, 20*, 709-734.

Mayring, P. (2007). *Qualitative Inhaltsanalyse. Grundlagen und Techniken* [Qualitative content analysis. Basics and techniques]. Weinheim: Deutscher Studienverlag.

Meindl, J. R. (1995). The romance of leadership as a follower-centric theory: A social constructionist approach. *Leadership Quarterly, 6*, 329-341.

Meindl, J. R., Ehrlich, S. B., & Dukerich, J. M. (1985). The romance of leadership. *Administrative Science Quarterly, 30*, 78-102.

Merton, R. K. (1948). The self-fulfilling prophecy. *The Antioch Review, 8*, 193-210.

Mintzberg , H. (1998) Covert leadership: Notes on managing professionals. *Harvard Business Review, 76*, 140-47.

Morrison, E. W., & Robinson, S. L. (1997). When employees feel betrayed: a model of how psychological contract violation develops. *Academy of Management Review, 22*, 226-256.

Mumford, M. D. (Ed.). (2006). *Pathways to outstanding leadership: a comparative analysis of charismatic, ideological, and pragmatic leadership*. Mahwah, NJ: Erlbaum.

Mumford. M. D., Zaccaro, S. J., Harding, F. D., Jacobs, T. O., & Fleishman, E. A. (2000). Leadership skills for a changing world: Solving complex social problems. *Leadership Quarterly, 11*, 11-35.

Orbell, J., Dawes, R., & Schwartz-Shea, P. (1994). Trust, social categories, and individuals. *Motivation and Emotion, 18*, 109-127.

Padilla, A., Hogan, R., & Kaiser, R.B. (2007). The toxic triangle: Destructive leaders, susceptible followers, and conducive environments. *The Leadership Quarterly, 18*, 176-194

Pelled, L. H., & Xin, K. R. (1999). Down and out: An investigation of the relationship between mood and employee withdrawal behavior. *Journal of Management, 25*, 875-895.

Peus, C., & Frey, D. (2009). Humanism at work: Crucial organizational cultures and leadership principles. In H. Spitzeck, M. Pirson, W. Amann, S. Khan & E. von Kimakowitz (Eds.), *Humanism in business: Perspectives on responsible business in society.* Cambridge, MA: Cambridge University Press.

Peus, C., Pawlowska, B., & Wesche, J. S. (2009, May). *Implicit leadership theories in academia*. Oral paper at the 14th European Congress of Work and Organizational Psychology (EAWOP), Santiago de Compostela.

Peus, C., Weisweiler, S., & Pawlowska, B. (2008, April). *Customizing Faculty Development: Faculty members' roles and skills.* Oral paper presented the 2nd CETL Conference: Preparing for Academic Practice - Disciplinary Perspectives. University of Oxford, England.

Phillips, J. S., & Lord, R. G. (1982). Schematic information processing perceptions of leadership in problem solving groups. *Journal of Applied Psychology, 67*, 486-492.

Pruitt, D. G., & Carnevale, P. J. (1993). *Negotiation in social conflict.* Belmont, CA: Thomson Brooks/Cole.

Pruitt, D. G., & Rubin, J. Z. (1986). *Social conflict: Escalation, impasse, and resolution.* Reding, MA: Addision-Wesley.

Raelin, J.A. (1995). How to manage your local professor. *Academy of Management Journal, Best Paper Proceedings*, 207-214.

Rahim, M. (2002). Toward a theory of managing organizational conflict. *International Journal of Conflict Management, 13*, 206-235.

Reeder, G. D., & Brewer, M. B. (1979). A schematic model of dispositional attribution in interpersonal perception. *Psychological Review, 86*, 61-79.

Ritter, B. A., & Lord, R. G. (2007). The impact of previous leaders on the evaluation of new leaders: An alternative to prototype matching. *Journal of Applied Psychology, 92*, 1683-1695.

Rokeach, M. (1980). Some unresolved issues in theories of beliefs, attitudes, and values. In H. E. Howe, Jr., & M. M. Page (Eds.), *1979 Nebraska symposium on motivation.* Lincoln, NE: University of Nebraska Press.

Ross, M., & Fletcher, G. J. O. (1985). Attribution and social perception. In G. Lindzey & E. Aronson (Eds.), *Handbook of Social Psychology* (pp. 73-122). New York: Random House.

Rost, J. C. (1993). Leadership development in the new millennium. *Journal of Leadership Studies, 1*, 92-110.

Schein, E. H. (1985). *Organizational culture and leadership.* San Francisco: Jossey Bass.

Schilling, J. (2009). From Ineffectiveness to Destruction: A Qualitative Study on the Meaning of Negative Leadership. *Leadership, 5*, 102-129.

Schwartz, S. H. (1992). Universals in the content and structure of values: Theoretical advances and empirical tests in 20 countries. In M. Zanna (Ed.), *Advances in experimental social psychology* (Vol. 25, pp. 1-65). Orlando, FL: Academic.
Schwartz, S. H. (1994). Are there universal aspects in the structure and contents of human values? *Journal of Social Issues, 50*, 19-45.
Schwartz, S. H. (2006). Les valeurs de base de la personne: Théorie, mesures et applications [Basic human values: Theory, measurement, and applications]. *Revue Française de Sociologie, 45*, 929-968.
Schwartz, S. H., & Bilsky, W. (1990). Toward a theory of the universal content and structure of values: Extensions and cross-cultural replications. *Journal of Personality and Social Psychology, 58*, 878-891.
Schyns, B., & Hansbrough, T. (2008). Why the brewery ran out of beer: The attribution of mistakes in a leadership context. *Social Psychology, 39*, 197-203.
Simons, T. (2002). The high cost of lost trust: When employees doubt a manager's integrity, the problem can show up on the bottom line. *Harvard Business Review, 80*, 18-19.
Sitkin, S. B., & Roth, N. L. (1993). Explaining the limited effectiveness of legalistic "remedies" for trust/distrust. *Organization Science, 4*, 367-392.
Smith, E. R., & Zarate, M. A. (1992). Exemplar-based model of social judgment. *Psychological Review, 99*, 3-21.
Staw, B. M., & Barsade, S. G. (1993). Affect and managerial performance: A test of the sadder-but-wiser vs. happier-and-smarter hypotheses. *Administrative Science Quarterly, 38*, 304-331.
Tekleab, A. G., Sims Jr., H. P., Yun, S., Tesluk, P. E., & Cox, J. (2008). Are we on the same page? Effects of self-awareness of empowering and transformational leadership. *Journal of Leadership and Organizational Studies, 14*, 185-201.
Tepper, B. J. (2000). Consequences of abusive supervision. *Academy of Management Journal, 43*, 178-190.
Tranfinow, D., Bromgard, I. K., Finlay, K. A., & Ketelaar, T. (2005). The role of affect in determining the attributional weight of immoral behaviors. *Personality and Social Psychology Bulletin, 31*, 935-948.
Ulrich, D., & Lake, D. (1991). Organizational capability: Creating competitive advantage. *The Executive, 5*, 77-92.
Weick, K. E. (1995). *Sensemaking in organizations.* Thousand Oaks, CA: SAGE.
Weiner, B. (1985). An attributional theory of achievement motivation and emotion. *Psychological Review, 92*, 548-573.
Yauch, C. A., & Wright, P. (2007). Studying the performance and agility of individuals using cooperative and competitive incentives. *Human Factors and Ergonomics in Manufacturing, 17*, 105-116.
Yost, D., Sentner, S., & Forlenza-Bailey, A. (2000). An examination of the construct of critical reflection: Implications for teacher education programming in the 21st century. *Journal of Teacher Education, 5*, 39-48.
Yukl, G. (1998). *Leadership in organizations* (3rd ed.). Englewood Cliffs, NJ: Prentice Hall.

CHAPTER 18

HEROIC ILLUSIONS

How Implicit Leadership Theories Shape Follower Attributions About Poor Leader Performance

Tiffany Hansbrough and Birgit Schyns

This chapter explores how implicit leadership theories shape follower perceptions of poor leader performance. We contend that followers' implicit leadership theories foster external attributions that provide leaders with some latitude for poor performance. Additionally, we consider how follower needs, the quality of the leader-member relationship and leader impression management tactics reinforce this tendency. Finally, the implications for the role of follower attributions in perpetuating leaders' power in organizations are discussed.

Traditional leadership research considers leadership synonymous with effective leadership. As Meindl, Ehrlich, and Dukerich (1985,) point out, "the romanticization of leadership is hinted at in the observations made by a number of social and organizational analysts who have noted the esteem, prestige, charisma, and heroism attached to various conceptions and forms of leadership" (p. 79). Recently our understanding of leadership has

When Leadership Goes Wrong: Destructive Leadership, Mistakes and Ethical Failures, pp. 513–524

broadened to include the dark side of leadership (Popper, 2001), abusive supervision (Tepper, 2000), "bad leadership" (Kellerman, 2004) and toxic leadership (Lipman-Blumen, 2005). Although research now acknowledges that leadership is not always positive, the leader remains the primary focus of such efforts. Yet the locus of leadership involves the behavior, traits and characteristics of leaders as perceived by followers (Lord & Maher, 1993). Based on these perceptions, followers bestow power and legitimacy upon leaders. Accordingly, it is imperative to understand the role of follower perceptions (Lord & Emrich, 2001). In this chapter we explore how followers make attributions for leader performance and how that process is impacted by follower needs and leader-member exchange. We contend that followers view leader performance though the lens of their implicit leadership theories. Moreover, leaders engage in impression management tactics that promote attributions consistent with leadership prototypes. To maintain their leadership images, followers are likely to attribute poor performance to external factors thereby holding leaders unaccountable for their performance. In this manner, followers foster heroic illusions about their leaders.

Leader Performance

The most commonly used definition of leader effectiveness is the extent to which the leader's organizational unit performs its task successfully and attains its goals (Yukl, 1998). Examples include profits, market share and meeting production deadlines. This definition allows followers to make different attributions for poor performance and is not a subjective measure such as follower satisfaction with the leader. Accordingly, we define poor leader performance as failure of the leader's unit to meet its goals. Our definition centers on leader ineffectiveness rather than unethical leadership. Further, in contrast to specific leader mistakes, poor performance is more of long term issue that can be due to many factors. As Schyns and Hansbrough (2008) observe, leader mistakes can be attributed to the leader or to external elements. Given that poor performance is likely influenced by a myriad of factors, observers may be more likely to simplify sensemaking by the use of cognitive shortcuts. Thus, poor performance lends itself very well to attributional processes.

Attribution Theory and Leadership

According to attribution theory individuals engage in sensemaking to provide causal explanations for events (e.g., Heider, 1958). Applied to a leadership setting, attributions account for a significant proportion of the variation in perceived leadership behaviors (Martinko, Harvey, & Douglas, 2007). Perhaps the most well-known application of attribution theory to leadership is the work of Green and Mitchell (1979) who examined how different factors influence leaders' attributions for subordinate performance. The authors conclude that extending attribution research to leadership studies has considerable potential for understanding leader-member interactions (Green & Mitchell, 1979). Despite encouragement to expand this line of inquiry, a recent review (e.g., Martinko et al., 2007) reflects that research still focuses primarily on leader attributions.

Green and Mitchell (1979) suggest that leaders make attributions about follower performance using controlled processing whereby they rationally weigh a variety of factors to determine the locus of follower performance. However, Lord and Maher (1993) contend "we suggest that the attribution processes described by Green and Mitchell are rarely used; rather attributional processes are linked to more schema driven processes." Schemas serve to reduce cognitive load and simplify information processing. As noted by Martinko et al. (2007), in everyday situations people do not generally exert the cognitive effort required to make causal attributions. Consequently, follower leader perceptions are likely governed by automatic processing such as implicit leadership theories.

Implicit Leadership Theories

Lord and his colleagues posit that leadership perceptions are driven by implicit leadership theories (Lord & Maher, 1993; Schyns, Felfe, & Blank, 2007). According to implicit leadership theory, the word "leader" serves as a schema that enables observers to classify individuals as leaders based on how well they resemble the prototype (Calder, 1977; Lord, Foti, & De Vader, 1984). The word "leader" is associated with traits such as intelligence, dedication, charisma, sensitivity, and strength (Offerman, Kennedy, & Wirtz, 1994). A recent study by Schyns and Shilling (in press) asked participants to name characteristics of leaders in general and rate them in terms of effectiveness. They found 58% of all characteristics were favorable and rated as effective while 6% characteristics were unfavorable but rated as effective. Thus, implicit leadership theories consist of primarily effective leader images.

Once activated, implicit leadership theories are subject to the same cognitive processing errors as other schemas including selective attention, encoding, and retrieval of schema consistent information as well as cuing schema consistent information where such information does not objectively exist (Phillips & Lord, 1982; Lord et al., 1984; Lord & Maher,

1993). Perceptions of leadership and leadership behavior are significantly influenced by information about leader performance (Lord, Binning, Rush, & Thomas, 1978; Phillips & Lord, 1981). Lord and Maher (1993) note success enhances perceptions of leadership while failure limits perceptions of leadership. Thus, leadership schemas provide information about what attributes generally go together. Individuals classified as leaders are presumed to be intelligent, dedicated, strong, and effective. Poor performance is inconsistent with such leader images. In order to preserve their leader images, followers will likely attribute poor leader performance to external factors, such as the situation or bad luck. As noted by Fiske and Taylor (1984) "if people can attribute inconsistent behavior to situational causes, they can forget the behavior and maintain their schema based impression" (p. 164). Here we suggest that being categorized as a "leader" provides superiors with some degree of latitude or protective halo for poor performance.

Proposition 1: Followers, consistent with their implicit leadership theories, will attribute poor leader performance to external factors.

Attachment Theory

Unmet follower needs may also impact perceptions of leader performance. Hunt, Boal, and Sorenson (1990) posit that individual differences in implicit leadership theories may be the result of early childhood experiences. In particular, parental models of leadership may play a pivotal role in shaping leadership schemas (Keller, 2003; Popper & Mayseless, 2002). As such, the leader-led relationship can be examined from an attachment perspective and depicted as a close relationship with attachment components (Popper, Mayselness, & Castelnovo, 2000). Further, attachment theory provides a theoretical foundation to examine how follower needs and motives might shape expectations of the leader-follower relationship (e.g., Keller, 2003) and leadership perceptions.

According to attachment theory, during childhood individuals form strong bonds with caregivers that promote survival of the species (Bowlby, 1977). Since infants cannot survive on their own, they are motivated to obtain proximity and protection from their caregivers. In the best case scenario, caregivers are lovingly responsive to their children's signals and provide a safe haven and a secure base from which children may confidently explore their environment. Interactions with responsive others promote the formation of attachment security characterized by comfort with closeness and interdependence (Mikulincer, Shaver, & Perge, 2003) as well as the expectation that partners are trustworthy and reliable (Shaver & Hazan, 1994). Yet not all caregivers consistently respond to their children's needs. Inconsistent caregiver responsiveness produces attachment anxiety characterized by a preoccupation with attachment (Hazan & Shaver, 1987), a strong need for closeness, worries about relationships and fear of rejection (Mikulincer & Nachshon, 1991). Finally, consistent caregiver unresponsiveness produces attachment avoidance characterized by defense self-reliance and preference for emotional distance from others (Shaver, Collins, & Clark, 1996).

In adulthood, the attachment system is activated during encounters with physical or psychological threats (Bowlby, 1969/1982). During such times, individuals seek proximity to supportive others, or turn to internalized representations of attachment figures (Mikulincer et al., 2003). In the work place leaders help followers cope with stress by providing a safe haven and thereby fulfill their attachment needs (Popper & Mayseless, 2002). However, the attachment system is chronically activated for individuals who score high in attachment anxiety (Mikulincer, Birnbaum, Woddis, & Nachmias, 2000; Mikulincer, Gillath, & Shaver, 2002). Instead of focusing on work, such individuals may be preoccupied with finding someone to meet their unmet needs (Hazan & Shaver, 1990).

Unmet attachment needs may have implications for cognitive processing. For example, it has long been noted that unmet needs can influence one's interpretation of ambiguous stimuli (Allport, 1955; Erdelyi, 1974). Moreover, since the attachment system is always primed in anxious individuals, it tends to bias cognitive processing in a self-sustaining manner (Mikulincer et al., 2003) whereby such individuals are biased to perceive proximity seeking as viable and search for even minimal signs of interest and availability. Thus, highly anxious individuals may be predisposed to view leaders as potential attachment figures and project their unmet attachment needs onto leaders with the hope that they will be fulfilled. Highly anxious followers may be especially motivated to maintain the perception that leaders are capable of meeting their needs. Indeed, highly anxious individuals may be motivated to see leaders as omnipotent and therefore capable of providing the save haven they so desperately crave. Since poor performance is inconsistent with leader images of the strong, heroic protector, anxious individuals may preserve their leadership schema by attributing poor leader performance to external factors. In this manner, unmet attachment needs may have important implications for leadership perceptions.

Proposition 2: Highly anxious followers will attribute poor leader performance to external factors.

Leader-Member Exchange (LMX)

According to leader-member exchange theory, leaders establish two qualitatively different types of relationships with followers. In-group members receive greater latitude in performing their tasks, as well as more time and attention from leaders. In exchange, in-group members provide leaders with greater loyalty and take on additional responsibilities. As noted by Graen (2003), in-group relationships are characterized by mutual trust, respect and commitment. In contrast, relationships with out-group members remain on an explicitly contractual level (Graen & Uhl-Bien, 1995). One predictor of group status is similarity. For example, Liden and his colleagues (1993) report that similarity between leaders and followers in terms of values, problem-solving, and demographic characteristics is positively associated with leader-member exchange quality.

Schyns, Kroon, and Moors (2008) contend that an idealized image of supervisors as considerate (Vecchio & Boatwright, 2002) is related to the perception of LMX and they report an interaction between idealized considerate leader images and a need for leadership (De Vries, Roe, & Taillieu, 1999). Thus when followers' ideal leader is considerate they feel more dependent on their leader and perceive more LMX. As those followers might feel dependent on their leaders, they will be less likely to blame their leader for poor performance. Thus, on the basis of their implicit leadership theories and their dependence on their leader, "in-group" followers will have a tendency to attribute poor performance to external factors.

Proposition 3: In-group members will attribute poor leader performance to external factors.

Leader Factors That Reinforce Follower Implicit Leadership Theories

Charisma. According to Meindl (1990), charisma is "hyper-romanticism" (p. 182), meaning that charismatic leaders are often regarded as larger than life. "Transformational leadership, with its emphasis on charisma and vision, is in part a matter of perception and attribution, myth and symbol that is likely to have a romanticized component to it" (p. 182). A recent meta-analysis found that people who romanticize leaders also perceive more charisma in their actual leaders (Schyns et al., 2007), meaning that charisma itself contains some form of idealized leadership image. Poor performance is at odds with such heroic leader images and inconsistent with followers' implicit leadership theories. Furthermore, followers of charismatic leaders report that their desire for leader approval was their primary source of motivation (Conger, 1989). Thus, charismatic leaders, by matching their followers' implicit leadership theories, on the one hand, and providing individual consideration (e.g., transformational leadership; Bass, 1985), on the other hand, provide followers with a greater sense of self-worth: Followers get attention from their idealized leader. Accordingly, it seems unlikely that followers will attribute poor performance to charismatic leaders as their self-worth is dependent upon keeping their leadership images intact.

Proposition 4: Followers will attribute the poor performance of perceived charismatic leaders to external factors.

Impression management. Leaders often seek to convey the message that they are important, competent and in control of events (Pfeffer, 1977, 1981). In an analysis of annual reports Salancik and Meindl (1984) found that top management consistently credited themselves with positive outcomes while blaming negative outcomes on the environment. According to Gray and Densten (2007), "leaders are motivated to transmit these images through impression management and 'woo' followers into constructing romantic images of leadership" (p. 558). Consequently, leaders reinforce their followers' romantic leader images and use the self-serving bias to make attributions for their performance. By making external attributions for poor performance, leaders promote effective leadership images consistent with followers' implicit leadership theories.

Proposition 5: Leader impression management tactics promote followers' tendency to attribute poor leader performance to external factors.

Status. The status of the leader may also reinforce followers' implicit leadership theories. Hollander (1992) suggests that leaders accrue status (e.g., idiosyncrasy credits) by fostering perceptions of their competence and conformity to group norms. Once earned, these credits allow leaders greater latitude for action. For example, charisma represents a great fund of idiosyncrasy credits (Hollander, 1992). It is possible that status provides leaders with greater latitude for poor performance as followers are more likely to view higher level leaders through the lens of implicit leadership theories. Since status is earned by perceptions of competence, followers have already made some positive assessment about leader performance. Accordingly, poor leader performance is inconsistent with existing leader images.

Proposition 6: Leader status promotes followers' tendency to attribute poor leader performance to external factors.

Prototypicality. As we have argued above, followers often evaluate leader performance through the lens of their implicit leadership theories. This may provide superiors categorized as leaders with a protective halo whereby leaders are presumed to be effective. However, implicit leadership theories may work against leaders who are "unusual" and do not fit the prototype (e.g., women, minorities; Schyns, 2006). Since these individuals were never presumed to be effective, intelligent, and dedicated, poor performance is consistent with their categorization as "non-leaders". In such cases, followers may readily attribute leaders' poor performance to internal factors.

Proposition 7: When leaders do not fit followers' leadership images, followers will attribute poor leadership performance to internal factors.

Discussion

In summary, followers may evaluate leaders through the lens of their implicit leadership theories. Leaders who fit the prototype are presumed effective. Poor performance is inconsistent with such leader images. To maintain their leadership schemas, followers may attribute poor leader performance to external factors. The use of automatic processes to evaluate leader performance has important organizational implications. Leaders may reinforce this tendency by the use of impression management techniques whereby they take credit for good performance while attributing poor performance to external factors. By sustaining follower leader images, leaders maintain power. Follower needs may exacerbate this problem. For example, highly anxious followers may assume emotional availability is tantamount to leader effectiveness. Thus, leaders who meet follower attachment needs are deemed effective. From the perspective of the leader-follower dyad, there are no performance problems; from the perspective of the organization there is an accountability problem. Indeed, the wide spread practice of evaluating leader performance by relying on follower perceptions could result in an organizational culture that fails to hold leaders accountable. As Nicholas Kristof (2009) laments,

> the marketplace of ideas doesn't clear out bad pundits because there's no accountability. We trumpet our successes and ignore failures—or else

attempt to explain that the failure doesn't count because the situation changed or that we were basically right but the timing was off" (p. A27)

While our focus centered on positive implicit leadership theories, some followers may harbor negative leadership images. As Schyns and Shilling (under review) note, while implicit leadership theories largely consist of positive characteristics, the leader images of some followers include negative characteristics such as unpleasant, individualistic, or stupid. In such cases we anticipate that followers will attribute poor leader performance to leaders. Thus we expect followers with negative implicit leadership theories will also make attributions that enable them to sustain their leadership images.

Limitations

Definition of leader performance. The definition of leader performance may have implications for followers' causal explanations regarding leader performance. Leader performance that directly affects followers seems likely to result in different attributions than outcomes that do not implicate the follower. Specifically, when outcomes are severe, such as organizational failure, followers lose their jobs. At this point, the protective halo of implicit leadership theories would seemingly backfire. Followers might feel betrayed by leaders, reasoning a "real leader" would have been able to protect us and sustain the organization. In such cases it seems likely that leaders will be held accountable for their poor performance as it is unlikely that they have enough idiosyncrasy credits for such a substantial withdrawal. Further, the defensive attribution hypothesis (e.g., Walster, 1966) suggests that observers attribute more responsibility for accidents that produce severe consequences. This is in line with Meindl et al.'s (1985) Romance of Leadership approach, stating that leaders are held responsible for company performance not only in times of very good but also in times of very bad company performance.

This contribution represents an important departure from previous research that focused on leaders' attributions for follower performance. We developed a theoretical framework that details how followers make attributions for leader performance. It is vital to understand these processes since leaders maintain their power and legitimacy through followers. The realities of leader performance can be obscured through imagery and self-presentation (Hollander, 1992). Followers may readily latch onto such explanations as they fit with their implicit leadership theories. This may have dysfunctional consequences where there is a disconnect between the perceptions of leaders and their followers and those outside the organization. Indeed, Hollander (1992) observes there is a pattern of excessively large bonuses and salaries paid to CEOs even in the face of lay-offs, declining earnings, and other poor performance outcomes for their firms. Recently, in the wake of the Wall Street crisis, the CEOs of failing organizations were rewarded with bailout funds and bonuses. To hold leaders accountable, we must first understand how followers evaluate their performance.

REFERENCES

Allport, F. H. (1955). *Theories of perception and the concept of structure*. New Work: Wiley.

Bass, B. M. (1985). *Leadership and performance beyond expectations*. New York: The Free Press.

Bowlby, J. (1977). The making and breaking of affectional bonds. *British Journal of Psychiatry, 130,* 201-210.

Bowlby, J. (1982). *Attachment and loss: Vol. 1 Attachment* (2nd ed.). New York: Basic Books. (Original work published 1969)

Calder, B. J. (1977). An attribution theory of leadership. In B. M. Staw & G. R. Salancik (Eds.), *New directions in organizational behavior* (pp. 179–204). Chicago: St. Claire Press.

Conger, J. A. (1989). *The charismatic leader: Beyond the mystique of exceptional leadership*. San Francisco: Jossey-Bass.

De Vries, R. E., Roe, R. A., & Taillieu, T. C. B. (1999). On charisma and need for leadership, *European Journal of Work and Organizational Psychology, 8*, 109-33.

Erdelyi, M. H. (1974). A new look at the new look: Perceptual defense and vigilance. *Psychological Review, 81,* 1-25.

Fiske, S. T., & Taylor, S. E. (1984). *Social cognition*. New York: Random House.

Graen, G. B. (2003). Interpersonal workplace theory at the crossroads: LMX and transformational theory as a special case of role making in work organizations. In G. B. Graen (Ed.), *Dealing with diversity, LMX leadership: The series* (Vol. I, pp. 145-182). Greenwich, CT: Information Age Publishing.

Graen, G. B., & Uhl-Bien, M. (1995). Development of leader-member exchange (LMX) theory of leadership over 25 years: Applying a multi-level multi-domain perspective. *The Leadership Quarterly, 6,* 219-247.

Gray, J. H., & Densten, I. L. (2007). How leaders woo followers in the Romance of Leadership. *Applied Psychology: An International Review, 56*, 558-581.

Green, S. G., & Mitchell, T. R. (1979). Attributional processes of leaders in leader-member interactions. *Organizational Behavior and Human Performance, 23,* 429-458.

Hazan, C., & Shaver, P. R. (1987). Romantic love conceptualized as an attachment process. *Journal of Personality and Social Psychology, 52,* 511-524.

Hazan, C., & Shaver, P. R., (1990). Love and work: An attachment—theoretical perspective. *Journal of Personality and Social Psychology, 59,* 270-280.

Heider, F. (1958). *The psychology of interpersonal relations.* New York: Wiley.

Hollander, E. P. (1992). The essential interdependence of leadership and followership. *Current Directions in Psychological Science, 1,* 71-75.

Hunt, J. G., Boal, K. B., & Sorenson, R. L. (1990). Top management: Inside the black box. *The Leadership Quarterly, 1,* 41-65.

Keller, T. (2003). Parental images as a guide to leadership sensemaking: An attachment perspective on implicit leadership theories. *The Leadership Quarterly, 14,* 141-160.

Kellerman, B. (2004). *Bad leadership: What it is, how it happens, why it matters*. Boston: Harvard Business School Press.

Kristof, N. (2009, March 26). Learning how to think. *The New York Times*, p. A27.

Liden, R. C., Wayne, S. J., & Stilwell, D. (1993). A longitudinal study on the early development of leader-member exchanges. *Journal of Applied Psychology, 78,* 662-674.

Lipman-Blumen, J. (2005). *The allure of toxic leaders*. New York: Oxford University Press.

Lord, R. G., Binning, J. F., Rush, M. C., & Thomas, J. C. (1978). The effect of performance cues and leader behavior on questionnaire ratings of leadership behavior. *Organizational Behavior and Human Performance, 21,* 27-39.

Lord, R. G., & Emrich, C. G. (2001). Thinking outside the box by looking inside the box: Extending the cognitive revolution in leadership research. *The Leadership Quarterly, 11*(4), 551-579.

Lord, R. G., Foti, R. J., & De Vader, C. L. (1984). A test of leadership categorization theory: Internal structure, information processing, and leadership perceptions. *Organizational Behavior and Human Performance, 34,* 343-378.

Lord, R. G., & Maher, K. J. (1993). *Leadership and information processing: Linking perceptions and performance*. Boston: Routledge.

Martinko, M. J., Harvey, P., & Douglas, S. C. (2007). The role, function, and contribution of attribution theory to leadership: A review. *The Leadership Quarterly, 18,* 561-585.

Meindl, J. R. (1990). On leadership: An alternative to the conventional wisdom. *Research in Organizational Behavior, 12,* 159-203.

Meindl, J. R., Ehrlich, S. B., & Dukerich, J. M. (1985). The romance of leadership. *Administrative Science Quarterly, 30,* 78-102.

Mikulincer, M., Birnbaum, G., Woddis, D., & Nachmias, O., (2000). Stress and accessibility of proximity-related thoughts: Exploring the normative and intraindividual components of attachment theory. *Journal of Personality and Social Psychology, 78,* 509-523.

Mikulincer, M., Gillath, O., & Shaver, P. R., (2002). Activation of the attachment system in adulthood: Threat related primes increase the accessibility of mental representations of attachment figures. *Journal of Personality and Social Psychology, 83,* 881-895.

Mikulincer, M., & Nachshon, O., (1991). Attachment styles and patterns of self-disclosure. *Journal of Personality and Social Psychology, 61,* 321-331.

Mikulincer, M., Shaver, P. R., & Pereg, D., (2003). Attachment theory and affect regulation: The dynamics, development, and cognitive consequences of attachment-related strategies. *Motivation and Emotion, 27,* 77-102.

Offermann, L. R., Kennedy, J. K., & Wirtz, P. W. (1994). Implicit leadership theories: Content, structure, and generalizability, *The Leadership Quarterly, 5*, 43-58.

Pfeffer, J. (1977). The ambiguity of leadership. *Academy of Management Review, 2*, 104-112.

Pfeffer, J. (1981). *Power in organizations*. Marshfield, MA: Pittman.

Phillips, J. S., & Lord, R. G. (1981). Causal attributions and perceptions of leadership. *Organizational Behavior and Human Performance, 28*, 143-163.

Phillips, J. S., & Lord, R. G. (1982). Schematic information processing and perception of leadership in problem solving groups. *Journal of Applied Psychology, 67*, 486-492.

Popper, M. (2001). The dark and bright sides of leadership: Some theoretical and practical implications. In J. M. Burns, G. Sorenson, & L. Matusak (Eds.), *Concepts, challenges and realities of leadership*. College Park, MD: Academy of Leadership.

Popper, M., & Mayseless, O., (2002). Back to basics: Applying a parenting perspective to transformational leadership. *The Leadership Quarterly, 14*, 41-65.

Popper, M., Mayseless, O., & Castelnovo, O., (2000). Transformational leadership and attachment. *The Leadership Quarterly, 11*, 267-289.

Salancik, G. R., & Meindl, J. R. (1984). Corporate attributions as strategic illusions of management control. *Administrative Science Quarterly, 29*, 238-254.

Schyns, B. (2006). The role of implicit leadership theories in the performance appraisals and promotion recommendations of leaders. *Equal Opportunities International, 25*, 188-199.

Schyns, B., Felfe, J., & Blank, H. (2007). Is charisma hyper-romanticism? Empirical evidence from new data and a meta-analysis. *Applied Psychology: An International Review, 56*,505–527.

Schyns, B., & Hansbrough, T. (2008). Why the brewery ran out of beer: The attribution of mistakes in a leadership context. *Social Psychology, 39*, 197-203.

Schyns, B., Kroon, B., & Moors, G. (2008). Follower characteristics and the perception of Leader-Member Exchange. *Journal of Managerial Psychology, 23*, 772-788.

Schyns, B., & Schilling, J. (in press). Implicit leadership theories: Think leader, think effective? *Journal of Management Inquiry.*

Shaver, P. R., Collins, N., & Clark, C. L., (1996). Attachment styles and internal working models. In G. Fletcher & J. Fitness (Eds.), *Knowledge structures in close relationships: A social psychological approach* (pp. 25-61). Hillsdale, NJ: Erlbaum.

Shaver, P. R., & Hazan, C., (1994). Attachment. In A.L Weber & J. H. Harvey (Eds.), *Perspectives on close relationships* (pp. 110-130). Boston: Allyn & Bacon.

Tepper, B. (2000). Consequences of abusive supervision. *Academy of Management Journal, 42*, 100-108.

Vecchio, R. P., & Boatwright, K. J. (2002). Preferences for idealized styles of supervision, *The Leadership Quarterly, 13*, 327-42.

Walster, E. (1966) Assignment of responsibility for an accident. *Journal of Personality and Social Psychology, 3*, 73-79.

Yukl, G. (1998). *Leadership in organizations*. Upper Saddle Hill, NJ: Prentice-Hall.

ABOUT THE AUTHORS

Merethe Schanke Aasland is a research fellow and a PhD-student at the University of Bergen, and a member of the Bergen Bulllying Research Group. Aasland is a licensed clinical psychologist and a former consultant in the field of work and organizational psychology, currently completing her PhD-thesis on destructive leadership in organizations. Other research interests are leadership, counterproductive behaviors and workplace bullying. Her work has appeared in journals such as *British Journal of Management, Leadership Quarterly, European Journal of Work and Organizational Psychology,* and *Journal of Occupational Health Psychology.* Contact: Department of Psychosocial Science, University of Bergen, Norway.

Mary Bardes has a PhD in business administration with a concentration in management from the University of Central Florida. She is an assistant professor of management at Drexel University in Philadelphia, PA. Mary's primary research interests include workplace deviance and destructive leader behaviors. She has published research articles in the *Journal of Applied Psychology, Organizational Behavior and Human Decision Processes,* and the *European Journal of Work and Organizational Psychology.* Mary teaches undergraduate and graduate courses in organizational behavior and leadership. Contact: LeBow College of Business, Drexel University; Philadelphia, PA, United States.

Michelle C. Bligh is an associate professor in the School of Behavioral and Organizational Sciences at Claremont Graduate University. Her research interests include charismatic leadership, interpersonal trust, and political and executive leadership. Her work has been published in *Jour-*

nal of Applied Psychology, Leadership, Employee Relations, Leadership Quarterly, Applied Psychology: An International Review, Group and Organization Management, Journal of Managerial Psychology, and *The Journal of Business Ethics.* She was awarded the 2007 SAGE Best Paper Award in Group and Organization Management and the 2003 SAGE Outstanding Paper Award for Research Methods. She also serves on the editorial review board of *The Leadership Quarterly and Leadership,* coedited a special issue of *Applied Psychology: An International Review* on follower-centric approaches to leadership, and coedited a recent book titled *Follower-Centered Perspectives on Leadership: A Tribute to the Memory of James R. Meindl.* Dr. Bligh has also helped a variety of public and private sector organizations assess and improve their effectiveness in the areas of leadership development, organizational culture, and change management. Contact: School of Behavioral and Organizational Sciences, Claremont, CA, United States.

Kathleen Boies is an associate professor of management at the John Molson School of Business, Concordia University. She received her PhD in industrial and organizational psychology from the University of Western Ontario. Her research focuses on leadership and, in particular, how leaders shape followers' thought processes and emotions. She teaches leadership in undergraduate, master's and doctoral programs. Dr. Boies' articles have appeared in journals including *Leadership Quarterly, Journal of Personality and Social Psychology, Journal of Occupational Health Psychology,* and *European Journal of Personality.* Contact: Department of Management, John Molson School of Business, Concordia University, Montreal (Quebec), Canada.

Susanne Braun is a PhD student and scientific associate at LMU Center for Leadership and People Management, Ludwig-Maximilian-University Munich, Germany. She received her diploma in psychology from University of Muenster, Germany. She holds a certificate in systemic management coaching and teaches other doctoral students in the fields of leadership and motivation, teamwork, communication and conflict management. Her research interests include women in leadership positions, transformational leadership, and leadership development in academia. Contact: LMU Center for Leadership and People Management; Ludwig-Maximilian-University Munich, Germany.

Diane J. Chandler (PhD, Regent University) is associate professor of leadership and formation at Regent University School of Divinity. She teaches graduate courses in leadership development, women in leadership, and holistic/spiritual formation. She has published articles in the areas of unethical leadership, leadership burnout, leadership self-care, and women in global leadership. She has served on various religious and nonprofit boards. Dr. Chandler participates in educational and service trips in various global locations, which have taken her to the United Arab Emirates, China, and Mongolia. She has served as a life coach, as well as a consultant for nonprofit organizations. Contact: Regent University, Virginia Beach, VA, United States.

Lily Cushenbery is a graduate student in industrial and organizational psychology at the Pennsylvania State University. Her research areas include leader error recovery and malevolent creativity. Lily is also a research assistant at the International Center for the Study of Terrorism and has managed several research studies and applied projects. Contact: Department of Psychology, Penn State University, PA, United States.

Marilyn Nicole Deese is currently a research analyst at Midwestern State University. After graduating from Centenary College of Louisiana, she earned a master's in applied psychology with an emphasis in industrial/organizational psychology from Clemson University. She has presented research at the Society of Industrial/Organizational Psychology and Work, Stress, and Health conferences. Ms. Deese's research interests include the study of positive organizational behavior, personal resources, work engagement, occupational health psychology, and destructive leadership. Contact: Department of Psychology, Clemson University, Clemson, SC, United States.

Bi-Hong Deng is a doctoral candidate in organizational behavior at the School of Behavioral and Organizational Sciences at Claremont Graduate University, and holds a BS in psychobiology from University of California, Los Angeles. Her core research interests are in positive leadership and followership, organizational learning, creativity and innovation, and knowledge management. Specializing in self-development and adult learning, she conducts training workshops for nonprofit organizations and is involved with the American Society for Training and Development, Academy of Management, and Center for Creative Leadership. Contact: School of Behavioral and Organizational Sciences, Claremont, CA, United States.

Jessica Dzieweczynski is a consultant at Federal Management Partners, a strategic human capital company dedicated to improving the effectiveness of the federal government. Dr. Dzieweczynski specializes in the areas of program evaluation, survey design and analysis, competency modeling, and workload analyses and forecasts. She has published in scholarly journals on topics including leadership, validity, and personality. Contact: Federal Management Partners Consulting, Alexandria, VA, United States.

Ståle Einarsen is professor in work and organizational psychology at the University of Bergen, Norway, and head of the Bergen Bullying Research Group. Einarsen has published extensively on issues related workplace bullying, leadership, and creativity and innovation in organizations. He is a founding member of the International Association on Workplace Bullying and Harassment, has acted as advisor to the Norwegian Government regarding workplace bullying, and has coedited three international volumes on bullying and harassment in the workplace. His work has appeared in journals such as *Journal of Occupational and Organizational Psychology, Leadership Quarterly, Work and Stress, British Journal of Management,* and *Journal of Occupational Health Psychology.* Contact: Department of Psychosocial Science, University of Bergen, Bergen, Norway.

Dawn L. Eubanks is on the faculty at the University of Bath in the School of Management. Her research interests focus on leadership and creativity. Her leadership research explores the characteristics of destructive leaders, how leaders respond to criticism, and how high level leaders interact with one another. Her creativity research focuses on identifying the ingredients necessary to foster an environment where creativity and innovation can occur. Her research findings appear in journals such as *Leadership Quarterly, Journal of Applied Social Psychology, Creativity Research Journal,* and *Human Resource Management Review.* She received her PhD in industrial and organizational psychology from The University of Oklahoma. Contact: Organization Studies Group; School of Management; University of Bath, United Kingdom.

Dail Fields (PhD, Georgia Institute of Technology) serves as a professor in the Regent University PhD program in organizational leadership. He is editor of the *International Journal of Leadership Studies,* a peer-reviewed research journal. Dr. Fields is the author of "Taking the Measure of Work," a reference guide to measurement in organizations published by SAGE Publications. He has published research studies in the *Academy of Management Journal, Journal of Management, Group and Organization Studies, Journal of Occupational and Organizational Psychology, and Leadership.* He has presented seminars and research studies at annual meetings of the Academy of Management, the European Group on Organizational Studies, and the European Academy of Management. Dr. Fields has been a guest speaker at Vilnius University, Henan University (PRC), the Singapore Institute of Management, the Malaysian Institute of Management, and the Human Resource International Convention in Guatemala. Dr. Fields has previously served on the faculties of George Washington University and the City University of Hong Kong. Prior to undertaking an academic career, he worked in business for over 20 years, starting a small business and holding management positions in such firms as Deloitte-Touche and MCI Communications Corporation. Contact: Regent University, Virginia Beach, VA, United States.

Dieter Frey is professor of social psychology and director of the LMU Center for Leadership and People Management at Ludwig-Maximilian-University Munich, Germany. In addition, he is academic director of the Bavarian Academy for Elite Training and member of the Bavarian Academy of Sciences. His research interests include basic social psychology (e.g., decision processes, information seeking, group processes) as well as organizational psychology (e.g., leadership and innovation) and behavioral finance. Contact: LMU Center for Leadership and People Management, Ludwig-Maximilian-University Munich, Germany.

Ellen Giebels (PhD, University of Groningen, 1999) is associate professor in the Department of Psychology at the University of Twente, the Netherlands and director of the Center for Conflict, Risk, and Safety Perception (iCRiSP). The center aims at advancing scientific knowledge on how citizens experience safety issues and risks, their receptivity to different types of influence and communication strategies, and the actual management of conflict and crisis incidents. Ellen is coauthor of numerous peer-reviewed articles and several books. Three of her papers received a best paper award, including her work on cultural differences in crisis negotiations, which won the 2007 Best Applied Paper award of the International Association for Conflict Management conference. Contact: Department of Psychology and Communication of Health and Risk, University of Twente, Enschede, The Netherlands.

Gina Grandy is an associate professor with the Commerce Department at Mount Allison University, Sackville, New Brunswick, Canada. Gina completed her PhD at Newcastle Business School, Northumbria University. Her research interests include competitive advantage, change, culture, dirty work, identity and leadership. Contact: Commerce Department, Ron Joyce Centre for Business Studies, Mount Allison University, Sackville, New Brunswick, Canada.

Tiffany Hansbrough is the director of the David Brain Leadership and Organizational Leadership Programs at Baldwin-Wallace College. She holds a PhD in organizational behavior from the State University of New York at Buffalo and has served as a faculty member at The Jepson School of Leadership Studies at the University of Richmond, Purdue University, and Arkansas State University. Her research focuses on implicit leadership theories, leader-follower relationships and level of analysis issues and has appeared in *The Leadership Quarterly, Human Relations, Organizational Research Methods* and *Leadership and Organizational Development Journal.* Contact: David Brain Leadership Program, Baldwin-Wallace College, Berea, Ohio, United States.

Sam Hunter is an assistant professor of industrial and organizational psychology at the Pennsylvania State University. His primary areas of research include leadership and innovation management. Within these areas, Dr. Hunter has published over 35 journal articles, books, and book chapters in outlets such as the *Leadership Quarterly,* the *Journal of Applied Psychology,* and the *Creativity Research Journal.* Dr. Hunter has also received funding for his work from agencies such as the National Science Foundation and the Office of Naval Research. Contact: Department of Psychology, Penn State University, PA, United States.

Karen A. Jehn is a professor of organization behavior at Melbourne Business School. Her research focuses on intragroup conflict, group composition and performance, and lying in organizations. Professor Jehn has authored numerous scholarly publications in these areas, including articles in the *Academy of Management Journal, Administrative Science Quarterly, Journal of Personality and Social Psychology, International Journal of Conflict Management, Research in Organization Behavior, Journal of Business Ethics, Business Ethics Quarterly,* and *Group Decision and Negotiation.* She has served on the editorial boards of *Administrative Science Quarterly, Academy of Management Review,* the *Journal of Organizational Behavior,* and the *International Journal of Conflict Management* where she was an associate editor. She was also a director of the Solomon Asch Center for the Study of Ethnopoloitical Conflict, the research director of the Alfred P. Sloan Foundation's Diversity Research Network, and the chair of the Conflict Management Division of the Academy of Management. She currently is the editor-in-chief of the *Conflict and Dispute Resolution Journal,* and the coeditor-in-chief of *Negotiation and Conflict Management Research.* Her two most recent research interests are in asymmetry of perceptions and member entitlement in workgroups. Contact: Melbourne Business School, Carlton, Victoria, Australia.

Jeffrey C. Kohles is an associate professor of management and organizational behavior in the College of Business Administration, as well as director and founding member of the Center for Leadership Innovation and Mentorship Building (CLIMB), at California State University San Marcos. Prior to his current position he was a Research Fellow at the Center for International Leadership in Buffalo, New York, as well as a research associate at the Kravis Leadership Institute in Claremont, California. His research interests include leadership, organizational communication, and the implementation of organization-level vision and strategy at the individual level. His research has been published in *The Academy of Management Review, Journal of Applied Psychology, Organizational Behavior and Human Decision Processes, The Leadership Quarterly, Leadership, Group & Organization Management, Journal of Managerial Psychology, Applied Psychology: An International Review, The Academy of Management Best Papers Proceedings, European Business Forum,* and *European Journal of Social Psychology.* He has also helped a variety of both public and private sector organizations assess and improve their effectiveness in the areas of leadership development, organizational culture, strategy implementation, and general product and service assessment methodology. Contact: Department of Management and Organizational Behavior, California State University San Marcos, San Marcos, CA, United States.

Robert C. Liden (PhD, University of Cincinnati) is professor of management and director of doctoral programs in the College of Business Administration at the University of Illinois at Chicago. He is the former chair of the Organizational Behavior Division of the Academy of Management. His research focuses on interpersonal processes within the context of such topics as leadership, groups, and career progression. Contact: Department of Managerial Studies, University of Illinois at Chicago, Morgan, Chicago, IL, United States.

Dirk Lindebaum is a lecturer at the University of Liverpool Management School. Coming from a structural engineering and project management background, Dirk completed his doctorate in organizational psychology at Manchester Business School (MBS) in 2008. Prior to moving into his current position, he was a postdoctoral research fellow in organizational psychology at MBS. Applying a more differentiated perspective, his present research interests center upon various aspects of emotion at work, ranging from emotional intelligence and leadership to issues of power and resistance. His research finds expression in several journal publications, featured, among others, in *Academy of Management Learning and Education* and *Journal of Management Studies.* Contact: University of Liverpool Management School, Liverpool, United Kingdom.

Daniel May is a PhD student and scientific associate at LMU Center for Leadership and People Management, Ludwig-Maximilian-University Munich, Germany. He also received his diploma in psychology from this university. He holds a certificate in systemic management coaching and teaches other doctoral students in the fields of leadership and motivation, teamwork, communication and conflict management. His research interests include constructive and destructive forms of leadership, group processes and selective exposure to information. Contact: LMU Center for Leadership and People Management; Ludwig-Maximilian-University Munich, Germany.

Dean McFarlin joined the School of Business Administration at The University of Dayton as a professor of management in 1999. Before that, McFarlin was on the faculty at Marquette University. Currently, McFarlin serves as both the chair of the Management/Marketing Department at the University of Dayton (a position he has held since 2004) and as the NCR professor of global leadership development (a position he has held since 2001). His current research interests include cross-cultural management, organizational justice, and executive influence processes on top management teams. McFarlin has over 100 publications and conference presentations to his credit, including several books with colleague Paul Sweeney. From 1998-2004, McFarlin served as a Consulting Editor for the Journal of Organizational Behavior. Since 2001 McFarlin has served as the research briefs editor for the Academy of Management Perspectives. And since 2005, McFarlin has served on the editorial board of the *Journal of Management.* Contact: Dept. of Management & Marketing, University of Dayton, Dayton, OH, United States.

Paul W. Mulvey is an associate professor in the Management, Innovation, and Entrepreneurship (MIE) department at NC State University in Raleigh. His research, teaching, and consulting focuses on leadership, reward systems, teams, recruiting, and retention. He has published articles in journals such as *Academy of Management Executive, Academy of Management Journal, Industrial Relations, Compensation and Benefits Review, Organizational Behavior and Human Decision Processes,* and *WorldatWork Journal.* Contact: Department of Management, Innovation, and Entrepreneurship, College of Management, NC State University, Raleigh, NC, United States.

Michael D. Mumford is the George Lynn Cross distinguished research professor of psychology at the University of Oklahoma where he directs the center for applied social research. He received his doctoral degree from the University of Georgia in 1983 in the fields of industrial and organizational psychology and psychometrics. Dr. Mumford is a fellow of the American Psychological Association (Divisons 3, 5, 14), the Society for Industrial and Organizational Psychology, and the American Psychological Society. He has written more than 270 articles on creativity, innovation, planning, leadership, and ethics. He serves as senior editor of the *Leadership Quarterly* and is on the editorial boards of the *Creativity Research Journal,* the *Journal of Creative Behavior, IEEE Transactions on Engineering Management,* and the

Journal of Business Ethics. Dr. Mumford has served as principal investigator on grants totaling more than $30 million from the National Science Foundation, the National Institutes of Health, the Department of Defense, the Department of Labor, and the Department of State. He is a recipient of the Society for Industrial and Organizational Psychology's M. Scott Myers Award for Applied Research in the Workplace. Contact: University of Oklahoma, Center for Applied Social Research, Norman, OK, United States.

Art Padilla is professor and head of the Management, Innovation, and Entrepreneurship (MIE) Department at NC State University in Raleigh. He previously served as academic vice president in the 16-campus University of North Carolina system and as a professor at UNC-Chapel Hill. He teaches and writes about organizational leadership and strategy. His latest book on leadership is scheduled for publication in 2011 by Wiley and Sons, Inc. Contact: Department of Management, Innovation, and Entrepreneurship, North Carolina State University, Raleigh, NC, United States.

Beata Pawlowska is a PhD student and scientific associate at LMU Center for Leadership and People Management at Ludwig-Maximilian-University Munich, Germany. She received her honours bachelor degree in psychology from the University of Western Ontario, Canada and a master's degree in psychology from Ludwig Maximilian University, Germany. She holds regular lectures and seminars on key topics in the area of leadership, social interaction at work, cross-cultural competence and work-life interference. Her research interests include leadership, crisis leadership and management and leadership development. Contact: LMU Center for Leadership and People Management, Ludwig-Maximilian-University Munich, Germany.

Claudia Peus is assistant professor of social psychology and executive director of the LMU Center for Leadership and People Management at Ludwig-Maximilian-University Munich, Germany. Before, she was a visiting scholar at the Sloan School of Management (Massachusetts Institute of Technology) and a postdoctoral fellow at Harvard University. Her research interests include leadership, leadership development, cross-cultural investigations of managers' career advancement and innovation. Contact: LMU Center for Leadership and People Management, Ludwig-Maximilian-University Munich, Germany.

Ronald F. Piccolo holds a PhD in management from the University of Florida. He is an associate professor of management and academic director of the Center for Leadership Development in the Crummer Graduate

School of Business at Rollins College, Winter Park, FL. Ron's primary research interests include leadership, motivation, and job design, and he has published research articles in the *Academy of Management Journal, Journal of Applied Psychology, Personnel Psychology,* and *Journal of Organizational Behavior.* Ron teaches graduate courses in leadership, policy, and organizational behavior, and serves on the editorial boards for *Organizational Behavior and Human Decision Processes* and *Leadership Quarterly.* Contact: Rollins College, Crummer Graduate School of Business, Winter Park, FL, United States.

Terry L. Price is professor and associate dean for academic affairs at the Jepson School of Leadership Studies at the University of Richmond, Virginia. He has a doctorate in philosophy from the University of Arizona, as well as degrees in philosophy, politics, and psychology from the University of North Carolina at Chapel Hill and the University of Oxford. He currently serves on the board of directors of the International Leadership Association and as a series editor of *Jepson Studies in Leadership.* Price is coeditor of *The International Library of Leadership, The Quest for Moral Leaders,* and *The Values of Presidential Leadership.* He is author of *Understanding Ethical Failures in Leadership and Leadership Ethics: An Introduction,* both on Cambridge University Press. Contact: Jepson School of Leadership Studies, University of Richmond, VA, United States.

Sonja Rispens received her PhD in social and organizational psychology from Leiden University (The Netherlands). She is currently an assistant professor of organizational behavior at Eindhoven University of Technology. Her work concentrates on conflict perceptions and individual and team effectiveness in organizations. Sonja published her work in several editorial books and outlets such as the *International Journal of Conflict Management* and *Academy of Management Journal.* Contact: Human Performance Management Group, Faculty of Industrial Engineering & Innovation Sciences, Eindhoven University of Technology, Eindhoven, The Netherlands.

Maria Carolina Saffie Robertson obtained her MSc in management from Concordia University in 2008. She is currently a PhD student in business administration, management option, at the John Molson School of Business, Concordia University. Her research interests focus on leadership and mentoring. In particular, she aims to identify the mechanisms that facilitate or hinder the development of successful mentoring relationships in the workplace. She is also researching the impact that culture and gender could have on the development of mentoring relationships. Contact:

Department of Management, John Molson School of Business, Concordia University,Montreal (Quebec), Canada.

Melanie Ann Robinson is a PhD candidate in business administration, management option, at the John Molson School of Business, Concordia University. She completed her MSc in administration in 2007 at Concordia University. Her research interests include leadership and forgiveness, as well as transformational leadership. Contact: Department of Management, John Molson School of Business, Concordia University, Montreal (Quebec), Canada.

Birgit Schyns is reader in organisational behavior at Portsmouth Business School. Her research interest focuses mainly on leadership, especially interactional theories such as leader-member exchange, as well as the perception of leadership and implicit leadership theories. Also, she is interested in career psychology. Birgit holds a master's (Diplom) degree from the Friedrich-Wilhelms University, Bonn and a PhD (Dr. rer. nat.) from the University of Leipzig, both Germany. In the 4 years prior to moving to the United Kingdom in 2006, Birgit has been an assistant professor at Tilburg University and the University of Twente, both in The Netherlands. Her work has been published, among others, in *Journal of Vocational Behavior, Leadership, Applied Psychology: An International Review.* She has coedited several special issues and a book on implicit leadership theories. Birgit is an associate editor for the *European Journal of Work and Organizational Psychology* and *British Journal of Management,* and is a member of several editorial boards. Contact: University of Portsmouth, Portsmouth Business School, Portsmouth, United Kingdom.

Anders Skogstad is professor in work and organizational psychology at the University of Bergen, Norway, and a senior member of the Bergen Bullying Research Group. Skogstad is also a licensed specialist in organizational psychology, and has worked extensively in developing monitoring systems for psychosocial factors at work. His main research focus has been on role stressors, bullying and destructive leadership. His work has appeared in journals such as *Journal of Occupational Health Psychology, Leadership Quarterly, Work and Stress, British Journal of Management,* and *European Journal of Work and Organizational Psychology.* Contact: Department of Psychosocial Science, University of Bergen, Bergen, Norway.

Paul Sweeney joined the School of Business Administration at The University of Dayton as a professor of management in 2001. He has also been a member of the faculty at the University of Central Florida and Marquette University, serving as department chair at both institutions. From

2003-2006, Sweeney served as an associate dean in the School of Business Administration—a role he again took on in Fall, 2009. As associate dean, his responsibilities include leadership of the MBA program and oversight of all SBA international programs and activities. His current research interests include international management, organizational justice, and executive influence processes on top management teams. Sweeney has over 100 publications and conference presentations to his credit, including several books with colleague Dean McFarlin. In 2005, Sweeney was named to the editorial board of the *Journal of Management,* a leading research journal in his field. Contact: Dept. of Management & Marketing, University of Dayton, Dayton, OH, United States.

Robert Sinclair is an associate professor of industrial/organizational psychology at Clemson University. He completed his PhD in 1995 at Wayne State University. Prior to moving to Clemson, he held faculty positions at the University of Tulsa and Portland State University. Dr. Sinclair is a founding member and past president of the Society for Occupational Health Psychology and he currently serves on the editorial boards of the *Journal of Occupational Health Psychology, Journal of Management,* and *Journal of Organizational Behavior.* His research interests include individual and organizational factors that contribute to occupational health and safety, employee commitment and retention, and the particular challenges faced by workers in nursing, retail, and military settings. Contact: Department of Psychology, Clemson University, Clemson, SC, United States.

Allison Starratt is a bachelor of commerce graduate from Mount Allison University, Sackville, New Brunswick, Canada. She is presently employed by Maple Leaf Foods as an assistant manager private label with the Maple Leaf Consumer Foods. Her interests lie in the broad areas of marketing and management. Contact: Mount Allison University, Sackville, New Brunswick, Canada.

Brian Tate is a research psychologist at the U.S. Army Research Institute for the Behavioral and Social Sciences. His research activities focus upon topics related to enlisted soldier personnel selection, assignment, and assessment, especially methods of noncognitive applicant testing, job analysis, and performance measurement. Dr. Tate has also published and presented research in leadership and personnel training. Contact: U.S. Army Research Institute for the Behavioral and Social Sciences, Arlington, VA, United States.

Suzanne van Gils is a PhD student at the Rotterdam School of Management, Erasmus University. In her project, she focuses ethical leadership and the role of leader-follower dynamics. Specifically, Suzanne is interested in the influence of self-construal on ethical behavior. Contact: Rotterdam School of Management, Erasmus University, Rotterdam, The Netherlands.

Daan van Knippenberg is professor of organizational behavior at the Rotterdam School of Management, Erasmus University Rotterdam, The Netherlands. His research interests include leadership, diversity, teams, social identity processes, and creativity and innovation. He is associate editor of *Organizational Behavior and Human Decision Processes* and *Journal of Organizational Behavior*, founding editor of *Organizational Psychology Review* (first issue February 2011), and cofounder of the Erasmus Center for Leadership Studies. Contact: Rotterdam School of Management, Erasmus University Rotterdam, Rotterdam, The Netherlands.

Niels van Quaquebeke holds a postdoctoral ERIM research fellowship at the Rotterdam School of Management. He is a member of the Personnel and Organization Management Department and the Erasmus Center for Leadership Studies. Likewise, he functions as the director of the interdisciplinary RespectResearchGroup. Niels specializes in leadership research with a particular focus on values and respect. More specifically, he investigates the logic by which respect functions as a lubricant for social systems. He was awarded repeated scholarships by the German National Academic Foundation as well as an award by the German government for the innovative approach of his research group. Contact: Rotterdam School of Management, Erasmus University Rotterdam, Rotterdam, The Netherlands.

Mo Wang, an assistant professor at University of Maryland, specializes in research and applications in the areas of occupational health psychology, retirement, cross-cultural HR management, and advanced quantitative methodologies. He has received Academy of Management HR Division Scholarly Achievement Award (2008), Careers Division Best Paper Award (2009) and European Commission's Erasmus Mundus Scholarship Award for Work, Organizational, and Personnel Psychology (2009) for his research in these areas. He has also received Early Career Achievement Award in occupational health psychology that is cosponsored by APA, NIOSH, and SOHP (2009). He currently serves on the editorial boards of *Journal of Applied Psychology, Journal of Management, Journal of Occupational Health Psychology*, and *Journal of Business Psychology*. He is also recently commissioned as the editor for the *Oxford Handbook of Retirement*. He has been contracted by several Fortune 500 companies and government agencies to provide consulting services related to workforce succession planning in both English and Chinese. Address: Department of Psychology, University of Maryland, College Park, MD, United States.

Jenny S. Wesche is a PhD student and scientific associate at LMU Center for Leadership and People Management at Ludwig-Maximilian-University Munich, Germany. She received her diploma in psychology from Bielefeld University, Germany. She gives university seminars as well as trainings in the field of leadership and organizational behavior. Her research interests include ethical behavior and decision making in organizations, leadership, and aspects job performance in particular citizenship and counterproductive behaviors at work. Contact: LMU Center for Leadership and People Management; Ludwig-Maximilian-University Munich, Germany.